St Laurence in Thanet

a parish history

Margaret Bolton

Ariana Press

The principal office of history I take to be this:
to prevent virtuous actions from being forgotten,
and that evil words and deeds should fear
an infamous reputation with posterity

Tacitus

Copyright © 2016 Margaret Bolton

Published by Ariana Press, Kent, England: 2016

ISBN   978-0952647430

All rights reserved. Neither this book nor any portion thereof may be reproduced or transmitted by any means – electronic, mechanical, photocopying, scanning, recording – or used in any manner whatsoever without the express written permission of the publisher except for the use of brief quotations in a book review or scholarly journal.

Margaret Bolton hereby asserts her moral right under Section 77 of the Copyright, Designs & Patents Act 1988 to be identified as the author of this work.

For details of her other publications, see https://ariesresearch.wordpress.com

Contents

Foreword	5
Acknowledgments	6
Introduction	7
Earliest Days	8
The Medieval Period	
The Building	11
Clergy and Staff	35
People, Events and Places	40
The Sixteenth Century	
The Building	47
Clergy and Staff	73
People, Events and Places	78
The Seventeenth Century	
The Building	88
Clergy and Staff	96
People, Events and Places	102
The Eighteenth Century	
The Building	124
Clergy and Staff	134
People, Events and Places	141
The Nineteenth Century	
The Building	164
Clergy and Staff	198
People, Events and Places	228
The Twentieth Century and Beyond	
The Building	281
Clergy and Staff	307
People, Events and Places	367
Appendices	
John Johnson alias Anthony	388
The Sum of the Whole Scripture	398
The Churchyard	401
World War One Roll of Honour	417
World War Two Roll of Honour	421
St Laurence and St Lawrence	424
Vital Statistics	426
Floor Plans	430
Hymns about the Church	432

Parish Magazine	435
Children's Services in the 1880s	452
Epilogue	455
Signing Out	456
Subject Index	457

Clergy

1535-1538 Young, John	73
1538-1557 Ming, Edward	73
1561-1567 Marsh, William	74
1567-1572 Coldwell, John	74
1572-1578 Stone, Simon	75
1584-1585 Shueler, Thomas	77
1595-1607 Kington, John	78
1607-1614 Cole, John	96
1614-1629 Turner, Thomas	97
1630-1644 Dunkyn, William	97
1653-1662 Johnson, Peter	101
1662-1699 Young, John	102
1699-1739 Bookey, Matthew	134
1740-1766 Tyler, Robert	135
1766-1793 Harvey, Richard, senior	138
1793-1836 Harvey, Richard, junior	198
1836-1880 Sicklemore, George	201
1880-1889 Molony, Charles	206
1889-1893 Fowler, Montague	209
1893-1899 Payne-Smith, Robert,	225
1899-1904 Crosse, Thomas	307
1904-1905 Oakley-Coles, James	310
1906-1907 Hughes-Games, Stephen	311
1907-1921 Bevan, Raymond	314
1922-1927 Wilcox, Alfred	318
1927-1942 Cowland-Cooper, Charles	320
1942-1961 Roundhill, John	335
1961-1965 Bird, Hartley	346
1966-1977 Yarker, Francis	350
1978-1988 Norwood, Philip	354
1988-1997 Cotton, Peter	358
1997-2002 Dewey, Peter	360
2003-2013 Ireland, Sharran	362
2015-date Jacobson, Andrew	364

Foreword

The English parish church holds a very special place in the heart of this nation. A place of worship where generations of families have been baptised married and buried. A sacred space offering peace and tranquilly, rich in history standing firm through times of war and peace, prosperity and economic depression. The Parish Church of St Laurence in Thanet is no exception.

Historian, Margaret Bolton's well researched and systematic account of the history of St Laurence Church provides a fascinating insight into its building, clergy and the wider community in which it is situated. Amongst other things, the research challenges the widely held assumption that the church was built in 1062 and proposes a more accurate date of 1090.

I highly commend this book which I am sure will attract a wide readership including social historians and visitors to the church.

The Reverend Andrew Jacobson
July 2016

Acknowledgments

I would like to thank for permission to use the following images:

- The Ramsgate Historical Society for the pictures of the bells in 1911, the interior of St Mary's church, of old St Lawrence schools and war memorial.
- Sheldon Goodman for the image of Montague Fowler's grave.
- Simon Cowland-Cooper for the images of Charles Cowland-Cooper
- Julian Roundhill for the image of John Roundhill.
- Peter and Timothy Yarker for the image of Francis Yarker.
- Dorothy Manning for the picture of Sharran Ireland.
- Mrs P Smith and her son Philip for copies of prints collected by the late John Smith and that of the choir in 1981.
- Lady Fowler, Mrs Newling and Peter Newling for additional information and images of Montague Fowler.
- Barbara Byne for additional pictures of the bells from 1911 and 1924. These were taken by Albert Siminson and copyright rests with his heirs until 2030.
- Brian Kennington for permission to re-use the graveyard images.
- The editor of the *Thanet Times* for the pictures of the parish hall fire in 1967 and the fundraising campaign of 1952 and for Peter Cotton from 1996. Copyright for these images rests with the *Thanet Times*, *Thanet Advertiser* and *Isle of Thanet Gazette* respectively.
- Jill Kensall for the images of the royal arms, the Norman head, the rood screen and the Robert Sprackling memorial.
- Julia Penn for the image of the Georgian font now at St Catherine's.
- St Laurence school for images of the modern school and Warre bust.

I would like to thank the Vicar, the Reverend Andrew Jacobson, for permission to reproduce the parish magazine extracts and for the opportunity to study church artefacts in depth.

I would also like to thank the Reverend Ivan Howitt for his help regarding the bells and his patience in answering questions, John Paramor for his time in showing me the church plate, and to thank too the ex clergy who gave so generously of their time in passing on memories.

Finally, I wish to express my gratitude to the staff of Ramsgate and Newington libraries and those of Canterbury Cathedral Archives for the way they obtained documents and did their best to provide a quiet place to work.

Margaret Bolton

Introduction

It was a warm summer's day in Rome in the year 258. A group of Roman soldiers burst into a church where a deacon named Laurence was working. "Give us the treasure" they demanded. The sight of armed soldiers must have been frightening but Laurence steadied himself and replied that he could not hand it over immediately but if they would give him a few days, he would collect it together. No doubt thinking he was an easy victim, the soldiers agreed and departed. On the appointed day they returned: "Give us the treasure" they repeated. They found the church full of people, old and young, rich and poor, sick and able-bodied, but no money because Laurence had given it all away to the needy. Laurence smiled gently and gestured at the congregation. "This is the treasure of the church," he said, "the people."

Laurence's response, which is inspiring to Christians today and which reflects the teaching of St Paul in I Cor. 12:27 that the church is the body of Christ on earth, failed to please the Roman soldiers. They took him outside and tied him to a hurdle or grid and set fire to him. It is for this reason that the symbol of St Laurence is the gridiron and that is why it can be seen today in various parts of the church such as on the weathervane and in the windows.

This book has been structured with this teaching very much in mind. The material is arranged chronologically and covers both the history of the church building and its use as well as life in the wider parish community. It seeks to explore how people lived through a variety of means including demographic analyses and vignettes of individuals. It also aims to show how the church has adapted over the centuries in terms of worship and mission.

Throughout this volume, modern spelling has been employed and English in place of Latin. Tradition has been followed in that the church is treated as St Laurence whilst the civil parish is St Lawrence. An appendix considers the history of the apparent spelling anomaly.

Prior to 1752, the year began on 25th March or Lady Day rather than 1st January. This was because it was presumed that as the calendar dated from the birth of Christ, so the year must begin with His conception nine months before. Dates here are shown according to the calendar in use at the time but with modern dating added for clarification. For example, in the Tudor period, 1st January 1536 followed 31st December 1536, but I have shown the date as 1st January 1536/7.

With regard to terminology, in the pre-Reformation period, the words priest and altar are used as this was in line with contemporary beliefs about the sacrifice of the mass. In the post-Reformation period, the words minister and communion table are used.

At various points in the book reference is made to monetary values then and now. Data is taken from the Economic History Association's calculator which can be found at http://www.measuringworth.com/ppoweruk/

Earliest Days

The ancient parish of St Laurence stretched from Cliffsend to Dumpton encompassing Manston and the whole of Ramsgate. People have lived within its borders for thousands of years. Mesolithic axes from around 6000BC have been found at Pegwell and Neolithic remains at Court Stairs and Nethercourt.[1] Pottery, knives, jewellery and burials associated with the Beaker period have been found at Cliffsend, Dumpton, Manston and on the West Cliff of Ramsgate. Dating from two thousand years before the birth of Christ, they suggest that people were starting to settle in the area rather than just travel through in search of fresh pasture. A particularly fine Bronze age flat axe was found at Ellington and there are signs of a developed trading community with engraved European manufactured jewellery existing between Hollicondane and Dumpton and suggestions of a market being held at Manston.[2] The road through Manston was further developed in the Iron Age showing its importance, although the enclosure found nearby showed no evidence of later occupation.[3] By this time, people were starting to settle on the coast and a number of Roman remains have been found over the years in Ramsgate and at Ellington.[4]

The coming of the Anglo-Saxons or Jutes in the early fifth century transformed the area. According to the Kentish Chronicle, the British king Vortigern "handed over to them the island that in their language is called Thanet, in ours Ruoihm."[5] That they settled here is demonstrated by the spectacular finds made at Ozengell. Burials in the cemetery there extend from the fifth to early eighth century.[6] Another cemetery of the

---

[1] Gerald Moody, *The Isle of Thanet from Prehistory to the Norman Conquest* (Stroud, 2010), pp.58, 65
[2] ibid. pp. 101-8
[3] ibid. p.134
[4] Charles Cotton, *History of the Parish and Antiquities of the Church and Parish of St. Laurence, Thanet* (1895) pp.261-7; K. B. Martin, 'Oral Traditions of the Cinque Ports' in *Yachting Magazine* vol 6 (1832) pp79-87; Moody op.cit. p.153
[5] John Morris, *The Age of Arthur*, (London, 1973), p.57. This volume contains a scholarly discussion of the dating of the landing, see pp. 55-86.
[6] C. R. Smith, *Collectanea Antiqua* vol.3 (London, 1854) pp.273-278

same period has been found at Cliffsend.[7] Evidence also exists in the form of place names, for example, Ellington, Manston, Dumpton, Newington and Haine.

The most momentous event of the Anglo-Saxon period was the arrival of St Augustine who was sent by Pope Gregory the Great to convert the English, allegedly after seeing some pagan slave children in a market in Rome whom he said should no longer be just Angles but "fellow-heirs with the angels in heaven."[8] It has been suggested that Augustine landed in 597 at either Pegwell or Stonar and that he waited for King Ethelbert of Kent at either Cliffsend or Ozengell.[9] Two of the stained glass windows in St Laurence church commemorate this event. The east window dating from 1902 shows the story from Gregory seeing the slave children to King Ethelbert's baptism whilst a window in the north aisle depicts the cross erected to mark what was believed to be the site of Augustine's first meeting with Ethelbert.[10]

According to legend, in the year 670, an evil man named Thunor who was advisor to King Egbert of Kent, murdered two of the king's nephews. The King offered to pay their sister compensation and she said that she would accept the amount of land on

---

[7] Moody op.cit. p.163

[8] J. A. Giles (ed.), *The Venerable Bede's Ecclesiastical History of the English People* (London 1854) pp. 36-9

[9] Gerald Moody, *St Augustine's First Footfall* (Birchington 2013), pp.61-63

[10] There has been some dispute over the exact location of the meeting over the years but it is impossible to know after the passage of over 1,400 years.

the Isle of Thanet which her pet deer could run round. Possibly hoping that the deer would simply go round the field, the King agreed, but instead, the deer ran right across the island from roughly Margate to Minster. Meanwhile the wicked Thunor, who was chasing the hind, was thrown from his horse and fell into a deep pit where he duly died. The tale does sound like a sketch from *Horrible Histories* and it is untrue: the story appears to have been created by Thomas of Elmham in the fifteenth century.[11] However, the story is important because of the impact it had on what would later become the parish of St Laurence. It meant that every inch of its land was now owned by the newly built Minster Abbey.

The ninth and tenth centuries saw the island come under frequent and severe attack by Danish raiders. The fact that archaeologists have barely uncovered any evidence of settlement on the island for this entire period reflects just how totally Thanet was destroyed. Minster Abbey itself was burnt to the ground. The population fled or was taken captive.

In 1027, King Cnut gave the rather desolate, and certainly no longer prosperous, eastern half of the island to St Augustine's Abbey in Canterbury. In theory, the gift was of the lands which had been held by Minster Abbey. It would be up to the Abbot to rebuild the area and St Laurence church would come into being as part of this regeneration.

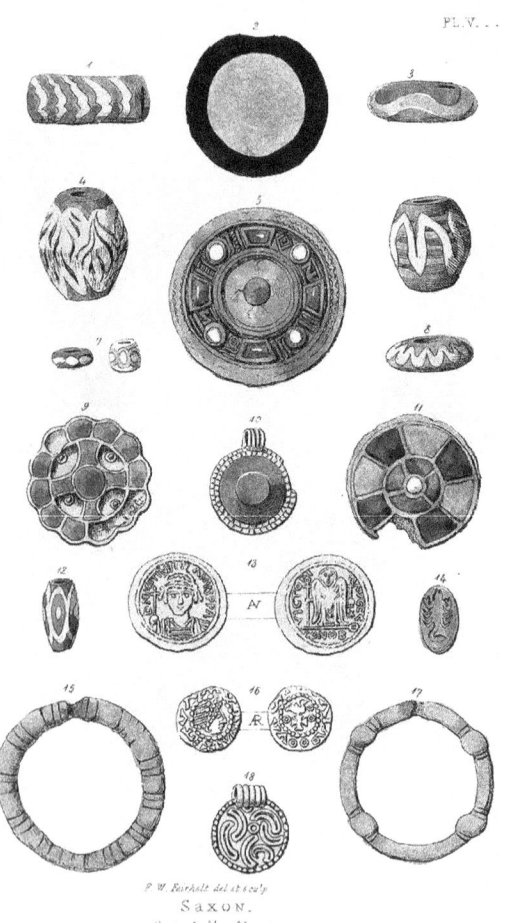

Finds at Ozengell as shown in *Collectanea Antiqua*

---

[11] For further discussion of the legend see, Beda Brooks, *Saint Domneva and the Foundation of Minster in Thanet* (Minster, 1991)

The Medieval Period

THE BUILDING

1062 and all that

In 1786, a local farmer named John Mockett, wrote a note between an account of different types of manure and a list of wheat prices. The note recorded that St Laurence church had been built in 1062. In 1805, he changed his mind and wrote that the church had been built in 1275 but this alteration has been generally overlooked and the date of 1062 has become firmly impressed in local folklore. It appears in guidebooks, websites and was made famous by Charles Cotton who quoted it in his *History and Antiquities of the Church and Parish of St Laurence in Thanet* (1895).

In order to consider the likelihood of 1062 being accurate, it is necessary to look at two things, the architecture and the source. John Mockett was not a historian and never claimed to be. He did not conduct research in libraries or examine documents. He liked to collect trivia and other dates in his notebook include 274 as the date the first candle was lit in a church, 98 for the first Christmas celebration, 1127 for the introduction of churchwardens, 481 for the first horse being shod and 742 for the first cemetery.[1] None of these dates can be substantiated. Whilst his interest was genuine, he also got confused about things such as claiming that Robert Sprackling murdered his wife in 1590 when it was Adam Sprackling who did so in 1652. This is not to denigrate him in any way. John Mockett was a good man, a successful farmer and hard working official at St Peter's church. The historical notes he wrote amid his jottings about agricultural developments and pricing simply reflected things he had heard as he remembered them. They were never intended to be the basis of future historical work. In his preface, he said his goal was "to entertain." If Charles Cotton had not chosen to take 1062 seriously, the entry would have faded into deserved oblivion.

---

[1] John Mockett, *Mockett's Journal* (Canterbury, 1836) reprinted by Michael's Bookshop, Ramsgate in 2006, pp. 3, 16, 35

So where did 1062 come from? There is nothing in the church building which would support such an early date. The answer most likely lies in the fact that most of Mockett's life was spent with the country either at war with France or about to go to war with France. Relations with the country had been strained for centuries and in 1785, France had banned most British imports causing distress to many in England who relied on the French market. A date of 1062 meant that the church could claim to be Anglo-Saxon and therefore English whilst a date after the Norman Conquest would indicate French involvement. Just as people with German sounding names sought to change them in World War One, so in the late Georgian period, there was a move to stress the Englishness of things and to downplay or disregard anything that could be construed as foreign. The Isle of Thanet was at the forefront of the conflict so anti-French feeling was especially intense. St John's was also given an unsubstantiated pre-Conquest date of 1050 by Mockett. The year of 1062, which appears to have been selected by someone at random reflects politics rather than historical fact.

The question of when St Laurence church was built is not a simple one. The building we see today dates largely from the thirteenth century but there are signs of the Norman core on the exterior of the back or west wall of the church. We can be sure that it did not exist before 1086 when the Domesday survey was written because it does not appear in that volume. Had the church been standing, it would have been listed under Minster in the same way that the church at Sarre was listed under Monkton. Instead, Minster is said to possess just one church which was in its own village. It follows that neither St Peter's nor St John's existed either. The Domesday survey was extremely thorough and organised primarily for the purpose of taxation although it aimed also to settle disputed questions relating to land ownership. The King, William the Conqueror, wanted to know the details of his resources so he could plan for tax revenue and assess the number of defenders that might exist in any given area in the event of war. Minster was said to contain: 150 villagers with 52 smallholders, one church with a priest, a salt house, two fisheries and a mill.[2] These possessions were spread across what is today Minster, Ramsgate, Broadstairs and Margate.[3] It is impossible to know the location of the items but it is quite likely that one of the fisheries was at Pegwell or Ramsgate. The population listed would have been men only so on the basis of each man having a wife and family, it is reasonable to multiply the 202 people listed by 4.5 to give an approximate population of around nine hundred. The value of the area was said to be £100 which made it the third wealthiest manor in the entire county and the most valuable of all the Abbey's possessions.[4] Moreover, it is made clear in the survey that the value had

---

[2] Philip Morgan (ed.), *Domesday Book Kent*, (Chichester, 1983) chapter 7 section 8

[3] Chislet held a small amount of land at Margate, see Rosemary Quested, *The Isle of Thanet Farming Community*, (Birchington, 2001) p.18

[4] By comparison, Rochester was valued at £20, Faversham £80, Sandwich £50, Canterbury £50, Chatham £15, Folkestone £145, Aldington £101, Chislet £78, Sturry £50, Northbourne £76, Dartford £60

increased substantially across the century rising by twenty-five per cent since the Conquest of 1066 and more than doubling since 1027 when the Abbey acquired the land from King Cnut.[5] This increase reflects the amount of rebuilding which had taken place, the value of the port and the investment in bringing land into cultivation. The manor of Monkton, which incorporated Sarre, Birchington and St Nicholas had also increased in value, doubling since the Conquest.

If St Laurence had been built in 1062 and there had been a community in the area, they would have been taxed. The only reason they would have been missed – and on an almost empty landscape, they would have been easily visible from Minster - would have been if the priest and reeves who were representatives of the Abbot of St Augustine's at Minster together with six villagers, all of whom were giving evidence under oath and under pain of death for falsification, had begged the surveyor to keep quiet about the St Laurence community because they wanted the pleasure of paying all the taxes themselves.   The utter improbability of this scenario, combined with the architectural evidence, suggests that a more accurate date for St Laurence church being built would be nearer 1090.

The decision to build the church would have been taken by the Abbot of St Augustine's at Canterbury. It was a period when a great many churches were being built and the monks would have been used to hiring workmen and arranging the importation of materials. It is likely that most of the stone used for St Laurence was brought through Pegwell.[6] The exact reason for building the church at this time is not certain. Obviously, all churches exist for the glorification of God but they were also built for the purposes of raising revenue. The more churches that the Abbot had under his charge, the more prestige he had and the more people he would have paying tithes. Of course, the cost of building a church was high so it would take some years before it earned money, but there was almost certainly a wealthy local landlord who contributed to the cost. The fact that the church was built either on or beside the estate of the St Laurence family would suggest that they were the benefactors and that they subsequently took their surname from the church.[7] For them too, this would have been a sign of prestige.

The first church at St Laurence was much smaller than the present one being a simple rectangular building on the site of the current nave. People would have gone in through a door at the west end and there are signs of this entrance on the outside of the building today. Small narrow unglazed windows on either side would have provided the only light so it would have been dark and cold inside. There would have been no permanent priest and few services initially as the church would have been dependent upon the services of a priest who would need to have travelled all the way from Canterbury, a lengthy journey by sea and land. Such a priest would have stayed

---

[5] Whilst modern historians agree this was a forgery, it was accepted as genuine at the time.
[6] Jonathan Foyle, *Architecture of Canterbury Cathedral* (London, 2013) p.36. This in itself would mean the building could not date before Archbishop Lanfranc 1070-1089.
[7] Surnames would not have been usual in the late eleventh century.

temporarily at Minster Abbey and probably travelled to St Peter's and St John's as well to take services. These would have been in Latin so not understood by those attending. The congregation would have been small too, most likely just the St Laurence family and those who worked for them. The altar would have stood against the east end wall which would have run just behind the present pulpit and lectern.

It is this church which is mentioned in a document issued by Abbot Hugh II when he declared that the income from the chapels of St Laurence, St Peter's and St John's should be appropriated for the sacristy of St Augustine's. This is the first reference to the church's existence but there has been confusion about the date. It is quoted twice in Thorne's chronicle, once under the works of the Abbot when it is undated but follows an entry for 1128, the second time as part of a papal bull which promises "all the pence which you were accustomed to have from the church of Thanet" are to be given "to the altar of the blessed apostles Peter and Paul and of St Augustine, for the repair and for the service of the monastery." This bull, however, is from Lucius II who reigned 1144-5 and even in the twelfth century it would not have taken sixteen years for a message to be taken from Canterbury to Rome and back again.[8]

Little remains of the original church saving the back wall of the nave and a short section before the first pillar at the south west end. Above the west window can be seen the earliest carving in the church, possibly meant to be a human face or maybe a protective angel or spirit.

Twelfth Century

This early church survived for almost a century at which point it was transformed by the addition of a tower and chancel. The date for this change has been estimated to be around 1175. This was a time when the authority of the Church was at its highest. Archbishop Becket had been murdered in 1170 and the resultant outrage had seen huge amounts being donated to the Church, some from the King who sought forgiveness having been blamed for the event, some from pilgrims who were crowding to Canterbury. It was the era of the Crusades also which signified the confidence of the Church. Aside from reflecting its growing status, the extension provided two major benefits to the community. It meant that bells could be installed which could be rung to warn people in time of trouble as well as summon them to worship and the tower could be used as a lookout over the sea and as a secure area for either possessions or people seeking refuge. Relations with France had been strained since their ruler had offered a home to the exiled Becket and, from 1173, to the Queen of England who was encouraging her sons to revolt against their father, Henry II of England. Having a good view of the

---

[8] A H Davis (trans), *William Thorne's Chronicle* (Oxford, 1934), pp. 68-9, 555. The pope in 1128 was Honorius II. Cotton's reference to 1124 is a simple error. 1144 would seem most probable.

Channel was particularly important at this turbulent time and this is why the tower was built at the east end rather than the west. The tower is unusual because the south and east sides both show arcading with five round headed arches whilst the north and west have one only. The most likely reason for this is that the village was located to the south and east which meant that the tower was normally seen from these angles. In order to save money, decoration was only applied to the sides generally visible whilst the other sides, which would only be seen by someone approaching from Manston, were left almost bare. There is evidence within the tower at ringing chamber level that there was a doorway on the north west corner which must have been accessed by a turret from the outside which would have been built at the same time. Access at this level would probably have been for storage or for maintenance of the bells with the actual ringers standing at ground level.

Within the church, the easternmost arch supporting the tower shows the typical zigzag decoration of the period. This was carved as a sign that beyond this point was a particularly special place because it was where the Mass was celebrated. Worshippers at this time would have had no access to the chancel which was purely the priest's domain. They were reminded of their place further by two carvings which can be seen to the right of the arch. These show a man in terror and the devil poised and ready to pounce on anyone who dares to defile the holy place.[9]

---

[9] The idea that only priests should enter the holy place and that the laity would be cursed if they presumed to do so comes from the Old Testament, see for example Num 18:22. For many years the pulpit stood at this point in the church so the vicar preached with the devil effectively looking over

To the right of the devil's head is a much defaced carving which shows an angel pointing at a building. It may be that this is a representation of the Christmas story with the angels pointing to the stable in which Christ was born. The incarnation of Christ is an essential element of the faith and was a reminder to worshippers that the Mass was not a celebration of some mere mortal but the very Son of God. Alternatively, the angel might be pointing to the empty tomb as a reminder that Our Lord rose from the dead.

Similar carvings existed on the pillar diagonally opposite but these were so defaced by coats of whitewash over the years that it was impossible to identify them which is why they were cut away in 1858. The present carvings were only cleared of whitewash in 1845.[10]

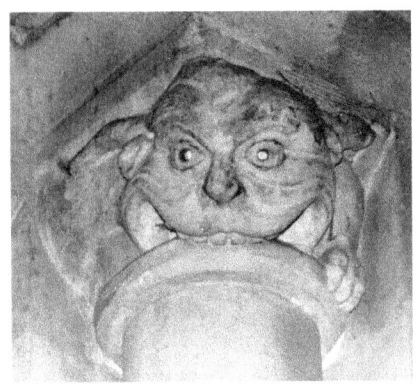

A further devil's head exists within the chancel itself on the north or left hand side. This head would only have been visible to the priest and acted as a warning of how they should, in the words of St Peter: "Be sober, be vigilant; because your adversary the devil, as a roaring lion, walketh about, seeking whom he may devour." (1 Peter 5:8)

The builders chose to use the transitional pointed style for these arches because it was believed this style was stronger and could bear more weight than conventional round headed ones. Further decoration was added in the form of foliage at the foot of the columns. Much of this has been worn away but some evidence can still be seen on the north side.

Naturally no picture exists of the church at this time but an artist's impression was drawn in 1933 based on architectural reports and this shows the nave to the left with its high windows which are matched by those in the chancel to the right.[11] The entrance

---

his shoulder.

[10] *Journal of the British Archaeological Association* (1847) pp. 48-49. Evidence of the existence of carvings opposite comes from the Reverend Charles Cowland-Cooper's interviews with parishioners who remembered the church prior to 1858.

[11] Drawn by Thomas Noyes-Lewis for the cover of the August 1933 Parish Magazine. The same artist provided a series of sketches which were prepared based on examination of the building and studies to be found in Canterbury Cathedral Archives. The work was supervised by the vicar of the

shown direct to the tower is presumed to exist although any evidence for this would have been destroyed when the church was widened. The tower is much shorter extending only just above the arcade. The chancel of this time would have reached only so far as the present choir stalls. There is some dispute whether it ended in a semi circular apse or a straight wall.[12] The artist has chosen the latter and shows it illuminated by just a small round east window and two round headed windows. The drawing is from the viewpoint of someone standing beside the present war memorial cross.

Not long after the completion of this work, the decision was made to extend the church in width. The walls of the nave were pierced to add two narrow side aisles. The purpose of these is uncertain but it is probable they were for the purposes of processions. Their width suggests they would not have added significantly to the area for people to stand in worship.[13] The columns are round with scalloped capitals and square abaci and although they appear to date from the same period, they are not in line with one another

---

period, the Reverend Charles Cowland-Cooper, a keen architectural historian. The single window over the arcade is probably incorrect and two should be shown.

[12] Robert Kennett, *The Church of St Laurence*, (Ramsgate, 1923) p.12

[13] Seats were only added in the Tudor period.

which suggests that one side was completed before the other.[14] Two crude heads appear on the columns to the south. Although these are now facing worshippers when they enter the church, at the time they were carved, entry was through the west door so the heads would have been facing away from the congregation and toward the processing priest. The heads are clearly the work of a different hand to those in the tower and chancel area which are much finer. The gagged head represents the message of St James in whose epistle comes the famous passage about the need to control the tongue (3: 3-10) and the warning: "If any man among you seem to be religious and bridleth not his tongue but deceiveth his own heart, this man's religion is in vain" (1: 26).[15] The second head shows a man gnashing his teeth and this is based on Our Lord's warning that those who fail to serve Him truly shall be cast into darkness "with the hypocrites: there shall be weeping and gnashing of teeth" (Matt. 24:51). The message of this latter is rather lost today for instead of being in shadow, the head is now in a brightly lit part of the church.

A similar process of expansion happened at St Peter's around this time and it is almost certain that the same masons were involved and they moved from one project to the other. What the congregation did meanwhile is also unknown. The church would have been a building site for a number of years and could not have been used for services. Those who were sufficiently fit would have gone to Minster but many would have not been able to worship as part of the church community.

Thirteenth Century

Around 1200, the chancel was extended to its present length. The remains of one of the original windows can be seen high up on the left hand side beside the communion table at the east end. The top of the priest's doorway from this time may be seen from within the vestry. It is likely that the east end was built with three narrow lancet windows rather than the one large window we see today. To the south of the chancel, or on the right as you face the communion table, can be seen the Early English piscina. This area was used for the washing of the communion vessels. The north and south walls of the tower would have been pierced at this stage too.

---

[14] It was usual for the north side to be cut first, see Grevile M. Livett, 'Early Norman Churches in and near the Medway Valley', *Archaeologia Cantiana*, vol. 20 (1893) p.147

[15] Psalm 39:1 also refers to bridling the tongue.

At this point, building work must have taken a break because the church was closed up from March 1208 to June 1214. This was the period of the interdict. Pope Innocent III had imposed this sanction on the whole of England because King John refused to accept his choice of Stephen Langton as Archbishop of Canterbury. For more than six years, every church in England was locked up and there were no services whatsoever – no masses, no baptisms, no weddings, no burials. Priests were to "abstain from all divine services except the repentance of the dying and their viaticum which with shut doors and the exclusion of lay persons may, by the favour of religion, be done privately if necessity requires it."[16] No work could be done on any church, neither minor repairs nor major alterations. The Abbot of St Augustine's thought this was a draconian response and decided to hold services within the Abbey for the next major festival, presumably Pentecost. The Pope's response was to suspend him and all those involved for disobedience.[17] What the people at St Laurence thought can only be imagined. Couples would have faced the prospect of delaying their weddings indefinitely or else indulging in fornication which they were taught would cause them to spend eternity in hell. Mothers who lost babies would have agonised over whether the infant would have been received in heaven without baptism. Families would have been left to bury their dead where they could. Although there would have been rejoicing and ringing of bells when the church did eventually re-open, many must have had their faith irrevocably damaged by the experience and some would only have returned under duress. Just two years later, in May 1216, when Prince Louis the Dauphin, heir to the French throne, landed at Stonar and claimed to be the rightful King of England the disgruntled parishioners were keen to support him. The Abbot promptly excommunicated Louis and threatened the same to all who assisted him which resulted in riots and thefts of the Abbot's food stores and livestock.[18]

The next major change to the church took place in the early 1270s. In 1275, St Laurence was made a parish in its own right distinct from Minster although all marriages, churchings and most burials still had to be held at Minster.[19] In celebration of this significant event, the church was expanded with the side aisles of

---

[16] *Thorne's Chronicle* op.cit. p.99
[17] ibid. p. 170
[18] ibid. pp.176-179. When King John died, the parishioners decided to support his brother Henry rather than the French claimant who departed home in 1217.
[19] ibid. pp.260-262

the nave being extended to their present width. The change in dimensions can be seen quite easily from outside the church on the west or back wall. The central wall of the nave has different stonework to that on either side whilst the stonework alters again just to the side of the round windows. The change meant larger windows could be added reflecting developments in glazing which would have made the building brighter.

Reflecting the new status of the church, a porch was built on the south side. This is the entrance generally used today although it is likely that most people continued to enter via the west door. The porch was two storeys high with the upper chamber being used either for storage or as a bedroom by one of the vicar's assistants. Robberies from churches took place in the middle ages and it was not uncommon for church officials to remain in churches overnight as security guards.[20] It could also have been used as a vestry. Signs of two original window sills to this upper room can still be seen. The room would have been accessed by a ladder either from within the church or from the corner of the porch behind the present hinge. An example of a two storey porch of this type can still be seen at St Nicholas-at-Wade. An image of St Laurence would have existed between the windows. A holy water stoup was placed beside the door into the church itself and this can still be seen beneath the notice board.

The porch in medieval times was not just the entrance to the church building but a place where important events took place. The first part of the wedding when couples would plight one another their troth signifying their willingness to enter into actual vows of marriage was said in the church porch. The first part of the baptism service also took place in the porch when the baby was signed with the cross using the holy water and the devil was exorcised. It was only after this that the service moved inside to the font where the child was actually baptised. Another service that often took place in the porch was the churching of women when a mother would go to give thanks for the fact that she had survived the ordeal of childbirth.[21] In some churches, meetings were held in the porch but the size of that at St Laurence would seem to preclude that. Whether

---

[20] Colin Platt, *The Parish Churches of Medieval England* (London, 1985), p.99
[21] In the later middle ages, many of these services moved into the main church.

there was ever a porch over the west door is unknown due to the changes made there over the centuries but it is quite likely, similarly with the north door.

Another artist's impression of the church at this time was drawn and this shows the church with the new porch, the main west door, and the new side aisles to the nave which were at this stage lower than their present height. The illustration shows the Abbot and his monks to the left and the Archbishop in the centre.

At the very end of the thirteenth century, the church was expanded again, this time at the east end of the church. The transept and chancel was broadened on the south side to create what is today known as the Becket Chapel. This name was only given to the area in the late twentieth century and was adopted due to the piscina therein which shows a tonsured head on the left and a cowled one on the right. These heads have

been interpreted as representing Henry II and Thomas Becket but in fact represent the apparition of St Francis to St Anthony at Arles in 1226.

It is sometimes said that the addition of chapels was thanks to the munificence of the Manston family but whilst this is possible, it is not at all certain and is certainly quite unlikely with regard the south chapel.[22] The building work would have required destroying one wall of the chancel and taking back some of the land which had been set aside as a churchyard. This could not have happened without the consent of the owners, St Augustine's Abbey. It is more likely that the process involved was akin to a modern shopping development. Certain groups or individuals would have made a petition to the Abbey which in turn would have made a decision about whether or not any extension should be made depending on how serious they felt the enquirers were. Whilst in theory churches existed solely for the glorification of God, in reality, they were a source of income. The Abbey would not wish to incur the considerable cost of building an extension if they were not going to find people willing to contribute, just as a developer today would want assurances that the units he was proposing would find buyers.

A key question would have been the purpose of the new space. If it was to establish a chantry which was a private chapel where members of the buyer's family would be buried and where a priest he had hired would say daily masses for the release of their souls from purgatory, then it is likely that most of the money came from one individual or family. However, if the space was to be used to set up a number of shrines where saints could be venerated and offerings made, the parish would have paid a greater part. Since there is no evidence of how the space was used prior to the fifteenth century and taxation records revealing the comparative wealth of parishioners at this time are scant, any comments about funding must be speculative. An undated return of Romescot taxpayers from around 1280-90 shows that the wealthiest parishioner was John of St Laurence. Behind him, but paying twenty-five per cent less, were Stephen Soldan, the heirs of Martin of Ramsgate, the heirs of John of Chilton, John Rosslin, the heirs of Martin of Nether Manston, Stephen Ligesy, Bertinus of Crawchopun, Stephen of Coleswood, William and John Brooman, Cecilia and Alicia Totterby.[23] This John of St Laurence had been the only person in the parish to hold the status of knight in 1253.[24] Thus, if the south chapel was established by an individual as a chantry, the St Laurence family would seem the most likely donors.

The new chapel was originally lower in height as can be seen clearly by looking at

---

[22] Cotton op.cit. p.188 propounds this theory based on an incorrect dating of the extension and a reference to Richard de Manston living in King John's day which he found in Philipot. What Philipott actually wrote was that he had found the name on an undated Pipe Roll which he thought might have come from King John's reign but the rolls have since been published by the Pipe Rolls Society and no such entry has been found for this time. Thomas Philipott, *Villare Cantianum* (London, 1659) p.388

[23] George Turner, Herbert Salter (ed.) *The Register of St Augustine's Abbey, Canterbury, commonly called the Black Book* (London, 1915) pp. 41-44

[24] James Greenstreet, 'Holders of Knights Fees in Kent at the Knighting of the King's Son' in *Archaeologia Cantiana* vol. 12 (1878) p.204

the outside wall. It was raised to match the height of the chapel built to the north (on the right as you face it from the church gate) some fifty years or so later.

Fourteenth Century

Around 1340, a chapel was built on the north side, the area today occupied by the vestry and organ. As part of this extension, the turret into the tower was demolished. Based on the evidence of memorials to the Manston family, it has been supposed that this chapel was set up as a chantry by them and this is possible, although a priest was not appointed by the Manston family to say masses until 1487 and the earliest surviving brass is dated 1444, a century later.[25] In 1631, Weevor recorded just one memorial to the Manston family existing, an undated one to Roger which disappeared in the course of the next century.[26]

There is a lay subsidy roll of 1334 listing all the taxpayers which provides a means of establishing the identities of the wealthiest people in the area who were most likely to have contributed to the building cost. The tax was calculated to represent a tenth of the value of the moveable goods of the householder. On this roll, William of Manston paid 13s 4d which placed him nineteenth in the list and meant he had goods worth the equivalent of around £5000 today.[27] The Manston family had clearly risen sharply in the fifty or so years since the Romescot tax assessment for then they had been charged sums from a halfpenny to a penny showing their moveable goods were worth around £100.[28] By contrast, the St Laurence family had fallen in status with their estate now valued at less than a quarter of the Manstons whereas fifty years before they had been worth almost

---

[25] PCC 11/2/324: a précis appears in Cotton op.cit. p254

[26] John Weevor *Ancient funerall monuments* (London, 1631) p.267. By the time Lewis wrote in 1723, the memorial was missing. Lewis was the first person to state that these memorials were in the North Chancel. John Lewis, *The History and Antiquities Ecclesiastical and Civil of the Isle of Tenet in Kent*, (London, 1723) Appendix p.97

[27] H.A. Hanley and C.W. Chalklin. 'The Kent Lay Subsidy Roll of 1334/5'. in *Kent Records* vol 18 (1964) pp 58-172

[28] Turner and Salter op.cit. pp.41-43. This increased wealth made them a target for attack. On Christmas Eve 1365, William Uncle broke into William Manston's home and stole linen, silverware and jewellery. He also beat the servants and raped Manston's wife. It would appear that Manston was not at home and that Uncle had accomplices. For his crime, Uncle was sentenced to death but he was pardoned by the King for an unknown reason. *Calendar of Patent Rolls* Edward III vol. 13 p.196. Uncle was clearly a wealthy man in his own right for in 1377, he and his wife, sold land they owned in St Laurence, Minster and Monkton for what would today be over sixty thousand pounds. Kent Archaeological Society *Kent Records: Feet of Fines Richard II*, vol 4 part 4 (2007) no 7.

eight times more. Other wealthy landowners in 1334 who may have contributed to the building cost include the widows of Robert of Dumpton and Robert Rosslin, Stephen Curling, Thomas Terry, Nicholas of Sandwich and Lawrence Craw.[29] However, there is a coat of arms at the west end just beneath the roof and this appears to belong to John Parys who in 1334 was the sixth wealthiest man living in the Thanet coastal towns.[30] He had no known connection to the Manston family but the presence of his arms suggests he was the major benefactor.[31] His family were prominent ship masters carrying troops to Crécy and Poitiers and commanding the 300 ton *Marie* for Richard II.[32] However, the cost of building made it unlikely that any one person or family was responsible. Over the centuries many medieval monuments have been destroyed or stolen or moved. For example, there were memorials to the Ellington family somewhere in the church, the existence of which we only know about from a chance comment made by an elderly resident to an author who decried "the injuries of time and barbarous hands."[33] There is no certainty that the Manston memorials were the only ones in this area and it is likely they were not.

One of the reasons that it was possible for such major construction projects to take place was that labour was cheap. This situation was about to change with the arrival of the Black Death in July 1348. Raging for two years, it is estimated to have killed between a third and half of the country's population and the Isle of Thanet was not immune. Communities such as those at Shuart and Woodchurch may have been wiped out either then or in the subsequent major outbreaks of 1361 and 1368. Most of the men who built the north chapel would have lived through it. The disease affected livestock as well as people and the reduced size of the labour force caused wages to increase dramatically. A Thanet ploughman prior to the Black Death earned 7s a year but 14s afterwards whilst a farm bailiff saw his earnings rise from 13s 8d per annum to 26s 4d.[34] The loss of stock combined with increased costs had a major impact on the lives of landowners and the amount of money they had available to give to the church. In 1300-1350, the period before the Black Death, it was possible to establish and equip a chapel within an existing building for around £75 which would be about £52,000 today. By the end of the same century, that cost would have increased to nearer £400 which would be over £270,000

---

[29] By the time of the Lay Subsidy, around 90% of the taxpayers had surnames. On the Romescot listing, only around 30% had recognisable surnames, the rest took their name from where they lived. This development suggests a period of population growth.

[30] The Lay Subsidy did not separate out the inhabitants of Ramsgate, Broadstairs and Margate but his arms in St Laurence would indicate that he lived in Ramsgate.

[31] John Papworth, *Ordinary of British Armorials* (London, 1874) p.377.

[32] Andrew Ayton and Craig Lambert, 'A Maritime Community in War and Peace: Kentish Ports, Ships and Mariners 1320-1400', *Archaeologia Cantiana* vol. 134 (2014) p.75

[33] Philipott op.cit. p.387. The speaker gave no details of the monuments merely said there had been a number of them which had all been removed, he thought because they were ancient and the family no longer existed in the parish. The Ellingtons ceased to reside at St Laurence around 1480.

[34] Quested op.cit. pp.32-33

today.[35]   It is not surprising that there were to be no further extensions to St Laurence church.

The new chapel was built taller than the south chapel which necessitated raising the roof of the latter. This roof with its four crown posts is still visible today almost seven hundred years later. The extent of the alteration can be clearly viewed from outside. Although the tracery is a nineteenth century reproduction, it will also be seen that the north and south chapels have quite different windows.

To the eastward end of the new arch built as part of the creation of the new chapel can be seen carved symbols of the Holy Trinity. This may indicate that the chapel was originally dedicated to the Trinity.

Some other work was done to the church building in the fourteenth century and this includes the enlarging of the west door, a sure indicator of its continued usage. Since this doorway was destroyed in 1858, our only representation of it comes from a sketch made by Miss Evans in 1817 in which, sadly, most of it is obscured by the graves in front. It is likely that this work was carried out either just before or just after the Black Death. The west door was clearly used at festivals and funerals and whenever there was a procession for in 1525 Robert Oxenden asked to be buried beside the west door "in the procession way."

Fifteenth Century

The fifteenth century saw a flowering of piety across the country and this was reflected at St Laurence. Fear of judgment and the belief that the recitation of masses would benefit the souls of the deceased who were in purgatory led to the creation of guilds which operated rather like an early twentieth century friendly society. A group of people would come together, often united by a shared occupation or interest in a particular saint, and they would contribute an amount of money each year into a general fund. That money would be used to pay for a mass when a member died and to provide a pall to cover the body. The guild would come together at least once a year for a special meal and a mass in whatever part of the church they had chosen to adopt and where they maintained lights in front of a particular image. Some guilds were particularly active as fund raisers for the church and they provided altar frontals and items such as communion

---

[35] Michael Hicks, 'The Rising Price of Piety in the Later Middle Ages' in Janet Burton (ed.) *Monasteries and Society in the British Isles in the Later Middle Ages* (London, 2008) p.97. The cost of building the actual chapel as well would have substantially increased these figures.

vessels. Others were more involved with charity seeking to help out the widows and orphans of past members when they were in need. We know from wills that a number of such guilds existed at St Laurence though we have no sets of their accounts or details of how they operated. Both men and women were involved in guilds, though it is unknown whether they were mixed or separate. Christianne Howglot in 1500, for example, spoke of being a "sister" in a number of guilds just as Richard Saunder in 1467 spoke of being a "brother" in several. It is possible that some of the guilds were related to localities for Thomas Knoller in 1501 made reference to the Hocktide taper maintained by East Cliffsend.[36]

It is from wills that we are able to form a picture of how the church was set out at this time and how it would have looked on the eve of the Reformation.

In addition to the main altar in the chancel, there were three chapels. These were dedicated to Our Lady (the Blessed Virgin Mary), to St Anthony and to St James. If the Manston family were originally laid to rest in the area now occupied by the vestry, this must have been the Lady Chapel because Joan St Nicholas, daughter of Roger Manston in her will of 1499 specified she wished to be buried there: "my tomb to be closed with a stone of marble with images thereupon graven of laton of me and of my husband and of the number of my children."[37] Her brass is still in the church though it was moved in the twentieth century but that of her husband disappeared centuries ago. Nobody else appears to have left instructions to be buried in this chapel in the fifteenth century which supports the idea that it had by then become a private chantry chapel.

By contrast, we have evidence of a number of people requesting to be buried in the chancel of St James which was on the opposite side of the church. These include Richard Saunder 1467, John Thatcher 1485, Collette Thatcher 1502 and John Pawlyn 1518.[38] There were also numerous bequests to maintain lights in this area, for example from Laurence Gibb in 1463, Stephen Grant 1474, John Walden 1477, Thomas Frost 1479, John Saunder 1502. The gagged head to be seen above the present font may have marked the entrance. Evidence was found during 1888 renovations of an interior wall or screen being erected part way down to separate this from the chapel to the east.

The chapel of St Anthony occupied the current side chapel. It was built to honour St Anthony of Padua who was a colleague of St Francis of Assisi and accepted as the patron saint of fishermen, sailors, pig farmers and horses. He was evidently popular at St Laurence where there were a number of bequests related to him such as Henry Pawlyn

---

[36] Hussey op.cit. p.270. Hocktide was the holiday immediately after Easter which was celebrated by fairs and church fundraising events.

[37] Arthur Hussey, *Testamenta Cantiana*, (London, 1907), p.268. Laton is the material we refer to as brass. The book was published after Cotton wrote which explains his incorrect assumptions about the layout of the church and dedications therein. The chapel was never known as either the Manston Chapel or St Catherine's.

[38] The Thatchers succeeded the Ellington family and it is likely that they chose this area because the memorials to the Ellingtons were there.

seeking burial in his chapel in 1501, Thomas Coppin leaving a pound of wax to make candles to be lit in his honour in 1474 and John Frost leaving money in 1484.[39] That a chapel was built to him in a church owned by a Benedictine abbey suggests that either the Franciscan friars were active in the parish at this time or that someone was particularly inspired by their work.

In addition to these formal chapels, there were a number of areas where images were displayed and which would have had lights burning in front of them. Lights could be purchased by individuals but were often maintained by guilds, much as today a particular group such as the Mothers' Union might accept responsibility for the flowers in a certain area. There were three images of the Blessed Virgin one of which was on the left hand side of the high altar. The other two celebrated her nativity and assumption. Sometimes the gifts toward these were made in cash such as the 4d left by William Taylor in 1473 and also by Stephen Grant in 1474, but often it was in grain which not only had a monetary value but could be used to make bread for the poor. Examples include the bushel of barley left by Richard Curling in 1463 and the bushel of corn from William Jenkin in 1485.

There were also lights to St George, St John the Baptist, St Catherine, St Margaret, St Michael, St Stephen and St Thomas (Becket) of Canterbury.[40] Some of these images would have adorned the early fifteenth century screen which today stands in the Thurstin room whilst others would have been stood in other parts of the church.

The choice of saints is interesting and says something about the interests of the parishioners. St George was associated with farmers, St John the Baptist with the sick, St Stephen with stone masons, St Michael with soldiers, St Margaret with pregnant women, St Catherine with millers and potters.

The most prominent images would have stood on the rood screen. This was erected in the early fifteenth century and would have been a much more substantial structure than the high beam seen today which dates from the 1930s. An ornately carved screen would have stood at ground level, painted and bedecked with images. Above would have been a wide platform or rood loft on which stood statues of Christ on the cross and St Laurence. The entire rood was covered in gold as was the statue of St Laurence. In 1515, Margery Byle left £2 for the re-gilding of both. In 1497, Edward Coppin left 6s 8d to paint the rood screen plus a further shilling provided that the painter inscribe his name on it as the giver. The fact that at least three people gave quite generous donations to the repair of the rood loft in the period 1498-1500 suggests that it was by then in need of restoration. Traditionally, the rood loft would have been used for the reading of the Passion just before Easter. At St Laurence, it was entered by a winding staircase to the north of the pillar behind the present pulpit.

The rood screen and loft would have effectively meant that the congregation

---

[39] St Anthony was not canonised until 1232 so the south chapel must have been built after this date.
[40] There is no evidence that the light to St Thomas received a particularly high amount of bequests and nothing to support the idea that there was ever a chapel named after him.

could barely see any of the service and this, combined with the fact that it was in Latin, gave rise to all sorts of superstitions and errors. The phrase "hocus pocus" still used today is a corruption of "hoc est corpus" said by the priest during the words of consecration. People had very little idea of participating in worship – most masses were said by the priest alone – and they were restricted in the parts of the church they could access by a variety of screens. The fact that they were so cut off from worship is one of the reasons they tended to show their devotion to the saints which were figures they could see.

A considerable amount of work was carried out to the church in this century to enhance and beautify the building. A new roof was installed in the nave in the middle of the century. Restored in the 1800s, this roof with its two crown posts, can still be seen. At some point, the great east window was altered from its original three narrow lancets to the single window of the size we see today, though the present window only dates from 1902. This would have substantially brightened the interior and was a work only made possible by the reducing cost of glass. Extra illumination would also have come from the addition of two small round windows in the gables of the north and south aisles at the west end. Also in this century, the upper chamber above the porch was demolished and the whole was remodelled. It may be assumed this last was done close in time to the work on the north door since they are almost identical in design.

The most significant work to the church related to the Tower. At the Privy Council meeting of 26th August 1439 it was reported that the bell tower of St Laurence in Thanet had been struck by lightning during a thunderstorm and had been ruined by the resultant fire.[41] Evidence of this fire can still be seen on the inside of the tower but the report is also significant because accidents to parish churches were not the sort of subject to ever feature on the agenda of a Privy Council meeting. The fact that it was mentioned shows that the church tower must have been used as a beacon by ships which is why its destruction would cause a problem. Troops were then gathering at Sandwich ready to go to France and they may well have witnessed the fire and reported it because they were concerned that its loss could affect their ships coming home. The tower was rebuilt with flint and the opportunity was taken to increase its height by almost six feet and to add battlements and carved heads. The difference between the old and new work is clearly to be seen on the tower which has a distinct two tone appearance. In 1888, one of the heads was removed as part of the restoration which enabled it to be seen clearly for the first time by parishioners.

It is possible that the new work replaced a wooden steeple. The first picture of St Laurence church was drawn by Thomas of Elmham just over

---

[41] Harris Nicolas, *Proceedings and Ordinances of the Privy Council of England* vol. 5 (London, 1835) p.386

twenty years before the fire and it shows St Laurence with a spire. There are two possible explanations for this. The first is that as Thomas was based in Canterbury, he did not know what the church looked like and so just assumed it had a spire. The second is that he had actually seen it and drew it from memory. It was not unknown for stone towers to have wooden steeples.[42]

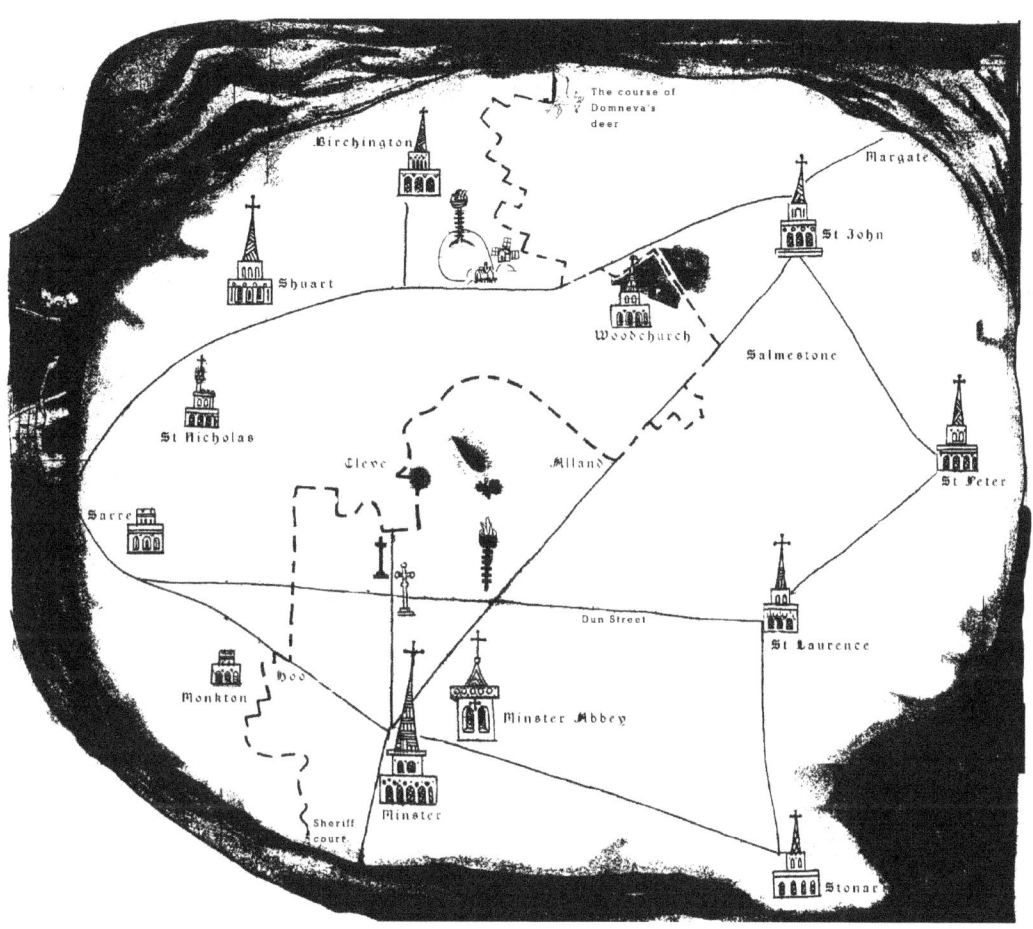

Possibly because the severe damage to the tower and its consequent rebuilding necessitated the clearing of considerable space on the north side of the church, or maybe in order to brighten what was a dark area, three of the windows on that side were replaced with wider and flatter topped windows. Only the window at the west end was left untouched in the Early English style. At the same time, a new north door was added. Having been sealed up, this door is only evident from inside the church and it is

---

[42] Platt op.cit. p.15

impossible to say whether it replaced an earlier door or was cut new. It is in line with the south porch so there have been suggestions that it could have been used during baptisms as a devil's door. There was allegedly a superstition which said that the devil, having been exorcised from the baby in the porch, would run into the church and that someone should therefore open the nearest door to let him out so that the child would have a trouble free life. This was not church teaching and it did not make much sense as an idea. Why would the devil not just run away from the church porch? Besides, the first recorded mention of this tradition dates from 1851, over four hundred years later.[43] The association of the north side with evil has long traditions stemming both from the Bible when Isaiah records Lucifer as saying: "I will sit also upon the mount of the congregation, in the sides of the north" (Isa. 14:13) through to folk memories of rampaging Vikings coming from the north. It would be easy, therefore, to see how such an idea could come about but it is more likely that the door was used simply as an extra entrance. The fact that the westernmost window was not altered supports the idea that this area of the church was set aside for some special purpose. The north side of a church was generally associated with women due to evil Eve being blamed for man's fall which is why Lady Chapels were usually on the north and why churchings (the blessing of women after childbirth) tended to be held there.[44] The most likely explanation for the

door is that the font stood in that corner of the church. The image of St Margaret may have stood here also.

Probably the last change made to the church in the medieval period was the new roof in the chancel. That is most likely to date from the reign of Henry VII (1485-1509) although it could be early in his son's reign. It is a barrel roof with finely carved bosses.

Memorials

Toward the rear of the south chapel can be seen two brasses. That on the left is of Nicholas Manston who died on 6th August 1444. It shows him in full armour This is

---

[43] R Hawkes in *Notes And Queries* (1851) no 46 p.251. Had the practice been a common medieval superstition, it would have been referenced in reformation sermons or articles and it is not suggesting that the idea originated with Victorian antiquarians.
[44] Even today at weddings, the bride's family sit on the left or north side.

plated with fashionable oreillets (ear covers) and a skirt made of metal bands called taces. The spurs are long as is typical of this period. On his right hip is a dagger and on his left is his sword with a jewelled pommel. Both are sheathed to show he is a man of peace, and this piety is further demonstrated by his hands being clasped together in prayer. Around his neck is a collar of esses, an item made famous by its depiction on the Holbein portrait of Sir Thomas More. This symbolised his allegiance to the Lancastrian dynasty, the three kings Henry IV (who usurped Richard II), Henry V (who won the Battle of Agincourt) and Henry VI (reputed to be a saint). The collars were the gift of the sovereign and the pendants varied according to the giver, thus those given by Henry IV bore a buckle, by Henry VII and Henry VIII a portcullis and rose and those from Henry V and Henry VI had a ring. Nicholas' collar has a ring and matches that which can be seen on the effigy of Queen Joan, widow of Henry IV, in Canterbury Cathedral which was made seven years before. This collar would ordinarily only have been worn in the presence of the sovereign.[45]

At his feet is a dog, probably not representing a real one but rather as a symbol of faithfulness. His status is further shown by the extreme length of the points on his shoes, sumptuary laws of the time defining the length a man could wear depending on his place in society. His age is unknown but it is likely that he was under forty.[46] There does not appear to have ever been a memorial to his wife so she may have remarried. Her name was Eleanor Haut and her father was one of the benefactors to the building of the nave at Canterbury Cathedral. The close similarity of Nicholas Manston's brass with that of John Frogenhall, who died in the same year, in Teynham church suggests that a standard pattern was used rather than the image being based on a personal likeness.[47] It is also interesting to note that although there are records of many of the Manston family serving in various conflicts from the 1360s to 1460s, Nicholas' name never appears. Perhaps he had a health impediment which prevented this. His decision to be shown in armour may therefore be aspirational rather than factual.

On the pillar to the right is the brass of his niece Joan who married Thomas St Nicholas. She is wearing a butterfly headdress which involved her hair being concealed in a cap which was then covered with a starched veil probably of a very fine silk. By the time she died in 1499, this was an old fashioned look suggesting that either she continued to wear the style because it suited her or, more likely, she chose to have herself portrayed

---

[45] J.G.N. 'On Collars of the Royal Livery' in *Gentleman's Magazine* (December 1842) pp. 595-597. The image of the collar is taken from p.597
[46] This is surmise based simply on the supposition that his father was a young man when he fought at Agincourt.
[47] The sketch of the Teynham brass is from *Archaeologia Cantiana* vol 1 (1858) p.89

as she had looked as a younger woman.[48] Her gown is simple and she is wearing fur cuffs which would have been detachable. These were a source of warmth and wealth. The neckline is more in line with Tudor fashions and there is evidence of a kirtle or under dress at both the neck and in the skirt where two different fabrics can be seen. Around her waist is a girdle which is highly decorated and seems to be studded with jewels. She is not wearing any personal jewellery. In her hands she is holding a sprig of something, probably rosemary which was the herb associated with remembrance. The brass therefore asks those who see it to remember her and – because this was erected in Catholic times – to pray for her.

These brasses were originally in the chapel which was converted into a vestry, approximately where the desk now stands. They were then moved to a screen which stood outside the vestry facing into the north transept. In the early twentieth century, they were moved to hang on the north wall of the high chancel just to the left of the communion rails. They were moved to the side chapel in 1970.

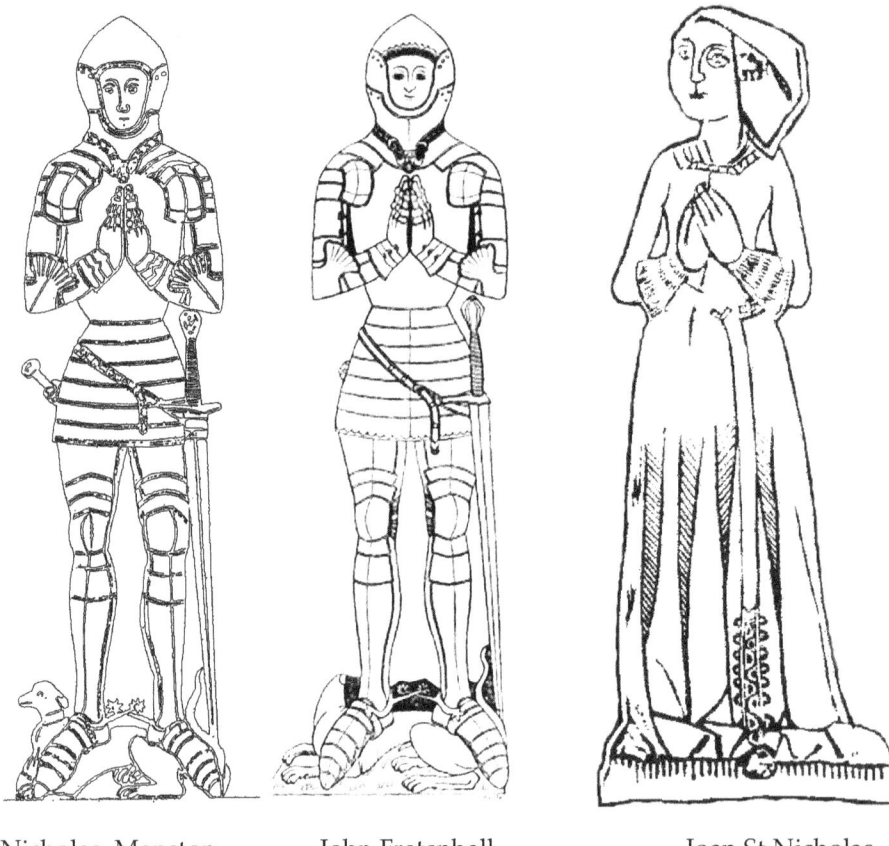

Nicholas Manston   John Fretenhall   Joan St Nicholas

---

[48] Her head-dress is identical to that shown on the brass of Lady Peyton in Isleham which dates from fifty years before.

Bells

Initially the tower probably had two bells. One would have been used to summon people for services on Sunday and another to toll for the dead. This latter would have been rung by the parish clerk when news was received of a death, the manner of ring denoting whether it was a man, woman or child who had passed.[49] There may have been a third bell to mark the start of curfew, the time at which fires were due to be covered, though one of the other two bells may have been used for this. Just as today, money and availability would have determined activity. If the church could afford to have different bells for different purposes, then they would have done so: if not, the same bell would have been used for everything.

A small sanctus bell was probably added in the late thirteenth century to mark the consecration of the elements during the Mass. This would not have been part of the main peal. In East Kent, the sanctus bell was often known as the wakerell and it is interesting that a family of that name still live in the parish. This bell, may also have been used for the angelus.[50]

Given that by the early seventeenth century, there was a treble, second, third and great bell as well as another small bell, it would appear that either in the middle ages or in the sixteenth century, more bells were added to the tower. It is totally impossible to say when this happened although it is likely that changes were made following the fire of 1439 and consequent rebuilding of the tower.

Music Book

On display on the southern side of the church is a fragment of a fourteenth or early fifteenth century service book. This was found only in the late 1880s when one of the churchwardens picked up the Elizabethan parish register and found the cover starting to fall off. He went to pull it together and discovered that the cover was in fact a piece of old vellum with musical notation scribed upon it. The document was removed and analysed by Father Egan of St Augustine's Abbey in Ramsgate who cleaned it and identified it as belonging to an ancient Antiphonary, a volume containing the Gregorian setting of the Psalms and Antiphons (sung responses).[51] The two pages found covered the Antiphon of the Benedictus sung at Lauds and that of the Magnificat sung at Vespers together with an Antiphon and Hymn to commemorate St Elizabeth of Hungary. Part of this reads:

> Thirsting for God alone and hastening forward with this thirst upon her, she learnt to thwart the lusts of the flesh. World without end, Amen

---

[49] J. C. L. Stahlschmidt, *The Church Bells of Kent*, (London, 1887) p.127
[50] It was sold in 1599 since the Reformation outlawed such practices.
[51] Father Egan's full report together with illustrations and translations appears in Cotton's *History* pp.113-123

Her home and goods being taken from her, she blessed the Lord whilst she begs for food and shelter in the furnace of poverty. World without end, Amen

For such great virtues of a faithful handmaid let every spirit bless the Lord from the heavens. World without end, Amen

Glory be to Thee, O Good Jesus, now and for evermore, Thou who aidest abundantly those struggling in the fight and givest a crown as a reward to him who conquers manfully.

Pray for us, O Holy Elizabeth, that we may be made worthy of the promises of Christ.

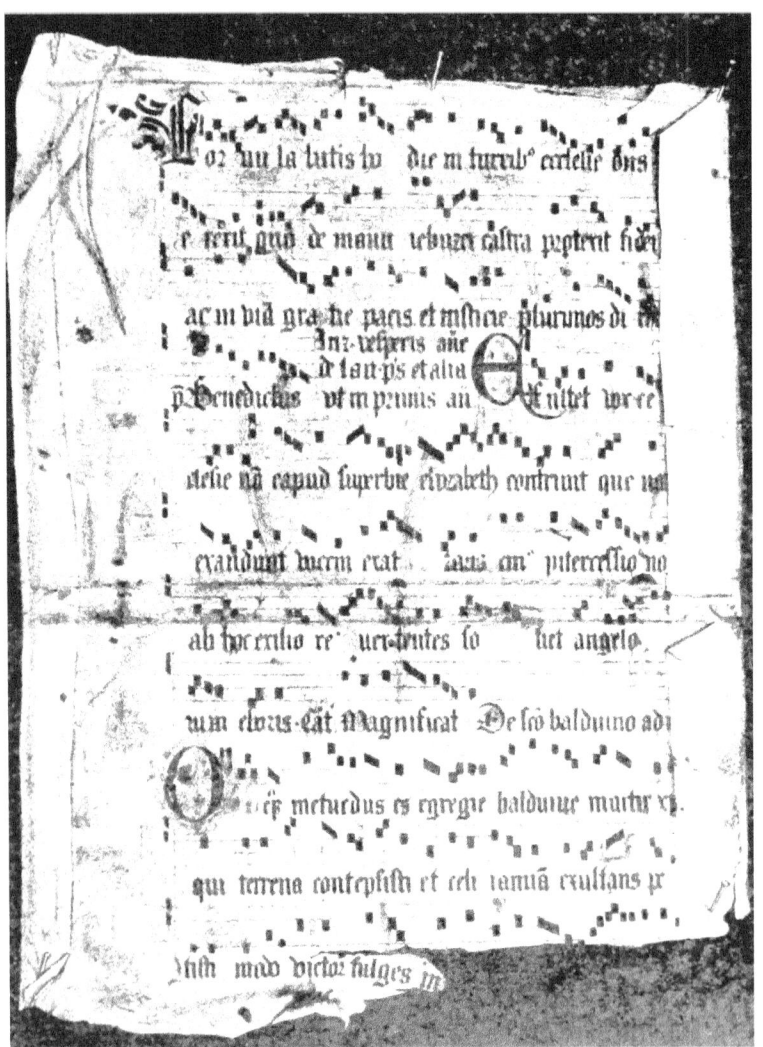

How the church came to have such a document is unknown. It may have been part of a book used in the church which was discarded at the Reformation but such a degree of choral singing would not normally be found in a parish church. It may have come from the library of St Augustine's in Canterbury or most likely was simply bought second hand as cheap wrapping paper and used without a second thought.

CLERGY AND STAFF

Very little is known about the individual clergy who served the parish in the Middle Ages. Even many of the names are lost so it is impossible to determine how many vicars the parish had during this time.

In 1301, the vicar's name was **Edmund** and he has the dubious distinction of being the only vicar to have been excommunicated. His crime was denying the authority of the Archbishop of Canterbury in favour of the Pope. The Archbishop promptly had him thrown in jail where he remained for two years until the Pope ruled in 1303 that vicars of churches belonging to the Abbey of St Augustine's were to be managed by the Abbot except in the area of spiritual jurisdiction where they were to be ruled by the Archbishop.[52] Edmund had been vicar since 1286 so he was probably not a young man by medieval standards. Presumably because his incarceration had lost him income and left him in distress, the Archbishop made a payment of five shillings to him in July 1305.[53]

John Blyce was vicar during the Peasants Revolt, arriving in 1370 and staying until 1395. He then exchanged livings with **John Wylly** of Reculver who stayed at St Laurence to 1409. This was a particularly difficult time with Richard II being usurped by Henry IV in 1399 and the subsequent political difficulties that followed.[54]

In 1416, **John Byfield**, vicar of St Laurence appeared in a court case at Canterbury in support of William Verich who had been accused of theft. His evidence saw Verich cleared and Verich later prosecuted Richard Cokelyn for falsely accusing him.[55]

It is possible, however, despite knowing little about the clergy themselves to imagine how they lived. Having taken vows of celibacy, they would all have been single men and most would have come from families who were based in East Kent. Some would have been educated but it is likely that others were barely literate. In 1188, Pope Celestine wrote to the Abbot of St Augustine's to complain of the practice whereby impecunious vicars were allowing totally unqualified people to take services in return for a fee. The Pope noted that churches were thus "defrauded of their rightful possessions and, what is worse, divine services are performed with the minimum of decency."[56] Whether this happened at St Laurence is unknown but it was clearly a common practice in the area. Although we have no images of clergy at St Laurence, Monkton church has a brass of one of their vicars which gives an idea of what they would have worn.

---

[52] David Oliver, *Late Medieval Thanet and the Cinque Ports*, (Broadstairs, 1997) p.33
[53] *Calendar of Patent Rolls - Edward I* vol.4 p.301. This was probably around a month's income.
[54] Cotton op.cit. p.158
[55] Brian Woodcock, *Medieval Ecclesiastical Courts in the Diocese of Canterbury*, (Oxford, 1952) p.58
[56] *Thorne's Chronicle*, op.cit. p.131

With regard to residence, the vicar would have been accommodated in a cottage to the side of the church, almost certainly on the site of the current vicarage.[57] It is impossible to know what this property looked like but in 1268, the vicar of Eynsham was given a house by his Abbey which consisted of a hall, a chamber for sleeping, a kitchen, a bakehouse, a larder and a latrine and it is reasonable to suppose that the vicar of St Laurence received something similar.[58] Probably a century or so later, a house was built for the chantry priest at Ellington and this building stood until 1892 and the vicar would have been at least as well accommodated as the chantry priest.

The vicar's duties would have involved:

- taking daily and weekly services. These would have included as a daily minimum Mass and the services of Matins, Prime, Evensong, Nones, Lauds, Vespers and Compline
- taking baptisms, funerals and weddings
- hearing confessions
- visiting the sick

---

[57] In 1993 the house was renamed The Rectory.
[58] Platt op.cit. p.58

- preaching four sermons a year covering the Ten Commandments, Seven Deadly Sins and Seven Virtues and the Seven Sacraments
- keeping the vicarage in good repair
- ensuring that both church and churchyard were treated reverently at all times and excommunicating any who played games or conducted business therein
- farming the glebe which was the land provided to sustain him
- maintaining hospitality at the vicarage
- collecting tithes and mortuary fees on behalf of the Abbey and reporting anyone who failed to pay
- investigating morals and reporting breaches to the archdeacon's court[59]

It was these last two functions which not only took a large proportion of his time but meant that he was often seen as the enemy of the people. Tithes were exacted not just on cash income but on wheat, wool, lambs, calves, geese, pigs, doves, cheese, milk, hemp, flax, merchandise, apples, pears, garden produce and eggs.[60] These items would have been handed over quarterly at Minster to the Abbot's representatives who would have come over to the Abbey for a few days for such a purpose. Had the parish had a rector instead of a vicar, the tithes would have been kept by him.

In the mid fifteenth century, a manual was published called *Instructions for Parish Priests*. In this John Myrc said that baptisms should only take place at Easter and Whitsun unless the child was at risk of death. The vicar should then spend eight days at these festivals performing one baptism after another. He also said that the priest should take steps to ensure that families did not allow their children to sleep together after the ages of seven lest there be encouragement to vice and offspring result.[61]

From 1237, the vicar himself would have received a salary or stipend of ten marks a year, the equivalent of £4000 in today's money and in line with the earnings of a craftsman such as a wheelwright.[62] This amount would have been confiscated if the said vicar was "proved for certain ever to have asked for more." [63] For additional income and food, he would have had to rely on gifts when he visited the sick and what he could earn from the small amount of glebe. From 1275, he would also have received a proportion of burial fees as well but the Taxatio shows that in 1291-2, his regular income was £5, still worth around £4000.[64]

---

[59] Platt op.cit. pp.48-49

[60] *Thorne's Chronicle* op.cit. pp.553-554

[61] Edward Peacock (ed.), *Instructions for Parish Priests by John Myrc*, (London, 1868) pp.5,7

[62] Hicks op.cit. p.98

[63] ibid. p.200

[64] http://www.hrionline.ac.uk/taxatio/benkey. The vicar of St Peter's received the same amount, the vicar of St John's received £5 6s 8d.

That the vicar was seen as poor can be seen from a 1385 tax return which enables a comparison to be made between the value of different vicarages. The vicar of St Laurence paid 5s which was a twentieth of his annual income. The vicar of St Peter's paid the same but St John's paid 5s 4d, Woodnesborough 10s, Monkton 10s, Reculver 16s 8d, Faversham £1 and Minster £1. He was, however, better off than the vicar of Sarre whose income was said to be so low that they could not even tax him. [65]

Even with a parish population of maybe five hundred[66], there would have been a considerable amount of work and the vicar would have had assistance. The number and nature of his helpers would have depended very much on what he could afford as he was generally responsible for hiring and paying them. There is no evidence that the Abbey ever supplied a chaplain or even a deacon so it is probable that he had just a parish clerk whose role would have been to:

- assist the priest by singing or reciting the responses in services
- read the epistle at mass
- clean the church including damping the earthen floor
- prepare the church for services including the communion vessels, censer, vestments, books, altar frontals and lights
- ring the bell for services and curfew
- accompany the priest to visit the sick carrying a lighted candle and ringing a bell whilst chanting
- carry the cross in processions at funerals and festivals[67]

He would also have had an informal, but vital role, at weddings. Prior to the Reformation, these were conducted in Latin which meant that neither bride nor groom would have been able to follow the service or had any real idea of what promises they were making. The clerk's job would have been to prod the said parties at the appropriate point so they could signify their assent. Depending on whether there was money to pay another wage, he may also have had to dig the ground for burials and set traps for vermin.

---

[65] ibid. pp.633-634
[66] The 1334 subsidy suggests a taxpaying population for the Isle of Thanet of around 3000. St Laurence would have comprised about a seventh of that suggesting that the taxpaying population was just over 400. Assuming that half the population was too poor to pay tax, the total just before the Black Death might be estimated to have been around 800 and after it, just under 500.
[67] Platt op.cit. pp.61-62. See also Myrc's comments in Peacock op.cit. p.60

In addition, churchwardens would have existed to assist with parish work. It is unknown when they were introduced and different parishes would have felt the need for them at different times, but it is likely that St Laurence had at least one from around 1275 and two by the fifteenth century. Their role would have covered:

- setting and collecting rent on church owned property including buildings and cattle
- handling money left to the church for masses
- purchasing raw materials for candles and arranging for them to be made in the church wax house
- keeping the church and churchyard in good repair (excepting the chancel)
- selecting craftsmen to work on the church and paying them
- ensuring the church had the correct mass books
- scheduling masses on the correct memorial days in line with bequests
- distributing alms to the poor
- raising funds for church repairs through collections and special events
- purchasing and maintaining vestments
- organising defences and maintaining arms

There would have been two further priests in the parish who were responsible for the two chantry chapels which existed. There was one dedicated to the Holy Trinity at Ellington on the site of what was for many years the girls secondary school, and another at West Cliffsend dedicated to the Holy Cross: Thomas Terry left two bushels of barley to the latter in 1500.[68] These chapels were independent of the church and their priests were privately paid out of money left by testators. It is unknown when either chapel was built or closed but both had disappeared prior to 1535.[69] Many such chapels closed in the late fifteenth century or early sixteenth as money to fund them simply ran out. Paying a priest to say a mass every day for your soul would have cost some £5 a year and there would also have been expenses associated with building maintenance, housing and feeding the priest and the cost of bread and wine. Moreover, costs naturally increased over the years. Inflation was rampant with prices more than doubling between 1480 and 1550. The fate of Holy Cross is unknown but Holy Trinity building survived into the nineteenth century although it was a ruin by 1646 and remained so as a drawing made in 1817 indicates.[70] Judging by the sketch, the chapel was built in the early fifteenth century although Dr Cotton believed the foundations were older.[71] It was a small building just ten feet by

---

[68] Hussey op.cit. p.270
[69] This is evident from the fact that neither was included in the *Valor Ecclesiasticus*
[70] Will of Robert Sprackling PROB11/199/141
[71] Cotton op.cit. p.218

fifteen and if this dating is accurate, it was almost certainly built by the Ellington family.[72]

The priest's house which was opposite the chapel was converted into a labourer's cottage and extended in 1640 but this was demolished in 1892 along with Ellington House when the park was created.

PEOPLE, EVENTS AND PLACES

Sheriffs of Kent

In the fourteenth and fifteenth century, the parish was home to three individuals who became Sheriff of Kent. They were:

    Ralph of St Laurence in 1327
    Thomas of St Laurence in 1333
    William Manston in 1436

The office of Sheriff was an ancient one and very prestigious. It involved a variety

---

[72] Zechariah Cozens, *A Tour through the Isle of Thanet* (London, 1793) p.67

of duties from assisting with tax assessments to empanelling juries and ensuring that judges' verdicts were carried out.

We do not know a great deal about these men. Ralph was a man clearly trusted by both Edward II and Edward III. In January 1326 he was made responsible for guarding the Thanet ports and for searching ships for letters "prejudicial to the Crown." Two years later, he was sent to value crops in Kent and then to sell them to raise money so that he King could pay back the loan he had accepted from bankers in Florence.[73] As a sign of favour, he was granted Stonar in 1325 together with the income from its crossing to Sandwich.[74] His main source of income remained land and he held property not just in this parish, but at Minster, Chislet and Swalecliffe.[75] In 1346 he was one of only five people in Thanet whose land holding was considered of sufficient value to create a liability to scutage or the charge levied by Edward III to knight the Black Prince.[76] This fee was £2 or around £950 in modern money so may have been an honour he would have liked to avoid.

His son Thomas is a more shadowy figure who appears only once in the records in 1343 when he was called upon to assist in the arrest of anyone "attempting to execute papal provisions to benefices in England after the proclamations against this."[77] This was a reference to the Statute of Provisors enacted against Pope Clement VI in Avignon by Edward III who was angry that money which should be used to support English churches and hospitals was being sent abroad leaving native souls at risk.

It was as Sheriff that William Manston attended the Parliament held in London for nine weeks from 21st January 1436/7. The king's mother, Queen Katherine, had died on 3rd January and William attended her funeral on behalf of the county on 9th February.[78] There was much discussion of issues relevant to the people of this area at that Parliament including coastal security and import and export duties. England had lost Paris to the French in 1436 and Calais was under threat which created fears of French raiding parties crossing the Channel to destroy property. Stonar had been annihilated by such a raid in 1385 so the parishioners would have been deeply concerned about their security. There were also worries about diminishing trade so the decision to charge merchants a shilling for every poundsworth of goods being either imported or exported but excluding exports of grain would have been particularly welcome to the local farmers.

Just over twenty years before becoming Sheriff, William Manston had served

---

[73] *Calendar of Patent Rolls* Edward II vol 5 p.208; Edward III vol 1 pp.344, 353

[74] *Calendar of Patent Rolls* Edward II vol. 5 p.25

[75] ibid. pp.63, 65, 129

[76] James Greenstreet, 'Assessments in Kent for the Aid to Knight the Black Prince' in *Archaeologia Cantiana* vol. 10 pp.115, 123. Nicholas of Sandwich was also listed as a major landowner in the parish.

[77] *Calendar of Patent Rolls* Edward III vol 6 p.100

[78] This is the French princess Katherine who features in Shakespeare's play *Henry V* trying to learn English. After the King died she married Owen Tudor from whom sprung the Tudor dynasty.

with his brother Roger at the Battle of Agincourt. As the elder brother, he had fought on horseback while his brother was an archer.[79] No memorial to William exists at St Laurence but he is remembered in Minster church where his arms appear on a misericord flanked by two fleur-de-lis.

It is uncertain whether the William Manston who was commissioned on 4th April 1451 to "array and try all men at arms, hobblers and archers within the Isle of Thanet and to lead them to the sea coast and other places in the island to resist the King's enemies and to take the muster of the same from time to time and to set up beacons in the usual places and to cause wards and watches to be kept, arresting and securing such as refuse to keep the same" was the man who had served as sheriff or his son of the same name.[80] The William who fought at Agincourt and served as Sheriff was probably born around 1390 so could have still been active in 1451. In 1450, a William Manston had been pardoned for his involvement in the rebellion led by Jack Cade[81] and although Henry VI was famed for his saintliness and forgiving nature, it would seem strange to entrust the defence of the island to someone who only months before had taken up arms against him and been involved in the pillaging of London citizens and murder of the Duke of Suffolk, effectively the country's prime minister. It is perhaps more likely that the son was the rebel and his father the trusted local administrator. Less than a year later, William received another commission on 17th February 1451/2 to "call together all the king's lieges of the county to publish and arrest certain who have conspired to subvert the realm as enemies and rebels."[82] The enemies referenced by these commissions were not the French but the Duke of York and his supporters. The petulant Duke was conducting a vendetta against the Duke of Somerset which had seen him raising thousands of men to march through London, demanding that he be recognised as Henry VI's heir and closest advisor, gathering an army at Blackheath and publishing letters of grievances. Although the Duke was defeated in 1452 he would rise again and start the Wars of the Roses.

As well as such special duties, William would have had the regular task of training local men to defend the region. The law requiring all men aged 15 to 60 to maintain a bow and arrows was passed in 1252 and communities were required to establish butts so that men could practice their skills. From 1363 until the end of Henry VIII's reign, it was compulsory for all men to attend the butts every Sunday after church. Boys were also generally taught the use of the weapon from the age of seven. Given the English reliance on the longbow which was so dramatically seen in battles from Crécy to

---

[79] http://www.medievalsoldier.org/Agincourt.php. It is likely that William was the son of either Edmund or Roger Manston who served as squires to Lord Cobham in the naval expedition of 1377-78.
[80] *Calendar of Patent Rolls* Henry VI vol 5 p. 443. A hobbler was a mounted soldier.
[81] William Durrant Cooper, 'Jack Cade's Followers in Kent' in *Archaeologia Cantiana* vol 7 (1868) pp. 268, 270
[82] *Calendar of Patent Rolls* Henry VI vol 5 p. 577

Agincourt, this responsibility of William Manston's was substantial.[83] The parish butts were opposite Lord of the Manor, close to the present Derwent Avenue.

Upper Court

In the middle ages, in addition to the area known as Nether or Lower Court, there was Upper Court. Prior to the Black Death, this was occupied by the St Laurence family but afterward it passed to the Criols or Kyriells. They built themselves a new manor house which was excavated as part of the preparations to build the Tesco superstore in Manston Road.[84] It was clearly a prestigious mansion with a moated orchard and its own chapel. Whether the family built the latter because they were very pious or because they had a difficult relationship with the vicar is unknown. It was quite common for manorial lords to build their own chapels if they lived some distance from the parish church but Upper Court was clearly close by.

The most famous member of the family was Sir Thomas Kyriell who was a noted military commander in France from 1428 to 1439 when he became Lieutenant of Calais.[85] He returned to England in 1444 only to be accused of corruption in that he had withheld wages from the garrison at Gisors. He returned to France in 1450 but was captured at Formigny. Back home, he served as MP for Kent in 1455 and 1460 and in August 1457 he led an attack on the French who were raiding Sandwich. Throughout his life, he had been a loyal Lancastrian but in June 1460 he decided to change sides and join the Yorkists. They promptly elected him as a Knight of the Garter although he never lived to be installed. Thomas had joined the Yorkists because he supported their desire to replace those whom they identified as being bad advisers of the Lancastrian Henry VI. Thomas' son in law, Sir John Fogge, was a keen Yorkist and would be Treasurer of the Royal Household for Edward IV from 1461-69. Yorkist policy changed in October 1460 when Richard, Duke of York, returned from exile and claimed the throne. Civil war resulted and Thomas served with the Yorkists. At the second Battle of St Albans on 17th February 1461, he was given responsibility for guarding the Yorkists most prominent prisoner, Henry VI , a position of great trust. He did this loyally but the Yorkists lost the overall battle. The newly released Henry VI promised Thomas a pardon in recognition of past services but his wife, Queen Margaret, was not so forgiving of a man she saw as a turncoat. She ordered his execution which duly took place watched by the eight year old Lancastrian Prince of Wales.[86]

---

[83] Margaret Bolton, *The Isle of Thanet: Its History, People and Buildings*, (Thanet 2006) p.39. The longbow was last used in the 1644 battle of Tippermuir.
[84] Phil Andrews et.al., *Kentish Sites and Sites of Kent*, (Wessex Archaeology Report, no 24, 2009) p.212. The house was demolished in the seventeenth century.
[85] Kyriell also held land at Sarre, Westenhanger and in Devon and Somerset so was unlikely to have been a regular worshipper at St Laurence.
[86] For a full account of the life of Richard, Duke of York and his claim to the throne see Margaret Bolton, *Seven Centuries of Service*, (Eire, 2013).

Henry of Newington

That the people of St Laurence detested the Abbey was a well known fact in the middle ages. They resented the fact that it owned its land and they had to pay taxes upon it. Some of these were in money but most were in goods or services. For example, for every suling of land they had to:

- plough an acre of Abbey land or pay a shilling
- provide two lambs each June 24th or pay 18d
- take two and a half loads of barley to Minster for collection by the Abbey at Christmas
- take a further two and a half loads of barley to Minster at Easter[87]

A suling was around two hundred acres so would have been a single estate for farmers such as the Curlings at Chilton or an area divided up into smaller plots by maybe a dozen families. These payments were in addition to the tithes they paid of grain, wool, fruit, eggs, garden produce, livestock and cheese to St Laurence church itself which collected them on behalf of the Abbey. There were also other levies made such as that raised in 1273 when the Abbot decided he wanted to buy a new palfrey. The animal cost around £2 but he collected £132 in taxation, £53 6s 8d of which came from Minster and its daughter chapels of St Laurence, St Peter and St John.[88]

Something else which made them angry was having to attend Canterbury for administrative and legal matters. This was a long journey. Parishioners had first to go to Sarre and then pay for a ferry journey to the mainland. It was expensive and time consuming taking normally two or three days for a return trip. Furthermore, for anyone with livestock – and that was virtually everyone except the very poorest in society – it was totally inconvenient. Animals could not be left unattended for a few days. In 1176, an appeal was made to Henry II that the Abbot should keep court at Minster instead but this was turned down. It became a much repeated request. In 1318, things boiled over into violence. Six hundred men attacked the Abbot's properties across the island with "bows, arrows, swords and sticks." They set fire to some buildings, cut down trees and assaulted everyone they could find who worked for the Abbey. One of their victims was Henry of Newington who was a monk working at Cliffsend. It is unknown what property the Abbey held there which required him being at least temporarily resident but it may have been a mill. They besieged him for six days before finally releasing him and selling him as a slave to Walter the chaplain for four shillings. The revolt lasted five weeks and it was said that over two hundred pounds worth of damage was done, around a hundred and thirty thousand pounds today. The Abbot had the rebels arrested and jailed and protested to the King about what he had been forced to endure. One can only imagine the

---

[87] *Thorne's Chronicle* op.cit. p.lxiv
[88] ibid. pp. xli, 259

Abbot's reaction when the response came back from Edward II pardoning the rebels "for the pity which we feel for the condition of the same people" and ordering their release.[89] What happened to Henry of Newington is unknown but it may be presumed that Walter was forced to return him to the Abbot. Whether he ever set foot again in Cliffsend after his harrowing experience cannot be said.

Peasants' Revolt

The basic story of the Peasant' Revolt is well known. In the summer of 1381, Wat Tyler led a revolt against the new poll tax taking his men to London where they met with the boy king Richard II on June 12th at Blackheath. The parish of St Laurence became involved in this event but the disturbances here related to local issues and were rather a case of people "jumping on the bandwagon".

The problems began on 10th June when four men broke into William Medmenham's home in Canterbury where they "feloniously trampled upon and carried away" goods worth ten pounds. The quartet included one man from Romney Marsh, one from Westgate plus John Read who was simply said to be of the Isle of Thanet and William Mund whose residence was not given.

Three days later, the sacristan and clerk at St John's, Margate, took advantage of having a crowd of people gathered for the festival of Corpus Christi, to call for a raid on the home of William Medmenham at Manston to "demolish his house and level it with the ground, and fling out the books and rolls found there, and to burn them with fire, and, if the said William could be found, that they should kill him, and cut off his head from his body."[90] The crowd agreed and duly made its way to Manston where they burnt the books and damaged property to the value of either one pound (the equivalent of almost two years wages for a labourer) or twenty marks which was over thirteen pounds and the equivalent of almost £9000 today.[91] The fact that witnesses disagreed so sharply about the value is evidence of the chaos that surrounded the attack. There is no evidence that any of the perpetrators were parishioners but the authorities were unable to identify all the members of the mob and only the leaders were prosecuted. It was said that the leaders had forced up to two hundred men to go with them.

The reason that William Medmenham was targeted was because he was a tax collector and steward of St Augustine's Abbey. He was also a Clerk of the Green Wax which meant that he collected fines levied by the Sheriff and justices.[92] He was presumably an elderly man by 1381 for almost forty years before he had been part of a commission to investigate arrears owed to the Abbot of St Augustine. His role was to report those who refused to pay, to issue fines, imprison anyone who stood in his way or

---

[89] ibid. pp.432-434
[90] W. E. Flaherty, 'The Great Rebellion In Kent Of 1381 Illustrated From The Public Records', *Archaeologia Cantiana* vol 3 (1860) p.72
[91] ibid. pp. 73, 76
[92] George Price, *A Treatise on the Law of the Exchequer* vol 1. (London, 1830) p.95

who took back property seized by bailiffs from those who had not paid.⁹³ Such a job made him a wealthy man but not a popular one. The rebels rallying cry was that "no tenant should do service or custom to the lordships." The leaders ordered that money be raised across the island to fund their revolt but only from those who held land from St Augustine's Abbey. All tenants of Christ Church were specifically excluded from the revolt – effectively everyone living in Monkton, St Nicholas, Sarre and Birchington. They burnt rolls and books because they thought that if there was no evidence on paper about who owned what, no taxes could be levied and no arrears charged but their hopes would have been in vain. Aside from the fact that copies would almost certainly have existed in other places, fresh officials were no doubt preparing new assessments only weeks later. The Peasants' Revolt here had nothing to do with the poll tax but was part of a long series of arguments that took place between parishioners and the Abbey.

It was not until 1441, sixty years after the revolt, that parishioners finally saw an end to doing service for the Abbey. In that year, the Abbot made an agreement with his tenants that they should pay him a fee of between 3d and 6d an acre. The list of tenants who signed the agreement represented many families who had enjoyed long histories with the parish and would go on to do so. They included James, John and Stephen Curling, William and Roger Manston, William and Nicholas Sprackling, John, Robert, Laurence, William and Thomas Saunders.⁹⁴

Church Wax House

At some point probably in the late thirteenth or early fourteenth century, the church built a wax house which was located to the south between the present war memorial and Tesco Metro. This would have been used for making candles, for the distribution of alms, for meetings, for cooking and for brewing ale. Each year at Whitsun⁹⁵, the church would have held a festival where there would have been minstrels, dancing and food and drink. This would have used ale brewed on the premises together with oxen or other animals roasted on spits inside. This event, known as a Church Ale, would have been the main fundraiser for the year. The church fair, held on St Laurence day, would have been held just outside along the High Street. In 1468 the profit on the fair sent to St Augustine's Abbey was just 6d (about £16 today) which suggests it was a small event.⁹⁶ If mystery plays were put on – and Biblical dramas were sometimes used for raising funds – they would have been held in the same spot most likely in June.

---

⁹³ *Calendar of Patent Rolls*, Edward III, vol 5, pp.504-5
⁹⁴ Lewis op.cit. 1736 edition, Appendix XXIII pp. 35-40
⁹⁵ The term Whitsun has largely been replaced by Pentecost today in line with Roman usage. It comes from the medieval English word "wyght" meaning spirit.
⁹⁶ Charles Cotton, 'St Austin's Abbey, Canterbury: Treasurer's Accounts 1468-9' in *Archaeologia Cantiana* vol 51 (1939) p.76. The holding of fairs in churchyards was prohibited by law in 1295. One of those responsible for enforcing this and other aspects of the Statute of Winchester was Ralph of St Laurence, *Calendar of Patent Rolls* Edward II vol.5. pp.369-370.

The Sixteenth Century

THE BUILDING

The Reformation

At the start of the sixteenth century, St Laurence church was a gaudy and cluttered place full of screens and barriers and redolent with the fragrance of incense. Within fifty years, it would become a bright open space in which worship reflected the Gospel of Our Lord.

To understand the changes brought about by the Reformation, it is first necessary to consider the basic history of this event. It began in 1517 when a German monk named Martin Luther nailed ninety-five theses on the door of the church in Wittenberg expressing his belief that the practice of selling indulgences was not in line with scripture. At that time, it was believed that at death a person went to suffer in purgatory whilst they were made fit to dwell with Christ. How long they spent there was dependent on their sins. As the prospect of years of torment was clearly unattractive, the Pope offered a solution. If people were to give the Church money – be that for masses, strips of paper called indulgences or as gifts – then he would reduce the time they had to suffer. His justification of this was that as Christ had promised Peter the keys to heaven and hell and he was the heir of Peter, he had authority to change sentences of judgment.[1] Luther noted that this practice was not in line with Biblical teaching. Had Jesus not told the thief on the cross, "today you shall be with me in paradise" not "today you shall go to purgatory for years"?[2] Did not the Bible teach that salvation came only from faith in Christ, not from donations or from works? To Luther, this sort of abuse meant the Church needed to be reformed. His ideas spread across Europe and the Reformation was born.

Response to Luther's ideas in England was initially muted. Henry VIII at this time was one of the Pope's most devoted followers and could not believe that the Pope could do anything wrong. Since childhood, he had owned a prayer roll which promised a

---

[1] Matt. 16:19
[2] Luke 23:43

remission of 52,712 years and forty days from punishment in purgatory every time Henry was to gaze at a particular image and recite the Lord's Prayer and Hail Mary five times, as well as his safety from all evil spirits, pestilences, fevers and all other infirmities on land and on water.[3] Indignant at the idea of anyone criticising the Pope, he wrote a book against Luther which resulted in Leo X giving him the title of Defender of the Faith for his devotion on October 11th 1521. It followed that English scholars reading Luther's works were liable to be accused of heresy and put to death, hence discussions of them had to take place in secret.

The situation changed in the early 1520s when it became obvious that Queen Katherine of Aragon was past childbearing. Henry was tormented about what would happen if he did not have a son. The last time a female had been due to inherit, the country had descended into civil war and the Wars of the Roses were still within living memory. As a child, Henry VIII himself had been forced to flee to the Tower with his mother as his father fought off insurrection. As the first duty of a king was to ensure a peaceful succession so that order was maintained and people could prosper, this meant Henry had failed. The Tudor dynasty would die with him and there would be rivers of blood in the streets. The only solution was for him to re-marry and have a son.

At the time that Henry proposed this idea, it did not seem unreasonable. Popes were normally amenable to political expediency. His sister as Queen of Scotland had just received such an annulment as had his brother-in-law Charles Brandon and so had Louis XII, King of France. All Henry needed, he thought, was a legal technicality or procedural abnormality and he thought he had this because the original papal bull allowing the marriage said Katherine was a virgin – despite her having been married to his brother for six months and by her own admission sharing his bed. Henry said she had not been so and hence the bull was invalid. Katherine protested she had been a virgin and her family located an hitherto unknown bull which covered the fact that she might not have been. Henry's lawyers demanded to see this, were refused, and denounced it as a forgery. Meanwhile, Katherine's nephew marched into Rome and took the Pope prisoner. It was clear that Henry's objective was not going to be as straightforward as he had anticipated.

At the same time, the harvests failed catastrophically for three years in a row. There was starvation across England and those who survived were scarred for life as can be seen by skeletal evidence for those men who served on the *Mary Rose*.[4] The Church as a major landowner was generally unsympathetic and anger against the Church grew. Typical of the mood was Simon Fish's pamphlet of 1529 *A Supplication for the Beggars* which talked of people dying of hunger whilst the clergy, whom he described as "ravenous wolves", "idle holy thieves" and "blood suckers", piled up extortions, led women astray and far from dispensing charity were quick to raise lawsuits against any who challenged them. This pamphlet was immensely popular going into multiple editions. Whether a copy found its way to St Laurence is unknown but given the centuries

---

[3] Bolton, *Seven Centuries* op.cit. pp. 167-168
[4] Ann Stirland, *The Men of the Mary Rose* (Stroud, 2005) pp.89-91.

long tradition of anger against St Augustine's, it is certain that it would have found a ready reception.

Whilst the Pope tried every delaying tactic he could imagine to avoid giving Henry his annulment, Henry decided to try and put pressure on him by assembling a body of learned opinion from across Europe which supported his case. As part of this, Henry purchased a copy of the new polyglot Bible which showed the Latin text with which he had grown up alongside the original Hebrew and Greek. To his surprise, it was demonstrated to him that the verse in Hebrew condemning those who married their brother's wife did not say they would be without sons but without heirs, *aririm*.[5] To Henry, a loyal son of the Church, the fact that the Pope had authorised a mistranslation was deeply shocking. It made him wonder what other errors there might be. Could it be that Luther and his fellow reformers actually had a point?

The climax came when after years of prevarication and lying, the Pope summoned Henry to Rome so the matter could be tried in court. Henry exploded. He was King of England, not some lackey. He broke off relations with Rome and declared:

> This realm of England is an empire, and so hath been accepted in the world, governed by one supreme head and king, having the dignity and royal estate of the imperial crown of England,…: he being also institute and furnished, by the goodness and sufferance of Almighty God, with plenary, whole, and entire power, pre-eminence, authority, prerogative and jurisdiction, to render and yield justice, and final determination to all manner of folk, residents, or subjects within this his realm, in all causes, matters, debates, and contentions, happening to occur, insurge, or begin within the limits thereof, without restraint, or provocation to any foreign princes or potentates.[6]

The cheers rang out across England in response. Henry had stood up to Rome and this appealed to latent English nationalism as well as xenophobic tendencies. From henceforth, the Pope would be known simply as the Bishop of Rome and neither he, nor any other person or body outside England, would have any say in her affairs. It was England for the English from now on.

Initially, Henry thought to just have Catholicism without the Pope but his ongoing explorations of the Bible caused him to adopt an increasing number of Protestant ideas, most importantly the need for an English Bible. The Reformation, as it progressed

---

[5] The Latin Bible translated Lev. 20:21 as *absque filii*, without sons not *absque liberis*, without children. *Aririm* is also used in Jer. 22:30 where it relates to a king who had children but whose heirs would not inherit. A paper on Henry's use of Hebrew by the author is forthcoming.

[6] Preamble to the 1533 Act of Appeals in Henry Gee and William Hardy, *Documents Illustrative of English Church History* (London, 1896) p.187

through the sixteenth century and the reigns of his children, may be interpreted as an ever greater attempt to bring religion into line with the Holy Scriptures.

Impact on St Laurence – Henry VIII's reign (1509-47)

Once Henry VIII was declared Supreme Head of the Church in England under Christ, it followed that changes could be made by him directly and by parliament. In 1535 he ordered that the Pope's name "be utterly abolished and razed out, and his very name and memory to be never more remembered except to his contumely and reproach."[7]

In the summer of 1536 came the first set of royal injunctions and these covered worship, clergy behaviour and made the first change to the church building.[8] The regulations included an instruction that vicars preach at least every six weeks on how:

> the Bishop of Rome's usurped power and jurisdiction, having no establishment nor ground by the law of God, was of most just causes taken away and abolished ; and therefore they owe unto him no manner of obedience or subjection, and that the king's power is within his dominion the highest power and potentate under God, to whom all men within the same dominion by God's commandment owe most loyalty and obedience, afore and above all other powers and potentates in earth.

They were also to teach the Lord's Prayer, Apostles' Creed and Ten Commandments and they were to do this by going through each a clause at a time and getting people to repeat them until they learnt them. The most important clause was number seven which stated that churches must obtain "a book of the whole Bible both in Latin and in English and lay the same in the choir for every man that will to look and read thereon and shall discourage no man from the reading of any part of the Bible."

In practice, this landmark regulation which for the first time allowed people to read the Word of God in English was barely followed due to the difficulty of obtaining the book. That was not rectified until early 1539 when the Great Bible was first printed and it took three years to print enough copies for there to be one in every parish church. By that stage the rule had been altered to say that the Bible must be situated in "some convenient place" where all could see it. This would have meant outside the chancel which was off limits to the laity. Failure to have a Bible was punishable by a fine on the parish of £2 a month until one was provided. In today's money, that would be £1150 or almost £14,000 per annum.[9] The cost of the Bible was to be shared equally between the vicar and the congregation. There are no records to show when St Laurence first obtained

---

[7] Walter Howard Frere and William Kennedy, *Visitation Articles and injunctions of the Period of the Reformation* vol. 2 (London 1910) p.109
[8] ibid. pp.3-10
[9] ibid p.35

one but there must have been some excitement. Previously to this, owning even a scrap of the Bible in English had been an offence liable to the death penalty.[10] Even those who could not read - and they would have been in the majority - would have been impressed by its size. Few would ever have seen a printed work before. The frontispiece showing the kneeling King at the top right receiving the Scriptures on behalf of the people directly from Christ draws a parallel with Moses receiving the Law from God on Mount Sinai. Along with the mountains, there is also the suggestion that the King has rescued England from the oppression of Rome just as Moses led the Israelites from Egypt. The King is then shown on his throne passing the Word on to Archbishop Cranmer on the left to share with the clergy and to Thomas Cromwell on the right to share with the laity. Henry quotes Moses as he does so (Deut 1:17, 16:18). The recipients are duly grateful and all cheer "vivat rex" or "God save the king!" Christ meanwhile proclaims Henry the true heir of David and "a man after mine own heart which shall do all my will" (Acts 13:22). Henry himself quotes King Darius who declared that all shall fear the living God after he had witnessed Daniel's miraculous survival in the lion's den, a further reference to Henry regarding himself as the saviour of his people from Rome (Daniel 6:26). The image is interesting also for recording the dress of the period, including the square caps worn by the clergy, and because it shows the Word being received by men and women, young and old, rich and poor. The central inscription stresses that the

---

[10] J.H. Merle d'Aubigne, *The Reformation in England* vol 1 (1853) translated by W.H. White pp. 459-468

volume has been "truly translated after the verity of the Hebrew and Greek texts by the diligent study of diverse excellent learned men expert in the aforesaid tongues."

A further change in 1536 banned the celebration of patronal festivals and celebrations of saints days which fell in the summer. As St Laurence day was August 10th, the church was directly affected. Events such as the annual fair could no longer be held at that time. The reason for the summer ban was because the authorities wanted to ensure that everyone was available to help with the harvest but the wider ban on patronal festivals marked the start of the reduction in role of the saints. In the medieval church, they had played a significant role with images being erected in their honour and prayers being offered to them. This happened at St Laurence where there is evidence of ten saints being so venerated. Instead, the King declared that every church would celebrate its dedication on the first Sunday in October.[11] This practice continued at St Laurence until 1978.

Two years later, further injunctions were introduced with regard to saints. These stated that all candles should be removed from in front of images and that there were to be no offerings made to them either of money, gifts or prayers. Images were to be allowed only for the benefit of those who could not read so that they might see an example of a godly life and be inspired to emulate it. Using an image for any other purpose was idolatry. Clergy were to preach this message clearly and if they had previously encouraged parishioners to donate money for lights or go on pilgrimage they were now to publicly apologise to their congregations and explain "you did the same upon no ground of Scripture, but as one being led and seduced by a common error and abuse crept into the Church, through the sufferance and avarice of such as felt profit by the same."[12] Medieval wills show numerous entries for people at St Laurence leaving money for lights before images and indicate guilds existed to maintain them so this would have been a startling change. It is likely that there was some anger, particularly from the descendants of those who had given money for such things in good faith. The extinguishing of lights would also have made the church suddenly much darker. Aside from the windows, the only lights allowed now were the two candles on the high altar and those in the rood loft which illuminated the figure of Christ. The gilded image of St Laurence was to be left in darkness. Whether the vicar made any public apology is unknown. The vicar at the time was John Young who had only arrived in the parish three years before so he might have argued that the donations were made before his time. The point of the regulation was to focus attention on Christ alone, a theme which was to be emphasised over coming years.

Another clause of the 1538 regulations was to compel parishes to keep registers of births, marriages and deaths. The early records of St Laurence have not survived and the first register actually dates from the end of Queen Elizabeth's reign. Presumably there had been some issue with the former volume, perhaps it had got damp or been damaged by vermin for at that time they purchased a new book but they copied in the entries only

---

[11] Frere op.cit. p.5
[12] ibid. p.39

back to "the beginning of the raigne of our Queene Elizabeth".[13] The first entries in each section were:

> John Sarles married Joan Wells on 28th July 1559
> Thomas Harris buried 5th August 1559
> Paul son of Vincent Colbrand baptised 6th January 1560/1

The registers were required to be kept in a chest with separate locks for the vicar and churchwardens who were to supposed to ensure that the events of the week were written up each Sunday or face a 3s 4d fine. It is possible that the church used the chest which they had purchased a century earlier and which can still be seen in the church.

There was one other clause in 1538 which would have affected St Laurence and that was a specific order to destroy any images of Thomas Becket and to utterly remove any references to him. He was not to be commemorated in any way but was rather to be proclaimed as a traitor.[14] Since the church had previously had an image of him, this would have been taken down and smashed.[15] Henry's proclamation here was based on historical evidence. Becket had been a drinking companion of Henry II and was only ordained on the day before he was made Archbishop having undergone no vocational training. He upheld the rights of clergy who were accused of serious offences such as rape and murder to be tried only in church courts where they might face a penance or fine only rather than the death penalty they would get in the civil courts.[16] Becket's stance angered Henry II and resulted in his exile. Becket settled in France at the court of Henry II's enemy which exacerbated the situation. He was martyred on his return but whilst Henry VIII did not condone his murder, he did maintain that Becket's disobedience was treason and would have merited judicial execution.

A year later, the King did something which must have delighted the parishioners - he closed St Augustine's Abbey. This was part of the Dissolution of the monasteries and one of St Laurence's own parishioners, John Johnson, was actively involved being an employee of Thomas Cromwell - see Appendix. It is sometimes suggested that the Dissolution caused great hardship as monasteries were valuable hospitals for the poor

---

[13] Her accession was 17th November 1558 so the start dates were almost a year later for marriages and burials and over two years later for baptisms.
[14] ibid. pp.42, 109
[15] The survival of the piscina in the south chapel is proof that the heads do not represent Henry II and Becket
[16] Frank Barlow, *Thomas Becket*, (University of California, 1990) pp.92-94

and they dispensed charity. This may have been the case and people in Canterbury might have felt upset by the loss but a sick or starving person at St Laurence would never have been able to journey to Canterbury for help and there were no nearer monastic establishments.[17] To the people at St Laurence, the Abbey was just a grasping and hated landlord. The change in structure also meant that for the first time, the church did not have to share a portion of its fees with Minster. It was now independent.

Towards the end of Henry's reign in 1544 the first service was issued in English. It was a Litany, a form of prayer to be used in procession. This included the famous line: "From all sedition and privy conspiracy, from the tyranny of the Bishop of Rome and all his detestable enormities, from all false doctrine and heresy, from hardness of heart and contempt of thy word and commandment. Good lord, deliver us." Although the wording of the Litany would vary across the years with the words "detestable enormities" being removed in 1553, this form of congregational intercession continued in use until well into the twentieth century when Holy Communion took over as the main service of the day. The Litany was important because it introduced the Lord's Prayer in the traditional format which we know today. For those with money before this, the English translation – only permitted for home use - had been rather less memorable:

> Father thou that art in heaven
> Hallowed be Thy name by meek voice
> Thy kingdom be for to come
> In us sinful, all and some.
> Thy will be doing in earth here
> As it is in heaven clear,
> Our each day's bread we Thee pray
> That Thou give us this same day
> And forgive us our trespass
> As we done them that guilt us has
> And lead us in no fonding
> But shield us all from evil thing. Amen.[18]

A year later, the King's Primer was issued. This included the Lord's Prayer, Hail Mary, Ten Commandments and Apostles' Creed in English with the King stating that those who did not know Latin should learn them that "they should be the more provoked to true devotion, and the better set their hearts upon those things that they pray for." The volume was aimed at all ages and included a variety of prayers for general use plus translations of the daily offices of prayer including Lauds, Matins, Evensong and Compline. It was the first time that ordinary people would ever have seen these services

---

[17] Since the Danish invasions, Minster Abbey had just been used as an occasional home for the Abbot or his servants
[18] Peacock op.cit. p.13

or a form of confession in English and was an important advance though the Mass remained in Latin. The goal was to create a manual of prayer in simple to understand language which was yet full of Biblical allusions as the two extracts show:

> Most dear and tender Father, our defender and nourisher, endue us with Thy grace that we may cast off the great blindness of our minds and carefulness of worldly things and may put our whole study and care in keeping of Thy holy law. And that we may labour and travail for our necessities in this life like the birds of the air and the lilies of the field, without care.

> Most merciful Lord God and most tender and dear Father, vouchsafe I heartily beseech Thee, to look down with Thy fatherly eyes of pity upon me, most vile and wretched sinner which lie here prostrate in heart before the seat of Thy bottomless mercy, for I have sinned against the throne of Thy glory and before Thee O Father insomuch that I am no more worthy to be called Thy son. Nevertheless, forasmuch as Thou art the God and Father of all comfort and desire not the death of the sinner but, like a true Samaritan, take thought of my silly wounded soul. Make me I pray Thee, by infounding the precious oil of comfort onto my wounds, joyfully to run with the lost son unto the lap of Thine everlasting pity.

With regard to doctrine, Henry VIII remained Catholic issuing articles upholding the benefits of confession, good works, prayers for the dead and maintaining transubstantiation.[19]

Impact on St Laurence – Edward VI's reign (1547-53)

The start of Edward's reign saw a national visitation to ensure that all churches were maintaining the regulations issued by Henry VIII. They also wanted to know if anyone was still using a rosary or was making superstitious use of church property such as sprinkling holy water on a crop, using a cross to fend off the devil or lighting candles to try and forecast whom a girl might marry. In this way, the regulations were extended from the church alone to people's own beliefs.

Edward issued his own set of injunctions in 1547 which followed on from those of

---

[19] Copies may be found in Charles Lloyd (ed.), *Formularies of Faith put forth by authority* (Oxford, 1856). The Litany excludes prayer for the dead but Henry requested this in his own will.

his father but included some important new clauses.[20] With regard images, they demanded that if anyone had made a gift to any, censed one or made a pilgrimage to it, the image must be immediately removed and destroyed as must any images in walls or windows. Processions were banned as were prayers for the dead. Where chantry priests existed, they were to "exercise themselves in teaching youth to read and write and bring them up in good manners and other virtuous exercises."[21] Guilds which had been set up to maintain shrines and images were to be disbanded and hand their funds over to the vicar for the use of the poor. A new chest was to be provided in the chancel to collect such donations. Clergy were to prohibit anyone whom they felt was not in love and charity with their neighbour from receiving the sacrament. It followed that clergy were to be more actively involved in trying to settle disputes and bring about reconciliations. They were to spend more time studying. They were to purchase their own copies of the New Testament in Latin and English and a copy of Erasmus' *Paraphrases*. The Archdeacon would then set them a section to learn by heart and work upon each six months and test them on it at the next visitation. They were also to memorise "sentences of scripture as do set forth the benefits, mercy and goodness of Almighty God towards all penitent and believing persons" which they could use to help people who were in despair. This was a clear call to a more pastoral ministry and so keen were the King and Cranmer for this to happen that they included some Comfortable Words in the new service book.

It was not only the clergy who had to own a copy of Erasmus' *Paraphrases* but churches also had to buy a copy and set it up near to the Bible. This book included the text of the New Testament together with simple explanations. In an age when the clergy were generally ill educated, it was an essential tool. In fact, as it is unlikely that the vicar of St Laurence could have afforded to buy his own copy of the New Testament and *Paraphrases*, it is more likely that he used the copy inside the church.

The reason the authorities were so keen to see the education of the clergy improved is made clear upon consideration of a survey made in 1551 of the clergy in Gloucester diocese. Of these, only a third knew the Ten Commandments. One in thirty-four did not even know that there were ten and one in six had no idea where to find them in the Bible. One in twenty-five could not recite the Lord's Prayer whilst one in ten had no idea it was actually by Jesus: a fifth could not find it in the Bible. Ninety-four per cent were able to recite the Apostles' Creed but only one in four was able to offer any scriptural proofs of any part of it. The remainder could not locate the creation story in the Bible nor the nativity nor even the crucifixion or resurrection.[22] If the ministers did not know the faith, how could they teach it to others? This need for the clergy to be educated reflected the change in belief about salvation. In the middle ages, a person could be saved

---

[20] Frere op.cit. pp.114-130

[21] The records show none existed at St Laurence at this time as the chapels at Cliffsend and Ellington had closed and the money left by the Manston family had either run out or been stopped.

[22] James Gairdner, 'Bishop Hooper's Visitation of Gloucester' in *English Historical Review* (January 1904) pp.98-124

by hearing masses and it did not matter a whit whether the priest saying them was godly or an absolute rascal. The Protestant understanding was that people were saved by faith as it said in the Holy Bible, and that meant they had to be taught. Being a vicar was not about being able to recite a Latin service but being a pastor.

Blessed be they that mourn, for they shall receive comfort
Lack of children or parents, and such other as we entirely love, commonly is counted a miserable thing, insomuch that some deprived of their affections do sometimes kill themselves for sorrow. Man's comfort intending to heal the grief, does often make it worse. But the spirit which is the true comforter does so inwardly refresh the mind being clear in conscience and ascertained of the rewards of the life to come, that in most grievous afflictions of their bodies, they think not themselves unfortunate, but rather do most joyfully rejoice. He will recompense their temporal wailing with inestimable hearts joy, and afterward they shall be translated unto everlasting bliss.

Blessed are the clean of heart, for they shall see God.
The common sort of men call them unhappy that be blind, and because they have lost their most pleasant sense, they say they be no longer alive, but that they abide in darkness like dead men. If it be a thing so much to be wished for to behold the sun with the bodily eye, how much more pleasant and blessed a thing is it with the eyes of the mind to behold God, the maker of the sun, and of all things? As a web is to the eyes, so are sins to the mind. Therefore blessed be they whose heart is pure and clean from all filthiness. For they shall have this gift, which is more to be desired than all the pleasures of the world. They shall see God

Blessed be the peace makers, for they shall be called the children of God.
The following of the fathers steps, declares a true and a natural child. God forgiving freely all offences, does stir and provoke all men which have offended him, to peace and amity. He offers himself of his own accord very merciful to all them that do repent. He will not acknowledge them for his children, which do not show themselves to their brethren, as he has showed himself towards all. Carnal fathers disinherit their sons, which do not agree with their other brethren, so the heavenly father will put away the haters of peace and the causers of discord, from the inheritance of heaven. The children of God is no vain title. He that is the son, must needs be heir also.

Extracts of Erasmus' *Paraphrases* on the Beatitudes

As a sign of the new stress on the ministry of the Word, the regulations further introduced a requirement that churches provide themselves with a "comely and honest pulpit." It followed – though no order was ever issued regarding this – that with services being extended by sermons which generally lasted an hour, that there was a need for seating. In the medieval church, a few benches had been provided at the back for the old and weak (hence the phrase 'backs to the wall' meaning those in trouble) but now pews were more generally introduced. As might be expected in a society which was very class conscious, differing types of seats were provided for working men and employers from high backed seats with cushions to rough benches. It was normal for congregations to be segregated according to gender with the women sitting in the north aisle and even for them to be divided into married women and single.[23] The cost of installing and maintaining pews was usually met by a system of charges with those nearer the front being more expensive than those further back. A standing area would have been left for those unable to afford the luxury of a seat.

1547 also saw the publication of the first Book of Homilies or Sermons. Since 1538, clergy had not been allowed to preach without a licence and it has been estimated that only a fifth of clergy had such.[24] The twelve sermons covered the doctrines of original sin and salvation, encouraged people to faith and good works and warned against the evils of anger and adultery. They were notable for their clear teaching of justification by faith alone, the key tenet of the Protestant Reformation. The following year, Cranmer ordered a visitation of Canterbury diocese which required every church – including St Laurence – to confirm that they had the book and that one was being read every week.

In January 1548, the use of ashes on Ash Wednesday, palms on Palm Sunday and candles at Candlemas were abolished on grounds they led to people putting their faith in the items as a protection against evil when their trust should only be in God. The use of holy water was banned a few weeks later.[25] The stoup in St Laurence porch has been disused since this time.

In 1549, the first Prayer Book in English was published. It was a milestone for it laid down the principle that people should talk to God in their own language.[26] It is hard to imagine the impact that this would have had on the congregation at St Laurence. For centuries, services had been held in Latin. Not only could people not understand them but they could not hear clearly because the vicar chanted the words from the high chancel. What had seemed like magical incantations was now laid bare and they could follow proceedings. This reflected the new Protestant understanding of worship as something which people engaged in rather than a spectacle which they watched. As the preface to the new service book made clear, the goal was that people "should continually

---

[23] Sedley Ware, *The Elizabethan Parish in its Ecclesiastical and Financial Aspects* (Baltimore, 1908) p.24
[24] ibid. p.34
[25] Frere p.184
[26] The laws all spoke of this as English for there was no concept of England as a multicultural society. The Welsh and the Cornish protested.

profit more and more in the knowledge of God and be the more inflamed with the love of His true religion."[27] To this end, everything was to be based upon the scriptures which were to be read in English according to a new Lectionary which ensured the entire Old Testament was read through each year, the New Testament twice a year and the Psalms every month. [28]

Something else which was new in 1549 was that both bread and wine were distributed to the worshippers at Holy Communion. Previously, only the priests had received both, the laity had simply had the bread. The logic was that employed by Portia in *A Merchant of Venice* who noted that since flesh must always contain blood, there was no need to distribute both. The change was made in line with Christ's own instruction.

The one change which may have disquieted some at St Laurence was that the singing of anthems was now prohibited because they interrupted the concentration. We do not know what singing took place in the pre-Reformation church but there are references in wills to singing clerks and sung masses which would suggest there was at least some music.[29]

In 1550, the problem of music was solved with the publication of John Merbecke's *Booke of Common Praier Noted*. This was produced in line with Cranmer's injunction that there should be one note per syllable so that the music did not detract attention from the words.[30] Almost five hundred years later, St Laurence church continues to use this setting, a powerful reminder of the roots of our church.

The first Prayer Book had been imperfect in many ways not least because much of it was a translation of the Latin and not truly reformed but this changed in 1552 with the publication of the second Prayer Book. Now it was made clear that clergy were to speak clearly and loudly and from such a position as all could hear. The greatest change was with regard the Holy Communion. The celebrant was now generally referred to as the minister rather than the priest and a communion table replaced the altar. These changes reflected the new understanding that the service was a memorial of Christ's once and perfect sacrifice ("Do this in remembrance of me") and not a re-enactment. The Mass had been understood as a sacrifice and so required priests and altars but Protestants saw Christ as the only great High Priest with the clergy being just ministers. Catholic belief was that at the consecration, the bread and wine became the true body and blood of Christ. It was now taught that the bread and wine remained unchanged but that the faithful believer would be fed and strengthened by Christ in their heart. It was, however, more than a change of terminology. Cranmer re-ordered the service so that people would receive immediately after Christ's words "Do this in remembrance of me" were read. There was to be no further talk which might suggest that something special was

---

[27] Joseph Ketley (ed.), *The Two Liturgies* (Parker Society, 1844) p.17
[28] Unlike today, full chapters of the Scriptures were read with no edits or deletions to remove verses which people might find uncomfortable.
[29] For example, William Saunders of 1538 and Roger Saunders of 1533
[30] John Cox (ed.), *Miscellaneous Writings and Letters of Thomas Cranmer* (Cambridge, 1846), p.416

happening to the bread and wine: people were simply to obey Christ's commandment. This pure order of service based on the Gospel remains in the Book of Common Prayer today and continued in use in the Church of England generally until the 1970s when there was a return to the structure of the Mass prompted by ecumenicalism and the repercussions of the Victorian Oxford movement.[31]

Even for those in the congregation who failed to appreciate the theology, there were dramatic visual changes. Firstly, an ordinary table covered with a simple linen cloth replaced the usually stone altar with its costly frontal. Secondly, the table was to be placed "in the body of the church" and not far away at the east end. This was to stress the fact that the service was by definition the Lord's Supper and meals were celebrated around a table. In order to place it there, the rood screen at had to be destroyed which meant that for the first time in its history, people could see and walk right through St Laurence church.[32] This removal of the screen was a powerful reminder of the Temple screen being ripped at the moment Christ died (Matt. 27:51). Stools would have been placed in the chancel facing the communion table to further stress this point. Thirdly, the minister was not to stand with his back to the congregation facing east as had always happened before but to stand on the north end like the host at a dinner table. The table itself was to be stood with the narrow ends facing the nave and east end. He was therefore physically between the congregation and God but not turning his back on either. Moreover, he was to be dressed plainly in a black gown and white surplice to demonstrate his humility and the simplicity of the Gospel rather than ornate vestments which bespoke pride and created a barrier between him and the congregation. Fourthly, ordinary bread was to be used rather than wafers on grounds that this was what Jesus had used. These changes must have been startling to the congregation but there are no records to say if they were welcomed or hated. The communion table beneath the tower at St Laurence only dates from the 1970s but it may be assumed that the Tudor table stood on the same spot, the difference being that distribution was made there too rather than at the east end which happens today.

Buying all these books – the Bible, Homilies, two Prayer Books, *Paraphrases* – must have caused difficulties for the churchwardens. St Laurence was not a wealthy parish. The cost of the 1552 Prayer Book was set at 2s 6d if sold as loose pages, 3s 4d if on parchment and 4s if bound with leather or board.[33] It may be presumed that the church would have needed to purchase at least one bound copy for the vicar and either a second bound copy for the clerk or loose pages. The Great Bible was sold for 10s.[34] The cost of the *Paraphrases* varied from 6s 2d for loose pages to either 10s or 12s 8d for a bound copy depending on

---

[31] For a full discussion on the structure of liturgy across the centuries, see Margaret Bolton, *The Book of Common Prayer and Worship Today* (2015)

[32] The rood was stored in the church and finally sold as scrap in 1636 for 4s 8d.

[33] Joseph Ketley (ed.), *The Two Liturgies* (Parker Society, 1844) p.355

[34] Derek Wilson, *The People's Bible.* (Oxford, 2010) p.56

the binding.[35] The cost of the Homilies is unknown but was probably similar. The total cost, therefore, must have been around £2 which would equate to about a thousand pounds today. Even if the Vicar had paid half as stipulated (and at a sixth of his annual income he may not have been able to do so) that represented a considerable investment. With so few people being able to read and take advantage of these texts, it is likely that there was some grumbling about having to spend so much. What cannot be known is whether the church received any of these volumes as gifts. It is entirely possible that John Johnson, who worked for Cromwell and who was committed to the Reformation cause, may have given the church its first Bible.

One way in which the church would have raised money toward such costs would have been through the sale of items no longer required or allowed. Images and screens could be sold as either firewood or melted down depending on their material. Vestments and altar cloths could be sold and cut up to make other items. Fabric was incredibly expensive at this time and highly valued.

Impact on St Laurence – Mary's reign (1553-1558)

The death of Edward VI at the tragically young age of just fifteen saw the accession of Mary Tudor, known throughout history as Bloody Mary. The impact on St Laurence was drastic. Everything which had happened in Edward's reign was undone. Services returned to Latin, altars were brought back and set up at the east end, the Bishop of Rome became known as the Pope again and only the bread was distributed at Holy Communion.

It is unknown if any parishioners suffered persecution during these years. Many were arrested and jailed and left to die without any record being kept. Forty-one people were burnt alive at the stake in Canterbury. After the first, John Johnson, who had been a parishioner of St Laurence but since moved to the city, was arrested for throwing street earth or dung at Cardinal Pole's home in the city.[36] He was a brave man.

As Ramsgate was linked to Sandwich in the Cinque Ports, it is possible that some men from here assisted those courageous men who were active in running messages between Protestants who were in hiding in England and exiles on the continent. Part of the work they did was smuggling the Holy Scriptures.[37]

Although Mary may have wanted a return to rood screens and images, it is unlikely that St Laurence invested in such. Even had they wished to do so, they probably could not have raised the money in the short period that she reigned. Evidence of a return to popery is slight but the will of James Harnett made on 29th December 1558 left money for a single mass to be said at the time of his death and another a month later. It is

---

[35] E. J. Devereux, 'The Publication Of The English Paraphrases Of Erasmus' in *E J. Bulletin of the John Rylands Library* vol 51 part 2 (1969) pp.363-4
[36] For full details of Johnson's remarkable life, see Appendix.
[37] A full account of their work may be found in Christina Hallowell Garrett, *The Marian Exiles* (Cambridge, 1938) pp. 258, 292, 342

unlikely, however, these were ever said since by then, Mary had died and the Protestant Elizabeth taken the throne.[38]

Impact on St Laurence – Elizabeth's reign (1558-1603)

Elizabeth's accession saw a return to life largely as it had been when Edward died. The church would have resumed services in English with the communion table still in the midst of the church and no side chapels around. In a bid to compromise with those of her subjects who had more catholic sentiments, Elizabeth ordered that the communion table be stood at the east end whenever it was not in use.[39] It is easy to imagine that the frequent moving of a heavy table must have caused some irritation to the churchwardens at St Laurence. In a similar compromise, she ordered that flatbreads be used for Holy Communion rather than Catholic wafers or the ordinary loaves favoured by the Protestants.

Other changes made by Elizabeth included the requirement for clergy to catechise every second Sunday and for people to kneel for prayer and bow their head each time the name of Jesus was spoken. For "the comforting of such that delight in music" she permitted a psalm to be sung at the start of the service. This was the only music other than the Gloria which was sung at the end of Holy Communion and once again had to be plainly sung with no descants, drawn out notes or any embellishments which would detract attention from the words. She also introduced the office of sidesmen although their role was a little different to that we see today. At this time, it was compulsory that

---

[38] PRC17/33/114

[39] Frere op.cit. vol 3 pp.27-28

everyone attend church each Sunday or else pay a fine of one shilling (around three days wages for a labourer or two for a skilled craftsman). The sidesmen were "to see that all the parishioners duly resort to their church upon all Sundays and Holy Days and there to continue the whole time of the godly service. And all such as shall be found slack or negligent in resorting to the church having no great nor urgent cause of absence, they shall straightly call upon them and after due admonition, if they amend not, they shall denounce them to the Ordinary."[40]

In 1561, a regulation was issued that churches have the Ten Commandments painted and displayed on the wall or a screen behind the communion table at the east end.[41] Such a display remained at St Laurence until 1902 when the current East Window was installed. The only other ornamentation in the church would have been the royal coat of arms which would have been displayed as a reminder that the Queen was Supreme Governor of the church and had been appointed by God. The church building in 1603 was much less colourful than it had been in 1500 but it was open and light and much more akin to what we see today.

The fact that there were regular visitations where checks were made that churches had conformed to all the various rules imposed means that we are able to get an idea of how St Laurence church fared during Elizabeth's reign. These show, for example, that in 1562 the chancel was in need of repair but that the church possessed all the books it should have done and showed no traces of the old chapels or images. Some repairs were clearly made for it is not until 1583 that another report appears that the chancel is "not sufficiently repaired" an allegation made again in 1584, 1585 and 1588. Initially the churchwardens blamed Robert Sprackling who was the farmer of the parsonage but he denied it was his responsibility. Meanwhile, in 1579 the church was said to be in need of tiling, which probably meant roof repairs although it could have referenced the floor. The churchyard wall was also said to be on the verge of collapse and the church porch so decayed that it could not be used. Work began on the porch in 1580 but was stopped when the masons were commandeered by the Queen for work on local defences. Following further complaints about the state of repair of the church and vicarage, more repairs were carried out to the former and the churchwardens told the Archdeacon in 1597 that they had completed them but added that unfortunately recent strong winds had broken the glass in some of the windows. For the rest of Elizabeth's reign, the reports were regularly the same that the church and churchyard both needed repairs and the parish intended to do them when they had the money, which they did not at present.[42]

At some point during Elizabeth's reign, the parish obtained a copy of Foxe's *Actes and Monuments* better known as the *Book of Martyrs*. The work told the story of the early Christian martyrs, including St Laurence, but concentrated in detail on the Protestants

---

[40] ibid. p.22
[41] ibid. p.108
[42] Hussey op.cit. pp.31-33. Given the west door was in use, there would have been little incentive to spend money repairing the south-west porch.

who had been martyred by the Roman Catholics in England and across Europe. It was the volume which impressed upon generations the horrors of Bloody Mary's reign of terror and which awakened people in this country to a sense of solidarity with their fellow sufferers in Europe. Foxe had been an exile himself and conducted thousands of interviews with people. His story of the composer and Biblical scholar, John Merbecke, whose setting of the Holy Communion remain in use at St Laurence almost five hundred years later, was one of those featured. Foxe did his best to check every source and his stories are simply told, designed not to elicit pity for the victims but admiration. It was made accessible to all by the illustrations which meant that even those who could not read, could see the way the Roman Catholics had tortured, maimed and executed people. Amongst the memorable stories was that of the martyrdom of Perotine Massey, a Protestant woman in Guernsey who was pregnant. This did not prevent her being tied to a stake and burnt alive in July 1556 alongside her mother and sister but as she burned, her belly split and the child dropped. It was reported that by a miracle, the child was not burnt for it fell on some dampened wood – a device often employed to lengthen the death pains of the victim. The child was retrieved but the order was given by the Roman Catholic in charge to toss the live newborn baby back into the flames. Another story told of William Hunter, a nineteen year old apprentice in London arrested after a Roman Catholic priest caught him looking at a Bible. John Tooly, meanwhile, was burnt for reciting the Litany in English. Then too there was Rawlins White, an elderly fisherman who was so keen to read the Scriptures that he saved up to send his son to school so that his son could teach him in turn. Having read the Scriptures, he refused to accept the idolatry of the Mass so was burnt in his wedding shirt. There was the heroism of Cranmer and Latimer at their executions and the horror of Bishop Ridley's botched demise. Bishop Hooper was imprisoned in a dungeon for eighteen months before being taken to his execution:

> Three iron hoops had been prepared to fasten him to the stake. There was a strong wind and the greater part of the faggots being green it was a long time before they caught fire. Three times they were lighted before they really began to burn up. He was heard to pray aloud: "Lord Jesus, have mercy upon me! Lord Jesus, receive my spirit" Those were the last words he was able to utter. He was black in the mouth and his tongue swollen that he could not speak. His lips went till they were shrunk to the gums and he knocked his breast with his hands until one of his arms fell off and then knocked still with the other while the fat, water and blood dropped out of his fingers' ends until... his hand did cleave fast to the iron upon his breast. In three quarters of an hour, neither moving forwards, backward nor to any side... his bowels fallen out, his body fell forwards and he

was released from his sufferings. He died as quietly as a child in his bed.

The question arises how St Laurence came to have the book and how it was used In April 1571, Convocation – the precursor of Synod – voted that cathedrals should all display a copy of Foxe's work alongside the Holy Bible. Parishes were encouraged to do so but visitation articles show this was not enforced. Since the accounts do not exist for St Laurence at this time, it cannot be known if the church bought a copy or was given it by a wealthy parishioner, one of the Johnson family perhaps. Its existence is highly significant as showing the parish's Protestant sympathies. Parishioners would have known all about the burnings in Canterbury, Maidstone and London and they would have heard about the atrocities in France and the work of the Inquisition because their position on the coast brought them into contact with Europeans. The fact that it was displayed alongside the Holy Bible gave the impression to worshippers and visitors that it was to be regarded almost as a sacred text. Vicars from Simon Stone onwards would have preached sermons that referenced the lives of martyrs and the church school would have used it as a textbook.[43] Some churches read extracts of it during services, either according to a schedule drawn up by the vicar or based on the calendar of martyrs included in the book and laid out like the Prayer Book lectionary. For ministers who could not preach, reading an inspiring story of courageous witness was not only easy but arguably relevant as it demonstrated faith in action. When there was no minister – as happened often in St Laurence – the clerk could read from Foxe or Erasmus in lieu of a sermon. It is certain that wet afternoons found people reading it for themselves or to others in the church and looking at the pictures with the sort of fascination always bred by horrific crimes. The importance of the work in formulating opinion cannot be over-emphasised.

The copy at St Laurence remained on display as late as the 1830s when it was to be found with the Geneva Bible in the north chancel just outside the vestry.[44] For over two hundred years it must have inspired parishioners but it was removed by the Reverend George Sicklemore for reasons which are unknown. It was a most regrettable loss.

It is impossible to say what became of most of the items made redundant by the Reformation. Part of one screen remains in the church recycled to create a vestry but other items would have been broken up or sold. The fate of one small twenty pound bell is known because at the end of Elizabeth's reign when there were fears of invasion, the Commissioners for Ramsgate asked that it be melted down with other metal to make a new bell for the watch-house on the shore which could then be rung in event of trouble.[45]

---

[43] For example, Edward Clark, *The Protestant Schoolmaster* (London, 1682)
[44] Stephen Glynne, *Notes on the Churches of Kent* (London 1877) p.38. Glynne's visit took place between 1829 and 1840 but the exact date is unknown. It is possible that the copy of Erasmus' *Paraphrases* was also still in the church as Glynne refers to other books of similar vintage being on display alongside.
[45] Hussey op.cit. p.34

Robert Sprackling monument

The main monument in the church to date from the Tudor period is to Robert Sprackling who died on May 15th 1590.[46] Situated now on the west wall of the south chancel, it shows him lying down with his hands in a position of prayer. He is fashionably dressed with a small ruff, doublet with slashed sleeves, velvet breeches and two designs of hose held taut by garters. A row of buttons can be seen around his waist and these were a male status symbol at the time often being made of precious metals or incorporating jewels. His outfit is fastened together with strips of leather known as points due to the metal rivets in the ends. His short beard is typical of the period and he is bare headed as a sign of humility. The memorial is a fine example of Southwark alabaster work.

It is unknown how old Robert was when he died but his will names three grandchildren as well as two surviving adult sons and three married daughters.[47] Robert's will shows him to have been a man of property for he leaves all of the following: Newland Grange, Ellington, a house and three acres at Newington, various properties in Cliffsend that realise an annual rent of £20, a farm at Haine, a house in Canterbury, two cottages at Sarre, woodland at Hoath, Ryders Wood plus marshes at Chislet and unspecified land at Minster. The Ellington estate alone was huge stretching as he noted from Thomas Terry's Way (Grange Road) to Southwood in one direction, to the vicarage in the north and out to Upper Court. In cash bequests, he left around £200 which would be over £50,000 today.[48] He left a young cow to his servant William Ewell and the use of the house and grounds at Newington for life to another servant named William Joy.[49] His eldest son Adam got Ellington complete with "plate and jewels" whilst his wife was given the house at Canterbury.[50] To the poor chest at St Laurence he gave £3 which would today equate to just over £800.

---

[46] The great-grandfather of the notorious Adam. Joan St Nicholas' is early Tudor, see pp.31-32
[47] PCC 11/75/466. The will was made fifteen months before his death.
[48] An exact figure is impossible because he left a certain amount to each godchild without saying how many he had.
[49] Robert's great-grandson attacked his servant Ewell just before murdering his wife in 1653 and it is likely that this Ewell was a direct descendant of the one mentioned in 1588.
[50] Robert had married Joan Lynch in 1576 when he was a widower.

Robert's monument was originally placed on the pillar which formed the north-east pier of the tower facing what was then the pulpit, presumably to indicate his attention to the Word. It was moved in the early nineteenth century to its current location.[51]

Geneva Bible

The greatest treasure possessed by the church is its copy of the Geneva Bible. This is not because of its financial value but because it represents a link to those courageous souls who fought for our faith and our right to read the Word of God in our own language.

The Geneva Bible takes its name from its place of printing. When Bloody Mary came to the throne and began her reign of terror, a number of Protestants agonised over what they should do. Should they stay and be martyred and so bear witness to God's truth or should they flee into exile and take their manuscripts with them so they could return at a later date? Those who escaped abroad included a number of scholars who set to work creating a new translation of the scriptures into English. Their aim was to produce something they believed would be more accurate than Henry VIII's Great Bible but also something which would be more accessible. In 1557, they completed the New Testament and in 1560, the entire Bible.

It was not long before copies of the new Bible began to reach England. Some would have been smuggled in locally through Sandwich and Ramsgate. Unlike the official Bible, the Geneva Bible was small enough to carry in a bag or even large pocket. The St Laurence Geneva is 16cm x 25cm x 8cm. The typeface was much clearer and easier to read. Words were included in full with none of the medieval contractions found in the Great Bible, such as thē for them. Most importantly, it contained notes to help the reader understand the text. Each book had an introduction and there were pages of maps and

---

[51] Lewis op.cit 1723 edition p.98 and Zechariah Cozens, *A Tour through the Isle of Thanet* (London, 1793). p.55 both refer to it in this location showing it was there for the entire eighteenth century. The painting of the south aisle which dates from c.1850 shows it in its present position. The exact date of moving and the reason is unknown but it may have been in 1837 when the church was redecorated.

tables of cross references. The Geneva Bible was the first to show the New Testament text divided into numbered verses, something we take for granted today. Sales soared and by 1644, it had run through 140 editions.

The St Laurence copy contains not just the text of the Holy Bible but a number of other documents. At the back is a copy of Robert Herry's 1578 *Two right profitable and fruitful concordances* as printed by Robert Barker in 1608. This includes not just references to words but notes on where to find verses relating to particular subjects or which can be used as reassurance in particular situations. For example:

> God will keep his saints from slipping away in temptation -
> 1 Sam. 2-9
> Prayer against pride – Eccles 23: 4-7, Prov. 30: 7-8

It also includes direct teaching such as:

> Against worshipping of saints – Judg 13:15-16, Ps. 19:1, 115:1, 81:9, Isa 42:8, Esth 13:13-14, Matt. 4:10, Luke 4:8, Acts 10: 25-26, 14:11, 1 Cor. 1:12-13, 3:5-6, Rev 22: 8-9
> The faithful are priests – Prov 19:16, Isa 16:6, 66:21, Jer 33:21, Ps. 13:1-9, 18
> Offering spiritual sacrifice – Rom 12:1, 1 Pet. 2:5, Rev. 1:6

At the front of the book is part of *The Whole Booke of Psalmes, Collected into English Metre* which was originally published in 1562. This was the only music allowed in English churches, other than Merbecke's settings, for centuries. The first fourteen pages are missing as is the second half and it is a sign of how much the owner valued the work that they chose to pay to have it bound in with the Geneva Bible despite it being incomplete. Amongst the psalms surviving is the twenty-third which is familiar to us today as "The Lord is my Shepherd." Two versions of this are included. One is by Thomas Sternhold and dates from 1548. It begins:

> My shepherd is the loving Lord
> Nothing whereof I need
> In pastures fair with waters calm
> He set me forth to feed
> He did convert and glad my soul
> And brought my mind in frame
> To walk in paths of righteousness
> For his most holy name

The second version comes from the book of worship used by the English exiles in Geneva and that begins:

> The Lord is only my support
> And he that doth me feed
> How can I then lack anything
> Whereof I stand in need?
> He doth me fold in coats most safe
> The tender grass fast by
> And after drives me to the streams
> Which run most pleasantly

A few of the psalms contain music but most are just words which can be sung to any tune. Both versions of Ps.23 shown are in double common metre so could be sung today to the same tunes as *I heard the voice of Jesus say*, *It came upon the midnight clear* or *Thine arm, O Lord, in days of old*.

The owner of the St Laurence Geneva Bible clearly enjoyed the psalms because a copy of Coverdale's Psalms from the Book of Common Prayer are also included. There is too a single page of the Commination against Sinners from 1559.

Three more complete documents appear at the front and these would have been sold with the Bible itself. The first is a set of Godly Prayers which appeared with the 1552 and 1559 Prayer Books and were first bound with the Geneva Bible in 1582. These include prayers for different occasions and days of the week: amongst them is the prayer against worldly carefulness first seen in Henry VIII's Primer of 1546. Typical is that provided for use at bedtime:

> O merciful Lord God, Heavenly Father, whether we sleep or wake, live or die, we are always Thine. Wherefore I beseech Thee heartily that Thou wilt vouchsafe to take care and charge of me and not to suffer me to perish in the works of darkness, but to kindle the light of Thy countenance in my heart that Thy godly knowledge may daily increase in me through a right and pure faith and that I may always be found to walk and live after Thy will and pleasure. Through Jesus Christ Our Lord and Saviour, Amen

Since the prayers reference King James I by name, it is evident that this section was printed between 1603 and 1625.

There is an introduction to the subject of Holy Scripture and what it means which is reproduced here in the Appendix. That is followed by a Question and Answer series about how to live a Christian life which includes:[52]

Q - I perceive that nothing is more necessary than the word of God : therefore I pray you, show me how I may attain to some knowledge and profit thereby.

A - By diligent hearing of such as preach it, by continual and orderly exercise of reading and praying

Q - What orderly exercise think you most convenient to be used herein?

A - That as every day, twice at the least, we most commonly receive food to the nourishment of the corporal life : so no day be let pass without some reading, in such sort that occasion thereby may be taken to speak again unto God by prayer, as he in his word speaks unto us: so that at the least two chapters would be orderly and advisedly read every day, all other business, impediments and lets set apart.

Q - This seems very easy to be done : what think you else required?

A - That some special places of Scripture be committed to memory, that the mind may ever be furnished with some good matter against temptations. to which end I note these scriptures

---

[52] This section was added into Geneva Bibles from 1583.

unto you, whereupon you may join your own choice : Psalms 139,37,51, Isa.53, John 17, Rom.8., I Tim.4

Q - But the scriptures are hard and not easy to understand
A - Discourage not yourself herewith : for God makes them easy to such as in humility seek him : and that hardness that you find, serves to move you to the more diligence and to make enquiry of such as have knowledge when any doubt arises. That which you perceive not at one time, God shall reveal at another : so that you shall have your growing in grace, knowledge and godliness, to God's glory and your own comfort in Christ, whose Name for ever be praised. Amen.

A simple prayer was then provided to assist the reader:

Give me grace to love thy holy word fervently, to search the scriptures diligently, to read them humbly, to understand them truly, to live after them effectually. O Lord grant me thus to do, for the glory of thy holy Name. Amen

Regarding the Scriptures themselves, the translation includes the famous reference to breeches which was introduced to Geneva Bibles from 1579, Genesis 3:7 reading as: "Then the eyes of them both were opened, and they knew that they were naked, and they sewed fig tree leaves together, and made themselves breeches." [53] It also includes the first use of the phrase "through a glass darkly" in 1 Cor 13:12, a phrase to become famous when it was adopted by the Authorised Bible in 1611.[54] In other places it follows Tyndale in the use of words which were selected to most accurately reflect the meaning of the original Greek although they were a little archaic, for example the use of "harberous" in 1 Pet. 4:9 meaning to provide a safe harbour, something later translations rendered as hospitable.

> 7 Then the eyes of them both were opened, and they ᵍ knew that they were naked, and they sowed figge tree leaues together, and made themselues †breeches.

The Geneva Bible version of Gen 3:7

---

[53] The note records that this was their interpretation of the Hebrew which meant "things to gird about them to hide their privities."
[54] In the Great Bible of Henry VIII it was aprons.

> that the same tre was good to eate, and lusty to the eyes, & that the same tre was pleasaunt to get wisdome) toke of the frute therof, and dyd eate: and gaue vnto her husband beynge with her, which dyd eate also. And the eyes of them both were opened: and they knewe that they were naked, & they sowed fygge leaues together, and made themselues aperns. And they heard ye voyce of the Lord God walkynge in the garden in the coole of the daye. And ☞ Adam & his wyfe dyd the

The Great Bible version of Gen 3:7

Since the purpose of the editors was to encourage study, each book of the Bible had its own introduction or Argument. That to The Epistle of Jude read:

> St Jude admonisheth all churches generally to take heed of deceivers which go about to draw away the hearts of the simple people from the truth of God and willeth them to have no society with such who he setteth forth in their lively colour, showing by divers examples of the Scriptures, what horrible vengeance is prepared for them: finally he comforteth the faithful and exhorteth them to persevere in the doctrine of the Apostles of Jesus Christ.

Notes appear throughout the text. Those to Revelation identify the "beast that cometh out of the bottomless pit" as "the Pope which hath his power out of hell and cometh thence". Regarding Rev. 11:9 it compares Papal jurisdiction with "Sodom for their abominable sin and to Egypt because the true liberty to serve God is taken away from the faithful." The earlier Geneva Bibles had been less explicitly anti-Catholic but in 1572 the Massacre of St Bartholomew's took place when it was said that a hundred thousand Protestants were murdered. This hardened attitudes and since refugees from this catastrophe would have come into the parish, it is easy to speculate that volumes condemning the Pope would have been welcome. The notes are, however, positive, for example saying regarding Rev. 11:15 "Albeit Satan by the Pope, Turk and other instruments troubleth the world never so much, Christ shall reign."

Other notes were less controversial such as that on Jesus' injunction to be the "salt of the earth" (Matt. 5:13) which read:

> The ministers of the word especially must needs lead others both by word and deed to this greatest joy and felicity. Your office is to season men with salt of the heavenly doctrine. Your doctrine must be very sound and good, for if it be not so, it shall be nought set by, and cast away as a thing unsavoury and vain.

Although it appears as a single book today, the St Laurence Geneva Bible represents a binding together of a number of different documents from the late Elizabethan and Jacobean periods. It was possible to buy the Geneva Bible unbound from as little as seven shillings (about £70 today) which put it within reach of poor clergy and devout laymen of the skilled craftsmen and yeoman classes. It is likely someone bought it thus and that another person later in the seventeenth century, who had a little more money, chose to have it bound properly with what remained of their copy of the psalms.

Like all good Bibles, the St Laurence Geneva shows signs of being well read. Between the Apocrypha and New Testament is a hand written copy of the hymn by Joseph Addison 'When all thy mercies' which first appeared in *The Spectator* on August 9th 1712. The handwriting would suggest a date in the first part of the eighteenth century showing that the volume was used for at least two hundred years.

By studying this Bible we not only learn about God but we are enabled to make a direct link with the earliest English Protestants and to see the message our parish clergy would have heard and based their ministry upon.

CLERGY AND STAFF

Our first record of a vicar in the sixteenth century is of **James Young** who was present at the valuation survey made at some time between February and May 1535. That survey showed that his income was £7 a year – the equivalent of around £3900 today. Of this sum, £4 was paid out of Newland Grange. This might be compared to the vicar of Monkton who got £13 8s 4d, St Peter's who got £8 17s 8d, St John's who got £8, Minster who got £33 3s 4d and St Nicholas who got £15 19s 4d.[55] Parliament implied that the minimum needed to support a clergyman was £8 per annum when they exempted those earning less from paying the subsidy.[56] Leaving the vicar deliberately in such poverty explains much of the resentment against the Abbey which, with an annual income of £1274 (almost three quarters of a million pounds today), could have afforded to give him an increase.[57] It should also be remembered that, as in the middle ages, the entire of the vicar's first year's income went in tax and ten per cent of every year thereafter.[58]

On August 15th 1535, he was replaced by **John Young**. The only thing known about him is that he played host to Archbishop Thomas Cranmer when he visited the church to preach.

He was followed in 1538 by **Edward Ming** who was one of those monks dispossessed by the Dissolution. As late as February 1556 he was receiving an annual

---

[55] John Caley (ed.), *Valor Ecclesiasticus* vol 1 (London, 1810) pp.34-35
[56] Michael Zell, 'The Personnel of the clergy of Kent in the Reformation Period' in *English Historical Review* vol 89 no CCCLII (1974) p.529
[57] Caley op.cit. p.89. Christ Church priory, which later became the cathedral, was worth £2289.
[58] These sums had been paid to Rome but after the Reformation went to the Crown.

pension of £6 8s 4d which effectively doubled his meagre salary.[59] Given his background in the Abbey and his evident Catholicism, it is perhaps surprising that he remained vicar here throughout the reign of Edward VI. Was he convinced by the new teaching or did he just pay it lip service? He stayed at St Laurence until March 1557 when he moved on to Hernehill. He died as incumbent of that parish in June 1567.

There is no record of there being a new vicar until the start of October 1561 when **William Marsh** was appointed. Services were probably taken between 1557 and 1561 by a succession of curates but it is likely that there were times when no minister was available. The religious changes had made men nervous about entering the ministry as a career and St Laurence was such a poor parish that it was an unattractive option. It is telling that William Marsh was also appointed vicar of St Peter's at the same time in order that he have sufficient income to live upon.[60] The income was still £7 per annum which might be compared to the £4 per annum plus food earned by labourers or £9 plus food earned by skilled craftsmen such as carpenters.[61] Convocation in 1562 recommended that £20 should be the minimum paid to clergy to attract quality candidates.[62] To the annoyance of the parishioners at St Peter's, Marsh chose to live at St Laurence which meant they did not get regular services or hear the Gospel and they complained at the lack of sermons.[63] Marsh was described as being a learned man who cared for the poor and he was also the first vicar to have been a married man.[64]

Marsh was followed by **John Coldwell** who was appointed on 27th December 1567, the day he was ordained. Coldwell was just twenty-four at this point and had spent eight years at St John's College, Cambridge. As such, he was the best educated vicar that the parish had ever had but his training had been in medicine. Since 1564, Coldwell had been a doctor in his native town of Faversham. This is why, despite being a graduate, Coldwell was not licensed to preach in his own right and had to stick to reading from the authorised Book of Homilies. In 1569, the St Laurence churchwardens denounced him for using ordinary bread for Holy Communion but this did not stop him being appointed chaplain to Archbishop Matthew Parker the same year.[65] This role probably limited the time he spent in the parish but boosted his income. In 1571, also whilst still Vicar of St Laurence, he became Archdeacon of Chichester. Evidently he could not carry out both

---

[59] W. E. Flaherty, 'The Pension Book of Cardinal Pole' in *Archaeologia Cantiana* vol. 2 (1859) p.58

[60] The appointment read: 'tam propter caritatem et paucitatem ministrorum idoneorum in hoc regno Anglie nunc existentem quam propter exilitatem et exiguitatem fructuum et proventuum dicte vicarie sancti Laurentii'

[61] Rev. C. Eveleigh Woodruff, 'Wages paid at Maidstone in Queen Elizabeth's reign', *Archaeologia Cantiana* vol.22 (1897) pp.316-319

[62] Christopher Hill, *Society and Puritanism in Pre-Revolutionary England*, (London, 1964) p.50

[63] Arthur Hussey, 'Visitations of the Archdeacon of Canterbury', *Archaeologia Cantiana* vol. 25 (1902) p.44. Marsh gave up St Peter's in 1564.

[64] Lewis op.cit. (1723 edition) p.128

[65] Hussey op.cit. p.31 It was from the Archbishop's frequent surveys that the phrase Nosey Parker stems.

roles which were far apart and this probably marked the effective end of his ministry in the parish. He left at some point prior to Whitsun 1572 when he moved on to become Rector of Tunstall.

Coldwell is notable for being the only vicar so far to have gone on to become a bishop. From Tunstall, he went on to become Dean of Rochester from 1581 to 1591 and he was then appointed Bishop of Salisbury. His time there was marked by a long running property conflict with Sir Walter Raleigh. He died on 14th October 1596 by which time he was so poor that his body had to be buried without honours in a previous bishop's tomb to avoid expense.[66]

A survey from 1569 when Coldwell was vicar shows that the parish then numbered 98 houses and had an adult population of around 400. If children had been included, the total would have been nearer 600.[67] Twenty-five of the houses were in Ramsgate.

Coldwell was succeeded by **Simon Stone** who was appointed on 30th May 1572, three weeks after his marriage. Once again, due to financial problems, he was also made Vicar of St Peter's though in this case, he received the second appointment in October 1573 and not at the same time. By 1578, Stone had moved to St Peter's which naturally angered the people at St Laurence. They complained that he did not preach quarterly, he failed to read the Litany on Wednesdays and Fridays, and when he did appear to take a service, he did not wear a surplice, though they added that this could be because the church did not own one.[68] They also advised that due to financial problems, they could not afford the required flat breads so he was using ordinary bread for communion.[69] He was more popular at St Peter's where he continued as vicar until his death in 1617.

Although Simon Stone may have been unpopular with the churchwardens, he was responsible for one of the most important developments at St Laurence, the foundation of the parish school. This would have been held in the church though it is not certain where. The side chapel represented a large empty space after the removal of the two altars and the existence of ledger stones in that area from 1694 to 1735 shows the area was not pewed at the same time as the rest of the church.[70] Alternatively, they may have used the back of the church. Cuts in the pillars on the south side show evidence of a screen between the aisle and the nave and just such a screen existed in this position at St

---

[66] Details of Coldwell's later career are taken from his entry in the *Dictionary of National Biography*.
[67] Hussey op.cit. p.31. The figure of 400 relates to communicants who would have been people of both sexes aged fourteen or more.
[68] Surplices were valuable items. It took 8 ells of cloth (10 yards) at 5s. an ell to make a surplice which cost £2 in 1578, around £600 today, See Ware op.cit p.18
[69] ibid. See also Claude Jenkins 'An unpublished record of Archbishop Parker's visitation of 1573' in *Archaeologia Cantiana* vol 29 (1911) p.288
[70] The later ledger stone of 1836 which commemorates the vicar's daughter was laid in front of the pews which faced the high chancel. It is under the communion rails on the left now.

John's in Margate to partition off their school.[71] It is possible they used both for two classes. Education was valued highly by the reformers and Henry VIII himself in 1545 had ordered that as soon as children had learnt their ABC, they should be taught to pray.[72] Indeed, the purpose of education then was simply to encourage people to read the Bible and so grow spiritually. It was not intended to further anyone's career prospects. If people wanted to know more than how to read, they had to pay.

Simon Stone started a school at St Peter's in 1575 and three years later did the same at St Laurence. The first teacher was John Cole. Four years later, John Hewitt took over, a father of five in his late forties and.[73] The school was to continue through to 1644.

The lack of any costs in the church accounts indicates that some charge must have been made for attending, though it is possible that poorer children – or certainly those who appeared quick witted - were subsidised from donations. The majority, would only have attended long enough to learn to read. This would have been taught by the teacher displaying the letters and encouraging the children to recognise them alone and in combination:

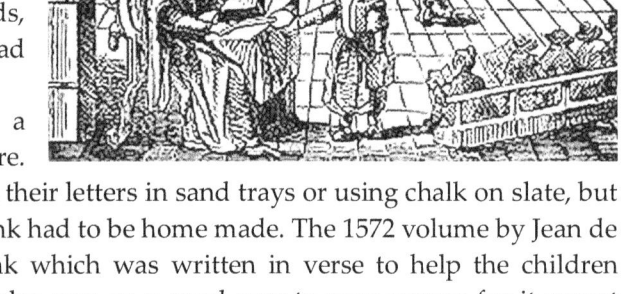

Dab, deb, dib, dob, dub
Dac, dec, dic, doc, duc
Dad, ded, did, dod, dud
Daf, def, dif, dof, duf [74]

As soon as they could form words, they would have been taught to read the Lord's Prayer from a horn book.

Writing would have been a separate subject and cost more. Initially children could learn to form their letters in sand trays or using chalk on slate, but paper was expensive and pens and ink had to be home made. The 1572 volume by Jean de Beauchesne contains a recipe for ink which was written in verse to help the children remember it. Learning by rote was also seen as a good way to save money for it meant that the school only required one book for the teacher.

> To make common ink, of wine take a quart
> Two ounces of gum, let that be a part
> Five ounces of galls of copperas take thee
> Long standing doth make it better to be

---

[71] Lewis op.cit. 1736 edition p.140
[72] Royal Injunction of 6th May 1545 introducing the *King's Primer*.
[73] A list of licensed teachers appears in Arthur J. Willis *Canterbury Licences (General) 1568-1648* (London, 1972) and online at http://db.theclergydatabase.org.uk
[74] Anon, *An ABC for Children* (1570) p.2

If wine ye do want, rain water is best
And as much stuff as above at the least
If ink be too thick put vinegar in
For water doth make the colour too dim[75]

They would have copied Biblical texts as writing practice.

Enter in at the straite gate for wide is the gate and brode is the waie that leadth to destructioun and many there be that go in thereat

The sons of the better off farmers and merchants would have been taught some mathematics. Simple addition, subtraction, multiplication and division could be practiced orally and then on slates or with counters arranged in rows representing value. The standard reference book for teachers through the sixteenth and seventeenth centuries was Humfrey Baker's *The Wellspring of Sciences* and that included practical exercises such as:

1. At 5d the yard, what will 49 yards amount unto?
2. When the quarter of wheat doth cost 6s 8d the cost of bread weighing 20 ounces is sold for a half penny. If the quarter of wheat did cost 10s, how much shall the loaf of bread be sold that weigheth 16 ounces?
3. If 1lb of cinnamon do cost me 8s ready money, for what price shall I sell 100lb to be paid a quarter at one month and the residue at end of three months so that I may gain £9 upon the 100lb in 12 months after the rate? [76]

The success of the school may be seen by the rising numbers of people who were able to sign their own wills as years went by. At the start of the seventeenth century, yeomen were frequently incapable of doing this but by mid century, even fishermen were more usually able to write their own name.

Simon Stone was followed by **Thomas Shueler** who was instituted on 19th March

---

[75] Jehan de Beauchesne, *A booke containing divers sortes of handes* (London 1571) p.3. The sample is in secretary hand, the most widely used Tudor hand.

[76] Humfrey Baker, *The Wellspring of Sciences,* (1564) pp. 151, 222-223. The counters are adapted from an image in Clement Francis, *The Petie Schole,* (London, 1587) and show £369 17s 10¾d

1584. He did not stay long and was regarded as totally unsatisfactory by the churchwardens. They complained that he did not catechise or wear a surplice and in 1585 noted that he had disappeared altogether.[77]

Nine years were to pass by before St Laurence got another vicar. Valentine May served as curate in the first part of that period and Daniel Pawson the latter.[78] The low remuneration was the main factor. The income remained £7 but due to the high inflation of the 1540s, much of which stemmed from the costs of the war in France, this had devalued over the years. In 1520, the £7 had been worth about £4000 in today's money, but by 1550 it was nearer £2500 and by 1580 just £2000. By 1600, the value was under £1400. That was barely enough for one man to live on let alone a family and the vicar had to return a tenth of it in tax. Recruitment cannot have been helped by the fact that the vicarage was said to be in ruins from 1573 onwards, hardly surprising since its maintenance was the responsibility of the clergy. This may have been a medieval building for in 1615, the vicar described it as "an old dwelling house with a little out room, one close with a small garden."[79] If so, it would have been uncomfortable because it would have had a central hearth rather than chimneys. Although many parishes had large amounts of glebe to generate an income, the Vicar of St Laurence had only two acres, just half that which a 1589 Act of Elizabeth I said was the minimum to be allowed for all new houses on grounds less than this could not offer subsistence to a man and his family. At St Laurence there was room for a vegetable patch and perhaps a fruit tree but not much more. Ideally, the Vicar would have wanted to keep pigs, chickens and at least one cow.

In 1588, a survey found there were 656 communicants.[80] Allowing for younger children who would not have been confirmed, that would suggest that the population had grown to around 800.

In February 1595, **John Kington** was appointed as vicar and he stayed until the start of 1607 when he moved on to become Vicar of St Dunstan's, Canterbury. Since no complaints were made about him, it must be assumed that he took services just as the Prayer Book demanded, that he preached regularly, catechised children and led a godly life.

All of the Tudor clergy would have been known locally by the title of Sir and their Christian name, hence Sir Thomas, Sir John etc. This was the customary mode of address for clergy at this period. They did not become known as Mr for another century.

---

[77] Hussey op.cit. p.32

[78] Pawson was at St Laurence for at least four years. He witnessed the will of Thomas West on 8th September 1589 and went on to become Vicar of Tonge in July 1593. He died a year later.

[79] Cotton op.cit. p155

[80] Edward Hasted, *The History and Topographical Survey of the County of Kent*, vol. 10 (London, 1800) p.405

PEOPLE, EVENTS AND PLACES

Thomas Cranmer

The most important visitor to the parish in the Tudor period was Archbishop Thomas Cranmer. The exact date of his visit is unknown but was almost certainly in either October or November 1535 while he was resident at Ford near Chislet.[81] The fact that he wrote a letter to Henry VIII on 26th August 1536 summarising the sermon he preached enables us to create a clear image of what happened when he came to St Laurence.

Cranmer's arrival in the parish would have been a spectacular affair. He probably journeyed from his home at Ford through Sarre to St Nicholas-at-Wade and then made his way across the island. He would have been accompanied by banners, the episcopal cross, by maybe a dozen or so priests and at least the same number of secretaries and servants plus an armed guard and herald at the front with a trumpet to sound his approach. They would have been mounted on horses of the best quality with coats of velvet embroidered with gold thread. The vicar and wardens would have gone to meet him at the parish border and accompanied him to the church where the bells would have been ringing. John Johnson would have been with them as he knew the Archbishop well from his work as Cromwell's messenger. Cranmer and his senior staff would have stopped at the vicarage for a meal and so that the horses could be tended. This would have been the Archbishop's opportunity to ask questions about the parish and the vicar's own ministry. Did he preach regularly? What did he teach the people about the Bible? Was he aware of anyone speaking against the King? As the vicar had only arrived a couple of months before, they no doubt discussed his future hopes and plans.

The rest of Cranmer's party would have been entertained at the Church House which would have been busy brewing ale and roasting meat for days beforehand. A visit of this nature would have created a huge amount of work both in the entertaining of the Archbishop and his party and in the preparation of the church. People would have been polishing every surface and piece of plate until it gleamed and strewing fresh rushes. There was probably some effort made to practice a suitable psalm so they could try to make a good impression. Everyone would have been in their finest clothes. It was known that the Archbishop was close to the King and to Queen Anne Boleyn and a visit from Cranmer was regarded as being like a visit from the royal couple themselves.

Cranmer's sermon would have taken place during a Mass. It is unknown whether the church had a pulpit at the time and there may have been some frantic activity to construct one for the Archbishop's use. This would have stood under the tower and been

---

[81] James Gairdner (ed.) *Letters and Papers, Foreign and Domestic, Henry VIII*, Volume 9 (London, 1886) document numbers 627 dated 17th October to 869 dated 22nd November. This date is supported by Cranmer's own letter where he refers to talking before Christmas to some who questioned his sermon, John Cox (ed.) *Miscellaneous Writings and Letters of Thomas Cranmer* (Parker Society, 1846) p.328

raised up as high as possible so everyone could see and hear him. Sermons were extremely rare so people would not have known what to expect. Would he speak to them in terms they could understand or would it be something only the most educated could follow? For those who had opposed the King separating from Katherine of Aragon, there would have been keen interest to see whether he would mention that or offer any explanation for his role in the affair.

Cranmer began by saying that the Bishop of Rome was not God's Vicar on earth but that he had usurped authority contrary to God's word. He referred to Jesus giving Peter the keys of heaven and said that this was a gift to the Church as a whole, not one man. He spoke about Rome saying that it was not a holy place and about the Bishop of Rome telling them that he did not live the life which would be expected of a holy father. As Cranmer told Henry VIII, rather "I took occasion to declare the glory and pomp of Rome, the covetousness, the unchaste living, and the maintenance of all vices." Cranmer had visited Rome himself and had considerable dealings with the Papacy so he could speak from experience here. He then went on to explain that that the Bishop of Rome's laws were not equal to the law of God but sometimes contrary to it. Those which were good were being maintained by the King and "therefore as laws of your realm they must be observed, and not condemned." He would have enlarged on this with examples of papal rules which conflicted with scripture such as those relating to indulgences. This

issue of whether the Pope had authority to over-ride the word of God had been at the heart of England's break with Rome for the Pope had said that he could allow a man to marry his brother's widow despite it being forbidden in Leviticus. Cranmer said he told them that he had seen "the see of Rome work so many things contrary to God's honour and the wealth of this realm, and I saw no hope of amendment so long as that see reigned over us" which is why everyone should be glad that King Henry VIII now controlled the church. Henry was a godly man and intent on reforming abuses. Cranmer admitted that his sermon had been long but said that he was told afterwards that his detailed explanation had been appreciated:

"I was informed by sundry reports, that the people were glad that they heard so much as they did."

It might be queried why Cranmer came when he did. The summer of 1535 had seen the Holy Roman Emperor defeat the Turks then make an alliance with France against England. A new pope had been elected - Paul III - and he was actively seeking support to remove Henry from his throne. There was therefore a real danger of invasion and Henry VIII invested considerable sums in fortifying Dover Castle at this time.[82] The Isle of Thanet was close to the continent and a potential landing area and the last thing which the authorities wanted was to have people living on the coast who were not fully supportive of Henry's policies. Bishop Fisher of Rochester and Sir Thomas More had been executed earlier that summer and the visitation of the monasteries was ongoing, John Johnson being one of those involved. Events had left many people confused and asking questions and that always created a potentially dangerous situation, especially with the harvest having failed. Cranmer's job was to justify the King's actions and to inspire the people to support the cause and their country.[83]

William Warham

Although less famous today than Cranmer, William Warham was his predecessor as Archbishop of Canterbury and he also visited the parish at the start of November 1512. His purpose, as he advised Thomas Wolsey, was to check coastal defences.[84] The visit was prompted by the fact that the King had joined a league against France and was planning to go to war. Warham's report does not survive but he took advantage of his tour to conduct a visitation which found that the church was in good order. The only problems reported related to two wills where it was noted that the executors were with-holding bequests from the church.[85]

John Johnson

John Johnson was born in Canterbury around 1497. His mother may have died soon afterwards as when his father died in 1508, John was placed in the care of a priest in Lyminge. He was later apprenticed to a haberdasher in Canterbury named John Anthony who made him his heir. In response, Johnson adopted the alias of Anthony. It was through his trade with Christ Church priory that Johnson came to the attention of Thomas Cromwell, Henry VIII's chief minister. For the next eight years he worked for Cromwell

---

[82] The death of the Duke of Milan in November 1535 caused France to separate again from the Empire but this was not known when Cranmer visited.
[83] For more on the political situation of this period see Margaret Bolton, *De Carles' Trial and Death of Queen Anne Boleyn translated into modern English* (Berlin 2015)
[84] J. S. Brewer (ed.) *Letters and Papers, Foreign and Domestic, Henry VIII*, Vol. 3 (HMSO, 1867) no 2647 letter dated 31sst October
[85] K.L. Wood-Legh (ed.) *Kentish visitations of Archbishop William Warham and his deputies, 1511-1512 Kent Records* vol. 24 (KAS, 1984) pp.75-76

being involved in the case of the Nun of Kent, the dissolution of the monasteries and the King's works at Dover. His service saw him working with Archbishop Cranmer, Attorney General Christopher Hales, the Boleyn family, Henry VIII's uncle the Lord Lisle and Dr Rowland Lee who was widely supposed to have conducted the wedding of Henry VIII and Anne Boleyn. He was also Receiver-General for the property confiscated from Bishop Fisher. By 1534, he was living at St Laurence and he expanded his interests in the parish over the coming years purchasing Upper Court in 1558. He was a committed Protestant and it is entirely likely that he gave the church its first copy of the Holy Bible in English. By the time he was sixty, he had moved to the mainland where he witnessed the horrific burning alive of Protestants in Canterbury which began in July 1555 and continued to 11th November 1558, just six days before the accession of Queen Elizabeth. He even protested against this barbaric process. Johnson died in Fordwich in 1566 leaving money for sermons and for the repair of Ramsgate pier.[86]

A detailed biography of him can be found in the Appendices.

Dr Cotton repeats the bizarre story that originated with Agnes Strickland that Johnson's grandson Silas married the grand-daughter of Katherine Parr and so achieved great wealth.[87] Silas married Priscilla Bix in 1639 and derived his income from his own mercantile activities and that which he inherited from his father Paul. Katherine Parr's only child died when she was less than two years old so clearly never married or had children.[88]

Statistics

It is possible from the parish registers to derive information about the lives of parishioners in the later Tudor period

Between 1560 and 1609, a total of 1, 533 people were baptised at St Laurence, an average of almost thirty a year. Of these 793 were female (51.7%) and 740 were male (48.3%). Of these, 517 of the males and 508 of the females can be traced through from cradle to grave representing 70% and 64% respectively. A further 124 men and 203 women can be traced through to marriage after which they appear to have moved from the area. This leaves just 13.4% of males and 10.3% of females unaccounted for.

Amongst the boys, 118 died in their first year of life compared to 86 girls. This is in line with other areas where infant mortality was highest amongst males. At St Laurence, 15.9% of boys died before their first birthday – around one in six – whilst 10.8%

---

[86] The pier then was quite small and "by no means adequate to afford security to the numerous vessels that were driven on this coast in tempestuous weather" according to Leland who visited on behalf of Henry VIII in the early 1540s. Arthur Montefiore, *The Isle of Thanet with historical and descriptive notes* (London, 1893) p.42

[87] Agnes Strickland *Lives of the Queens of England* vol V (London, 1899) p.129

[88] The inscription for the child's burial was composed by Katherine Parr's chaplain, John Parkhurst and located by Professor Janel Mueller of Chicago University. The wills of Silas and his father are PRC17/52/127 and PRC17/69/175.

of girls did so – about one in nine. Children born in May and June were most at risk with a fifth dying in infancy whilst those born in July and August fared best with less than one in nine perishing. This pattern reflects the fact that mothers were most likely to be at risk of malnutrition in the late spring as the food from the previous harvest was almost exhausted and the new harvest was not yet in. Children who lost their mother during their first two years of life when they were most likely to have been breast feeding were significantly more at risk of early death. Almost a third of children who lost their mother during this time themselves died as infants.

Looking at life expectancy overall, just one person in fifty lived to see their eightieth birthday. Women were more likely to die as young adults due to risks associated with childbearing. Just over one in sixty births saw the mother die shortly afterwards, possibly from the results of complications.

Age at death	Male %	Female %
Infant	22.8	16.9
1 to 9 years	11.6	16.3
10 to 19 years	7.0	4.7
20 to 39 years	17.0	23.0
40 to 59 years	19.5	20.5
60 to 79 years	18.6	16.1
80 years or more	3.5	2.4

Amongst those who reached forty or more, 62% of men and 56% of women remained in St Laurence parish until their death. A further 29% of men and 37% of women moved but lived within five miles of their place of birth.

The low life expectancy affected family structure. A fifth of children were born without any grandparents and more than a third had just one. By age ten, over half had no grandparents and just one in three hundred had all four still alive. Yet those who had even one surviving grandparent aged ten could expect to live nine years longer than those children who were born without any. Whether this was due to genetics or the fact that parents could seek the childcare advice of their own parents is unclear.

Of those who married, 45% of women and 39% of men wed at St Laurence. A further 25% of women and 21% of men married elsewhere on the island. That left 29% of women and 39% of men forced to travel to the mainland to find a spouse. It does not follow that those who married away from home stayed away. Two thirds of those who married in Canterbury, for example, settled afterwards and died in St Laurence. Of the men, 23% married more than once and 14% of women. These were all after being widowed. The average age at first marriage was 24 for women and 27 for men.

A total of 398 couples married at St Laurence during the reign of Queen Elizabeth. Fifty per cent of grooms and fifty-nine per cent of brides had been born in the parish: just one in seven of either sex had been born on the mainland. Excluding couples where the wife was past childbearing, four in every five had children. The average family size was four with a quarter of couples having six or more. Less than one in five had two or less and in the majority of cases, these small families reflected the death of one of the parents not deliberate limitation which was seen as sinful. Of the couples who had children, almost half (45%) saw at least one of their children die in infancy. One family in twenty lost every child they had.

With regard to weddings, October and November were far and away the most popular months with more than a third of marriages taking place at that time. Less than 1% married in March due to the restriction on marrying in Lent. One in ten brides was pregnant. The stigma attached to illegitimacy is evident in that 99.74% of children were born in wedlock. This is the more impressive because the fee for a wedding and banns was 3s 6d – about two weeks wages for a labourer, a significant amount to save.[89]

With regard to names, over two thirds of boys shared just seven names – John, William, Thomas, Robert, Richard, Nicholas and Stephen. Almost a fifth of boys were called John. Bible names used included Moses, Mesach, Barnabus, Aquila, Samuel, Zachariah, Solomon, Nathaniel and, surprisingly, Manasses. Amongst the girls, fifteen per cent were named Mary with Elizabeth, Anne, Margaret, Joan, Alice and Katherine also being very popular. Together these six names accounted for sixty per cent of female names. Traditional Catholic names such as Mildred disappeared and were replaced by Biblical and faith related names such as Priscilla, Godly, Repentance, Rachel, Abigail, Abisag and Lydia.

Just over a quarter of the parish population shared one of just ten surnames – Coppin, Curling, Saunder, Bennett, Jenkin, Knowler, Johnson, Mockeness, Troward and Sprackling. The first two surnames represented more than a tenth with 5.2% of people named Coppin and 5.1% Curling.[90]

Visitations

It was the duty of churchwardens to present people who had failed to observe the royal laws regarding the church at the Archdeacon's court which sat twice a year in Canterbury at Easter and Michaelmas. They also had to report on the state of the church building.

In the reign of Queen Elizabeth (1558-1603), thirty-one cases were presented by the churchwardens.[91] They represented:

    7 complaints about individual vicars – as shown above
    7 cases where people owed the church money – total value £2 3s

---

[89] Lewis op.cit. 1723 edition p.103. This was the fee at Margate but it would have been general in the area.
[90] The next most common names were Bing, Bayley, Fairman, Martin and Colbrand.
[91] Hussey op.cit. pp.31-33, Jenkins op.cit. p288

- 8 people who refused to attend church regularly – including Gregory Curling who also owed the church money, George Mullet who preferred to spend his time in the alehouse, and Richard Wright who not only failed to attend but refused to keep his wife and demanded that she pay him rent for the pleasure of sharing his home
- 2 cases of suspected witchcraft – the first case was of Alice Bush, a widow who had recently arrived in the parish from Margate. She admitted that she did "use charms, sorcery, enchantments, invocations, circles, witchcraft, soothsaying or like crafts or imaginations invented by the devil" and was sentenced to do penance in the market place on July 3rd 1560. She did not turn up to do this and was excommunicated. This would have prevented her attending church in future, selling goods, being buried in consecrated ground and eating with other people.[92] Why she confessed to the crime is unknown. She appears to have left the parish again and her fate is uncertain.[93] The second case was of a married woman named Sybil Ferris who must have been around sixty. She was not convicted but she was charged with the same offence at a later date.
- 2 cases of immorality – Leonard Sprackling was reported to be living in sin with Julianne Saunder whilst a maid named Mary was pregnant out of wedlock. Leonard and Julianne paid a fine and moved to Canterbury where they married in 1562.
- 1 woman for blasphemy – Mrs Knowler was reported on a number of occasions for not attending church, for blasphemy, for being a drunkard, for being a common scold and generally not living in charity with her neighbours.
- 4 miscellaneous cases including a dispute about the burial of William Troward's father and John Duckett who was accused of teaching children without a licence. John Hewitt, who later served as official schoolmaster, was reported in 1578 for saying Morning and Evening Prayer in church in the absence of the vicar and also without any congregation. The authorities were keen to prohibit services held without a congregation lest they be compared to the Roman practice of masses being said by a priest alone under the belief that this would benefit the soul. The final case was of Robert Brown, a lighterman at Ramsgate, who was reported in 1581 for having observed when being told he must attend church on 20th October and thereafter: "It was never merry England since we were impressed to come to the church." The fact that he was not presented again indicates that Brown did as the law required until his death in 1598, albeit probably with an ill grace.

---

[92] Arthur J. Willis, *Church Life in Kent 1559-65* (London, 1975) p.39
[93] She may have been the Alice Bush buried at Faversham on 6th February 1560/1.

Poverty

One of the most famous changes made during Elizabeth's reign was the passing of the 1601 Poor Law. This made parishes responsible for the appointment of two overseers to establish and maintain records of land ownership in the parish and to use these to levy a rate to raise sufficient funds to care for the poor. They were then to make payments to the infirm and hungry according to need, make provision for orphans to be clothed and apprenticed and to organise basic medical care for those unable to purchase the service from an apothecary or midwife. The overseers were based in the church wax house which had declined in use following the Reformation. There was no longer such a great need for candles to be made and the ales had been stopped as they encouraged disturbances and rowdy behaviour.

Payments to the poor had been made before the Act and a list of those made in 1589 was found folded within the Churchwarden's accounts.[94] This shows eighty-four people received money totalling £8 17s 6d. Twenty-six of the recipients were women with twenty-two being shown as widows. Five of the women received aid on more than three occasions. Of those who could be traced, all were aged fifty or more and two-thirds died within five years. The average payment was 1s 3d. By contrast, three quarters of the male recipients received aid only once suggesting that they were not in long term ill health but rather plunged into unexpected need by maybe a delayed ship or weather affecting the harvest.

In order to assess the value of the average payment, it is worth considering current wages and prices. A table of wages from Maidstone in 1563 shows a labourer earned around three pence a day where his employer provided food and drink, or eight pence if he had to find his own food. Women domestics earned on average a penny a day whilst male servants got fifty per cent more. Boys and apprentices got less than half a penny a week. Skilled craftsmen such as carpenters and plasterers would have earned around a shilling a day.[95] Some price information exists in the local assize records and although there was considerable regional and seasonal variation, common costs included a penny for a loaf of bread or for six herrings, a penny ha'penny for a dozen candles, six pence for a cheese, fourteen pence for a loin of mutton, one shilling and sixpence for a shirt, two shillings for a petticoat and four shillings for a blanket,.[96]

Lifestyles

It is from the Elizabethan period that we get our first account of how parishioners lived. William Camden in 1586 wrote:

---

[94] CCA-U3-19/5/1
[95] Woodruff, 'Wages Paid' op.cit. pp.316-19
[96] J. S Cockburn (ed.), *Calendar of Assize Records* (HMSO, 1979) cases 12, 627, 700, 888, 945, 1645, 2786, 2881

> They are passing industrious and are, as it were, amphibious that is both land creatures and sea creatures, and get their living both by sea and land….They that hold the plough tail in clearing the ground, the same holds the helm in steering the ship. According to the season of the year they knit nets, they fish for cod, herring, mackerel, they sail and carry forth merchandise. The same again dung and manure their ground, plough, sow, harrow, reap their corn and they inn it. Men most ready and well appointed both for sea and land and thus go they round and keep a circle in their labours.[97]

This lifestyle can be confirmed through wills made by parishioners. For example Stephen Sampson of Ramsgate in 1592, who described himself as a fisherman, owned a third share in a boat named *The Thomas* plus various items of fishing equipment and a sea chest as well as a house in Ramsgate with a garden and twenty acres of land. He also owned a second house in Ramsgate with two acres of land attached which he rented out.[98]

In 1566, there were seventy men employed on fourteen vessels of between three and sixteen tons which were used in fishing and the carriage of corn.[99] This would have represented virtually the entire male population of Ramsgate plus maybe a fifth of those living in St Lawrence village.

Crime

The crime rate at this time appears to have been very low with just four cases in the entire of Queen Elizabeth's reign. Two of these were dismissed outright but Agnes Cutborne in 1586 was found guilty of murdering her newborn baby daughter by initially trying to strangle it and then cutting its throat. Agnes was a single woman and sentenced to hang. In the final case in 1601, two labourers were convicted of stealing three bushels of wheat from John Johnson. One of them absconded and the other was sentenced to be whipped until it was found that he had committed a burglary only the week before at Alkham whereupon he was hanged.[100] Unlike Agnes, neither of the labourers were parishioners. However, the true crime rate was undoubtedly higher than this. As a limb of Sandwich, Ramsgate cases would have been heard there but no records of these survive, something which should not be interpreted as meaning an absence of lawbreaking.

---

[97] William Camden, *Britannia* translated by Philemon Holland (London, 1610) p.340
[98] PRC 17/49/244
[99] J. M. Gibson, 'The 1566 Survey of the Kent Coast' in *Archaeologia Cantiana* vol 112 (1993) p.345
[100] Cockurn *Assize Records* op.cit. Case numbers 1475, 2788, 2826, 2916

The Seventeenth Century

THE BUILDING

The church is fortunate to have a set of churchwarden's accounts which cover the period 1613-47 and 1689-1721.[1] These make it possible to see some of the changes that took place to the building and with regard to worship over the century and to see the cost of those alterations. In 1614, for example, the church spent £1, around a twelfth of its total income, to buy a pulpit. A year later they spent a further 2s 4d for some decorative ironwork above it. Although we do not know what the pulpit at St Laurence looked like, a new one was purchased at St Nicholas-at-Wade about this time and that still exists and it is likely that the two were similar.

The pulpit at St Laurence was purchased from William Kennard who was a 38 year old joiner whose roots were in the parish although he then lived in Eastry. The cost of £1 would be equivalent to around £185 today. In 1638, an hour-glass was purchased and

---

[1] CCA-U3-19/5/1-5

fitted at a cost of 8d. This was not simply so that the preacher did not go on too long but was so that the congregation could see that they were getting the full hour of sermon which they believed was their entitlement.

One of the biggest areas of expense was always the bells. From the early seventeenth century, the church had what it termed the Great Bell, the Small Bell, the treble, the Second Bell and the Third Bell. Ropes were purchased almost every year, for example 1614, 1615, 1618, 1620, 1621, 1622 etc. at an average cost of 6s 4d per annum. Then there were gudgeons – 13s 8d in 1615 – and baldricks[2] which needed replacing every year or two at a cost of 2s 6d per bell. Mending the clappers was another regular expense, for example 10s in 1613, 8s 6d in 1614, 13s 6d in 1619, 11s 8d in 1620. In addition there were the occasional costs such as making a new wheel in 1624 for £1 5s, recasting a bell in 1641 for £14 9s and general repairs.

Although it cannot be known which foundry did the work in 1641, it is probable that it was Joseph Hatch of Broomfield. The amount paid in carriage is very close to that paid a few years earlier by Birchington church to have their bells transported there.[3] Hatch's foundry had operated since at least the mid Tudor period and given that Henry Hatch was a business partner of John Johnson of St Laurence, it is likely that this foundry was used in the Tudor period and that reliance on it would have continued into the 1640s unless there had been any dispute about workmanship or bills. Given the difficulty of transporting the bells, location would have been a key issue in selecting a supplier. In 1704, the bells would be sent by sea up to London from Margate but the lack of any references in 1641 to wharfage fees or ships suggests that they were moved by land. The fact that Hatch made bells for St Nicholas, Minster, Monkton and Margate as well between 1615 and 1636 also supports the belief that he was involved in 1641.[4]

Other bell related costs included work on the tower itself, or steeple as it was then called, and the provision of ladders for people to reach the bells in order to carry out the work. There were payments to the bell ringers for ringing to mark significant events such as November 5th and the King's birthday. In 1689, 7s was paid for ringing to mark the coronation of William and Mary. In 1694, 2s 4d was paid for them ringing when the King returned home from Europe, landing at Margate.[5] In 1688, it was reported that "the bells of the steeple are very much out of repair and want new casting; and the frames of the said bells want mending also" but despite an order from the Archdeacon to attend to this, it was not until 1704-5 that the work was done.

Another area of significant expense was the roof. Various sections were replaced in 1614, 1621, 1629, 1694 and 1698. These were occasions when at least two thousand tiles

---

[2] The leather lined strap from which the clapper was hung
[3] J. C. L. Stahlschmidt, *The Church Bells of Kent*, (London, 1887) p.176
[4] ibid. pp. 170, 349, 355, 357, 388. Alternatively, another foundry had opened in Canterbury around 1636 operated by John Palmar so this may have been used, ibid. p.83
[5] They also rang for his arrival in Margate in 1691 both events being referenced in William John Hardy (ed.) *Calendar of State Papers Domestic: William and Mary, 1690-1* (HMSO1898), p.223, 547

were used and it must be presumed that other work was done in the period 1648-88 for which we have no records. Inside the church, on the westernmost beams above the windows on each side, can be seen inscribed the date of the new roofs in those areas – 1687 in the north aisle and 1689 in the south.

As well as the church, the wardens had to maintain the Church Wax House and in 1637 this had its roof repaired whilst in 1619 the oven was rebuilt by the mason at a cost of 5s 6d. They had to contribute to the cost of repairing the pier as well, spending £3 9s 6d in 1637 for fresh planks and timber, probably after a storm.

The church windows too saw regular expenditure with the glazier being employed each year to carry out repairs at an average cost of 15s.

Other details to be found in the accounts include the laying of paving tiles throughout the church in 1616 and the extension of these into the vestry in 1617.[6] A mat was purchased to go round the font in 1699 and a gallery was erected at some point in the 1660s or 1670s as there was a payment to remove it in 1697. In 1694, a sundial was made and fitted to the church tower at a cost of £1 15s 10d (about £300 today). This can be seen in some old pictures of the church. A standing sundial in the churchyard was fitted in 1620. In 1619, work was done on the tower as the date was found carved on the bottom of the north-west pier during restoration in 1888.

It is not always possible to determine what work has been carried out because often the entries simply record that the churchwarden has paid the bill received from the carpenter, mason, glazier, smith etc. with no further details. There is only one explicit reference to work being carried out on the Church Wax House in the later period which suggests that either it was left to fall into disrepair after the Civil War or that the expenses were included in general bills for the church.

There are a number of references to books being purchased such as:

1627	Book of Common Prayer	8s
1633	The King's Book of Lawful Sports	6d
1634	Book of Common Prayer	3s 8d
1634	Book of Homilies	8d
1635	Holy Bible	£2 14s 4d[7]
1637	Book of the 39 Articles	1s 10d
1694	Prayers in memory of Queen Mary	1s 2d

The *Book of Lawful Sports* had originally been published in 1618 by James I but was re-issued in 1633 by Charles I. It said that after church, people should be allowed to dance, leap or enjoy archery but that there should be no bear baiting or bowling on that day.

---

[6] Dr Cotton's statement that the vestry was created in 1733 is erroneous as there are references to it in the accounts from 1616 and it is clear that it already existed by this date.

[7] This item was bought in Canterbury when the Vicar and wardens attended the visitation to avoid the extra expense of transporting it to the parish. The old one was sold to Mr Evers for 15s.

Only people who had attended church should be allowed to indulge in such activities. The reason given was that prohibiting such things prevented "the conversion of many, whom their priests will take occasion hereby to vex, persuading them that no honest mirth or recreation is lawful or tolerable in our religion, which cannot but breed a great discontentment in our people's hearts, especially of such as are peradventure upon the point of turning: the other inconvenience is, that this prohibition barreth the common and meaner sort of people from using such exercises as may make their bodies more able for war."[8] The real reason was that many churches had sermons on Sunday afternoons and the government wanted to suppress them for fear they would spread seditious ideas. Many people were upset by this document which the King required to be read from every pulpit in the country. One minister read it as ordered then recited the Ten Commandments and invited his congregation to choose whether they would rather obey God or man.[9]

Amongst some of the more unusual entries in the accounts are:

1615	3d to mend the stable
1618	£1 0s 10d to purchase a disused mast from a ship at Sandwich (7s 6d) for Nicholas Dason to make into two ladders to reach into the tower (13s 4d)
1628	2s 6d paid to John Francis, mariner, who had great loss by the Spaniards and Dunkerquers
1637	7s paid to 71 Christians redeemed out of Turkey
1689	5s to fifteen sailors who lost their ship
1694	5s sent to the victims of the great fire in York
1695	6s paid to the minister to redeem a slave
1696	1s 6d to set up a beacon on the church
1697	1s to William Fagg for setting up a dragnet

This last was a device for catching birds. Churchwardens were not only responsible for the church building but for vermin control across the parish. This was considered an important part of their job because if the crops were destroyed, people would starve. From the late seventeenth century and into the early eighteenth, regular payments were made to people – mostly teenage boys – for hedgehogs (4d each), sparrows (1d a dozen), polecats (4d each) and rooks (1d each) they had collected. In the early eighteenth century, the children of Robert and Jane Maxted appeared to be in contest with one another the following payments being reported:

---

[8] The reference to conversion here is interesting and indicates that notwithstanding the Reformation, there were still those who had yet to make a personal commitment to Christ.
[9] Richard Culmer, later Vicar of Minster, refused to read the Book of Sports and was one of those suspended by Archbishop Laud – Richard Culmer, *A Parish Looking Glasse* (London, 1657) p.8. For details on other clergy reactions including the minister quoted see B.M. Gardiner and J.S. Phillpotts *King and Commonwealth* (London, 1874) p.74

> John Maxted (age 15) 2d for a weasel
>
> William Maxted (age 7) 2d for a dozen sparrow's heads, 6d for half a dozen sparrows
>
> Sarah Maxted (age 11) 1s for 4 dozen sparrows and a hedgehog
>
> Mary Maxted (age 10) 4d for a polecat, 10d for 2 ½ dozen larks
>
> Robert Maxted (age 14) 3 ½d for 7 rooks heads

Their father at the time was parish constable and their uncle the churchwarden.

Although most of the expenses related to repairs and the church itself, there were occasions of community rejoicing. Faggots were bought each year for a bonfire on November 5th. In 1637, the amount spent was 3s 4d, about £25 in today's money.

Security was important with new locks being purchased for the church in 1616 and 1695, the vestry in 1618, the chest in 1698 and the church gate in 1633, 1639 and 1698. Vandalism and theft would have existed in the seventeenth century and the church would have contained not just silverware and cloth but weapons. The churchwardens were responsible for organising musters of men for local defence. In October 1614 they raised from Ramsgate alone fourteen armoured men, thirty-seven musketeers, eleven pikemen and ten men with billhooks. Sadly the records of what they raised from St Laurence have been lost.[10] It is likely these items were stored in the tower but they may have been kept in the porch which could be used as a strong room.

The accounts show as well the employment of different people about the parish. In 1622, the parish appointed a dog-keeper at 1s 8d to make sure dogs did not get into the church. The sidesmen were paid at 10s a year (approximately £70 in today's money). The parish clerk earned £4 a year from 1637 after the rates were increased by a groat per house to fund the increase. That fell at some point during the Civil War or Interregnum so that when the accounts resumed in 1689, the rate was £3 3s. In 1695 it rose again to £4 14s. The constable's rate varied slightly across the century but was normally about £3.

Various expenses appear relating to worship such as the purchase of bread and wine for Holy Communion At the start of the century, Holy Communion was celebrated only at Easter, Whitsun and Christmas but this increased steadily from the early 1630s. In 1631, Holy Communion was celebrated each week during Lent. In 1634, it was additionally celebrated each week during Advent. In 1637 a further celebration was added on the first Sunday of every month.

With regard the cost of communion bread and wine, the churchwardens did have an additional source of income which was known as communion pence. This was the

---

[10] SP14/78/18. The armoured men were generally yeomen or landowners with more than twenty acres of land. The muskets were used by men with around ten acres, the pikes by people who paid just a few pennies in rates and who did not hold much land, most being fishermen. The bills were in the hands of those at the lowest end of the social scale, men of good character but who probably rented rather than owned land or who were employed on the properties of other people.

voluntary contribution all worshippers were invited to make toward the cost of the elements. Such a contribution had existed in the middle ages when it was often called Paschal pence. The church was not allowed to charge for the sacraments but it may be certain that most people regarded communion pence as the price for taking Holy Communion and that they were discouraged as a result. The amounts collected normally exceeded the cost of the bread and wine, for example £2 8s 6d in 1618, £2 13s in 1624 and £2 2s 8d in 1631 whilst the cost was about 5s per celebration.[11] There are no entries for communion pence being paid after the Civil War.

Also present each year were the costs of the churchwardens and the vicar attending the Archdeacon's visitation at Canterbury each Easter and Michaelmas. The costs of this were significant and represented a tenth of the church's income most years. The process involved paying the vicar to copy out the entries in the parish register since the last visitation, the purchase of ink and paper for him to use, the hire of horses for the journey, food and drink when they got there, and if they were presenting anyone for breaching regulations – such as reporting someone who had missed church – there were the costs of writing out the case details, hiring a lawyer and taking oaths.

Something else which is evident from the churchwardens' accounts is the financial risk which people took when they accepted the role. In theory, churchwardens were to set a rate which meant they would collect enough money to keep the church in good repair and to pay its necessary expenses. In practice, this did not necessarily happen. A bad storm might destroy windows which were costly to repair and so destroy the budget. In such circumstances, the warden had to pay the additional expenses out of his own pocket and then wait for the church to pay him back at a later date in a year when the churchwardens might have a surplus. Examples of some of the deficits are shown below with the approximate modern value in brackets:

Anthony Curling owed £4 4s 10d in 1623 (£740)
John Curling owed £4 15s 4d in 1631 (£700)
Richard Langley owed £11 16s in 1642 (£1840)
Thomas Goldfinch owed £4 4s 4d in 1689 (£650)

The accounts show that it often took a number of years before the amounts were paid back and some never were. The financial realities meant that churchwardens had to be selected from the more wealthy farmers and merchants and it may be presumed that few of them ever sought the task. One warden was supposed to be selected by the vicar and the other by the people but it was common for the matter to be decided by the drawing of lots with it being compulsory that the person chosen take the role unless ill health prohibited.

---

[11] The amounts collected in communion pence would suggest around four hundred people took the sacrament each Easter. From 1577 at Margate, parishioners were charged 6d every Easter as their offering, a sum equivalent to around two days' wages – Lewis op.cit. 1723 edition p.103

Worship

For most of the seventeenth century, the Book of Common Prayer was in use but there was an interval of around seventeen years when this was not the case.

In 1645 it was replaced by the Directory for the Public Worship of God. This prohibited bowing to the communion table and required that people pay full attention to the service – not talking, not sleeping, not reading and not watching their neighbours. Ministers could select their own readings but had to read at least two chapters per service and cover the whole of the Holy Bible each year. The sermon would follow and then the confession. There would then be the general intercessions on behalf of the church and the world. The service was, therefore, very similar to the Prayer Book except that ministers could employ their own words for the prayers. The services of baptism and Holy Communion were almost unchanged except that actions such as making the sign of the cross and kneeling to receive the sacrament were removed. With marriage, the giving of a ring was removed and so was the requirement for someone to give the bride away. The biggest change was with funerals. The Directory said that because "praying, reading, and singing, both in going to and at the grave, have been grossly abused, are no way beneficial to the dead, and have proved many ways hurtful to the living; therefore let all such things be laid aside" though it did allow ministers to lead a meditation on the Christian hope with the mourners. The singing of psalms was much encouraged, the Directory recommending:

> That the whole congregation may join herein, every one that can read is to have a psalm book; and all others, not disabled by age or otherwise, are to be exhorted to learn to read. But for the present, where many in the congregation cannot read, it is convenient that the minister, or some other fit person appointed by him and the other ruling officers, do read the psalm, line by line, before the singing thereof.

There was nothing in the Directory to arouse objections and there is no reason to suppose that the congregation at St Laurence had any problem using it. In 1662, the Book of Common Prayer returned and this remained the service book in use at St Laurence until the mid twentieth century.

Memorials

There are a number of memorials to people dating from the seventeenth century both within the church and in the churchyard. Directly in front of the communion table at the east end is the brass to Sir Adam Sprackling who died in 1610. He was grandfather of the murderer of the same name. His son died five years later and his brass is in the chancel floor just beyond the tower arch. The Sprackling brasses were all moved in the late Victorian period due to changes being made about the church which is why they are separate from one another and in some cases share their space with the Abbott family. The Sprackling memorials are the only ones in the church to use the dating phrase *Salutis nostrae* meaning year of our salvation rather than the more usual AD or year of Our Lord.

Beside Sir Adam's brass is a memorial to Thomas Gillow who died aged 49 on 23rd November 1678. His is the largest ledger stone in the church. Gillow farmed Newlands Grange and in 1668 was taken to court by the churchwardens for his failure to repair the chancel. It was admitted in court that whilst the parishioners were responsible for the repair of the nave and side chapels, the chancel was the responsibility of those who farmed Newlands and Ozengell, the two granges which had once belonged to St Augustine's Abbey. Gillow replied that he was willing to do his share but that Robert Maxted, who farmed Ozengell, refused to pay his share. Maxted confirmed this was the case.[12] The court ordered Gillow to have work commenced up to the value of half the estimated total and to pay the costs which he duly did. Whether Maxted ever paid up so the work could be completed is unknown but the inconvenience and cost probably explained why Gillow felt he deserved such a prominent monument.

The most remarkable memorial is to Frances Coppin who died in 1677 age 54. This is in the corridor behind the organ so almost impossible to see today but at the time it was erected, it would have been just outside the vestry door. Before the organ arrived, the north side of the church was open like the south. The full inscription reads as follows and is an interesting example of the style of preaching at that time. Frances and her husband were resident in London when the Civil War broke out

> This faithful stone records her praise,
> to make additions to her days;
> Know then, you strangers to her life,
> she was a truly virtuous wife.
> Adorned with graces was her breast, *1 Tim. 2:9*.
> As by the Apostles she was dressed, *1 Peter 3:4*.
> In duties, or in recreation, in house and
> in conversation, in all relations such she was,
> as for a pattern she may pass,
> with love and honour crown'd she dies; *Prov.11:16*.
> And leaves us these dear legacies.
> Here let the precious dust take rest,
> till Christ shall come,
> with 'Come ye blest', *Matt. xxv.34*.
> And then, all tears, wip'd from her eyes.
> She to eternal joy shall rise'.
> 'Jesus said unto her, I am the resurrection
> and the life' *John xi.25*

---

[12] Hussey op.cit. p.38

A memorial which dates from 1836 but which refers to the civil war can be found on the wall just behind the communion table in the side chapel on the left hand side. The stone remembers the then vicar's father but notes "In the Parliaments of 1654, etc. his ancestors represented the County of Suffolk, and Borough of Ipswich, and were faithful supporters of the Monarchy."

Within the churchyard, the earliest named person is George Skinner who died on 11th May 1656 but this is actually a later monument, the original having been damaged during building work. Skinner was a yeoman who owned property in both St Laurence and St Peter's parishes.[13] The oldest genuine monument is a red sandstone headstone to George, twenty-four year old son of Richard and Mary Bennett who died on September 17th 1683. The next oldest is a sandstone headstone to four year old Mildred Sanders which has a motif of two bells with coiled rope. The earliest born person to have a monument is "Old Alexander Long the fisherman" who was baptised at St Laurence on 17th September 1615 and lived through six reigns and the Civil War to die at the age of ninety-three on September 8th 1708. He is remembered on a brick based vault on the north side of the church just past the vestry door. His wife had died six years earlier aged eighty-eight. On 7th June 1690, when the parish had a house to house collection for the relief of poor Irish Protestants, he gave five shillings.

CLERGY AND STAFF

John Cole was the first vicar to be appointed in the seventeenth century. He succeeded John Kington in 1607 and stayed seven years before departing to Hougham where he died a few months later. Complaints were made about him that he had not kept the vicarage in good repair and that he failed to preach or even read from the Book of Homilies.[14] This last was particularly ironic given the church bought a pulpit during his incumbency. He appears to have been a litigious individual because he sought to prosecute the parish schoolteacher Lewis Rogers in 1612 for teaching without his consent which he said reduced his "small means of maintenance." This complaint was dismissed and Rogers' licence confirmed. Cole then presented Rogers as "a common alehouse haunter and gamester," a complaint which may have had some merit since Rogers was replaced in 1614. Cole also reported Margaret Hall in 1608 for "evil demeanour and shameful speeches" complaining that she had called him a "knave" for not attending quickly enough when her husband was ill. Given that Margaret had married in 1575, it must be assumed that she and her husband were around seventy at this point. She was not punished but Thomas Pamphlet was, being forced to stand in the centre of the church on 24th May 1613 wrapped in a white sheet and to say:

---

[13] PROB 11/256/162. His cash bequests in today's money were about £80,000. He gave his address as "St Lawrence in the field"

[14] A report in 1616 confirms that the vicar still resided in the medieval house.

> Good Christian people, whereas I, through the temptation of Satan and frailty of mine own flesh, have committed the sinful act of incontinency to the offence of Almighty God and breach of the King's Majesty Laws, do here before this present congregation confess this my fault and am heartily sorry therefore, praying you to forgive me, and those that I have offended thereby to be with this my humble confession satisfied, and wishing to lead the rest of my life more honestly and chastely, which God grant I may perform.[15]

Cole swapped livings with **Thomas Turner** who also seems to have had a temper. In 1616, he was reported to the Archdeacon by the churchwardens following a brawl he had in the churchyard with William Nethersole on Saturday 23rd March 1615/16. Turner's relations with his wardens and sidesmen were generally fraught. The new pulpit had arrived only a few months before Turner arrived and the old pulpit was still in the church. Turner demanded that the latter be set up as a chair under the tower for his wife to sit in. This was done but the location caused problems for the bell ringers who rang from the floor and who were unable to reach the ropes due to her head being in the way. A complaint was duly made and the seat removed which then led to William Curling being presented to the Archdeacon for removing the seat without consent of the vicar. Curling must have felt he could not win. Another parishioner Robert Widdett, called Curling "a peevish fellow" and expressed contempt of the vicar which resulted in another court case. It was clearly not a happy parish.[16]

Turner was an interesting man, however, being also a licensed physician giving him cure of souls in more ways than one. He left St Laurence in 1629 to go to St. Nicholas-at-Wade where he died in 1630 aged fifty-eight.[17]

Turner was followed by **William Dunkyn** who was also a man of letters. He received his BA from Clare College, Cambridge in 1620 and his MA in 1623, the year he was ordained. He came to St Laurence on Palm Sunday 1629/30 and in November of that year took over teaching in the parish school. How he could have found time for this is a mystery but he was probably attracted by the fact that teaching provided much needed extra income.

It is probable that William Dunkyn was also Chancellor of Canterbury Cathedral from 17th November 1638. This is a curious appointment made by Archbishop Laud and it

---

[15] Hussey op.cit. pp.33-35. Pamphlet was a twenty-five year old labourer who was married but had fathered an illegitimate son. He regularly worked for the church doing odd jobs such as cleaning up after the mason.

[16] ibid. pp.35-36

[17] Ian Mortimer, 'A Directory of Medical Personnel Qualified and Practising in the Diocese of Canterbury, circa 1560-1730', *Archaeologia Cantiana* Vol. 126 (2006) p.191

is impossible to know what was involved since there were no previous or later holders of the post.[18] Its chief interest is that it would indicate that Dunkyn was favoured by Laud, something further suggested by his appointment as one of the Six Preachers of Canterbury five months later and his licensing as an approved preacher throughout the whole of Canterbury and London dioceses on 26th September 1634.

It is said that a man can be judged by his friends and if that is true, Dunkyn must be regarded as a man of little judgment.

Archbishop Laud was incredibly unpopular in Kent. He attacked the overseas Protestant refugees which had settled particularly in Canterbury and Sandwich but also across Thanet. He stopped the printing of Foxe's *Book of Martyrs*, the popular account of how Protestants had suffered under Bloody Mary. He discouraged lectureships. These had been set up in many churches, including Margate, so that congregations might have more detailed and more frequent teaching about the Bible. He even objected to people leading prayers and discussing the Scriptures in their own homes. Where groups banded together to finance the provision of educated ministers, he took legal action to confiscate their assets.[19] He promoted a return to services in Latin. He took little interest in his diocese and when he did deal with ministers, he displayed intolerance, impatience and bad manners. He was behind the 1640 Canons which ordered that once every quarter, every minister should preach in support of the Divine Right of Kings and teach that disobedience to him or his Church was "treasonable against God, as well as against the King." People were further to be taught that it was their God given duty to pay taxes and that taking anyone resisting any decree was doomed to damnation. Any minister who failed to so preach was to be suspended.[20] The same canons also declared that everyone must spend the entire morning on the anniversary of Charles I's accession in church in "humble gratitude to God for so great a blessing, and dutiful affections to so benign and merciful a Sovereign" or else face a fine. In an attempt to further restrict freedom of opinion, the Canons prohibited all "makers, importers, printers, and publishers, or dispersers of any Book, writing, or scandalous Pamphlet devised against the discipline and government of the Church of England" on pain of excommunication. The Canons went on to say that communion tables should be called altars, that people should bow to them and that the tables should be railed in case anyone might sit on them or cast their hat upon them.[21]

---

[18] Joyce M Horn (ed.), *Fasti Ecclesiae Anglicanae 1541-1857* vol. 3 (London, 1974), pp. 21-22. The appointment is listed as William Dunlyn, M.A. but this is likely to have been a transcription error since no such person as Dunlyn has ever been traced.

[19] Christopher Hill, *Society and Puritanism* (London, 1964) pp.72, 112, 192; Christopher Hill, *The World Turned Upside Down* (London, 1972) p.96; Hugh Trevor-Roper, *Archbishop Laud* (London, 1962) pp.197-202

[20] With many churches only having a sermon once a quarter, this meant that no teaching about Christ was offered at all, just political hectoring in favour of the unpopular Charles I.

[21] Church of England, *Constitutions and canons ecclesiasticall; treated upon by the Archbishops of*

For those accustomed to the existence of rails, it may be hard to understand why they aroused such fury in the seventeenth century. There were a number of objections. Firstly, they implied that something special was happening at the communion table and that somehow Our Lord was more present there than in other places when the Holy Bible taught He was omnipresent. Secondly, they were openly called altar rails and the word altar meant a place of sacrifice yet Anglican teaching was that Our Lord's sacrifice on the cross was sufficient and that the Holy Communion was a memorial not a sacrificial act. Thirdly, they separated the minister from the congregation when the Bible taught that all were equal before God. Fourthly, they destroyed the sense of Holy Communion being a remembrance of a shared meal with friends. Jesus had not enjoyed the Last Supper behind rails and nobody set rails round their dining tables at home. The Vicar of Minster, who was brother-in-law to the Johnsons of Nethercourt described the scene in Canterbury Cathedral where "at the East end they have placed an Altar (as they call it) dressed after the Romish fashion, with Candlesticks and Tapers, for which Altar they have lately provided a most Idolatrous costly cloth; towards which Altar they crouch and duck three times at their going up to it." This practice had spread so that: "all the Communion Tables in the said City, have lately been removed, and set up to the East end of the Chancels, and railed in." [22] Prynne, in a separate account, spoke of Laud altering " the ancient Communion Table; standing with the ends East and West, some distance from the Wall Table-wise, even from the beginning of Reformation till his coming to the Arch-Bishopric without any Rail about it, into a New Altar placed Altarwise against the Wall, with the ends North and South, hedged in with a new costly Rail."[23] Milton described such as "a table of separation." [24]

Not only was Laud hated for his innovations but also for the way he enforced them. He had Lady Davis committed to a lunatic asylum for criticising his return of images at Lichfield, had the Reverend Peter Smart fined £500 (over £75,000 at today's value) and jailed for more than five years for disagreeing with them and had churchwardens heavily fined and jailed for a year apiece if they refused to convert their communion tables into altars.[25]

Canterbury and York, (London, 1640)
[22] Richard Culmer, *Cathedrall newes from Canterbury*, (London, 1644)
[23] William Prynne, *Canterburies Doome* (London, 1646) p. 81, 83.
[24] Christopher Hill, *The Century of Revolution* (London, 1961) p.70; Prynne op.cit. p.65
[25] Prynne op.cit. p.108. The image is from Anon, *Of the Life, Reigne, and Death of William Laud,*

It was popularly believed that Laud was a papist and the Pope did actually offer him a cardinal's hat but there was never any likelihood that either the King or Laud would surrender English independence in favour of Rome. However, Laud was firmly of the medieval tradition in that he believed worshippers should simply attend services and that was all. He saw people discussing the Holy Bible or thinking about faith for themselves as dangerous. The favour that Laud showed Dunkyn would indicate that the vicar of St Laurence shared his views, though not in everything. Richard Culmer saw Dunkyn as politically "neuter."[26]

Dunkyn's other friend was none other than the wife-beating, heavy gambling drunkard, Adam Sprackling. It was reported that he would spend time carousing with him in local alehouses where Sprackling was wont to provoke fights.[27] Another eye-witness described Dunkyn as "a drunken, scandalous, railing Priest."[28] The congregation were not impressed but knowing that there was no point in raising a complaint against one of Laud's men, they were forced to keep quiet.

The fall of Laud presented the opportunity that the churchwardens had been waiting for. Although no copy of the complaint exists, they clearly did protest to Parliament about him. Since Parliament received in 1641 alone over nine hundred petitions from parishioners who were unhappy about their minister, it did take some time for a response to be received.[29] However, the fact that Dunkyn's handwriting ceases abruptly in the parish register in April 1644, directly after an entry in the churchwarden's accounts noting that 8d was paid to a messenger from Greenwich about the minister shows he was sacked.

Despite his ejection, Dunkyn refused to leave the vicarage. He argued that since he had been appointed by a bishop, only a bishop could eject him, but Parliament abolished bishops the same year. Dunkyn remained in the parish until at least 1647, effectively squatting at the vicarage, his presence known because he continued to witness wills such as that of John Tickner. His action effectively prohibited the hiring of a replacement but ultimately the parish succeeded in getting him out. Dunkyn went on to Reculver where he died in May 1658.

His absence caused real problems as there was nobody to take services. The churchwardens spent ten shillings hiring two ministers to give a sermon each but that still meant there was little teaching and no celebrations of Holy Communion. In 1648, the parish clerk was given a book and sent round all the houses in the parish to collect subscriptions for a new minister. Meanwhile, those who had the means went to Minster where they were able to hear the renowned puritan Richard Culmer. One parishioner

---

Archbishop of Canterbury (London, 1644)

[26] Culmer jr. op.cit. p14

[27] Calamy op.cit

[28] Culmer jr. op.cit. p18

[29] Christopher Hill, *The World Turned Upside Down* (London, 1972) p.30

openly said that they would praise God if they had such a minister.[30] Some others who lived on the other side of the parish may have gone to St Peter's but most would have gone without.

In 1654, the parish finally obtained a new vicar in the form of **Peter Johnson**. Pressure to appoint someone had been spearheaded by Edmund Calamy who wrote the pamphlet about the Sprackling murder as an example of what would happen in a community where there was no godly minister. Calamy was a member of the Westminster Assembly of Divines, a London clergyman and the man who had ordained Peter Johnson. He knew the family well and there can be no doubt that he was behind the decision to appoint him.

Johnson was twenty-five when he returned to the parish as vicar and had an MA from Corpus Christi, Cambridge. There are no churchwarden's accounts for his time here so it is impossible to say what he achieved. He would have used the Directory rather than the Book of Common Prayer and he almost certainly taught school because he continued to do this after his ejection in 1662. He was a godly man who endeavoured to live his life according to the Holy Bible, doubtless using the Geneva edition. He was described as living an "unblamable life" and showing "diligence and proficiency in his studies."[31] He was evidently popular because when in 1662 he was dispossessed for refusing to deny the validity of his ordination, a number of the congregation went with him to set up a new church in the town.[32]

Until 1662, Johnson resided in the vicarage but it is unclear where he lived for the remaining forty-two years of his life. The Nethercourt estate was owned and occupied by his brother John. In 1664, Johnson occupied a modest two hearth house in St Lawrence street. Thereafter, there is no evidence from the rates or hearth tax of Peter Johnson living there or anywhere else in either Ramsgate or St Lawrence.[33]

Johnson continued to attend St Laurence occasionally and his children were baptised there: two were also buried there in infancy. Johnson ultimately went blind and became housebound due to ill health. He died in 1704 and was buried at St Laurence close to the entrance to the vestry where generations of the Johnson family had been interred. His memorial shows the family arms which includes a pelican vulning itself. This emblem

---

[30] Culmer jr op.cit p28
[31] Testimony of Calamy quoted in Cotton op.cit. p.184
[32] Johnson had been ordained by Calamy and four others in a service that was legal according to contemporary law. However, the Archbishop in 1662 ruled that because Calamy was a member of the Westminster Assembly and not a bishop, the ordination was invalid. This effectively denied Johnson's vocation which understandably upset him deeply. He was offered the chance to retrain and be ordained but he declined, preferring instead to continue his ministry outside the Church of England.
[33] The suggestion that he owned Nethercourt is erroneous. His brother paid rates there until his death whereafter the estate was sold. Peter Johnson was never a ratepayer in either Ramsgate or St Lawrence though he did pay Hearth Tax for Nethercourt in 1667. The fact that he did this for one year only suggests his brother was away on an extended trip at this time.

also appears on the arms of Thomas Cromwell, the man who did so much to advance the Reformation under Henry VIII and whom Peter Johnson's great-great-great-grandfather had served. It was recorded that Peter was "a man of good parts and learning and very useful gifts."[34]

Following Johnson's departure, the parish seemed destined for another long period without a vicar due to the income available. Prices had risen by 40% since 1620 but the pay had not altered. Archbishop Juxon resolved the problem by more than doubling it from £16 to £40.[35] This enabled the parish to secure the ministry of **John Young,** a man about whom almost nothing is known because almost all the records from his incumbency are missing.

PEOPLE, EVENTS AND PLACES

The Spracklings

Although a certain notoriety has attached itself to Adam Sprackling, he was but one member of the family who owned Ellington from the mid sixteenth century onwards.

The Robert Sprackling whose monument appears in the south chancel was followed by his son Adam who died on the 6th April 1610 aged 58. He had been knighted on 12th June 1604 at Greenwich by James I although it is unclear why. He appears to have been a charitable man, however. In 1587 he provided money to apprentice Ralph Hale, son of the widow of John Hale who had kinship links with the Thatchers who had owned Ellington prior to the Spracklings. In 1608, Adam wrote with other Justices of the Peace to petition for assistance to the poor who were starving as result of high prices following a poor harvest:

> Since our last letters we have received no order for provision of corn for the poorer sort at prices reasonable, or for furnishing the markets which are now badly served and the prices increased extremely without just cause to 48s and 50s the quarter in the markets, and four marks and three pounds already demanded by private persons. We pray that stay be made of transportation of corn out of these parts, and that a survey be taken of the store in these parts, and a proportion made (for the poorer sort) of wheat, barley, beans and oats as they may be able to buy it; and for the residue that the markets may be served therewith, and example made of such as set extreme and unconscionable prices without cause. [36]

---

[34] Samuel Palmer, *The Nonconformist's Memorial* vol 2 (London, 1777) p.77
[35] John Ecton, *Thesaurus rerum ecclesiasticarum:* (London, 1742) p.17
[36] M S Giuseppi and G Dyfnallt Owen (ed), *Calendar of the Cecil Papers in Hatfield House*, Vol. 20,

It is probable that he did not receive the response he required for in 1609, he gave £2 to the poor box in order to meet the urgent need, it having proved impossible to raise sufficient in tax. In 1598, he increased the Vicar of St Laurence's income by allowing him a further five shillings a year out of the income of Newland Grange.[37] His brass can today be seen in the chancel floor directly in front of the East Window with that of his son Adam who died in 1615, situated behind it and between the choir stalls.[38]

Sir Adam's heir at Ellington was Robert who was born in December 1577. He clearly made changes to the house because when it was demolished, a tablet showing the date 1613 was found.[39] He was regarded as a trustworthy man for Edward Harnet, a yeoman at Spratling Street, left him in charge of the charity he set up when he died. Harnet gave £5 to Sprackling to hold and invest so that the interest on the sum should be given to the "head churchwarden" each St Andrew's day and thence distributed to eight poor people.[40] Robert married Margaret Moyle and had two sons and four daughters. His eldest daughter died when she was seven but the other three survived to adulthood. His second daughter, Maria, was married when she was just twelve to a kinsman in a clearly arranged dynastic alliance though she did not take up residence with her husband (who was almost twenty years older) for another five years. The two girls were followed by two boys, Adam in March 1605/6 and Robert in 1608. Two more girls completed the family, Margaret who married the lawyer Matthew Hadd in 1631 and Margery who wed Robert Knowler in 1644. Of these children, Adam is undoubtedly the most famous.

Nothing is known about Adam's childhood though it must be assumed that he received a good education. His mother died when he was eighteen so he had a settled family life up to that point.[41] On 12th July 1631 when he was twenty-five, he married seventeen year old Katherine Lewkner from Acrise. His father settled twenty-nine acres of the Ellington estate upon the couple though it is unclear whether they lived in a home of their home or with his widowed father. In November 1633 they had a son Robert who was followed by a daughter Margaret in August 1635 and another son Adam in August 1637.[42] Their fourth child Mary was born in the summer of 1638 but died after only six

---

(HMSO, 1968) p.175

[37] Mary Anne Everett Green (ed.), *Calendar of State Papers of Elizabeth I: 1598-1601* (HMSO, 1869) p.530. The increase was about a pound a week in today's money.

[38] All the Sprackling monuments were originally on the wall between the high chancel and vestry and along the front where the communion rails now sit. They were moved to other locations about the church when the high chancel was remodelled.

[39] It cannot be known what changes he made. He may have totally rebuilt the property. He did refer to a gallery in his will and since these were popular at this time, he may have added a wing with a long gallery.

[40] PRC17/70/378. Worth around £750 today.

[41] She was originally buried in the high chancel under the present communion rails.

[42] That he named his first two children after his parents suggests he had positive childhood memories.

months and Adam's life started to deteriorate shortly after. He bought a further fourteen acres in 1639 but within two years he was forced to sell up. His debts were so bad that he was forced to flee with his wife to London where they settled to the west of the Tower and just north of Billingsgate. Their final child, Nicholas, was born there at the start of May 1642. Presumably Adam ran into more trouble there because in 1643 he returned to his father's house only to be excused paying rates on grounds he had no resources. For a gentleman, such a situation was shameful indeed and he did not pay rates in 1644 or 1645 either.

At some point in this period, he was jailed in Canterbury though whether for debt or affray is unknown. He had already been involved in a number of alehouse brawls drawing his sword to attack John Simmons and Henry Giles at St Peter's and attempting to cleave the head of William Grant in two with a cutlass at St John's. In a fight that spilled over into the street at St Peter's, a shoemaker had been run through the bowels, though whether by Adam or his henchman was unknown due to the confusion. In one fight, Adam had been bested by Robert Lister so he sent his man to break Lister's jaw with a cudgel the next day in revenge. He was in modern parlance, a vicious thug with no respect for life.

In November 1646, Adam's father died and this transformed his fortunes. He inherited Ellington with its stables and orchards, the lease of Newlands, marshland at Chislet with a flock of sheep thereon plus silver, armour, weapons, books and furnishings. His father had clearly been concerned about Adam's ability to handle money because he created a trust fund in his will for Adam's children which he left in the care of his daughter Margery rather than Adam himself. It is likely that Adam was unhappy about this. He also left a series of financial gifts locked in a chest in his closet which he wished to be distributed privately, probably to ensure Adam was unable to take them.[43] Adam's father was laid beside his mother under the present communion rails but the memorials were stolen in the early nineteenth century. That to Adam's father has never been recovered but the brass to his mother was found in 1891 and is now under the tower.[44]

Returned to freedom and with money in his pocket, Adam set about spending his fortune which would have been considerable even after his debts were paid. He did some major work on the house in 1649 and he also purchased books, but most of the money went on drink and gambling. Within four years, the 172 acres which his father had left him had been cut to 90 acres as Adam was forced to sell off land to pay his debts. One who knew him said he "wanting the grace humility, exalted himself above measure, affected pre-eminence in all companies, used in his braveries long hair &c. to ride about the island and frequent tap houses and there to rant and roar, game and swear exceedingly, upon the least provocation and used to quarrel and draw his weapon &c. He regarded not the Sabbath but profaned it at home. The public worship of God and

---

[43] PROB/199/141
[44] Robert Sprackling's memorial was recorded in Cozens op.cit. p.54.

preaching of the Word he seldom or never attended."[45] This failure to attend church resulted in fines that cost him the equivalent today of over a thousand pounds a year. Another person who knew him recorded him as: "a great jeerer at praying by the Spirit, a condemner of public Ordinances."[46] Nor was he content to confine his opinions to himself. Adam travelled to Minster to publicly harangue their vicar who was preaching to a crowd of hundreds.[47]

In 1648, Adam decided to take revenge on Richard Langley whom he blamed for having had him arrested and placed in jail. He no doubt also hated him for his role in obtaining Dunkyn's dismissal, it being said that Langley had "procured the casting out of the unsavoury salt."[48] Adam's decision to do this some three years after the event was taken in cold blood. Twice he drew his sword on him in public and threatened him but Langley refused to fight. Langley by then was fifty-six and a twice married man who had fathered thirteen children. He was a maltster who lived in Ramsgate and was a highly respected member of the community who served in various official capacities and who was a devout Christian. On 22nd May, Sprackling sent two of his men to Langley's house. They were armed with guns which they brandished as they shouted at him through the door. Langley escaped through the back and made his way to Nethercourt to Mistress Johnson's house.[49] She lent him a mare and Langley set off toward Minster. Her twenty year old John saw him go and then witnessed a few minutes later, Adam's two henchman galloping past with their pistols held at the ready. Two miles on and Langley was shot through the chest, falling in a hail of bullets and being left for dead. Langley was buried at St Laurence on 25th May. Meanwhile, Adam had joined his two henchman and they rode on to Canterbury where another fight was brewing in which Adam was keen to play his part.

This was the era of the civil war and Kent was a troubled place in the spring and summer of 1648. On 18th May a petition had been raised against Parliament which soon boasted twenty thousand signatures, including Adam Sprackling's. This was rejected by Parliament prompting a gathering at Canterbury on 23rd May to raise a rebellion in support of King Charles I who was then incarcerated on the Isle of Wight. A number of cavaliers, Adam amongst them, mustered at Barham the next day where his cousins, the Oxindens, lived.[50] They started a series of attacks on various Parliamentary strongholds in East Kent including Dover Castle which they were unable to take. At one point, Adam kidnapped some men and held them prisoner – illegally - in his home.

On 27th May, by which time the Barham brigade was a thousand strong, a

---

[45] Calamy op.cit
[46] Richard Culmer Jr, *A parish looking-glasse* (London, 1657) p.31
[47] ibid.
[48] Edward Calamy, *The Bloody Husband* (London, 1653).
[49] She was the widow of Henry Johnson who was Adam's first cousin.
[50] Adam's first cousin Henry was a respected man of letters and a Parliamentarian but his son Thomas was a highwayman. See Antonia Fraser, *The Weaker Vessel* (London, 1984) p.330

Declaration was issued stating that they would defend their petition "with our lives and fortunes" regarding any opposition as provocation and taking "refuge to our Arms, from which no threats or face of Soldiery shall drive us." They claimed they were fighting "for the defence and preservation of the King's Majesty's royal person, the privileges of the subjects, and the laws and liberties of the free-born people of this nation."[51] In truth, they were less interested in the King's freedom than their own and their enemy was not Parliament but the committee set up to run the county which they described as imposing an "intolerable yoke of slavery" which "would have shamed the most notorious tyrants" and which had imposed excess taxes.[52]

At this point, the navy in the Downs mutinied and went to Holland where they were joined by the Prince of Wales and his brother the Duke of York both of whom were in exile in France. This led to even more confusion and excitement with there being rumours that the Duke had landed at Margate, though this was untrue.

Eventually, there was a showdown between the cavaliers and the parliamentary forces in Maidstone on the 1st of June. The cavaliers were heavily defeated in a particularly ferocious and bloody battle and the survivors fled. Whether Adam Sprackling was at the battle or still with forces at Barham is uncertain but he definitely decided to flee at this point. He went to join the naval mutineers taking the following oath:

> I, *Adam Sprackling*, do in the presence of Almighty God the Searcher of all hearts, solemnly vow and protest, that in the first place I shall heartily endeavour the freedom and Restoration of my Sovereign Lord King Charles to all his full and just Rights: and will behave myself faithfully in the service of His Highness the Prince of Wales. Next I do vow all true obedience to my Lord High Admiral the Duke of York, and that I will conform myself cheerfully to all his Highness' lawful Commands which shall be for the service of his Royal Father: That I will hold no correspondence with the Enemy, but shall faithfully discover all Designs that I can come to the knowledge of, of that nature; and shall endeavour with the utmost hazard of my life to defend and protect his Highness' Person from all danger; nor will ever give consent to deliver him up without the King his Royal Father's command, or his own consent. And as I shall be faithful and just in the performance of all this; so help me God.[53]

He remained with them for some two months during which the Revolted Ships, as they were known at the time, engaged in various acts of piracy and a number of

---

[51] Anon, *The declaration and resolution of the knights, gentry, and free-holders of the county of Kent* (1648)
[52] Quoted in Alan Everitt, *The Community of Kent and the Great Rebellion*, Leicester. 1966) pp.220-221
[53] Anon, *The oath taken by the seamen of the revolted ships* (1648)

skirmishes and failed invasion attempts. When the revolt failed, Sprackling returned home where his life continued to spiral out of control. On 27th April 1649 he was declared delinquent which meant that his estate was now forfeit to Parliament unless he was prepared to renounce his royalist sympathies and pay a huge fine.[54] He was forced to shut himself up at Ellington to avoid his creditors which left him "sad, choleric and petulant and full of rage in his house."[55] He took his temper out on his innocent wife, his violence toward her being such that she at times had to lock herself away in another part of the house to avoid his fists. Wife beating may not have been illegal in the mid seventeenth century but it was strongly frowned upon. The Homilies which were required to be preached in each church at least twice a year included strong condemnation of this and the message was repeated at every wedding. A man who beat his wife was compared to the devil, a Bedlam man (i.e. a madman), said to be vile and told it would be better for the earth to swallow him than he were to continue to live. The sermon said: "A man may well liken such a man (if he may be called a man rather than a wild beast) to a killer of his father or mother….It is the greatest shame that can be, not so much to her that is beaten, as to him that doth the deed."[56]

In January 1651/2, Adam and Katherine Sprackling faced another blow when their youngest child Nicholas died aged nine. It cannot be known what impact that had on the marriage but it cannot have helped.

By December 1652, things had reached a point where the Spracklings only had two servants and they were unable to afford fuel to heat the main house. On the night of Saturday 11th Adam and his wife were trying to keep warm in the kitchen. Their servant Ewell was with them and a friend named Laming.[57] Adam was drinking and in a belligerent mood. His daughter Margaret, then seventeen, decided to shut herself in an out building for the night with the other servant who was female. She had seen her father in such a mood before and it scared her.

Laming left and Adam sent for a tenant of his named Moses Martin to join them. Martin had been a tenant of the family for over twenty years and held just under five acres not far from Newlands. The exact location is uncertain but it was probably close to where the viaduct is today. Martin was then sixty-seven. As soon as he arrived, Adam told Martin to sit Ewell on the ground and bind him up. This Martin did thinking it was better to humour his landlord than criticise.

As the evening wore on, Adam got steadily more abusive. He accused his wife of deliberately leaving doors open so that those after him might come and take him away

---

[54] Mary Anne Everett Green (ed.) *Calendar of the Committee For the Advance of Money*: Part 2 (HMSO, 1888) p.1062

[55] Calamy op.cit

[56] Church of England, *Sermons or Homilies appointed to be read in Churches in the time of Queen Elizabeth*, (Oxford, 1816) pp. 428, 433, 434

[57] Adam's brother had married Rebecca Laming and he may have been a kinsman. Ewell was a tenant of the Spracklings farming eighty acres.

and said this was proof of her disloyalty. At one point he pulled a dagger and struck her in the jaw but she did not respond.

In the early hours of Sunday 12th Katherine rose to leave the room. She may have hoped that Adam was falling into a drunken stupor but if so, she was disappointed. He turned on her swiftly and as her hand tried to move the handle, he sliced it off with a chopping knife. The terrified Martin went to her and tried to bind her wrist with a napkin, all the time urging her to be quiet and hope that all would be well.

Time passed and it was almost dawn. Adam remained abusive and his wife, who had lost a lot of blood, duly kept quiet. Finally, he picked up a cleaver and struck her on the forehead with such force that she fell to the floor. She struggled to her knees covered in blood and started to pray. She recited the Lord's Prayer and asked that God forgive her husband as she forgave him. As she did so, Adam took the cleaver again and with an almighty blow, simply sliced her head in two. She dropped dead instantly.

Ewell and Martin must have been scared almost witless themselves by now but the horror was not yet over. Adam then killed his six dogs, which had presumably been in the kitchen all this time, with a knife and threw their bodies beside his wife's. Roger Strivern, who later escorted Adam to jail, testified that he claimed he did this so that people would say he was mad. It may also have been a reference to Jezebel or Ninevah.[58]

Adam was still not finished with his orgy of violence. He pulled his wife over and lifted her skirts right up in an act designed to deliberately dishonour her. He hacked at her legs and ordered Martin to spread her blood across his own face then his and Ewell's. Martin obeyed though his hands were probably shaking by this point.

What happened next is unclear. It may be that Adam left the room and Martin released Ewell and raised the alarm. It could be that Adam's daughter and the maid came in for breakfast and uncovered the horrific scene. What is certain is that Adam was arrested on Sunday evening and taken to jail in Sandwich. He was still brandishing a pistol and had a dagger in his belt.

The remains of thirty-nine year old Katherine Sprackling were buried at St Laurence on Wednesday 15th December in the family vault in the high chancel. It may be assumed that the church was full. Her sons were away and would have missed the funeral and it is unlikely that her daughter was there either. She must have been deeply traumatised. It cannot be known what happened to her in those first few days. She may have been taken to stay with the Johnsons, the only other gentry family in the parish, or she could have been taken in by her aunt Margery or her uncle Robert in Canterbury.

Adam's trial took place on 22nd April 1653 in Sandwich and an eyewitness account was published just three weeks later on 13th May by Edward Calamy, a friend of the Johnsons. The purpose of the tract which was reproduced in Cotton's *History* was not to encourage prurient interest in the disaster but stated to be threefold. Firstly, it was to pay tribute to Katherine Sprackling and the way she had withstood the persecution of her husband. She was seen as a model of Christian fortitude, a woman who had suffered

---

[58] Nahum 3:45, 1 Kings 21:23

martyrdom for her faith and who would be rewarded as Our Lord promised in the Beatitudes.[59]

Secondly, the tract was designed to celebrate the fact that God was just and the wicked would not be allowed to prosper for ever. This was a warning to those who sought to spend their time drinking, gaming and fighting, but was also a reassurance to the godly.

Thirdly, the author argued that the case showed the need for changes to be made to the way the Isle of Thanet was governed. If a crime was committed in Ramsgate, it was necessary for someone to sail to Sandwich to rouse the Deputy and then to return with him. By that time, the criminals would have fled. Calamy argued that the island should be made a county in its own right with its own law enforcement agencies because it was "so far from justice that it is full of profaneness. …Not a year passeth there but a drunkard breaks his neck off his horse or over the cliff. Two have hanged themselves within a year last past, one on Easter Monday last being actually drunk hanged himself."[60]

Calamy's account of the trial showed how Adam remained totally unrepentant of his actions. He tried to delay proceedings by objecting to the first twenty jurors but was told he would have to accept those appointed by the judge since he could present no reasons. Neither of the two lawyers he had vowed would defend him turned up and the two doctors he hired to say he was mad at the time actually admitted to the court that he was perfectly sane and just of an habitual violent temper. When invited to give his own account, Adam simply said: "No man can judge between man and wife but God alone." He was found guilty of murder and sentenced to hang in five days time. Adam only made two requests, the first that he be left alone, the second that his body be delivered into the hands of four women whom he named. The reaction to the names and the fact that their identities were deliberately excised from the record suggests that he named four prostitutes whom he had been apt to frequent, a further and final insult to his wife and the mother of his children.

On Wednesday 27th April, Adam was taken out to be hanged. A crowd of almost two thousand had gathered and a preacher was there to highlight the fate of the wicked and to call sinners to repentance. He called out to Adam as he approached the gallows and invited him even at this late hour to cast himself on God's mercy. Adam replied: "Sir I

---

[59] Matt. 5: 10-11. The homily on marriage which so condemned wife beating had advised women who found themselves living with such a monster to "take it not too heavily but suppose that thereby is laid up no small reward hereafter and in this lifetime no small commendation if thou canst keep quiet." *Sermons or Homilies* op.cit. p.433

[60] That the Isle of Thanet was seen as separate and remote is also reflected in William Lambarde's *Perambulation of Kent* in 1576 which deliberately excludes it and remains a study of mainland Kent.

have made my confession to God, I pray trouble me not: man hath nothing to do with it. O pray speak no more of it."[61]

Towards evening the next day, Adam's body was taken to the Three Kings in Sandwich to be stripped and recoffined. It was carried by sea to Ramsgate then taken on men's shoulders to St Laurence church. That night, with no ceremony, he was buried beside his wife. Cotton suggests that an unidentified body found under the tower in 1888 might be his but that is far from certain. Six such bodies were found at the time and given that all the other burials in the tower area dated from 1791 onwards, it is most likely that those six were of similar or later date. There is no reason to suppose that those who brought his body back would have started digging out a new area to place his body when there was a family vault and contemporary evidence is clear that he was buried beside Katherine. After all, his wife had forgiven him and he was still a child of God.[62]

What impact did the incident have on his family? Adam and Katherine's eldest son, Robert, was away at university when the murder took place studying for his MA. He qualified as a doctor and went to practice in Angers, France. He returned to England around 1665 when he wrote *Medela Ignorantiae*, a book upholding the humoural theories of Galen and the idea that plague stemmed from bad air against those physicians who were advocating a new theory that disease was contagious. He refused to live at Ellington due to its unpleasant associations and sold it at the start of 1655. Keen to get far away where the family shame was unknown, he settled in Lancashire where he became a Catholic for a while and was renowned for leading a "drunken and debauched life." He was described by one who knew him as having a "morose and cloudy" demeanour.[63] He died at Preston in 1670 when he was thirty-six years old.

The second son, Adam, died in London in 1668 aged thirty-one. He had not married and there is no evidence of him achieving anything of note in his life. He had been fifteen at the time of the murder and living away from home, probably in education.

Almost ten years after the murder, the only daughter, Margaret, married Isaac Taylor at St Bartholomew the Less in London. Although he was, hopefully, a good and kind man, he was not from the sort of class that would have been expected for one of her pedigree but her father's behaviour had made her unattractive to gentry suitors. Like her brothers, there is no evidence of her ever returning to St Laurence parish.

Adam's sister Margery, who had been left trustee of the fund set up by their father for Adam's sons, was widowed and in 1660 remarried Roger Strivern who had given evidence against him at his trial. She lived her entire life in the parish and died aged sixty-five in 1680.

The greatest support shown to Adam was shown by his brother Robert who had

---

[61] The image is not of Sprackling's execution but is contemporary coming from James Cranford, *The Teares of Ireland* (1642).
[62] Cotton op.cit. p.81. The full report of the 1888 excavations is CCA-U3-19/6/B/10.
[63] Antony Wood, *Athenae Oxonienses* (London, 1690) p.800; Edmund Borlase, *Latham Spaw in Lancashire*, (London, 1672) p.13

his infant son christened in Canterbury Cathedral just days after Adam was convicted and the day before his execution. The name he chose, which must have raised eyebrows, was Adam.

As to Moses Martin, the unwilling witness to the murder, he died in the summer of 1666 aged eighty-one.

The Mystery of Thomas Trice

In 1727, Adam Sprackling, nephew of the murderer, left thirteen and a half perches at Southwood to the church so that it might be used to support the sexton on condition that the sexton agreed to maintain the grave of Thomas Trice.[64] Dr Cotton says that he did this because Adam had once fallen into a coma and been pronounced dead. He had been coffined and the funeral held when he was suddenly woken by the sound of Thomas Trice digging his grave. Adam duly started knocking on his coffin lid and shouting and Trice – rather than fleeing or collapsing with shock – quickly opened the coffin and let him out. Adam was so grateful that he promised to look after Trice ever more and that including arranging for his grave to be tended.

It is a great story but cannot possibly be true because Trice died in 1643 ten years before Adam was even born. It is possible that Trice had saved the life of his father Robert who would have been thirty-three when Trice died or even the life of his uncle Adam, though many would not have thought saving his life was a cause of celebration. Even then, it would be exceptional to remember someone almost eighty years on. As is evident in churchyards and cemeteries across the country, few graves are maintained for even ten years never mind eighty. Besides, there is no evidence that Trice was ever the sexton. If he had been, he would have been paid both a regular wage and extra for digging graves inside the church and the churchwardens accounts show no payments to him whatsoever. Nor was Trice ever a tenant of the Spracklings: he lived at Newington and then held six acres in Church Hill. There is no evidence of him being related to them in any way, either himself or through his wife. Why then did Adam Sprackling, who lived his whole life in Canterbury and quite possibly never even visited the parish of St Laurence, make such a bequest? We simply do not know but there must have been some reason the family felt indebted to Trice. Unfortunately, by this stage it was too late and Trice's grave could not be found. The ground, however, remained in the hands of successive sextons of St Laurence into the twentieth century, the last holder being Arthur Startup who tended his allotment there. There being no replacement for Mr Startup, the land was auctioned on 1st November 1972 when it raised £4156.42 for church funds.[65]

---

[64] PRC/32/60/308. Adam Sprackling is buried in the cloisters of Canterbury Cathedral where he has a large ledger stone recalling the virtues of himself and his ancestors.

[65] It was located in Chapel Road.

Richard Coppin

In the late 1640s and early 1650s, a radical thinker and preacher emerged whose name was Richard Coppin. It is certain that he came from Kent but he does not say where in his autobiography. However, there are reasons to suppose that he came from St Laurence.

Alexander and Agnes Coppin had a son Richard in 1613 who was followed by a brother Thomas in 1614 and two girls Martha and Mary in 1616 and 1619. Richard married for the first time in 1637 but his wife died shortly after giving birth to their only child. He remarried in 1640 and had four more children with a significant gap between the third and fourth which corresponds to the period when the preacher Richard was in jail. Richard's brother Thomas went to London and preacher Richard refers to spending two years in London. Both Thomas and his wife are buried at St Laurence, the wife with an incredibly long inscription on her tomb which is in the style of preacher Richard's writings, though this could be argued to be contemporary puritan style. Preacher Richard disappeared from public life at the end of the Commonwealth period and Richard Coppin returned to St Laurence in the late 1650s. Richard's wife died in the summer of 1665 and he died on Christmas Day 1676. Both lie buried in the churchyard.

If preacher Richard was the man born at St Laurence, we have through his autobiography, an interesting account of church life during the incumbency of William Dunkyn. Richard writes:

> I heard of a God afar off, one that lived above the skies, sitting in a golden chair, and was like myself, which the Priests and people did talk of, as one that loved those that did well, and hated others that did ill; and would at the last day come to judge me and all men according to their works and that his worship consisted in mens and womens going to Church, and such like service (but not childrens) and that this holiness consisted in abstaining from swearing, drunkenness, thieving, whoring, and such like sins; which sins being not committed by me, I thought sufficient to save me, being taught so by the Priests of those times, who themselves, as well as others, committed all manner of sin and wickedness, and who deceived both me and many thousands of souls by their delusions, but never taught us of a Jesus, all this while, neither could they, because they knew him not themselves.

Disillusioned, he turned first to the Presbyterians but he found them too legalistic. He then tried the Baptists but rejected them as too superstitious. He spent two years studying the Bible, spending hours in prayer and attending up to five sermons a day but found "I knew no more of it then I did when I was under the Prelates Ministry;

only that there was a God afar off and not within me." At this point he had a life changing encounter with the risen Lord and "all my prayers which I made, books which I had read, sermons which I had heard, besides and below Christ, all now appeared to be of no worth unto me; for I had found one Jesus."[66] He set off as a preacher spending time in Oxfordshire, Berkshire, Gloucestershire and Kent. At one time he was in Westwell, another in Rochester. His sermons attracted controversy for he taught that since God dwelt within all, whatever a man did – be that commit adultery or give alms – such must be the will of God and he denied the existence of heaven and hell and the resurrection of the body. He was jailed several times. Around the time that Oliver Cromwell died, he became disillusioned with the struggle and retired from public life.

The Compton Census

In 1650, Parliament passed the Toleration Act which allowed people for the first time to worship somewhere other than their parish church. They were only allowed to worship in another Protestant church, not Catholic, and they still had to attend worship, but it was a measure of freedom. The Act reflected a change in the understanding of worship. Kings and Parliament had no compunction about forcing people to go to church, not because they were interested in brain-washing, but because they firmly believed that if people did not worship God then God would punish them with plagues, war, poor harvests etc.[67] Attending church was therefore a patriotic duty and part of being a member of the community. Yet the idea that people could make their own decision about worship was new and the authorities were worried about the results. Hence, in 1676, a survey was carried out to find out more about people's habits in worship.

In that year, St Laurence had a congregation of 1200 people whilst the Congregational church in the town had fifty. The vicar of St Laurence, John Young, wrote on his form: "most of the inhabitants come to church for prayers and sermons but few of them will be induced to receive the communion by any argument or persuasion."[68]

His response was very similar to that of the Vicar of St John's in Margate who had noted that although he had around a thousand in his congregation every week, barely ten per cent took Holy Communion even at the major festivals of Easter and Christmas. He said of the people's attitude to church that they were "not very comfortable in it, rather out of a rude clownishness than any fractious or peevish opposition."[69]

---

[66] Richard Coppin, *Truths Testimony* (London 1655) pp.10-14

[67] Even in the twentieth century, this attitude existed with people being confident they would win the war because God was on their side and talking about AIDS as God's judgment on homosexuality.

[68] Anne Whiteman and Mary Clapinson, *The Compton Census of 1676 : a critical edition* (Oxford 1986), pp.22-3

[69] C W Chalklin, *Seventeenth Century Kent* (London, 1965) p.224

Shipping

Being a coastal parish, the sea continued to play a significant part in people's lives. At the start of the century, none of the locally owned vessels had exceeded eight tons and they were used for fishing and short journeys to places such as Sandwich.

A quarter of a century later in 1626, Ramsgate had twenty-one ships registered. They were:

Vessel	Tonnage	Owner(s)
Alivant	24	Robert Sprackling esq, Richard Bassett, Griffin Hollam
Blessing	56	Henry Fairman, Thomas Fairman, Widow Culmer, William Evans
Elizabeth	20	George Curling, Stephen Golding
Gift of God	18	Thomas Coppin, Widow Mockeness
Greyhound	8	William Coppin, Widow Holt
James	18	Richard Bassett
Mary	22	Richard Hougham, William Coppin, Robert Coppin
Mary & Frances	22	William Knowler, Anthony Knowler, Thomas Deveson, Richard Martin
Mary & John	18	George Long, Thomas Curling
Mary Fortune	45	Nicholas Spencer, Vincent Underdown
Mayflower	16	Paul Wastell
Nicholas	10	Roger Eason
Nightingale	26	William Saunders
Primrose	22	Richard Saunders
Primrose	20	George Bennett, Richard Hougham
Richard	16	Richard Barber, William Coppin, John Fairman
Roger	20	Stephen Golding
Speedwell	18	John Eason senior, John Eason junior
Thomas	24	Thomas Fairman senior, Thomas Fairman junior
Vineyard	26	William Evers, Widow Culmer
William & Anne	30	William Fairman[70]

These vessels were a little larger and would have been engaged in local fishing but also the carriage of beer to Sluys and goods to London. Many had multiple owners as people sought to lessen the economic risk of investing all one's money in one vessel. Twenty men were qualified ship's masters and a further twenty-eight served as regular crew meaning up to a fifth of the adult male parish population may be estimated

---

[70] National Archives E190/648/18

therefore to have been sailors.[71]

As the century progressed, the size of ships grew and the pattern of trade changed. In the early part of the seventeenth century, around a twelfth of the locally grown corn exported to London went from Ramsgate. This would have included that grown in the parish at Chilton, Ozengell, Manston, Haine, Newington etc. By 1666, Margate had secured 98% of the trade and by the 1690s, Ramsgate had no involvement at all.[72] This forced parishioners to look elsewhere and the market they moved into was the Baltic. This required still larger vessels and more hands. By 1701, Ramsgate had forty-five ships with a total tonnage of 4,100 and these provided employment for 388 men – around two thirds of the adult male parish population.[73] It was the fifteenth busiest port in England and now exceeded Margate by some degree. The change was to have a significant impact on the parish because it generated wealth which would subsequently transform the church building and introduce a more cosmopolitan congregation. It also led to the transformation of Ramsgate from a minor fishing village where just a small proportion of the parish lived to a large town which would become independent of its mother parish and eventually dwarf it.

Witchcraft

In 1611, Sybil Ferris was accused of being a witch and causing the sickness of Jane Northcliffe nine months earlier, an illness which lasted three months and ended with Jane's death. Sybil had been presented by the churchwardens for witchcraft back in 1597 but the case had not progressed as she had denied the charge and no proof had been submitted. This case was more serious because she was being accused effectively of murder. Sybil by this time was around seventy and had been widowed three months earlier. In many ways, therefore, she fitted the contemporary stereotype of a witch in that she was old and alone and this made her vulnerable. The case was dismissed but it is interesting to note the impact it had on her family: her children fled to Cambridgeshire.

---

[71] National Archives SP16/39/28

[72] Stephen Hipkin, 'The conduct of the coastal metropolitan corn trade during the later seventeenth century', *Agricultural Historical Review* vol 61 no 2 (2013) pp.241-2

[73] John Andrews, 'The Thanet Seaports 1650-1750', *Archaeologia Cantiana* vol 66 (1953) p.39

Such a journey was unusual and indicates the shame and embarrassment they must have felt at their mother being so accused not just once but twice. [74]

Poverty

As well as people being expected to pay a rate set by churchwardens toward the maintenance of their parish church, they were expected from 1604 onwards to pay a rate or sess towards the relief of the poor. This was set by overseers and there were normally two rates a year although more could be levied in times of need, such as when the harvest failed or there was disease. For example, there were five sesses in 1646 and 1649 and four in 1667, years of hunger and typhus. The role of the overseers required them to maintain those in need whether they were elderly, sick or orphans. In the case of the latter, they had to provide homes for them and clothing until they were of an age to be apprenticed. St Laurence is fortunate to have the records of the overseers for the poor from 1604 to 1672 after which there is a gap until 1693.[75]

A considerable amount of the money went in keeping widows who were unable to work and in paying their rent. Women were very vulnerable to destitution when their husband died because wages were set at a subsistence level which meant most men were unable to save money to leave to their wives. A typical example is the case of Susan Woolton née Curling. She married John Woolton in April 1633 when she was twenty-five years old. He was a widower, ten years older than her, with two daughters of twenty months and three months respectively. Susan went on to have seven children of her own over the next thirteen years, at least one of whom died in infancy. Her husband died in April 1647 and she was immediately plunged into poverty. Over the coming year, the parish paid out:

	£	s	d
Cloaks for her children	1	10	6
Making clothes for her children	1	2	8
Coal		6	10
Meat		7	6
Rent		7	
Clothes for the Widow Woolton		14	6
Cash payments		16	7
Wool to make a pair of hose		3	8
Mending a pair of hose			8
Hose for the children		8	10
Buttons and thread		2	6

Susan became ill which resulted in more cost:

---

[74] Image from Anon, *A Most Curious Strange and True Discovery of a Witch* (London, 1643)
[75] CCA-U3-19/12/1 to CCA-U3-19/12/5

	£	s	d
To women tending her		15	
Costs of medicine and caring for her		11	
Linen for sheets and clothes		11	

She died and was buried on the 4th March 1648/9 but the costs did not end there for the parish still had to take care of her children who were too young to work and pay for her funeral.

	£	s	d
For a coffin and tolling bell		10	8
Given in bread and beer to those who carried her to church for burial		3	10
Keeping the Widow Woolton's children for one week		9	6

The four children were divided and sent to live with various people often for just a few weeks at a time. These included Michael Yoakely, Goodwife Fagg, Goodwife Frances, Goody Dabson, John Hills, Widow Doust and Widow Webb. In 1649, her son William was apprenticed to Augustine Hills, the parish spending 13s 4d on clothes for his new life and a further 2s 6d to the lawyer for drawing up the papers. There were similar costs as the others grew up. In today's money, the parish spent some £1500 on her and her family in the two years which elapsed between her husband's death and her own. Each sess raised around £25 at this time so expenditure on the Wooltons took almost half a sess.

Another example is the Widow Terry who died in November 1668 age 75. Her husband had been a husbandman and he died in 1649. In the last month of her life, the parish spent 3s on medicine for her, 5s 6d on bedding, 1s 11d on coal to keep her warm, 4s to the Widow Dowling for laying her out and disposing of her few goods and 8s 6d on a coffin.

The fact that the overseers spent so much is an indication of the care they took. In the same period, they took charge of Susan Curling who was lame and whose widowed father was unable to cope with looking after her and working. They bought her clothes, paid for her keep and bought medicine when she was ill. They also cared for Katherine Yoakely, who lost her mother at nine and her father at sixteen, purchasing for her when she started domestic service two coats, three aprons, a pair of stockings, a change of underwear and two waistcoats.

Another child whose care fell to the parish was James Groves. His father had been a shoemaker who had married twice and had six children, two of whom had died in infancy. James lost both his parents within a month of each other in January 1648/9 just when he should have been celebrating his fifth birthday. His eleven year old oldest sister died a day after his mother. Clearly there had been some health problem in the household although no other home in the parish was affected. James was immediately separated from his nine year old brother and seven year old sister and cared for by a succession of people in the parish. In 1650, for example he spent five weeks with Widow Hogbin before being transferred to Widow Gibbens who it seems was not happy about the condition in which he arrived since she immediately applied for, and received, 5s 4d to buy a yard and a half of jersey, some thread and some buttons to make him a short coat to keep him warm. James grew up and died aged thirty-eight in Minster. He never married.[76]

A study of children born in the parish from 1600-20 showed that one in ten children lost both parents before their twelfth birthday which gives some indication of the potential costs on St Laurence.

Organising the collection of money and controlling its expenditure was a responsible job and the role was rotated like that of churchwarden between those of mainly yeomen status. There is evidence that they tried to run the process like a business. They would buy wool and give it to widows or disabled single women to spin so that it could be sold and the money returned to the poor fund. In the late 1640s, for example, women were being paid 2d per pound of spinning completed. They also tried to do similar for men offering them weaving or stone breaking work. Wherever possible, they gave orphan children into the care of widows which not only secured the children but gave the widow an income rather than leaving her simply living on alms. Examples in 1671 include Widow Bennet receiving ten shillings a month for Fairman's child, Widow Curling getting eight shillings a month for Norman's girl and Widow Martin getting ten shillings for the Parker child.[77] They bought loads of coals from Margate for distribution to the poor and also bushels of wheat and barley when there was expected to be a shortage. Such items were stored in the Church Wax House where the overseers kept their office.

Further evidence of poverty can be found in the Hearth Tax returns. These recorded the number of hearths in each home in the parish and whether the person was able to pay the tax levied. In 1664, a total of 138 homes were listed in two regions. St Lawrence East covered Ramsgate, St Lawrence village, Southwood, Chilton and Dumpton and 49 of the 93 homes there (53%) were judged too poor to pay tax. Westborough covered Nethercourt, Manston, Cliffsend and Haine and there 17 of the 45 homes were excused payment on grounds of poverty (38%). In 1667 and 1673, the tax list was made out as Ramsgate and St Lawrence but the results were similar with Ramsgate having 44% excused on grounds of poverty on both occasions and St Lawrence 54% and 52% respectively.[78] They were the highest rates on the island.

---

[76] His older brother died aged twenty-four. His sister married when she was twenty-eight. She named her first child after her brother James indicating some fondness but he died after a few days.
[77] CCA-U3-19/12/5
[78] National Archives EXT 6/100 (previously E179/249/37, E179/129/746, E179/330/14 and 15). 1673 figures are from Alfred Walker, *The Ville of Birchington*, (Ramsgate, 1991) p.82

Wills

Between 1600 and 1699, 303 parishioners made a will. They represent a variety of the population and show something of the standard of living and how people made their money. For example, Richard Fowler who was a slaughterman spoke in 1651 of his long period of sickness which had damaged his savings but noted that his wife had her own shop and went regularly to London to buy supplies for it. William Jenkin was a fisherman who lived at Hereson. In his will of 1647 he spoke of the equipment of his trade such as herring nets, barrels and ropes but also of owning two cottages at Upton which he rented out. Another fisherman, Thomas Bassett, also had two houses in Ramsgate plus a boat named the Mary Frances. John Sea, a fisherman in 1682 had a house in Ramsgate but also owned a shop in the town which was rented out. He further left herring and mackerel nets plus shares in a yawl, a pink and a North Sea boat. Richard Underdown, a husbandman, had a two bedroom house when he died in 1616. Lewis Rogers, at one time schoolmaster at St Laurence, left in 1642 a variety of books including a Bible to his daughter plus a considerable amount of bedding and a black doublet and breeches. George Grant, a yeoman at Newington, spoke of his house complete with orchard, barn, malthouse and garden. Since wives could not make wills without their husband's consent, almost all the wills are made by men. Of adult women buried, 4.7% made a will; of adult men 32.9%.

Patterns of Death

It is popularly supposed that the lives of those in the seventeenth century were short and that prior to the 1660s, outbreaks of plague were common. An analysis of the burial registers shows that this is not entirely true in the case of St Laurence parish.

Between 1600 and 1699, a total of 3108 burials took place. Of these, 23 were of people for whom no details were recorded, mostly shipwrecked sailors or soldiers. Of the remainder, it has proved possible to trace 90.4% of the males and 83.5% of the females which creates a database of 2686 people.

Of the burials, a fifth were of infants less than a year old and a further one in ten were of infants aged one to five. One in six burials involved a person over the age of sixty. The Vicar could expect to bury just one person aged eighty or more every two years. A fifth of burials were of people we would regard as young adults, those aged twenty to forty, and the same proportion again were aged forty-one to sixty. Thus, in rounded terms, for every ten children born, two would die before they were ten, one would die in their teens, one would die in their twenties, two would die in their thirties or forties, two in their fifties, one in their sixties and one would reach seventy.

Infant mortality was higher amongst boys than girls. 12.9% of boys died in their first year of life compared to 10.6% of girls. After this, mortality rates were very similar with around 6% of each dying aged one to five and 2% aged six to ten. Overall, 21.5% of boys and 18.5% of girls failed to survive to their tenth birthday. Since baptism ordinarily took place on the first Sunday after birth, or sooner in the case of a sickly child, it is possible to assess the proportion of deaths which were neonatal, i.e. within a month of birth. Boys proved more vulnerable at this stage with around one in thirteen perishing within thirty days of birth compared to one in twenty girls. For babies generally, the most dangerous time was the summer, the season of diarrhoea.

In demographic terms, crises appear when the number of burials in a single year are double that of the average for the preceding decade. St Laurence experienced three such years during the century - 1625, 1638 and 1690. A lesser crisis was also evident in 1669. The year 1625 saw high mortality across England. Margate and Birchington were affected and St Peter's to a lesser degree. Plague existed in Canterbury, Dover and Sandwich but there is no evidence that it spread to St Laurence where deaths were concentrated in the winter and included a high proportion of the over fifties. Such a pattern is not consistent with bubonic plague which occurs in the summer, is concentrated in families rather than scattered cases, builds slowly to a peak then falls rapidly, and is particularly likely to attack children from around five to fifteen. Nor is it consistent with pneumonic plague which occurs in the winter, again in households, but has a much higher mortality and a sharper peak. It could not be a waterborne disease either where deaths rocket overnight in a particular locality. The pattern would suggest a viral infection of some type. Similarly in 1638, deaths were high but this was in the winter after the harvest had failed. Malnutrition made people susceptible to illnesses from which they might otherwise have recovered. 1669 saw a number of child deaths during the very hot summer and the likelihood is that these were due to smallpox or measles. The worst year for burials in the century was 1690 when over half the burials occurred in a space of ten weeks. This was the year of the Battles of the Boyne and Beachy Head when typhus broke out amongst the soldiers. Bodies from the ships were brought ashore at Ramsgate and Margate for burial and sadly some inhabitants were affected.

The lack of plague over the century is significant. As a port with trading links to London, Dover and Sandwich, it might have been expected that the parish would have succumbed quickly in each epidemic. That it did not do so indicates the vigilance kept and the speed with which trading links inland and coastal were closed when news of an outbreak began. At such times, the parish had to become self-supporting for food. Another factor which probably helped was the fact that so many parishioners were fishermen. Presuming they consumed part of their catch and allowing for much of that being mackerel which has anti-parasitic qualities, they may have had some immunity.[79]

William Joy, the English Samson

Born at St Peter's at the end of February 1672 was William Joy who was to achieve great fame and some wealth as "The English Samson" or "Kentish Samson." He was the son of Robert Joy, a husbandman and began life working on the land. The second of eight

---

[79] For a full discussion of the spread of plague and recent medical research see Margaret Bolton, 'The Experience of Plague in East Kent, 1636-38', *Local Population Studies*, (Spring, 2016) pp. 9-27

children and oldest son, his father died when he was fifteen leaving him the responsibility of providing for his mother and younger siblings. The family moved to St Lawrence where he trained as a ship's carpenter and in his own day, Joy was known as a man of Ramsgate.[80] He went to sea and served in the Nine Years' War being captured by the French off Spain. It was on his return to England that he began performing as a strong man. His authorised biography, written in 1699, describes a street fight which he had in Southwark with a carter. Not only did Joy have the man begging for mercy after being almost suffocated but he threw the man's horse on its back with such a force that onlookers thought at first the animal was dead. He then snapped a two inch thick rope in half before acknowledging the onlookers. The reaction clearly suggested to him that performing would be a good way of making money.

>Behold this William Joy by name
>Of late he into Southwark came
>where he by strength does far outdo
>Not only men but horses too.[81]

He rented the Dorset Garden theatre in London in September 1699. Billed as "The Strong Kentish Man" he attracted much attention and some scandal, particularly after a letter was found addressed to him by a Countess who said she had watched him "with satisfaction exerting your parts" and comparing his wonders favourably with the conquests of Caesar and the labours of Hercules. She went on: "It grieves me to see so noble a talent mis-employed and that strength thrown away upon undeserving horses that cannot reward your labour which might better divert the requiting woman. Meet me therefore, thou puissant man, in another garden on a better theatre where you may employ your abilities with more profit to yourself and satisfaction to the expecting Melisanda."[82] Whether he accepted the lady's offer is unknown.

Amongst those who went to see him were Ned Ward and the philosopher John Locke who wrote: "The performances of the Strong Man now in London would be beyond belief were there not so many witnesses of it. I think they deserve to be communicated to the present age and recorded to posterity." His image was engraved and circulated on handbills including one by Berge in 1699 which described him as "William Joy, the English Sampson."[83] He became the subject of investigation by doctors of the day who sought to understand his abilities. Those who saw "Billy the Kentish Samson" as he was also known, noted he was "fair of complexion, slight of limb" and thought his feats utterly "miraculous" because "he is not of the breed of giants being lean

---

[80] His mother, Widow Joy, appears in the rate books throughout this period living at Church Hill, now High Street St Lawrence. Her poverty is evident as she was either excused rates or paid 1d.
[81] Anon, *The Kentish Sampson* (London, 1699)
[82] Tom Brown, *Amusements Serious and Comical* (London, 1715) pp.147-148
[83] Henry Bromley, *A Catalogue Of Engraved British Portraits* (London 1793) p.202

and spare."⁸⁴ Daniel Defoe who saw him agreed and described him as "a fellow of gigantic strength, though not of extraordinary stature."⁸⁵ He said that Joy "suffered men to fasten the strongest horse they could find to a rope, and the rope round his loins" then "sitting on the ground, with his feet straight out against a post, no horse could stir him." Dr Desaguliers noted imitators were few and far between because "He was very strong in the arms and grasped those that tried his strength that way so hard that they were obliged immediately to desire him to desist." However, he did not think him actually that strong but rather that he was able to achieve his feats due to a greater understanding of how to position his body.⁸⁶

In November 1699 Joy was invited to appear before the King at Kensington and he decided to have new portraits etched and to restyle himself 'The English Sampson'. His claim to this title was opposed a fortnight later by the Derbyshire Sampson and Joy seems to have dropped it. Audiences fell so that by the end of his run in January 1700, ticket prices had been cut by 70% notwithstanding his efforts at trying to increase interest by adding other members of the family to the act. By the following year he was performing solo again on the fairs circuit alongside attractions such as three breasted ladies, dwarves and sacrificial virgins.⁸⁷ Not long after, Joy left London to go on tour overseas with his new wife. Returning to England some years later, he sought new ways of making money and seems to have descended into the world of crime. The area in which his theatre had been situated was close to Alsatia, a notorious haunt for criminals. We also know from his biography, as well as his communications with people such as Farquar, that his temperament from quite a young age had inclined toward fighting and gambling. He became a smuggler and drowned in 1734. His death was recorded by the Thanet clergyman and historian John Lewis who probably got the news from his brother. A couple of decades earlier, Defoe had visited Ramsgate and asked after the Samson only to be told "he disappear'd, and we heard no more of him since."

Harry Houdini later investigated his methods and provided an explanation of how some of the feats were performed.⁸⁸ It would seem likely that some trickery was involved for Joy was said to have lifted a ton (2240lbs or 1016kg), which is more than double the record of Zydrunas Savickas, the World's Strongest Man of 2009, 2010, 2012 and 2014. Not only was he said to have lifted this amount but the print shows he did it with one hand! He was also supposed to have carried 112 stone or 1568lb on his back from St George's in Botolph Lane to the Monument, half a mile away. Hafthór Björnsson's record is 1433lb for five steps.

---

⁸⁴ Anon, *The Kentish Sampson* (London, 1699)
⁸⁵ Daniel Defoe, *A Tour through the Whole Island of Great Britain* vol.1 (London, 1724) p.45
⁸⁶ John Theophilus Desaguliers, *A Course of Experimental Philosophy* (London, 1745) p.265
⁸⁷ Henry Morley, *Memoirs of Bartholomew Fair* (London, 1859) pp.326-327, 351-352
⁸⁸ Harry Houdini, *Miracle Mongers* (London, 1920) p.105

Curiously, St Peter's churchyard has a gravestone which reads:

> In Memory of Mr Richard Joy
> (called the Kentish Samson)
> who died May 18th 1742 aged 67.
> Herculean Hero famed for strength
> at last lies here Breadth and Length.
> See how the mighty is fallen.
> To death ye strong and weak are all one.
> And the same Judgement doth Befall,
> Goliath Great and David Small.

Richard was William's brother, born in 1673. His will, made shortly after William's death and including an allowance for William's son, shows him to have been a violinist with a substantial collection of musical instruments and some minor land investments. The age shown is wrong but happens to match the false age given by William on a handbill and in his authorised biography "Kentish Samson" which is held at the British Library. Richard lived in Ramsgate and his wife was buried at St Laurence. The churchwardens at St Peter's were keen to use the gravestone to attract visitors having it painted in 1828.[89]

As an example of how the myth grew, in 1871, the local paper wrote a feature on William Joy the English Sampson where they claimed he was born at St Lawrence and that he was 7'9" tall and weighted thirty stone, claims totally disproved by not only reason but contemporary documents.[90]

---

[89] Mockett op.cit. p.32
[90] *Thanet Advertiser*, 5th August 1871.

The Eighteenth Century

THE BUILDING

There are two principal sources for information about the building in the eighteenth century. Churchwarden's accounts exist for the period up to 1721 and vestry minutes from 1733 onwards. The earliest faculty for work in the church dates from 1715.

Galleries were first erected in the church at the end of the seventeenth century. An account of the church from 1719 describes it as: "large and handsome with a tower in the middle and several galleries in it."[1] These were increased in the early 1730s. The vestry had noted in 1730 that the parish now numbered between two and three thousand souls and there were insufficient pews to seat them all. For this reason they sought a faculty to build a gallery between the second and third arches at the west end on the south side of church 23' broad and 15' 8" high from the floor. A faculty was granted for this in 1732.[2] A curious case emerged in May of 1752 where it was reported that a gallery had been erected at the west end of the south aisle without the consent of the churchwardens. They demanded that the person responsible pay £2 2s compensation or else demolish the gallery. Presumably the person paid because the gallery can be seen in the painting of the church made a century later but it must be wondered how it ever came to be built. The church was opened each day by the sexton and the carpenters would have come in. It seems unlikely they could have finished the job in one day so surely the sexton would have noticed the work that had been done when he went to lock up and reported it. It might have been thought that someone would have seen people taking lots of wood and ladders in to do the work and queried this. The last gallery to be added was that above the site of the present pulpit (no. 4 on plan), permission being given to Mr Townley by the vestry on 3rd April 1809 with the work to be done at his expense.

---

[1] John Harris, *The History of Kent* vol 1 (London, 1719) p.174
[2] CCA/DCb-E/F/St Lawrence in Thanet/ 2

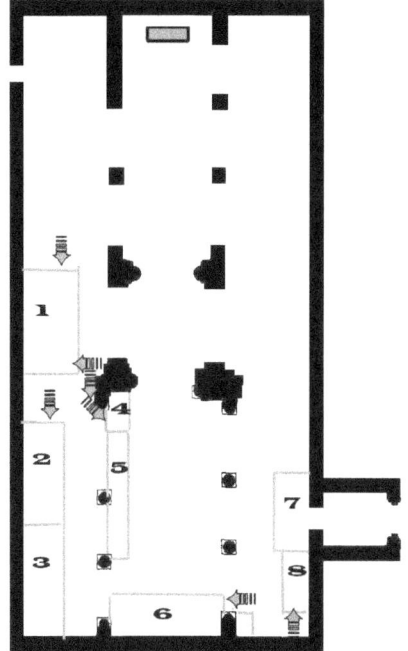

The galleries were erected over the porch, across the back or west end of the church, along the north side of the nave and down the north aisle. Some of the galleries had names such as that in the north transept which was called the Manston gallery and which housed the Ringers' Pew and one for churching. Access to the galleries was by a variety of narrow spiral staircases and there is evidence that they were not always entirely safe. In April 1799 it was decided to demolish and rebuild the north gallery (no. 5 on plan) due to it being in such a poor state that it was felt to be hazardous. In order to light and ventilate the galleries, a dormer window was cut into the roof of the nave and two small windows either side of the west door, remains of which can still be seen.[3]

On 3rd October 1758 it was agreed to raise the back part of the west gallery for the benefit of the singers. This is the earliest reference to there

---

[3] The Reverend Charles Cowland-Cooper who arrived in 1927 recalled speaking with the man who removed the dormer window.

being a choir at St Laurence. As the regulations regarding church music had not changed, they would still have been working from the Book of Psalms. An account of how choirs worked in the early nineteenth century appears in Thomas Hardy's *Under the Greenwood Tree* where he talks of the choir being accompanied by local musicians on fiddles, horns and flutes and them having to buy tunes from wandering pedlars. A child who was a member of the congregation at the end of the century and who did play the flute was Henry Maxwell Lyte who grew up to write *Abide with Me* and *Praise my soul, the King of Heaven* though whether he was ever in the music group is unknown.[4]

On 3rd August 1769, the following minute was entered: "upon representation being made that the parish church of St Lawrence is very large, high pitched, not ceiled and being situated on an eminence is exceedingly cold in the winter season to the great detriment of the health of numbers of the said parishioners and inhabitants and especially to the aged and infirm. It is hereby agreed unanimously at the meeting of the vestry with the consent and approbation of the minister and churchwardens that they the said churchwardens do cause to be made screens or inside doors to keep out the cold…this whole to be done in a workmanlike manner with plain yellow deal boards to be painted." It was further decreed that the work was to be done by parishioners as part of their policy of giving work to their own before those outside the parish. As part of this work, the west door which had been used as an entry to the church for almost seven hundred years was closed off.

On 16th September 1772 it was decided to demolish the ancient Church Wax House and to use the materials to repair the parish church. Dr Cotton later described this as a "barbarous" act of vandalism but the building had fallen into disuse since the erection of the parish poorhouse in 1724 and it was expensive to keep paying window tax on it.

The work carried out in 1773 included

- raising the roofs of the western aisles on either side of the church
- removing the old belfry and making a staircase into the loft immediately over it then painting this
- repairing the windows and interior tiled floor
- adding ceilings throughout the church to cover the medieval roofs
- re-glazing the window at the east end of the south chancel (now the side chapel)
- making a new window and frame at the east end of the vestry (now the kitchen)
- re-whitewashing the entire church
- covering the pulpit cushion and hanging the pulpit and desk with

---

[4] *The Beacon*, April 1954. A descendant had letters from Lyte's mother written at Ramsgate. Henry Lyte was taken from his mother at a young age by his father so it is unlikely that he performed at the church.

new crimson damask or velvet and to ornament it with gold lace or with fringe

One of the means adopted by the churchwardens to raise the cash for these alterations was to strip and sell the lead.

In 1774 the church also got a new font, presumably replacing the medieval one. It was very small which fitted in with the space constraints that resulted from the growing congregation. Since there is no record of the church buying the font, it must have been a gift. Today, the font is at St Catherine's, Manston. It is not clear whether the font was left in the north-west corner or moved although the fact that churchings were still held in the north side would suggest it remained there.

Not mentioned in the accounts or vestry book but clearly dating from the eighteenth century was the wooden reredos which can be seen in the Victorian painting of the church. The tendency for the accounts to just include names of bills rather than details of work is the reason for this. For example, in 1715, the carpenter was paid £3 11s for his work and the wood he had used but there is no indication of what he did. He may have been building a screen, making seats, repairing existing furniture or stairways. It is impossible to tell. With a modern equivalent of almost £450, it was a large sum.

The reredos contained the Ten Commandments, Lord's Prayer and Apostles' Creed in red Italian characters on a black background. It had four carved ionic columns and a pediment and it was painted white to match the surrounding stonework. The Palladian styling would suggest that it was probably added during the incumbency of the Reverend Robert Tyler (1740-66). It was much taller than the present stone screen and would have finished approximately in line with the knee of the central angel in the present East Window.

The two decker pulpit which can be seen on the mid nineteenth century painting was made of wood, probably oak, and stood under the tower against the south-east pillar. The parish clerk stood at the reading desk which formed the lower part of the structure and from there he would lead the worship and read the lessons. Given the vast majority of the congregation could not read, he would have "lined out" the psalms and versicles, reading out each line for the people to repeat. A curved staircase led up from the present choir stalls on the right to the hexagonal pulpit which had decorated panels around the top. It is impossible to identify these from the painting but it is likely that they were fairly plain, the fashion being for classical understatement. A cushion on a stand would have held the preacher's notes if he used any and his Holy Bible. The structure would have left his head approximately level with the devil's head, something which probably caused some amusement to younger members of the congregation. Although the date is unknown, it is likely that this was constructed in the first quarter of the century since one of the chief aims would have been to allow those sitting in the galleries to see the preacher. It may have been what the carpenter made in 1715.

Worship

The pattern of worship in the eighteenth century continued on from the seventeenth. It was much plainer than is the case today. The minister wore a simple black cassock and surplice, the latter of which he removed when he preached. Candles were lit about the church but only if it was dark, their purpose being purely practical and not symbolic. He entered the tower area behind the parish clerk but there was no procession and no cross. The service would have lasted around three hours. Matins would have been said first and then the Litany. The first part of the Holy Communion service would then have been used culminating in the sermon. By this stage, the congregation would have heard an entire chapter of the Old Testament and another of the New at Matins plus two readings as part of the Holy Communion. The service would not have been sung or chanted and there were no hymns but there were singers to help with the metrical psalm. From toward the end of the century, there would have been some musical accompaniment for this in the form of locally available instruments such as flutes or violins. On the occasions when there was to be a celebration of Holy Communion, those who wished to receive would go and stand in the chancel whilst everybody else left. The minister would go to the north side of the communion table which was probably turned for the purpose given the amount of space available at St Laurence. Communicants would have received kneeling, rails to support the infirm being provided from 1750.

Church Plate

It is unknown what items of silverware were owned by the church at the start of the eighteenth century. A communion cup was purchased in 1700 for £1 16s and another in 1718 for £5 6s 6d but it must be assumed that the first replaced an earlier cup and that the second was bought because of the increase in communicants. Both appear in the inventory of 1733 but they were replaced by a pair purchased in 1833.[5]

In 1733, the church also had three silver salvers or patens. Two of these still exist being a pair given by Thomas Tomson in 1721. He died on the 8th September of that year and it would appear that he did not live to see his order completed for the silversmith has inscribed them Thomas Thomson in error. The rate books show Tomson derived most of his income from his farm in King Street but he also owned a brewhouse for which he was

---

[5] CCA-U3-19/8/A/1

rated a shilling. In later years, this was to become the famous Tomson and Wotton brewery. The size of the patens show regular bread was then in use not wafers.

The third salver was sold in 1739 by the churchwardens to buy a silver flagon and this, dated 1742, is still in regular use at Holy Communion.

A further paten was made in 1722 although it was only given to the church in 1840. Another paten was bought in 1798 and remains in use. Other expenditure included 2s to gild a candle stick in 1709 and £1 to buy two candlesticks with snuffers in 1721.

This group of expenses suggests a clear move on the part of the then vicar, Matthew Bookey, to enhance the act of Holy Communion. It also reflects the growing population which was resulting in an increased congregation. When Mr Bookey arrived, the church averaged fifty-eight baptisms and thirty-nine burials a year. By the time he died almost forty years later, that had increased to seventy-three baptisms and fifty-five burials, an overall increase of around a third.

Royal Arms

Above the porch inside the church is the coat-of-arms of King George II dated 1729. Since the mid sixteenth century, churches had been obliged to display the royal coat of arms as a reminder that the monarch was the Supreme Governor of the Church of England. This remains the case and Queen Elizabeth II, as part of her coronation oath, vowed to defend the church.

The arms show a shield which is divided into four parts. In the top left or first quarter can be seen the three lions of England. Next to that can be seen the fleur-de-lis for France. The English claim to France dated back to the reign of Edward III whose mother had been the last surviving child of Philip IV. French law stated that a woman could not inherit so the crown passed to her cousin but English law had no such limitation so Edward claimed it on her behalf in 1340. The harp representing Ireland is in the third quarter and the fourth shows George II's German inheritance of Brunswick, Luneburg and Hanover with the crown of Charlemagne for the Empire in the middle.

On either side of the shield are the English lion and the Scottish unicorn. A rose can be seen beside the lion's feet and a thistle beside the unicorn's. The unicorn is chained symbolising the union of 1707.

Above the shield is the helmet which has cloth of gold and ermine tied to the top, both signs of prestige. At the top is the crown.

The shield is surrounded by the blue garter which has the words *Honi soit qui mal y pense* which means 'Shame on Him who thinks Evil of it'. This is the motto of the Order

of the Garter, the highest order of chivalry in the United Kingdom.[6] Beneath is the royal motto, *Dieu et mon droit* meaning 'God and my right.'

Churches were meant to have the arms repainted whenever there was a change of monarch but cost meant this rarely happened. It took until 1700 for St Laurence to set up the arms of William III who came to the throne on 13th February 1688/89 and they paid James Moses £2 12s for his work in painting them, around £300 in today's money. There is no evidence that they had them repainted for Queen Anne but they were done for George I in 1714. The parishioners were no doubt delighted that George III had the same arms as his father which meant there was no need to repaint them in 1760.[7]

It is uncertain where the arms were originally hung. Throughout the nineteenth century, they were on the north wall of the south chapel but they would have had a more prominent position previously, probably in the nave.

A note in the vestry minutes records the fact that when George II died, black cloth was purchased and draped from the pulpit as a mark of respect and across the communion table. George II is most famous today for having been the last British monarch to personally lead his troops into battle and for starting the tradition of people standing during the *Hallelujah Chorus*.

Bells

Just as in the previous century, the bells continued to be a source of major expense to the church. As well as the regular expenses for replacement ropes, clappers and baldricks and maintenance items such as oil, there was the cost of re-casting. In 1704-1705, this constituted a major project as the following expenses show.

---

[6] Despite the legend that this motto relates to Edward III chivalrously saving a lady's embarrassment when her garter fell, it is more likely to be a reference to the English claim to France and a warning that those who did not support it would be shamed.

[7] George III's arms changed in 1801 when the French fleur-de-lis was dropped. The royal arms were restored in 1994 by A. R. Goulden.

	£	s	d
Paid to Mr Paramor for drawing up the copy of the articles with the bell foundry		2	6
To Moses Martin for helping to take the bells down		2	6
To Jeremiah Parlow for carrying bells to Margate and home		13	6
To George Kennard for carrying the bells to Margate and home again		13	6
To John Wootton for use of his waggon		1	6
Spent at Margate when we carried the bells		4	
For weighing the bells	2	11	2
To John Turner for carrying the bells to London and down	3	14	
To Mr Pargrave for his expenses with the bell foundry	1		
To Richard Phelps for casting the bells in London	128	14	8
To John Goatham for timber and boards	7		
To Thomas Railton for the new frame and hanging of the bells	62	10	
For bringing bell ropes from London		1	6
To Zaram Basden for bell rope		6	6
	210	11	4

It may be wondered whether there was some sort of problem since two of them were recast just twenty years later and a third five years after. Having spent the modern equivalent of almost thirty thousand pounds in 1704-5, the church would probably not have anticipated having to spend further large sums so soon afterwards. Interestingly, they chose to use a different foundry for the work – Samuel Knight. A clue is given by the Vicar of Minster who noted in 1723 that a local church in Thanet – which he did not name - "having cast their old bells anew, to save charges have made candlesticks of them as to sound."[8] By contrast, Samuel Knight's bells were famed for being "sweet in tone."[9]

It is presumed that five bells were re-cast since in 1773 the church possessed five bells and there is no evidence of any being purchased between 1704 and 1773. This raises the question of the origins of the bells. Seventeenth century records, created after the sale of the angelus, refer to a treble, second, third, great and small bell. This last may have been the said treble since vestry minutes of 1773 refer to the "first or little bell" as well as a fourth bell which is not specifically mentioned in seventeenth century accounts, probably because it did not require special work during the period for which records existed. Such a bell would either have had to be created before 1613 when records began or between 1642 and 1687, the years for which records are missing. Minster and

---

[8] Lewis op.cit. 1723 edition p.97
[9] Stahlschmidt op.cit. p.108

Birchington both carried out major work just after the Restoration but did not buy new bells. Although it cannot be known for certain, the probability is that the fourth dated from the earlier rather than the later period because bequests suggest the parish contained more wealthy people at that point.

In 1734, a ringers chamber was created with its own floor to save the ringers from ringing at ground level.

In October 1773, the vestry agreed to "remove the old belfry and make a staircase into the loft immediately over it."

During the eighteenth century, the ringers customarily rang on what were described as "rejoicing days." These included on a regular basis the King's birthday, the anniversary of his accession, Gunpowder Plot (November 5th), St George's day (April 23rd) and Christmas. They also rang to proclaim news events such as when British armies had achieved a significant victory or when a new royal prince was born. There is no record of them ever ringing when a princess was born suggesting that this was not seen as a cause of rejoicing!

Monuments

The eighteenth century was a period of transition in the style of monuments within the church as murals replaced ledger stones. In the first half of the century, ledgers outnumbered murals seventeen to seven but in the second half of the century they were equal in quantity. By the first half of the nineteenth century, there were five times more murals than ledgers. The style of design also changed as the century developed reflecting new fashions and changing ideas about the world.

One of the finest ledger stones is beside the vestry door and it remembers Robert Eason who died on Boxing Day 1718 aged 59. Rate books show that he had lived in what was then called West End but is now the High Street. His home was seven doors down from Nathaniel Austen's so probably close by Chatham Street and it was the third highest valued property in the area. Robert Eason had married Mary Long in 1694 and was a sea captain travelling across Europe. His stone shows a skull on top of crossed thigh bones which represents mortality. Behind the head is a scythe which is a reminder of death as the grim reaper. The head, however, is decked with a laurel

wreath symbolising the victory that Christians believe they have through Our Lord over death. It is surrounded by a garland to show that Robert has passed to new life.

Imagery relating to mortality was typical of the period because it was a time when people inevitably felt vulnerable. Medical knowledge was slight and recovery from sickness often owed more to luck and constitution than to medicine whilst a failed harvest would lead to hunger and death. People felt powerless to control their fate. As the century progressed, scientific advances led people to feel slightly better and mortality symbols were shunned in favour of modern classical styles. Instead of skulls and bones, there are plaques, pillars, Grecian urns and pyramids, reflecting the growing interest in Ancient Egypt.

On the right hand side of the arch from the side chapel toward the south aisle is an oval memorial to the wife of Francis Freeling. She had come to Ramsgate in the hope that the sea water and fresh air would cure her but this was not to be. She died on the 4th May 1796 aged 33. The stone records that she "sustained a severe illness of considerable duration, with the fortitude and resignation of a true Christian." Unusually, the memorial also refers to his place of work. The General Post Office in London was then seen as a prestigious employment and Freeling rose through the ranks and was responsible for a number of reforms such as the use of steam ships and trains to speed up deliveries, achievements which later earned him a baronetcy. Almost fifty years later, the parish was to have another link with the mail system when Sir Thomas Wilde, who is buried in the D'Este Mausoleum in the churchyard, presented Rowland Hill's scheme for the introduction of postage stamps to the House of Lords. [10]

---

[10] The Freeling memorial was originally on the inside of the arch toward the tower but moved in 1888 during restoration work.

On the opposite side of the church in the north transept can be seen the memorial to William Rogerson. The large tablet includes a glowing eulogy by his wife which says:

> In the relative duties of life, as a husband, parent, and friend, he acquitted himself with singular tenderness, probity, and honour.
> In his attention to business, he was indefatigable.
> In his commerce with mankind, strictly just and upright.
> It pleased the Almighty to afflict him with a long and painful illness, which he sustained with a pious resignation and manly fortitude, and on the 9th of November 1782 resigned his soul to his blessed Redeemer in steadfast hope of a glorious immortality aged 60 years.

The parish register reveals that he disappeared one day and his body was found washed up on shore shortly afterwards, evidently drowned: at this time, the cliffs were unfenced. Rogerson was a highly successful woollen draper with a shop and warehouse near the Royal Exchange in London and a home in Broad Street Buildings. His estate in today's values was worth almost three quarters of a million pounds which explains the richness of his monument.[11]

To the rear of the church can be seen the 1754 memorial to Captain Thomas Redwood and his wife. It contemplates the issue of the Last Judgment and warns: "reader, thou and I shall hear our doom from Christ our Judge, whose sentence then shall be eternal bliss, or endless misery! Consider well this truth, and hourly pray, That you may happy be in that last day."[12]

CLERGY AND STAFF

The first vicar of the eighteenth century was the Reverend **Matthew Bookey** who arrived aged thirty-four at Christmas 1699 and stayed until his death on 15th March 1739. One of his first acts was to have a new vicarage built, a house described by the Reverend John Lewis of Minster as "a handsome and commodious dwelling."[13] No image survives of this building but it may be supposed that it was similar to other Queen Anne houses in the parish such as those at Chilton and Ozengell. It was Matthew Bookey also who agreed to try and exorcise the ghost at Ellington. Inexplicable sounds of banging had been heard there, allegedly since the murder of Katherine Sprackling in 1652. Bookey's efforts

---

[11] PROB 11/1098/199

[12] Redwood was a sea captain and merchant travelling between England and Spain in his ship, *Union*.

[13] Lewis op.cit. 1736 edition p.181

had no effect on the apparent ghostly activity which was only ended when the stables were moved, it being discovered that the banging sounds were actually echoes of the horses hooves who were stabled over cavernous cellars.[14]

Matthew Bookey died on 15th March 1739 aged 73 having served as Vicar for almost forty years. He was buried in the vestry with his son Matthew by his side. It is this location which has caused his grave to be arguably the most visited in the church for in 1994 a lavatory was installed in the middle of it. This astounding example of disrespect demonstrates the change in attitudes to the dead across the centuries. When the Victorians wanted to use a space occupied by a memorial or a vault, they took the time to move it first. The Parker ledger stones on the floor of the chapel are an example of this as are the various Sprackling memorials. Little did Mr Bookey think that he would be laid to rest in what was to become a public lavatory. His daughter in law is laid behind him under the flower arrangers cupboard.[15]

He was followed by the Reverend **Robert Tyler** who served from 1740 through to his own death on 10th June 1766. It was during his ministry that the vestry decided on 3rd June 1750 to provide a "decent rail round the communion table." This was over a century after the Laudian reforms which suggests that the parish had been committed to the low church tradition long after the resignation of Peter Johnson.

In 1758, Tyler prepared a report on the parish for the benefit of the Archbishop. The original is held in Lambeth Palace Library and shows his answers to questions about such issues as population, worship and education:

> *What is the extent of your parish? What villages or hamlets, and what number of houses doth it comprehend? And what families of note are there in it?*
> The topography of the parish is about 3½ miles from east to west and nearly 3 miles from North to south. There are fifteen villages and hamlets with about 650 families as the total inhabitants. They are St Laurence, Southwood, Chilton, Courtstairs, Cliff End, Manstone, Pole Ash, Spratting Street, Coleswood, Hain, Northwood, Allicondean, Newinton, Easton, Ramsgate. At Ramsgate some part of the summer resides Lord Conyngham, William Bookey, Esq,: and Mrs Abbot all the year.
>
> *Are there any papists in your parish? And how many, and of what rank?*
> There is no Papist nor Popish priest in the Parish.

---

[14] Cotton op.cit. p.209

[15] The Parker ledgers were originally part of a chest tomb which had to be moved so the remains were re-interred and the panels turned into ledgers.

Are there in your parish any Presbyterians, Independents, Anabaptists, Methodists, or Moravians? And how many of each sect, and of what rank? Have they one or more meeting-houses in your parish, and are they duly licensed? What are the names of their teachers and are they qualified according to law? Is their number lessened or increased of late years, and by what means?

Ramsgate has about 500 houses. About a twelfth of the population is chiefly Presbyterian and the rest Anti-paedobaptists. These Dissenters have two meeting houses in the town but I do not know if they or their teachers are qualified according to law. The Presbyterian minister is named Spence and comes from the Orkneys and is a modest inoffensive man. The Baptist minister is called Matthews, a cooper residing at Birchington. The Presbyterians are a declining sect owing in part to the women marrying with Churchmen who generally attend their husbands to the established worship. The anti-paedobaptists seem to keep their ground.

Are there any persons in your parish, who profess to disregard religion, or who commonly absent themselves from all public worship of God on the Lord's Day? And from what motives and principles are they understood so to do?

The parishioners in general frequent the service of the church and behave with great decency. The few who absent themselves pretend that they have not room. It must be confessed our church is too small for the number of inhabitants.

Do you reside constantly upon your cure, and in the house belonging to it? If not where, and at what distance? And how long in each year are you absent? And what is the reason of such absence? And have you a licensed curate residing in the parish?

I reside upon my cure and in the vicarage house about eleven months in the year and do the duty of the cure without the help of an assistant. The other month is spent in some years in or near my other parish of Tunstall where I officiate when in that part of Kent.

Is public service duly performed twice every Lord's Day in your church, and one sermon preached? If not, what is the reason? And on what days besides are prayers read there? Is there any chapel in your parish?

Every Lord's Day we have a morning and afternoon service with a sermon at each. I read prayers on Litany days from the start of Lent until Michaelmas and on all festivals throughout the year. Children are catechised on Wednesdays and Fridays in Lent sent from the schools. The Sacrament of the Lord's Supper was held nine times in the past year – six occasions with at least seventy communicants and the three grand festivals with over one hundred communicants. No unbaptised person attends church and it has no chapel of ease.

Is there any free school, hospital or alms-house in your parish?
There is no hospital, almshouse or free school in the parish

Is there any voluntary charity school in your parish? And for how many boys or girls? And how is it supported? And what are they taught? And are they also lodged, fed, or clothed?
There is a charity school within these few years set up for the instruction of the poor boys in reading and writing and as many girls in reading, knitting and sewing supported by contributions of the parishioners and a charity sermon but they are neither fed or clothed. When they leave the school they are presented with a Bible and some little useful tracts given to the school by Archdeacon Denne.[16]

The report is fascinating in many ways. He does not state when the six celebrations of Holy Communion were held other than Easter, Christmas and Whitsun but it is likely that they were in Lent. Morning Prayer or Matins was then the main service on Sunday mornings, a situation which would continue until the second half of the twentieth century. Holy Communion was seen as something special which required considerable prayerful preparation so not something to be held repeatedly when it might appear ordinary. The number of communicants is also interesting. Fifteen years after his report, the parish population was said to be just over 2,700. Tyler's 650 families would suggest that it was close to the same figure when he wrote. That would indicate that his regular congregation, allowing for absentees and Dissenters, was close to two thousand. Clearly, when there was a celebration of the Lord's Supper, less than one in twenty chose to partake. An additional point which he does not mention in the report but which clearly formed part of his workload was that he performed on average sixty-eight baptisms, eighteen marriages and fifty-nine funerals every year.

Robert Tyler died on 10th June 1766 age 65 and he was buried in the vestry where

---

[16] Lambeth Palace Library MS 1134A transcribed in *The Beacon*, March and June 1963. The spelling of place names has been shown in the original. Easton is Hereson, Allicondean is Hollicondane.

his memorial can still be seen just beside the door.

The remainder of the century was dominated by the Harvey family. The Reverend **Richard Harvey** arrived age thirty-one in October 1766 and served as Vicar until 1793 when he resigned in favour of his son of the same name who was then twenty-six. Richard senior continued to work in the parish taking services as late as May 1820 which was fourteen months before his death aged eighty-six.

The arrival of Richard Harvey senior saw a number of changes being made to the church as well as the erection of a new vicarage. A hand written marginal note by the Reverend William Abbot who lived in the parish in his copy of Hasted's history said that the old building had been irrevocably damaged by fire although there is no mention of this in the surveyor's report.[17] Floor plans of the new vicarage show it had three bedrooms upstairs which were about fourteen feet square plus a smaller room which was nine by fourteen. Downstairs, there was a fourteen by fifteen feet study to the right of the entrance door with a parlour behind that which was eighteen by fifteen. On the left was a store room which was nine feet square and a stairway. A small pantry the other side of the stairs bordered the kitchen which was also about fourteen feet square. All the rooms throughout were eight feet six inches high. A wash house for laundry and a brewhouse were erected in the grounds. As was usual at this time, there were no indoor toilets just an earth closet outside but it is interesting that no stables were provided suggesting that the parish either anticipated that the vicar would walk everywhere or else were trying to save money. The property was really quite basic, especially since a clergyman might be expected to be married with half a dozen or more children and to maintain a spare room for visitors. He would also have had domestic staff. Images of the vicarage, which stood on the site of the current one until 1880, show it to have been very plain.

One of Mr Harvey's earliest innovations was the creation of a scheme to provide medical assistance to the poor. Messrs Daniel and Grigson would be paid £4 each a year to treat cases referred to them by the vicar, churchwardens or overseers. Both men were surgeons and they would work alternate weeks. It does not say how many hours they would serve in return for this sum (worth just over £1000 today) but it is likely that it was no more than a morning a week and

---

[17] ibid. p.153 , CCA/DCb-E/F/St Lawrence in Thanet/3

probably less.[18] Interestingly, they agreed to double up as apothecaries, a lesser ranked profession. With no other means of medical help, the poor were otherwise limited to home-made herbal cures and the potions on sale at Peter Burgess' library in the town which were almost certainly ineffectual and priced beyond their reach. For example, Dalby's Carminative which was advertised as a cure "for the wind, colic, fluxes, and other disorders in the bowels of infants as well as of adults" cost 1s 9d a bottle at a time when the average labourer earned around ten shillings a week.[19]

Richard Harvey was responsible for the building of a chapel of ease in Ramsgate which would later be known as St Mary's, and for extending the churchyard in 1766. He also instituted the enhanced record keeping system which has made him so beloved of demographic historians and shows him to have been a true man of the enlightenment.

In addition to being vicar of St Laurence, he was vicar of Eastry from 1772 until his death in 1821 from apoplexy. Although not distant in the era of the car, it is certain that Mr Harvey did not officiate at both churches. A look through the registers for Eastry shows that a curate was employed to carry out most of the work. He would have had two parishes for the same reason that some of his Tudor predecessors did, the income from St Laurence was insufficient. The situation in this regard was helped at the end of the century by a growing population and the war with France which led to more weddings and burials and consequently an increased revenue from fees. Before that he was helped by a gift made by the Reverend Gilbert Bouchery who left an investment to Canterbury Cathedral on condition that the annual interest be paid to the Vicar of St Laurence. Richard Harvey received the first payment in 1788 when it was worth £67.10s (about £7500 today). In thanksgiving for this munificence, a huge tablet was erected in memory of Gilbert Bouchery in the chancel, though it is now to be seen hidden behind a cupboard in the store room known as D9. The bequest was still being paid out until the 1920s when it was absorbed into the Ecclesiastical Commission grant and at that point, it represented a fifth of the vicar's income. In the mid nineteenth century, it had accounted for forty per cent. When Harvey received it, the sum would have doubled his previous income.

It would seem that from this and maybe other means, Richard Harvey was able to sort his finances for in his will made in 1818, he admits to having £600 in cash and £6000 of shares, two houses in Meeting Street which were rented out plus other "household goods and furniture, books, pictures, wines, liquors, plate, linen, china, wearing apparel, ready money."[20] This would equate to an estate worth well in excess of half a million today.

Richard Harvey is remembered by a memorial in the vestry which reads:

———————————————

[18] Tyro Grigson died in July 1793 aged 65 and is buried in the churchyard as is Edward Daniel who died in January 1811 age 86. Grigson has a headstone and bodystone (518), Daniel a table tomb with railings (858).
[19] *Kentish Gazette* 9th December 1808. The mixture was opium and castor oil dissolved in weakened wine.
[20] PROB 11/1647/214. He made no bequest to the church in his will.

> Near this place are deposited the mortal remains of the Revd. Richard Harvey, A.M., Vicar of Eastry and Worth. One of the six preachers of the Cathedral of Canterbury, Curate of Ramsgate Chapel, formerly Vicar of this Parish and a Magistrate for the County of Kent and the liberties of the Cinque Ports, who closed a long, useful and exemplary life, and a ministry of sixty three years (fifty-five of which were dedicated to this Parish) on the 29th day of July 1821 aged 86 years. In grateful testimony of whose worth as a Christian Pastor, upright Magistrate, and benevolent neighbour, this tablet was erected by his numerous friends, as a sincere (though inadequate) memorial of his virtues and their loss

In fact he is not buried very near to his memorial at all. The tablet in the vestry is just part of a much larger monument which was originally in the High Chancel just to the right of where the church banner hangs. When the area was redeveloped in the twentieth century, the monuments therein were all moved. In Richard Harvey's case, the rest of the memorial with the urn and coat of arms was discarded.[21]

It is impossible to know much about the churchmanship of the eighteenth century clergy but all of the vicars were Cambridge men, Bookey having an MA from Queen's, Tyler from Caius, the Harveys from Corpus Christi. Traditionally, Cambridge educated clergy were lower church than those from Oxford and there is nothing in church furniture to indicate otherwise. It may be assumed that none of them wore vestments and that there were no processions.

The clergy were supported as always by the churchwardens and parish clerk and the parish also employed a sexton. In 1773, the position of sexton became vacant and the following job description was agreed. The appointment was made following an election which took place in the church on 4th September. After nine hours the poll was closed. John Smith was found to have defeated the other four candidates having 124 votes from 217 cast.

1. to clean the church once in every fortnight throughout
2. to dig common graves to the depth of four feet and a half and the fee for the same to be one shilling and sixpence.
3. to dig double or deep graves at the rate of one shilling per foot after the above mentioned four feet and a half
4. In ringing knells to charge for the first or little bell one shilling, for the second bell two shillings, for the third bell three shillings, for the fourth bell four shillings, for the fifth or great bell six shillings and eight pence, one half of which

---

[21] An account of his funeral appears in the *Kentish Gazette* 7th August 1821. He died in Chapel Place

> (three shillings and four pence) to be paid to the churchwardens
> 5 To toll the great bell at the rate of one shilling for the first hour and four pence for every hour afterwards
> 6. To open the casements of the church every fine day
> 7. To clean the churchyard, on which account the salary is raised from seventeen shillings to one pound one shilling per annum
> 8. to live as near the church as possible

In 1794, a new sexton was needed and the same procedure followed. The rate of pay remained the same and now he had to provide his own tools but the following changes were made to the job description:

> 9. to regulate the time exactly by the pier clock
> 10. to begin tolling the first bell on Sundays at seven o'clock in the morning from Lady Day to Michaelmas

For all this work, he earned the modern equivalent of £125 per annum.

The work of the churchwardens continued to be varied as their accounts show. In 1702 they spent 6d on a white stick to be used when a member of the congregation who had committed some dire sin came into church to publicly repent and ask forgiveness from God and his fellow Christians. In 1710 they spent a shilling having someone named Johnson arrested and committed to jail. The fact that they had to do this would suggest that his crime was against the church itself, perhaps he had been disturbing worship or vandalised property. The wardens continued to pay for the destruction of creatures thought to be vermin and they were responsible for maintaining the roads. They established a separate set of accounts for this which includes payments such as 6d for a boy picking stones out of the road, 2s to the town crier for making announcements and £1 11s 10d to gravel New End, later known as York Street. At this time, every man in the parish was meant to spend four days a year working unpaid to repair roads or else send an able bodied man in his place. An inventory in 1777 revealed that the parish owned two wheelbarrows, two shovels, two rakes, two scrapers, two rammers and two mattocks.

PEOPLE, EVENTS AND PLACES

Daily Life

Just as Camden wrote an account of the parishioners in the Elizabethan period, so the Reverend John Lewis, vicar of Margate and Minster, wrote an account of how they lived in the first couple of decades of the eighteenth century. He described the seasonality of their lives:

They go to catch whiting and herring and to the north seas whither they make two journeys a year and come home the latter one soon enough for the men to go to the wheat season and take a winter's thresh: which last they have done time enough to go to sea in the spring. Besides this here are there two seasons for the home fishery. The first of these is the mackerel season which commonly is about the beginning of May when the sowing of barley is ended. The other is the season for catching herrings which begins about the end of harvest and ends soon enough for the wheat season, the time of sowing which is here about November… Those of them who occupy farms are often persons of good substance for they live in a very generous and hospitable manner. They who live by the seaside are generally fishermen or those who go voyages to foreign parts or such as depend upon what they call foying, i.e. going off to ships with provisions and to help them in distress. .. It is a thousand pities that they and the country people are so apt to pilfer stranded ships and to abuse those who have already suffered so much.[22]

He spoke of the great fruitfulness of the area, the amount of wheat grown as well as fruit, barley, fennel and beans. He noted how the farmers used seaweed as a fertiliser and how poor people would gather that from the seashore for sale. He described the life of the ploughman as working from six to ten in the morning and two to six of an afternoon with the time between spent having a meal and caring for the horses.

For the women, life revolved around looking after their children and menfolk. Quite aside from the very hard graft which this involved in the days before running water, labour saving devices, wipe clean surfaces and easy care fabrics, many women worked. Fishermen's wives made and mended nets, sorted and gutted fish and oiled sails and clothing. Farm labourer's wives might tend chickens or a pig and help with the harvest or take in extra laundry from larger houses.

Population Growth

The first census was carried out in 1801 with detailed household information only being available from 1841. This means that ordinarily it is impossible to assess the size of a population prior to that date except by the statistical means employed by demographic historians. However, the parish is particularly fortunate to possess in its registers tables of population data compiled by the vicar, the Reverend Richard Harvey, and continued by

---

[22] Lewis op.cit. 1736 edition pp.32-34

his son. These cover the years 1773-1800 and show the number of houses in each road, how many were inhabited and the total people living there. The survey was made each year in April and it took three days to complete. It shows, for example, that in the 1770s, there was very little growth. That increased in the 1780s, particularly at Ramsgate and this trend was accelerated in the 1790s. Harvey's figures show:

Population size	1780	1790	1800
St Lawrence	914	1070	1208
Ramsgate	1841	2213	2831

Inevitably this increased his workload. In the first decade of the eighteenth century, the vicar had performed an average fifty-eight baptisms, thirteen marriages and thirty-nine funerals every year. By the 1750s, it was an average of sixty-nine baptisms, eighteen marriages ad fifty-nine funerals. In the years above he performed:

Event	1780	1790	1800
Baptisms	74	112	164
Marriages	15	29	44
Funerals	51	118	178

Comparing Harvey's data with earlier periods is inevitably difficult but it is likely that the population at the start of the century would have been around two thousand which means that it doubled across the century. [23]

It is the detail, however, in Harvey's data which is so valuable for giving a picture of which parts of the parish were growing fastest, where population density was highest and the proportion of empty homes. At any one time, one in ten homes in Ramsgate was empty while only one in twenty-five was unoccupied in St Lawrence. Household size was highest in the farming districts due to the custom of farm hands living in and lowest in what was then considered the most desirable part of Ramsgate, Effingham Street.

	1795					change from 1791	
	houses inhab.	empty houses	total houses	inhab-itants	per house	total houses	inhab-itants
Ramsgate							
West Street (High St)	196	26	222	841	4.29	24	74
South End (Queen St)	63	8	71	272	4.32	10	28
Brick St (Effingham St)	23	10	33	74	3.22	0	-22
Hole (Prince's St)	32	1	33	136	4.25	-2	-19

---

[23] Harvey's data for the 1770s and 1780s shows a steady rate of 3.7 baptisms per thousand which would indicate a higher fertility rate than in the 1670s when there was 2.8 per thousand. The situation is made more complex by the rise of nonconformity and later age at baptism.

	houses inhab.	empty houses	1795 total houses	inhab- itants	per house	change from 1791 total houses	inhab- itants
New End (York St)	50	7	57	234	4.68	3	9
East End (Harbour St)	81	21	102	338	4.17	17	8
North End (King St)	134	8	142	603	4.50	39	118
	579	81	660	2498	4.31	91	196
St Laurence							
Hereson	26	2	28	98	3.77	1	-36
Dumpton	6	0	6	37	6.17	0	12
Hollicondane	7	0	7	42	6.00	1	19
Whitehall	3	0	3	15	5.00	0	3
Puddledock	4	0	4	14	3.50	0	0
Newington	7	0	7	20	2.86	0	-2
Northwood	7	0	7	38	5.43	0	2
Haine	6	0	6	32	5.33	0	-6
Coleswood	3	0	3	18	6.00	0	2
Spratling Street	2	0	2	21	10.50	-1	0
Poleash	2	0	2	8	4.00	0	0
Manston	19	2	21	92	4.84	2	5
Cliffsend	8	0	8	43	5.38	0	-2
Little Cliffsend	6	0	6	26	4.33	1	0
Chilton	4	0	4	27	6.75	0	-11
Southwood	19	2	21	123	6.47	0	5
Courtstairs	14	0	14	48	3.43	1	-1
St Laurence Street	90	7	97	332	3.69	18	13
Jackey Bakers	9	0	9	59	6.56	0	0
	242	13	255	1093	4.52	23	3
Totals	821	94	915	3591	4.37	114	199

In 1793, the following account appeared describing the two areas:

> Ramsgate, since the rage for sea bathing hath taken place, has had its share of visitants and consequently is every year much improving in its buildings and other accommodations. Here are many good lodging houses, several hotels, inns &c, a handsome assembly room, a very good library, coffee rooms, warm salt-water baths…The town being well paved is very clean and its commodious basin and magnificent pier, two striking objects to

an eye unused to such expensive scenes, cause it to be particularly pleasant. …Upon the hill about half a mile from the extremity of the town is St Lawrence a pretty little village which commands one of the most extensive prospects in the island having a fine view of the Downs, the French coast, the towns of Sandwich and Deal at a few miles distance and Ramsgate close under the brow of the hill as well as a scene of luxuriant cornfields and fertile meadows.[24]

Health

The late eighteenth century saw the rise of sea-bathing and an increased interest in scientific study. The Reverend Richard Harvey clearly enjoyed such debates and alongside his statistics of population decided to record details of causes of death. Such information in a register is extremely rare and is of immense value, even though it must always be remembered that Harvey wrote down what people told him was the cause of death: he was not a doctor himself.

Between 1774 and 1812 inclusive, the causes of death recorded were:

	Infant	*Age 1-9*	*10-19*	*20-49*	*50-69*	*70+*
Accident	2	22	12	43	7	8
Bowels	66	22	1	20	10	2
Cancer	1	0	0	5	10	1
Childbirth	0	0	1	42	0	0
Convulsions	171	55	5	10	2	0
Decay	393	188	50	4	249	478
Dropsy	10	18	8	33	44	24
Epilepsy	12	9	2	4	1	0
Fever	31	75	32	60	27	5
Heart	23	5	4	32	56	28
Infectious disease	135	312	6	11	3	0
Internal failure	0	0	0	2	3	1
Lunacy	0	0	1	2	0	0
Respiratory	5	13	54	385	91	4
Self-indulgence	1	0	0	2	4	0
Skin diseases	3	4	2	7	8	5
Stroke	0	0	0	7	22	10
Teeth	26	17	2	2	1	0
Weather related	9	7	2	6	5	2

---

[24] Cozens op.cit pp. 60-61.

Evidently the causes of death reflect the state of medical knowledge at the time. Lunacy, for example, is not a fatal disease though it can be a late onset symptom of syphilis. Decay is a wide term covering babies who failed to thrive, some cancer and a lot of tuberculosis. The stethoscope had yet to be invented so doctors were unable to identify lung disease easily. Infectious diseases were understandably highest amongst children with whooping cough, measles and smallpox all in evidence. The parish saw smallpox epidemics in 1784, 1790, 1799, 1807-8 and 1810. The weather related deaths show vulnerability in times of severe winter. The winter of 1794-95 was the coldest on record and bread and coal had to be distributed to the poor across the parish.[25] Amongst the women who died in childbirth or from related complications was Thomasine Curling née Holman who died in 1778 aged thirty-five when giving birth to her tenth child in fourteen years. She was the wife of Daniel Curling of Chilton, a wealthy landowner so she would have had medical attendance which most women would not. Her tombstone in the churchyard notes that she was laid with three of her children who had died before her as well as the infant whose arrival occasioned her own demise. Daniel's first wife had probably died from the same cause. Amongst those who died of accidents were two of the twenty-three victims of the 1802 hoy boat lost off Reculver, Elizabeth Tatnell who has a grave in the churchyard (no 1227) and a teenage American sailor named James Sheppard who was buried in an unmarked grave.[26]

Mercantile Development

The eighteenth century was a period of extreme growth for the parish. In the early part of the century, this stemmed from the development of trade; toward the end of the century, the growth resulted from the influx of servicemen who either passed through or were stationed here during the wars with France.

One way in which it is possible to assess the changing trade patterns is to look at the records of Seamen's Sixpences which are held at the National Archives. These reveal the names and owners of vessels, the tonnage and crew and the journeys made.[27] Taking three periods of five years as a sample, it can be seen how the size of vessels increased as vessels travelled ever further. At the start of the century, the main trade was with Russia and the Baltic ports. Ramsgate was one of the earliest trading partners of St Petersburg which was developed in the first quarter of the eighteenth century but her ships also travelled up into Archangel as well as to Narva and Viborg. They brought back lumber from Riga which was used to build homes and also by the Royal Navy to build ships, some of which finding its way no doubt into Nelson's fleet. They brought back tar from Stockholm for both the Royal and Merchant Navy as well as for roads and waterproofing

---

[25] For a full analysis of the data see Margaret Bolton, 'Causes of Death in Ramsgate 1774-1812', *Archaeologia Cantiana,* vol. 137 (2016) pp. 17-36
[26] *Kentish Gazette*, 10th February 1802. Seven died from the parish but only two bodies were recovered for burial.
[27] ADM68/194-208

homes and clothing. There were journeys to Danzig (now Gdansk) and Koënigsberg (now Kaliningrad) as well. An average of twenty voyages a year went to Russia and eighteen to the Baltic ports in ships that were some 140 tons and had ten crew. Later in the century, the trading focus shifted to North America with increasing traffic in tobacco but also in the carrying of troops to serve in the War of Independence. These vessels were even bigger at an average 170 tons. Meanwhile, small vessels of some 80 tons brought coal from Newcastle and ships of around 30 tons went fishing in the North Sea for months at a time. Yet it was the deep sea vessels that traded internationally which were the major source of wealth and employment and this is evident in memorials to be found at St Laurence church.

To the right in the side chapel beside the porch can be seen a huge monument remembering Captain Martin Long (1686-1751) of Pysons. This records his journeys to Russia and the Mediterranean but he also journeyed to China in his ship, the *New Ramsgate*. Long set up a charity when he died to feed the poor which was administered by his nephew, the Reverend William Abbot, whose monument can be seen just to the left of the communion table in the same chapel. A ledger stone under the communion rails remembers John Moses (1697-1736) whose vessel the *Endeavour* made regular journeys to Stockholm. Another ledger nearby remembers John Evers who sailed his ship the *Hannah* to St Petersburg but also to Maryland and Carolina. On the wall to the left is a memorial to Adam Spencer who worked the St Petersburg route in his ship the *Greyhound*. Originally a tomb but now a ledger, is the memorial to Captain Robert Parker (1691-1740) who made numerous journeys to Riga in the *Resolution*. He also left money to the church to pay for a sermon each Good Friday and to provide almost five hundred loaves of bread to feed the hungry.[28] Their work was supported by the Austen family who are remembered by two large monuments in the same area, a black one on the back wall and a marble one to its side. Both recall men named Nathaniel Austen, father and son. The Austens were ship owners, made ropes for ships as well as St Laurence bells and they had a bank in York Terrace. Nathaniel's son Edward had two ships which journeyed to St Petersburg and the Baltic ports named the

---

[28] PRC/32/61/1201b

Society and the *St Laurence*. Their ropewalk in Ramsgate is now Cannon Road.[29]

Other memorials to Ramsgate's mercantile past can be found beside the vestry door where Captain Robert Eason (1697-1747) is remembered. He owned three ships, the *Gillow*, the *Friends' Adventure* and the *Providence* which between them covered most of Europe. Near to him is Richard Tomson who undertook the very dangerous voyages to Archangel in his ship, the *Success*. His son married into the Rainier family, some of whom are buried in the churchyard, and whose most famous member was Captain Peter Rainier after whom Mount Rainier was named. Meanwhile, at the western end of the south aisle where the missionary literature can be seen are memorials to John Coxen (1682-1764) and to Captain William Abbot, (1685-1755) brother in law of Martin Long. There is also a stone to Captain Stephen Hooper who died on a voyage from Jamaica in 1767.

Yet more shipowners are remembered in the churchyard. These include Anthony Bayley (1689-1774) who not only had two ships trading with Russia and various ports around the Baltic but had at least one ship built in St Petersburg. A table tomb remembers Christopher Bircham of the Icelandic trade. There are memorials to at least eight sea captains of the Hooper family. Their ships included the *Charming Peggy*, the *Thanet*, the *St Lawrence*, the *Royal Ann*, the *Owners Supply*, the *Unity* and the *Speedwell* and between them they travelled the globe as it was known at the time. George Dear who ran colliers is remembered on a stone which shows Old Father Time. Representing the American trade is John Maxted (1729-1803) who owned the *Ann* and John Joad (1691-1757) who had the *Benjamin*, both with vaults plus John Brathery (1676-1756) who sailed to Maryland, Virginia, Staten Island in the *John and Robert* and who endowed the churchyard with its famous Adam and Eve stone. George Curling, who also traded with America in the 237 ton *Dorothy* is buried beside the Hoopers. Stood beside the vestry door and decorated with skulls is a reminder of John Redwood (1685-1737) who married the daughter of Nathaniel Austen and who owned ships going to Malaga, Riga, St Petersburg and America. Along the wall opposite are memorials which were once part of the Abbot mausoleum erected by Captain Thomas Abbot (1690-1750)

The *Dorothy*

---

[29] Nathaniel (1745-1818) married Sarah Cobb and details of their banking business can be found in the Cobb papers held at Kent Archives Office. His home, Monkton House or 124 High Street, still stands. His son and heir, Nathaniel Austen, went bankrupt in May 1840, the failure of his bank causing the family to leave town. *Thanet Advertiser,* 12th February 1898

who was the considered so important in 1735 that his house was featured on the map of Ramsgate, the only individual so honoured.[30] In the churchyard too is Henry Darling (1689-1749) whose ship named the *Kent* travelled to Scandinavia but also to America. It is likely that he returned with slaves since the baptism register shows two negro servants who worked for his family being christened as adults in St Laurence church.[31]

The churchyard is further home to both the celebrated maritime artist Francis Holman(1729-1784) and his seafaring father of the same name (1697-1739) who owned the *Happy Return* and who had married Ann Long. The artist Francis married Jane Maxted, an example of the high rates of intermarriage amongst the merchant families,

The quantity and value of these memorials are not just a reminder of a number of extremely brave men who journeyed across the world, often having only the stars as their guide, but of the importance of their work in the economic development of the town and beautification of the church.

Percentage of trade by region	*1726-30*	*1746-50*	*1766-70*
Russia and the Baltic	41.8%	58.6%	17.2%
Scandinavia	20.5%	9.0%	1.6%
UK	15.0%	2.1%	6.3%
North America	9.7%	9.0%	25.0%
Iberian	7.9%	13.1%	6.3%
Mediterranean	1.8%	1.4%	4.7%
Northern France	1.5%	4.8%	9.4%
Caribbean	1.3%	1.4%	29.7%
Far East	0.5%	0.7%	0.0%

In 1885, Dr Charles Richardson made the extraordinary claim that these men had "made off with easy fortunes." He was evidently neither a sailor nor a businessman.[32]

Poverty

Throughout the century, St Laurence appointed overseers who were responsible for setting and collecting a rate from the houses in the parish and for distributing the money raised to relieve the poor. In the first quarter of the eighteenth century, each rate or sess raised around seventy pounds.[33] A look at the overseers' accounts shows the variety

---

[30] Lewis op.cit 1736 edition p.175
[31] Elizabeth 29th June 1748 and John North West 11th February 1762.
[32] Christopher Richardson, *Fragments of History pertaining to the Vill or Wille or Liberty of Ramsgate*, (Ramsgate, 1885), p. 194
[33] In 1714, for example, there were 371 ratepayers, ten of whom paid over one pound and 151 who paid less than a shilling with thirteen being excused. The wealthiest inhabitants were Thomas Garrett of Nethercourt, Peter Harnett of Spratling Street, Robert Maxted of Ozengell, William

of expenses they faced in the days before any welfare state.

They paid pensions to widows who were unable to work and who lacked children who could support them. Varying from three to twelve shillings a month, in 1720-21, there were eighteen such widows on their books. In many cases, they also paid the rent for these widows too in order that they were not left homeless.

They maintained men and women who were too sick to work either due to old age or because of some temporary or long term health problem. Widow Stace, for example, received five shillings in 1731 because her wrist was out of joint which prevented her from spinning while John Panel received 2s 6d after an accident at the malt house burnt his hands. A number of payments were made to men who were lame and unable to work on the land. In 1762, the Danson family received two shillings to assist with the care of their children who had smallpox.

They paid parishioners to do jobs for each other and did all they could to keep people in their homes. In 1701, Robert Wagers was paid 1s 4d to mend Widow Forman's shoes. Thirty years later, Richard Paramor was paid £1 15s for ploughing and tilling the Widow Mills' land and Thomas Woodman earned 9s 1d for thatching Elizabeth Moses' house. The Widow Taylor was given three shillings worth of straw to enable her to keep her cows alive through the spring while John Hills earned money collecting dung and delivering it to farmers. Edward Troward meantime had his windows mended to prevent his death from cold.

The cost of caring for the poor rose sharply in the late 1720s and 1730s. The reality of the suffering can be seen by entries such as 2s 6d given to Mother Welby "for a shift, she not having one to her back." The case of Widow Curling who was in her early seventies showed just how many people might get involved when someone's health failed as hers did in the spring of 1728 and the cost to the overseers. There were payments direct to her to alleviate her hunger and for coals to keep her warm. A girl received money for going to draw water for her from a well. Goody Payne and Widow May were both summoned to nurse her and paid by the parish for their work. Doctor Fuller was hired to treat her and on 15th July he sent in his bill of £3 13s 6d. In modern terms, this would be about £500; at the time it was around four per cent of the overseers' total income for the year. All their efforts clearly failed to have the desired impact and on 4th October, the overseers spent five shillings to have the Widow Curling and her things taken to the poorhouse. She died there a few weeks later and was buried in the churchyard on 21st November, again at the parish expense. George Knowler received eight shillings for making her a coffin and Mistress Read got 4s. 6d for providing her with a shroud. In addition there were fees for the pallbearers, vicar and sexton and money spent on refreshments for them.

A key change in this period was the fact that Ramsgate took responsibility for its own poor. They built a poorhouse in Sussex Street and St Laurence built one in Chapel

---

Cooper of Cliffsend, John Curling of Chilton and William Belsey of Ramsgate. Thomas Tomson, who presented the silver paten to the church in 1721 was thirty-seventh on the list paying 4s 4d.

Road next to the sexton's land. This survived until the establishment of Poor Law Unions in the 1830s when the vestry sold it together with its garden and two cottages.[34] The records show regular payments for supplies of soap, herrings, peas, beans, cheese, mutton and suet as well as straw to make mattresses, coal and a variety of linens and shoes to clothe the inmates. By 1762, a shilling a month was being spent on tobacco for pauper men. It would appear that by the 1750s, sties had been built as there were a number of purchases of live pigs, some of which seem to have been used for breeding to generate extra income. On 1st July 1778, the *Kentish Gazette* carried an advertisement

> SAINT LAURENCE IN THANET
> *WANTED at MICHAELMAS next*
> **A MASTER and MISTRESS,**
> For the **POORHOUSE**
> For further Particulars apply to the CHURCHWARDEN
> or OVERSEERS as above.
> N.B. Two girls and a Boy to be put out Apprentices, apply as above

The Church Wax House continued to be used as the overseers' office for some thirty years after the poorhouse was built. Hops and malt were bought for it showing it clearly remained in use as a brewhouse and the repairs to the frying pan in 1725 indicate the kitchens still functioned, though the poorhouse later took on the manufacture of its own bread and beer. The building was used to store the supplies which the overseers bought for the poor to work upon. Spinning and weaving tasks were still carried out in private homes using materials bought by the overseers who would then pay for the labour and either sell on the produce to raise further funds or use the goods to maintain the poor in the parish. Shrouds, for example, could be woven and stored for pauper funerals. The overseers kept a stock of shoes and some basic clothes at the house ready for those in want or for orphans starting their apprenticeships. They also stored tools there. In 1723, for example, Thomas Newson was paid 9s 8d for sharpening four mattocks. Whether these were used for highway repairs or about the church is not known. At this time, the parish was responsible for both.

Although poverty always existed, it is worth noting that by the end of the century with the growth of the area brought about by sea bathing and shipping, poverty was substantially lower at St Laurence than elsewhere on the Isle of Thanet. A table of costs for 1791-93 shows that the rural areas were suffering badly with Monkton spending over one pound per head on average in poor relief. Minster, St Nicholas, Sarre and Woodchurch varied from nine to thirteen shillings whilst St Laurence was bottom of the table at under one shilling.[35] Unemployment was clearly very low at this point.

---

[34] Vestry Book 10th March 1836
[35] John Boys, *General View of the Agriculture of the County of Kent*, (Brentford, 1794) p.30. The per capita expenditure is based on total spent compared to population.

It does not follow that because people had work, they necessarily lived well. Wages in Thanet were a bit higher than the national average which is one of the reasons why people moved to the area but they were still poor as prices were also higher. For example, on 23rd November 1795 farmers in Thanet agreed to increase wages from 1/6 to 2/- a day which was above the 1/2 elsewhere but wheat in Thanet was £5 4s 2d per quarter compared to £3 15s 2d nationally.[36] Butter was 1/6 per pound compared to 10d nationally.[37] If a man's wife was able to do any work such as mending nets, laundry, helping with livestock, the family income might rise by another two or three shillings and older children might bring in a few pence more, however, for most people, wages were day rates and there was no security of employment so a man might earn 11s one week but 3s the next. A 1795 study of labourers across England showed that if a man had a wife and three children and wanted to feed each of them a minimum of 4 fl.oz milk (about 125ml) and 1 oz cheese (about 25g) per day and two rashers of bacon a week it would cost him:[38]

	s	d
Bread and flour	3	6
Meat and fish		8
Rent		9
Clothing and work tools		5
Tea and sugar		4
Milk		8
Candles		3
Soap		3
Fuel		3
Cheese		10
Salt and yeast		2
Beer and gin		2
Butter		8
Thread		2
	9	1

Many people had a lot more children and the budget made no allowance for taxes, medicine, extra milk for babies and nursing mothers, eggs, or any emergencies. The food allowances given were also very small and most people would have required more

---

[36] John Mockett, *Mockett's Journal*, (Canterbury, 1836) p. 36; J M Stratton, *Agricultural Records* (London 1969), 253. In 1724, farm labourers earned 1s 2d per day in summer or 10d a day in winter. In 1770, it was 1s 6d per day in summer and 1s 4d in winter – Quested op.cit. pp.73, 82

[37] Anon, *The New Margate and Ramsgate Guide in Letters to a Friend* (London 1780), 29.

[38] David Davies, *The Case of Labourers in Husbandry*, (London, 1795). Daily wheat consumption is based on Elizabeth Gilboy, 'Wages in Eighteenth Century England', *Journal of Economic and Business History* vol 2 no 4 (August 1930) p.612

to eat. Whilst farm labourers may have generally had a small garden to grow vegetables and possibly some fruit, town dwellers would have had to purchase these items which would have further added to the costs. People should have earned enough to prevent them starving but they were inevitably malnourished and this is further suggested by mortality patterns as the following demonstrate.

John and Elizabeth Meader married at the end of July 1785 when they were both 20 years old. John was the eldest son in a family of six and had a difficult childhood because his father died when he was just nine which means he would have been sent to sea as soon as he was able. John and Elizabeth's first daughter Lucy was strong and healthy but a son born just under two years later failed to thrive and wasted away, dying aged two months. Another two years went by and a second son was born, a healthy child this time who was named after his father. In 1795, Elizabeth had what was to be the first of eleven more children, nine of whom were to die in their first three months of life. Her last was born when she was 42 and this daughter perished of a bowel infection before she could even be baptised. The children were born at the rate of one a year and one can only speculate on what went through Elizabeth's mind when she was carrying each child and going through the anguish of childbirth, wondering how long it would be before the new infant was laid in the churchyard. Being almost constantly pregnant meant that she would rarely have been able to work or contribute to the family finances. John and Elizabeth themselves lived to 56 and 58 respectively and saw two of their surviving children married.

Although the Meaders had a particularly bad record, they were not unique. William and Rebecca Emery had nine children in fourteen years from 1782 to 1794. Five died in their first year of life and their eldest daughter succumbed to smallpox when she was eight. William died of consumption when he was thirty-one. Robert and Ann Lancefield had eight children between 1790 and 1800, five dying at under six weeks and another daughter aged fourteen of consumption. George and Ann Poole had ten children and lost five at less than two months old, one to whooping cough, three to general decay and one perished from the cold because her parents were unable to keep her warm. Samuel and Sarah Terry had eight children between 1793 and 1807 and lost all but the first within a few weeks of life. Poor hygiene, ignorance, lack of medical knowledge, genetic weaknesses may all have contributed to such tragedies but poverty is likely to have been a factor. It must have tested the pastoral abilities of the Reverend Richard Harvey to the limit to minister to people in such circumstances and to reassure them of God's love.

Bastardy

It is not easy to assess the impact of the Church in people's lives. The building might have been full on Sunday but that does not mean that the entire congregation spent each day in godly pursuits and that everyone had a living relationship with Our Lord. It is impossible to know the extent of practices such as drunkenness, wife beating, child abuse or gambling from a perspective of over two centuries but some idea can be gained of fornication for it often led to consequences.

From 1560 through to 1740, one in every two hundred and fifty babies was born out of wedlock: a vicar could expect to see one bastard every five years or so. The situation changed from the late 1740s and between 1746 and 1800, there were only ten years which did not see a single illegitimate child. The last decade of the century saw on average five bastards every year and the first two decades of the nineteenth saw that rate increase to six and eight respectively. From the late 1740s through to the start of the 1790s, one in fifty babies brought to baptism was a bastard, afterward it was one in thirty-three.

With regard to brides being pregnant at time of marriage, in the Elizabethan period, one in ten were in this condition: under the Stuarts it was one in seventeen. By the 1790s, it was one in four.

Of course, such figures cannot tell the whole story. Not every bride who was not pregnant was a virgin and there is no way of knowing the numbers of children conceived out of wedlock but lost by natural or unnatural means prior to birth. However, it is the only data available and, no matter the interpretation put upon it, there is a clear pattern. The Reformation and rise of puritanism resulted in people at least trying to espouse the Christian lifestyle. In the eighteenth century, many stopped doing so.

What happened to cause this rise in promiscuity? The late 1740s saw troops stationed in the town and so did the late 1770s and early 1780s.[39] From the mid 1790s, the town was full of soldiers due to the war with France. There can be little doubt that some of the local girls fell prey to a uniform. There was also the growth of the town due to increased trade. In the sixteenth century, the population was so small that girls would have known every boy of similar age in the area and they would have been related to quite a few of them too which would have ruled out sexual relations in most cases. The burgeoning population weakened family ties and broadened horizons. It is clear too that the church's message on the need to "be ye therefore perfect even as your Father which is in heaven is perfect" was not getting through.[40] Morality declined during the years that Richard Harvey senior and junior served as vicar. In their defence, it might be noted that the same trend occurred in other places and that St Laurence's rates remained much lower than the national average.[41] Yet the behaviour was indicative of a changing understanding of God. Previous generations had wanted babies baptised within a week of birth, partly due to a superstitious fear that an unbaptised child might not go to heaven. The late eighteenth century saw parishioners discard that fear and the interval between birth and baptism increase. That suggests either a lack of belief in hell and judgment or the growing idea that everyone will be saved regardless by a loving God, both theories which tend to distract from a concept of sin, and without sin there is no

---

[39] Evidence of this can be seen through the parish registers.
[40] Matt 5:48.
[41] Peter Laslett, *The World we have Lost* (London, 1971) p.142

need for a Saviour and no reason to avoid fornication other than peer pressure and economic factors.

Notwithstanding the abolition of the church courts which meant that church attendance and behaviour were no longer subject to legal action, as late as 1758, the vicar was able to report that almost everyone attended a place of worship on Sunday and that Anglicans were educated in the Christian faith via the catechism. A century later and the picture was very different with non-attendance in the parish up twelvefold and the Church of England's share of worshippers almost halved. It cannot be known when the decline took place or how many of the mothers of the bastards had been brought up in the church and therefore should have known better. The fact that the children were brought for baptism might be interpreted as a sign of repentance, but it remains impossible to view the growing bastardy rate as anything but a failure for local Church teaching and witness in the eighteenth century.

St Mary's Chapel

The pressure on St Laurence church as a result of population growth and increased pastoral demand let to the creation of an additional place of worship in the town itself. Erected off the High Street, the building would eventually take the name of St Mary's Church and the approach road would become Chapel Place. Yet this was not a daughter church of St Laurence in the way that the later churches of St Catherine and St Christopher were to be. The chapel was built by the vicar and his friends John Fagg, John Holman, John Horn and Joseph Norwood. They took on the cost of building and furnishing the chapel and they recouped their expenses through fees and the rental charges on pews.

At the chapel's centenary in July 1891, the Reverend Alfred Whitehead, who had been vicar there from 1861 to 1871 and was by then Rural Dean said: "a church should be built for the salvation of souls and the spiritual profit of the masses and not for the pecuniary benefit of shareholders and for large returns on money expended….It would have been better at once to have built a good parish church and separated Ramsgate from St Lawrence one hundred years ago. The dullest eye can see the irreparable mischief to church interest which has accrued though the plan that was then pursued. The plan was wrong in principle, miserably inefficient in extent and fatally exclusive as regards the masses. Before St George's church was finished and consecrated, the population of Ramsgate was fourteen thousand or more and where was the provision for any of the poor to worship? It is easy to let people drift away from the church but it is hard, very hard, to win them back and recover ground that has once been lost."

Whilst his comments were undoubtedly true and the idea of building a church as an investment does seem repugnant to the Word of God, it may be that Harvey knew that there was no money available to set up a church in any other way. The nineteenth century saw government and diocesan encouragement to plant churches but this was not the case

when Ramsgate Chapel was built. The five men even had to pay to get an Act of Parliament to allow them to build it, something which added considerably to the expense. It is also unlikely that they received much return on their investment for some time. The new church cost £2550 15s (around £275,000 today) and was designed to hold 662 people. Fee income would have been low because baptisms were free and they had no burial ground. Pew rental varied from four to ten shillings a year according to the location just as prices vary on theatre seats today depending on the view, but even if every seat was filled, it would have taken at least forty years to recover their money with no allowance being made for inflation or any requirements for repairs.[42] Due to the wars with France, prices rose by almost thirty per cent per cent between 1790 and 1820 so the investors certainly did not see "large returns."

The new chapel was designed with galleries like St Laurence and built in the classical style. Services were taken by a minister who was technically curate of St Laurence but whose position was more akin to that of a priest-in-charge. His income was set at £10 per month (just over a thousand pounds today). He was to take Morning and Evening Prayer each Sunday and preach at both except for the three festivals when he would celebrate Holy Communion and preach only once. A clerk was also to be appointed to clean and tend the building and to unlock the pews for the respective owners at a salary to be determined.[43] For the role of curate, Richard Harvey selected his son of the same name.

Ramsgate Chapel remained part of St Laurence parish until the establishment of St George's in 1827 but it continued financially in the hands of the descendants of the original investors until the 1860s. Given the name St Mary's in 1867, the church was destroyed in the Second World War. Over its century and a half's existence, it had won fame for the quality of its music and was unashamedly ritualist.

Richard Harvey, who contributed 45% of the project costs, died in 1821 and left his share of the Chapel to his widow Judith.[44]

John Fagg, gentleman, who donated the land and paid 20% of the costs died aged 67 on the 27th December 1795 and was buried in a tomb in the churchyard just beyond the east window. When Newington Road was widened in the early 1960s, his remains had to

---

[42] Charles Busson, *The Book of Ramsgate* (Buckingham,1985) p.37
[43] The full Act was transcribed and appears in Cotton op.cit. pp.268-274.
[44] PROB 11/1647/214

be moved and reburied in the south-west corner in the area later occupied by the Garden of Remembrance.⁴⁵ This requirement to move him presented an almost unique opportunity to view a late eighteenth century burial vault. It was found that his original tomb had been buried eight feet down with two black plaques portraying a white angel and an hour-glass, symbols frequently seen on memorials of this era above ground. A memorial tablet to him can be seen on the north side of the side chapel.

Joseph Norwood, a retired Royal Naval captain and who also paid 20%, died 10th May 1793 aged 66 and is buried at St Laurence.

John Holman, shipowner and brother of the artist Francis, contributed 10%. He died in May 1816 aged 82 and was buried just to the north side of the path that led to the west door of St Laurence where his tombstone and bodystone can still be seen. His granddaughter, Jane, had been the first infant baptised in the new chapel on 6th August 1789.⁴⁶

John Horn who contributed 5% and who was the youngest contributor, died in 1819 at the age of sixty-eight and was buried at St Peter's.

Lady Augusta Murray and family

The church of St Laurence is home to a number of monuments to Lady Augusta Murray and her family. There is a tablet to her in the north aisle, a hatchment to her mother in the nave, a ledger to her father in the north aisle as well as a monument in the nave, a hatchment to her son in law Baron Truro plus a mausoleum to them all in the churchyard.

On both Augusta's memorial and the Mausoleum it states that she married H.R.H. Prince Augustus Frederick at Rome on 4th April 1793. On the mausoleum it also states that she married him again at St George's, Hanover Square but gives no date. It then claims "both marriages were held invalid in England as contrary to an Act of Parliament entitled the Royal Marriage Act."

Augusta was the daughter of the Earl (shown left) and Countess of Dunmore. She had spent the early part of her childhood in America where her father was Governor of New York and Virginia. His time there was controversial with him waging war first against the Indians and then the Virginians. At one point, he had to evacuate his family to a hunting lodge whilst he took refuge on a ship. George Washington advised: "I do not think that forcing his lordship on shipboard is sufficient. Nothing less than depriving him of life or liberty will secure

---

⁴⁵ PCC minutes 14th December 1961
⁴⁶ Entries relating to the chapel are included in the St Laurence parish register marked CH. The dates show that the chapel was opened prior to the Act being obtained.

peace to Virginia." Dunmore was forced to release slaves so they could join the British army and continue the fight but to no avail. In 1776, the family fled back to England although Dunmore remained officially Governor of Virginia until 1783 when their independence from Great Britain was recognised. He later became Governor of the Bahamas but it is unknown if Augusta travelled there. In the winter of 1792-3 whilst he was there, she was in Italy with her mother and sister and it was at this time that she met the twenty-year old Prince who was the sixth son of George III and who had been sent south on account of his asthma.

That Augusta and the Prince formed an attachment was never disputed. In 1844, after both of them had died, some of their letters to one another were published in *The Times*. It was revealed that the Prince called her Gussy and that he had threatened to starve himself to death if Augusta refused to marry him. On March 21st, the couple declared their intentions to one another and recorded them on paper:

> On my knees, before God our creator, I, Augustus Frederick, promise thee Augusta Murray, and swear upon the Bible as I hope for salvation in the world to come, that I will take thee Augusta Murray for my wife, for better, for worse, for richer, for poorer, in sickness and in health, to love and to cherish till death do us part, to love but thee only and none other and may God forget me if I ever forget thee. The Lord's name be praised! So bless me! So bless us, O God. And with my handwriting do I, Augustus Frederick, this sign, March the 21st at Rome

> On my knees, before God my creator, I, Augusta Murray, promise and swear upon the Bible as I hope for salvation in the world to come, to take thee Augustus Frederick for my husband, for better, for worse, for richer, for poorer, in sickness and in health to love and to cherish till death do us part, so Bless my God and sign this Augusta Murray.

Augusta wrote in her diary "I must record this day as the forerunner of perhaps many happy ones."[47]

The Prince first approached a Roman Catholic priest but he refused to marry two Protestants. He then made contact with the Reverend William Gunn who was on holiday from England. Gunn was very reluctant to get involved and for good reason. The great romance was being conducted behind the backs of both sets of parents. As the Prince admitted in a letter to Lord Erskine in 1798, "I offered her my hand unknown to her family being certain beforehand of the objections Lady Dunmore would have made me had she been informed of my intentions." Gunn was also aware that under the Royal

---

[47] *The Times*, 24th May 1844

Marriage Act, anyone who aided a descendant of George II in marrying without the consent of the King was liable to have all their goods confiscated and face transportation. Indeed, since 1753, any clergyman who married a person under the age of twenty-one without parental consent was liable to fourteen years in an overseas penal colony.[48] The couple, however, effectively bullied him into submission by promising not to reveal his identity, a promise which they kept because it was not discovered until after their deaths. Thus, late in the evening of April 4th, Augusta was married to the Prince in the Sarmiento Inn where she and her family were staying, a building not authorised for marriages. There were no witnesses because Augusta had made sure all the servants had been sent out. Her mother had not gone out until nine o'clock and the Prince had been forced to hide until her carriage was out of sight. The couple had no licence. There had been no banns. There was nothing in writing to say that the marriage had taken place.

A few weeks after the event, Augusta and her mother went on to Florence and in August, the Prince left Rome for Windsor. The holiday romance would almost certainly have faded without trace had Augusta's mother not noticed that her daughter was suffering from nausea in the early morning and she was putting on weight. The discovery that Augusta was pregnant created havoc and Augusta's story about marrying the Prince must have seemed beyond belief. The family sailed for England arriving back in November.

It was agreed by both the Prince and Lady Dunmore that they needed to make certain the marriage was legal before the child was born. As a result, Augusta summoned her mantua maker, a lady named Mrs Jones, and asked her to rent a four roomed house in St George's parish on her behalf and to arrange for banns of marriage to be called. She told Mrs Jones that she was going to marry a gentleman from Devon who was related to Sir John Frederick, M.P. Augusta arranged for herself and the mysterious Mr Frederick to live with the Jones family during this period so she could claim residency in the parish. Mr Jones was a coal merchant so this must have been a novel experience for the Prince.

The banns having been called on November 10th, 17th and 24th, Augusta and the Prince married at St. George's, Hanover Square on 5th December 1793. Augusta wore a "common linen gown" and black cloak and took a hackney carriage to the church. The Prince dressed "as plain as possible in a greatcoat like a common shopkeeper." They gave their names as Augusta Murray and Augustus Frederick and the certificate was made out in this form. Augusta's mother was at the service but her father could not be there because he was still in the Bahamas. Another couple was married at the same time. Afterwards, the couple left the church for the property which Mrs Jones had rented for them and set up home. Their son Augustus was born on January 13th.

On January 22nd, the press got news of the nuptials and the King's new grandson and the horrified King immediately ordered an enquiry. The Privy Council met on January 27th and 28th and interviewed those involved. The Reverend John Downes of St George's said he had acted in good faith and "the parties were not at all distinguished by

---

[48] Terms of the 1753 Marriage Act.

their dress from the appearance of persons in trade." Mrs Jones said she had accompanied Augusta to the church and had no idea that the groom was anything other than a West Country gentleman. She had been astonished when Augusta told her the truth a few days afterwards. Augusta's mother admitted that she had known nothing about the Rome wedding at the time but said that she had been worried when Augusta told her there was no certificate and there had been no witnesses. She claimed that the Prince had written to her about it but when asked by the Privy Council to produce the letter, she suddenly remembered that Augusta had burned it. In another display of memory loss, she said that she could not remember how old her daughter Augusta was "past thirty-one but I do not just at this moment precisely recollect how much." The Privy Council immediately declared that the first alleged marriage was null and void because there was no evidence that it had ever taken place (other than Augusta's word) and the second was invalid because the Prince was under the age of twenty-one and did not have parental consent.[49] Seven months later, the Prerogative Court formally annulled it, this time for breaching the Royal Marriages Act. [50]

Whether from love or just some romantic idea of being star-crossed lovers, the

---

[49] The minutes of the Privy Council meetings are in Anthony Aspinall (ed.) *The Later Correspondence of King George III* vol.2 (Cambridge, 1963) pp. 157-170. Augusta's age does not appear on her monument. In the *Dictionary of National Biography* she is listed as being six years younger than her mother said.
[50] *The Times*, 8th March 1794

Prince announced that he would stand by Augusta. However, since he was abroad for most of the time, they scarcely saw one another until five years later. In the autumn of 1799, the Prince was in Berlin where he was taken seriously ill, so much so that he made a will. In this, he acknowledged that his union with Augusta was invalid but wrote: "I consider and ever shall acknowledge our son Augustus Frederick who was born after both these marriages as my true legitimate and lawful son." Augusta begged to be allowed to go and nurse him but this was refused. In the end, she had to use a false name to obtain a passport. The Prince recovered and returned with Augusta to England and for a few weeks lived with her at Lower Grosvenor Street. The result was a second child, a daughter whom they named Augusta.

Augusta must have thought all her problems were over. The people around her addressed her as Princess Augustus Frederick and in January 1801, the Prince addressed a letter to "My dearly beloved son, Prince Augustus Frederick."[51] Nonetheless, within weeks of their daughter's birth, the Prince accepted a twelve thousand pound grant from his father on condition that he depart from Augusta and start living as a prince. On 27th November, the Prince became Duke of Sussex; he never saw Augusta again.

The years that followed saw a number of lawsuits between the couple. In 1806, the Prince sought to stop her using the royal arms and his name. That case was settled by Augusta accepting the title of Lady D'Ameland and an allowance of four thousand a year to maintain herself and the children. In 1809, he united with his brother the Duke of Cambridge to try to have the children taken from her if she did not cease from telling them that they were a prince and princess by right. She agreed to back down but still had to face her son being moved from Winchester to Harrow school against her wishes.[52] That she remained feisty is made evident by a letter she wrote in 1811 which appeared after her death. She said that she had never given up her claim to be known as H.R.H. the Duchess of Sussex and "had I believed the sentence of the Ecclesiastical court to be anything but a stretch of power, my girl would not have been born. Lord Thurlow told me my marriage was good abroad, religion taught me it was good at home, and not one decree of any powerful enemy could make me believe otherwise or ever will. They have forced me to take a name but they have not made me believe I had no right to his. My children and myself were to starve or I was to obey and I obeyed but I am not convinced. …The moment my son wishes it, I am ready to declare that it was debt, imprisonment, arrestation, necessity which obliged me to seem to give up my claims and not my conviction of their fallacy." She goes on in the letter to discuss the activities of her son whom she deliberately references as Prince Augustus rather than Augustus d'Este.[53]

Augusta settled at Ramsgate taking a property on the east cliff known as Mount

---

[51] *The Times*, 14th June 1844
[52] *The Times*, 5th August, 1809
[53] *The Times*, 19th May, 1843. Her claim to being left destitute may be regarded as histrionics. Her allowance was worth the equivalent of £280,000 which should have been sufficient to feed and house her and the children quite easily.

Albion. She probably chose the spot because her parents had once lived at Southwood House and the town had happy associations for her.[54] After her death in 1830, her daughter continued to live there and she gave the land for Holy Trinity church. Many of the roads around that area are named after them.

The Prince died in 1843 without legitimate issue which meant that the title of Duke of Sussex died with him. Augusta's son decided to appeal to the House of Lords for recognition of his claim to the title. His case was put forward by Sir Thomas Wilde but failed on grounds that the marriages were invalid and he was therefore a bastard. The grant of titles to his father had been, like all titles, made hereditary only to legitimate sons.

Augusta's son died in 1848. For the last twenty-two years of his life he had suffered from multiple sclerosis and his diary of the disease is one of the earliest accounts of it.[55] The illness would not be defined for another twenty years. The onset of the disease came just after his ill fated attempt to woo Princess Victoria'a half sister, Princess Feodora. He declared to her: "I need not tell you I am as legitimate a prince as any to be named in ether of our houses." She knew it was untrue and dismissed him as "pretty and conceited."[56]

Augusta's daughter died in 1866 having spent much of her final years abroad due to asthma, something she had inherited from the Prince. She was described as "a thorough business woman though somewhat reserved in manner." Her funeral at St Laurence was attended by H.R.H the Duke of Cambridge and his wife.[57] She had married Sir Thomas Wilde shortly after her brother's case was heard. He went on to become Lord High Chancellor. Wilde died in 1855 and is remembered by a hatchment on the north side of the nave just to the right of the west window. It shows his motto *equabiliter et dilgenter* and is beside the one to Augusta's mother.

The mausoleum was erected by Augusta's son in 1847 and her body and her mother's, both of which had been buried in the church, were moved into it.[58]

---

[54] Her mother died at Southwood, *The Times* 14th November 1818

[55] D. Firth (ed.), *The Case of Augustus D'Este* (Cambridge, 1948), Anne-Marie Landtblom et.al.,'The first case history of multiple sclerosis: Augustus d'Esté (1794–1848)', *Neurological Sciences* vol 31 (February 2010) pp.29-33

[56] Princess Feodora was daughter of the Duchess of Kent by her first marriage. The correspondence of Augustus d'Este and Princess Feodora is stored at the National Archives, PRO 30/93/22.

[57] *Kentish Gazette*, 5th June 1866

[58] *South Eastern Gazette*, 16th November 1847

The reference to the marriage on the mausoleum and Augusta's memorial is telling. There is absolutely no doubt that there was no valid marriage and that her children were bastards. Augusta refused to accept that. She called herself a Duchess even though she had no entitlement to the title. Her father's monument is in the same vein. Its lengthy inscription notes he was fourteen generations removed from Edward III of England and nine from Charlotte of Bourbon. It would seem likely that Augusta composed the epitaph in a bid to show that her ancestry meant she was a worthy wife for a prince. Unsurprisingly, it neglects to mention the fact that his father was held in the Tower for treason after supporting Bonnie Prince Charlie at Culloden.

The Nineteenth Century

THE BUILDING

The church as it existed in 1800 would have been very unfamiliar to us today but by 1899 it had been transformed into something we would recognise. Most of the work was done in the incumbencies of two vicars, the Reverend George Wilson Sicklemore who served 1836 to 1880 and the Reverend Montague Fowler who served from 1889-1892. To enable us to chart the changes we have a wider variety of sources including newspapers, sketches, paintings, photographs, vestry minutes as well as annual reports from 1881-99 and from 1890-91 parish magazines. There are, however, no accounts so we are unable to see the cost of the alterations or to chart the smaller items which are so often indicative of how the building was being used.

Exterior

The earliest known drawing of the church dates from 1805 and was prepared to accompany a map showing the extent of the churchyard in that year. It is not entirely accurate for it only shows three windows on the north side instead of five but it does show the north door which was then in use, the covered over arcading on the tower and a dormer window on the north transept which was created to illuminate the gallery below. Also of interest are the buildings which are shown about the church on either side.

The first picture published of the church was in the *Gentleman's Magazine* of January 1809. It is clear that the artist made preliminary sketches at the church but only completed the drawing off site because there are some glaring errors. For example, he shows the Norman arcading on the west side of the tower when it only appears on south and east. He also has a round window in the porch over the door where there has only ever been a niche. He shows too a door on the south east corner when the vestry door is on the other side of the building. He does, however, show the two sundials, one on the ground beside the porch and the other on the south side of the tower. The dormer window which would have been opposite the present pulpit can also be seen sticking up from the roof. To the right can be seen the entrance gate which was then beside the buttress, not at the corner as it is today.

Late in 1810 an image was published by Messrs. Arch in London which was clearly more accurate. It shows the west door flanked by two small windows and the great west window without any tracery at all. The window has been glazed in the domestic style. It shows the dormer window as wide open. The two windows in the gables are plain and circular with no medieval or modern quatrefoil tracery. The church yard wall can be seen running along the right with various buildings close by. The large structure to the left is part of the old churchyard wall.

In 1817, a third view of the west end of the church was drawn by Miss J Evans and published in the first volume of William Deeble's *Delineations Historical and Topographical of the Isle of Thanet and the Cinque Ports*. This shows the west door more

clearly and the presence of tombstones in front of it.

On 18th November 1811, the church vestry committee "resolved unanimously that the Government be informed that they may have full liberty to make use of St Laurence church steeple to erect their signals on, upon condition that all expenses for the erecting such signals be paid for by Government and that it be left, when done with, at the expense of Government in the same state that is at present." This was the time of the war against Napoleon and evidence of the Navy Board's work can be seen in a further print by Miss Evans from 1817 and published in the same book. St Peter's church was used for the same purpose. The Reverend Charles Cowland-Cooper found the seat for the signalman still in place on the tower roof when he arrived more than a century later.

A fourth print exists which is undated and unsigned but appears to date from only a few years later. The artist's angle is curious because the west door appears almost buried and practically level with the bottom of the side windows which is an exaggeration. This print shows a chimney at the west end and the Skinner tomb beside the buttress to the right of the door. The other stones which stood in front of the west door have been omitted. The print was prepared for the benefit of tourists and clearly aimed at showing a romanticised image.

A print from the 1830s shows the west end complete with flagpole. It was customary for the flag to be raised each Sunday morning prior to service until 1846 when a vestry minute records that the Vicar stopped the practice. It shows the south side clearly before the creation of the second porch and gives the lie to the previous print which suggested the west door was almost buried. At the Archdeacon's visitation in 1824, the church was ordered to open up fully the round windows in the western gables which had been partially obscured.

The tower was restored in 1888 and the first photograph of the church from this angle shows it before the arcading on the west end was uncovered.

An image of the church published on the cover of the July 5th 1891 copy of *Church Bells* shows the restored tower as well as a chimney over the porch. New heating was installed in November 1889, the gridiron weathervane on 19th September 1890.

A similar image from a little more to the north shows a second chimney by the old north door which stemmed from the same heating installation.

A further sketch from 1891 shows the external staircase to the tower on the north side which was erected in 1848.

Images of the east end of the church start later than those of the west end. The following two show elements of the High Street with the Ladies' Academy on the right.

Another print which is dated 3rd June 1874 shows the churchyard wall and gates which were removed in 1883 and replaced with a lower wall and iron railings. The clock can be seen on the east end. This is the original clock which had one face only and which was installed in honour of Queen Victoria's accession in 1837.[1] The chimney to the right is

---

[1] A note inside records the first winder was appointed in January 1838. His name was Edward Petts (1810-52). Vestry records show it was repaired in 1850.

evidence of the heating in the vestry. The buildings in front appear closer because this print pre-dates the road widening by almost a century and the graveyard then extended further out across the present roundabout.

A photograph from the 1890s which was taken from almost the same viewpoint shows the old clock even more clearly plus the railings and lamp post.

The south east porch was added around 1861. Dr Cotton gives a date of 1858 but this is incorrect Not only do none of the newspaper reports which detail the 1858 alterations mention there being a new porch but the curate who was responsible for arranging the work specifically said that it was carried out as part of the window restoration campaign of 1860-65.[2] The objective was to create a fine new entrance, the medieval porch being in a state of extreme dilapidation. Being substantially taller than the

---

[2] Cotton op.cit. p.48. The earliest reference to it is in the *Thanet Advertiser* 28th September 1867 when it is mentioned in passing as the accepted principal entrance but there are no Thanet newspapers prior to 26th November 1859. The Reverend Haslewood's comments about his role in the new porch appear in the *Thanet Advertiser* 15th April 1876. He did not arrive in the parish until 27th December 1857 and said that the porch was added after lengthy correspondence and fund raising..

earlier entrance, it was much easier to get biers through for funerals, also to get furniture and building materials through and for processional use. Although a very handsome addition, the new porch soon proved troublesome as the large doors let in a considerable amount of cold air. As a result, it was decided in 1892 not to use it as the main entrance but rather to restore the medieval porch which had been in a poor state for many years. The church had been ordered to repair it in 1832 but only minimal work was done and areas were boarded up rather than mended.[3]

A sadly disfigured postcard of around 1890 shows the railings and the south east porch plus the area which would later be occupied by the war memorial.

In honour of Queen Victoria's Diamond Jubilee in 1897, a new clock was installed with four faces so that the time could be seen from whichever way one approached the church.

Interior

The church is fortunate to have two paintings showing how the church looked in the middle of the nineteenth century. They were painted by the then Vicar's daughter, Miss Sicklemore, and bought for the church from the estate of her mother in 1891.[4] Today, the painting looking east hangs in the vestry whilst the view of the south aisle is in the Thurstin Room. They both date from between 1842 and 1858 with the eastward view being later.[5]

The image of the nave shows two galleries on the left. That nearest the tower was occupied by the Townley family which is why the Townley hatchment can be seen hanging above it. Entrance to this gallery was by a winding staircase round the pillar

---

[3] CCA-DCb-V/A/2/4 p.208
[4] *Parish Magazine*, December 1891
[5] The south view shows the Clements memorial on the right which was erected in 1842 whilst that of the nave shows the Massey monument set up in 1846.

which came out using the medieval doorway into the rood loft. At the east end can be seen the high reredos which was in the Greek style and showed the Lord's Prayer, Ten Commandments and the Creed. The entire ceiling in the chancel is boarded over. To the right, against the south east pier of the tower is a two tier pulpit, the lower section being used as a lectern or reading desk. At the top right can be seen a window which had been inserted into the roof to aid lighting. The pews are very high, almost five feet tall, and boxed in with gates on the end. These would have had locks so that only the family who rented them could use them. During this period, the vestry records show that it was customary for different types of people to sit in different parts of the church and even to use different entrances. The opening of St George's in 1827 meant that some worshippers left St Laurence and that the seating plan was consequently re-organised. Tradesmen sat on the south side of the nave while servants occupied the area under the west gallery and beside the north door, this being the entrance they had to use whilst their employers entered via the south-west porch. The singers were moved into the north gallery where they occupied three pews suggesting that there must have been just over a dozen of them.

The painting of the south side shows the galleries which were built out over the porch and the facing gallery with stairway up. There are pews all the way up where now the font, Burma Star cabinet and side chapel stand. Curtains can be seen at the clerestory window top left and on the great west window. The west gallery and the top of the medieval west door can also be seen just above and to the right of the man in the picture. The Townley gallery is shown on the far right together with its entrance. On the  arch behind the people, the Sprackling memorial is on the left and the Wilson one on the right. On the inside of the arch can be seen the Freeling monument which was moved during work on the Tower in 1888 and re-sited beneath the Wilson one.

The Sicklemore era

The arrival of Reverend George Wilson Sicklemore in 1836 saw the start of a process to transform the church. A man of tremendous energy who was profoundly interested in church design and who valued practicality, he altered almost everything over the coming forty-four years.

In April 1837, the church was shut for two weeks so it could be repainted. Mr Sicklemore wanted to replace the pews next but the collapse of Austen's bank in Ramsgate meant that there was no money for this as a number of parishioners had been ruined. The newspaper reported: "Long and severely will this most extraordinary and unexpected event be felt in the town and its vicinity. Not an individual from the most affluent down to the humblest mechanic or labourer but either directly or indirectly is a sufferer. The deposits in the Bank, added to the numerous notes in circulation, amount to a very large sum and the difficulties and stagnation to business arising therefore are of course proportionately great."[6] Early in 1842, the two decker pulpit was dismantled and a temporary one erected in its place while it was rebuilt closer to the nave but still on the right hand side. A year later, the vestry toilet was removed on grounds it was not required and improvements were made to the heating system.[7] In 1848, the internal stairs to the ringers' floor were replaced with an external staircase. Yet the greatest changes came in the major restoration a decade later.

In 1858 the church was closed for ten weeks so that major alterations could be made. The galleries were all demolished and all the high pews removed. The present pews were installed which were open-ended. This was a significant move because it meant that all seats were now technically free so people could sit where they chose. In practice, a number of pews were still reserved and remains of the nameplate boxes can still be seen on some seats.[8] These changes necessitated laying a new tiled floor and moving a number of the wall mounted monuments so they were more evenly spread, particularly in the nave. A new pillar had to be built behind the present pulpit because the removal of the gallery at that point involved removing part of the medieval wall and so altering the width of the arch. The organ which had been in the gallery was re-positioned in the south chancel. The two decker pulpit was replaced with a single level stone one which was the gift of a young man in the congregation who wished to remain anonymous. A new reading desk was given also and set on the other side. The west window was extended downwards to give more light at the expense of the medieval west doorway which was filled in with flint on the exterior. This new west window was filled with plain glass and had Early English style tracery. The north door was blocked up. The Archbishop came to re-open the church and it must have seemed ironic that having removed the galleries on grounds that with St George's, Christ Church and Holy Trinity now existing there were less people, so many people turned up that the sidesmen and churchwardens had to raid the school for extra seats! [9]

A curious incident occurred in 1864 with regard to the new pews. Colonel Nedham took out a private prosecution of a thirty-six year old gentleman named Henry

---

[6] *South Eastern Gazette*, 14th July 1840

[7] The Vestry Book CCA-U3-19/8/A/2 records the removal of the toilet but makes no mention of its installation or precise location. It was only for clergy use, not the laity.

[8] The loss of pew rents would have been quite significant to the finances. Although no figures are available for St Laurence, at St Peter's, the pew rents accounted for almost £90 a year income, around a quarter of the total. Mocket op.cit. p.36. The churchwardens of St Peter's so admired the new pews at St Laurence that they voted to remove their own high pews and galleries and install "seats like those lately erected at St Lawrence's." Peter Hills, *The Parish Church of St Peter-in-Thanet* (1970) p.25

[9] *Kentish Gazette*, 19th October 1858

Curtis whom he alleged had conducted himself improperly on Sunday 11th September. Colonel Nedham had four daughters at this time namely Eleanor aged 25, Lucy aged 18, Blanche aged 16 and Alice 14. He also had a younger son and a wife. On the Sunday in question, Curtis had apparently reached over the pew and asked if he might share the prayer book held by his one of his daughters. When she either failed to reply or else fluttered her lashes, Curtis stepped nearer. At this point Colonel Nedham lashed out and the result was that Curtis was removed from the church. He subsequently apologised to Colonel Nedham who refused to accept this and insisted on taking the matter to court. It took some time for the magistrate to persuade Colonel Nedham to accept the apology but eventually he did so on the proviso that Curtis pay all the costs – and one imagines agreed never to sit anywhere near his family in future. As Nedham observed, such a case could not have happened in the old pews.[10]

1860 Chancel restoration

Never one to rest on his laurels, the Vicar next turned his attention to the High Chancel. The old east window was completely removed and replaced. No illustrations exist of the pre 1860 east window but it was probably without tracery in the same way that the west window was until 1858. Just as the new window at the west end, this was created in plain glass but with medieval style tracery. The wooden reredos was replaced with a stone one with cinquefoil arches with the Lord's Prayer, Ten Commandments and Creed all in illuminated characters. The arches and columns were based on those to be found in the cloisters of Canterbury Cathedral. Similarly, the wooden communion rails were replaced with stone and a mosaic was laid. The entire cost of this work – which must have been considerable – was paid by the Vicar in memory of his parents. A brass commemorating his generosity can still be seen on the left hand side. [11]

The first photograph of the interior of the church dating from 1881 (overleaf), just after the arrival of the Reverend Charles Molony, shows the new east end together with the 1858 pulpit and reading desk. Notice also the pews in the transepts facing into the tower area, the server pews beside the pulpit and the large amount of empty space which would later be occupied by the choir stalls. The transept pews faced into the tower because that was where the pulpit stood and the main services were non-sacramental.

1887-88 Tower Restoration

Major changes were made to the church when the tower was restored. The need for this was made evident by cracks appearing inside the chancel over the eastern tower arch and ringing chamber. The church called upon the architect John Loughborough Pearson to give them his report. Pearson was a man with exemplary credentials having been architect at Westminster Abbey and the cathedrals of Lincoln, Rochester,

---

[10] *South Eastern Gazette*, 18th September 1864.
[11] *South Eastern Gazette*, 18th December 1860.

Peterborough. Exeter and Truro. In March 1887 he reported that: "One great cause of the weakness of the tower is the absence of lateral support. The removal of the eastern walls of the original transept deprived the eastern tower pier of all support on their north and south sides and the support which the western piers derive from the nave arcades is very indirect. This accounts for the slight twist which the tower arches present, and although the tower has for 400 years or more been without transepts, I cannot but feel that their reconstruction would add greatly to its stability." He advised underpinning the foundations of the piers and replacing the ceiling of the tower and beams of the ringing chamber. The estimate was £400 but it was admitted that this might increase depending on the extent of damage which might be found when the piers were excavated.[12] He further recommended removing the cement which covered the flint exterior and repointing it.

    The church decided to undertake the restoration in honour of the Queen's Diamond Jubilee in 1887 and the two new arches created on either side to strengthen the church can be seen today, the one to the north filled with organ pipes and the back entrance to the vestry and that to the south immediately behind the chairs in the side chapel. In celebration, the tower was illuminated.

    However, as Mr Pearson had predicted, further problems were found. Mr Port

---

[12] He was asked about providing improved access for the ringers and recommended recreating the medieval turret on the north side but this suggestion was not taken up. At the vicar's request, he also quoted for repairing the roof and south porch at £1340.

later wrote:

> On examining the foundations of the tower piers they were found to be not more than eighteen inches below the church floor and the ground around and close up to the footings had been removed for burial purposes to a depth of six to ten feet and on the east side of the tower a wall had been removed. This removal had caused a great pressure to be put on the piers on that side. The south east pier was found to be so much damaged necessitating its being carefully underpinned from quite four feet below the footings…The east arch had to be nearly all removed and re-set together with the circular shafts under it. …When the old plaster and cement on the outside of the tower was removed the cracks on the east face were found to reach up to the parapet and through the full thickness of the wall. The parapet was in such a dangerous state that it required to be rebuilt and the cornice beneath with the battlement had to be nearly all renewed.[13]

Faced with the need to raise a further £500 for this work, the vicar sent out an appeal in September 1888 urging people to donate urgently. Perhaps unsurprisingly, he neglected to tell them about the eighteen inch foundations for fear that the more nervous members of the congregation might flee.

---

[13] *Kent Coast Times,* 22nd November 1888. Mr Port's building firm at St Lawrence carried out the work.

The strain of raising such large sums of money clearly had its effect on those involved and the organising committee descended into chaos. At one point, one churchwarden was so exasperated that he placed the following advertisement in the *Kent Coast Times* of 6th September 1888:

> Estimates are required from persons willing to undertake the covering of the whole of the exterior walls of the Tower of St Laurence church with coal, tar and road grit.
>
> Lowest tender may be accepted.
>
> Payments made by annual instalments over fifty years.
>
> Full particulars of
> William Mascall
> CHURCHWARDEN
>
> Whitewash or other unsuitable material might be accepted if cheaper than tar.

The vicar was absolutely furious and the following response appeared two days later in the *Thanet Advertiser*:

> The undersigned members of the Committee for the Restoration of St Laurence Church Tower hereby give notice that in consequence of the unwarrantable and insulting advertisement bearing the signature of W. Mascall, Churchwarden, inserted in the *Kent Coast Times* of Thursday last, the 6th instant, the meeting of which notice was given in the same paper will not be held and that they repudiate all liability for any orders that may be given by Mr Mascall.
>
> Signed   C. A. Molony (Vicar)
> H Weigall   B Hodges
> J W S Howe (curate)   W G Lawrence
> W G Lewis (Hon. Sec.)   W Perkins
> J Frost (Churchwarden)   J Kennett
> The Hon. Treasurer K. W. Wilkie esq is absent from England and therefore been unable to sign the foregoing

Mr Mascall made his response in another open letter saying that: "I have had to fight the Committee almost unsupported. I endeavoured to impress on the Committee a sense of their duty by reasoning, failing which I tried satire, but both failing I beg to tender my resignation to the parishioners." The public squabble may have entertained the local population but it was hardly edifying and the deep seated divisions caused were to be the subject of further problems in years to come. Nonetheless, the work was completed and a plaque put up on the south side of the tower which included Mr Mascall's name so presumably some degree of peace was made.[14] The cost in today's terms was over £107,000 of which some £24,000 was still owing in November 1888 when the tower was re-opened.[15]

One of the corbels removed from the tower during the course of the work was placed on display in the vestry presenting a rare chance to see an almost six hundred year old carving close up.

1890-92 Refurnishing

Although the church building had been restored by the end of 1888, there had been scarcely any changes to the interior since 1858, other than the pulpit being moved from the right hand side to the left in 1887. A further campaign relating to furnishings took place between 1890 and 1892.

The high chancel was transformed by having the sacrarium raised and inlaid with walnut and oak to make the communion table more prominent. This reflected two new ideas. Firstly, there was the desire to focus attention on the sacrament rather than the pulpit, but also it was to restore the unity of the church. Since Laud had returned communion tables to the east end, there had been a tendency to view the church building as a suite of rooms with different functions, one area being for baptism, another for communion and another for preaching. The new layout symbolised how all areas of worship and life came together in Christ. The medieval waggon roof which had been boarded over was opened up and restored. An ornate screen and sedilia was erected in the archway to the side chapel. The stone communion rails were replaced by oak with a brass standard. The whole area was carpeted and two new brass lights were added. A variety of new frontals and linen were given for the communion table and Miss Sale gave a new silver paten and chalice. Two sets of crosses and candlesticks were donated, one in oak, the other in brass as well as the brass alms dish used today. The chancel re-opened on 11th December 1890.[16]

During the course of the work, evidence was found of windows either side of the chancel though they were not fully excavated. Signs were also found of a wall to the north which may have been used during construction of the church centuries before. The tomb of Captain Robert Parker was uncovered and the slabs converted to ledgers in the south chancel. A temporary communion table was purchased so that Mr Fowler could celebrate whilst the work was taking place and the area under the tower was cleared of pews so that he could do this. The table was subsequently used in the side chapel.

---

[14] There had been further issues between the vicar and Mr Mascall in 1884 because his house was found to encroach eighteen inches into the vicar's land. Eventually, it was decided not to prosecute, see CCA-U3-19/6/7. Mascall had taken over Newington Mill in 1874, *Kent Coast Times*, 23rd May 1874
[15] The faculty includes a map of the graves found during excavations, CCA-U3-19/6/B/10.
[16] The communion rails were replaced in 1932. The sedilia is the triple seat for officiating clergy, not used since celebrations under the tower began. Another chalice had been given in 1873.

On Sunday 19th July 1891, the choir stalls and matching clergy desks were dedicated. Given by Mrs Frances Barber in memory of her music loving son William who died aged thirty-six, they were carved from Riga wainscotting oak by Mr J T Wilson of Hampstead Road, London who also made the pulpit for the church on behalf of Miss Ellerm later in the same year and the oak litany desk. The choir stalls were originally positioned nearer to the sacrarium leaving just a narrow passage through to the south chancel which had yet to be set up as a chapel. Although handsome, the stalls caused problems as books kept falling off them. To avoid this a raised edge was added in 1900. To further assist the choristers, an upper stand for music was erected in 1971.[17]

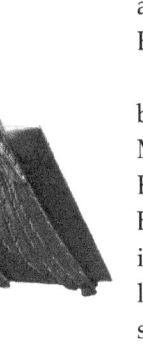

The processional cross was given by an anonymous donor and shows the Lamb amid the symbols of the Evangelists.

Within the nave, the brass lectern was given by Miss Astle and first used at Easter 1890. It was made by Benham and Froud. The eagle is the traditional shape for lecterns because it is the symbol of the Gospel writer, St John. The eagle is associated with strength and the ability to cover long distances. Legend claimed that eagles renewed their strength by flying close to the sun which Christianity interpreted as a reminder that our strength comes from the Son of God. The eagle was also sometimes seen as a symbol of the Ascended Lord being free from earthly constraints of space and time and so accessible to everyone. He stands on a globe which represents the Word being spread throughout the world.

The churchwarden's wands were given by Mr Guillum Scott. As with the processional cross, they show the symbol of resurrection above a globe.

The pulpit shows the figures of the four evangelists, each character quite distinct and beautifully carved, beneath gothic tracery and intricately carved vine leaves. At the time it was installed it was to the side of the pillar because the pews extended right down the nave. Later the front pews were removed and the pulpit moved in front of the pillar. It was dedicated on 17th December 1891.[18]

---

[17] PCC Minutes 15th March 1971, Vestry Book 17th April 1900

[18] Being a gift, no receipt exists for the pulpit but Mr Fowler had budgetted £60 toward purchase of

Font

In October 1861, the church was given a new font by a group of friends who chose to remain anonymous. It was made of stone and octagonal in shape with deeply carved lilies on the sides and the words "Suffer the little children to come unto me" (Mark 10:14). The first child to be baptised in it was Alfred, son of the artist Philip Calderon. Calderon was a leading pre-Raphaelite who had already exhibited both Biblical and historical works and would later become Keeper of the Royal Academy. Some of his work today can be seen at Tate Britain. The fact that his child was the first could suggest that he had been involved in the font's design although there is no evidence of him working in sculpture.

The cover shown in the photograph was made in 1900 by Dr and Mrs Worsley who were members of the congregation. The carvings showed the Jerusalem Cross

a pulpit before one was donated which would be about £7000 today.

surrounded by palm branches representing victory and the Star of Bethlehem symbolising baptism as the start of the Christian journey.[19]

The font was installed beside the arch between the high chancel and side chapel as can be seen from the following photograph (left) taken in 1886. At this time, the big south east porch was the main entrance to the church and fonts are traditionally located beside an entrance to symbolise how baptism is the entry to Christian life.

In 1890 it was moved to sit just to the left of the medieval porch beneath the Garrett memorial. Dr Cotton congratulated the vicar on restoring it to what he believed was its original position.[20]

Church Clock

For many years, the parish had been reliant on the clock at the pier yard in Ramsgate. It was part of the sexton's job to listen for that and then to toll the bell at St Laurence to mark the hour.[21] In 1810, a clock was purchased for the church but it was not until 1837 that one was installed in the tower when it was decided that this would be a suitable way to honour Princess Victoria's accession to the throne. The clock had a blue face and was on the east side of the tower so that people approaching from Ramsgate could see the time but anyone else would have to walk round. It was reasoned that it would be a waste of money putting a clock face to the west since the deceased had no need or ability to see the time.

In 1897, the church decided to get a new clock in honour of Queen Victoria's Diamond Jubilee. They decided to do this because they felt that the old one was no longer

---

[19] *Parish Magazine*, June 1900
[20] Cotton op.cit p.35. Dr Cotton refers to "the present vicar" who at time of publication in 1895 was the Reverend Robert Payne-Smith but the move is recorded in the Reverend Montague Fowler's *A Record of Church Work* (1890) p.17. Evidence suggests the font was actually in the north aisle rather than the south from the thirteenth century onwards.
[21] *Vestry Book*, 26th October 1794

accurate and it did not show up sufficiently.[22] However, it was admitted at the dedication on 20th October that given most people now had watches, there was really no need for the church to display the time. The Archdeacon said that instead "the clock would teach them to regulate their consciences, to discriminate between right and wrong. While the clock proclaimed the passing hours of day and night and other times for refreshing the soul as well as the body, it would remind them of the day of rest." The four faces, each 6' 6" across, were said to symbolise how the British Empire under Queen Victoria stretched to all four corners of the globe, to north, south, east and west.[23] The clock itself cost £230 and was purchased from John Smith and Sons of Derby who had made the clock for St Paul's Cathedral. The mechanism was designed by Lord Grimthorpe who had designed the clock at the Palace of Westminster popularly known as 'Big Ben' and involved three weights which worked by gravity, one controlling the quarter chimes, one the hour and the third the actual time. This constituted a major advance in accuracy as it regulated the pendulum and linked it to the hands.[24] Until 2000, the clock was wound by hand every three days. The clock occupies the second floor of the tower and the hour chime is sounded by the third bell.

Church Music

The decision to replace the musicians in the west gallery with an organ was taken on 24th November 1841 and the instrument must have been purchased and installed soon afterwards for on 14th December, the church vestry voted to invite Mr Bloxham to play it from Easter onwards for the sum of £15 per annum (about £1200 today). No details are known of the weight or dimensions of the instrument so it is impossible to say whether it played any role in the virtual collapse of the west gallery just six years later.[25]

In the summer of 1848 with the west gallery duly reinforced and repaired, a second organ was purchased from Bishop's of London for £250 and this was installed on 30th August 1848. The original price had been £270 but the church were able to get £20 off by letting Bishop's take the old organ away. This was a two manual organ and had been previously owned.

When the gallery was removed in 1858, the organ was moved to the side chapel where it sat on the site of the present communion table. An appeal was launched in 1873 to repair the organ but notwithstanding the completion of the work in August 1874, problems evidently remained according to a visitor to the church in 1876 who wrote: "The music of the church is quite in the old style and I pitied the organist who had such an instrument to deal with. If he wanted a piano passage the older part of the organ had to be used and when a loud passage was required it seemed to burst from some portion of

---

[22] Major repairs had been made in 1850, 1888 and 1895.
[23] *Thanet Advertiser*, 23rd October 1897; *Vestry Book* 20th April 1897
[24] For more details, see *The Engineer*, May 1905.
[25] Margate, St Peter's and Monkton already had organs, the former since 1797, Stephen Glynne, *Notes on the Churches of Kent* (London, 1877) pp. 35-37.

the organ so ill adapted to the other parts it was stunning and not musical."[26] Money for the 1874 alterations had been raised single-handedly by the organist and the work involved mending two large holes in the bellows, adding twenty pipes to bring the total to seven hundred and fifty four, taking the swell down four notes and cleaning and re-lacquering the entirety.[27]

In 1883 it was enlarged by a pedal organ at a cost of £240 and in 1885 it was moved to its present position in the north chancel. By this time the organist earned £60 per annum (about £5400 today). Although people were presumably keen to see the organ improved, they were not keen on paying for it and the then vicar, Charles Molony, was forced to use his own money to pay the bill. The *Parochial Report 1888-89* reveals that he was still owed £57 18s 6d (almost £5700 today). It may be no coincidence that Mr Molony decided to retire that year saying he could not afford to continue as vicar.

In 1891, the Reverend Montague Fowler made an appeal in the parish magazine for money to restore the organ. He noted that the mechanism was worn out and the bellows were liable to give way at any moment. He said that dust from the 1888 tower restoration and 1890 chancel restoration had choked the pipes and marred the tone and that the bottom octave was deficient. He further commented that the case was shabby and that the organ was too exposed. An estimate suggested that the church would need to raise £140 per annum for the next four years to rectify this but the sum was not forthcoming and no further work was done to the organ in the nineteenth century although a fund was started.

The decision to replace the amateur musicians with a professional organist was one which was being made in churches across the country around this time. It is not known how the change was regarded at St Laurence but it is easy to imagine that there must have been considerable hurt experienced by those who had given their best for possibly many years. In his novel *Under the Greenwood Tree* written in 1872, Thomas Hardy imagines the reactions of just such a group saying: "the venerable body of musicians could not help thinking that the simpler notes they had been wont to bring forth were more in keeping with the simplicity of their old church than the crowded chords and interludes of the organ." In his introduction he went further and spoke of "the professed aim of the clergy to increase control and accomplishment" and noted the "indirect result being to curtail and extinguish the interest of the parishioners in church doings."[28]

It would appear that the organ replaced both musicians and singers for it was reported in 1873 that the organist, Valentine Barton, had formed a thirty strong choir to enable the church to have sung evening services.[29] This supposition is supported by the fact that when the church was re-opened in 1858 after restoration, the music was supplied

---

[26] *Thanet Advertiser*, 13th May 1876, *Kent Coast Times* 27th August 1874
[27] *Thanet Advertiser*, 22nd August 1874.
[28] Hardy op.cit. Part 4 chapter 5
[29] *Thanet Advertiser*, 8th November 1873

by the choir from St George's.[30] The new St Laurence choir was defined as the men and boys but there were also ladies who sat apart but sang with them in support. The 1876 visitor who criticised the organ said of this arrangement: "the choir was supported by some middle aged ladies whose round mellow tones did not mix well with the shrill, infantile voices of the children." George Burton, one of the congregation replied that the singing at St Laurence was "never good. The authorities do not encourage it."[31]   Three years earlier, another person had reported: "Anything more slovenly than the style in which the congregation of this church as a rule perform their worship it would be hard to find. A dropping fire of muttered responses can alone be heard on ordinary occasions whilst the praises appear to be left to the organ. Viewed spiritually, much is left to be desired. We were glad to see a body of some thirty singers which may in time have the effect intended viz. to tempt the congregation to sing also."[32]

It is not known where the choir sat at this time because the choir stalls did not arrive until 1891 when Mrs Frances Barber gave them in memory of her son, William, who was a keen singer. Prior to 1884, the various groups of men, women and children evidently sat in different parts of the church because the vicar listed amongst his achievements of the year bringing them together in one place.[33]   It is likely that some had sat in the side chapel near the organ, some in the north chancel where the organ was subsequently placed, and possibly some at the back of the church in their traditional location. In 1887, they were given surplices for the first time. Made for fifteen boys and twelve men, the costs were

	£	s	d
Linen (72 ½ yards)	3	12	4
Making up	9	9	0
Press	2	19	0
Rail	1	10	6
Fittings for rail		10	3
Curtain for rail (9 yards)	3	7	6
	21	8	7

At this stage, the surplices were worn over ordinary day clothes. It was not until 1889 that cassocks were bought. By 1890, the church choir consisted of twelve men and eighteen boys. A separate ladies choir was set up in the same year for the benefit of women's

---

[30] *South Eastern Gazette*, 19th October 1858

[31] *Thanet Advertiser* 20th May 1876. At the 1874 Harvest Festival, the new choir was still not in evidence, music coming solely from the organ – *Kent Argus* 5th September 1874 – so their appearance at morning services must have commenced around 1875.

[32] *Thanet Advertiser* 6th December 1873

[33] *Parochial Report 1883-4* p.3

services only.[34] In 1891 they gave their first recital of Stainer's *Crucifixion*.

At Christmas 1889 *Hymns Ancient and Modern* was introduced, a volume which remained in use in the church until 1996, although the revised edition was implemented in 1950. This replaced *Church Hymns* from the SPCK which had been introduced at Advent 1881. The donor of the new hymnbooks was William Barber, the man in whose memory the choir stalls were given.

On 5th October 1890, whilst the vicar was away visiting his parents in Scotland, a most extraordinary thing happened – the choir walked out in the middle of Matins. Work had been taking place within the church and for some reason, the ten men of the choir found that their psalters were not in their usual place, When the curate announced the psalm, rather than use their Prayer Books which had the words but not the music, they simply stood up and processed out, leaving the bewildered choir boys to do the best they could. Presumably the books were found because later that day Evensong was sung without incident by boys and men. The curate had, however, reported the incident to the Reverend Montague Fowler who was horrified. He immediately wrote a letter of apology and sent it to the church saying that he expected every man who had walked out to sign it. The curate went to choir practice and read it out and the men decided it was altogether "too abject" and departed. Their view was that Mr Fowler was making a mountain out of a minor incident whilst he regarded their behaviour as indicating a lack of reverence for God and His church. On the following Sunday, none of the men turned up and the boys were left to take the musical lead. At the end of the week, Mr Fowler returned and met with the men. Accounts of exactly what happened next varied but the result was that all the men either resigned or were dismissed and Mr Fowler set about forming a new choir. The newspaper reported:

> No choir could have acted in a more childish spirit. The boys had more sense of propriety about them….The recalcitrant old choirmen have had their places filled by men of well tried vocal ability who will think twice before deserting their church in the absence of a Vicar who has done nothing to merit their discourtesy.

In an effort to make amends and salvage their reputations, the old choir decided to reunite to go carol singing two months later though they chose to give the money raised to Lady Rose Weigall's Soup Kitchen rather than the church.[35]

---

[34] The Reverend Montague Fowler, *A Record of Church Work,* (St Lawrence, 1890) pp. 19, 31, hereafter referred to as *Parochial Report 1890*
[35] *Thanet Advertiser*, 18th October 1890; *Kent Coast Times*, 16th October, 30th October 1890, 22nd January 1891; *Kent Argus* 25th October 1890, 1st November 1890

Windows

At the start of the nineteenth century, all the windows were in plain glass. The existence of galleries made this imperative as light was at a premium. Moreover, with the exception of the two side windows at the rear of the church, most were glazed in the style of a country house with regular square panes and no tracery. The windows opened for ventilation and many had curtains to prevent glare in the summer. The removal of the galleries in 1858 generated an opportunity to restore the windows to their medieval form and to add some colour. For many years, the criticism had been made that the church with its whitewashed walls was garish and dazzlingly white.[36]

The window restoration fund was started immediately after the 1858 changes were complete. The curate Frederick Haslewood was put in charge of superintending the work and carrying out necessary correspondence. He served eighteen years in the parish before going on to become Vicar of Chislet. The fund raising was left to a committee composed exclusively of women, the first time in the church's history that such a demonstration of female involvement was made. They organised sales of works and teas busily but it was expected that it would take at least a generation to raise the hundreds of pounds needed - some forty thousand pounds today. The likelihood of this being the case can be seen by looking at the bazaar held in 1865 which raised £130 with a further £7 a few days after when the leftover goods were taken to the school for sale.[37] It was destined to be a very long project.

The first window to receive stained glass was the west window which had been enlarged and given Early English style tracery in 1858. The vicar, George Wilson Sicklemore, donated the figure of Christ for the central panel. It signified that not only was Christ central to our lives and worship but that He was always behind us to support us. Our Lord is shown holding an orb to represent his role as Saviour of the world. Mr Sicklemore also donated the tracery together with Mr Smith. When the window was unveiled in June 1859 the hope was expressed that other people might follow suit and provide stained glass for other windows in memory of loved ones and this did indeed happen. Two years later the figures of the four evangelists with their symbols below – Matthew with a winged man, John with an eagle, Mark with a lion and Luke with an ox – were added to the window. These were given by Thomas Noel Harris of Pegwell in memory of his father who, as the memorial beneath states, "served and bled for his country in the glorious campaigns of the Peninsula, Germany and France from 1811 to 1814, and at the famous Battle of Waterloo, 18th June 1815". Harris was a generous man who also gave to the Methodist Mission Room at Cliffsend (now St Mary's) and St Catherine's church at Manston, thereby following his father who had been a substantial benefactor of Holy Trinity Church at Ramsgate.[38]. Chairman of the local Conservatives, he

---

[36] Glynne op.cit. p38
[37] *Canterbury Journal*, 24th June 1865
[38] *Thanet Advertiser* 28th October 1871, 8th February 1873, *Kentish Gazette* 17th June 1845

derived money from slavery having over three hundred on a plantation in Barbados.[39] The figures were designed and manufactured by Messrs. Smith and Son of Ramsgate. The glass above remained clear for almost seventy years until the addition of a set of angels designed by Henry Weigall. The West window is unique in having been filled in three separate stages.

Other donations followed. The next was in the north aisle in memory of John Ashley Warre who died 18th November 1860. He had served as a Liberal MP since 1812 being an active speaker and supporter of Palmerston. In 1816, he had memorably described taxation as "the great and permanent cause of the misfortunes of the country." He described himself as "a warm supporter of the principle of civil and religious liberty" and "a strenuous advocate for the most rigid economy in every branch of the public service."[40] Locally, he was the benefactor of the church school and Holy Trinity Church as well as first President of Ramsgate Hospital. He was also a magistrate, Deputy Lieutenant of Kent, Sheriff of Kent and President of the Isle of Thanet Agricultural Association and of the Ramsgate Cinque Ports and County Permanent Building Society. This window was destroyed in the Second World War and remained plain glass until 1998 when one showing St Augustine's cross was inserted.

Five more windows followed in the 1860s. Two were to the Garrett family and they can be seen in the south aisle at the back of the church. The third was to Anthony Crofton and in the vestry but this was also destroyed in the Second World War. The fourth is beside the font and was given by the Vicar in memory of his daughter Catherine who died aged thirty-three in 1869. It depicts Our Lord healing the sick and welcoming children. The fifth is to the Mayhew sisters and is at the back of the church on the north

---

[39] On 24th April 1836 he received compensation of £6736 11s 9d when they were freed, claim no 2016 ref. T71/897, see https://www.ucl.ac.uk/lbs. In today's money, that would be aroud £540,000
[40] http://www.historyofparliamentonline.org/

side. By the end of the decade, the church had seven stained glass windows, three of them depicting Mary Magdalene going to the tomb on Easter day (Warre, Mayhew and Garrett).

Two windows were given in the 1870s, that in the north transept beside the organ pipes which remembers John and Esther Vinten and the one at the back of the church on the same side which remembers seventeen year old Emily Jane Moses who died in 1877. The former showed the occasion when Our Lord was asked about the tribute money and was a reminder of His removal of the merchants from the Temple on grounds it should be a house of prayer and not a market place. The latter illustrated two of Our Lord's parables, that of the good shepherd and that of the sower.

A further two windows were given in the 1880s. The first is in the south transept behind the server stall and remembers George Wilson Sicklemore who served as vicar for forty-four years. The money for this was raised by public subscription, his parishioners wishing to give thanks for his life. It shows Our Lord's injunction to Peter to "feed my lambs" and "feed my sheep", a reminder of the need to minister to adults and children alike. The final window is to the left within the side chapel. Made by the highly respected firm of Clayton and Bell, it was erected in memory of Caroline Warre, widow of John Ashley, who was a benefactress of the parish school as well as active parish worker.[41] Given her love of children, the family chose images of Our Lord's nativity and childhood.

Hatchments

The church has eleven hatchments of which nine date from the nineteenth century. Originally the hatchments were placed near the relevant family memorials but they were moved in 1907 when the roof was restored to create a regular distribution. Thus the Townley hatchment which used to hang over the pulpit above the seat where Townley sat was moved to hang on the left of the west window and over the Spencer monument whilst the Spencer hatchment was moved to the south aisle above the Garrett window. The Austen hatchment which used to hang above his monument in the side chapel was moved to the nave.

The present layout of the hatchments is:
North aisle
From the west or rear of the church
Captain John Pettit, died 1723
Mark Sellers Garrett of Nethercourt, 1779

Nave
North side from the west or rear of the church toward the pulpit
Sir Thomas Wilde, Lord Chancellor, 1855

---

[41] *Thanet Advertiser* 5th July 1888. Clayton and Bell had created the West Window at King's College Cambridge, the mosaics for the Albert Memorial and all the glass for Truro Cathedral.

Elizabeth, Dowager Countess of Dunmore, 1818
John Sicklemore, father of the vicar, 1837

South side from lectern to rear of church
Samuel Winter of Southwood, 1842
Nathaniel Austen, banker, 1818
James Townley, lawyer, 1817

South aisle
From the font to the rear of the church
Ellizabeth, Baroness Conyngham, 1814
Charles Jolliffe of Southwood, 1870
Lieutenant George Spencer, RN, 1809

The hatchments reflect a much later desire to recreate a touch of the medieval. In the middle ages, when a knight or lord died, his body was taken to the church together with his shield. After the service, the shield was returned to the house and mounted with a black border where it would stay for a year before being taken back to the church to rest on his tomb which would by then have been built. In the eighteenth and nineteenth century, the arms were painted with a background which showed the status of the deceased. If only the left side was black, it meant the deceased was either a bachelor or that his wife was still alive: when she died, the right hand side would be blacked out. It will be noted that a number of the hatchments at St Laurence are only black on one side although it is certain that the wives are long dead. Presumably having gone to all the effort of getting the hatchment up to the roof, they decided against bringing it down to repaint it later.

In most cases, the hatchment was erected as an additional monument to the deceased. Wilde and Dunmore are remembered in the D'Este Mausoleum in the churchyard where Townley also has a vault. Austen, Sicklemore, Conyngham and Spencer all have tablets on the walls of the church. On 23rd March 1848, the church vestry set a fee of £1 5s to erect a hatchment in the church which compared to £4 4s for a vault.

Monuments

The most notable memorial of the nineteenth century – and possibly the best in the church – is the marble relief to Henrietta Froude which can be seen on the south wall of the Side Chapel. It was made by the pre-Raphaelite sculptor Thomas Woolner who was elected to the Royal Academy in the same year. Amongst his more famous works is the bust of Tennyson to be found in Westminster Abbey. Lord Tennyson was a friend of his as was Carlyle and Charles Darwin. The monument was unveiled in December 1875 and shows Henrietta reclining on a couch as if asleep.[42] She is dressed in a light robe rather than a shroud which drapes realistically about her figure. Henrietta was the daughter of John Ashley Warre and wife of the historian James Anthony Froude. She died on 12th February 1874 aged 49.

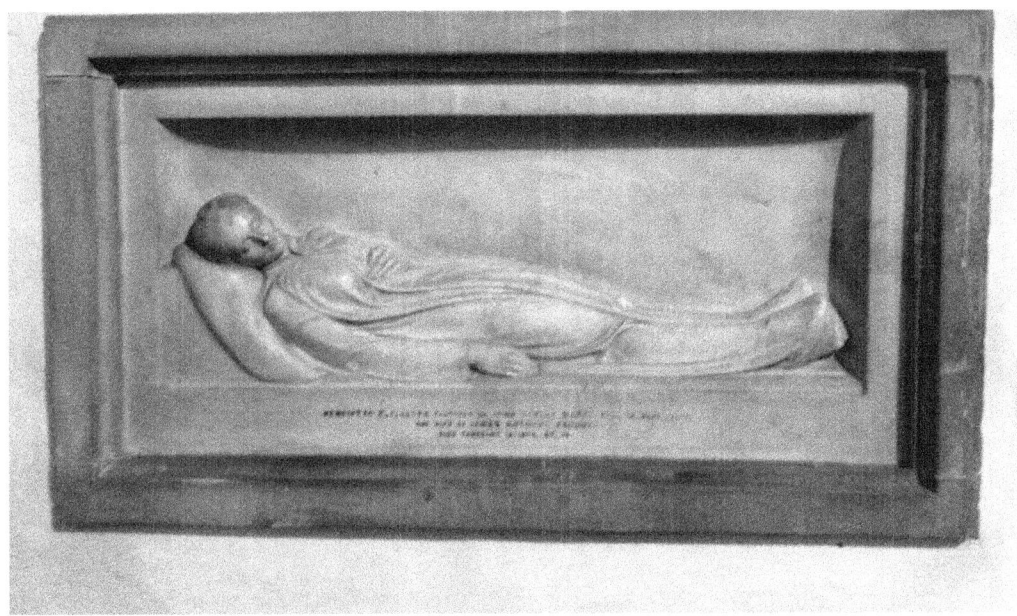

At the west end of the church in the south aisle is the memorial to Samuel Vince. He was born on 9th April 1749 in Suffolk, the youngest of three children born to the village bricklayer. As soon as he was old enough, he started working with his father. One day, when he was twelve, the vicar spotted him taking a break and reading something. Surprised to see a labouring child doing this, the vicar went across and started to talk to him. Finding he was intelligent and keen to learn, the vicar offered to lend him books which Samuel could then study at night. This continued for some time until the vicar was able to secure an opportunity for Samuel to teach in another village. This work enabled him to earn money to help his parents but also to pursue his education. Having been found to be exceptionally good at mathematics, certain generous sponsors came together to send him to St Paul's School in London. From there, he went on to Cambridge where he earned his degrees and carried out research eventually becoming Plumian Professor of Astronomy and Experimental Philosophy in 1796. Samuel's study of nature strengthened his faith in God. He wrote:

> What must be the power of that being who formed and gave motion to the vast bodies which compose the universe? If we

---

[42] *Kent and Sussex Courier*, 17th December 1875

consider the laws by which these bodies are regulated and the admirable harmony and simplicity of the arrangement, we cannot less admire the wisdom than the power of the same Being.

Whoever will examine the structure of the universe, the construction of the animal and vegetable creation and the wonderful provisions that are made for their subsistence, will see such marks of power, design, wisdom and goodness as must force him to acknowledge "This hath God done for us, it is marvellous in our eyes."[43]

Ordained in 1784, Samuel served in various parishes in Norfolk and Lincolnshire before being appointed Archdeacon of Bedford in 1809. He wrote a number of scientific works and lectured extensively on astronomy, hydrostatics, electricity and physics creating works which were to be standard reference sources for generations. A colleague described him as accomplished mathematician and amiable man.[44] He died 28th November 1821 aged 72, a powerful example of how a working class child could advance if given the opportunity and a testimony to the vicar who first took time to help him on his way.

Bells

In 1808, one new bell was purchased from Messrs. Thomas Mears and Son in London and the existing five bells were recast to create a peal of six. They were rehung in September by Messrs. Sweetlove using rope from Nathaniel Austen in Ramsgate and dedicated by the vicar, the Reverend Richard Harvey. The expenses were:

	£	s	d
Bells	144	18	
Hanging	72	10	
Rope	2	2	
Carriage	8	11	
Weighing		5	6
Correspondence		10	
Wharf fees		6	
	229	2	6

The modern equivalent would be around £15,000.[45]

---

[43] Samuel Vince, *The Credibility of Christianity*, (Cambridge, 1798) p.11
[44] Gilbert Wakefield, *Memoirs* vol. 1 (London, 1792) p.134
[45] The figures appear in Cotton op.cit. pp.27-28. He quotes a churchwarden's account which no longer exists so it cannot be seen if there were any other expenses in the project.

On Friday 15th February 1867, during bell ringing practice, the largest bell slipped from its bearings and tumbled to the belfry floor. The newspaper rejoiced in the fact that nobody was hurt and attributed the accident to rotten bearings.[46] Curiously, there is no evidence of work being done to repair or re-hang the bell although this clearly happened.

It may have been safety fears which caused the parish to adopt what was known as the Ellacombe chime system. This meant that the bells were kept permanently up with hammers in each which were connected by rope to a frame. The advantage of the system was that it meant only one person was required to ring as many bells as were connected to the chiming apparatus. This saved the need to find volunteers and reduced the costs to the church since paying one man to ring was clearly cheaper than paying half a dozen. Two accounts exist of this, both from the 1870s. In May 1876, an unimpressed visitor wrote: "Before the commencement of the service the tones of the bells from the old fashioned tower struck on my ears. I thought the frantic bell ringer who tries to play hymns on old, worn out and cracking bells had much better have left that part to the organist and choir inside." His comments elicited an angry response from one of the congregation who said that the single ringer did his best but six bells represented six notes and most hymns used more than that so he just had to try and select the nearest. He added that it was "a thing that is not done on the same principle anywhere else in Kent."[47] Just under a year later, another visitor wrote: "What chimes they are ! Clear and sweet in tone, the bells ring out a joyous welcome to God's house. I may say, without exaggeration, that, with the exception of some of the finer carillons in the old cities of Belgium, it is long since I have heard such ringing. Some three or four hymns are given and are given with faultless precision as to time and tune; not a flat note is to be heard."[48] Whether it was the same ringer is not known but there is no record of any work having been carried out in the intervening time.

The arrival of the Reverend Montague Fowler in 1889 saw renewed interest in the bells.[49] He was an enthusiastic ringer and would later go on to edit the magazine *Church Bells* from 1895 to 1903. In November 1889, just three weeks after his induction, he wrote a letter to the local paper explaining how the church only had five working bells due to the fourth being cracked and saying how they needed money to repair them. He added optimistically that it would be really nice if they could purchase two more bells at the same time:

> The parishioners have borne their part nobly in restoring the
> church and tower and as St Laurence is the mother church of

---

[46] *Kentish Chronicle,* 23rd February 1867, *East Kent Times* 21st February 1867
[47] *Thanet Advertiser,* 13th and 20th May 1876
[48] *Thanet Figaro,* 16th June 1877
[49] His predecessor had shown no interest and was the only clergyman in Thanet to refuse assistance to Stahlschmidt in his study of church bells, Stahlschmidt op.cit. p.387

> Ramsgate and the only church in the immediate district which has a peal of bells, I venture to ask for the assistance (and I feel sure I shall not do so in vain) of all those in Ramsgate and elsewhere who are proud of St Laurence church which had its place in history for centuries before there existed a house between it and the sea.[50]

Mr Fowler did receive one substantial donation in response to his appeal as well as a number of smaller ones and there was the usual range of fund raising activities such as bazaars, concerts and special collections.

In September 1890, he published an update saying that the repairs would cost £120 and they had £85 toward this; two new bells would cost £115 and they had £50 toward that.[51] More money came in but then Mr Fowler had a shock. The estimate had been increased after a further crack had been found in the third bell and changes to the frame would be required to accommodate the additional bells on the same level. The new costs were said to be:[52]

	£	s	d
Bell frame	85	10	0
Rehanging the six bells	36	10	0
Re-casting the cracked fourth	26	10	0
Re-casting the cracked third	23	3	0
Two new bells	75	15	6
Fitting of the new bells	16	0	0
Chiming apparatus	10	0	0
	273	8	6

Undaunted, Mr Fowler continued his fundraising and on May 1st 1891, the entire work was complete and the two new bells were dedicated by the Dean of Canterbury. The new trebles from Messrs. Mears & Stainbank were the gift of John Tyzack Hedley of Durham, a bank manager with no link to the church but who loved bells. The prayer written for the occasion was:

> Grant O Lord that whosoever shall be called by the sound of these bells to Thine house of prayer may enter into Thy gates with thanksgiving and into Thy courts with praise; and grant that they who ring them may give the full services of heart and life and, together with the congregation they summon, may be

---

[50] *Kent Coast Times*, 14th November 1889
[51] *Kent Coast Times*, 11th September 1890
[52] *Kent Coast Times*, 27th November 1890. In today's terms, the amount would be about £27,000

numbered among those blessed ones who, having washed their robes and made them white in the blood of the Lamb, stand before Thy Throne and serve Thee day and night in Thy Temple, through Jesus Christ our Lord.

The next day, the St Laurence ringers together with guests from Faversham, Canterbury and Boughton rang a Thurstans' peal of 5040 Stedman Triples in three hours and eight minutes which *Church Bells* reported was "The first peal in the method by a band resident in the county."[53] Despite having an enlarged peal, it remained the practice to only ring on the first Sunday of the month.

As well as using the church bells, in 1845, the ringers borrowed the handbells from the Six Bells public house and went to the top of the tower where they rang 250 changes bob major style from the battlements to celebrate the anniversary of Queen Victoria's accession. Whether they could be heard at ground level was open to question but they certainly attracted attention as a curious spectacle.[54]

Charities

One feature in the church which is almost totally impossible to see is the list of charitable benefactions. The display of such information is customary and boards were regularly erected from the eighteenth century onwards, not only to highlight the generosity of those who had made bequests but so that the churchwardens could be reminded of their responsibilities and the poor be reassured that the money donated was not being used in other ways. When the Archdeacon visited on June 8th 1824, he was unhappy that no such board existed at St Laurence and he ordered that one be erected in "a prominent place in the church." The board was indeed set up a few weeks later, although whether the porch constituted "a prominent place" is open to question.[55]

Vestry

Although the area once occupied by the Lady Chapel had been turned into a vestry at the Reformation, it was not until 1809 that the room was fully enclosed. On 21st June that year, the church voted to create a fireplace in the south-east corner and to set up

---

[53] *Church Bells*, 15th May 1891.
[54] *Kentish Gazette*, 1st July 1845. In 1902, the Kent County Association of Church Bellringers visited St Laurence to ring 600 Stedman quatres and 364 Stedman cinques on the church's handbells which would suggest that they bought their own set in the late nineteenth century, *Thanet Advertiser* 5th April 1902
[55] Vestry Book

a screen to prevent people walking through. Prior to that date, the vestry would simply have been a curtained off area at the end of the north chancel with people able to walk through as they do today from the side chapel into the high chancel. There was no organ at this date to restrict the view.

Worship

Not only did the church building change dramatically within the nineteenth century but so did the form of worship. In 1800, the church was Protestant, Evangelical and proud of it. The windows were plain glass and aside from a few monuments, there was nothing to distract the attention from the Word of God. The minister wore a plain black cassock to preach. There was no organ or choir, though a group of singers and musicians sat in the west gallery to lead the singing of a metrical psalm at the end of Morning and Evening Prayer. Services otherwise were said rather than sung. The Lord's Supper or Holy Communion was celebrated rarely and when this happened, the minister donned a surplice and stood at the north end of the communion table. The celebration would have followed Morning Prayer and the Litany and those who wished to stay would have stood in the chancel for this part of the service. Not only would getting people to and fro galleries have been impractical but in the days before the railways, few people were eligible to receive due to the difficulties faced by bishops in getting to parishes to confirm them.

By the end of the century, the scene was very different. The service was sung and led by a surpliced choir. Music was provided by the organ and prayers were interspersed with hymns. The pulpit was to the side and the focus was on the communion table which was now adorned with an embroidered frontal and candles and raised up. The minister wore a surplice and stole throughout the service and he entered, together with the choir and Holy Bible, behind a processional cross. The east end of the church was now fully lit and its importance shown by the quality of its furnishings – gleaming brass rail, ornately carved sedilia and painted reredos.

What had happened to cause these changes ? The simple answer is that the church was imbued with Tractarianism, a philosophy that emerged in the 1830s and seeped through the Church doing its best to replace the purity of Reformation worship with revived Catholic ritual. The controversy almost tore the Church of England apart in the nineteenth century and the local papers are full of anti-Catholic and anti-Ritualist protests and meetings. A number of the Tractarian leaders such as Newman decided to join Rome, thereby confirming the fears of Evangelicals that this had been their goal all along. Meanwhile, many disgruntled Evangelicals seeing the Ritualists successfully flout the law without censure from the bishops, joined the Methodists or other Nonconformist churches.

At St Laurence, the first vicar of the nineteenth century was Richard Harvey and he was an Evangelical. He was followed by George Sicklemore who stayed forty-four years. He does not appear to have made many changes in worship, other than introducing an organ, but he did seek to beautify the church with stained glass and gothic features as part of a desire to stress the catholicity of the Anglican faith. Charles Molony introduced a surpliced choir, one of the hallmarks of Tractarianism, but because he was aware that this was not a popular idea, he bizarrely had the surplices worn over ordinary clothes. His successor, Montague Fowler, put the choir into cassocks and implemented considerably more ritual including lit candles on the communion table, frontals and processions.[56] He brought in the Tractarian hymnbook, *Hymns Ancient and Modern* and sung services to Merbecke. He wrote "the dignified ceremonial of the worship of the Anglican church is not a modern innovation but has its origin in the magnificent Jewish ritual, every detail of which was arranged by God Himself." Yet he upheld the Prayer Book regulations with regard to north facing celebration rigidly and condemned the ministers who were prepared "to overstep the limits laid down for the conduct of the services and to go beyond the formularies which have been handed down and endorsed by those who are responsible for the spiritual government of the church." He opposed Roman Catholicism with its confessional, "modern and unscriptural dogmas, claim to spiritual autocracy" and its "false worship and idolatry." Both at St Laurence and in his many books, he always referenced the communion table rather than the altar.[57]

His successors showed less respect for Prayer Book regulations and at the end of the century brought back eastward celebration, something which had not been seen since the middle ages. In the twentieth century, the ritualist trend was to continue with a Sung Eucharist taking over as the main Sunday service and ministers adopting vestments. It reached its zenith in the 1997 Good Friday service at St Laurence advertised as the Mass of the Pre-Sanctified, something definitely not found in the Book of Common Prayer or any other Protestant liturgy.

In 1872 the Act of Uniformity Amendment Act allowed clergy for the first time to hold services which were not in the Book of Common Prayer and this allowed the creation of special afternoon services for different groups.[58] From 7th November 1875, an afternoon service was started at St Laurence by Mr Sicklemore, something made possible not only by the Act but by the installation of gas lighting which enabled Evening Prayer to be said outside the hours of daylight.[59] It is not certain for whom this new service was intended but it is likely that it was children. Mr Fowler, vicar from 1889 to 1893, had services for women on the first Sunday, men on the third and children on the other weeks. His predecessor and successors both had monthly children's services only. Mr

---

[56] Candles were permitted for the purpose of giving light but the introduction of gas lighting had rendered them superfluous in most churches.
[57] Montague Fowler, *Christianity through Judaism* (London 1901) pp. 3,19, 20. His book shows his belief in progressive revelation which explains the apparent paradox of an animal lover praising Temple ritual which was dominated by animal sacrifice.
[58] The same Act also allowed for Holy Communion to be said without Matins and the Litany.
[59] *Thanet Advertiser* 8th November 1873, 23rd October 1875. Evening Prayer was standardised at 6:30pm rather than the previous 3 p.m.

Crosse introduced weekly children's services in the last year of the century. The clergy were restricted to elements of worship which were in either the Holy Bible or the Prayer Book. An example of a children's liturgy is given in the Appendices to show how this worked in practice. Such a restriction did not apply to the Church Army.

CLERGY AND STAFF

At the start of the nineteenth century, the vicar was the Reverend **Richard Harvey**, who until 1821 signed himself as junior to avoid confusion with his father of the same name who had been his predecessor. Richard was born on 5th June 1767 in the vicarage at St Laurence and baptised in the church on 8th June, being thus the second incumbent to be born in the parish.[60] He became vicar of St Laurence a few days after his twenty-sixth birthday in June 1793 following the resignation of his father and held the post until his death aged sixty-eight. The first two decades of his ministry were dominated by the wars with France which totally transformed the parish and his work.

With the arrival of peace, Mr Harvey was able to consider other projects. In 1820, he established a group of subscribers and set up the Ramsgate and St Lawrence Dispensary. This important body survived until the creation of the National Health Service in 1948 and was responsible for the saving and improvement of thousands of lives. In 1824, it was visited by the Princess Victoria and her mother and so became the Royal Ramsgate and St Lawrence Dispensary. By 1857, it had helped over 33,000 people and by 1875, over 58,000. The scheme was a development of that set up by his father in 1767 and involved the more able members of the congregation subscribing a particular sum which was used to secure the attendance of medical practitioners at an office at a certain time. Those who subscribed were given the right to send parishioners to be treated and those in need of medical help had to apply to the subscribers. Not only were poor patients treated for free, but they received medication and the loan of essential items such as spectacles and walking sticks, products which could not only enhance the quality of life but often enable someone to work again.[61] The system was later changed so that application could be made via the office and a small charge was made for medicines. In 1871, a surgeon attended the office in Cavendish Street at 10am each day from Monday to Saturday and a dentist was available from 9am on Wednesdays and Fridays.[62] Regular collections in aid of the Dispensary were held at St Laurence church. It was undoubtedly one of Richard Harvey's most lasting legacies.

A further scheme of his which benefited many and saved lives was the establishment of the Ramsgate and St Lawrence Maternity Charity. The purpose of this

---

[60] The first was Peter Johnson.
[61] *Kentish Gazette*, 4th August 1857, Kent Archives Office R/Ch1
[62] *Thanet Advertiser*, 4th February 1871

was to provide practical assistance to resident married woman who were in need. It loaned clothes and equipment and provided some very basic medical assistance. By the time of its centenary in 1900, it had helped more than ten thousand women.

In 1829, Mr Harvey decided to set up a lending library. This was arranged through the auspices of SPCK and day to day management was vested in the curate. The cost of the books was borne by subscribers, notably William Garrow and John Ashley Warre. They purchased one hundred and twelve books each of which could be borrowed for two weeks and the register of loans shows that most volumes went out around fifteen to twenty times a year. The most popular books were *Travels in Africa*, *Christmas Stories*, *Natural History of Insects*, *Death Bed Scenes* and *Lessons for Young Persons in Humble Life*. Bible commentaries and books about prayer were noticeably less read. The library represents a real attempt to provide reading material for those who were unable to afford books of their own although, in practice, most of those who used the service were gentry and farmers.[63]

Just as his father had recognised the need for greater church provision in the rapidly expanding parish, so Mr Harvey pressed for a new church in Ramsgate. The arrangements for its building understandably occupied the vestry committee for months. Not only were there issues such as how many seats to include and what proportion should be rentable, there were all the complexities of creating a separate parish which would be accountable for its own roads, poor relief and so forth. St George's opened in 1827.[64] The Act of Parliament which established the new parish confirmed upon Mr Harvey the right to receive all fees from the new church, excluding pew rents, for the remainder of his life. He also had the right to appoint the first vicar which he did selecting his son, another Richard Harvey, for the position. The fees would have proved quite lucrative as there were over a thousand burials and five hundred marriages in this period.

Other achievements associated with his ministry include the organisation of Ramsgate's Golden Jubilee celebrations to mark George III's fifty years on the throne, the recasting of the bells in 1808 and the addition of a sixth bell. It is almost certain that he started the Sunday School and quite possible that he introduced hymn singing, previous generations simply having metrical psalms. The chalices used at Christmas Holy Communion also date from his incumbency being a pair from 1833.[65]

In 1806, Mr Harvey had the interesting experience of having the Archbishop of Canterbury resident in his parish for a month's holiday. It must be assumed that the Archbishop worshipped at St Laurence during this time and that Mr Harvey took special care with his sermons on those weeks. Other summer visitors who would have worshipped at St Laurence included in 1805 the Earl and Countess Spencer, g-g-g-

---

[63] CCA-U3-19/7/5. A similar library was set up in the 1968 called the Bray library.
[64] In 1826, the vestry decided to have 2000 seats of which 1200 would be free.
[65] It is unknown how the church came to have these. There is no reference to their purchase in the Vestry Book. It is possible that they were the gift of the Bedford family who are remembered by two tablets on the chancel walls, Thomasine dying in 1833.

grandfather of Diana, Princess of Wales and therefore g-g-g-g-grandfather of HRH Prince William, our future king.[66]

In addition to being vicar, Mr Harvey served as domestic chaplain to the Conyngham family. Baroness Conyngham died in 1814 and is remembered at St Laurence by a tablet now in the Thurstin room and by her hatchment, which is that nearest the font. Her daughter-in-law was the mistress of George IV and her grandson was the man responsible, together with the Archbishop of Canterbury, for breaking the news to Princess Victoria that she was now Queen.[67]

No image of Richard Harvey exists and only one direct comment exists made about him as a person and that stems from Samuel Wesley, nephew of John.[68] He visited the area in 1812 and asked permission to use St Laurence church for a recital. He says that Mr Harvey refused because he was: "afraid of offending the tight-laced part of his congregation by this novelty."[69] Whether Mr Harvey thought the use of the church for a secular concert was likely to be objectionable or the problem was that Wesley had become a Roman Catholic is unknown. The notion of allowing a Catholic within the church would have been deeply unpopular. Catholic emancipation was still some years away and the abuse later heaped upon Pugin showed the level of local hatred. Alternatively, he may have been concerned about the disruption which Wesley would cause bringing in and setting up his organ.

Richard Harvey died on 11th February 1836 in Walcott, Somerset. He had been ill since at least 1824 when the Archbishop permitted him to appoint a curate to minister to the parish on his behalf for two years.[70] An "unfortunate accident" saw him on long term absence again in 1828 and there is also no sign of him taking regular services in the parish between 1829 and 1832. He is remembered on a ledger stone at the rear of the church directly under the west window, though part of it is covered with the wooden platform supporting the pews. Two of his three children died in infancy and are also buried in the church, Richard who died aged ten months having never thrived and William who passed away before he could even be baptised. Another son whom he named Richard survived and went on to become the first vicar of St George's, Ramsgate.

---

[66] *Kentish Gazette* 14th June 1805, 9th September 1806

[67] For a courtier's account of George IV's mistress, see Charles Greville, *A Journal of the Reigns of King George IV and King William IV* (London, 1875) vol 1 p.46

[68] The illustration shows a contemporary clergyman named the Reverend Thomas Stock and gives an idea of how Harvey might have dressed.

[69] Letter from Samuel Wesley to Vincent Novello, dated October 1st. Wesley was staying at 7, Harbour Street and was not impressed by the town. He continued, "all the fine folk being in the habit of prancing about of their palfries and bowling about in their tumbrils for two or three hours after scrubbing their mangey carcases in the sea ... do away any reasonable expectation of their coming to hear our quaverings before dinner time." British Museum in Addit. MSS. 11729

[70] CCA-DCb-F/L/251

Less than a month later, a thirty-year old minister arrived who was to dedicate the rest of his life to the church, **George Wilson Sicklemore**.[71] Information about the changes made to the building under his direction has already been given but we are fortunate in having two accounts of church services during his incumbency. The shorter of the two dates from 1876 when the visitor described the curate's style as "somewhat curt and abrupt but he had a good voice for reading and making himself heard. The whole of the service was conducted by the curate until the communion when it was much relieved by the grand and noble voice of the Vicar who read the Communion and one or two more short prayers in good style. He did not preach the sermon in which I was somewhat disappointed as the monotony of the curate's voice palled on the ear."[72]

Criticism of the curate was also made in the longer account which dates from 1877 which recounts a visit made on June 10th:

> There is a very fair - indeed large - congregation today. Noticeable is the quiet, decent and orderly behaviour of all. True that by the door is a crowd of small children who, after gazing out through the portals upon the bright morning are reminded of flowers to be picked and birds nests to be rifled and are disposed to much blowing of noses and much clattering of feet, but their noise is not obtrusive. The farming element is strongly represented; brown faced hard handed, yet withal well dressed folk, have come in from the country; the neighbouring tradesmen are present with their families; there is a good sprinkling of visitors; and the fair, fresh faces of the girls' school form a pleasing part of the satisfactory congregation.
>
> The chiming of the bell ceases. The organ peals. From the vestry the curate and vicar enter. The former rises in his place: "When the wicked man." Then we rise also. The curate, who wears a moustache, has not a very sympathetic voice. He gets through the service in that perfunctory way to which we have become accustomed, and, which makes even an intoned service a relief. When however, the vicar delivers the first verse of the first lesson, the attention is aroused. There is something in his manner which at once arrests. The lesson for the morning lends itself to dramatic effect. The reader is

---

[71] The speed of his appointment suggests that the demise of Richard Harvey was expected and that the Archbishop had already spoken to George Sicklemore about the role. Mr Sicklemore later arranged a meal for twenty-five elderly parishioners to mark the silver anniversary of his arrival, *Thanet Advertiser*, 2nd March 1861

[72] *Thanet Advertiser*, 13th May 1876

evidently excited by the narrative. He sees the action of the story. He understands the character of the actors. He is with the jaded Sisera when he enters the tent of the deceiver. He anticipates the climax and sees the nail driven through the head of the sleeping victim - through his head and into the ground. There is nothing of the actor in this. The reading is natural and easy. An unsuspected emphasis, an unusual inflexion of the mellow voice, all add to the effect. The second lesson describes Christ's appearance before Pilate. Whether it was my imagination or not, I cannot say, but it appeared to me that the venerable vicar, by a judicious use of emphasis, became the apologist of Pilate. The impossibility of acting in opposition to the demands of the domineering Hebrews seems more evident than it usually does. The magisterial instincts are strong in him now. In Pilate's place he feels he could scarcely have done otherwise. And when the final shout of "Away with him ! Crucify him !" is sent up, the reader raises his voice and produces a dramatic and even sensational effect.

I have not yet seen the vicar. An inconvenient pillar is between me and him. When he ascends the stone steps of the pulpit, however, I have a full view. The Rev. G. W. Sicklemore, M.A., the Vicar of St Laurence, is a man who has passed the grand climacteric of life. His face is benevolent. As a Justice of the Peace one would expect his sentences to be tempered with mercy. He has a clean shaven and ruddy face. There is an appearance of health and an enjoyment of the same about him. Here clearly is no ascetic - not one given to deplore the fact of living among a perverse generation and in a wicked world; but, rather, one who can give thanks for God's good gifts and enjoy them. His manner in the pulpit is at once easy and dignified. There is a dash of the old school about him - of the best characteristics of the old school. If I were asked by an artist or novelist to point out to him my *beau idéal* of a village pastor, I would conduct him to this old church with its memories of centuries upon it, and tell him to study for his canvas the clergyman who is now talking to his flock about the "ministry of reconciliation."

The merit of the vicar's sermon is its simplicity. There is no attempt at startling effect. Once, and once only, does he indulge in a figure of speech. The intense pathos of that sad wail raised by the Israelites who sat down by the waters of Babylon, he compares to the song of the nightingale when robbed of its young. His quotations are nearly all from the Bible or from the Liturgy. Once he quoted from the "judicious Hooker." and once he alluded to St Ambrose and St Augustine. His style is flavoured by a study of the Fathers. Phrases like "comfortable privilege" are frequently put into requisition. His hatred for the Arians is undisguised. There is no laboured argument - no metaphysical subtlety - no polemical hair-splitting. It is simply an appeal to his congregation to study the form of worship prescribed for them. He dwells on its beauty. He points out its sufficiency. Emotionally he prays that the Church may never be robbed of it. There is, perhaps, no brilliancy about this, but it is easy to understand.

Having urged the claims of the Liturgy, he leans over the pulpit. There is a necessity for pecuniary support, or a weekday service will have to be abandoned. This appeal is pleasantly put, without any of that objectionable hat in the hand business so common now in appealing for charities. The work of supporting the church is not only a duty, but a comfortable privilege even. Such is the view submitted to the parishioners of St Laurence.

Now the scriptural encouragements to subscribers are read from the altar. As the congregation stands, as the silks rustle, as the collectors go round with their little money bags. The congregation kneels. Again the impressive and mellifluous tones of the vicar succeed to the less successful elocution of his martial looking curate. The benediction. The devotional pause. The burst of the Hallelujah Chorus from the organ. We emerge from the dim light of the church and stand once more in the little graveyard, with the summer scents all about us, and the hot reflection of the sun dazzling our eyes as it is flung back from the chalky road.[73]

The cartoon published with the account represents the first published image of a Vicar of St Laurence.

With regard to worship, Mr Sicklemore introduced Harvest Festival to the church, although the stress seemed to be less on giving thanks for God's gifts to humanity and more about preparing for the

---

[73] *Thanet Figaro*, 16th June 1877. The readings show it was the second Sunday after Trinity.

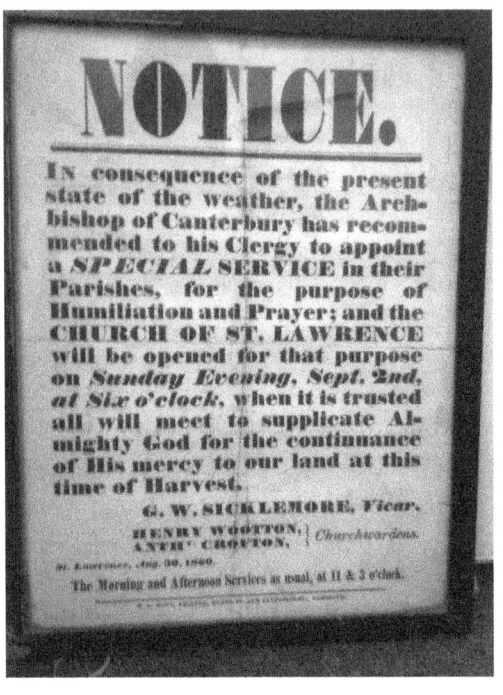

final harvesting of souls and the need to be prepared for judgment.[74] There were also occasional days of prayer, some set up locally and some nationally. A flyer for one of these hangs in the vestry today. Another was held on Friday 14th August due to "prevailing sickness and mortality."[75]

Not content with his work at St Laurence, Mr Sicklemore planted churches in other areas which resulted in changes to the parish boundary. They included Holy Trinity in 1845 and St Luke in 1875. He also gave the land for a church at Manston and a school as well as land for the Methodist Chapel at Acol.[76] In addition, he was a busy magistrate and a substantial landowner. His wife Catherine had inherited Cleve Court and Nethercourt and on 28th January 1853, he received permission to move to the latter which was within the parish.[77] He remained at this address for the rest of his life, the vicarage being let.[78] Census returns show that his household staff generally consisted of two housemaids, a cook, a coachman, a footman, as well as various nursery staff when his children were younger. There was also a lodge keeper, gardener and an array of agricultural staff. Ever the keen builder, Mr Sicklemore added orchards and a conservatory to Nethercourt and before that, stables to the vicarage.

The breadth of the vicar's role at this period was much wider than it is today since the parish was an active unit of local government. The vestry book shows considerable time being spent discussing the roads, drainage, what to do about crumbling cliffs at Pegwell and street lighting. This last issue created a controversy which ran for some months and generated considerable coverage in the newspapers as people argued about where it might be needed, what sort of lights to buy, and who should pay for it. Residents of Manston and Haine, for example, objected to being charged for a service they did not want and no change could be made to the rate without a vote being held and at

---

[74] *Thanet Advertiser*, 28th September 1867. The services took place annually, ordinarily mid September though sometimes at the end of August.
[75] *Kentish Gazette*, 18th August 1849
[76] *Thanet Advertiser* 16th February 1867, CCA-U3-239/6/B/1, *Whitstable Times* 24th April 1875
[77] CCA-DCb-F/L/699
[78] It was rented for some years by the barrister and JP Anthony Crofton to whom a memorial window once existed in the church but this was destroyed in the Second World War.

least two thirds of the ratepayers giving their consent.⁷⁹ There were disputes about pavements and where to put them, how wide they should be, and how much to spend. In 1875, a group was set up particularly to look at sanitation, it being said that the parish was a risk to health. The vestry was also involved in arranging rosters for constables, dealing with break ins, preservation of the sea wall and in January 1845 debated the likelihood of accidents as horses were being frightened by the new trains. The parish was involved in poor relief and barely two months after Mr Sicklemore's arrival, it voted to set aside £30 "for defraying the expenses of emigration of poor persons having settlement in this parish and being willing to emigrate."⁸⁰

With regard to personality, Mr Sicklemore seems to have been a kind man. He opposed the idea of closing the churchyard because he said that it was important that the poor should be able to bury their dead locally – where he had discretion with regard to fees – and so they had no expense in visiting their graves. In September 1871, he arranged for a man who was too ill to continue work to have an exhibition of models he had made at the parish infants school with a view to raising enough money to keep him and his family out of the workhouse. He persuaded the vestry to accept a change to the rating system so that bills for lower value properties were sent to the owners rather than the tenants which meant that poorer people would not have to suddenly find a single large sum for rates and risk high court fees for non-payment, but rather that the charge would be factored into their weekly rent.⁸¹ He opened his gardens at Cleve Court on one day a year to raise money for charity.⁸² He also gave up an area of his glebe and had it transformed into allotments so that poor working men could have a chance to grow food for their families.⁸³

George Wilson Sicklemore died early in the morning of 19th February 1880 aged seventy-six. He had been vicar of St Laurence for forty-four years and Rural Dean for seven. His death was not unexpected. He had had a stroke in the summer of 1879 from which he had appeared to make a good recovery but there had been a relapse just before Christmas. His funeral saw the entire village come to a standstill as the shops closed and crowds came out to watch the lengthy procession wend its way up the hill from Nethercourt. There were representatives from the judicial bench in attendance, from the Liberal party of which he was local chairman, from the Freemasons and the Foresters of which he was an active member. The obituary recalled his "sound judgment and practised common sense" and spoke of the miles he would go to do a kind deed and the fact that nobody had ever heard him speak ill of anyone. The vicar of St Peter's said that

---

⁷⁹ In particular see *Thanet Advertiser* reports of 29th May, 5th June, 24th July and 21st August 1869
⁸⁰ Vestry Book, 28th April 1836. There is no record of any payments being made from this fund. The expectation was that it would be cheaper to pay a family to leave than to maintain them for many years, something that would have been inevitable in the case of those too sick ever to work.
⁸¹ *Thanet Advertiser*, 16th September 1871, 8th February 1873, 1st April 1876
⁸² *Thanet Advertiser*, 12th June 1875
⁸³ CCA-U3-19/6/7

"to young and old, rich and poor, high and low, he was ever the same, ever courteous and kind, ever affable and sympathetic, ever genial and ready to cheer."[84] He was laid to rest in the new part of the churchyard against the wall in a plot which was once part of his vicarage garden. His parishioners were so upset by his loss that they raised funds to erect a stained glass window in his honour, something he would have been sure to appreciate.

Mr Sicklemore had once said that he loved St Laurence so much that he was sure that if they opened him up after death, they would find it written on his heart – an allusion to Bloody Mary's claim to have Calais on hers. He said that there was no life, in his opinion, so blessed as that of a "quiet, peaceful country clergyman" and that he gave thanks daily that "his lot had been cast among those who would listen to God's servant when he exhorted them to pray to Him."[85]

The task of following a vicar who was so much loved and who had been incumbent for so long, was not going to be an easy task for anyone. The person appointed was the Reverend **Charles Molony**, aged 53, who arrived in May. One of his first tasks was to find somewhere to live since the vicarage was said, after years of being rented out, to be in too bad a state of repair to be habitable. He moved into 14 West Cliff Terrace with

his young wife and three children where his fourth child, a daughter, was born only a few days later. The old vicarage was demolished and a new vicarage built at the bottom of Manston Road, the site now occupied by St Lawrence Court. The new property was larger than the old one with fifteen rooms.[86] It was built of red brick and had a tiled roof.[87]

---

[84] *Kent Coast Times*, 26th February 1880
[85] *Thanet Advertiser* 27th May 1876, 28th September 1867
[86] 1911 census. This excluded bathrooms, lobbies and offices.
[87] It was said on 19th June 1958 that it had been built "by an Irish parson with fourteen children" but this was untrue. Molony was not Irish and he had four children when he arrived in the parish. He went on to have three more, one of which died aged eleven months. The source for the statement

Mr Molony set about modernising the parish. In 1881, the church signed a twenty year lease on two rooms in 8 Hart Terrace which were set up as the Parochial Office. This was used by the overseers for the poor as well as by the churchwardens for the storage of records and completion of registers and accounts.[88] In 1885, the Parish Hall was built and also a new infants school.

In his first year in the parish he started the Parochial Report. This was an annual publication which included the vicar's review of the year showing what had been achieved and his goals for the coming period. It also contained details of services, numbers of communicants and a full set of accounts for each of the parish funds.

He set up a branch of the Church of England Missionary Society in December 1881. A lover of music, he established two bands for boys, one being for school age children in 1882 and the other, a drum and fife band for working lads, in November 1881. During 1883 he set up Bible study classes for young people. In order that these classes be conducted in an orderly manner with members not being distracted from their studies, the boys and girls met on different days and in different places. Classes for adults began a year later, also single sex with the women meeting in the vicarage whilst the men were in the church. In February 1883 he began a branch of the Church of England Temperance Society complete with Band of Hope for children at St Laurence and another at Manston, the former attracting 115 members in its first year, the latter 21. He was also happy to report that these initiatives had resulted in more children becoming associated with the church and that the Sunday School had grown from 210 members at the start of 1884 to 297 in 1885.

He started a fund to improve the organ in 1881, work completed eighteen months later. He had new hymnbooks bought and had the organ moved from the side chapel to the north chancel. The choir were also brought together instead of sitting in different parts of the building and surpliced.

Mr Molony devoted considerable effort to improving and maintaining the church building. In 1883 the high churchyard wall was replaced with an iron fence whilst funds were raised for the lower wall seen today and for new railings which cost £145.[89] New paths were laid out in the churchyard and a new gate at Manston Road for £25. It was said that the churchyard was so overgrown that it was impossible to even see where the paths had been earlier in the century and which appear so clearly on prints of that time.

His major project was the tower restoration of 1887-88. The opportunity was taken of the church being closed to re-plaster the naves and aisles, to clean and repair the pillars and mural monuments, to re-stain and varnish the pews, to re-lay floor tiles and some of the ledger stones, to re-set the font, to clean and repair the clock and to install new gas heating. In line with parish policy as much as possible of the work was done by firms within the area. The builder and the stone came from St Lawrence, the clock repairs

---

which was made by the Diocesan architect in the Dilapidation report is unknown but totally untrue.
[88] Vestry book, 6th January 1882.
[89] The railings were removed in the summer of 1942 as part of the war effort.

and gas installation from Ramsgate.[90]

Keen to ensure that the Gospel was spread throughout the parish, Mr Molony began working with the deaf asylum located in the house known as Upper Court in High Street, St Lawrence. On 19th October 1886, the church presented thirty-five candidates to the Bishop of Dover for confirmation eight of whom were totally deaf and dumb and gave their assent through sign language and nine of whom were able to follow the service by lip reading and speak for themselves.[91]

To the same end, he also introduced a visitation system. In the early nineteenth century, a minister named Thomas Chalmers had been concerned at the lack of church contact amongst his parishioners in Glasgow. He devised a scheme whereby the area was divided up into twenty-five sections which each contained sixty to a hundred families. To each section, a visitor was appointed who would call house to house on a weekly basis – or more frequently depending on need – to ascertain requirements and to spread news of church activities. Chalmers system was later described in detail in his book, *The Christian and Civic Economy of Large Towns*, and became very influential. Mr Molony based his system at St Laurence on this although he found it difficult to obtain the necessary volunteers for it to work effectively.[92] The District Visitors would continue to function in the parish until the late 1920s when they were replaced by a Relief Committee barring a spell during the incumbency of the Reverend Robert Payne-Smith from 1893-1899.

Acutely aware of the poverty in the parish, Mr Molony set up a series of Provident clubs most of which were to last until the Second World War. These all operated on the same principle in that a person contributed a certain amount each week and at the end of the year, the parish rewarded them with a dividend which was funded by the donations of other members of the congregation. For example, members of the clothing club got two pence for every shilling deposited up to a maximum of two shillings. The system enabled the worst off in the parish to save for expensive items like coal and shoes.[93] Such clubs were made possible by the Parish Hall which acted as the receiving centre for members and in some cases the distribution centre. Supporting her husband's efforts, Mrs Molony set up a maternity charity to help expectant mothers and a blanket charity to loan blankets to those who might otherwise perish from hyperthermia. The Molony family's arrival in the parish co-incided with that of Lady Rose Weigall and together they set up Mothers' Meetings which took place weekly from November to March in Manston and at the Parish Hall with the view of educating mothers on how best to care for their babies. Although sometimes decried by modern liberal historians as paternalistic, there is no doubt that they filled a need. Lower life expectancy meant many

---

[90] *Kent Coast Times* 22nd November 1888, *Thanet Advertiser*, 17th November 1888.
[91] It is possible that one of his family was deaf which would explain his ministry in this area, though there is no such evidence on any census return. None of his predecessors or successors seem to have had the same communication ability.
[92] He refers in his first *Parochial Report* to the vacancies. Chalmers book was published in 1826.
[93] Parochial Reports show the clubs each had between one and two hundred members each year.

women started a family without having their own mother to help and a lot of women could not read even if they had been able to afford childcare books. Particular attention was focussed on issues like the need to settle baby down separately, even if that meant in a drawer or a shoebox, since countless infants were smothered every year by their mother taking them into bed then accidentally rolling over on top of them.[94] Another subject was trying to help the mothers learn how to interpret and deal with a crying infant, the usual solution otherwise being a dose of opium which was cheap and easily available.[95] The meetings were not only educational. They began with prayers, a hymn and a Bible reading which gave women who might not be able to attend church on Sunday morning an opportunity for worship. They included the reading of a novel whilst the ladies sewed or knitted, providing them with some entertainment. They offered fellowship to the women and gave the church a chance of encouraging them to bring children for baptism or to family services or Sunday School and to tell them about other projects such as the provident clubs and the maternity charities.[96]

Mr Molony was a keen historian and spent considerable time trying to map the churchyard and record inscriptions. In 1886 he came up with the theory of the sculptured legend at St Laurence, a notion his friend Charles Cotton loyally supported, despite nobody else being convinced that heads carved in different centuries and different parts of the building were designed as part of a sequence.[97] He was also the man supposedly responsible for the town motto *salus naufragis, salus aegis* i.e. safety for the shipwrecked and health to the sick.

In 1889, Mr Molony announced that he was retiring to Canterbury. He was sixty-three at the time and wrote that the previous two winters had shown him that the parish needed a younger man. He spent his retirement in historical research and working for the Church Defence Institution, a Tory group committed to opposing political interference in church matters.[98] He died in May 1894 and was buried at St Martin's.

The Archbishop did indeed select a younger man for St Laurence, his very own chaplain, the Reverend **Montague Fowler**. Known as Monty, he was then thirty years of age and a newly married man. Ordained at Canterbury Cathedral in 1883, he had no experience of working in parish ministry other than the year he had spent in Kensington as a deacon, but his knowledge of the international Christian community and church politics after ten years travelling the world with the Archbishop was unrivalled. What he

---

[94] Elizabeth Hansen, 'Overlaying in 19th Century England', *Human Ecology* vol.7, no.4 (1979) pp. 333-352; Deborah Gorham, *The Victorian Girl and the Feminine Ideal* (London, 2012) p.67

[95] Anthony S. Wohl, *Endangered lives: public health in Victorian Britain* (Harvard, 1983) pp.34-36

[96] For more on mothers' meetings in general see F Prochaska, 'A Mother's Country', *History* vol. 74 (January, 1989) pp.379-399

[97] Charles Molony, 'A Sculptured Legend at St Laurence Church', *Archaeologia Cantiana* vol. 16 (1886) pp.207-208

[98] *Thanet Advertiser*, 19th May 1894; M. J. D. Roberts, 'Pressure Group Politics and the Church of England', *Journal of Ecclesiastical History* vol. 35 no 4 (October 1984) pp. 560-582.

lacked in pastoral experience he made up for in enthusiasm and he was to give St Laurence a new breadth of vision. Years later, Canon Norwood was to say of him: "a most remarkable man. I'm surprised they did not make him Prime Minister!"

Mr Fowler's induction took place on October 24th 1889. The Rural Dean referred to the recent troubles in the parish and told the congregation: "There has been far too much dissension and standing aloof. A house divided against itself cannot stand. Be at peace, be at unity, work together, strive together, pray together: do everything in common to the glory of God. Rally round your new vicar, help him and co-operate with him. He has a difficult post to fulfil and will need all your sympathy and help." He then described Monty as "a young man full of earnestness and zeal" before announcing the hymn, 'Through the night of dark and sorrow.'[99]

Mr Fowler was aware of the hornet's nest he was inheriting and had already sent a letter at his own expense to everyone which read:

> By the time that this letter is in your hands, I hope to be in a position to call myself your Vicar. This will be the case as soon as I have been instituted to the living by the Archbishop. The Institution is not merely a legal ceremony, It is a solemn commitment of trust by the bishop of the diocese to the Incumbent. To your pastor is committed by the bishop the "cure and government of the souls of the parishioners." It is in the strength and with the promised support of the great head of the Church, Our Lord Jesus Christ, that I undertake a charge so grave, so solemn, so full of responsibility. It will be my constant aim and my earnest prayer, as long as I am permitted to remain among you, to be in the true sense of the word, your minister. I shall strive in the words of the Prayer Book to be a "messenger, watchman and steward of the Lord: to teach and to premonish, to feed and provide for the Lord's family: to seek for Christ's sheep that are dispersed abroad and for His children who are in the midst of this world that they may be saved by Christ for ever." It will be my aim to preach and to teach the faith of Christ crucified and to show how, through the guidance of the Holy Spirit, that faith has been handed down to His Church through centuries of vicissitudes and difficulties.
>
> I shall be always ready to see and advise, to the best of my ability, any parishioner who seeks my counsel, in temporal as in spiritual affairs. I shall look to you, and I know I may do so with confidence, to give me your hearty and loyal support and co-operation. I know how many among you have for years

---
[99] *Kent Coast Times*, 31st October 1889

devoted time and strength to the work of the church in this parish but I need hardly remind you that there is always room for those who are willing to do something for Christ among their neighbours and I look forward to the time when nearly everyone in the parish will be in some way employed in working for the Master.

It may be that certain alterations in the services and modifications of the existing use will be made. I shall take care at the proper time to explain the meaning of such changes and to show you the reasons for making them.

We all know how from time to time dissensions among Church people have given occasion to the enemies of the Lord. The greatest source of weakness in the Church today, which counteracts so much of her noble and self-denying work, is want of unity. I look to you to join with me in showing to the diocese and to the Church at large, the power and influence of a parish united around the cross of Christ: united in the acceptance of one Lord one faith, one baptism: united in one holy bond of truth and peace, of faith and charity: so that we may with one mind and one mouth glorify our Heavenly Father.

I hope as soon as I come among you to sketch out a plan of work, classes and such for the winter but it will not be necessary to trouble you with any details in this letter.

My dear wife is looking forward with interest to her share of the work and she hopes, as I do, that before long we shall know each parishioner personally. But I am sorry to say that for some time she has been in the doctors' hands. Her own medical man and a London physician whom I have consulted about her both insist that for the next two months she must avoid all fatigue and anxiety and keep absolutely quiet. This is a great disappointment to us both but if she neglects their warning there is a danger that her heart, from which she is at present suffering, may be permanently affected.

Believe me always your affectionate Vicar and friend

Montague Fowler[100]

---

[100] *Thanet Advertiser*, 19th October 1889. His wife Ada was twenty-five. The couple had married on 8th January 1889.

It was a letter which was to prove typical of the man demonstrating his determination, energy, genuine care for people and own powers of articulation. He intended to lead from the front.

Less than three weeks after arriving in the parish, Monty launched an appeal for money to restore the bells. As a keen ringer himself, he had been horrified upon ascending the belfry a few days after moving into the vicarage to find that the bells were not in sound condition, despite having a beautifully refurbished tower in which to hang. By 1891, the church had two new bells, a new frame and the cracked bell had been recast.

Something else which he said struck him forcefully when he arrived was that there was no meeting place for men or boys. Instead the boys "seemed to have escaped the hold of the church and taken possession instead – often at very late hours of the evening – of the streets of the village which did not tend much to the comfort of the inhabitants." He suggested establishing something and was told by senior members of his congregation that he had no chance of raising the money so soon after the tower restoration and he should leave the idea. Monty prayed about it and decided to go ahead in faith. Having raised £40 in the first week, he ordered an iron building from Humphrey and Co in London for £191 10s which was duly delivered in January 1890. The building was erected on the ground in front of the Parish Hall and had a room for men at one end, for boys at the other and a reading room between. A coffee tavern was attached between the new building and the hall.[101] Donations of board games and books were made, Monty

---

[101] The iron building covered the site later occupied by the Fire Escape building and must have extended up to the Hall itself with the coffee tavern probably being linked to the plumbing there.

and Mr Lawrence clubbed together to buy a stove, and various people gave subscriptions to different newspapers ranging from the *Morning Post* to the *Illustrated London News*. The parish Temperance Society gave an urn whilst ladies contributed a wide range of cups, saucers, milk jugs etc. The clubrooms were opened on 28th January by Countess Granville and soon proved very popular – too popular in fact. The men who joined seeking the chance to go to read and smoke found themselves interrupted by the noise being made by the lads at the other end with their bagatelle and boisterous games and in October 1890, the boys were removed.[102] The project was significant not just for demonstrating what the *Kent Coast Times* called Mr Fowler's "indefatigable energy" but because it was aimed at meeting the needs of the users instead of merely providing church literature. It provided regular daily newspapers rather than just missionary magazines, books about mechanics and history and good quality novels instead of Bible commentaries and volumes of sermons. With no public library at the time, it provided an excellent way for a working man to better himself as well as find some peace and quiet in a warm, teetotal atmosphere.

The issue of what to do with the boys was regarded as urgent. Mr Fowler would have been aware of the report published the year he came to the parish which reported that seventy per cent of young people left the church when they reached thirteen and left school.[103] Nationally, concern had led to the formation of the Boys' Brigade in 1883 and the rise of the Muscular Christianity movement which sought to portray the man of faith as being strong and rugged rather than emotional and weak, characteristics which were then associated with effeminacy and Catholicism. It also had the goal of encouraging boys to take an active part in building up their community and country through service rather than retreating into asceticism or a life of dissipation.[104] Mr Fowler's response to the problem at St Laurence was to occupy the boys in two ways, through music and sport. Both activities involved discipline and working together in a team and were seen as encouraging respect for self and others, an appreciation of God's gifts and the development of character. Mr Molony's drum and fife band was enlarged and re-organised and a brass band started in 1889. In 1891, the former had twenty members and the latter ten. Instruments were purchased by the church and remained their property though uniforms were bought by the boys if they were able or subsidised by the church if not. To avoid disturbing local residents, they practised at Southwood in the iron building which doubled up as a soup kitchen in winter. At Easter 1892, Mr Fowler started a bugle

---

Although no floor plans or photographs exist, it must have been a reasonable size since it was also used for Sunday School classes where some forty to fifty children were present.
[102] Montague Fowler, *A Record of Church Work*, (Ramsgate, 1890) pp.42-43. The building was finally paid for in 1893.
[103] *Thanet Advertiser*, 9th November 1889
[104] For further discussion on this see Nick Watson et.al. 'The Development of Muscular Christianity in Victorian Britain and beyond', *Journal of Religion and Society* vol.7 (2005) pp. 1-20 and Michael Rosenthal, *The Character Factory*, (London 1986)

band and set up a branch of the Church Lads Brigade which formed a further brass band of its own, raising all the money for its own instruments. The bands put on concerts and took part in civic events such as the November 5th town carnival where they marched proudly through the streets with the vicar at their head.[105]

Of the Lads Brigade, Mr Fowler said: "It aims, by means of drilling, cricket and football clubs, gymnasium, dumb-bell exercise, to provide healthy and attractive amusement for the members and by means of Bible class, church parade and personal intercourse with the vicar and officers to help the lads spiritually."[106] Eighty lads turned up to the first meeting and within six months numbers had doubled and there were three companies. In establishing the organisation in the parish, Mr Fowler was showing his awareness of national developments for the Church Lads Brigade had only been formed in October 1891.[107] The parish corps was one of the earliest in England.

Girls were clearly not regarded as a problem so no similar group was established for them. Both boys and girls were able to join the Band of Hope which aimed at promoting the teetotal lifestyle through a range of educational activities, songs, magic lantern shows and excursions. When Mr Fowler arrived, the Band of Hope had ninety members and the adults branch – the Church of England Temperance Society – had forty-six. A year later and the adult members had risen to fifty-four and the children to one hundred and ninety-one.[108]

There was also a new branch at Manston. Given that Mr Fowler himself took an active role in the meetings, much of the credit for this belongs to him. The reason why abstinence was seen as so important was not simply because everyone was aware of the families blighted by alcoholism, the wives and children battered by drunken fathers, but because it was believed that the money saved could be used for good. The local newspaper explained that Ramsgate spent £87,300 per annum on alcohol each year - £10,300,000 in today's terms. This would:[109]

---

[105] *Kent Coast Times*, 5th November 1891; *Parish Magazine*, July 1892

[106] *Parish Magazine*, May 1892. The drilling was to be with rifles although the parish did not immediately have the funds to provide these having chosen to spend the money on sports equipment and musical instruments first.

[107] It was started by Walter Gee in Fulham.

[108] *Parochial Report, 1890* p.50. In 1891, the Band of Hope passed the two hundred mark.

[109] *Thanet Advertiser*, 9th November 1889

	£
Keep 150 publicans in comfort for one year	30,000
Employ 50 men for one whole year	15,600
Provide 1000 suits for men, 1000 for women, 1000 for boys and 1000 outfits for girls	8,500
Endow 12 churches	6,000
Provide a park to benefit all	5,500
Provide a pension for 200 old people for a year	5,200
Provide school education for everyone in Ramsgate	5,200
Give to 1000 poor families – a ton of coal, a sack of potatoes, a sack of flour and a blanket each	4,850
Pay the rent of 155 houses	2,825
Feed 1000 children for the three months of winter	1,625
Maintain the Infirmary and Sailors' Home for a year	1,000
Total	87,300

Other groups meeting in the parish included the Sunday Schools, Bible classes and groups for mothers. In a move to support men or boys who sought to better themselves, he volunteered to arrange classes in any technical subject if requested. He also set up a Help Yourself Society the members of which contributed a sum of their choosing each week and at the end of the year received 2s 5d for every pound deposited – a very generous rate of 12% interest at a time when inflation was under 1%. The Society also offered small loans to people in temporary distress, for example when sickness prohibited work or a death created a sudden need for money for funeral expenses.

He continued the restoration of the church and much of the furniture seen today dates from his time. This includes the lectern, pulpit, choir stalls, litany desk, churchwarden's wands, processional cross, weathervane as well as the crosses and candlesticks which ordinarily stand on the communion tables. He was responsible too for purchasing the two paintings of the church interior created by Miss Sicklemore around 1850 plus the table used in the side chapel and for exposing the fine waggon roof in the chancel. In order to create a clearer vision of the east end from the nave he removed the pews from under the tower. The font was moved from its position beside the south east door near the side chapel to stand on the left of the south west porch. Within the said porch, the medieval windows which had been bricked up were opened out and glazed, a light was fitted and the cupboard which had effectively blocked its usage was removed. This work, in September 1892, saw the medieval porch become the main entrance to the church, something which it had not been for three decades.[110] His expressed aim was: "To restore to a condition in which for many centuries to come St Laurence will stand a living and speaking witness to the continuity of our branch of the holy catholic Church and of the abiding presence of the Son of God within her."[111]

This same objective affected his outlook on worship. At his direction, frontals were made in different liturgical colours for the communion table. From the Reformation until 1880, it had just been covered with a fair linen cloth, and since then with a plain dark cloth.[112] He introduced *Hymns Ancient and Modern* and cassocks for the choir at Christmas 1889. Something which is taken for granted today but which was seen as radical at the time was his introduction of a processional cross. Processions had been banned at the Reformation and they remained forbidden outside the confines of cathedrals except where the Bishop had given permission. Since the Reverend Charles Cowland-Cooper applied for a faculty to retrospectively allow the use of a processional cross in 1928, it may be assumed that Monty either never asked the Bishop or he did not get consent in writing.[113] In 1891, he thanked church members who had accepted the changes having been "accustomed to greater simplicity in the service."

With regard to services, he introduced an 8a.m weekly celebration of Holy Communion from Lent 1890 in place of the usual once a month evening service. This early celebration of the eucharist on Sundays has been held ever since and is regarded as normal although it was not so at the time. Mr Fowler said that it was the duty of every confirmed person to avail themselves of the opportunities of receiving the Holy Comunion, to say prayers morning and evening, to attend church at least once very Sunday, to kneel during the prayers, to join heartily in the singing and responses, and to be quiet and reverent throughout the service. Regarding the time of day, he asked: "Which practice is most likely to conduce to a worthy reception of this highest Christian privilege, coming to the Holy Communion with the mind fresh and undisturbed by the worries and anxieties of the day or coming with brain and spirit alike weary when the mind is worn out and distracted. The essence of the service is sacrifice – the offering of ourselves, body, soul and spirit to Almighty God. Ought we to give Him of our best or to offer only that which remains after the world has claimed its share of our spiritual life?"[114]

He decided to have Matins and Evening Prayer in the church daily so that all

---

[110] *Parish Magazine*, October 1892

[111] Miss Astle had promised to donate an east window also but she died in the 1891 influenza epidemic which also killed the widow of Mr Sicklemore. Mr Fowler also planned to re-establish the side chapel but both of these ideas were to be implemented by his successors.

[112] The re-introduction of altar frontals was regarded as a revival "after the Roman use" and not universally popular, *Kent Coast Times*, 9th January 1890. The red frontal was restored in 1970 and continues to be used.

[113] CCA/DCb-E/F/St Lawrence in Thanet/ 20

[114] *Parochial Report, 1890* pp.8, 29, 60. His sentiments reflect Oxford Movement influence but he remained an Anglican, always for example referring to the communion table and not the altar and celebrating in surplice and stole not vestments. Evening celebrations were regarded as Low Church.

could come to pray rather than these rites just be part of the vicar's own private devotions. This decision met with objections to which he responded: "It is difficult to realise the point of view of those who not only abstain from coming themselves but criticise us for offering our daily sacrifice of prayer and praise to Almighty God."[115] Another innovation was the prayer meeting designed "to strengthen our hands for the conflict with vice and indifference by the force of intercession." He spoke of the "evil influences" that surrounded the parish and noted how some "of those who come forward to seek the sevenfold gifts of the Spirit have to meet with considerable opposition. A terrible responsibility rests on all who thus place a stumbling block in the way of those who are striving after the truth." He wrote:

> I would urge all Church people and especially our Communicants to remember that their lives cannot be hidden and that a solemn responsibility rests upon them to show forth in their daily walk and conversation the example of a life lived in the presence of the Lord Jesus. Let them be regular in attending the house of God and reverent in their worship: let them avail themselves of the opportunities of receiving the Holy Communion: let their conduct throughout he week be consistent with their profession of Christianity. This can only come by the strength granted us through regular and heartfelt prayer. Our morning and evening prayers must never be omitted or shortened.[116]

Nor did he confine his attention to St Laurence. He increased services at Manston and established in December 1889 a Church Club and Reading Room in the old armoury of the Coastguard Pegwell for worship, talks and entertainments. Concerned about the ability of people to get to church in bad winter weather, at Lent 1890 he began services at Haine using a Mission Room built for the purpose by Mr Warre at the bailiff's house, something which lasted until the First World War.

The impact of his work could be seen in the size of the congregation which it was noted had greatly increased. During the winter months, the congregation was around three hundred but during the warmer weather, it was between four hundred and fifty and five hundred with there being standing room only some weeks. Communicants had more than doubled although it remained the case that less than ten per cent of the congregation took communion.[117] There were a number of reasons for this. Some people did not receive because they had never been confirmed but others preferred the simplicity

---

[115] *Parochial Report, 1890* p.6
[116] *Parochial Report, 1890* pp.8-9
[117] Parochial Reports show 85 communicants per month in 1888, 189 in 1892. Of the approximately forty people who received each week, over two thirds did so at 8a.m.

of Matins to the ceremonial of Holy Communion. Many people seem to have believed that taking Communion was an act so holy that it should only be a once in a lifetime experience. Both the Book of Common Prayer and 1 Cor 11:27-29 did warn that those who received unworthily were making themselves as guilty as those who had called for Our Lord's crucifixion and were eating and drinking their own damnation so it is not surprising that many were unwilling to take the risk. Probably the majority saw no reason to either get up early and go to two services on Sunday morning or stay after Matins when they wanted their lunch. Anglican teaching had always said that only those intending to receive should attend Holy Communion because worship was a participative act not a case of watching others.

Just two months into his ministry and it was reported: "The services at the old church are now greatly improved in many features." They added: "the new vicar has attracted large congregations by the able and eminently practical style of his discourses."[118] It is possible to get some idea about the content of these from his later book, *The Morality of Social Pleasures.* In this he seeks to answer the question of how the Christian can live in the world but refrain from being of the world, how they can bear witness without being priggish and so deter others from coming to Christ. For example, he says that it is morally wrong for a person to play sport on Sundays when he has the opportunity to do so on one of the other six days of the week. However, for the labourer who works six days a week, sport on a Sunday after church is permissible and beneficial, though only in parks or public grounds. It would be wrong to play at a club which would involve somebody else having to work.[119] He urges employers to require just the very barest minimum of service from their staff on Sundays and to eschew all luxuries and frivolities themselves so that their servants might be free to worship and not be set a bad example. He encourages people to take an interest in sport but not to bet on results writing: "What right have men in order to satisfy their craving for excitement or to pander to the spirit of greed and covetousness, to bring their nearest and dearest to want and perhaps penury if they lose or to reduce another to the same condition if they win?" He says that theatricals can be great entertainment and can amuse, educate, edify and build confidence but they should never take place on a Sunday and those which fail to meet this criteria should be avoided. Dancing should only be undertaken by the pure in heart and not for sensual expression or for the arousal of others. He offers traditional wisdom such as the need to ask oneself before telling a story about someone whether it is kind, wise or necessary, and if it not all three, to desist. He advises couples to idealise each other and never to let pride prevent a rapprochement, even when a person is not at

---

[118] *Thanet Advertiser*, 14th December 1889

[119] In his *Christianity through Judaism* (London, 1901) he wrote that opening shops and places of amusement on the Sabbath was a Roman Catholic idea and "contrary to the Divine will" but added that provided a person had attended church on Sunday "it cannot be wrong to indulge in such recreation as is not inconsistent with the professions of repentance and faith which have been made so long as such recreation does not involve the labour of others or animals." p.24

fault.[120]

To spread the message further, Monty started the parish magazine. It began in December 1889 just two months after his arrival as a four page *Parish Paper*. Within a year it was selling on average 240 copies a month but it was losing money as the account shows:

Expenditure	£	s	d	*Income*	£	s	d
Printing costs	27	17	0	Sales	28	7	10
Church Monthly inset	5	5	0	Advertisements	1	14	0
	33	2	0		30	1	10
				Deficit	3	0	2

Given that it had been his idea to start the publication, the churchwardens felt that he should pay the shortfall, something he was forced to do every year of his incumbency.[121]

The issue of money was to be a regular problem throughout Mr Fowler's time in the parish. The cost of running the church was about £250 per annum. That figure covered heating, lighting, the organist, church cleaning, service books etc. Average collections were 5s at 8 a.m., £2 4s 10d at 11 a.m. and £1 at 6.30 p.m. total £3 9s 10d a week or £181 14s 8d a year. Some weeks the total was less than £2 10s. Clearly many people were giving less than a penny a week.[122] Part of the problem was that people erroneously believed that their rates should cover this but the other issue was poverty. The level of need in the parish can be seen by the fact that in January 1891, porridge suppers were served free to sixty people who would otherwise have gone without any hot meal, by Sunday School children getting gloves and socks rather than books or cakes for treats and ninety families being fed by the soup kitchen at St Lawrence and twenty-one at Manston – this from a population occupying 536 homes over a third of which had less than five rooms.[123]

A famous study made by Benjamin Seebohm Rowntree demonstrated very clearly the reality of poverty then by contrasting the diet of the poor with those of the servant owning class. For the latter, a normal breakfast was porridge followed by bacon and eggs then marmalade on toast washed down by coffee with cream and sugar. Dinner was roast meat, potatoes, carrots and turnips followed by roly-poly pudding or fruit and custard or blancmange. Tea was sandwiches followed by cake and accompanied by tea. Supper was cold meat or fish followed by oranges and biscuits with a mug of cocoa made with hot milk at bedtime. For the labourer it was bread and butter for breakfast with tea, then bacon with bread and potatoes for dinner, followed by bread and jam for tea and more bread and butter for supper. If they were fortunate in maintaining work and thrifty,

---

[120] Montague Fowler, *The Morality of Social Pleasures*, (London, 1910) pp. 35, 51-2, 60, 91, 110-3, 134
[121] *Parochial Report, 1890* p.32. This amount is equivalent to £360 today.
[122] *Parish Magazine* May 1891. The £250 would be about £29,000 today.
[123] The 1891 census showed 27.9% of homes in St Lawrence Intra and 42% of those in Extra had less than five rooms. The average household contained 5.1 people.

there might be an egg at weekends or a little cheese. Whilst high in fibre, the diet was woefully deficient in protein and fresh produce.[124]

Mr Fowler re-organised the District Visitor system started by his predecessor and by 1891 the population of 2,536 was divided into twenty districts each of which had its own visitor. Aside from Colonel Lowe at Pegwell, all the visitors were women. They included, Lady Rose Weigall at Haine, Spratling Street, Coleswood and Ozengell, Mrs Fowler at Manston, Miss Sale at the almshouses and Mrs Port at Ellington. Their job was twofold. They were to represent the church and to spread news about its activities, for example, inviting women to mothers meetings, telling parents about Sunday School and clubs, selling the parish magazine. They were also to offer practical help. If a family was poor and in need of food, they could apply to the vicar – who was available every day from 11:30 a.m. to 12.30 for this purpose – to issue a relief ticket. These varied in value and type and could be redeemed at local stores for meat, milk, bread, basic groceries or flannel. If a woman was expecting a child, they were to ensure she had everything she needed and if her husband was unable to provide this, they were to raise her case with the parish maternity charities. If a family was found to be cold in winter, they were to make application for coal or loan blankets. In 1891, 645 people received food vouchers through the scheme, 172 received gifts of coal or soup, 348 received clothing or shoes and a further 311 people received discretionary payments due to hardship.[125]

Although not part of the team himself, Mr Fowler undertook a lot of visiting believing that the personal touch was important too. His declared aim was to visit every house in the parish and the fact that he carried out a thousand home visits every year suggests that he succeeded in his aim. His devotion to this work was remarkable because this was an era when the clergy were regarded as gentlemen and not expected to converse with the lower classes, let alone enter their homes or shake their hands. Mr Fowler himself had come from a privileged background. His father had been Chief Engineer of the London underground railway, the first of its kind in the world and was Engineer in Chief of the Forth Bridge at the time Monty came to St Laurence.[126] As a child, Mr Fowler had a fully staffed nursery and he went on to be educated at Harrow and Trinity College, Cambridge.[127] His holidays were spent on the family yacht or at their 57,000 acre estate of Braemore in Ross-shire where he rubbed shoulders with the artists Landseer and Millais as well as being introduced to royal circles and luminaries such as Thomas Carlyle. Yet he did not let this stand in his way. He was not content to spend his days in the vicarage and was often to be found in the local soup kitchen serving meals or taking his dog out as a means of exercise and meeting people. He demonstrated the same level of concern in a

---

[124] Benjamin Seebohm Rowntree, *Poverty - A Study of Town Life* (London, 1908) pp. 234, 252

[125] *Parochial Report, 1891* p.30. Mrs Fowler started a maternity charity for women at Manston and Cliffsend who had not been covered by the previous one.

[126] His father became a baronet on 15th April 1890 and visited Monty at St Laurence shortly afterwards. The Forth Bridge opened the same year.

[127] He read mathematics and theology and achieved excellent results in both.

later parish where he spent a year getting up before dawn and travelling on filthy third class trains so that he could talk to the men who used them and find out their needs and, being concerned about the homeless, he even went so far as to spend a week on the streets and in dosshouses. He was to write extensively on unemployment in later life.[128]

Mr Fowler clearly had some success in his outreach work and he was particularly touched by the donations he received from working class families such as the men who contributed a quarter of their week's wages to support the building of the Church Club.[129] He was not, however, insensitive to the problems which the Church as a whole had in terms of reputation, being seen as out of touch in some quarters and elitist. To try to counter this he chose to introduce the Church Army in February 1890. They were regarded as the Church of England's attempt to copy the Salvation Army which had proved very successful in its attempt to reach the working class in particular. A unit had been formed at St Lawrence in 1886 though it had faced problems. A series of letters to the local press in 1888 had decried it as "maniacal" and fairly typical was:

> Why should these people be allowed daily to annoy residents living in the thoroughfare through which they bellow their salvation songs. Is it that their lungs are stronger than the law? That they are a nuisance I believe nine tenths of the inhabitants would testify to. … Their outside processions are unseemly and irreverent and the holding forth by illiterate men and women in the streets causes obstruction and often scenes which must shock the ears and eyes of persons who use a more serious and less sensational form of religious worship.[130]

Mr Fowler's move was no less controversial. He reflected in his parochial report of 1891:

> The criticisms which poured in upon me, often from the most unexpected quarters, would have been amusing had it not been for the element of regret at the loss of one or two workers for a time. I was accused of introducing a Jesuitical agency into the parish for the purpose of leading the people to Rome! I was reproached for introducing a Dissenting schism into the midst of a united Church parish! The variety and strength of the criticism neutralised one another and having secured the services of an able, energetic and earnest young Captain, J R

---

[128] Further details of his work and how he sought to alleviate poverty are available in Montague Fowler, *A History of All Hallows* (London, 1909), also *Home Words,* March 1908 pp.62-64
[129] *Thanet Advertiser*, 30th January 1890
[130] *Kent Coast Times*, 17th May 1888

> Matthews, we have gone forward with most happy results and the assurance of God's blessing.

Nonetheless, division still existed and a year later, he was defending his position:

> My sole object in introducing it in St Lawrence was by its agency to win over men and women to membership of the Church. The moment it ceases to do this and threatens to become an independent organisation it ceases to meet the object for which it was founded.

In January 1892 he warned people in the parish magazine to: "be on their guard against allowing themselves to look upon the Mission Hall as their goal. This work is only a means to an end, that is to win people to Christ and then hand them over to be built up in the doctrines of the church and lead them to become communicants." Miss Mascall, one of those who laboured there, wrote: "we would fain hope that many who may not see eye to eye with us in our methods will at least, in considering the results, be kind in their criticism and wish us God-speed."[131]

The Church Army was based in Southwood Mission Hall, a building since demolished but which stood on the corner opposite the Australian Arms. They held two services each Sunday and mission services on four evenings a week. During the summer, they set up a tent in the High Street and evangelised from there. Regular attendance for prayer meetings and Bible study varied from thirty to forty and on Sunday evenings it was reported "the hall is filled to overflowing." At least two people came forward to train as evangelists and over a dozen were confirmed in its first year of operation. The fact that the Church Army had the hall was due entirely to Mr Fowler who actually bought the premises for £170 with a personal loan and allowed the church the use of it rent free.[132] This was extraordinarily generous for a newly married vicar whose stipend was low. He wrote: "I was unwilling to add an additional burden to the weight of debt which we have inherited and was anxious after the great strain that has been put upon you in recent years to avoid the necessity of appealing to you for help in raising the amount required but, at the same time, I felt that its importance as a centre of Church work in the heart of the parish was so great that I must secure it for spiritual purposes. The Hall is in constant use and the wonder is that we could ever have done without it."[133]

In addition to his church related work, Mr Fowler was involved in wider activities that related to the parish. He served on the organising committee for the 1892 Ramsgate and St Lawrence Arts and Industrial Exhibition and contributed a prize for the

---

[131] *Parochial Report 1891* p.38
[132] *Parish Magazine*, February 1891. In today's values, it would be just under £20,000.
[133] *Parochial Report, 1891* p.3, 1890 p.5

best mechanical apparatus. He took part in a debate about Sunday observance.[134] In 1891 he became Chaplain of the 1st Volunteer Battalion East Kent Regiment (The Buffs) something which he said he enjoyed having served with a similar regiment whilst at Cambridge. He carried out many public speaking engagements and was an active supporter of local flower shows.

During his time here the parish saw many important visitors including both the Archbishop of York and the Archbishop of Canterbury. The former was Mrs Fowler's uncle and he died on Christmas Day 1890, Monty receiving the telegram at breakfast after taking two services and before the third. After pealing merrily for Christmas, the bells were half muffled and rung in honour of the late Archbishop. The latter was the man most famous for devising the Nine Lessons and Carols service. The actor, Sir Henry Irving, a personal friend of Monty's for many years, also came to stay.

In autumn 1892, Monty's health collapsed and the doctor advised a period of complete rest. Not only had he been working at a tremendous pace, his wife had been seriously ill for some months and he had been forced to send her to London for treatment. As he observed, this separation was not sustainable long term. He also had financial worries because his income as vicar of St Laurence was insufficient to keep him or pay Ada's medical bills. His gross was £306 but the amount he was forced to spend in essential expenses such as taxes, combined with necessary costs of maintaining a curate (the parish had not collected enough to pay one so Monty was not only accommodating him rent free at the vicarage but was subsidising his stipend), repairing the vicarage (at over £100), plus all the other costs he was expected to take on from having the churchyard grass cut to printing the parish magazine, meant his actual income was just £19 a year – or 7s 4d a week, less than labourers in his congregation.[135] By the end of 1892 he was owed £18 16s 11d – almost £2200 today – and that excluded the cost of the Mission Hall. It was a sad state of affairs and Monty would later observe that any vicar at St Laurence would "not only have to live upon his private income but be in a position to spend a not inconsiderable portion of that private income upon the parish."[136] He departed the parish in December 1892 hoping that he would be well enough to return six months later but Ada contracted influenza and her illness prevented him getting the rest he needed. In April 1893 he was forced to resign. He reported in his final *Parochial Report* that in his capacity as vicar he had each year received seven thousand letters and sent five thousand, relieved 1,300 cases of poverty, visited a thousand homes, preached two hundred

---

[134] *Kent Coast Times,* 11th June, 18th June 1891

[135] The day rate for labourers was 2s 6d, *Kent Coast Times,* 26th November 1891. The census for that year shows that Mr Fowler had his mother-in-law living with him and that he employed a cook, footman and three housemaids. This was one less member of staff than Mr Sicklemore. In 1911, Mr Bevan would employ the same number. The vicarage contained fifteen rooms excluding bathrooms, lobbies and offices so the staffing level was not unreasonable. As vicar, Mr Fowler would have had no say in the size of house he occupied.

[136] *Parochial Report, 1892* p.6

sermons, held eight hundred meetings with individuals at the vicarage and three hundred with groups. He had been treasurer of twenty-eight separate funds and in the space of three years had raised almost £4000 – about £460,000 in modern values. It was an extraordinary achievement. His final words were: "It is, however, the growth and deepening of the spiritual life of my parishioners which has been my first care and to this end I have laboured to the utmost of my strength. I earnestly pray that my efforts have not been in vain."

He did not return to parish ministry until 1900 when he became rector of All Hallows, London Wall, a position he held until his death. Whilst there he implemented many social relief schemes as well as introducing services in French and Greek for the benefit of visitors. During the First World War he was a fire watcher in the City, something which exacerbated the breathing difficulties which would ultimately kill him.

He also remained characteristically productive with his life. His father had been president of the Egyptian Exploration Fund and General Engineering Advisor to the Egyptian Government and Monty had visited the country with him in 1877. He returned in 1900 when he was able to use his language skills – Monty spoke fluent French, Greek, Arabic, Hebrew and Aramaic – to investigate inter-faith relations. He lectured extensively on this subject and believed that the Church should cease trying to export Catholicism or Presbyterianism to the Middle East and instead should support the native Orthodox churches and work toward the reunification of Christendom.[137]

He continued to write, his volumes including *Christianity through Judaism*, *Church History in Queen Victoria's Reign*, *Christian Egypt* and *Some Notable Archbishops of Canterbury* all of which are eminently readable and worth study today. He edited *Church Bells* and *Crockford's Clerical Directory*. He played golf to relax, being a founder member of a club at Trouville, and enjoyed watching and playing cricket and playing the piano.[138]

---

[137] Monty was offered the first Anglican bishopric in Egypt but refused due to his wife's ill health. For an interview with him regarding the subject see Charles Dant, *Distinguished Churchmen and Phases of Church Work* (London, 1902) pp.246-265. He had discussed the issue at length in his 1901 book *Christianity through Judaism*

[138] *Golf Illustrated*, 8th September 1899

In 1913, he founded the Church Imperial Club at Artillery Mansions, Victoria Street, London to provide clergy visiting the capital with a place to stay and study.[139] In 1910 he spearheaded a movement to teach voice production to ordinands and established clergy so that congregations would be better able to hear services.[140] He was well qualified to do this having acted on the West End stage under the name of Montague Mazeran.[141]

He was passionate about animal welfare. For many years he was secretary of the RSPCA fund for Sick and Wounded Horses and their Educational Secretary and he campaigned against the idea of animals being taken to abattoirs further from the farm which was a cause of distress to them.[142] Particularly devoted to dogs, he was on the committee of Battersea Dogs Home from 1900.[143]

In 1911, his wife Ada died aged just forty-six. He remarried a French lady in February 1915 and five months later became the fourth baronet after his nephew, a captain in the Seaforth Highlanders, was killed in action. He had two daughters with his second wife.

Montague Fowler was one of the most able vicars that the parish was blessed to receive. His dedication and faith shine through his work and writings and so does his sense of humour. Newspaper reports frequently mention laughter at his meetings. His wife told the Reverend Philip Norwood a story he had told her about how he had taken on a maid when at St Laurence. He had commented that he was sorry she had to take the room overlooking the churchyard and hoped she would not find it depressing. The young maid, still in her 'teens, responded solemnly: "Given a choice betweens looking at the dead and the livin' round 'ere, sir, I'd as soon look on the dead."

Monty passed away on April 1st 1933 at the age of seventy-four having been ill for a few days with bronchitis. His second wife died in 1993 aged one hundred.

He was succeeded by the Reverend **Robert Payne-Smith**, son of the Dean of Canterbury. For those who had regarded Mr Fowler as over enthusiastic, Mr Payne-Smith seemed a return to a safe pair of hands.

---

[139] *Sydney Morning Herald*, 1st November 1913. The club was still there at the outbreak of the Second World War at number 77.
[140] *Hartlepool Mail*, 30th July 1910
[141] A scrapbook relating to his acting and his wife Ada's writing has been kept by his family. She wrote novels as Dayrell Trelawney and plays as Gaston Gervex. Her dramas were performed in London at the Coliseum, Court and Ambassador theatres as well as in Manchester and were sufficiently respected that Sarah Bernhardt herself selected one of them for a performance in 1911.
[142] *Glasgow Herald*, 20th December 1932
[143] Garry Jenkins, *A Home of Their Own*, (London, 2011) pp.147-8

Aged forty-one when he arrived, his ministry was to be singularly devoid of initiatives and his time in the parish was marked more by things closing than starting. These included the suspension of Church Army work in 1895 and the closure of the Church Club, the latter being sold to pay off the debt on the Parish Hall and the space it occupied being given over to development.[144] The adult temperance society and the communicants guild were also closed.[145] It is noteworthy that the annual Parochial Reports for his incumbency are barely a twentieth the size of his predecessors.

It was during Mr Payne-Smith's time that Queen Victoria celebrated her Diamond Jubilee. Mr Payne-Smith served on the town committee organising the celebrations declaring that it would be "barbaric" if people were to spend their time "eating and drinking all day." He advocating giving everyone some improving literature instead. Other committee members were more sensitive to the desire for a party and the fact that many of the poor would welcome a meal with treats like meat, cake and fruit, but it was agreed that older children would get a volume about the advances made during the Queen's reign.[146] Mr Warre chose to give the town a piece of land on Newington Road which could be used as a recreation ground. A trust of seven members was set up to lay out the grounds and Mr Payne-Smith was one of these. The committee met regularly to debate the benefits of cricket, football, tennis, whether there should be a cycle track or not, what sort of pavilion should be built, and their deliberations went on for so many months that they became the butt of a number of pointed comments in the local press. Mr Payne-Smith was more successful with celebrations at St Laurence where the decision to install a new clock was made and implemented without argument.

Mr Payne-Smith's biggest achievement was the creation of the cemetery in Cecilia Road as an extension to the churchyard. The original plan had been to purchase five acres next to Ramsgate Cemetery for the use of parishioners plus two acres next to the churchyard but the latter scheme had been discarded following opposition from the Sanitary Authority who said it would mean corpses being laid too close to the water supply. Early in 1898 the church bought the land and by the end of August, the new cemetery was laid out. The costs of the project were:

	£	s	d
Land for burials	1270	10	0
Land for road	200	10	0
Walls	441	0	0
Road	204	0	0
Laying out grounds	427	0	0
Architect's fees	102	0	0

---

[144] The fire service were there from 1897 and the accounts show them paying ground rent to the church. Since then, the building has been occupied by a florist's business and a hairdresser.
[145] Both were restarted by his successor, the Reverend Thomas Crosse.
[146] *Thanet Advertiser*, 5th June 1897. One parishioner still has a copy of the book given.

	£	s	d
Legal fees	200	0	0
Lodge and chapel	938	0	0
Bier and furnishings	59	10	0
Postage	2	6	3
	3844	16	3

To fund this, they originally borrowed £3000 from the Ecclesiastical Commissioners at an interest rate of 3.125% over thirty years but that proved to be insufficient so they borrowed a further £1100 taking their monthly repayment up to £18 8d. In order to raise this, burial fees were set as: 7s per adult or teenager, 5s per child aged four to twelve, 3s per child aged three or less and 2s 6d for a stillborn baby. The amount was the same whether the burial took place in the consecrated or non-consecrated sector but if the consecrated ground was used, a further 3s was due to the vicar for each burial. For those who wanted a permanent place of their own rather than to see their loved one buried with strangers in an unmarked grave, the following charges applied:

> to purchase the plot was £1 for a single space, £2 10s for a double
> to register the purchase was 2s 6d
> to erect a headstone on said plot was 15s
> to erect a bodystone was a further 15s
> to erect a single vault was £1 or £3 for a double vault
> to erect kerbstones was £1 10s
> to have the grave maintained was 5s per annum[147]

These were only the cemetery fees and the family would have faced extra bills from the funeral director and stonemason. Over the first five years, the average number of burials was 91 with numbers in St Laurence churchyard declining by a quarter.[148] The cemetery was only created for those who lived within what was known as St Lawrence Intra which was the village or urban part of the parish. Those who lived in Manston or Cliffsend which were classified as St Lawrence Extra had to either pay double the fees or go in the churchyard.[149]

Mr Payne-Smith was responsible too for the extension of both boys and girls schools and the erection of the board in the porch which contains the names of past vicars as researched by M.B. Phillips and published by Charles Cotton.

---

[147] CCA-U3-19/8/A/3 Vestry Book, 3rd April 1898. For families who owned a plot and wanted to bury another member in the same, the fee was 10s 6d to open the grave. Two thirds of the land was consecrated, one third was not. The chapel was never consecrated.
[148] 78 consecrated, 6 unconsecrated, 7 stillborn.
[149] *Thanet Advertiser* 13th April 1901. Manston sought to create their own burial ground but did not do so.

During his incumbency, his income was £322 gross or £224 net. This was made up of £10 from the Ecclesiastical Commissioners, £3 from Queen Anne's Bounty, £71 from fees, £65 from the Bouchery benefaction made to the parish in 1788 and the remainder from commuted tithes. His gross was equivalent to an income of £38,000.[150] In addition, he had income from the £420 of Great Western Railway shares left to him by his father.

In November 1898, it was announced that Mr Payne-Smith was to go to a church in Taunton and his wife arranged a farewell party in the Parish Hall in January 1899. In fact, he did not leave until April 2nd. He died suddenly in January 1917 in Somerset aged sixty-four.

PEOPLE, EVENTS AND PLACES

War with France

The war with France began in 1793 following the new republic's decision to invade Belgium and execute the deposed king Louis XVI. Aside from a brief peace in 1802, the war went on until 1815. During this time it had an immense impact on the parish. It vastly increased the population: effectively, one soldier was stationed on the island for every three locals. It made fishing and maritime trade – both major sources of employment – extremely dangerous. Mariners no longer had to contend with the weather but also the possibility of being shot by the French or taken captive: twenty vessels were taken in November 1796 alone. In 1800, four hundred prisoners of war were landed at Ramsgate an observer noting: "they made a very miserable appearance having been very badly treated."[151] Between 1803 and 1806 when invasion seemed likely, the war reduced the number of visitors which in turn affected incomes both for individual parishioners and for the church as it reduced collections. The need for people to get involved in war work also affected congregations and saw men who would normally have served as parish officers called away.

Initially, the presence of the troops added colour to life. Crowds came out to see the men marching through towns and to hear the bands. Many of the soldiers wore scarlet uniforms, the artillery and light dragoons were in blue, and there were several battalions from the Highlands in kilts. Most of the troops were foot soldiers but there was also cavalry with their roman style crested helmets and great horses. Nothing like it had ever been seen before. The impact was such that even over fifty years later, eyewitnesses were able to describe the scene in Ramsgate quite vividly:

---

[150] In 1912, the Reverend Francis Bevan had the same income but inflation meant it was worth the equivalent of £34,000. A report of the same year showed that this meant he earned three times as much as a trained nurse and two thirds as much as a doctor. *Thanet Advertiser*, 21st September 1912. Details of clergy incomes appear in the annual editions of *Crockford's Clerical Directory*.
[151] *Kentish Gazette*, 28th January 1800

> Barracks were constructed in all directions and improvised wherever needed, and on high and spacious levels of our cliffs and their slopes, canvas was visible, and far and near and all around were to be seen the attributes and appendages of active camp life. Parade grounds were formed whereon houses are now closely packed. East and west, nothing but the entailments of military occupation, in its peaceful form, were to be met with. Men marched into town to await or to receive their orders to embark... Upon one occasion a body of six men deep marched into the town, and they extended from the pier gate to Nethercourt toll bar, their destination being Belgium, then the seat of the war. Throughout the day men were to be seen in our streets marching to and from their respective parades. Our sands at low water were swarming with troops - infantry, cavalry, artillery surged and galloped and wheeled in all directions charging and recharging with swords in hand and bayonets glittering in the sun, whilst others further along the shore were occupied with single file firing practice into the face of the cliff for hours daily. To complete the hubbub and din, trumpets blared, buglers practised their calls, and signals and drums of all kinds and sizes, with the shrill fifes added their portions to swell the noisy doings.
>
> So too... with the piers and harbour, bustle and activity prevailed on all sides in preparing vessels with their respective freights... Stores of all kinds blocked the pathways in endless confusion of piles and heaps. Horses and oxen stood in tethered strings, with heads to the parapet of the pier, waiting to be swung on board their respective ships.
>
> At certain hours of the day, the military bands were wont to play in various parts of the town, rivalling each other in their efforts to please... Balls, parties, dinners and fetes of all kinds were the order of the day at all seasons of the year.[152]

Yet the war brought more than just spectacle and entertainment. Local people were expected to get involved and two means were provided for them to do this. The first was through the Volunteer companies. These were land based and consisted of foot soldiers with a separate battalion of mounted troops taken from the local landed gentlemen and yeomen farmers. The Ramsgate division of Kent Volunteer Artillery Corps was under the command of Captain Austen. There were also three volunteer infantry

---

[152] Richardson op.cit. pp.63-4.

companies, commanded by Captains Grey, Gibson and Mayhew.[153] In September 1797 Mrs Townley presented to them the colours she had painted.[154] In 1793, sixty gentlemen of the leading local families were formed into the Isle of Thanet Yeomanry with Thomas Garrett of Nethercourt as captain. His brother, John Garrett of Ellington, was appointed lieutenant in 1794 and captain in 1814. By the time the regiment was disbanded in 1828, Thomas had risen to Colonel of the entire East Kent Yeomanry.

The second option, from 1798, was the Sea Fencibles. Their role was to keep watch on the coast and to help protect merchant vessels from armed attack. As with the infantry Volunteers, members got a shilling a day and were expected to serve at least one day a week or two in the summer. In return for their work, they were safe from the press gang and exempt from tax on hair powder. One hundred and forty-two parishioners joined the Sea Fencibles including five members each of the Meader, Bayly, Forwood, King and Cooper families.[155] Those who had not volunteered for either faced forcible means when the order went out across Ramsgate in March 1803 to impress men for the Royal Navy under the Defence of the Realm Act. Parishioners living in the rural districts of St Lawrence should have been exempt from the order but it is unlikely that the press gang stopped to ask too many questions. Quite aside from the life threatening conditions on ships, the men taken faced the worry about what would happen to their family. Left without a breadwinner, women were forced to take drastic means to feed their children and if their husband was a farm labourer in a tied cottage, they could be rendered homeless as well. The parish overseers must have dreaded the financial consequences of a sudden rise of people in need.

The need to defend the coast together with the requirement to house large numbers of troops and equipment resulted in a number of changes to the parish. A battery was built on the East Cliff at Ramsgate. Barracks were built on the south cliff at Ramsgate in 1799. Military Road was constructed in 1805 at Ramsgate to ease embarkation of troops and supplies. In addition, warships were stationed around the coast such as the Texel of 74 guns which arrived in 1803. Most of the gates to the sea which existed around the coast were sealed up with high walls and preparations were made to seal the rest in less than an hour. A powder magazine was built at Ramsgate in 1802. In November 1803, Admiral Keith had four 68lb howitzers placed on Ramsgate pier and a chain and boom to secure entrance to the pierheads. St Laurence church tower was used as a signalling station as was St Peter's.

Amongst those parishioners who chose to serve with the regular services, three were at Trafalgar – Henry Blackburn, George Everett and Thomas Poole. One of the longest serving men in the Royal Navy was James Fegan who served forty-six years

---

[153] Captain Mayhew was brother-in-law of Thomas and John Garrett.

[154] *Kentish Gazette*, 23rd September 1797

[155] ADM 28/36

reaching the rank of gunner. In 1798, he was on HMS Swiftsure at the Battle of the Nile, one of Nelson's greatest victories. Daniel Curling from Ramsgate also served as a gunner for much of the war. This was a key role on the ship, an opportunity for skilled working men to become officers and earn good money. Responsible for the guns and ammunition, they needed to be able to read and to have strong mathematical abilities. Failing to calculate the range or amount of powder needed could result in many fatalities. They also needed to be extremely strong.

For the vicar, Richard Harvey, there was not only the additional work which came from a larger population but there was the need to involve himself in civilian matters because the parish was still the main unit of local government. In 1803, Sir William Pitt, ex-Prime Minister and Lord Warden of the Cinque Ports, visited the island to discuss defence and what should be done in event of invasion. The vicar and wardens had to prepare a report showing the numbers of horses, waggons, spades, cattle, sheep and livestock they had as well as armed men. They were required to count people who were capable of removing themselves from the area and those who would need assistance. They further had to report on the identities of skilled personnel who would need to be moved out, the form being more interested in bakers and millers than surgeons. Having gathered all this information, they were to prepare an outline plan of how to arrange the evacuation.[156]

At the consequent meeting in Margate it was agreed that all main roads should have ten men guarding them with pikes and shovels, all roads to and from the island being capable of closure. Plans for the evacuation of troops meant that each area had to supply a set number of waggons, each with four horses and two drivers. Ramsgate had to supply eight. Should the invasion signal sound, the waggon teams were to repair to the field at Nethercourt complete with three days' provisions for the drivers, two trusses of hay and eight bushels of oats for the horses.[157] Groups of armed men would then patrol the area whilst the troops left before the evacuation of the population began. Harvey, just twenty-six, had only become vicar four months after the war began so this was a baptism of fire.

The bell ringers would also have been kept busy as they rang to notify the population of both victories and disasters. On 20th December 1805 they rang to announce the appearance of HMS Victory off the coast containing the body of Lord Nelson en route from Trafalgar to London for burial. Nelson had accompanied his mistress, Lady Hamilton, to visit Lady Dunmore at Southwood in 1801. [158]

The arrival at Thanet ports of wounded soldiers served as a stark reminder to those living in the area of the nearness of the war. The fact that prior to 1805, the only hospital facilities for them were at Deal or on the hospital ship Spanker at Sheerness, meant the wounded had to be taken across the island in wagons for all to see. Even the

---

[156] *Kentish Gazette*, 5th July 1803
[157] Peter Bloomfield *Kent and the Napoleonic Wars* (Maidstone, 1987) p.157
[158] Bob Ogley, *Kent 1800-1899 A Chronicle of the 19th century* (Westerham, 2013) p.20

villages could not escape the sights of war. Public concern about the large numbers of wounded led to a national Patriotic Fund being set up to support disabled ex-servicemen and the widows and dependent children of those who had died. A collection at St Laurence church on the 17th December 1805 raised £23 8s 6d. Ramsgate Chapel raised £45 6s and Burgess' Library in the town £106 6s 6d. This total of £175 1s represented just over seven per cent of the national total, indicative of how strongly the parishioners felt about the subject.[159]

In 1809, a total of 168 servicemen were laid to rest in St Laurence churchyard from a total of 312, the highest number of burials in a single year ever. Of these, 88 died after contracting typhus on their return from Portugal. A graphic account of his experiences was given by one officer arriving in January:

> After a most tremendous passage and a most disastrous and ill fated expedition, I am once more safe arrived in my native land but in a very exhausted state of body from excessive fatigue and hardship such as I did not imagine my constitution capable of enduring. I have not been out of my clothes for a month nor sheltered more than four nights in that time. The scenes of horror that have taken place beggar all description; ten thousand men will not make good our losses in killed, wounded and prisoners. Men, women and children with horses, mules, asses, strewed the road during the last fortnight which died through the severity of the weather, hunger and fatigue….Our marches were generally in the night over mountains covered with snow after ascending from valleys drenched through with rain, without food and numbers barefoot, and no other shelter than the canopy of heaven. My eyes were like salamanders for want of sleep and my legs reduced to the size of drumsticks, my joints benumbed and swelled that we could not march more than a mile per hour through roads knee deep in mud. All the treasure and baggage was destroyed for want of means of conveyance….In this state we reached Corunna…I am sorry to say that numbers of our wounded were unavoidably abandoned as we finally retreated in the middle of the night to the shipping in a most distressed and sorry state.[160]

The burials all took place between 15th February and 16th April, just sixty days. A memorial erected just above the lectern in St Laurence remembers:

---

[159] *Morning Advertiser*, 14th January 1806
[160] *Kentish Gazette*, 31st January 1809

> Sacred to the memory
> of Charles Smith esq.
> of Richmond in Surrey
> late Surgeon of the Royal Surrey Militia
> who died at Ramsgate on the 23rd of February 1809
> of a fever brought on by his kind and
> unremitting attention to
> the sick soldiers landed there from Spain
> aged 30 years
> This stone is erected by his brother officers as
> a testimony of their great regard

Just three months later, hundreds lined the cliffs to wave off the thousands of men who were departing for Flushing.

> Thousands of spectators at this place and along our coast have been gratified this morning with the most pleasing sight imaginable…Ramsgate Pier was crowded with persons of various descriptions and on the cliffs also innumerable beholders were assembled to view the fleet then proudly passing by. It was indeed grand beyond description. Here and there appeared towering above the rest lofty ships of war and at regular intervals between them, smaller vessels, transports, gunboats. The sea was, as it were, covered by them. In this manner the first line of the Grand Expedition under an easy sail passed Ramsgate bearing along with it the most sincere prayers and wishes for success for many here - whilst they looked on with heartfelt satisfaction in the national pride - could not fail to be reminded that they had a father, son or brother among those gallant defenders of our country.[161]

Six weeks later, the men from this expeditionary force started to return. Ninety per cent had fallen ill, mostly with a form of malaria. On 17th September, a correspondent from Ramsgate told the *Kentish Gazette*: "We have upwards of 300 in our barracks sick, some desperately so, but the fever is not contagious as first feared. On Thursday, thirteen had died at our barracks since their arrival and nine bodies are now lying in the dead room." Once again, Richard Harvey arranged collections for the sick at the church.

The total number of soldiers buried at St Laurence during the war was 293. Of these 196 were from infantry regiments, 13 Light Dragoons, 3 Heavy Dragoons, 9 Guards, 31 from county militias, 11 from the King's German Legion, 1 from a Veterans battalion, 5

---

[161] *Kentish Gazette*, 28th July 1809

from the Waggon Train, 4 Royal Artillery, 1 Royal Marine, 2 Royal Staff Corps and 17 were simply listed as serving soldiers with no regiment specified.

St. Laurence churchyard contains nine memorials to people who fought in the Napoleonic War. The most spectacular is that to Thomas Steed, Quarter Master with the 15th Light Dragoons who died suddenly aged fifty-one in March 1804. It shows a range of musical instruments. Another remembers John Woolward who served under Nelson at Aboukir Bay before going on to become Harbour Master at Ramsgate for twenty-six years.[162] A stone near the mausoleum refers to George Wood who died after nine years as a prisoner of war in Verdun in 1811. There are also two stained glass windows which remember veterans of the war, Robert Garrett who served in the Peninsula and Thomas Noel Harris who served in both the Peninsula and at Waterloo.

Amongst those buried who had no memorial was Private George Gregory of the 2nd Dragoons who was laid to rest on 26th March 1814. His regiment had been ordered to leave their Ramsgate Barracks to join Wellington but at the time of departure, Gregory was found to be drunk and ordered to ride at the rear as a prisoner. Gregory strenuously denied that he was drunk and argued with Major Gordon who decided to disarm him. The Major struck Gregory's horse with the flat side of the sword whereupon the horse turned and Gregory fell back on to the sword tip, bleeding to death within minutes from his wound. The Major was subsequently fined £50 for manslaughter.[163] Also unlawfully killed was Private Michael Latimore of the Leitrim Militia who was buried on 21st April 1812. He fell victim to a hatchet blow by a sailor named Mark Austen who was consequently jailed.[164] On 23rd November 1799, Thomas Peebles, a fourteen year old drummer boy with the 63rd Foot Regiment was laid to rest in an unmarked grave. He had fallen over the unfamiliar and unfenced cliff edge while drilling.

The Townley family lost two sons in the war. James died aged 32 after entering a decline following service in the Peninsular Campaign which caused his resignation from the 1st Foot Guards. He died at Townley House (now Farley's in Chatham Street) and was buried in the vault which would later hold his parents. His younger brother, a Lieutenant in the Royal Navy, was killed in action off the French coast in 1810 and buried at sea.

Sunday School

It is impossible to know when the first Sunday School was established at St Laurence church. The first definite reference to its existence is in 1851 but it is likely to have been founded earlier. The Post Office Directory of 1845 stated that three Sunday Schools existed in the Ramsgate and St Lawrence area but did not give their names. Since

---

[162] As Harbour Master he earned £200 p.a. the same as Nathaniel Gott who is remembered by a monument in the north transept, HMSO, *Parliamentary Papers, House of Commons and Command*, Volume 19 (1816) or pp xxxi-xxxiv. That equates to about £16,000 today.
[163] *Kentish Gazette* , 28th March and 12th April 1814.
[164] *Kentish Gazette,* 21st April 1812

in 1851 there were eleven - of which just two were Anglican - it may be suspected that the figure of three was erroneous. Whilst it is possible that the Reverend George Wilson Sicklemore founded the Sunday School, it is more probable that it was an innovation of the Reverend Richard Harvey, junior and that it began during the time of the wars with revolutionary France.[165]

The first Sunday Schools were formed very much on the same lines as the Tudor school in that they aimed to teach people to read so that they could study the Bible and join in worship. The vicar of Boughton-under-Blean who set one up in 1785 explained that it was "to furnish opportunities of instruction to the children of the poorer part of the parish without interfering with any industry of the week days and to inure children to early habits of going to church and of spending the leisure hours on Sunday decently and virtuously. The children are to be taught to read and to be instructed in the plain duties of the Christian religion with a particular view to their good and industrious behaviour in their future character of labourers and servants."[166]

The creation of the parish Infants School in 1841 altered the nature of the Sunday School so that it ceased to teach literacy and devoted itself to religious instruction. This was a topic on the day school curriculum and the fact that children received teaching about the Bible and catechism in the parish schools may account for why the church Sunday School was so poorly attended by comparison with other churches. For example, the local Congregationalists and Methodists had Sunday Schools in 1851 which were almost double the size of St Laurence's but they had no day schools of their own. However, the nature of the teaching did differ between parish school and Sunday School. In the former, the children were primarily taught facts, Biblical geography and recitation whilst the Sunday School aimed at fostering a personal relationship with God.[167] Whether the children or parents were fully aware of the distinction is uncertain and it seems evident that a number assumed that having had religious instruction during the week, there was no need to go for any more on Sunday.

Two further changes in the nineteenth century which affected Sunday Schools were the growth of understanding about child development which started to affect teaching methods toward the end of the century and the rise of incarnational theology. This last, whilst never denying the atonement, moved the stress from original sin and the need for personal regeneration to a focus on Jesus' humanity and the collective witness of the Church. In practical terms, it changed the impression of children from the

___

[165] In June 1813, there were at least 513 children attending Sunday School across the entire island, *Kentish Gazette,* 15th June 1813.

[166] J Henry Harris (ed) *Robert Raikes: A Man and His Work* (London, 1899) p.330

[167] The Diocesan inspector in 1890 reported of the parish girls' school: "The instruction is given carefully. There is an evident aim to improve the moral tone of the girls as well as to instruct them in portions of Christian doctrine. In both divisions the subjects of instruction are well remembered. The portions of the Catechism written from memory were well done. The repetition was good." – *Parochial Report, 1891* p.36

Augustinian miserable sinners en route to perdition unless they acknowledged God to the cherubic little innocents that adorned millions of chocolate boxes. In time, this new philosophy would lead to modern liturgies with their watered down confessions and selective lectionaries and to liberal theology which Niebuhr famously condemned as teaching: "A God without wrath brought men without sin into a kingdom without judgment through the ministrations of a Christ without a cross." In 1884, Archbishop Benson specifically denied that conversion was a goal but said that rather Sunday Schools existed to mould character, particularly the development of humility.[168] The danger of this was that people might then interpret this as saying the way to heaven was in being good – the heretical doctrine of justification by works rather than the Biblical teaching of justification by faith.

Our first information about how the Sunday School was organised dates from the time of the Reverend Montague Fowler, vicar from 1889-93. He met with the Sunday School teachers fortnightly to go through the lessons with them. This direct involvement of the vicar was recommended by the Lambeth conference though it was a far from universal practice. In 1890 there were three Sunday Schools with the infants meeting in the Church Club and the boys and girls at separate ends of the Parish Hall.[169] They met morning and afternoon and the average attendance was:

		Morning			*Afternoon*		
Day School	*Sunday School*	*1890*	*1891*	*1892*	*1890*	*1891*	*1892*
76	Infants	51	37	52	74	38	62
130	Boys	45	35	36	48	46	41
61	Girls	50	58	31	58	69	48

It is impossible to know how many of the children attended both morning and afternoon and which attended the parish school but the data suggests that around three quarters of day school infants probably attended Sunday School, a third of the boys and almost all the girls. In addition, forty children – who may or may not have been Sunday Scholars – attended the Church Army service on Wednesdays at 6 p.m. If these figures are related to the census for 1891, it can be seen that 42% of all infant school children in the parish (excluding the Manston and Haine area) attended St Laurence Sunday School, 25% of junior aged boys and 39% of girls. Nationally the rates were 29%, 30% and 35% respectively.

The pupil-teacher ratio was good with six teachers to each school meaning one teacher per ten infants or one per seven juniors. Only three of the teachers were male (16.7%) two of them being the vicar and his curate. Nationally, the official *Church of England Yearbook* for this time showed Anglican Sunday Schools averaged almost fourteen pupils per teacher with just over a quarter of teachers being male. Involvement with

---

[168] *Church Sunday School Magazine,* vol.20 May 1884 p.389
[169] Prior to the Parish Hall and Church Club, the parish schools had been used.

Sunday Schools was regarded as a particularly suitable role for women and was an important step toward acceptance of their ministry outside the home. None of the fifteen ladies was married and only five worked, two being dressmakers, one a laundress, one running a guest house and the last being headmistress of the parish girls school. The others lived on private means, though one had been a day school teacher in her youth. The teachers therefore represented a cross-section of the community and must have made an interesting social mix at meetings. The average age of the teachers was 38 for the boys, 36 for the girls and 26 for the infants. Each school had one teacher in their sixties whilst three of the infants' teachers were teenagers and one each in the girls and boys. Almost a third of the teachers lived outside the parish.

What format did Sunday School take? The session would have lasted about an hour and begun with a formal act of worship which involved a hymn, the Lord's Prayer (which was recited kneeling) and a Collect. Excluding the infants class, the Apostles Creed was then said. The lesson itself would have taken half an hour and the session would have ended with a further short act of collective worship involving a hymn and closing prayer.[170] The content of the lesson would have varied according to age group but would generally have begun with a question, then a pertinent reading followed by explanation with the teacher then asking questions of the children to make sure they understood it. The application of the teaching to daily life would be drawn out and the children given a text to memorise - a single verse in the case of infants, two or three for older children. There was no set syllabus but lessons revolved around the church year. It

---

[170] *The Church Sunday School Magazine* vol. 29 (1889) p.289

was expected that a quarter of the year would be spent studying the Old Testament, half the New Testament, and the other quarter would be taken up with studying the catechism and the liturgy, with most attention being given to Matins and the Litany.[171] The accounts show that at St Laurence money was spent purchasing text cards for children to take home. The Reverend Montague Fowler also invested £2 16s 9d on books on his arrival.[172]

Children generally attended Sunday School from the age of four until they were thirteen or fourteen when they left school. At that stage, they were considered ready to join in the main worship of the church and encouraged to attend Bible Classes to deepen their faith. Although occasional classes were started for girls, there seems to have been no pastoral impetus to this work. This may have been because more girls than boys stayed on as church members after leaving Sunday School or it could reflect the fact that they were regarded as better behaved and less in need of further character building classes. It could also have reflected a practical difference in that boys were more likely to be employed on local farms or in businesses and so be free in the evenings to attend a class whilst girls tended to go into service where they did not have such freedom. The fact that the St Laurence clergy were generally disinclined to give numbers of young people attending these classes suggests that they were not particularly successful. Late in the century, membership of the parish football club and gymnasium was made dependent upon attending Bible class which boosted numbers and led to more confirmations, though whether it produced lifelong Churchmen is unknown. The bribe technique has its risks.

William Fox

Very little is known about William Fox's early life. He was born around 1733 and joined the Royal Navy serving in the Seven Years' War and War of American Independence. In 1780, he was captain of the *Prince George*, a warship of ninety-eight guns. He reached the rank of Rear-Admiral before retiring to Ramsgate where his sister lived. Mary Fox had married the brewer Richard Tomson in London in 1762 and the couple had five daughters and one son to whom William was clearly very close. He signed as the witness to the marriage of four of the children and they were the chief beneficiaries in his will.

Ten months after his death, St Laurence church received a surprise visit in the form of HRH The Duke of Clarence, third son of King George III. The Duke said that he wished to pay respects to the grave of his friend William Fox. The sexton duly took him to the appropriate place in the churchyard. The Duke asked why there was no stone. Was there a tablet inside? The sexton said that none had been erected and the Duke asked why. The sexton said that the family could not afford it – a statement which was probably untrue. William had left hundreds of pounds and the family included the most prominent

---

[171] General Committee of the Church of England Sunday School Institute Minutes 3rd February 1891
[172] *Parochial Report, 1891* p.32. In today's money, this would be about £330

businessmen in town – Richard Tomson, Peter Burgess, and George Hooper. However, the sexton had been put in a very difficult position. The Duke replied: "then send for a mason and I will order and pay for one." He promptly took a pencil out of his pocket and some paper and wrote the following inscription which was duly carved on a marble tablet and erected on the north wall of the north chancel:[173]

> This monument to the memory of the late Rear Admiral William Fox, who died 3rd December 1810 aged 77 years, is erected by His Royal Highness Prince William Henry, Duke of Clarence and St Andrews, and Earl of Munster, K.G. & K.T., Admiral of the Red Squadron of His Majesty's Fleet from a sincere regard for the character of the late Rear Admiral, and from an uninterrupted friendship which subsisted for 31 years. October 11th 1811

William Fox lived in Effingham Street on the site of the fire station with part of his land later being used to build Ramsgate Public Library.[174]

Jane Austen

It is likely that Jane Austen visited the church since she stayed in Ramsgate during the summers of 1802 and 1803. Whether she came as a visitor or worshipper cannot be known. By that date, Ramsgate Chapel was in existence and that was closer to where she was staying. Her brother Francis married Mary Gibson at St Laurence on 24th July 1806 but she was not in attendance at that time as her diaries prove.[175] A memorial to his mother in law, Mary Gibson née Curling, can be seen on the south wall near the font.

The fact that Jane Austen's brother adopted the same arms as Nathaniel of Ramsgate would indicate a familial link but the alleged shared ancestor lived in the reign of Henry VII. If the tree was to be authenticated, it should show they were fifth cousins three times removed, which almost certainly means that they would have been unaware of it.

Royal Links

The most famous visitor to the parish in the nineteenth century was undoubtedly Princess Victoria, the future Queen. She first came to the church in 1823 when she was just four years old and as late as 1890 there were members of the congregation who remembered her sitting with her mother and governess and peering over the high pews

---

[173] *Imperial Magazine* (1833) p.200. The monument is now behind the organ.
[174] His will shows he owned property in Queen Street as well PROB 11/1518/133
[175] She was at Bath until 22nd July then went to Clifton. The witnesses to the marriage were Caroline Townley (daughter of James and Mary) and Harriet Bentinck (sister-in-law of Robert Garrett)

to look back at the congregation.[176] She returned in 1825 and 1827, staying again at Townley House on both occasions. Her tutor described her as "volatile" but "very good tempered and very affectionate" noting how she was particularly gentle with all animals.[177] In 1830 and 1835, she stayed at Albion Place, although illness prevented her being seen much in 1835. In 1836, she stayed at West Cliff House, home of the Warre family. It was noted that not only did she attend church in the parish but she visited its attractions such as the tea gardens at Pegwell and she enjoyed walking about the village.[178]

On September 30th 1836, the year of her last full visit, the wardens stood on lookout at the top of St Laurence church tower to see the coach carrying the young Princess and her mother, the Duchess of Kent, entering the parish. Immediately, the bells were rung and the Royal Standard was raised whilst the Vicar sped down to the seafront in his own coach so that he would be there to greet them.[179]

As confirmation that the Princess enjoyed her time in the parish, in November 1842, she brought her new husband, Prince Albert, to see Ramsgate. Although they did not stop at St Laurence church, they drove past it on the way to the seafront and no doubt waved at the crowds who had gathered with their flags as the bells rang out.

When Victoria became Queen in 1837, the parish installed a clock to mark the occasion. Eight years later on the anniversary of her accession, the bell ringers took a set of handbells up to the top of the tower where they rang 250 changes bob major style from the battlements.[180] In 1887, for her Golden Jubilee, they restored the tower. In 1897, for her Diamond Jubilee, they installed a new clock. When she died in 1901, the Parish Magazine was issued with a black border and a collection was started for a memorial window.

In 1803, the Princess of Wales, took Albion House then East Cliff Lodge as her summer residence which caused her to worship at St Laurence church. This was the

---

[176] Montague Fowler, *A Record of Church Work* (Ramsgate, 1890) p.17
[177] *Kebles Gazette*, 3rd February 1917
[178] *Kent Coast Times*, 22nd November 1888
[179] *Canterbury Weekly Journal*, 8th October 1836. The Royal Standard would have remained flying as long as the Princess was in the parish. It was kept in the church tower but stolen in May 1984. The fact that it was flown was controversial for it should only have been used when the reigning monarch was in the parish, not the heiress presumptive.
[180] *Kentish Gazette*, 1st July 1845

unfortunate Caroline of Brunswick who would later face the indignity of being shut out of Westminster Abbey when her husband became George IV. The couple had separated by this stage and it is significant that other members of the royal family chose to support her.[181]

The parish was staunchly royalist and in March 1863, when Princess Alexandra arrived off the coast of Margate from Denmark on her way to marry the Prince of Wales, not only were the church bells rung but the anvils of St Lawrence forge were struck twenty-one times in lieu of guns as a salute.[182] In 1821, the High Street at St Lawrence was festooned with garlands and a triumphal arch was erected for the passage of George IV through the village en route to Ramsgate where he dined with his friend Sir William Curtis, the man to whom the phrase "three Rs" is attributed.[183] He arrived almost three hours late by which time it was dark so it is unlikely any parishioners would have seen him even if he had opened the carriage window. George IV was so touched by the display of affection by the inhabitants that he bestowed the title of Royal Harbour on the town. It was unusual. George IV was one of the most unpopular monarchs which the country has ever had. Nathaniel Wraxall said he was:

> A most fascinating and accomplished gentleman, but he wanted all the qualities of a wise or of a great prince : self-command, application, economy, activity, firmness, and above all, economical principles….There was from head to foot a flaccidity of muscle and a rotundity of outline inimical to our conceptions of masculine strength or beauty…His person had, something diffused over it indicative of repose or of sloth, rather than of energy or activity.[184]

Moore meanwhile claimed that: "I am sure the powder in His Royal Highness's hair is much more settled than anything in his head."[185]

In 1817, the country was shocked by the death of Princess Charlotte, sole child of the future George IV. Richard Harvey decided to hold a funeral service at St Laurence simultaneously with the actual burial. The bells were tolled duly half muffled and crowds arrived to take their seats. Just as the vicar was about to start, the sound came of a pack of hounds accompanied by horseback riders. He hurried outside and remonstrated with the sportsmen severely ordering them to either dismount and come into church and show

---

[181] *Kentish Gazette* 15th April and 12th May 1803; John Marshall, *Royal Naval Biography* (London, 1830) p.409. For further information see Bolton *Seven Centuries* op.cit. p.340.
[182] *Thanet Advertiser*, 18th March 1863
[183] *Kentish Gazette* 24th September 1821.
[184] Henry B Wheatley (ed.), *The Historical and the Posthumous Memoirs of Sir Nathaniel Wraxall*, vol. 5 (London, 1884) pp.353, 363.
[185] Spencer Walpole, *The Life of the Right Honourable Spencer Perceval*, vol 2, (London, 1874) p.226

their respects like gentlemen or else to go home and have their sport at a more suitable time.[186] It is not clear which option they chose but the service went ahead without further interruption.

In January 1892, the church held a memorial service for H.R.H. the Duke of Clarence, elder brother of the future George V. As with the service for Princess Charlotte, the service was held simultaneously with that taking place at St George's Chapel, Windsor. The service was not taken by the vicar, however, for the Reverend Montague Fowler was actually attending the main event in Windsor itself.

Cromwell Massey

A monument on the south side of the wall of the nave remembers Cromwell Massey who died in 1845. He had served with the Honourable East India Company which operated as the British Army in India. In 1780, he was a Lieutenant in Captain Phillips company of European grenadiers when Haider Ali invaded the Carnatic. Haider's army consisted of sixty thousand cavalry and fifty thousand infantry all under the command of French officers. A British observer reported his army occupied an area seven miles by three.[187] He was supported by his son Tipu Sahib who attacked Colonel Baillie's detachment at Perambaucum on 5th September with thirty thousand cavalry and eight thousand infantry.[188] Severely outnumbered and under equipped with his troops facing wholesale slaughter, Baillie sent for help and Captain Phillips troop was one of those sent to the rescue.

Having relieved Baillie, they started back to Conjevaram fourteen miles away but they were attacked en route first by Tipu's cannons to the left and then Haider's cavalry to the front. Within minutes, they were surrounded and disaster struck when two of Haider's rockets succeeded in blowing up the British ammunition tumbrels. This caused huge casualties and broke the British line. Baillie took the four hundred or so men he had left to a mount and formed them into a square. With no ammunition left, the men - most of whom were wounded - tried to fight off their attackers with bayonets. They repelled thirteen separate charges. One officer wrote: "History cannot produce an instance for fortitude, cool intrepidity and desperate resolution to equal the exploits of this heroic band."[189] He described the scene:

> The field presented a picture of the most inhuman cruelties and
> unexampled carnage. The last and awful struggle was marked
> by the clashing of arms and shields, the snorting and kicking of
> horses, the snapping of spears, the glistening of bloody swords,

---

[186] *Thanet Magazine*, November 1817 p.247
[187] Innes Munro, *A Narrative of the Military Operations on the Coronmandel Coast* (London, 1789) pp.144-145
[188] Also known as the Battle of Pollilur
[189] Munro op.cit. p.155

> oaths and imprecations ; concluding with the groans and cries of bruised and mutilated men, wounded horses tumbling to the ground upon expiring soldiers, and the hideous roaring of elephants stalking to and fro, and wielding their dreadful chains alike amongst friends and foes. Such as were saved from the immediate stroke of death were so crowded together that it was with difficulty they could stand: several were in a state of suffocation ; while others, from the weight of the dead bodies that had fallen upon them, were fixed to the spot at the mercy of a furious foe.[190]

Eventually, Baillie had to admit defeat and he raised the white flag. Haider's cavalry leader said they should lay down their arms which they did but then, to British horror, the enemy continued the assault. His men rode through the British ranks on elephants and horses slashing out at the now unarmed men. Of eighty-six officers, only sixteen escaped unhurt. The situation was made worse by the fact that there had recently been heavy rain so there was suffocating mud everywhere. It was reported that "in a few seconds, Baillie's little body of Europeans was cut to pieces."[191]

Haider Ali was encamped six miles away and he offered rewards to his men who would bring him the heads of British officers. Massey's commanding officer Captain Phillips was beheaded in the field and his head taken as a trophy.[192] Eventually, the killing stopped and Haider's troops decided to strip the wounded and stretch them out in the sun and leave them to die. Massey's fellow Lieutenant, Phillip Melville, described the experience:

> I was lying naked on a bank of scorching sand, fainting from time to time with loss of blood, and from the severity of my wounds unable to move. By day I was assailed with the rage of intolerable thirst, and if at times I opened my eyes to surrounding objects, the countenances of such as were suffering in the agonies of death increased the horrors of my mind while my ears were tortured with their dying groans. By night, the same doleful sounds mingled with the howling of beasts of prey.[193]

Massey was wounded but the details of his injuries are unknown. He clearly

---

[190] ibid. p.156
[191] Robert, James and John Lindsay, *Oriental Miscellanies*, (Wigan, 1840) p.139
[192] Anon, *Historical Record of the Honourable East India Company's First Madras European Regiment* (London, 1843) pp. 276-280
[193] Philip Melvill, *Memoirs of the late Philip Melvill* (London, 1812) p.49

survived the two days that the prisoners were left exposed without water amid foxes, jackals and tigers because he was next taken on the journey to Arnée. Those who could walk were left to do so, chained in pairs and with no medication and being beaten if they flagged by their guards. Those unable to walk were put in cages just three feet by two feet across and dragged through the villages, their open wounds bumping against the bars and the cart all the way, this so they could be taunted and abused by the inhabitants as well as the guards who poked sticks at them. They not only sat in their own excrement but they had it thrown at them.[194] On 14th September, they were given small pieces of coarse cloth each and some dry cold rice soaked in water whilst a heavy rain shower brought brief relief from the sun. During the course of the journey, Lieutenant Knox died leaving Massey as the sole surviving officer of Captain Phillips company.

The men arrived at Arnée on 16th September. They still had no shoes or proper clothes but they did receive the ministrations of a surgeon who had some rusty instruments and they tore the cloth they had been given into bandages. Their daily food allowance was a little rice, a spoonful of ghee, half a spoonful of salt, a little curry powder plus twice a week some mutton.[195] On November 1st, Massey, with eight others, was considered fit enough to be taken on to Seringapatam, an island fortress some three weeks walk away. The dungeon there was to be his home for the next three years and seven months. On December 23rd ten more officers joined them from Arnée.

Three detailed accounts of the time spent at Seringapatam exist. One was published by William Thomas who shared Massey's cell and Massey himself kept a diary which is now held by the British Library.[196] It is in two volumes and just 4" by 2" and it was hand sewn using ink he made by mixing soot from the wick of a lamp with gum water. Part of the diary is in code. It includes letters received from other captives about the prison. Referring to the forced circumcision of the prisoners which is described in lurid detail, the most memorable entry in the diary is "Terribly alarmed this morning for our foreskins."[197] Another journal was kept by John Lindsay and was published under the title of *Oriental Miscellanies* in 1840.[198] Lieutenant Melville, who had been with Massey at Arnée was sent to a dungeon at Bangalore where he describes very similar conditions.

All of the accounts all speak of the physical and mental anguish suffered by the prisoners. They were chained in pairs which left them barely able to walk. Each set of irons weighed almost nine pounds.[199] The prison doors were kept closed during the day which left them sometimes gasping for air. Many of them died and their bodies were then thrown outside for the tigers to eat.[200] Access to medicine was almost non-extant and they

---

[194] William Thomas, *Memoirs of the Late War in Asia* vol. 2 (London, 1788) pp.19-20
[195] ibid. op.cit pp.23-24
[196] MSS Eur B392
[197] Linda Colley, *Captives* (London, 2002) p.289
[198] Lindsay was also in the same cell, Thomas op.cit. p.203
[199] ibid. p.47
[200] ibid. p.43

were in constant fear of being poisoned or mutilated. At various points, their food allowance was reduced. Despite this they showed ingenuity and courage, concealing letters and diaries in their clothes or in holes in the ground. They passed messages to captives in other parts of the prison by hiding them in rice cakes or rolling them up in cigars. They sent money hidden in buttons.[201] They did this despite being warned that if they were discovered communicating they would have their noses and ears cut off. They made a pack of cards, a chessboard and backgammon set from bits of bamboo and decorated them with paint made from indigo and turmeric. They earned money by

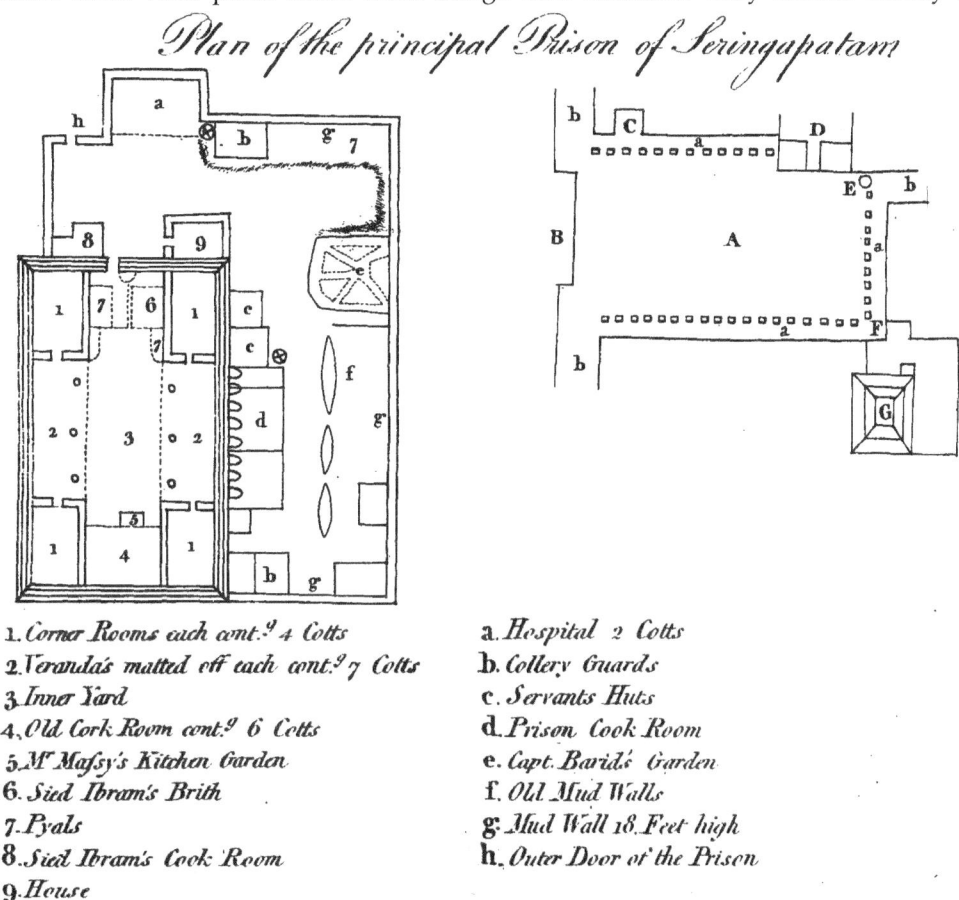

Plan of the principal Prison of Seringapatam

1. Corner Rooms each cont.g 4 Cotts
2. Veranda's matted off each cont.g 7 Cotts
3. Inner Yard
4. Old Cork Room cont.g 6 Cotts
5. Mr Massy's Kitchen Garden
6. Sied Ibram's Brith
7. Pyals
8. Sied Ibram's Cook Room
9. House

a. Hospital 2 Cotts
b. Collery Guards
c. Servants Huts
d. Prison Cook Room
e. Capt. Barid's Garden
f. Old Mud Walls
g. Mud Wall 18 Feet high
h. Outer Door of the Prison

trapping rats in their cell and selling them to the natives for curry.[202]

In October 1782, Massey was taken seriously ill and released from his irons as it was expected he would die. This was due to an outbreak of fever which was exacerbated by poor sanitation, the cells being regularly flooded and left with stagnant water. He

---

[201] ibid. p50, 57, 157
[202] Lindsay op.cit. p.217

recovered and was returned to them on 6th February 1783.[203]

In August 1783, Massey and Thomas witnessed a visit by Tipu's eight year old son and gasped as they saw:

> The young Sultan was mounted on a beautiful managed Arabian horse, finely caparisoned. He was attended and preceded by a number of people, some of whom bore up his umbrella, others fanned his face, others proclaimed his rank and high descent. Two elephants were stationed to pay their compliments to the young prince among the rest of his adorers. The creatures were not only taught to kneel at his approach, and mew other marks of obedience, but to fan his face as he went along, with fans which they grasped and wielded with their trunks.[204]

On March 22nd 1784, the men received news that peace had been agreed between Great Britain and Tipu Sultan, his father Haider Ali having died. They prepared themselves a banquet of plantain fritters and sherbet and waited. The next afternoon, their irons were knocked off and they were taken outside. Over the next few days they were allowed to walk in the bazaar and bathe in the river but they were unable to enjoy this as much as they had hoped because the long months in chains just eight inches long and scant diet had left them very weak. Thomas said they stumbled around like cripples "No effort of our mind, no act of volition, could, for several days, overcome the habit of making the short and constrained steps to which we had been so long accustomed."[205]

By April 15th, all the prisoners from Seringapatam and Bangalore were reunited and their complete freedom soon followed. Massey chose to stay with the East India Company and remained in their service until his retirement on 1st October 1800. He married Frances Bamford of Meath a month later.[206] She died on Valentine's Day 1834 in Sloane Square, London.

The monument in St Laurence tells the story of Massey's survival using the wording of his obituary in *The Illustrated London News* and adds that "He resided at St Laurence for the last 11 years of his life, where he was greatly respected for his benevolence and his many acts of charity to the poor and to the public institutions of the place."[207] It is not known how the monument came to be erected. Massey left no money to

---

[203] ibid. p.234, Thomas op.cit. p.90, 122
[204] ibid. p.136
[205] ibid. pp.207-208. See also Lindsay op.cit. p.216
[206] *East India Register 1845* p146. He was clearly in Europe at the time he retired because he could not have sailed from Madras to Ireland in a month.
[207] *Illustrated London News* September 20th 1845 p.187

the church and his estate was left to his housekeeper, his family having died.[208] An incised sandstone chest tomb to him can be found in the churchyard.[209]

Massey's age at the time he died on 8th September 1845 is shown as 103. On the 1841 census, where he appeared living between the church and Ladies' Seminary, he was listed as being one hundred years old. Given that his birth and early army records are missing, it is impossible to verify this, though the fact that he died sixty five years after being taken prisoner indicates that he was of very advanced age.

Augustus Welby Pugin

It is likely that Pugin's first visit to Ramsgate took place in 1832 when he was twenty years old and newly widowed with an infant daughter. His aunt, Selina Welby, lived at Rose Cottage and he stayed with her for a while before returning to work in London. He must have liked what he saw for a year later he returned with his new bride and settled at Ellington Cottage. Whether he ever attended worship at St Laurence is uncertain but it is possible as he did not join the Roman Catholic church until 1835 although he was taking instruction from 1834. It is likely, however, that he visited as he was interested in church architecture, going so far as to say that a true sense of the sublimity of God could only be generated through buildings.[210] His new home was beside the old chantry chapel and he clearly enjoyed exploring the ruins and excavating for he wrote to a friend on 21st January 1834:

> I am now settled at Ramsgate in Kent where I live in a small retired house with a magnificent view of the Channel and well calculated for study and which I have filled with antiquities of various sorts from William the Conqueror to Henry the Eighth – a collection which it would afford you as much pleasure to see as me to show you. In my garden I have the ruin of a chapel dedicated to St Laurence and in digging have discovered the great part of the tracery etc."[211]

It is likely that Pugin would have been regarded as something of a character by the locals. An eyewitness account describes him as "beardless with long, thick, straight black hair, an eye that took in everything…a striking figure though rather below ordinary stature and thick set." They added that he wore wide skirted black dress coats, loose trousers, shapeless shoes "tied anyhow" and black silk handkerchief at his neck. The

---

[208] PROB 11/2024/209. The will was written on 14th September 1836.
[209] Grave no. 468
[210] Rosemary Hill, *God's Architect*, (London, 2007) pp. 101, 121, 127, 138, 157
[211] Margaret Belcher, *The collected letters of A.W.N. Pugin*, Vol. 1 (Oxford, 2001) p.20. The chapel was dedicated to the Holy Trinity not St Laurence. Pugin kept no records of what he found thus denying historians the opportunity to learn more about the building.

overall effect, they claimed, was a cross between a dissenting minister and a sailor. Another person added that he had "a sonorous trumpet voice" and was prone to sing operatic arias as a baritone when happy and when not, was liable to turn the air blue with his language.[212] His neighbours must have been delighted.

On 15th June 1834 Pugin's son Edward was baptised at St Laurence by the curate. Augustus was absent being overseas at the time. He was described in the register as an architect although he had completed little work by this time and was best known for his work as a set designer for London theatres and for the furniture which George IV had commissioned for Windsor Castle. Following the death of his aunt and a bequest which enabled Augustus to pursue his career, the family left the parish in May 1835.[213]

In May 1843, Pugin bought an area of land on the West Cliff on which he built his new home, The Grange. By this time, he had become famous for his books, such as *True Principles* (1841) and for his church designs. A year after his arrival, he began work on the Houses of Parliament, many of the drawings for which were created in Ramsgate. Pugin died at The Grange on 14th September 1852 aged forty. On the afternoon before his death he had gone for a walk with his wife as far as St Laurence church making it one of the last places he would have seen.[214]

In 1850, Pugin's daughter Ann married a stained glass artist and settled at Southwood Terrace where her next door neighbour was the vicar of St Laurence's widowed mother, Mrs Ann Sicklemore.

William Garrow

Within the churchyard to the south-west of the church and in front of the Garrett memorial wall and old boiler-house, is the tomb of Sir William Garrow. Born on 13th April 1760, he was the son of a vicar and schoolteacher who chose to educate him at home rather than send him to public school. It was evident that William had a gift for words and for logic so he was encouraged to consider a career in the law. With no family connections, this was thought to be a considerable ambition but William joined some debating societies where his successes helped him attract patronage. He went to London and after training at Lincoln's Inn, commenced his career as a barrister in 1783. It was said of him that: "His acuteness in examining witnesses and his dexterity and judgment in seizing and discussing points of law raised for him a distinguished character and most favourable public opinion." In short he possessed "the acquisitions of a scholar and the manners of a gentleman."[215]

Garrow's work as a lawyer featured in the 2009-2011 BBC series *Garrow's Law* though in a fictionalised form. For example, in the first episode of the third series, he was shown heroically defending a man traumatised by war who had fired shots at the King. In

---

[212] Hill op.cit p.178, 325
[213] Pugin's wife remained an Anglican until the summer of 1839. Hill, op.cit. p.210
[214] Caroline Stanford, ed. *Dearest Augustus and I* (Reading, 2004) p.76
[215] *The Times*, 7th November 1840

 reality, Garrow was part of the prosecution team who far from wishing to see James Hadfield escape the noose by plea of insanity, urged his immediate execution.

Yet, Garrow was a man of principle. When invited to take on the representation of a company of slave traders he responded: "Sir, if your committee would give me their whole income and all their estates, I would not be seen as the advocate of practices which I abhor and a system that I despise."

His legal work caused him to enter politics. He joined the Whig Club in 1784 and became a supporter of Charles James Fox, the confidante of the Prince of Wales who tried to bring down the government during George III's first bout of mental illness in order to gain the profligate, debt-ridden prince, a bigger allowance. Garrow went on to serve as Solicitor-General to the Prince and became an MP in 1805 at his encouragement. He admitted that he regarded himself as the Prince's servant rather than the ministry's or his constituents.[216] As an MP, he opposed Catholic relief and liberty of the press and he encouraged the severest punishment of machine breakers. He claimed the utmost rigour was required for the sake of society. The only bill which he ever instituted related to the speed of stage coaches which he sought to limit but in this he was unsuccessful. William Deeble commented: "His abilities as a statesman are far less eminent than his talents as a counsellor and pleader at the bar."[217] Unsurprisingly, he also spoke on various occasions in defence of the Prince and his behaviour, including supporting him in his treatment of the Princess. When the Prince became Regent, he rewarded Garrow by appointing him Attorney General. When George IV visited Ramsgate in 1821, Garrow was invited to dine with him and he also delivered the loyal address on behalf of the town.[218]

It was whilst he was a barrister that Garrow purchased a property at Pegwell which he demolished to build a new villa for himself.[219] He showed his involvement in the parish over the years by contributing to various charitable causes including the establishment of the SPCK library.[220] He was clearly a regular worshipper for on 13th December 1827, the vestry voted to allow him six feet of space in the pew directly below the Townley gallery which means he would have sat directly next to the present pulpit.[221] Even when his work kept him in London, his children remained and in 1802, his daughter

---

[216] http://www.historyofparliamentonline.org/
[217] William Deeble, *Delineations Historical and Topographical of the Isle of Thanet and the Cinque Ports* Vol.1 (London, 1817), p.117
[218] *Kentish Gazette*, 24th September 1821
[219] Hasted op.cit. p.378. He was said at the time to be earning 300 guineas a case, around £30,000 today.
[220] CCA-U3-19/7/5
[221] This was the second pew back from the pillar. Samuel Winter of Southwood sat behind in the third pew and Mr Warre in the fourth.

Eliza married William Lettsom, son of the founder of the Royal Sea Bathing Hospital at Margate.[222]

Garrow served as a judge for fourteen years and was knighted in 1817. He retired to Pegwell in 1832 where he died aged eighty on 21st September 1840. He was laid to rest at St Laurence despite him stating in his will that he wished to be buried with his uncle in Hadley.[223]

The Church Schools

During the nineteenth century, the parish established four schools. The infants school in Newington Road was built by John Ashley Warre and opened in 1841 when it was described as a "neat and elegant" building. It was set up for the poor to provide the children with their basic ABC free of charge.[224] The land was given by Warre specifically for this purpose and the original trustees were Warre and his wife Caroline, his two sons Arthur and John, and the vicar and his wife. By 1844, it had two hundred pupils in two rooms which were about twenty feet square.[225] The school operated on what was known as the Bell and Lancaster system which meant that the teacher concentrated on teaching the older pupils and the ablest of these in turn taught the younger ones in small groups about the same room. This saved money because it meant less teachers needed to be employed and it could be argued that it encouraged responsibility and clarity of thought since instructing others requires a good level of understanding. It did, however, limit the amount of education which a child could get but this was a charity school designed to teach the basics not prepare children for further study. It was considered modern at the time because it taught children to read syllables and use them to form words rather than simply to recognise word forms. It advocated learning multiplication tables before addition and subtraction and recommended short lessons to maintain attention and a rewards system to encourage, instead of maintaining discipline through fear. The founder of the system said that religion must be taught to encourage "habits of diligence, industry, veracity and honesty" though one might have hoped that the church's aim was to spread the Gospel and that these virtues were a by-product not the end game.[226]

It is unknown when the girls school came into being but given that it was not listed in the *Post Office Directory* of 1845 and was in *Bagshaw's Historical Directory and Gazeteer of Kent* in 1847, it must be presumed that it opened in 1846.[227] In 1847, there were

---

[222] John Whyman, *The Early Kentish Seaside* (KAO, 1985) p.348
[223] Richard Braby, *Sir William Garrow: His Life, His Times and Fight for Justice*, (London, 2010) p.158.
[224] *Canterbury Journal*, 30th January 1841. The request for tender had been published in the *Kentish Gazette*, 10th March 1840 which indicates how swiftly the builders worked.
[225] *Kentish Gazette*, 3rd September 1844.This clearly included children who were beyond infancy.
[226] Andrew Bell, *The Madras School or Elements of Tuition*, (London, 1808) pp.64-82, 153. Bell's work was the basis for all National Society schools and introduced to the army by the Duke of York.
[227] Bagshaw vol. 2 p.146. The lack of any entries in the church accounts relating to its erection would

said to be ninety infants and forty girls with the girls school standing behind the infants.[228] Plans were being drawn up to erect a school for boys.

By contrast, the boys school which stood opposite, beside what is now the Warre Recreation Ground, was built by public subscription. Donors included: the Vicar £50, John Ashley Warre £35, Sir Moses Montefiore £35, Thomas Noel Harris £35, the Dowager Countess of Ashburnham £27, the National Society £20, Cobb's Bank at Margate £10, Bethlehem Hospital £10, the Archbishop of Canterbury £10, Daniel Hooper £5. The government made a grant of £58 toward the project and the architect contributed £10, the solicitor £5. Other donors included Gilbert Bedford whose memorial can be seen just above the choir stalls in the high chancel of the church. The vestry book records the start of building work in February 1850 on ground had been given by George Wilson Sicklemore and was part of the parish land or glebe. [229] The costs were as follows:

	£	s	d
Building	385	14	
Architect fees	20		
Legal fees	19	1	
Stove	5	6	
Books	2	13	4
carpentry work	2	19	
Green baize blinds	3	1	3
Printing costs	1	6	1
	440	0	8

In today's terms, this would be £42,000. As the parish had collected £443 1s 6d, this meant that the new school started life with £3 0s 4d in hand. On 18th May 1860, it became a National Society school which meant it was subject to both HM Inspection and Diocesan Inspection and liable to grants. Within twenty years of opening, the number of boys had outgrown the school

---

suggest that it was built by the Warre family.
[228] This small structure appears on the 1860 Ordnance Survey map. It was demolished in 1885.
[229] The plans are held at Kent Archives Office DE/S315/1. The land was not part of the ancient glebe but formed part of that added under the Queen Anne's Bounty scheme.

and funds were being raised to extend it but the rate of collection was poor.[230] Finance was a continual problem. From 1875 to 1880, the school was running at a deficit with the vicar having to pay £10 to £30 a year from his own income simply to keep it open.[231] Pupil numbers continued to rise and by 1896, forty of the boys – just over a quarter of the regular pupils - were having their lessons in the Parish Hall. As a result, in 1898, over thirty years after the extension fund opened, an additional classroom was added for £376 10s and by 1900, there were 214 boys attending.[232]

In 1885, owing to pressure of space in the Warre building, a new infants school was built opening on 30th November 1885. Costing £335, this was built of red brick and barely thirty feet by twenty, the children being taught in the one room. The girls moved into the original building and new toilets and a playground were added.[233] The infants was incorporated with the National Society on 31st August 1888.

As well as the schools, there was a house which had been erected for the head teacher of the girls school and which provided two key benefits. It meant that the school had no need to provide a staff room or toilet since the teacher could simply walk across the playground to make her tea or use the facilities. It also generated a small rent which contributed to the running costs. In 1891, the census shows that the head teachers of the girls and infants schools were sharing the property, both being single ladies. In 1861, the property had been occupied by the head teacher of the infants and her assistant.

A further parish school was built at Manston in 1875. It had been intended that St Catherine's church would operate as a school Monday to Friday and as a church on Sunday and the Ecclesiastical Commission had made it a condition of their grant toward

---

[230] *Thanet Advertiser*, 29th August 1868, 18th September 1869

[231] *Parochial Report, 1881* p.3 The vicar's annual income in the 1870s was £162 gross so this donation was a considerable percentage, equivalent to around £2000 a year today, *Crockford's Clerical Directory* 1874. His successor declined to continue this practice and raised the fees.

[232] In 1882 a new lobby was added on the northern side. *Parochial Reports 1882-3* p.3, *1897-8* p.2, *1898-9* p.13

[233] The final bill was £479 13s 6d to which Mr Warre gave £150 and the diocese £50. Work on the old infants school, which was now the girls, cost £97 of this. The remaining sum related to fees from the architect, lawyers and correspondence expense. The total would be about £54,000 today.

the new church in 1873 that this would be the case.[234] However, that soon proved impossible and in 1874, the Vicar, Mr Sicklemore, gave land for a new school to be built. It was designed by Mr W. V. Green and built by Mr W. H. Port at a cost of £360.[235] This school was affiliated to the National Society in 1876.

In addition to these, a school was erected for the 1300 strong population in the area of Holy Trinity which was still part of St Laurence parish. This was built by W. E. Smith who was also carrying out the restoration of St Laurence church at the same time. The school cost £900 to build and equip and consisted of two rooms, each of which was able to seat sixty children with boys being on one side and girls the other. It was designed as a multi-purpose building with the screen that created the two rooms being removable to leave a large public meeting room. Mr Warre and his wife were generous benefactors to that school also.[236]

Prior to the Education Act of 1880, it was up to the parents to decide whether or not they wished to send their children. This voluntary principle was regarded as being very important for two reasons. Firstly, it meant that the church maintained control of the schools whereas a compulsory system meant government control. Secondly, it was recognised that in a poor parish such as St Laurence, many parents were dependent upon the money their children earned. In May 1874, the Reverend J. Gilmore of Holy Trinity noted that few people were in regular work and that the three or four shillings a week which children might earn was the difference between hunger and the family having a hot meal once a day.[237]

Having built the schools, the parish did its best to make use of them. Prior to the erection of the Parish Hall, they were used for a variety of meetings and in 1853 they were opened in the evenings to provide classes for older teenagers. The newspaper said that it trusted they would be "the means of keeping out of the streets many children who have been idling about" but this seems not to have been the case and the experiment was not continued in subsequent winters.[238]

From 1890-93, the Reverend Montague Fowler published the reports on the parish schools. They revealed that the boys school had 147 on its registers but an average attendance of only 130 each day – suggesting about one in eight on any given day was either working or sick. This was possibly just as well since the school only had desks for 140 children. Each boy paid 4d a week for their education with the Poor Law Guardians paying this sum on behalf of a tenth of them. The school's income was £246 of which £113 came from a grant, around £75 from the weekly pence paid by the children, and the rest from gifts or parish fundraising. The expenditure showed £192 13s 3d went on salaries,

---

[234] *Thanet Advertiser*, 8th February 1873
[235] *Thanet Advertiser*, 17th April, 1875. The site is now the Village Hall.
[236] *South Eastern Gazette*, 19th October 1858. The school was opened on the Friday and two days later came the grand re-opening of the restored St Laurence church.
[237] *Kent Coast Times*, 18th May 1874
[238] *Kentish Gazette*, 29th November 1853

£8 2s 8d on books, £12 2s 4d on fuel, £3 15s on furniture, £3 on rent, 6s 3d on insurance and £3 16s 4d on prizes giving them almost £20 left over for contingencies and school development. HM Inspector noted in 1891:

> The boys are well disciplined and their class subjects generally creditable, though grammar might be improved in the fourth standard. Reading on the whole is satisfactory and intelligent and spelling accurate. Writing in copybooks deserves great praise. Arithmetic is good in the four lower standards and very fair in the upper part of the school but the processes adopted are unnecessarily lengthy and more briskness should be shown both in dictation and working sums. If this is unattended to I shall be unable another year to recommend the higher grant.

The infant school had 106 on its books with an average attendance of 76. Having space for 120, there was plenty of room. Parents paid 2d a week for children aged three to five and 3d a week for children over five. Almost a third of the infants had their fees paid by the Guardians. The low numbers were causing financial difficulties, however, with the income of £78 6s 10d only just covering the salaries of £75: the total cost being £103 15s 11d. An endowment by the Warre family helped but the school could clearly not afford to lose money at such a level. Of this school, the Inspector said: "The infants are in good order and have received satisfactory instruction both in object lessons and elementary subjects.

The girls school was funded differently to the boys and infants in that it received no grants and that the total costs were met by the Warre family saving the money raised by the children's own school pence. There were 74 girls on the list but the average attendance was 61. Each paid 2d a week, half the rate of the boys. The Diocesan inspector reported:

The lower group seemed to be well acquainted with the subjects though there was some haste and thoughtless answering which detracted from their merit. The older girls were generally well versed in their work and the instruction had evidently been given with care and precision. The repetition throughout was very creditable.[239]

Presuming the costs of running the girls school were similar to those of the boys and infants, it would appear that the Warres were funding some ninety percent of the total which, together with their endowment to the infants school, suggests they were spending around ten thousand pounds a year in today's money on education – a very handsome benefaction. A bust of Caroline Warre made by the sculptor Henry Weekes who created the Manufactures group for the Albert Memorial in London was given to the Infants School as the gift of Sir Moses Montefiore in 1876 as a tribute to her generosity.[240] In 1896 the situation changed and the girls school became liable for grants and government inspection.

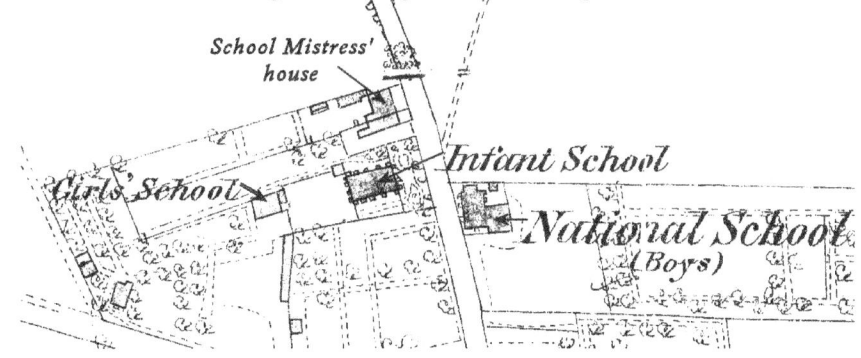

In all cases, it is evident that substantial numbers of parents were not sending their children to the parish schools. The 1891 census shows that the area about the church contained 146 infants, 163 junior aged boys and 116 junior aged girls. The percentage registered were 71%, 91% and 68% respectively with attendance being 51%, 77% and 52%. In the case of girls and infants, an alternative school was available, namely the Ellington Iron School on the corner of Crescent Road and this attracted an average of 70 girls and 38 infants each day bringing the total numbers of girls and infants in school to 78% of infants

---

[239] Montague Fowler, *A Record of Church Work* 1891 and 1892. Fees ended in 1902.
[240] *Thanet Advertiser* 7th October 1876

and virtually all the girls.[241] By this stage, the Education Act had made schooling compulsory but economic necessity meant some parents preferred to send their boys to work instead. At Manston, 90% of the available children were in the church school each day. The impact of the schools on the parish can be demonstrated by comparing the number of people who were able to sign their own name when they married. At the start of the 1860s, 64% of grooms and 77% of brides could do this: by 1900, everybody could.

No set of regulations survives for the parish schools but it is likely that they were very similar to those for St Nicholas at Wade's church school which showed that pupils attended from 9am to noon and from 2pm to 5pm from March to October with the afternoon being 1.30 to 4.30pm in winter. It was expected that children would go home for lunch though those who travelled in from Haine and Cliffsend could bring their own. Attendance twice a day at Sunday School was considered part of regular attendance. Children had a month off each harvest tide so they could work, plus a week at Christmas, two days at Easter, Whit Monday, May Day, the Queen's Accession, Michaelmas Day and every Saturday for holidays.

1851 Religious Census

In 1851, for the first and only time, a religious census was taken alongside the regular household one. This showed the following:[242]

St Laurence church
800 seats available of which 300 were free and 500 were rented
Attendance at morning service   347
Attendance at afternoon service   317
Sunday School attendance morning   117
Sunday School attendance afternoon   118

The survey is interesting because it provides our first firm evidence of the existence of a Sunday School in the parish.

Holy Trinity was then part of the parish and their figures were

Holy Trinity church
700 seats available of which 300 were free and 400 were rented
Attendance at morning service   500
Attendance at afternoon service   240

No figures were provided for Sunday School attendance, presumably because none existed.

---

[241] Figures from *1887 Kelly's Directory*. A small number of parents would have had the money for private governesses.
[242] Data from Margaret Roake, *Religious Worship in Kent: the census of 1851* (KAS, 1999)

In addition to the two Anglican churches, there were two Wesleyan Methodist chapels in the parish, one having only a morning service and the other an afternoon one, presumably because the same minister served both.

St Lawrence Methodist
125 seats available of which 100 were free and 25 were rented
Attendance at morning service   40
Sunday School attendance morning   70
Sunday School attendance afternoon   50

Manston Methodist
60 seats available of which 30 were free and 30 were rented
Attendance at afternoon service   40
Sunday School attendance morning   21
Sunday School attendance afternoon   40

The census can only be regarded as a snapshot. In order to have accurate data, it would have been necessary to repeat the exercise over several weeks. The survey was taken on Mothers' Day which may not have been representative as a number of people would have been away visiting their mother that day who may have been in another parish. Also, it was a very wet day which may have reduced attendance. The results are hard to analyse because it is impossible to tell the actual number of people who attended since many of those who attended morning worship or Sunday School also did so in the afternoon. The fact that so many churches reported numbers which were in multiples of ten also suggests that some rounding up or rough guessing was involved. There may also have been people who attended a church outside their own parish. Despite all these reservations and difficulties, the census remains the only set of figures available to enable us to gauge the outreach of the church in the mid-Victorian period. The population of the parish at this time was 3,015 with around 660 being aged four to fourteen and so of Sunday School age and 400 being younger.[243] If it is estimated that some 410 different adults and 120 children attended St Laurence and about 548 adults went to Holy Trinity, that meant that 49% of adults and 18% of children were practising Anglicans.[244] The Methodists were attracting about 4% of adults and 17% of children.

Today, we would rejoice in the thought of having a congregation which was so large but the Victorians were absolutely horrified by the results - almost half of all adults and two thirds of children were untouched by Christian worship. The fact that the vicar of St Laurence decided to abolish pew rents and make all seats free shortly afterwards was almost certainly prompted by the fear that there were people who wished to attend church but who felt they could not afford to do so. The decision to plant churches at Manston and St Luke's was another response to improve access.

---

[243] E. A. Wrigley and B .S. Schofield, *The Population History of England* (Cambridge, 1981) p.529.
[244] Based on a fifth of the afternoon congregation not having attended in the morning.

Cholera Epidemic

In 1854, an outbreak of cholera struck the town. During August seventy-six deaths were attributed to the disease in Ramsgate and eighteen at St Lawrence: in September, forty-one died in Ramsgate and twenty-three in St Lawrence. The first burial took place at St Laurence on August 10th itself and from then onwards there were almost daily burials until September 26th. From September 5th to 7th, there were five funerals every day and all of them were taken by the curate, James Boucher. Indeed, owing to the vicar's absence, he took sixty-four funerals in two months, something which must have been both physically and emotionally exhausting. The Barton family of Ellington lost four members – the mother and three children – in just a few days. Ten of the deaths occurred in Castle Cottages with more in nearby Boundary Place and Hereson, yet the disease was also active in Southwood which was on the other side of the parish. The rural parts of the parish were not affected and nor was the village High Street where there would have been many deaths had it taken hold. Given that cholera is a waterborne disease spread generally through polluted drinking water and shared cesspits, it is curious that there were so few families which lost more than one member and that the households affected were so far apart.

Understanding of the disease was still in its infancy since the disease had only appeared in England in 1831. In 1849, John Snow had published his seminal *On the mode of communication of cholera* which hypothesised that it could be spread by infected water but he was not able to prove his theory until he was able to analyse the 1854 outbreak which covered much of the country. Until then, the theory had been that it was caused by bad air and the *Kentish Gazette* reflected this in their guidelines on how to avoid cholera which advised removing foul smells with zinc or chloride of lime and making complaints to the authorities if the drains were noxious. They also printed the Medical Council of the Board of Health's advice which alleged that eating raw vegetables or the over-consumption of alcohol were likely causes and warned against getting the feet wet.[245]

The epidemic caused burials at St Laurence to rise by two-thirds. Proportionally, deaths were slightly higher than in the town – 1.4% compared to 1%. This, together with the spread of cases, is indicative of the poverty which existed at that time since susceptibility to death was directly affected by nutritional status.[246]

1861 Census

The first detailed census of the population was taken in 1841 and with the exception of 1941, a census has been conducted every ten years since. Each provides a snapshot of the parish on a given day and enables us to gain new insights into the work of the parish clergy of the time. 1861 was in the midst of the incumbency of the Reverend

---

[245] *Kentish Gazette*, 26th September 1854. The cholera bacillus was discovered in 1854 by Filippo Pacini but his work was not accepted for a further thirty years.
[246] Masimo Liv-Bacci, *Population and Nutrition* (Cambridge, 1991) p.38

George Sicklemore and it shows that notwithstanding the arrival of the railway and the growth of Ramsgate town, the parish was still very rural.

The total population was 1,926 of whom 90 lived at Cliffsend, 218 at Pegwell and Chilton, 269 at Haine and Manston and the remainder in St Lawrence village and environs. This last group, generally known as St Lawrence Intra comprised 324 in the village High Street, 419 in Southwood, 389 in Ellington, 113 in Newington Road, 22 at Nethercourt, 18 at Northwood, 29 at Whitehall and 34 at Ozengell.

The people occupied 408 houses, so average occupancy was 4.7 people per house. However, in eighteen cases, the householder was away. For example, there were servants who were awaiting the return of masters and wives whose husbands were absent at sea on the day the census was taken. With the exception of one boarding school at Ellington which housed forty-three females, all the houses were family homes. Just sixteen houses had a single occupant – 4% - eight being widows, one a widower, four unmarried women and three unmarried men. Of 228 married couples, just 18 - 8% - were without children. The average number of children at home was three, although more than thirty households had six or more children in them.

With regard to age, the structure was very different to the parish today. Over a third of the population was aged twelve or less and less than one in twelve was over sixty. Only one in thirty-six was over seventy. The oldest parishioners were two women aged eighty-eight and one of those was still working as a barmaid at the Sportsman Inn. Overall, three quarters of the population was under forty which explains why Victorian clergy were so active in relation to youth and there were no organisations for the elderly.

1861 was before the Education Act which made schooling compulsory so it is interesting to see how many children went to school. The Warre family had established a free school for infants from poor families but most people had to pay. Parents, therefore, had to make a decision as to whether to send their children to school or to work and to determine how much education they might actually need. Literacy was not necessary for many workers so was it a waste of time? Were there any opportunities if they could do more than read and do basic sums? The table shows the proportion of boys and girls at school and at work in the parish and shows that whilst parents were less likely to invest money in educating daughters, those who did kept them at school longer. In both cases, as soon as a child was able to work, he or she was likely to be removed from school. Perhaps unsurprisingly, school attendance was highest amongst those who lived nearest to the schools. Only just over a third of girls who lived at Manston went to school and less than half of the children in Pegwell received an education.

Age	Boys in school	Girls in school	Boys at work	Girls at work
3	23.5	29.2		
4	44.4	53.6		
5	63.2	56.4		
6	75.0	69.6		

Age	Boys in school	Girls in school	Boys at work	Girls at work
7	88.9	76.7		
8	83.3	76.9		
9	95.0	74.1		
10	75.0	88.2	6.3	
11	59.1	73.7	27.3	
12	55.2	75.0	20.7	
13	43.5	55.6	43.5	5.6
14	14.3	30.0	57.1	10.0

The youngest worker was a ten year old boy who worked as a labourer in the brickfields. Other boys were employed as bakery assistants or in shops whilst seventy per cent of boys were employed on farms. The census only records the usual occupation of the children and it is certain that many of those listed as scholars were in fact only part time students and that they were absent whenever there was work to be done such as helping with ploughing, harvesting or scaring birds away from the newly sown crops. For the girls, there was only one occupation usually open on leaving school, domestic service.[247] Going to work at a young age should have created children with a sense of responsibility and the parish had one twelve year old orphan working as a farm labourer as well as looking after his younger brother and sister, desperately trying to earn enough to feed them and keep them out of the workhouse.

Amongst adults too, agriculture remained the biggest employment source for men whilst women were most likely to be either servants in a private house or, if they were widowed, charwomen or laundresses. Unemployment was almost non-existent and office work was so scarce that it is easy to see why parents saw no reason to encourage their children to learn more than the basic "3Rs".

Occupational group	Male	Female	% male	% female
Agriculture	227	4	44.2%	1.6%
Domestic service	45	118	8.8%	45.7%
Crafts e.g. blacksmith	58	18	11.3%	7.0%
Charring and laundering		50		19.4%
Retail	30	6	5.8%	2.3%
Labouring – unspecified	32		6.2%	
Living on pension or alms	20	10	3.9%	3.9%
Teaching	3	19	0.6%	7.4%
Renting out homes/ land	11	11	2.1%	4.3%
Brickmaking	19		3.7%	
Transport	17		3.3%	
Living on means	4	11	0.8%	4.3%

[247] Later in the century, shop work would be an option but the hours were long, from 9am to 9pm in winter and 9am to 10pm in summer with just a short break for lunch, *Kent Argus* 3rd June 1875

Occupational group	Male	Female	% male	% female
Coastguard Service	13		2.5%	
Seafarers	13		2.5%	
Miscellaneous[248]	7	2	1.4%	0.8%
Nurses		5		1.9%
Professional	7		1.4%	
Unemployed	3	2	0.6%	0.8%
Office workers	4		0.8%	
Lodging house keepers	1	2	0.2%	0.8%

The rural parts of the parish such as Manston, Haine and Cliffsend were inevitably almost entirely occupied by farmers and their staff but many agricultural workers lived along High Street, St Lawrence whilst Newington Road and Whitehall were centres of cow keeping.

What impact did this have on ministry in the parish? The low number of professional workers meant there were few candidates for roles such as churchwarden or Sunday School teacher. The majority of the population was on a low income so fund raising was difficult. Most would have worked extremely long hours so evening meetings or services would have been poorly supported. With most wives not working outside the home, there were opportunities for pastoral work amongst mothers.

The census forms did ask about people who were disabled in some way but not a single person in the parish was listed as blind, deaf, lame or mentally ill, something which suggests a failure on the part of the census enumerator.

Robert Garrett

Toward the back of the church, just past the porch on the left hand side, is a window which shows the centurion kneeling before Our Lord to ask that He will heal his servant. He says that as a man who has men under authority, he knows that if Our Lord merely gives the word, his servant will be healed. Our Lord, he says, has no need to come to his house and he is not worthy for this to happen. In healing the servant, Our Lord pays tribute to the centurion's faith (Matt. 8: 5-13) This text was selected deliberately on behalf of Robert Garrett who was an important military man in the nineteenth century.

Garrett was born on September 18th 1791 at Ellington, son of John and Elizabeth. Following his education at Harrow, he chose to pursue a career in the army becoming an ensign in the 2nd Foot in 1811.[249] It was with them that he went to Spain in 1811 and his letters home describing the action were published in 1934.[250] Amongst the incidents he

---

[248] Includes a fish sauce manufacturer, piano tuner, police constable and a tollhouse keeper.
[249] Now the Queen's Royal Regiment (West Surrey)
[250] A. S. White (ed.), 'A subaltern in the Peninsular War. Letters of Lieutenant Robert Garrett, 1811-1813', *Journal of the Society for Army Historical Research*, Vol. 13 (1934). The sixty-two originals are in Kent Archives Office R/U888/C11/3-62

describes was one where he was seriously ill and stumbling badly as he tried to make his escape on foot from a Spanish village which was about to be taken by the French. He was spotted by an officer who had met Garrett at his uncle's house in Nethercourt and who promptly found Garrett a horse on which he was able to flee and save his life.[251] Another time, he had to fight off attackers with the butt end of the company colours, something that was discussed so much it is said to have been incorporated into *Yeomen of the Guard* in the character of Leonard Merryll.

Garrett was in Hinde's brigade, part of the 6th Division under Clinton at the Battle of Salamanca on 22nd July 1812 where Wellington was said to have defeated forty thousand Frenchmen in forty minutes. This victory was not achieved without high cost. Garrett, just twenty, was the sole surviving officer of his party and he was wounded twice. His bravery in fighting on was commended and he was created a Lieutenant a year later and transferred to the Royal Fusiliers in Portugal. Garrett's courage at Salamanca even won the respect of the French, their commanding officer General Marmont sending him a dog afterward which went on to become his family pet.

Garrett served with the Royal Fusiliers for almost two years. On 25th July 1813 he was severely wounded at the hill of Oricain in the Pyrenees almost losing his left arm. From 1814 to 1818 he served in Ireland with the 97th. This posting also almost cost him his life when he became seriously ill with typhus. Between being wounded and going to Ireland he married Charlotte Cavendish-Bentinck, niece of the ex-Prime Minister and sister of one of Wellington's closest staff, but they had little time together as she died in November 1818 after a tragic accident when she fell over their dog and damaged her spine.[252] In 1821 he married the widow Louisa Devaynes.

The bulk of Robert's career was spent with the 46th Foot where he went from Major in 1834 to Brevet-Colonel in 1854. He was sent to the Crimea that year where he commanded the 4th division. The situation there was difficult. The Charge of the Light Brigade at Balaklava which took place while he was still at sea may have been heroic but it had been a major defeat. Garrett's men landed three days after the Battle of Inkerman

---

[251] D.C. Gibson, 'General Garrett', *Archaeologia Cantiana* vol. 81 (1966) p. 126
[252] Her uncle, the Duke of Portland, was Prime Minister 1807-1809

which was a victory but achieved at a loss of thirty per cent of the men and it was clear that the Russians were far from defeated and were digging into Sevastopol. The siege would last until September 1855 and conditions were difficult. A hurricane struck their supplies just six days after they landed. Thousands died as a result of sickness and cold. Boots fell apart Sevastopol was described as a "slough of despond intersected with ditches and dotted with holes" so deep in mud that each man had become a "pedestal of mire." A journalist wrote:

> Imagine the bleakest common in England, the wettest bog in all Ireland or the dreariest muir in all Scotland, overhung by leaden skies black as ink and lashed by a tornado, sleet, snow, pelting rain – a few broken stone walls and roofless huts here and there, roads turned into torrents of mud or water…The hospital tents are all down and the wounded have to bear the inclemency of the weather as best they can…. About forty of our horses have died from the cold and wet….Dead horses and cattle lie all over the country and here and there a sad little procession might be seen with the burden of some inanimate body. [253]

Yet not all was doom and gloom. His son, who served with him, formed a "Theatre Royal" in a tent with makeshift props and instruments to entertain the men appearing himself in two farces, as a servant in "Phenomenon in a Smock" and as a lawyer in "The Moustache Movement."[254]

After the fall of Sevastopol, Garrett went on to Balaklava. On behalf of the British, he returned the town to the Russians before departing on the *Argo*, the last British soldier to leave the area.

Following his time in the Crimea, for which he was knighted and received the Légion d'honneur, Garrett continued his military career in Gibraltar, China and India. [255]

---

[253] *The Times*, 12th December 1854
[254] *The Times*, 26th January 1856
[255] *The Times*, 17th July 1856, *London Gazette* 2nd January 1857 p.12

From 1862 onwards, he worked as a JP in Kent. He died at his home in Pall Mall, London on 13th June 1869 and his body was returned to St Laurence for burial on 17th June 1869.

St Laurence Fair

A fair had been held on St Laurence day in the middle ages with proceeds to the monks of St Augustine's Abbey in Canterbury. It had been a small affair. A fair was also held in the Georgian period as is attested by the records of the local constable who attended it.[256] These records have since been lost so details cannot be given or verified. The first evidence for there being a fair comes from 1804 when the *Kentish Gazette* carried an advertisement for it. By 1868 it had become a regular event though it was not seen as a particularly prestigious event the local newspaper observing: "the annual collection of gingerbread and toy stalls usually called the fair were pitched in this village on Monday last and attracted the customary motley collection including a great number of children with whom the toy stall keepers did a great trade."[257] The following year, the local authorities began prosecuting hawkers and traders for obstructing the highway which effectively stopped the fair. The triumphant newspaper reported: "As the motley collection of stalls, shows, drinking booths etc. tends to do more harm than good the Isle of Thanet Highway Board have issued instructions to the County Surveyor which will check if not totally do away with the fair altogether."[258] There is no evidence that the fair was ever organised by the church or held for its benefit though it must be presumed that retailers had made a contribution to the rates like modern pitch fees at boot fairs.

The church did, occasionally, have bazaars when it needed to raise money for a particular purpose such as restoring the windows or building the Parish Hall. These could be quite elaborate. as the report on one in 1891 held to raise money for the Church Club showed:

> The scene inside the Parish Hall was rendered very brilliant by the array of bright colours, various nations being represented by their national costumes. Amongst them we noticed an Algerian family attended by Moorish and Arab servants in an Algerian room at the west end of the hall fitted up under the supervision of Mrs Fowler. a Bedouin chief, Bas-Breton peasant, Boulogne fisher girl, Brittany peasant, Chinaman, Spanish gypsy queen, Indian lady, Spanish picador and some ten or eleven other costumes. In addition there was a gypsy tent, bran pie, parcels office, art museum etc.[259]

---

[256] Cotton op.cit. p.166
[257] *Thanet Advertiser*, 15th August 1868
[258] *Thanet Advertiser*, 21st August 1869
[259] *Kent Coast Times*, 13th August 1891. The bazaar raised about £100 according to the November 1891 *Parish Magazine* and was held over two days. The modern equivalent would be about £11,600.

St Catherine, Manston

The 1870s saw St Laurence church give birth to its first daughter church in the modern sense.[260] The Methodists had begun their work at Manston in 1856 and by 1868 were attracting crowds of three hundred to their meetings which meant that almost all the village was there.[261] The prospect of losing influence in a key area of the parish prompted St Laurence to plan its own outreach to the village. In February 1873, the Ecclesiastical Commissioners agreed to give £120 per annum to the parish – enough to pay for a curate - provided that it undertook the costs of building the church, equipping it, and holding services therein every Sunday and utilising it as a school Monday to Friday.[262] A collection was promptly started and generous donations were made by the vicar and Mr Thomas Noel Harris and also by Sir Moses Montefiore. The former two names might have been expected to contribute given their positions within St Laurence but it was extraordinary that a Jew should be so generous in supporting Christian mission and his gift was a powerful testimony to his humanity and the reality of inter-faith relations.

Just five months later, on 18th July 1873, the foundation stone was laid by the Dean of Canterbury. In a cavity beneath was placed a glass bottle containing a copy of the day's programme, a copy of each of the *Kent Coast Times* and *Thanet Advertiser* for that week and some coins. Drawings of the new building by the architect W. E Smith of London were put on display and they showed a building sixty feet by thirty with a porch

at the west end and a hammer beam roof, the whole to be built in the Early English style in line with the contemporary fashion for all things Gothic. Land for the church had been given by the Reverend George Sicklemore from his personal estate and there was sufficient space to permit a chancel to be built at a later date if money was forthcoming. In accordance with the policy of employing local firms, bricks made in the parish were to be used faced with Bath stone and with additional Staffordshire blue bricks to decorate. The actual building was to be erected by Smith and Sons of Ramsgate. There were to be enough pews to seat 250 adults on a Sunday or the

---

[260] St George, Holy Trinity and St Luke's were all created out of St Laurence but as fully fledged parishes and not as dependent daughters. Ramsgate Chapel, alias St Mary, had been privately built.
[261] *Thanet Advertiser*, 18th April 1868. The Methodist church at Manston closed on May 21st 2006.
[262] *Thanet Advertiser*, 8th February 1873

same number of children as a school.[263]

The church was licensed for services on 20th May 1874 and in September 1874, the first harvest festival was held. A Sunday School was formed and in January 1875, the children therein went on their first Christmas treat.[264]

For reasons which are unclear, the building was never used as a school. There may have been fears that the children would vandalise it, there being concerns about "the great amount of vice and depravity at present existing amongst the children of the district." In the week before the church opened, a meeting was held regarding building a new school and Mr Sicklemore said he would give land for this on condition that it was established as a National Society school rather than a secular one. In the spring of 1875, it was announced that Mr Port had won the contract to build the school at a cost of £360. It would have room for 120 children aged from three to thirteen. The architect was W. Vincent Green who also lived in the parish.[265]

As a new church there was little requirement for major work to be done in the remainder of the century though there were enhancements. In 1890, new brass communion rails were installed and the church was given the stone pulpit from St Laurence to replace the plain wooden one which it had used since 1874. It already had the Georgian font.

In the wider field of mission, an SPCK lending library was established in the church in 1881 and a Band of Hope started in 1882. In February 1890 a church choir was formed with twelve men and boys. This was started by Mrs Ada Fowler, wife of the vicar, who accompanied her each week for practice sessions. From Easter 1890 the choir was surpliced. Mrs Fowler also began a Sewing Class in the village in 1889 and set up a maternity charity to raise money to support poor women. In a major expansion of services, the Reverend Montague Fowler introduced Holy Communion three times a month alongside the weekly 11a.m. Matins with Litany and 6:30 p.m. Evening Prayer plus children's services twice a month, all with sermons. His efforts saw the church average six confirmation candidates a year and the congregation double.

The church at Manston was named after St Catherine, not because of any ancient link with the medieval Manston family, but simply because Catherine was the name of Mr Sicklemore's wife and he loved her and wanted to honour her. This romantic reasoning led to some problems in the twentieth century when the idea emerged of having a patronal festival. Was it meant to honour St Catherine of Alexandria whose day

---

[263] *Thanet Advertiser*, 19th July 1873. The same architect also designed St Luke's in Ramsgate two years later. The land on which the church was built was formally given to St Laurence parish on 17th May 1882 having previously been held on a "rose rent" basis.

[264] *Thanet Advertiser*, 30th January 1875. It was not until the 1970s that the practice began of school Christmas parties or treats taking place before Christmas. Previously, they were always held around Twelfth Night rather than in Advent.

[265] *Kent Argus*, 16th May 1874, *Thanet Advertiser*, 17th April 1875, *Parochial Report 1891* p.55. The school opened in 1876.

was 25th November or St Catherine of Siena whose day was 29th April or even St Catherine of Vadstena on 24th March, of Bologna on 9th March or Genoa on 15th September?. There was also some confusion about the spelling with the name appearing as St Katherine in 1887 and again in 1905 when the author was none other than the vicar.[266] For the most part, it was just known as Manstone Chapel, the 'e' at the end not being dropped until 1908.

John Collis Browne

John Collis Browne was born in Maidstone on 18th June 1819, the son of Captain William Browne of the 13th Light Dragoons. In 1845, he joined the army as an assistant surgeon and he travelled with the 98th Foot to India where he devised a compound of chloroform and morphia which he used successfully to treat cholera in 1846. It was when he was back in England in 1857 that he decided to start marketing this as chlorodyne. Unbeknown to him at the time, a London chemist was also selling a product of the same name and had been doing so since 1844 and this led Browne to take out three lawsuits against him, all of which he lost. The exasperated judge in the last suggested that Browne was simply taking the actions to generate publicity for his product. It was pointed out to him that he could not patent a name like chlorodyne, which simply meant a compound of chloroform and an anodyne, any more than one could patent a combination like ham and eggs.

Browne's version of chlorodyne was sold for many years and given the advertising suggested it could cure almost everything, this was not surprising:

> Advice to invalids. If you wish to obtain quiet refreshing sleep relief from headaches, relief from pain and anguish, to calm and assuage the weary achings of protracted diseases, invigorate the nervous media and regulate the circulating system of the body, you will provide yourself with that marvellous remedy discovered by Dr John Collis Browne (Member of the College of Physicians, London) to which he gave the name chlorodyne and which is admitted by the profession to be the most wonderful and valuable remedy every discovered.
> CHLORODYNE is the best remedy known for coughs, consumption, bronchitis, asthma
> CHLORODYNE effectively checks and arrests those often fatal diseases diphtheria, fever, croup, ague
> CHLORODYNE acts like a charm in diarrhoea and is the only specific in cholera and dysentery

---

[266] *Parochial Report 1904-5* p.2, Stahlschmidt op.cit. p.387

>CHLORODYNE effectively cuts short all attacks of epilepsy,
>   hysteria, palpitations ad spasms
>CHLORODYNE is the only palliative in neuralgia, rheumatism,
>   gout, cancer, toothache
>Sold in bottles at 1s 1 ½d, 2s 9d, 4s 6d[267]

It was even prescribed to Queen Victoria in the last week of her life to help her sleep when the pain of her osteoarthritis and cerebro-vascular disease prevented this.[268]

The formula for chlorodyne changed several times over the years. In 1898 the *British Pharmacopoeia* gave the following instructions:

>Chloroform 1 ½ fl. oz.
>Morphine hydrochloride 87 ½ grains
>Diluted hydrocyanic acid 1 fl. oz.
>Tincture of capsicum ½ fl.oz.
>Tincture of Indian hemp 2 fl.oz.
>Oil of peppermint 14 minims
>Glycerine 5 fl.oz
>Alcohol 90 per cent 9 fl.oz.
>
>Mix the chloroform, tincture of capsicum, Indian hemp and glycerine with the alcohol and dissolve the morphine hydrochloride in the mixture. Add the diluted hydrocyanic acid then mix with enough of the alcohol to form one pint of the compound tincture.[269]

The hemp or cannabis could be omitted to create a clear liquid, liquorice added to darken it or cochineal added to turn the mixture red and make it attractive to children.[270]

The product was highly addictive and was implicated in a great many deaths. Collis Browne threatened to prosecute for libel anyone who made such a claim but tests were made and confirmed the problem.[271] In 1892, the government successfully prosecuted the manufacturer for selling what they regarded as a poison without labelling it as such.[272] This case resulted in a further change to the formula. In 1924 the Rolleston

---

[267] *Thanet Advertiser* 16th May 1874. Two years earlier, his chlorodyne had gone on sale in Japan under the name of Shinyaku meaning divine medicine
[268] Robert Abrams, 'Sir James Reid and the Death of Queen Victoria', *The Gerontologist* (2014), p.3
[269] Medical Council, *The British Pharmacopoeia* (London, 1898) p.343
[270] William G Sutherland *Dispensing Made Easy* (Bristol, 1922) pp.28-29
[271] *Medical Times,* 1st January 1870
[272] `Important decision under the Pharmacy Act 1868', *Pharmaceutical Journal*, 3rd ser. 22 (1891-2), pp. 928-40. For more on this see 'Poisoning by chlorodyne', *Pharmaceutical Journal*, 3rd ser. 20 (1889-90),

report noted its addictive qualities and Viscountess Lady Astor asked that it be brought under the control of the Dangerous Drugs Act but nothing happened.[273] Medical tests in the 1960s showed that all those who took it regularly suffered peripheral neuropathy and marked physical and mental deterioration with periods of acute psychosis. In 1967, following pressure by the BMA who wished to see it made a controlled substance, the chloroform content was reduced from 17% to 5% and the morphine was eliminated but it remained addictive and studies showed widespread dependency amongst people of all ages. Further deaths were ascribed to it, crime was committed in order to obtain it, and severe mental and gastric problems were associated with it. For those who became addicted, the prognosis for recovery was stated to be "very poor."[274] For John Collis Browne, however, the compound was a money-spinner with annual sales regularly reaching the equivalent of £300,000 in today's values.

Less controversially, Browne's other medical interest related to beards. He wrote extensively on the subject and claimed beards filtered out bad air and germs thereby preventing sore throats and making men healthier than women. He recommended them for warmth and said they were necessary to regulate the body's natural rhythms. In advertising, he was always shown with a beard.

John Collis Browne moved to Ramsgate late in life being attracted by the sea. A keen sailor, he had a yacht called the *Kala Fish* which he moored in Ramsgate Harbour. In 1873 he took his steam yawl to Dover to join the flotilla assembled to welcome the Shah of Persia. The local press wrote that his vessel "resembles the shoe in which Old Mother Hubbard lived, if one may believe the illustrators of fairy story books."[275] A year later, he was chairman of Ramsgate regatta.[276]

Browne was one of the founding members of the Ramsgate Improvement Society and was influential in ensuring the completion of their project to develop the area in front of Nelson Crescent into a promenade and gardens. Browne happened to be living there at the time.

He died at Mount Albion House in Victoria Road on August 30th 1884 aged sixty-five and was buried in St Laurence churchyard. His epitaph reads "If thou shouldst call me to resign what most I prize, It ne'er was mine, I only yield Thee what is Thine." It refers to him as a doctor and Browne did use this title himself although no evidence has ever been found to show that he actually qualified as such.[277]

---

p. 1035; 'The consumption of chlorodyne and other narcotics', *British Medical Journal*, r (1891), p. 817
[273] *Hansard* 13th March 1929 c.1125
[274] R.R. Parker, J. P. Cobb, P.H. Connell, 'Chlorodyne Dependence', *British Medical Journal*, (March 1974) pp.427-429
[275] *Kent Coast Times* 20th June 1873
[276] *Thanet Advertiser* 5th September 1874
[277] Surgeons were trained by apprenticeships, usually for five years, after which they were referred to as Mister. An examination was set for those wishing to become Members of the Royal College

Edmond Regnier

A set of kerbstones just to the left of the Collis Browne memorial marks the last resting place of Edmond Regnier, a Frenchman who led an adventurous life before settling in the area.

Regnier was born on February 11th 1822. He trained as a doctor and served as a surgeon with the French army in Algeria and also worked as editor of a democratic newspaper. He was a gentleman of means with landed estates in England as well as near Paris.

On 19th July 1870, a war broke out between France and Prussia but France fared badly being outnumbered almost threefold and was defeated at Gravelotte and Sédan. With the Prussian army approaching his home, Regnier took his wife and three daughters to England where they arrived on 31st August. He was followed a few days later by the Empress Eugenie of France who arrived at Hastings. Regnier promptly sent the Empress a letter then went to see her and was met by her courtiers who asked him "Who are you Sir who allow yourself to interfere in these matters not being of our set?" Regnier replied that in military terms, Prussia was bound to win and for the defence of Paris, action was needed. He said: "to make no effort to win it becomes more than a fault, it is almost a crime." He recommended that he be sent "secretly and confidentially" to communicate with Bismarck and said that he was ready to start the next day if desired. A ruse was dreamt up whereby Regnier would carry to France a picture of Hastings signed by the Empress' son Louis Napoleon and addressed to his father. Instead Regnier went to Meaux where talks were to be held with Bismarck about an armistice. Delays meant he arrived after Bismarck had left so he chased after him. When they did meet, Bismarck told him that his goal was to avoid any future wars with France and that meant "an alteration of the frontiers of France is indispensable" Regnier conveyed what he claimed were the secret instructions he had been given by the Empress and Bismarck gave him safe conduct to get to the French army in Germany, though Regnier had to travel wrapped in a shawl to hide his face. At Metz, Regnier swapped identities with General Bourbaki who returned to Hastings to await the Empress' instructions. Aware that his papers could be seized at any time by the Prussians, Regnier wrote a glowing account of how well the French were, even though he knew they were so hungry they were slaughtering their own horses to eat. His goal was to see the 120,000 French troops currently in Germany allowed to return to France to form the nucleus of a new force able to fight on at a better time, something he believed could be

---

and Browne passed this in 1842. By contrast, physicians trained in medical colleges to become doctors. Browne was licensed by the Royal College of Physicians in 1845 but not listed as a full Member in the *Medical Directory*.

achieved by their surrender. The situation meanwhile was complicated by the fact that following the fall of Sédan, the French government had declared a republic and deposed Napoleon III which left Regnier as the emissary of a non-person. Or was he? When Bourbaki reached Hastings, the Empress denied having sent Regnier at all. Was he a spy or was he acting on his own initiative from a desire to save his country and see the return of the Imperial family? Regnier wrote that Bourbaki was upset at leaving Metz and "every other consideration vanished from his brain" and said that he later hastened to Chislehurst where the Empress was then living in exile to explain.[278]

For days, Regnier continued to try and mediate between the French and the Prussians, often travelling under the guise of a Red Cross representative concerned about care of the wounded. He later wrote a detailed account of his actions and the terms he was proposing but his efforts were frustrated by problems with papers and arguments about authorisation as well as the pride of the French officer in charge at Metz who seemed to believe defeat was more the more honourable course.[279]

At this point, the English newspapers got involved, the *Pall Mall Gazette* of 5th October publishing a feature entitled 'A Very Strange Story' which recounted how Regnier - who was referred to merely as Monsieur M - was acting and claiming that he was working for the Prussians and that his motive in sending General Bourbaki to Hastings had been to weaken the French army so that they could be more easily defeated.[280] *The Standard* of the same day, suggested Regnier's motive was to encourage civil war between the Imperialists and Republicans in France which would also be to the benefit of the Prussians though the article ended:

> We are reluctant to say that it was anything but the desire or the hope of achieving something useful and profitable for both countries. It seems to have been mediation of a spontaneous kind by someone without authority and without power. Time, perchance, will clear up the mystery.

In fact, time did nothing of the sort. Prussia won the war and a peace treaty was signed on 26th February 1871. Regnier was arrested but freed after three months for reasons that have never been satisfactorily explained. Some time later, a new arrest warrant was raised but he fled to Switzerland. Unable to try him, a Parisian court martial condemned him to death in September 1874 on grounds that he had maintained relations with the enemy and provided them with information.[281] Having had all his property in France confiscated, Regnier made his way to England and in 1875 he moved to Southwood Lodge where he rebuilt his life by opening a laundry in Ashburnham Road.

---

[278] Napoleon III would settle at Chislehurst following his release by the Prussians in 1871
[279] Edmond Regnier, *What is Your Name*? (London 1870)
[280] An argument also made by *The Times* of 20th October.
[281] *The Times*, 19th September 1874

Was Regnier a spy or a double agent or was he simply a patriotic man who made extraordinary efforts to defend his homeland and took seriously Our Lord's statement "blessed are the peacemakers"? Certainly he was disappointed by the reaction of the French to his work noting sadly: "It has been only amongst our adversaries that I have met with those gentlemanly dealings to which I have all my life been accustomed." "Why do we suffer ourselves to be guided by what anyone may think or say of us preferring our miserable personality to the general good? We witness in the enemy, from the corporal to the generalissimo, a patient and persevering individuality which has no end but the interest of all."[282]

He was buried at St Laurence on 23rd August 1886 though this too became the subject of legend. The *New York Times* claimed his demise had been "disproved" and was merely a ruse to enable him to escape his difficulties and that someone else had been buried in his place.[283] *The Times* referred to him as a man of legend, "something like the Man in the Iron Mask" and said that this "curiosity of the world" would forever have "a little corner in history."[284] His wife and one of his daughters subsequently joined him in the grave.

Parish Hall

The need for a parish hall was first raised in 1875 by the Reverend George Sicklemore. At the time, meetings were being held in the parish infant school.[285] He died before this could be achieved but his successor, the Reverend Charles Molony and his churchwardens set about the project with enthusiasm visiting thirteen sites before finding one beside the church in 1883. Their first intention was to erect an iron building and they purchased one from Westgate-on-Sea in 1884 complete with fittings for £180, but they soon decided that it would be better to build in brick since this would be more permanent. Nonetheless, it was an expensive project and some of their original plans had to be discarded for reasons of cost. As a result, they decided to build a smaller hall than first envisaged but to place it back from the road so that there was room for expansion when funds allowed.

The new hall was opened by Caroline Warre on 5th June 1885 as the bells rang. The newspaper reported:

> The hall which is erected on a site previously occupied by two or three dilapidated and untenanted cottages has a somewhat unimposing exterior. The interior, however, has a most comfortable appearance and is capable of seating 250 persons. Excellent workmanship has everywhere been put in by the

---

[282] Regnier op.cit. pp. 65, 68
[283] *New York Times*, 25th January 1894
[284] *The Times*, 20th October 1873, 15th December 1873
[285] *Thanet Advertiser*, 13th March 1875

builder Mr Port and great attention has been paid to light and ventilation.[286]

It was put to use immediately as a temporary school whilst the new infants school was built.[287]

The total cost of the build was:[288]

	£	s	d
Site	226	0	0
Legal fees	90	1	6
Architect fees and building costs	415	0	0
Furniture and fittings	37	6	10
Iron railings and gate	15	18	0
Harmonium	30	0	0
Insurance	3	1	6
Total	817	7	10

Of this sum, just over £567 was raised by parishioners. To have achieved this in two years – and the sum was equivalent to almost £65,000 today - was extraordinary. This was a poor parish where many relied on the soup kitchen and other parish charities and there were no grants available. It was also remarkable because when the first parish meeting was held to discuss the project, only ten people bothered to turn up, a display of interest which meant that Mr Molony had chosen to proceed on faith rather than on pledges of support. The vicar was also pleased to report that all the work had been done by firms based within the parish using local labour. The new hall was to be managed by a trust in the same way that the boys school was run. The six trustees were the vicar and two churchwardens, plus Messrs, Warre, Weigall and Wilkie and they would appoint a small management committee to take care of routine daily business.

Financing the hall proved extremely difficult. In 1890, the accounts showed:

Expenditure	£	s	d	*Income*	£	s	d
Gas and water	4	13	3	Hire charges	6	6	3
Cleaning and heating	1	17	9	Donations	3	5	0
Interest on mortgage	10	19	6	From entertainments	4	7	11
Rates	1	9	0				
Repairs	7	2	9				
	26	2	3		13	19	2
				Deficit	12	3	1

---

[286] *Kent Coast Times*, 11th June 1885
[287] *Kent Argus*, 14th September 1889
[288] *Parochial Report*, 1886-7 p.6. In current values that would be about £90,000

In today's terms, the deficit would be £1,410 and that was without the actual mortgage itself which had to be paid off, a further £250 in 1890 values, £29,000 in today's. By 1900 it was already recognised that: "this important adjunct to Parish work cannot be self supporting" so the church would have to raise money to fund its continuation.[289]

Although no images exist of the Victorian parish hall, the size was the same as today. The roof was evidently high as there was room for young men to exercise on a high bar installed in there. The stage was taller than now with a fair degree of storage beneath and children sometimes got inside to play. Behind the stage was a separate room which could be used for meetings.[290] There was also a kitchen and outside toilets.

Sarah Noel

Sarah Noel was one of many Nonconformists to be buried in the churchyard prior to the creation of the civil cemetery in Cecilia Road. On Sunday 14th May 1893, she had eaten lunch with her husband who was a Sunday School teacher at St Lawrence Methodists. She then stayed home while he went back to take his afternoon class. When he returned home, he found the door locked and thinking his wife might have decided to take a stroll along the seafront, he went in search of her. He could not find her so returned home. The door was still locked so he went to his neighbour who had not seen or heard her. Together they got some steps and it was then that William Noel saw his wife on the floor apparently unconscious. He broke the window and climbed in whereupon he found that she had been shot in the head, this evidently after some struggle as her blood was found across the room and there were other contusions. The police were alerted and Charles Cotton was one of the doctors summoned to examine the body and provide crucial information about time of death. He arrived at the house at 4.40p.m. and said Sarah had been dead for two hours: her husband had arrived at Sunday School at 2.35pm having left his home in Grange Road between 2.20 and 2.25pm. [291]

Sarah Noel, aged fifty-three, was buried at St Laurence on 18th May being laid to rest with her father-in-law, Benjamin Noel, whose funeral the Reverend Montague Fowler had conducted in 1891.

William Noel was charged with his wife's murder and the affair attracted considerable coverage, not just locally, but nationally. Lurid stories were told of his relationships with younger women though the consensus was that he had lived happily with Sarah. There were arguments about whether there really had been a robbery or if Noel had just emptied a few drawers to give that impression. Particular attention was focussed on the fact that the family labrador had not barked and it was thought that he would have created considerable noise and probably attacked any stranger who had

---

[289] *Parochial Report 1899-1900* p.4. The mortgage was paid off in 1895.
[290] The Bible Study class which had almost thirty members met here in 1903 showing this room was of reasonable size as did the PCC through to the 1960s.
[291] *Canterbury Journal*, 27 May 1893. *Thanet Advertiser*, 1st June 1893

entered the house, especially since he had been with Sarah at the time. The idea of a murderer being unmasked by a dog who failed to bark had been used five months earlier by Arthur Conan Doyle in his story *Silver Blaze* so was current in people's minds.[292] It was also curious that Noel did not seem to have a key. In July, just two months after the murder, the case opened in Maidstone whereupon Chief Justice Grantham launched a withering attack on the local police saying that "in the whole course of his experience he had never come across a case in which there was on behalf of the prosecution so much incompetence, impropriety and illegality. During the sixteen days the case was before the magistrates, there was not adduced as much evidence as might be compressed into one small piece of paper… There was not enough evidence to hang a dog much less a man." He dismissed the statement of Dr Cotton regarding time of death as just an opinion and not proof. He recommended that the bill be thrown out so that if evidence was forthcoming later, there could be a trial whereas if they continued and acquitted him, Noel could never face prosecution for the murder. The jury followed the directive and Noel walked free.[293] He sold the Ramsgate butchery business and set up in Maidstone where he traded under a different name. Just eight months later, he attracted scandal when there were rumours that he was to marry his young book-keeper.[294] The couple departed to London where they married and started a family. Noel died in 1938.

Nobody was ever convicted of murdering Sarah Noel who continues to lie in a grave toward the Manston Road end of the churchyard. The inscription, no doubt composed by her husband, describes her as a "devoted wife" who simply "passed away" claiming "she was spared the pain of parting tears, she was spared all mortal strife. It was scarcely dying - She only passed in a moment into endless life." It was an interesting way to describe a bullet through the brain.

---

[292] *The Strand Magazine*, December 1892
[293] *Reynolds Newspaper*, 16th July 1893
[294] *Maidstone Journal*, 22nd March 1894

Charles Cotton

Dr Cotton, parish historian, was born on 7th February 1856 in Twickenham, the sixth child of Hugh Powell Cotton, a Treasury clerk, and his wife Eliza.[295] He grew up in Kensington and attended Kings College School. He went on to study medicine at St George's Hospital, Westminster and became a member of the Royal College of Surgeons on 28th January 1879 and a member of the Royal College of Physicians in Edinburgh in 1881. He settled at 42 Spencer Square shortly afterwards where he worked for many years, serving at Ramsgate General Hospital and the Seamen's Infirmary in particular. Despite living in Christ Church parish and worshipping at St Mary's in Chapel Place which he preferred as having a more Roman style of worship[296], he developed a keen interest in St Laurence church and became close friends with the vicar Charles Molony. They shared a love of old books and archaeology. In 1895, aged thirty-nine, he wrote his first book, *The History of the Parish and Antiquities of the Church and Parish of St. Laurence, Thanet.* The book reflects his antiquarian interests and remains valuable for the details of gravestones and monuments which he recorded. He would later write a study on the *Bardon Papers as they related to Mary, Queen of Scots* (1907) and on the *Grey Friars of Canterbury* (1924).

Dr Cotton married Adelaide Leigh and the couple had two sons, Charles Leigh Stephen and Robert Hugh Alban who were baptised at St Mary's, Ramsgate on 10th September 1885 and 2nd December 1888 respectively. His eldest son was ordained in 1910 and spent his career in various Cornish parishes except for two years spent in Chatham as chaplain to the St John's Ambulance Division, a move he probably made in support of his parents. He died in 1977 at Sutton in Surrey. Dr Cotton's younger son followed him into the medical profession and qualified as a doctor in 1905 and worked in Reading. However, he too felt a call to the ministry and he became a priest serving as curate at Holy Innocents, Hammersmith. He joined the Royal Army Service Corps and was a Second Lieutenant at the time of his death in Italy on 12th October 1918, a month before the Armistice. [297] He is remembered on a monument in Lincoln Cathedral because he had trained for the priesthood in Lincoln Theological College. His parents refurnished the side chapel at St Laurence in his honour in 1920 and a brass at the east end to the right of the window records this gift.

During the Great War, Dr Cotton was responsible for thirteen auxiliary hospitals and Commissioner for the St John Ambulance Brigade in Kent, Surrey and Sussex. In

---

[295] Curiously, he was not baptised until he was two years old on 7th April at Mortlake.
[296] His interest in the Oxford movement and Anglo-Catholicism is discussed in his obituary in the *Church Times*, 6th October 1930
[297] Amongst the books left by Robert Cotton was a 1540 copy of Erasmus' *Novum Testamentum Annotationes* which his father presented to Canterbury Cathedral Library.

1920, he received the O.B.E. in recognition of his services. He was also created a Knight of Grace of the Order of the St John of Jerusalem in 1905.

Dr Cotton retired to live at 11d The Precincts, Canterbury where he died on 28th September 1939. He was buried at St Martin's.

Bertie Ayton

Baptised on St Laurence day 1873 was Bertie Henry Ayton, son of a shopkeeper in the parish. He joined the army and served in the 21st Lancers at the Battle of Omdurman on 2nd September 1898 when the British army under General Kitchener together with their Egyptian allies inflicted a major defeat on the Sudanese who outnumbered them two to one. The 21st had been sent in ahead to clear the plain and it was not expected that the four hundred strong regiment would have a great deal of difficulty but unbeknown to them, there were 2,500 infantry lying in wait. They eventually fought their way through and drove back the enemy but not without some fierce fighting. One of the officers in the regiment was the young Winston Churchill. Bertie Ayton was a private and his bravery on the day saw him Mentioned in Despatches and there was discussion whether he would be awarded the Victoria Cross though this did not materialise. Bertie's letter home dated 6th October told of his experiences just before the battle and during it:

> I got into camp about four and tied my horse up to a tree till the regiment came in for I was sent on with the Major's baggage. While I was attending to this duty someone said "horse overboard" and I found my horse in the Nile in about twelve feet of water. Of course I made a rush to get him out and we had a good struggle with him. I once got him half out but he made a bit of a plunge and back he went and in about five minutes he was at the bottom. Within two days march of the Dervishes and my horse, saddle, sword, carbine, change of clothing, in fact almost everything I had, gone. But it is no good looking on the dark side of things and the next morning they gave me another horse. A bright thing he was too for as soon as we got into a gallop he would bolt. But anyway that was all there was so I had to put up with it.

On the day of the battle

> Our Colonel wheeled us into line and we went at the enemy like lightning. Then the fun came. There was not much time to think for it was fighting for life. How I got through I never seemed to know and never shall. It was hard fighting for the Dervishes are very strong and their cuts need a lot of guards. I had one cut my

haversack from me and another made a dive at me with a big spear but I managed to dodge it and at last got out. I now found myself at the other end to which the Regiment was for my horse bolted and I could not guide him with the regiment. I then galloped up to the flank of the enemy when I found one of our men with his arm almost cut off. He has since lost it. He asked for help so I gave him my horse and just as he was getting up the Dervishes saw us and opened a strong fire upon us. If they had made a bit of a run they could have had the two of us as easily as could be but they only kept firing and I don't know how it is they did not hit us. I at last got him out of danger and managed to stop the bleeding till he was got to hospital.[298]

Winston Churchill in his account noted that "Riderless horses galloped across the plain. Men, clinging to their saddles, lurched helplessly about, covered with blood from perhaps a dozen wounds. Horses, streaming from tremendous gashes, limped and staggered with their riders. In 120 seconds five officers, 66 men, and 119 horses out of less than 400 had been killed or wounded." Afterwards:

> Close to, the scene looked like a place where rubbish is thrown, or where a fair has recently been held. White objects, like dirty bits of newspaper, lay scattered here and there---the bodies of the enemy. Brown objects, almost the colour of the earth, like bundles of dead grass or heaps of manure, were also dotted about---the bodies of soldiers. Among these were goat-skin water-bottles, broken weapons, torn and bedraggled flags, cartridge cases. In the foreground lay a group of dead horses and several dead or dying donkeys.[299]

The experience did not deter Bertie Ayton from pursuing a career in the army although he subsequently settled in Liverpool. He served at Cape Colony, Tugela Heights and in the Relief of Ladysmith. During the First World War, he was a Sergeant in the South Lancashire regiment. He died in 1938.

---

[298] *Thanet Advertiser*, 15th October 1898; *The London Gazette* 30th September 1898 p.5729
[299] Winston Churchill, *The River War*, vol. 2, (London, 1899) pp. 138, 144

Landscape

The development of the print market, precursor to the postcard, makes it possible to see just how rural the parish was at the start of the century.

Southwood above. Pegwell below.

Newington Road

As surveyed 1860

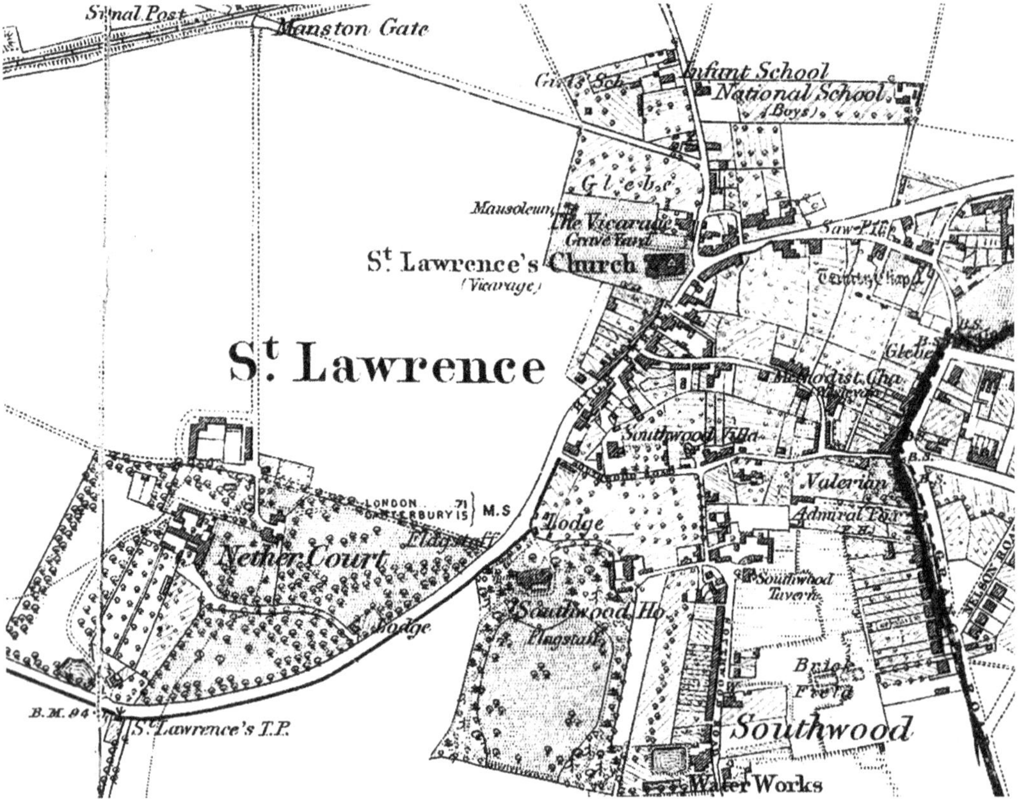

The Twentieth Century and Beyond

THE BUILDING

Although the church which can be seen today is very similar to that seen by the Victorians, there have been some major changes.

East Window

The east window was installed in 1902 in memory of Queen Victoria who used to worship in the church when she was a little girl which is why the royal coat of arms appear in the bottom left hand corner. The large panels show the Easter story when the women went to the tomb to prepare Jesus' body and they were told by the angels that He had risen. The bottom panels tell the story of how Christianity came to England. Beginning on the left, you can see Pope Gregory seeing some slave children in Rome and asking their identity. He is told that they are Angles and pagans, whereupon he is said to have punned, then they shall be angels! He decided to send Augustine to convert the Angles and the next panel shows him arriving in this country. Tradition says he landed at Ebbsfleet but most modern scholars think it was Pegwell. The third picture shows Augustine preaching the Gospel to the King of Kent whose wife, Bertha, was already a Christian. The last panel shows Ethelbert being baptised. Above left, you can see St George of England and at the top is Our Lord in judgment surrounded by angels. The reason why these two incidents were chosen – Mary at the tomb and the conversion of King Ethelbert – was explained at the sermon when the window was unveiled on Sunday 5th April:

> The window upon which you will look Sunday after Sunday gives you an instance of how a good woman's influence can be exercised quietly, consistently and in the fear of God....Who can

estimate the influence of Queen Bertha or gauge the value of her prayers in the little church of St Martin in bringing about the establishment of Christianity in this part of England? ... If courage, integrity, truthfulness and simplicity are qualities which the manliest man may recognise in the example of our beloved Queen and be proud to imitate, it must ever be to women that her life appeals with more direct and intimate influence – a dutiful daughter, a loving wife, a devoted widow, a wise and exemplary mother... a pattern of what an earnest Christian woman may be and do.... And as the model life of Queen Victoria, so is the remembrance of Queen Bertha an inspiration and an encouragement to every woman which is living the Christian life in her own quiet home and thereby influencing husband and children and neighbours by her faithfulness and devotion... It is a protest against the carelessness and godlessness of the world around.[1]

The window was designed by Hemming of London and cost £291 14s 4d which was met by public subscription. In today's money, that would be about £29,000, an impressive sum to raise in such a short period and indicative of the great affection in which the Queen and Empress was held.[2]

---

[1] *Parochial Report 1902-3* p.19. The window cost £235, plus £7 for wire guard, £34 13s to alter reredos, £10 5s for architect fees, £3 for faculty, £1 6s 4d for postage and printing. Mr Hemming also designed the east window for St Catherine's, Manston – *Parochial Report 1904-5* p.2. The January 1901 edition of the Parish Magazine shows that it was the intention to fill this window with stained glass before the Queen died but her demise provided the impetus for the project to be completed. The newly painted reredos appears on the cover of the 1903-4 Parochial Report.

[2] Together with the west window, it was restored in 1989.

In order to install the window, the reredos installed in 1860 had to be cut down. This meant removing the illuminated texts and creating the arches we see today. This work was done by Elliott, the Ramsgate stonemason who created chevron carvings to mirror that on the chancel arch. The stone heads either end represent King Ethelbert and Queen Bertha and relate to the window above.[3] The altered reredos was considered too plain and as a result the screen was painted shortly afterwards with the Christogram IHS in the centre, alpha and omega either side, and two flanking figures to left and right representing the Evangelists. This artwork, the work of the artist Henry Weigall, did not last long being removed in 1928. Depending on the light it is still possible to see traces of the figures on the screen today.

The east window was damaged by enemy action during the Second World War which caused its removal for a year and replacement with plain glass. The restored window was returned at Christmas 1948.

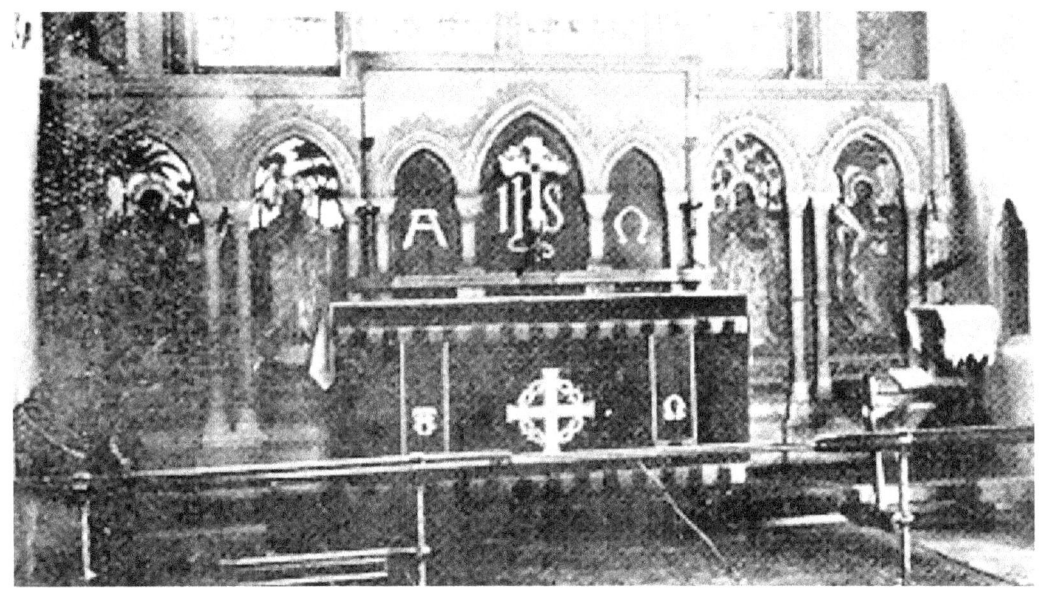

Chancel

The arrival of Charles Cowland-Cooper marked a major change in the churchmanship of St Laurence. An Oxford educated man, he was imbued with the Oxford movement and one of his first acts upon arrival was to arrange for the creation of

---

[3] *Parish Magazine*, February 1902

what was known as an English altar.[4] The philosophy behind this was explained by Percy Dearmer, head of the Warham Guild's advisory committee, who said they were really Catholic altars because they wished to go back to the situation before the Reformation. Instead of having a plain table around which the Christian family would gather to share the meal of bread and wine as Our Lord instructed, there would be a railed off, screened off altar which was decorated with angels like the Ark of the Covenant and gilded to focus attention on the sacrament instead of the Word. The northward celebration as directed by the Book of Common Prayer was rendered impossible by the design forcing the minister to face eastward as in the Middle Ages. In introducing this change, Mr Cowland-Cooper became the first vicar in almost four hundred years to use the word altar, something that was anathema to Protestants due to its association with sacrifice. As the Thirty-Nine Articles and the Book of Common Prayer clearly taught, the only sacrifice was made by Our Lord on the Cross. The 1928 English Altar was designed by James Swan of Birmingham and memorialised in a painting by the church secretary Charles Armstrong. Its erection involved the destruction of the paintings in the reredos lest they form a distraction. It remained in place until the late 1960s.

In 1932, the present communion rails were given in memory of John Coussmaker Anderson. They are carved in oak and show Tudor roses with pearl centres, the design being selected to fit in with the roof above. Anderson had been born in 1852 and studied law in the Inner Temple before spending much of his professional life in India and Europe. As with the altar posts, they were designed by James Swan.

The ornately carved chair was bequeathed to the church by the Reverend Harry Wagstaffe who died in 1979. He had served as a curate in the parish from 1930 to 1933 and then as a retired priest in the 1970s.

The votive candlestick holder was given by Alex Hallier in December 1995.

---

[4] CCA/DCb-E/F/St Lawrence in Thanet/ 19

The medieval chest was moved to this part of the church in 2012.

The early window which can be seen high up on the left hand side was fully uncovered in 1931 as part of the church restoration project of that year. It had been located in 1890. In 1969, a glass cover was placed over the opening to preserve it.

Lower down the chancel near the tower, the credence tables were given in 1997 in memory of Harold Bull, a long serving churchwarden and editor of the parish magazine.

Rood Beam

The bar across the tower arch which contains the figures of Our Lord on the Cross between his mother and St John is known as a rood from the Middle English word *rode* meaning cross. It was erected in 1936 in memory of Harry Howard Gilliat who had left a hundred pounds to the church and the same to the churchyard. The church secretary, Mr Armstrong, proposed that a rood be purchased and the PCC on May 25th 1935 agreed. It was designed by James Swan of Birmingham and sculpted by Celestino Pancheri of Bromsgrove, an Italian sculptor and woodcarver who created many beautiful works of art in English churches from the 1920s onward.[5] Gilliat was an American who had been sent to school in England and who stayed to marry an English girl. He worked in insurance and only came to the parish after his wife's death in 1931. He settled in Chapel Place and joined the church having made friends with Ernest Spencer-Payne who was treasurer.[6]

---

[5] CCA-U3-19/6/19
[6] Spencer-Payne was executor of Gilliat's will.

The location of the rood at this point of the church is significant. It reminds Christians that they must pass through suffering and death in order to reach the new life which is represented in the High Chancel by its window that portrays the resurrection. It is also designed to encourage meditation upon the Passion. Consider, for example, Mary's eyes raised in faith, Our Lord's concern for her suffering despite enduring His own, John's downcast eyes as he struggles to come to terms with the enormity of what is happening. The letters INRI above Our Lord's head represent the Latin inscription which the Romans put up saying "Jesus of Nazareth, King of the Jews." The text below comes from John 3:16 which reads in full: "For God so loved the world that He gave His only begotten Son that whosoever believeth in Him should not perish but have everlasting life."

Side Chapel

The area occupied by the Chapel of St Anthony in the Middle Ages had ceased to be used as a chapel at the Reformation. It was used as a school until the mid seventeenth century and later for storage but from the eighteenth century onwards it was filled with seats and from 1858-85 the organ.[7]

It was the Reverend Montague Fowler who originally proposed that the area be returned to its original use. He suggested setting it up as a Morning Chapel so that the small congregation which attended the daily offices would be in closer proximity to one another. He left before that could happen and it was left to the Reverend Raymond Bevan to re-establish the chapel. In 1911, he turned the pews from facing the high chancel to face each other and set up a reading desk between. This is the stall that can now be seen to the left and was given in memory of Arthur Guillum Scott who died in 1909. In 1920, it became a more conventional chapel when the claw foot table purchased second hand for use as a temporary communion table in 1890 when the

---

[7] See image in the previous chapter under Font

chancel was being restored was moved in, rails were added, a curtain set up behind the table and a stove was affixed beside the south-west porch.⁸ The work was mostly paid for by Dr Charles Cotton who furnished it in memory of his eldest son who died in the Great War. Mr Bevan confirmed in the faculty application that there was no intention of using the chapel for celebrations of Holy Communion but only for the daily offices and the faculty was granted on this basis, although the addition of a communion table was clearly unnecessary to such an objective.

In May 1968 the decision was made to place an aumbry in the chapel and this work was done the following year. The idea of reserving the sacrament had been proposed by the Reverend Hartley Bird in 1962.

In 1970, the church purchased a set of wooden chairs to the same design as those to be found in Coventry Cathedral from money left to them by Mrs Hudson. The chairs remained in use for almost forty years until they were replaced with the padded seats at which point some of them were moved about the font. Kneelers were made by parishioners in the Embroidery Group showing the arms of ancient manorial families from 1971 onwards but these were also removed as the new design chairs did not include any storage section for them. From 1972, it became customary to use the chapel for early morning celebrations of Holy Communion.

When the chapel was re-established in 1920 it was known as the Side Chapel. Every PCC minute or Parish Magazine reference refers to it as this. When Mr Bird arrived in 1961, he initially decided to call it the Lady Chapel but six months later, changed his mind and decided to call it the Becket Chapel just prior to the start of the 1962 celebrations.⁹ This was not entirely popular and a number of people preferred the title Lady Chapel which was used up to 1978, creating some confusion as the Lady Chapel in the Middle Ages was on the other side of the church. The reason for the change can be traced back to Dr Cotton who announced in his 1895 history that since the south chapel was the most ornate, it must have been in honour of Thomas Becket who was much honoured at this time. Indeed, he optimistically gave a service book inscribed to the "Chapel of St Thomas." Nonetheless, medieval wills conclusively prove that the church never had a chapel dedicated to Becket. The name is totally modern and has no historical validity whatsoever.¹⁰

The east window in the side chapel is unusual in that it was given by Mr and Mrs Guillum Scott in thanksgiving for the safe return of their son from the Boer War. Unveiled on 21st April 1901 it shows the Resurrection of the Just from Rev. 14:13 with the dead

---

⁸ CCA-U3-19/6/B/2

⁹ Mr Cowland-Cooper had attempted to introduce the name Lady Chapel in 1931 but failed, CCA-U3-19/8/A/6

¹⁰ Cotton was confused by Lewis' *History* which erroneously said that wherever there was a light to a saint, there must have been a chapel. In fact, the church had many images in different parts of the church but only three chapels.

rising from their tombs assisted by angels.[11] The window to the side also shows angels, Gabriel and Michael, and was given in memory of Arthur Warre in 1932.

The sanctuary lamp was given in 1932 by Mrs Thomson. The dark wooden cross inlaid with mother of pearl which stands at the eastern wall was given in the same year in memory of Francis Murray. They were part of an improvement scheme for the area which was begun in 1931 and included the replacing of the pews with wooden chairs and the erection of a short oak screen at the back.[12]

The beautiful carved oak litany desk to the right was that given by Miss Ellerm in May 1890 and originally stood under the tower. It was moved after the cessation of reading the Litany.

At the rear of the chapel, moving toward the font, is the book of remembrance recalling the names of the faithful departed. It was set up in memory of the Reverend Harry Wagstaffe who died in 1979.

Bells

The twentieth century opened with St Laurence church having eight bells and no ringers. In October 1900, the then vicar, Mr Crosse, announced that he wanted to "revive the custom of ringing the bells for service on Sundays." Some young people came forward which enabled a muffled peal to be rung in 1901 when Queen Victoria died. However, owing to weaknesses in the frame, the tenor and number seven could not be used. At the start of 1902, numbers seven and eight were lowered for new stocks and the frame was strengthened with twelve iron brackets at a cost of £35. The work carried out clearly failed to solve the problems for on 21st April 1908, the vicar noted that none of the bells could be rung because the frame was unsafe and moreover, the ringers floor was in urgent need of repair with five beams totally rotten. At the time, the roof in the north and south aisles was letting in water and the vicar insisted that this must be completed first. The Reverend Francis Bevan was keen to see the bells in use but he took his role as steward of the church's finances seriously and he refused to countenance expenditure without supporting income. When the necessary roof repairs were made, it was discovered that the cost of rehanging all eight bells and recasting three of them would be £398 and there was a great rush to raise this sum in order that the bells should be able to be rung in time for the coronation of George V. The vicar had suggested that if it was not, conscience would prevent them ringing all the bells. Work in the tower itself was a further £56 10s.

In 1910, the bells were all removed and three of them were recast being returned at the end of March 1911. The event was photographed by Albert Siminson for the newspaper and church but the bell fund – known as the Edward VII memorial fund – was still short. The vicar made an appeal from the pulpit and at the end of the service, Mrs

---

[11] The Parish Magazine records it was made by Lavers and Westlake
[12] CCA/DCb-E/F/St Lawrence in Thanet/ 22

Mary Holman of Southwood Road approached him with a blank cheque to cover the money owing. As a result, the bells were pealed for the first time since their return on 22nd June 1911 for the coronation.[13]

Mr Bevan's successor, the Reverend Alfred Wilcox, was a keen bell ringer and it was at his initiative that two new bells were added to the tower in 1924. Their arrival was also photographed by Albert Siminson who sold copies in his shop beside the church. Dedicated by Dame Janet the inscription on the first was: "The Great War 1914-18. To the Glory of God and in thanksgiving for peace. This bell was dedicated Armistice Sunday November 9th 1924." The second, dedicated by Mrs Wilcox on behalf of the bereaved families, read: "The Great War 1914-18. To the Glory of God and in Remembrance of Britain's sons who laid down their lives by land and sea. This bell was dedicated Armistice Sunday November 9th 1924."

The bells are the smallest in the tower weighing around 5cwt each and having diameters of 27" and 28⅜" respectively. They cost £232 17s 10d (about £8400 today) the money being raised by donations, concerts by the St Lawrence Orchestra and choir and various bazaars.[14] After a full peal, they were rung half muffled for the Armistice.

---

[13] Vestry meeting 19th April 1911; *East Kent Times*, 29th March 1911; *Thanet Advertiser*, 13th April 1912. Mrs Barker had paid for the new floor in memory of her parents. At the time the work was done, the 2nd, 7th and 8th bells were recast but subsequent renumbering means that these are now the 4th, 9th and 10th. The image shows in the background the alpha and omega of the reredos.
[14] CCA-U3-19/5/5

Bell ringing remained popular over the decade which followed. In 1930, there were eighteen ringers and two conductors. The second world war put an end to this since not only was ringing forbidden by the government from 1940 to May 1943, but most of the ringers were themselves serving as part of the war effort. In the early 1950s, the bells were still not being regularly rung each Sunday due to lack of ringers but they were rung for special occasions such as Princess Margaret's visit to Newington in 1950, the return home by the Queen and Prince Philip from their Commonwealth tour in 1954 and the birth of Prince Andrew in 1960. An appeal by Stan Gee, Tower captain, in June 1956 produced four probationers which doubled the team. For various reasons, this did not solve the problem and in August 1963, the Reverend Hartley Bird admitted to the ambition that he would be able to "revive the lost art of bell ringing and once again use them to summon worshippers." It was not, however, until a campaign of 1970 generated a team of twenty ringers in 1971 that regular and complex peals proved possible.

In January 1995 an appeal was launched to have the bells tuned as a complete peal for the first time, to have fittings replaced, the frame reinforced and the bells re-hung. The estimated cost was £45,000, equivalent to around £80,000 today. An extraordinary campaign of fund raising began with the majority of the money being raised within the church itself and £15,400 was saved by volunteers doing part of the work themselves.[15] On 13th September the bells went to Whitechapel and on 15th November they came back being put on display in the church. They were re-dedicated on 17th January and two plaques commemorate this event in the church, one to the south of the tower and the other on the stairs leading to the belfry.[16] Now tuned to E and re-weighed, the bells were listed from treble to tenor as:

Bell	Weight lb	Weight kg	Tuned	First mention	Date Added	Recast
treble	514	232.8	G#		1924	
2	581	263.2	F#		1924	
3	575	260.5	E		1890	
4	605	274.1	D#		1808	1911
5	657	297.6	C#	1617	Before 1613	1704, 1729, 1808
6	737	333.9	B	1637	Before 1613	1704, 1724, 1808
7	906	423.1	A	1624	Before 1613	1704, 1724, 1808, 1890
8	1155	523.2	G#		1890	
9	1295	586.6	F#		Before 1613	1704, 1808, 1890, 1911
tenor	1615	731.6	E	1615	Before 1613	1641, 1704, 1808, 1911

---

[15] St Laurence DCC Minutes 8th January 1998. The final bill was £29,608
[16] It had been intended that their last peal before being taken away would be to welcome the new vicar, the Reverend Peter Dewey, but the sudden death of Diana, Princess of Wales a few days before meant that they were rung half-muffled on 6th September.

Bell ringing was also affected by changes made to the tower during the twentieth century. In spring 1979 the external stairs were removed and an internal stairway established. New galvanised beams were installed in 2015.

On February 3rd 1985, a set of seventeen hand bells from Whitechapel Bell Foundry were dedicated.

Roof

At the start of the twentieth century, there were ceilings throughout the nave, aisles and over the side chapel which covered the timbers. The process of removing these was commenced in 1906 and at the Annual Vestry Meeting of 1909 it was reported that "an immense improvement has been effected; there has been no extravagance and the whole thing has been done well."[17] Opening up the timbers not only allowed them to breathe but acted as a reminder of the antiquity of the church, the original work in many cases dating back to the era of the Black Death.

Later in the twentieth century, the roof became a subject of much fundraising as it was found to be infected by death watch beetle. It was first reported in 1958 and the nave and south aisle were treated in 1963, the north aisle in 1968.[18]

Porch

The front door was given by Mrs Tucker in 1906 and made by her son-in-law Albert Rutter. It has a Charles Collinge hinge with its unique hemispherical pin as invented in 1851. The medieval door had been deemed beyond repair so was discarded.[19]

On the right is a Portland stone war memorial erected in 1923 and dedicated on Armistice Day.[20] This was felt necessary because the war memorial cross in the churchyard contained no names. On the left opposite is a rare example of a wooden war shrine. These were first introduced in Hackney in August 1916 and quickly became popular. They were ordinarily erected in the streets and provided an important unifying point where people of all faiths, or none at all, could share in remembering those who were serving. The triptych form was usual and it was normal for the names of serving soldiers to appear across the top panels whilst the bottom section showed those who had died and included a space for flowers. Some were home made but most were professionally created. That at St Laurence is believed to have come from Strange and Sons in Tunbridge Wells.[21] By April 1917, the parish had two war shrines, one being in

---

[17] *Thanet Advertiser* 17th April 1909. Faculty CCA/DCb-E/F/St Lawrence in Thanet/ 10
[18] CCA/DCb-E/F/St Lawrence in Thanet/ 32 and 39
[19] CCA/DCb-E/F/St Lawrence in Thanet/ 10
[20] CCA/DCb-E/F/St Lawrence in Thanet/ 16. The churchwarden's accounts, CCA-U3-19/5/5, show it cost £43 5s, about £1550 in today's money
[21] An advertisement exists in the parish archives but no order.

Southwood Road beside the water tower.[22] The one in the porch matches its description but was clearly created at the end of the war because it only lists the names of the fallen. It must have been set up in the early summer of 1919 since no later names are included. Twenty one names appear on the stone memorial which are not on the wooden and four on the wooden which are not on the stone.

Fonts

At the start of the twentieth century, the church had an early Victorian font situated to the left of the porch. That changed in 1972 when a new font was installed. Designed by the Warham Guild in Norman style and to proportions that matched the pillars, it was not a universally popular addition. Some loved the stark simplicity which fitted with the purity symbolised in baptism whilst others thought it too large and out of style with the Victorian and Gothic interior. The Diocesan Advisory Committee had expressed their disapproval of the design but the PCC sent a letter back saying that they had approved it and would have it.[23] Money for the font came from that left by Lionel Siminson who wanted a "tangible memorial" to his parents Albert and Anne. Albert had been a chemist and photographer with a keen interest in both the church and the village. The font was given a new position in the south aisle just to the right of the lectern. The objective of this move was to give it greater prominence and to enable everyone to see when a baptism was celebrated as part of a family service. It was also, as the vicar said, to prevent people leaving their hymn books on it when going out of church. In order to place the font here, a number of pews had to be removed and a new floor laid.[24] The cost of creating the new baptistery was £2427. The bill would have been higher but the church chose to use the cheaper option of reconstituted stone rather than real stone to save almost £200, a decision which was to cost them dearly in later years.[25]

At the start of the twenty-first century, the 1972 font was replaced due to cracks. The current font arrived in 2005 from Lydd on Romney Marsh. It is of fourteenth century style being octagonal with a deep bowl and supported on four pillars. There are carvings on four of the sides. Lilies represent the Virgin Mary and are a reminder of the importance of motherhood. The christogram IHS used since the eighth century, represents the first three letters of the name of Jesus in Greek. The dove is a symbol of the Holy Spirit and a reminder of how the dove appeared at Our Lord's

---

[22] *East Kent Times* 11th April 1917
[23] PCC Minutes 21st September 1971.
[24] The Warham Guild was paid to remove the Victorian font at time of installation.
[25] CCA/DCb-E/F/St Lawrence in Thanet/ 41

baptism (Luke 3:22). The cross reminds us not only of Jesus' death and resurrection but the Trinity itself because the ends of each arm are split into three.

The statue of the Blessed Virgin with Our Lord in her arms which sits on a ledge nearby was added in 1933. It was the gift of Mrs Hooper in memory of her father who had been a Sunday School teacher and based on a painting by Murillo.[26]

Server Stalls

Beneath the tower can be seen the oak stalls purchased from the legacy of Sarah Page who died in 1922. They were originally for the use of the choir which was much larger at that time and divided into men, women and boys. Their original location was behind the choir stalls and parallel to them in what is now the side chapel. Dedicated on 9t March 1924, they were designed and manufactured by J. Wippell and Co in Charing Cross. The stalls are used today by the servers.[27]

Thurstin Room

The twentieth century saw considerable developments within the vestry area and the tower as needs changed. Initially the church had considered building an extension to the rear or north to house a parish office, meeting room and toilets but this proved expensive and complicated due to the burials which would necessarily have been disturbed. The area in question included many listed monuments. Instead the church decided to develop the north-east corner. A lavatory was installed in the Bookey grave and a small kitchen area also. A meeting room which doubled up as the choir vestry was set up on the floor above. Various monuments were moved. Given that the project was largely funded by the bequest of Edward Thurstin who had died in April 1994, the new area was named the Thurstin Room. Edward had been a server at the church since Whitsun 1942 together with his younger brother Victor who died in 1993. It was dedicated on 17th July by the Reverend Philip Norwood.

---

[26] CCA/DCb-E/F/St Lawrence in Thanet/ 24
[27] CCA/DCb-E/F/St Lawrence in Thanet/ 16, *Church Times* 14th August 1931

Banners

The church has a number of banners on display. The main church banner is stored on the left hand side of the High Chancel. It was designed by Noyes-Lewis for the 1934 town pageant and depicts St Laurence with his gridiron with Rome behind him on the left and St Laurence church on the right. It was renovated in 1973 by the Warham Guild for £84.64.

The Mothers' Union banner opposite dates from 1937.

In the Tower area can be seen two youth banners. That to the left was designed and made by Ellington School in 1979 in memory of Mollie Thurstin whilst that to the right was made in 2012 by the 6th Ramsgate Brownies and Rainbow Guides. A further youth banner, also from 2012, exists in the south transept and this incorporates the Olympic rings, a reminder of London hosting the games that year.

Model

The scale model of the church on display in the south transept was started by Miss Dorothy Healey at the start of 1950 and completed in February 1951. Miss Healey was a member of the Ramsgate Model Club as well as an active part of the congregation for many years. She served on the PCC, was Sacristan, and taught fretwork to a group of choristers in 1949 so that they could make models and a doll's house to sell for church funds.

North Transept

Prior to 1928, this area contained pews which faced the tower area where the pulpit had stood prior to 1888. The Reverend Charles Cowland-Cooper decided to have the pews removed as they were not only surplus to requirements but they now only faced the choir stalls. In their place, he obtained a faculty to set up a children's corner.[28] The purpose of this was to have a place where children could go to read Christian books – many families in the parish were too poor to buy them – and to pray. At various times, the area was used by the Sunday School and the Kings Messengers' and it was also sometimes used as a quiet area by parish children who wanted time away from their families, perhaps to think, perhaps to do their homework.

In 1969, the corner was dismantled and the 'altar' sold to St Barnabas' church in Gloucester. In its place was set up the Bray Library, a collection of Christian books which church members could borrow for a small fee. In 1976, the pews were turned toward the tower area where the new communion table stood and mounted on a low platform so that the children from the Sunday School could watch the service. In 1994 the area was largely cleared to make way for the passage through to the toilet. A prayer corner was subsequently created using the 'altar' which had stood in the missionary corner opposite until 1970 when it was removed to make way for a Christmas tree.

---

[28] CCA/DCb-E/F/St Lawrence in Thanet/ 21

Icon

One of the newest additions to the church is the copy of Andrei Rublev's Icon of the Trinity which is displayed above the doorway into the vestry. One of the most famous works of Russian art, the original is in the Tretyakov Gallery in Moscow and dates from around 1411. The icon depicts three angels who visited Abraham at the Oak of Mamre (Gen. 18:1-8) to tell him that his wife was to have a son who would be the father of many nations. The angels are sat in a circle with a cup in the centre of the table which contains a calf's head, a reference to the calf which Abraham gave them to eat. All wear blue which is a colour traditionally associated with spirituality. In the background is a house, the oak tree and Mount Moriah. Focus in the icon is drawn to the cup which acts as a reminder of Holy Communion. Since the sixteenth century, the icon has been interpreted in light of the Holy Trinity with the angels symbolising the Father on the left, the Son in the centre and the Spirit on the right. This leads to other layers of meaning such as the tree representing the Fall in the Garden of Eden and also new life through the Cross, the mountain representing the Law or Creation and the house signifying the Church. The icon was a farewell gift from the Reverend Sharran Ireland in July 2013.

North Window

Just to the right of the blocked up north door can be seen the newest window in the church. Designed by the artist Denys LeFevre, an active member of the congregation, it shows the cross erected at Ebbsfleet to mark the arrival of St Augustine in 597AD. The window was given in memory of Lloyd Butcher who was a Lay Reader in the parish and unveiled by the Reverend Philip Norwood on 21st June 1998.

Organ

At the start of the century, Henry Abram, organist since 1885, died. The position was advertised and over eighty people applied. The person selected was Dr Arthur Froggatt, ex organist of Kilkenny Cathedral, and he started at Easter 1900 just in time to oversee the major rebuilding of the organ for which the parish was then collecting. The work was done by Hele Organ Works of Plymouth and the new organ dedicated on 7th June that year. Dr Froggatt's account in the Parish Magazine explained what had been done:

> The Organ erected by Bishop, in our Church in 1848, consisted of a Great from GG, with 8 stops, and a Swell from tenor C, with 5 stops. A very good Open Diapason of 30 notes was subsequently added as a Pedal: but unfortunately no addition was made to the wind supply. Various alterations had been made in this Organ, some stops having been taken from the Great and placed in the Swell and *vice versa*. The total number of pipes was only about 800; and the organ was out of date.
>
> The recent re-building has been entrusted to Messrs Hele & Co., a firm which has during recent years attained a considerable reputation. Of course it is premature to speak of the mechanical part of the work, the action, blowing apparatus etc.; but there can, we think, be only one opinion as to the excellent manner in which the old pipe work and the new have been combined. The Organ now comprises three complete manuals with pedal, and contains 1398 pipes. While every feature of the old Organ has been retained, the practical resources of the instrument have been considerably more than doubled.
>
> Of the Great Organ, the Open Diapason, the lowest seven pipes of which were formerly of wood, has now been carried down in metal, and the nineteen largest pipes form the Chancel front. The Claribel is the original Clarabella of Bishop, and is continued below middle C by a stopped Diapason. The Harmonic Flute is entirely new. Every stop, with the exception of the Dulciana (Bishop), runs through.
>
> There is of course a much greater amount of new work in the Swell, inasmuch as every stop, with the exception of the Voix Céleste, is carried down to CC. The 12 lowest pipes of the Lieblich Bourdon are placed outside the Swell Box.
>
> The Choir Organ of five stops is an addition of the utmost value. Messrs Hele are certainly to be congratulated on the excellence of the Gamba, the "strong toned" quality of which is most effective. The Gedact is the original Stopped Diapason of the Swell Organ, carried down in stopped wood; the present Stopped Diapason in the Swell being entirely new. The Flute is also in part derived from the stop of the same name in the old Great Organ. With the exception of the Clarinet, every stop on the Choir runs through.
>
> To the Pedal Open Diapason have now been added a Bourdon (wood) and Violoncello (metal). The pipes of the latter stand on the west screen.
>
> To the usual five couples of a three-manual organ has been added a sixth, namely, Choir Sub to Great. In the absence of a Double on the Great Organ, this coupler becomes of great value. By its means, a Contra Gamba and Bourdon, both of 16 feet-tone, are added to the Great Organ down to tenor C.; while, for solo purposes, the Clarinet becomes a Contrafagotto to middle C.
>
> The cost of the Organ is £462 10s. There is still £60 owing. The Vicar will be glad to receive further subscriptions.

The cost of the work was £462.10 and at the time of the dedication, the parish was still £130 short. The vicar accepted the need for the work but after so much fund raising in the previous few years thought it was a lot to ask. He wrote "it was not a task of my choosing being part of the jubilee scheme and I hope that those who attend the church will take their share in paying for it."[29] The final payment was made in November that year, the work costing in today's terms around £50,000.[30]

The work carried out was presumably successful for aside from adding an electric

---

[29] *Parochial Report, 1899-1900* p.4
[30] CCA-U3-19/6/29 Three payments were made: £196 5s on 2nd May and 16th June and £70 on 24th November 1900. Mr A. Warre donated £100 to the fund.

blower in 1914 at a cost of £29 to end the laborious process of hand pumping, no further work was done until the 1970s. The estimate for restoration then was £5300 and with inflation then running at around nine per cent per annum, the fund raisers were in a hurry to get the work started.[31] They received £2277 from the Siminson bequest but the rest was raised by fairs, sponsored events, concerts and coffee mornings.[32] Work began a year later and took a year. During this period, music was provided by Graham Richards at the piano, the choir moved under the tower and consecration of the elements took place at the tower communion table. In addition to adding a new drawstop console, adapting the soundboards for the benefit of electric action, thoroughly cleaning and restoring the organ, the pipes were painted a bluish grey, this last at the direction of the Warham Guild upon whose aesthetic judgment the PCC of the time was heavily dependent. The final bill was £7022.50, equivalent today to over £75,000.[33]

Memorials

There are few memorials from the twentieth and twenty-first centuries though there are some brasses in different parts of the church such as one remembering the chorister Stanley Gee in the choir stalls, another to the organist David Brewer in the north transept and one to Bill Cox, bell ringer, on the stairs up to the Tower. The most prominent memorials are those to the Great War, two in the porch and one in the churchyard.

Burma Star

The Burma Star cabinet was dedicated on 21st March 2006 and remembers those who served in Burma during the Second World War. The Thanet branch of the Burma Star was formed in 1972 and a memorial garden for those killed was established at Cliftonville in 1991. The cabinet contains memorabilia relating to the conflict and service personnel. The banner is green and gold to represent the forests and beaches of the East.

Choir

The choir has been an integral part of the worship at St Laurence since the 1880s but the size and format has changed dramatically over the years. At the start of the century, there were approximately twenty boys and twenty-five men. During the First World War, the young men left and the Vicar noted that in 1917 the age of the choristers

---

[31] The estimate from F.H. Browne and Sons of Canterbury was accepted by the PCC on 13th November 1972.
[32] *The Beacon*, May 1973
[33] CCA/DCb-E/F/St Lawrence in Thanet/ 42. In 1982, the organ was valued for insurance purposes at £40,000 (£135,000 today), *PCC Minutes* 6th May 1982.

now averaged almost sixty. They did, however, while the vicar was absent serving overseas have the benefit of the head of Westminster Abbey's choir school to lead them.[34]

During the 1930s, the numbers were pretty stable with around thirteen men, sixteen women and an unrecorded number of boys. On 11th August 1936 the choir was affiliated with the Royal School of Church Music which had been founded by Sir Sydney Nicholson whose brother designed the War Memorial cross at St Laurence. From 1938 onwards it developed its plainsong repertoire thanks to Alf Miller who had taken over as organist.

The involvement of women in church music has been variable. They first appeared in 1890 as a separate choir but this was only for women's services and it was disbanded in 1893 when these services ceased and they did not re-appear until the end of the First World War when they were allowed to sing at the main service. They did not wear cassocks and surplices like the men or boys, however, but rather full length white albs like the servers with dove grey veils like nuns. In 1923 choir stalls were established for them, partly because there was no room in the existing choir stalls but also it was felt that it would be indelicate to have the two genders sitting together lest either be distracted from the solemnity of worship. Indeed, the ladies stalls which were originally placed behind the stalls in the Side Chapel were soon moved to sit under the tower which was further away and more decorous. Perhaps surprisingly, the women left the choir during the war and it was not until August 1948 that ladies were once again invited to play their part in church music. They were then formed into an auxiliary choir which sat under the tower but did not process. By January 1949, there were eleven men (eight bass, two tenor, one alto), twelve boys and ten ladies.

The 1950s saw five different choirmasters but numbers remained reasonably stable. The ten men, twelve ladies and seventeen boys of 1956 was typical. The boys were numerous enough to field sports teams and twice to set up their own magazine, *The Warbler* in 1949 and the *St Laurence Choirboys Chronicle* in 1955. From 1968 to 2005 the

---

[34] CCA-U3-19/8/A/3

choirmaster was Tony Roach who encouraged new heights of excellence.

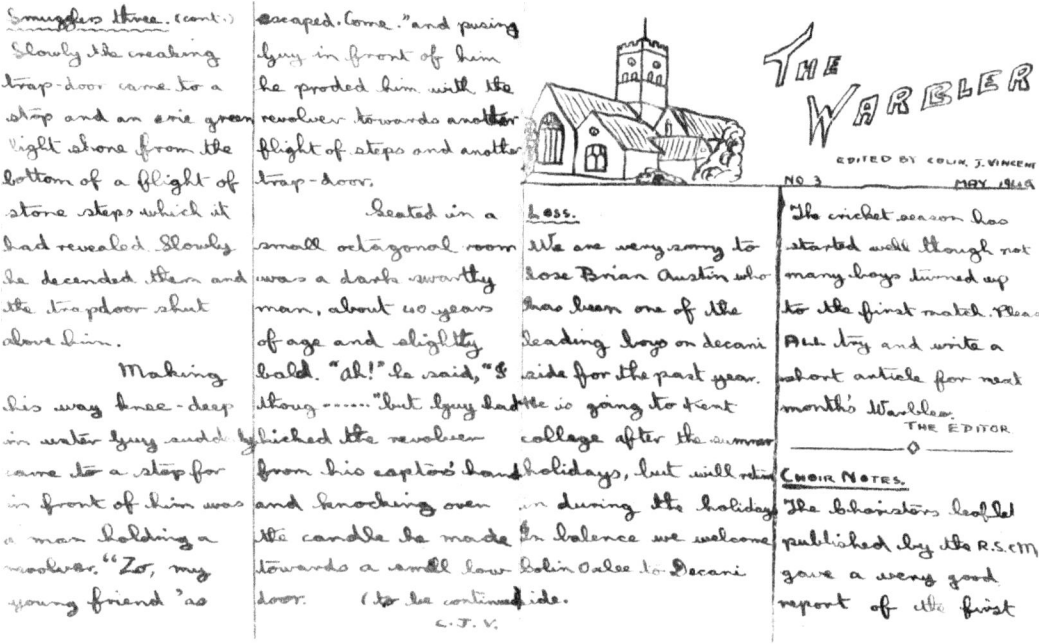

The repertoire of the choir has not changed a great deal. Throughout the twentieth century, the setting for the Sung Eucharist was Merbecke, except for the weeks when the new rites were trialled. Hedley Steward, choirmaster from 1951, enthused about the value of tradition: "Boys may come and boys may go but St Laurence Church goes on for ever. We can imagine the Eucharist being sung here centuries ago, the same music by Merbecke that we still sing on Sunday mornings." For Mr Roundhill, who had himself been choirmaster from 1942 to 1945 and who continued as a tenor soloist, the reason for keeping the setting was because "otherwise: the service tends to become a special performance by the choir and the congregation just listeners. This is entirely opposed to the purpose and meaning of the service. It is our Lord's own service in which all have a share."[35] In 2016, David Thorne's setting was adopted despite it being for a mass.

A performance of Stainer's *Crucifixion* was given almost every Easter during the twentieth century and the Nine Lessons and Carols started in 1953. The fact that the choir averaged between thirty and forty members meant that they were able to put on a Handel festival in 1951. One of the most memorable performances of the *Crucifixion* was when Stan Gee – a long serving chorister whose name is recorded on the choir stalls by a brass plaque – decided to turn the lights out for dramatic effect just as the bass intoned "there was darkness over all the earth." The effect was ruined by a lady of rather nervous disposition screaming!

---

[35] *Parish Magazine,* October 1947; *The Beacon,* July 1952

Worship

The twentieth century has seen considerable change in worship but in order to understand this, it is necessary to briefly look back at the previous nine hundred years.

From the eleventh century when the church was built through to 1549, services were in Latin and people went on Sunday morning to hear mass. They did not understand it and the service took place behind a screen out of sight. In 1549, worship was transformed by being put into English but this first Prayer Book was largely a translation of the earlier services with just the worst medieval accretions removed. It was not until 1552 that the Church of England adopted a truly reformed rite, one which was scriptural and enhanced by the majesty of Archbishop Cranmer's prose. The Archbishop had visited St Laurence in 1535. The accession of Bloody Mary saw the Latin Mass revived for five years but Queen Elizabeth then re-introduced the 1552 Prayer Book with a few minor amendments. This continued to be used in all parish churches up and down the country until the Civil War of the 1640s when the Directory was introduced. This was not dissimilar but the authors worked on the principle that unless something was specifically recommended in the Holy Bible, it should be omitted whereas the Prayer Book had sought to base its ceremonies on wider scriptural practice. For example, the Bible did not require the giving of a ring in marriage so the Directory cut this from the wedding service. The Prayer Book included it because the Bible had spoken of gifts being exchanged at marriage and the English tradition was that the gift was a ring. Similarly, when instituting the Lord's Supper, Our Lord did not say, "Kneel, do this in remembrance of me" but just "do this in remembrance of me." The Directory therefore excluded kneeling whilst the Prayer Book required it on grounds that Our Lord Himself knelt to pray. The Directory banned funerals because there was nothing in the Bible to show either Our Lord or any of the apostles or patriarchs attending such whilst the Prayer Book included them because Our Lord had told people to bury their dead and since the Holy Bible taught life was a gift from God, it was appropriate to thank Him for this at time of burial. In 1662, upon the return of Charles II, the Prayer Book was restored and this continued to be the service manual at St Laurence until 1966.

The 1928 Prayer Book, introduced by the Reverend Francis Yarker in 1966 was a volume born in controversy. From the late nineteenth century, there had been demands in the Church at large for the 1662 Prayer Book to be updated but since the volume was authorised by Parliament, it could only be amended by Parliament and when the Church of England presented its proposals in 1928, Parliament rejected them. In a move of dubious legality, the Church then decided to permit its use anyway although the volume was never authorised. Only the 1928 version of the Holy Communion service was used at St Laurence, Evensong remained according to the 1662 Prayer Book. The chief changes in the new volume were:

- o the recital of the Ten Commandments was made optional
- o the use of Kyrie Eleison was permitted (despite Article 24 which states

- that it is "plainly repugnant to the Word of God" to have any part of the service in a language which is not native to the worshippers.)
  - the exhortations were omitted
  - the distribution of the elements followed the Lord's Prayer and prayer of oblation rather than immediately following Our Lord's command to do this in remembrance of Him

The 1928 service was to be embodied as Series 1 in the same year but further change was to take place the following year with the birth of series 2 which was was used at St Laurence from January 1st 1968. This introduced the idea of having an Old Testament reading as well as an Epistle and on 21st May 1968, the PCC voted that this should be read by one of the laity. The Prayer Book had required that all lessons be read by the clergy and had not included an Old Testament reading because the authors had presumed people would hear that when they attended Matins each Sunday. Series 2 also moved the Gloria from the end of the service where it was a thanksgiving to the start as a hymn of worship.

Series 3 appeared in 1973 and was tried at St Laurence but not popular. It was the first modern language rite using the second person plural "you" instead of the singular "Thou" for God. It specified sitting for the Bible readings other than the Gospel. It used "we" in the creed and allowed for the laity to lead the intercessions, although this did not happen at St Laurence until the summer of 1982. It further introduced the idea of sharing the peace. This first happened at St Laurence on 4th August 1974 but after two months, it was agreed to stop the practice as it was disruptive and embarrassing. It was not until the adoption of the Alternative Service Book (ASB) in 1980 that it re-appeared. Series 3 itself was rejected by the congregation, by votes in the church schools and at PCC level. The church settled for Series 2 and when the ASB appeared, opted for Rite B which was closest in form to it.

The 1980s saw considerable battles across the parish over Rites A and B which were roughly equivalent to series 2 and 3. St Mary's and St Catherine's adopted Rite A in 1985 as part of their preparation for the Down to Earth Mission, believing that it would be easier for all the new converts to understand. St Christopher's held out against Rite A until 1988. Their minister from 1981 to 1984, the Reverend Tony Christian wrote: "We once had a liturgy of elegant simplicity and it's replaced now by the humdrum and mundane." Comparing the volume to a "civil service manual", he said it represented "a loss of order, a valued framework replaced by hotch-potched devotions."[36] St Laurence never made the change and when Common Worship appeared in 2000, selected the traditional version of Order One. This clearly met a need in the area as the electoral roll showed that some forty per cent of worshippers came from outside the parish. The arrival of the Reverend Andrew Jacobson saw the use of modern language services for three weeks of every month but kept Order One. However, Order One is far from being simply

---

[36] *The Beacon*, September 1983

a modernisation of Prayer Book forms, it is a conscious return to Roman Catholicism. The liturgical order is based on the Mass. The addition of "Blessed is He that cometh" and eucharistic prayers which include an epiclesis tend to support a doctrine of the real presence and suggestion that the elements are being transformed in some way. Confession appears at the start rather than as a response to the Word.

This same trend toward Rome is evident in ceremonial changes. The medieval custom of ringing the bell at consecration was re-introduced by Mr Roundhill in 1948 From 1928, it became the practice for the minister to wear vestments rather than a simple cassock and surplice and processions became more common. Mixing water with the wine was also introduced.[37] Mr Yarker began the idea of having the bread and wine brought up during the service arguing that it was inappropriate to have great ceremony for the collection whilst the elements were just set aside: "The bread and wine stand for all God's gifts to us and for all our life and work. We do not just offer money; we offer ourselves." He also started the tradition of the Gospel being read from the nave. Previously, the procession had gone to bring the Bible from the sacrarium and carried it down to read under the tower. He introduced the idea too of the minister facing the people during Holy Communion. Clergy at St Laurence had celebrated facing east from the start of the century despite the Prayer Book requiring a northward position. Although the PCC was happy in February 1967 to accept that change, they were less happy about his attempts to celebrate at a table under the tower, even though Mr Roundhill had done this during the winter in the late 1950s. It was not until 1976 that the PCC finally agreed that the tower communion table, used since September 1974 due to restoration work being carried out on the organ, should become permanent

Until 1966, people knelt from the start of the service through to the reading of the Gospel, as directed by the Prayer Book. Mr Yarker stopped this as being "too much" and allowed people to sit after the Collect for the epistle. They also knelt from the confession through to the actual receiving of Holy Communion. From Series 2 onwards, no directives were issued about posture except for kneeling for confession and standing for the Gospel and the former of those requirements was omitted in the ASB. *Common Worship* does say: "on occasions, the congregation should kneel for prayers of penitence." In recent years, kneeling for confession has ceased and the prayers of preparation and humble access have been largely omitted in line with the options in *Common Worship*.

The Authorised Version of the Holy Bible was used until 1969, the PCC voting on 16th June that year to use the Revised Standard Version except where the clergy deemed the Authorised an improvement, such as having the traditional version of John 1 at Christmas. In 1976, an extraordinary resolution was passed to shorten the length of services by reducing the scriptural content by cutting out the Old Testament reading. The present incumbent, the Reverend Andrew Jacobson, is to be praised for not only restoring this but also incorporating a psalm.

---

[37] This is justified by John 19:34 where blood and water are said to have flown from Christ's side but it contradicts the instructions of Our Lord at the Last Supper in Matt 26:27, Mark 14:23, Luke 22:20

From 1967 to 1987 there were no collections during services, simply a plate at the door for those who were not members of the Planned Giving scheme. There were several reasons behind this. Firstly, the sight of people wandering round with collecting bags was not considered to paint a good image particularly to visitors who might regard it as proof that the church was only after money. Secondly, the rooting around in pockets for coins and the movement of people about the church distracted attention from the hymn and the worship of God. Thirdly, the church wanted to encourage Planned Giving to make budgeting easier. Collections were re-introduced because it was thought that some people were reluctant to put money in a plate which was visible to all, unlike bags which were more private, and also because some were failing to contribute at all.

In terms of occasional services, Mr Cowland-Cooper introduced the Midnight service on Christmas Eve whilst Mr Roundhill started the Nine Lessons and Carols in 1953.[38] Mr Norwood began the Christingle in 1981. The imposition of ashes, outlawed at the Reformation, was first requested in 1970. Rogation processions were revived in 1976.

The pattern of Sunday service has varied across the century. The 8 a.m. weekly celebration of Holy Communion has been a constant. Prayer Book Evensong was held generally at 6:30 p.m. each week until 2008, though war caused it to be brought forward for a while and there were occasionally other forms of service at this time. The Reverend Charles Cowland-Cooper re-introduced an additional noon celebration of Holy Communion once a month in the 1930s – this having been stopped in 1907 - but the main morning service remained Matins until the time of his successor. The Reverend John Roundhill initially had Matins at 10:30 and a weekly Sung Eucharist at 11:30 but he swapped these over at Easter 1947 to focus on the Holy Communion. Matins ended at Easter 1960 and was never resumed. Since then, the Sung Eucharist at either 9:45 a.m., 10.00 a.m. or 10:15 a.m. has been the principal service. A non-eucharistic praise service was started in April 1986 at 11:15 which formally ended on 25th November 1989 though the slot has been used since 1991 for family services, parade services and baptisms at a variety of intervals.

It is impossible to know the exact numbers attending at the start of the century. At Easter 1902 there were 402 communicants at St Laurence from a total population of 2,507 and it must be assumed that there were also many present who did not receive. There were over two hundred in the Sunday School who were almost certainly there and they would not have taken communion. It may be concluded therefore that at least a quarter of the inhabitants were in church that morning. Across the parish, the figure would be higher if the non-conformist worshippers were known. Being a festival, Easter is not representative and the regular number of communicants was 51 of which 30 were at the early service and 21 the late. However, the main morning service was Matins and

---

[38] Prior to the mid 1970s, carols were always sung after Christmas but since then they have been usually sung from the last Sunday in Advent, though some carol services were held earlier in the twenty-first century.

that attracted over 250 people.[39]

Service registers, extant from 1916, until recently only recorded communicants so numbers at Matins are unknown but they do show the changing pattern of attendance:[40]

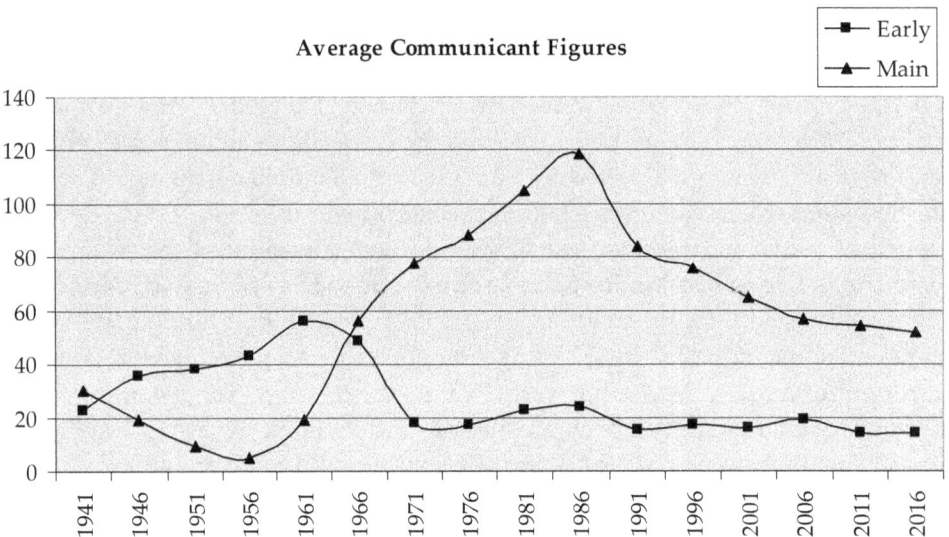

Children were expected to attend the Sung Eucharist with their parents in Mr Roundhill's time. Mr Bird moved the Sunday Schools back to Sunday morning meaning that children no longer attended the Sung Eucharist. Concerned at this practice, Mr Yarker introduced the idea of the children being brought in after the sermon in 1976. The north transept was adapted for their seating and the Bray library moved. The practice of them coming in at this point of the service has continued although they now sit at the front in the nave and generally arrive after the consecration. In the early part of the century, they attended the first part of Matins then went out to Sunday School prior to the sermon.

The idea of allowing children to attend the Sung Eucharist which is so generally accepted and encouraged today was highly controversial when first suggested. The Church's position had been that Matins and Evensong were designed for everyone but the Eucharist was just for church members which is why only those who had been confirmed could receive. Given the stress on worship as participative and not a spectacle for people to merely watch or hear, it followed that only those who wished to receive

---

[39] *Parochial Report 1902-3*, p.3. Manston had 61 communicants from a population of 565.
[40] CCA-U3-19/1/H/1-11. A further forty to fifty attended the non-eucharistic Morning Praise service in the 1980s and 1990s. However, attendance is not necessarily the best indicator of a church's health. As the Reverend Hartley Bird said: "Head countering is but pandering to our pride and our Heavenly Father is no celestial schoolmaster ticking off the register and marking down the absent.", *The Beacon*, April 1962

should attend. Children, being too young for confirmation, were never allowed in except usually on the week before their confirmation as part of the preparation. Interestingly, Mr Roundhill introduced family communion based on his tractarian views whilst Mr Yarker encouraged it, despite coming from a liberal tradition.

Although the norm has been for formal worship to be led by a surpliced choir and organ, in the 1920s, Mr Wilcox started a men's orchestra to provide accompaniment to men's services. A similar idea was repeated with Morning Praise sixty years later although the band represented both sexes and all ages.

CLERGY AND STAFF

The vicar at the start of the twentieth century was the Reverend **Thomas George Crosse** who had arrived in May 1899 when he was forty-seven. He was a family man who delighted in spending time with children. He went into the parish schools on four days a week and saw the teachers on the fifth. He also devoted time to building up the Sunday School which had over two hundred members. A firm believer that it was the vicar's job rather than the curate's to welcome people into the church, Mr Crosse was exceptional in that during his five and a half years of ministry, he took almost every baptism in person – over 250 of them.

The time he spent visiting families convinced him of the need to obtain the services of a nurse for the parish. This was some fifty years before the National Health Service and families were totally reliant on the care of relations unless they had the resources to employ staff. A fund was started and in October 1900, Nurse Laura Dowker arrived, a forty-five year old widow who lived with her mother in St Mildred's Road. Her services were provided free to parishioners in need but they were unable to call on her themselves. The scheme was organised so that when a doctor saw a parishioner whom he felt was in need of a visit from a district nurse, he would contact Mr Crosse and he would arrange it with Nurse Dowker. The system worked well but the parish could only afford to employ her for six months of each year from mid October to mid March.[41] As a result, Mr Crosse devised a scheme whereby St Laurence would unite with St Luke's, Christ Church and Holy Trinity to share the services of a district nurse who would work all year, the contribution from St Laurence being £25. This started in 1902 and Mr Crosse was able to report that between November 1902 and May 1903 she had made 450 visits to fourteen parishioners.[42] The church was to continue paying for this service for over thirty years.

A Lads Club was set up in February 1900. Seventeen attended the first meeting but by December it had grown to sixty. Members had to be between fourteen and twenty

---

[41] The nurse cost St Laurence £46 in salary and £1 19s in equipment, *Parochial Report* 1901-02 p.17. This would be equivalent to around £5,600 today.

[42] *Parish Magazine*, July 1903. This was around a third of her visits in total. The nurse was provided by the St John's Ambulance Association, Dr Cotton's wife acting as co-ordinator.

and they paid 6d a month. Meeting four times a week, their programme was varied. They had debates on resolutions such as "smoking is a habit which ought to be discouraged" and "trade unions are not necessary." There were various games to play and in 1902 they fielded a team for the local draughts league. On Wednesdays, the Parish Hall was turned into a gymnasium with high bar and parallel bars and a professional instructor came in. The vicar noted it was: "very popular and doing the young fellows a great deal of good."[43] In the summer, they went swimming. On Saturdays, they had special permission to use the Warre Recreation Ground which opened on 29th November 1900 for football. They set up a negro minstrel troupe which was in great demand for shows and raised a considerable amount of money from February 1901 onwards including all the costs of their own gym equipment. On Sundays there was a Bible class and in 1901, thirty-five of the fifty-two confirmation candidates from the parish were club members. The Club was similar to the Church Lads' Brigade started by Mr Fowler and closed by Mr Payne-Smith but less militaristic which was curious given the fascination at the time with army life engendered by the Boer War.

During Mr Crosse's incumbency, the parish was very active. A cricket club was set up in 1901 meeting on Tuesdays and Fridays in the Warre Recreation Ground. For girls, the Girls Friendly Society existed to provide games, country dancing and handicrafts. For women, there was the Bible Class with Mrs Crosse and the Ladies Home Mission Association. Children had the Band of Hope and it was noted in November 1902, they had been given a demonstration of a gramophone "which greatly astonished and amused the children." The Parish Hall was used as a lending library one day a week where adults could borrow a book from Miss Warre for 1d a fortnight and children could do the same for ½d.[44] On Tuesdays, Dr Froggatt's new Choral Society met there. From 1903, a wood carving and fretwork class met on Thursdays in the boys school. Thanks to the generosity of Mr Weigall who offered them six acres at Southwood, an allotment association was formed in April 1901 which soon had seventy members who put on their own annual flower and produce show from 1902 onwards. A branch of the Oddfellows had 242 members. The District Visitor scheme was restarted.

Manston also flourished at this period, largely due to the influx of a hundred children in January 1900 when the Isle of Thanet Union workhouse at Minster moved the younger paupers out into the Cottage Homes. As a result, 1901 saw a new choir formed, a branch of the Girls Friendly Society, extra pews added and a Band of Hope set up Communicant numbers rose almost sixfold and numbers in the Sunday School reached 133. In 1902 a library was set up and clubs for boys and men. Mr Crosse advertised for a curate but reported "the response to my appeal was not what I looked for."[45]

Mr Crosse was remembered as a very kind man. A parishioner writing in October 1981 described how he would visit his mother and take her tickets which she could

---

[43] *Parochial Report 1902-3* p.3. The instructor was paid £3 per annum.
[44] This library incorporated that set up by Mr Fowler in the men's clubroom.
[45] *Parochial Report 1901-2* p.3

exchange locally for a shillingsworth of groceries or coal At the time they were a family of four living in just two rooms, one above the other. Mr Crosse's generosity was the more remarkable because the children were illegitimate and churches usually refused to help the mothers of bastards.

Major changes made to the church during his time included the installation of the great east window in 1902, the east window of the side chapel in 1901 and the rebuilding of the organ in 1900. He also had the rendering removed outside at the back of the church to show the remains of the old west door and the buttresses repaired. In addition, he had the bell frame strengthened. A safe was purchased for parish records.

The fact that parish magazines exist for four of the years he spent here and also parochial reports enables us to get an idea of Mr Crosse's personality. He was clearly an optimist. Talking of how some people see a rose as a beautiful shrub marred by thorns whilst others saw it as a thorny bush sometimes improved by flowers, he wrote: "Go where Christ would go, act as He would act, speak as He would speak, let others see that He is your friend and master, that He indeed abides with you, then you will see roses on every thorn bush and happy indeed will be all the days of your life."[46] He was also, as might be expected, a man of faith writing: "Apart from God there can be no life. Actions speak louder than words. We write our own lives and they are read as an open book by all who see them. Let our mottoes be constant prayer, constant Bible reading, constant Church, constant holy communion. Then will God not only direct us on our road but at the journey's end give us rest and peace."[47]

Mr Crosse had no wish to leave the parish but he was advised by the Bishop that a man of his talents was needed elsewhere. At his farewell party in the parish on 12th October 1904 he was given a new bicycle. It was noted how he had cycled out to Manston in all weathers at least twice a week to take the children's service he had started there and to visit the Cottage Homes.

---

[46] *Parish Magazine,* January 1903
[47] *Parish Magazin,e* January 1902

He was praised for never asking others to do what he would not do himself and for always leading by example.[48] That his parishioners remained fond of him is shown by the fact that years later, he was the man chosen to dedicate the war memorial at Manston.

He went on to minister at Faversham and then Ickham where he gave an oak reredos to mark his fifty years in the ministry. His two sons were killed in the First World War but his daughter maintained a link with the parish taking children from St Lawrence schools on tours of Canterbury Cathedral every year. Mr Crosse died on 3rd January 1931 lamented by all the parishes where he had served.

Mr Crosse swapped livings with **Canon James Oakley-Coles** of Faversham who arrived in the parish in November 1904. The Canon was an older man being sixty years old and the move had been recommended for his health. His institution had to be delayed for several weeks until he was well enough to start work but he then pronounced that the sea air was doing him a great deal of good: "We came as invalids, my dear wife suffering from long continued illness and myself broken down simply from overwork and anxiety. The air of Thanet has done wonders for both of us by God's blessing."[49]

The Canon was unusual amongst ministers of this period because he had had a career before entering the ministry. Most clergy then went from school to university and then into the Church. By contrast, the Canon had qualified as a dentist and was the author of a number of standard reference works used in medical schools.[50] Experience of running his own practice had given him a better grasp of finances than some of his predecessors and he set about reforming the parish system. Instead of having over forty separate funds for different ends, he consolidated them into a more manageable group. He also insisted that the laity take charge of the finances rather than expect the vicar to be treasurer.

At Easter 1905, the annual vestry meeting took place. It offers a rare glimpse of the Canon as a man. The people's churchwarden Mr Eastes stood up and said that people had said the Canon's sermons were too long. Such a statement created a furore with some agreeing, some disagreeing, and even more thinking that the annual meeting was not the time or the place for such a discussion. The Canon was quite upset but remained articulate and determined asserting that his job was to elucidate God's Word and that as a matter of principle, he would not cease from this or reduce the educational and exhortatory content of his addresses.[51]

The Canon issued just one annual report and since he had only been in the parish for a few weeks at the time, much of it was taken up with his hopes for the future. He wrote that "it is the spiritual work that is important and that with which I am most

---

[48] *Thanet Advertiser*, 15th October 1904
[49] *Parochial Report 1904-05* p.3
[50] They include *The Mechanical Treatment of Deformities of the Mouth* (1868), *On Deformities of the Mouth, Congenital and Acquired* (1870), *A Manual of Dental Mechanics* (1873), *The Dental Student's Note Book* (1876)
[51] *Thanet Advertiser*, 29th April 1905

anxiously concerned." He wanted to start some Bible study classes and said that the Sunday Schools were in need of more teachers if they were to achieve their goals. At this time, the Sunday School was almost two hundred strong. He also established groups to review the state of the churchyard and to investigate the "foul air" that emanated from the north aisle of the church.

His hopes and plans were largely disappointed. At the start of October, the Canon was taken ill and forced to retire to his bed. He died in the Vicarage on Christmas morning having been vicar for barely a year. He was remembered for his "versatile eloquence and brave enthusiasm."[52]

After the demise of Canon Oakley-Coles, the parish needed the services of a good pastor who would help them come to terms with their loss and restore continuity. They got the Reverend **Stephen Hughes-Games,** a forty-four year old man who delighted in writing religious verse such as his address to a dead baby: "Sleep, sleep: thy days were few, Why should they be many? We with more have oft to rue that God gave us any." He was instituted on 1st May 1906 and although his incumbency was to prove the shortest in the church's history at just nine months, he certainly made an impression.

Our knowledge of his ministry stems from two sources, local newspapers and the yearbook which he prepared before his left. A month after his arrival, he announced that he wished to extend the churchyard. He wrote in the June issue of the Parish Magazine: "The vicar and churchwardens have to protect the dead as well as the living. …The poor would suffer most if the churchyard was closed and it is just the poor whom we are bound most of all to consider." Since the parish had only recently invested in creating a cemetery in Cecilia Road on which they still owed thousands of pounds, this was a controversial intention although very sound ethically.

The most telling impression of his character stems from his letter to the yearbook in which he writes:

> We ought not to introduce into our religion the partisanship of secular life. We cannot expect our work to prosper unless we can make up our minds to forget our differences and unite, heart and soul, in doing all for the glory of God. The spirit of self assertion is absolutely opposed to the spirit and mind of Christ. In all ages the spirit of self has been the greatest hindrance to the work of the Christian Church. It has taken many forms but it always ends and must end in disaster and disruption.
> There are matters of principle which I cannot submit to a Church council but there are a large number of other matters which are questions of expediency, convenience, taste etc which I shall always be willing and am desirous of

---

[52] *Parochial Report 1905-06* p.2

> submitting to the judgment and decision of a really representative Church council.

He went on to explain that two curates were not enough and he felt that he needed three assistants. He was commencing fund-raising to that end:

> Our ancestors have done much for us and we are most grateful to all our benefactors, known and unknown: but they could not foresee and were not able to provide for all the needs of the twentieth century. We must do something for ourselves….There are very few clergymen who can live on their stipends… I am sure the laity do not realise the drain on a scanty income of dilapidations, repairs, cases of distress, hospitality, subscriptions and all the other claims the clergy are expected to satisfy. They cannot like other people choose their places of residence but often have to live in houses ludicrously beyond their means and their wishes. And it is very difficult for a man to do good work with constant financial anxiety to face and meet.

Yet, he added "the main and most important work of any parish must be done by the laity….The responsibility rests chiefly on the vicar but.. there are but twelve hours in the day and a vicar's time is necessarily much taken up by meetings, correspondence and all the countless business arrangements of a parish."

His letter ended with him expressing his opinion on people's offerings to the church:

> I wish to make it quite clear that we cannot accept gifts for our church simply because they are given. Such gifts must be worthy of our church and God's glory. 'Neither will I offer burnt offerings unto the Lord my God of that which cost me nothing.' To buy in the cheapest market is always a mistake but to do it for God's house is a profanation.

Declaring that the church was in need of major restoration since the quality of furnishings were not to his standard – a statement which must have upset all those who had given so much - he concluded by stating that

> The church door given by Mrs Tucker in memory of her late husband and made by Mr Rutter is an excellent example of what gifts to the church ought to be. Every part was chosen and

> worked with the greatest care without any consideration as to cost and for many generations will survive as a beautiful specimen of honest and painstaking craftsmanship.[53]

Mrs Tucker must have felt most honoured to have had her gift deemed acceptable by Mr Hughes-Games.

The tone of the letter suggests an autocrat and it is clear that he was not happy in the job. Given he would have seen the church building and known the income and help available when he came, it is hard to understand why he agreed to become vicar in the first place. At the end of January 1907, he simply resigned and left without any apparent notice. There is no evidence that anyone in the parish regretted his departure or that there was any collection or farewell party.

At the Easter vestry meeting held a few weeks later, there were the most extraordinary scenes. All the local papers devoted almost an entire page to the event. Normally such annual meetings merited just a paragraph or two as the churchwardens were chosen, the accounts summarised and the vicar thanked all those who had helped during the year. In 1907, there was no vicar and the meeting descended into complete shambles which almost saw the police being called to restore order. People, including wardens, were shouting at each other across the Parish Hall and calling names which the newspaper had to indicate with dashes as they were unfit for a lady to hear or read. There were disputes about graves being dug without authorisation and someone brandished a letter from the Archbishop saying: "grossly illegal. Might just as well have started building a cottage in the churchyard." A lengthy debate followed on exactly what Mr Hughes-Games was said to have known and approved. One churchwarden revealed that he had been told by Mr Hughes-Games that "the servants are trying to take over from the masters" and they must unite to stop this. Even something as ordinarily innocuous as the building report created furore with allegations that the choir were left so cold that they were unable to walk out of church at the end of the service because their feet and legs were numb, the suggestion being that the new radiators had been deliberately badly chosen and positioned, There was such a row about the electoral process that the meeting had to be disbanded to take legal advice as it was now "a bear garden." It was clear that Mr Hughes-Games had not left a happy parish. One editorial noted: "Rumours had long been current that matters did not run smoothly in the ancient parish and from yesterday's proceedings is it apparent that there are many disturbing influences."[54] A week after the meeting, one of the curates resigned saying that these were "troublous times" and he was conscious of his inability to cope. He departed praying that God forgive the church officials.

In such a circumstance, it was important that the next vicar be a man of good character who would be able to take charge and mend fences. The parish was blessed

---

[53] *Parochial Report 1905-6* pp.2-4.
[54] *Thanet Advertiser*, 3rd April 1907, *Kent Coast Times*, 6th April 1907

that the man appointed to the task was **Raymond Francis Bevan**. Arriving on 15th June 1907, he was ten days short of his forty-first birthday and the son of the first chairman of Barclays Bank by his second wife who was the daughter of Sir James Hogg. Most importantly, he was an experienced minister who knew how to bring people together and to lead them effectively.

The early years of his ministry were taken up with major work on the church. He inherited a project started by Mr Hughes-Games which was to remove the ceilings from across the church to reveal the timbers and this took two years to complete as Mr Bevan insisted that they could not start work on the next area until they had the money to do so. At the Annual Meeting of 1909 it was reported: "an immense improvement has been effected; there has been no extravagance and the whole thing has been done well." From this he moved on to tackle the issue of the bells. They needed to be re-hung but that would cost £265, almost £25,000 today. Having just completed the roof which had cost almost as much, this was a serious undertaking. The Fabric Fund had been left £100 toward the work by Mr Vivian but the need for urgent repairs to the Parish Hall meant this money had been borrowed for that which left them £63 in the red. The fund raising campaign was launched by a revival of St Laurence summer fair in 1909 and continued for more than two years. In 1911 he also started the process of removing pews from the south chancel and turning the area into a space suitable for reading the Litany.

With no parish magazines or annual reports from his incumbency, it is very difficult to gain any impression of Mr Bevan as a person. One man who remembered him in the 1970s recalled him as "a wonderful man" and praised his dedicated support to those who served in the war. He understood the hardships they had faced through personal experience and was on hand to help them come to terms with the difficult transition to civilian life afterwards. For the most part, the men did not feel able to share the horrors they had seen or their doubts and fears with their wives and families and this left many feeling frustrated and alienated, especially as the home fit for heroes promised by Lloyd George failed to materialise. When war broke out in 1914, Mr Bevan was one of those appointed to the Ramsgate Recruiting Committee and he spoke out in favour of conscription saying that it was right to "allow all our youth to enjoy the privilege of bearing arms and enjoying a share in the protection of their country."[55]

We have just one sermon of Mr Bevan's to give an impression of him and it dates from Christmas 1916:

> To the great majority of Christians the need for a saviour from sin and of the perpetual consciousness of His presence is more apparent than ever… This world is in Browning's phrase, like the antechamber leading to another and (to paraphrase his language) the wise who view it thus can tell by the glories which adorn it what royalties in store lie one

---

[55] *Thanet Advertiser*, 5th December 1914

step past the entrance door for whom is reckoned not too much this world's munificence…Those who are disappointed in Jesus Christ are asking Him to give what He never promised. The peace He promised is not the peace of immunity from trial. He bade his followers prepare for conflict. Roast beef and plum pudding at Christmas may be very agreeable but they are not part of the Gospel offer. The peace of which Our Lord speaks is peace with God, the peace of a good conscience, the assurance that we are working with the will that rules the universe, the will of Him who has revealed Himself as a loving Father. There must be peace within before there can be peace without. When the nations of Europe have really enthroned Christ as King they may hope for the fulfilment of these ancient words: "They shall beat their swords into plough shares and their spears into pruning hooks: nation shall not lift up sword against nation, neither shall they learn war any more.[56]

A visitor to the church in 1914 had previously described Bevan as being "of the Dean Farrar type, a little sharp in feature," possessing "a terse voice of a cultured and scholastic type with the charm of a certain conversational directness and the defect of periodical indistinction." He did not say much about the sermon on that day, merely that it was long but able. He did note that Mr Bevan did "scold" his congregation for "squatting" when they should be kneeling.[57]

The war inevitably caused many difficulties. The choir was depleted by men going away to serve. The organist joined up. With young men away, the harder physical jobs such as maintaining the churchyard simply lapsed. The Band of Hope closed for want of leaders never to re-open. Services at Haine stopped. The various groups representing women were re-organised and used to instruct people on how to cope with the novelty of rationing. Members of the Women's Bible Class were encouraged to knit balaclavas as they studied the Word. For the first time ever, parishioners came under aerial bombardment with bombs and shells landing across the parish and damage being caused by zeppelins and aircraft. The church clock itself was damaged and not repaired until 1919. The Parish Hall was used by the War Savings Association with adults raising £48 and the church school £9 toward the war effort. In 1916, the Royal Naval Air Service – soon to become part of the Royal Air Force – set up a base at Manston which not only affected the population but the parish boundaries since part of the land used was within the borders of Minster. Military hospitals were set up, one in 1915 within Nethercourt

---

[56] *Thanet Advertiser*, 23rd December 1916
[57] *Thanet Advertiser*, 5th December 1914

House.⁵⁸ This had room for eighty patients, one of whom was the ex-footman from 10 Downing Street who was able to entertain his fellows with accounts of events there. Lady Rose Weigall was a constant visitor and set herself the task of knitting special gloves for men who had lost fingers or deformed hands. In July 1916, the first men to arrive back from the Battle of the Somme were brought in. The local newspaper reported:

> Those men must be suffering untold agonies but there is not a sound to be heard from any of them. The faces of most are set like a mask: faces which resemble each other in one particular for several days growth of beard gives them the appearance of 'wild men of the woods.' These very quiet heroes who are as unlike the battle hero of postcards as can be.
> It is a curious sight. A row of men in filthy tattered garments lying on these neat white cots, labelled like parcels, human freight gazing helplessly straight up a the ceiling above them each grasping a pathetic little bag given him at some base hospital. In this repose all the belongings to which he has managed to cling. And some are almost empty.
> All is quietness in the ward save when some dreamer starts up and grabs the air for his rifle, but these hallucinations will disappear together with the war talk. Next week they will be talking of any subject under the sun except war.
> From the silent ward we go out into the sunshine flooded grounds of beautiful Nethercourt and see men who were brought in under similar conditions, practically healed and enjoying a game of tennis or bowls. Soon they will be ready to leave Nethercourt, ready to go back to the place where they were snatched from the jaws of death, ready to have another game with fate. This is war.⁵⁹

For Mr Bevan, the war created new challenges. He had to minister to families torn apart by bereavement. Mrs Southey, for example, lost her second son and brother the same day.⁶⁰ Children were also showing behavioural problems as a result of the war which created difficulties in the school and in their homes.⁶¹ He had to take on work in other parts of town as other clergy either went away or collapsed under the strain.

___

[58] One set up for Canadians employed Frederick Banting who earned the Nobel prize in 1923 for discovering insulin.
[59] *Thanet Advertiser*, 8th July 1916
[60] *Thanet Advertiser*, 9th November 1918
[61] *St Luke's Parish Magazine*, November 1917

Although the St Laurence parish magazines have been lost, those from St Luke's show that Mr Bevan spent a considerable amount of time working there. He told the 1917 Annual Meeting: "It is hard for those who have extra work but when we see how our soldiers and sailors are doing their work, we must bravely face our task."[62] As the war went on, Mr Bevan felt increasingly frustrated that he was not with the men on the front line. Despite being told that he was doing a vital role here, he volunteered and in 1916 went to serve as a chaplain with the YMCA going to France in April 1918.[63] From October 1918 to March 1919 he served with the army in Russia and it was almost freezing to death there which ever after affected his health causing him hearing and nasal problems.[64]

Mr Bevan missed the celebrations of the Armistice which was declared while he was away. The news was received at Ramsgate at 9:15 on the morning of November 11th, being picked up by boats from Dover and proclaimed by loud and constant blasts from the ships in the harbour.[65] The bell ringers immediately went to ring the bells and the Union Jack was hoisted on the flagstaff. The children of the church schools received a day's holiday.

During the post war period the south chancel was set up as a chapel using money given by Dr Cotton for the purpose. This was a memorial to Dr Cotton's son but it was obvious that the parish needed a more general memorial. Mr Bevan favoured establishing a social club for men so that something for the living would come out of all the death but the parish opted for a war memorial cross, the same as St George's.

Other changes in this period included the birth of the Parochial Church Council or PCC in 1921. Initially, membership was selected to represent the various groups within the parish. There were two sidesmen, two from the Sunday School, one each from the Bible class, Men's Society, Relief Committee, Social Work Committee, District Visitors, Provident Clubs, Mothers' Union and the bell ringers plus four representatives from the choir and four from Manston. The Young Person's Welfare Officer was also a member as was the Vicar and his two curates. In subsequent years, membership was by election.[66] Women were allowed to serve on the PCC having won the right to attend vestry meetings for the first time in 1919.

Youth work was another area of concern for him, particularly the need to keep boys off the street and gainfully occupied. To this end, St Laurence Athletic Club was formed in 1919 with the specific goal of uniting all the lads in the parish into a league of sportsmen and friends. This was clearly successful for by 1925 the club had over a hundred members and six senior football teams which were all active in local leagues plus a junior team. There was also a billiard team, at least one cricket team and a tennis

---

[62] CCA-U3-19/8/A/3
[63] *Keble's Gazette*, 22nd January 1916
[64] In 1920-21, the parish collected £7 14s for the relief of those affected by the famine in Russia.
[65] *East Kent Times*, 13th November 1918. The news was thus received an hour earlier in Ramsgate than in London.
[66] *East Kent Times*, 6th April 1921

team. Their motto was "I serve not myself." The club was very actively supported by Mr Bevan's successor as well who saw it as a means of developing good character saying: "lose or win, I know St Laurence will play the game."[67]

During the school holidays most years, Mr Bevan was visited by his nephew Jack who loved playing on the sands, going for long walks, and most of all playing cricket with his uncle, initially in the vicarage garden and later on, when he was older, in the Warre Recreation Ground. Jack went on to play for Somerset, Cambridge University and for Minor Counties. He also became a keen educator founding Millfield School in 1935 where he promoted academic and sporting excellence but also the need to give talented boys from disadvantaged backgrounds a chance. In 1980, aged seventy-five, he founded another school in Athens which he named St Lawrence College, the name being as he said, a tribute to the many happy days he had spent in the parish.

Mr Bevan retired from St Laurence at Whitsun 1921. He was only fifty-three but his health had never recovered after his experiences in the First World War. He died at Knebworth on 25th November 1940.[68]

Mr Bevan was succeeded by the Reverend **Alfred George Wilcox** who arrived in February 1922. He was a man in his early sixties who had many years of pastoral experience and who had also served as a chaplain in the First World War when he was mentioned in despatches. One of his tasks in the last had been to bury his only son, Second Lieutenant Kenneth Wilcox, who was killed in action at Ypres on 8th November 1915. His experiences of war gave Mr Wilcox a great understanding of the men who had served and of the problems they faced. One of his most successful ventures at St Laurence was his revival of men's services.

Something which appalled Mr Wilcox upon his arrival was the state of the churchyard which he described as a "wilderness". He set up a Churchyard Care Committee in 1922 and organised a scheme of work to turn the area into an appropriate place of rest for past parishioners. Grass was cut, brambles cleared, paths laid out and money collected for flowers, trees and shrubs. An avenue of remembrance comprised of one hundred and seventy one roses was laid in 1923. Much of the work was done by volunteers but sufficient funds were raised to add an increment to the sexton's remuneration in return for maintaining the site.[69] Thanet Board of Guardians, who had

---

[67] *Thanet Advertiser*, 6th September 1924

[68] His estate was valued at almost £29,000 which would be worth £1.4 million today indicating that he had resources far beyond those he would have earned as a clergyman. *Crockford's Clerical Directory* of 1908 shows that he earned £320 per annum gross, £260 net of which £58 was generated by fees and £65 came from the Bouchery bequest. His father had died in 1919 leaving an estate worth £410,879 (£21 million today) and it is likely that Mr Bevan received a share which allowed him to take early retirement.

[69] This was Arthur Startup, sexton from 1925 to 1956. An allotment in Chapel Road went with the job which Mr Startup tended until he died in 1969, there being no sexton appointed following his retirement. He was a veteran of the Gallipoli landings and had been mentioned in despatches.

sent many paupers from the workhouse to be buried there, donated forty pounds to the project in 1924. Mr Wilcox regarded the care of the churchyard as important because to him, the inmates were "guests of Our Master" and they should as such be honoured and treated with dignity, not left to rot and ruin.

A small but significant change made by Mr Wilcox related to the vicarage. Previously, each new incumbent had been expected to purchase the fittings from his predecessor. Mr Wilcox duly bought them from Mr Bevan and then gave them to the parish arguing that they should go with the job rather than be an additional expense.[70]

There were several additions to the church during his time. The stone war memorial was placed in the porch in 1923 and a set of stalls for the ladies choir arrived in 1924. A rail was added to the lectern in 1925. The biggest change was the addition of the two new bells which brought the total in the tower to ten. Other changes included the inauguration of a Christmas fair in the Parish Hall and a summer fair in the vicarage garden. In 1926, the summer sale raised £150 4s 6d and the winter one £71 3s 7d, which was equivalent to a year's collections in church and more than four times the quota.[71]

Although no sermons survive from his incumbency, Mr Wilcox was remembered by parishioners as a man who was always immaculately dressed in highly polished gaiters with a fresh flower in his buttonhole and who walked with a very upright gait. He was a creature of disciplined habits. Every afternoon as the church clock struck three he would leave the vicarage to go for a walk, sometimes to visit someone in particular, sometimes just to stroll through the parish talking to people to find out how they were doing. As the clock struck six he would return to the vicarage in time for a cup of tea before Evening Prayer. Afterwards, when he had no Bible class to teach, he would attend choir practice or join the bell ringers. By his own admission, he loved the job. On April 22nd 1924 he said: "I am a very happy Vicar in a very happy parish."

Mr Wilcox was also a man sensitive to the circumstances of his congregation. He set up book clubs where twelve people could band together to purchase a Christian related volume and then pass it round for a month each. After a year, groups might exchange volumes. For those who could not afford that, there were magazine clubs where six people could each contribute 2d toward the cost of an annual subscription and then pass the magazine on weekly. Meanwhile, a group of parish ladies met weekly to mend and recycle clothes for the benefit of the poor with better items being sold to raise funds.

On 24th November 1926, the parish had a royal visitor, although not one who chose to enter the church. H.R.H. the Prince of Wales, later to acquire infamy by his dalliance with Mrs Simpson, arrived outside what is now Ellington Infants School where he was greeted by the Lord Lieutenant of Kent and other dignitaries. It was a sign of the changing position of the church in society that the Reverend Alfred Wilcox was not invited to be amongst them even though they were standing within yards of St Laurence church. The children from St Lawrence boys and girls schools did, however, have a

---

[70] *Thanet Advertiser*, 26th April 1922
[71] CCA-U3-19/5/5

chance to sing *God bless the Prince of Wales* before he got in the provided car and departed for Government Acre to commence a series of engagements.

In August 1927 Mr Wilcox took the bell ringers to Belgium. They saw the famous bell tower at Bruges before going to visit war graves at Passchendale, Tyne Cot, Hooge Crater and Renninghelst where Mr Wilcox's son was buried. They attended a service at the Menin Gate before sailing back to Dover where they were able to ring a peal. They returned home on Monday 15th August but during the evening, Mr Wilcox started to feel unwell. Despite it being summer, he was shivering and he had a blinding headache. He went to bed early but his condition deteriorated during the night and his wife sent for the doctor. Mr Wilcox was admitted to Ramsgate Hospital where he died on Friday just after one in the morning of double pneumonia aged sixty-nine.[72]

His demise shocked everyone and the funeral was a very big affair. His body was brought into the church the night before the funeral festooned with wreaths. Ordinarily a clergyman would rest in the chancel but he was laid under the tower which housed his beloved bells. An early morning service of Holy Communion was celebrated the next day with his funeral following mid afternoon. So many people attended that even with them standing in the aisles and side chapel, there were still people left outside in the churchyard waiting to pay their respects. Mr Wilcox's three brothers, all clergy, took part in the service and trumpeters from the RAF base at Manston played the Last Post. The PCC decided that in future the eleventh Sunday after Trinity should be kept as a special

day of thanksgiving for all those who had laboured for God's kingdom in the parish of St Laurence. The parish magazine was issued edged in black. His curate, the Reverend Alexander Weemyss wrote in tribute: "He had the primary and essential qualifications of a Pastor, an internal and living sense of the Good Shepherd as the Shepherd of his own spirit. It was He who soothed and healed hourly and gave His servant that smile of peace so integral to our memories of him."[73] The Archdeacon said Mr Wilcox was : "a true man of God – a true shepherd to his flock. He knew his sheep by name, tending to them in sickness and in health."[74]

After the sudden death of the popular vicar it required a sensitive man to pick up the pieces and that task fell to the Reverend **Charles Paul Cowland-Cooper,** a man described as "a keen churchman of the modern type" who preached "with frankness and outspokenness with a broad and tolerant vision.". He was a man who knew the area well having served as curate at St Andrew's, Reading Street and his pastoral credentials were exemplary but he was perhaps a surprising choice for St Laurence since he was

---

[72] He would have been taken by the ambulance which had moved into the Fire Escape building next to the Parish Hall in 1925.
[73] *Parish Magazine* , September 1927
[74] *Thanet Advertiser*, 27th December 1927

significantly more High Church than any of its previous clergy. Mr Cowland-Cooper would re-introduce private confession, the word altar, vestments and the title Father, none of which had been seen or heard since the Reformation, and the erection of the English altar with its riddel posts, curtains and angelic supporters was one of his first innovations. In fact, Mr Cowland-Cooper almost did not come to the parish. When he visited the church with his wife having been approached by the Archbishop about the opportunity, he was horrified to discover that there was no cross to be found in the building and not a single candle. He said that there was nothing to indicate the building was a church at all. It was only when he went outside and saw the war memorial cross that he agreed to come. He was inducted on 18th December 1927.

Just twelve parish magazines survive from Mr Cowland-Cooper's fifteen years in the parish but they show him to have been a good humoured man. The August edition each year included anecdotes and jokes such as:

> Patient: "Just dropped in Doctor to tell you how much I've benefited from your treatment."
> Doctor: "I'm glad to hear it. What was the trouble?"
> Patient: "None. It was my uncle's. I'm his heir."
>
> A lawyer named John Strange chose as his epitaph "Here lies an honest lawyer." His wife objected that it did not include his name. He replied that it did as anyone seeing it would say "An honest lawyer? That's strange."

The idea of injecting humour into the magazine was entirely his and he justified it saying that laughter was as much part of summer as sunshine: "Let us capture as much of the holiday spirit as we can because it will do us a world of good and make us more amiable and friendly and wonderfully improve our minds and bodies."[75] It was not to make a repeat appearance in the magazine until the early 1990s.

Mr Cowland-Cooper was a great enthusiast for the history of the parish and even wrote a book about it so it is ironic that he is behind one of the most famous myths about the church.

In 1934, the Borough of Ramsgate decided to hold a pageant in Ellington Park to celebrate fifty years since its incorporation. Such an event, which was due to last days and involve three thousand people, clearly took a long time to plan and Mr Cowland-Cooper was an active member of the planning committee. Originally, it was hoped to portray Queen Victoria spending time in the area whilst a Princess but the Lord Chamberlain's office told them that showing the Queen in this manner was forbidden. The council was upset because the intentions were very respectful. In order to get round the ban on depicting a monarch who had died in recent memory, Mr Cowland Cooper proposed a

---

[75] *Parish Magazine,* August 1936

new scene showing Queen Elizabeth attending St Laurence fair in 1571. It meant they could still have a colourful display with a royal character. Three hundred parishioners duly dressed up to perform the fifth scene of the town pageant which was described in the programme as:

> A gracious scene. Whispers of smuggling based upon the "free traders." Fishermen in almost familiar clothes. Folk dancers and then Queen Bess and her court in a glory of jewellery and lace.

Mrs Cowland-Cooper took on the heavy duties of Costume Mistress whilst Mr Armstrong was the producer and Mr Spencer-Payne the prop master. The cast included:[76]

Mr Robert Spracclynge	E. Spencer-Payne
Mr Thomas Johnson	C. Armstrong
Sir John Roper	E. W. Barnes
Lady Roper	Mrs Philpott
Queen Elizabeth	Mrs Brangwin
Earl of Leicester	Charles Sutton
Sir Richard Manwood	Mr Pryor
Lady Manwood	Mrs Price
The Reverend William Marsh	The Rev. Charles Cowland-Cooper
Mrs Marsh	Mrs Cowland-Cooper
Parish beadle	A. Startup
Constables	Messrs Oliver and Curling
Fortune tellers	Miss Huggard and Miss England
Singing Clerks	L. A. Bolton, S. Gee, D. Cunningham, J. Wightman
Stallholders	Mrs Curzon, Mrs Freeman, Miss Jessie Waters
Jugglers and wrestlers	Ramsgate Sea Cadets
Lord of Misrule	Mr Smithyman
Lord Warden of the Cinque Ports	Captain Paul Irven
Fishermen	C. E. Hawkins, R. W. Hawkins, Frank Small
Smuggler	Mr Munday
Villagers	Mr Waters, Mr Matson, Miss Sparkes, Miss Vane R. Solly, J. Hartley
Crowd	various members of the Darby, Griggs, Isaacs and Mirams families, Miss Dora Waters

---

[76] *East Kent Times*, 14th July 1934 p.12

As part of their performance, the Singing Clerks sang the Hymn to St Laurence and the 1594 madrigal by John Morley *April is my mistress*.[77]

It was only ever meant as a piece of fiction. On the date in question Queen Elizabeth was in Essex at Hatfield.[78] She never set foot on the Isle of Thanet at any time in her reign, let alone attended the church fair. The image which adorned the parish magazine cover was drawn to celebrate the pageant not the fictitious visit. That anyone since has regarded it as history would undoubtedly have amused Mr Cowland-Cooper greatly.

---

[77] *East Kent Times* 18th July 1934 p.3
[78] John Nichols, *The Progresses and Public Processions of Queen Elizabeth* vol. 1 (London, 1824) p.279. She was at Hatfield from 7th August to 2nd September.

Life changed a great deal during Mr Cowland-Cooper's incumbency. A survey found that of all children born in England 67% were baptised, 34% attended Sunday School, 25% were confirmed but just 9% grew up to receive Holy Communion even once a year, and less than 2% became regular communicants.[79] Despite the recession which followed the Wall Street Crash which took place two years into his ministry, people were generally better off than in the Victorian period. They had more disposable income and there was more to spend it on. Fifty years earlier, people had worked longer hours and the church represented almost the only source of entertainment and education. By the 1930s, this was different and people's expectations changed. A study of wages, prices and entertainments on offer from the Ramsgate newspapers of 1935 demonstrate this.

---

[79] *The Window*, March 1951

Item	£	s	d	Value today
Children's Toys				
Box of building bricks		2	0	6.48
Box of toy soldiers			6	1.62
Child's bicycle	2	5	0	145.80
Nurses outfit			7	1.76
Wooden painted truck		6	6	21.06
Deluxe teddy bear		5	11	19.17
Hornby train set		4	0	12.96
Meccano set		1	0	3.24
Teddy bear			11	2.84
Clothes				
Girl's gymslip		9	2	29.70
Man's black mourning suit	2	2	0	136.08
Man's coat	3	3	0	204.12
Man's flannel trousers		14	9	47.79
Man's pyjamas		6	6	21.06
Man's shirt		4	9	15.39
Man's socks, pair		1	0	3.24
Man's suit	3	10	0	226.80
Man's tie		1	0	3.24
Man's wool pullover		5	11	19.17
Woman's blouse		4	6	14.58
Woman's coat		18	0	58.32
Woman's girdle		6	11	22.41
Woman's handbag		3	11	12.69
Woman's hat		9	6	30.78
Woman's print summer dress		9	11	32.13
Woman's silk stockings, pair		2	0	6.48
Woman's skirt		3	0	9.72
Woman's slippers		4	6	14.58
Woman's suit	2	9	6	160.38
Woman's watch		5	0	16.20
Woman's wool dress		15	9	51.03
Drink				
Bottle of brandy	1	4	0	77.76

Item	£	s	d	Value today
Bottle of champagne		7	6	24.30
Coffee, per pound		5	0	16.20
Bottle of orange squash		1	0	3.24
Bottle of sherry		4	6	14.58
Tea, per pound		2	0	6.48
Tomson and Wotton ale, two pints			10	2.70
Entertainment				
Admission to Marina Bathing Pool			6	1.62
Cinema ticket			6	1.62
Dancing at Grand Hotel with live band		2	6	8.10
Day cruise to Southend		4	0	12.96
Dinner and dance at Grand Hotel		9	0	29.16
Flight over Isle from Northwood		4	0	12.96
Four course lunch at Lewis and Hylands		2	0	6.48
Return sailing to Ostende		10	6	34.02
Three course lunch at the San Clu		1	9	5.67
Food				
Back bacon, per pound		1	2	3.78
Biscuits, per pound			6	1.62
Strawberry jam, per pound			7	1.89
Brisket, per pound		1	2	3.78
Butter, per pound			10	2.70
Cheese, per pound			6	1.62
Chicken and ham roll, per pound		1	0	3.24
Chocolate, per pound		1	0	3.24
Corned beef, per pound			7	1.89
Sultana cake, per pound			6	1.62
Raisins, per pound			6	1.62
Margarine, per pound			4	1.08
Marmalade, per pound			5	1.22
Granulated sugar, per pound			2	0.54
Pork sausages, per pound		1	2	3.78
Porridge oats, per pound			5	1.22
Custard powder			5	1.22
Dundee cake		1	0	3.24

Item	£	s	d	Value today
Eggs, dozen		1	6	4.86
Fish paste, small jar			3	0.81
HP sauce			9	2.43
SR flour, three pounds			8	2.16
Tin of apricots			10	2.70
Tin of herrings in tomato sauce			4	1.08
Tin of peaches			10	2.57
Tin of pears			11	2.84
Tin of peas			5	1.22
Tin of salmon, small			7	1.76
Tin of soup			6	1.62

Household

Item	£	s	d	Value today
21 Piece tea set		7	6	24.30
26 Piece dinner set		19	6	63.18
4' mattress	1	5	9	83.43
4' oak bedstead	4	6	6	280.26
Single blanket		4	11	15.93
Pillowcase			6	1.62
Double blanket		19	11	64.53
Carpet sweeper		15	6	50.22
Double blanket		8	11	28.89
Electric fire	1	7	6	89.10
Electric iron		8	11	28.89
Electric radio	6	6	0	408.24
Rediffusion radio weekly rental		1	6	4.86
Fireside chair	1	15	0	113.40
Gas iron		10	0	32.40
Gramophone	1	17	6	121.50
Three piece suite	3	3	0	204.12
Upright piano	6	6	0	408.24
Vacuum cleaner	5	3	0	333.72
Wardrobe, dressing table and chest of drawers	10	15	0	696.60

Miscellaneous

Item	£	s	d	Value today
Accordion	2	8	9	157.95
Arch lever file		1	6	4.86

Item	£	s	d	Value today
Basic camera		5	0	16.20
Christmas crackers, dozen		1	0	3.24
Cigarettes, twenty		1	0	3.24
Coat fabric per yard		4	0	12.96
Course of driving lessons	2	2	0	136.08
Dress fabric per yard		2	6	8.10
Fox terrier puppy		10	0	32.40
Gold wedding ring		17	6	56.70
Hot water bottle		2	6	8.10
Library - borrowing fee per book			2	0.54
Lilo airbed		14	11	48.33
Mints per pound			6	1.62
Permanent Eugene wave		25	0	81.00
Pram	1	19	6	127.98
Printed Christmas cards - 1 dozen		3	0	9.72
Sewing machine	11	0	0	712.80
Shampoo and set		5	0	16.20
Tobacco per ounce			8	2.16
Typewriter	15	17	6	1,028.70
Umbrella			5	1.35
Property				
Bungalow in Newington Rd	495	0	0	32,076.00
House in London Road	665	0	0	43,092.00
Flat rental per week		14	0	45.36
House rental per week		16	0	51.84
Transport				
Bicycle	3	19	6	257.58
Bicycle rental weekly		2	0	6.48
Hillman minx	159	0	0	10,303.20
Morris saloon	182	0	0	11,793.60
Vauxhall saloon	205	0	0	13,284.00
Motorbike	29	0	0	1,879.20
Ramsgate to Canterbury train day return - 2nd class		2	3	7.29
Ramsgate to London train day return - 2nd class		9	6	30.78
Ramsgate to London, coach day return		7	6	24.30

Item	£	s	d	Value today
Taxi per mile			3	0.81
Weekly wages				
Part time home help (25hrs) with lunch		5	0	16.20
Live in waitress with meals and board		10	0	32.40
Junior clerk		12	6	40.50
Cook, small household		15	0	48.60
Senior housemaid		16	3	52.65
Shorthand typist		17	6	56.70
Waitress	1	0	0	64.80
Gardener	1	3	0	74.52
Cook, cafeteria	1	15	0	113.40
Agricultural labourer	1	14	3	110.97
Caretaker	2	0	0	129.60
Swimming instructor	2	2	0	136.08
Shop assistant	2	3	6	140.94
Carpenter	2	13	4	172.80
Railway ticket collector	3	5	4	211.68

Yet at St Laurence, the work of worship and witness went on. Two comments from visitors give their impressions. A journalist noted the huge amounts raised for charity by the weekly whist drives in the Parish Hall and praised "its atmosphere of friendly geniality."[80] The Archdeacon on 16th July 1936 reported: "The church is in beautiful order and it is a pleasure to visit a church so lovingly cared for and so well furnished with devotional intention."

A number of changes were made to the church during Mr Cowland-Cooper's time. The rood was given in 1936, a children's corner was set up in the north transept in 1928, pews in the side chapel were replaced by chairs and the present communion rails were given. The two banners of the church and Mother's Union were made in 1934 and 1937 respectively. He also had four banners made showing what Dr Cotton claimed were the arms of the four manors – Manston, Nethercourt, Ellington and Uppercourt – and these were hung beneath the tower, one against each pillar. In 1931, a major restoration project was started at a cost of £600 and it was during the course of this that the early thirteenth century window was uncovered in the high chancel. Strip lighting was installed on the tower but discontinued due to cost in 1938. Radio was installed also so that the congregation might sit and listen to the BBC evening service after Evensong. A missionary area was set up in the south transept in 1936 which housed a triptych made by

---

[80] *East Kent Times*, 24th December 1935

the sisters at West Malling Abbey and purchased using funds raised by the King's Messengers. This was moved to the children's area in 1961. [81]

With regard to activities, the Churchyard Care Committee set up by his predecessor still operated and so did the District Nurse Fund. There were afternoon Sunday Schools for children and a midweek King's Messengers group which learnt about the work of the Church overseas and raised money for it. For women there was the Mothers' Union and the Women's Fellowship. Bible classes existed for girls and women. The Provident Clothing and Coal Clubs were closed during his incumbency and replaced by a Relief Committee. A Soup Kitchen operated in the winter for four days every week providing up to nine thousand meals a year to the elderly, infirm and pauper children who would not otherwise have a hot meal. In 1938 he set up the Guild of Divine Healing whose members undertook to pray for specific sufferers by name each day. In the autumn of 1937 he introduced a breakfast of boiled egg, bread and butter and a cup of tea for 4d in the parish hall for those who had attended the 8a.m. Holy Communion service and wanted some sustenance before Matins.[82]

One of his key concerns was the need to extend the church's ministry to the more outlying parts of the parish. On September 2nd 1934 he commenced services in the Upper Room at Ebbsfleet. It was the birth of what would later become St Mary's Church, Cliffsend. A year later, the PCC considered a proposal to buy some land from Bethlehem Hospital to build a new church at Cliffsend but with no money for so large a project, services continued in the Upper Room.[83]

The Reverend Charles Cowland-Cooper in WW1

---

[81] It is now in D9.
[82] This was an idea made popular in Arthur Hebbert (ed.), *The Parish Communion* (London, 1937).
[83] PCC Minutes 15th October 1935

Parish of S. Laurence in Thanet.

"*Peace be to this house, and to all that dwell in it.*"

Book of Common Prayer.

To the Church Residents at Cliffs' End.

In addition to the regular services of worship held in the Parish Church, we are now enabled (by the courtesy and goodwill of various friends) to hold a service of

THE HOLY COMMUNION

on the First Sunday in each month (beginning on September 2nd) at 9.15 a.m., in the "Upper Room" of Mr. Hogbin's Barn.

We extend an earnest invitation to all Church people to join with us; and for those who have been Confirmed to receive the Sacrament of the Lord, if they so desire.

Why was the Sacrament of the Lord's Supper ordained?
For the continual remembrance of the sacrifice of the death of Christ, and of the benefits which we receive thereby.

Church Catechism.

C. COWLAND COOPER, Vicar.
T. R. ELY, Sidesman.

A considerable amount of Mr Cowland-Cooper's time was spent in the church schools. He was very much aware of the need for modernisation and in 1938, both schools were extended. As vicar, he was expected to give religious instruction and this he did with enthusiasm though he was not one to tolerate inattention. If he caught a child yawning, talking or looking out of the window, he would flick a piece of chalk at them. His aim was excellent and on one occasion he managed to get the chalk direct into the mouth of a girl who was gazing open-mouthed into space!

In June 1935, Mr Cowland-Cooper took the boys from the parish school to the local railway station to see the newly built train which had been named "St Lawrence." It ran on the London to Portsmouth line and continued in service until 1962 despite being damaged in an air raid at Cannon Street station on 11th May 1941.[84]

When he was not working, Mr Cowland-Cooper enjoyed gardening, tennis and painting. One of his artworks was given to the Sailors' Church in Ramsgate and some of his sketches were used as parish Christmas cards and magazine covers. He enjoyed company and one of his friends was Lawrence of Arabia, a man whom he had met when serving with the Egyptian Expeditionary Force in the First World War. After the war, Mr Cowland-Cooper had lectured extensively for Lowell Thomas Travelogues on Allenby's campaign and Lawrence's work.[85] Lawrence would regularly come to the vicarage on his motorbike and the two men would go off for the day to explore the local countryside.

---

[84] *East Kent Times*, 22nd June 1935; Alan Earnshaw,. *Trains in Trouble*: Vol. 8. (Penryn, 1993) p.20. A Hornby model was later released of the locomotive.

[85] Available at http://library.marist.edu/archives/lttravelogues/travelogue/travelogue.html

St Laurence in Thanet.

Above all, Mr Cowland-Cooper was a true pastor, always keen to encourage and support but also to teach and instruct. Examples of this include:

> It is when we keep religion wrapped up in a napkin, so to speak, as something separate from life like a medicine to be taken occasionally that it becomes such a dead, useless and unattractive thing. The very essence of religion is salt and salt needs contact, needs to be rubbed and worked into the substance if it is to be any good and find its true function and usefulness….So carry your religion about with you in your ordinary life. Keep it working as well and as regularly as your watch or your liver. Just as your watch has to be taken sometimes to the watchmaker and your liver to the doctor so, if your religion is to do its work satisfactorily in everyday life, you will have to take it to the repairer and restorer so that it may be kept up to the mark, recharged and renewed. That is why we Christians must have our regular place in the fellowship of Christ's church and in its worship in order that our religion may be kept going strong and reliable in our ordinary everyday life.

> There are parents who care not a rap about their children beyond their possible ability to earn a few more pence to swell the revenue – it would be a waste of time to talk to such as those. But to you who realise that your children are a trust from God to carry on your name and history after you are dead and for whom you rightly feel that every effort must be made to fit them to take their place in the battle of life- well, please don't cheat them out of that one little hour a week which is practically their only chance of learning those facts and truths and ideals which have been the very foundation stone and maintenance of every great and noble life.
>
> We are living in an age of confusion and perplexity where for many it appears a sort of Blind Man's Buff existence! But for those who have the inner light of the Spirit there need be no sense of darkness or groping.[86]

This aspect of his ministry was to be especially important in 1938 and 1939 as the country teetered on the brink of war and through the early days of the war when our forces faced considerable odds. When the Parish Hall was taken over for gas mask distribution in 1938, he stayed all day to help the officials and to reassure some of his more nervous and elderly parishioners. He worked with the authorities to review the shelter provision for the church schools. He made arrangements for how the church was to cope with the impending crisis. Services at Ebbsfleet ceased and those at Manston were reduced. Despite his own fears – and having experienced war and having two sons of twenty-seven and twenty-three respectively he must have been worried – he tried to keep spirits up: "This troubled and distracted world should not be allowed to occupy our whole attention nor become a daily nightmare to paralyse activity and overwhelm our spirits. The Christian takes God for his trust and will not fear what man can do unto him.[87]"

Ordinarily, the main Sunday service in church began at 11.15a.m. but on September 3rd 1939, the BBC had advised that an important announcement would be made at eleven. As a result, Mr Cowland-Cooper had the radio turned on and so it was in church that most people heard Mr Chamberlain's words: "this country is at war with Germany." The radio was turned off and a few minutes silence followed. A few people left. The organ then struck up the National Anthem and, slightly late, Mr Cowland-Cooper began Matins preaching, what must have been, one of the most difficult sermons in his life.

---

[86] *Parish Magazine,* August 1936, June 1938; *East Kent Times,* 7th April 1915
[87] *Parish Magazine,* July 1939

When war broke out, the Sunday Schools were closed but a Young People's Fellowship was started to give teenage children a place to go and relax amid the turmoil. This provided coffee and a range of games from cards to darts with tennis in the summer. Service times were altered to fit with blackout regulations and the needs of war workers whom it was recognised would not necessarily be available to join in Sunday worship. Mr Cowland-Cooper also increased his availability. Previously, he had been at home to parishioners from five to six each Monday to Saturday but those times were now extended to cope with the greater needs.

1940 saw the children evacuated, the church schools closed and the cessation of the parish magazine due to paper shortages. Also a victim of this was the annual report published each year since 1881 which contained the vicar's review of past achievements and plans for future work, inspection reports on the church schools and the accounts of the various funds. Sadly, it was never re-started. One of Mr Cowland-Cooper's last messages was on the eve of the evacuation of Dunkirk when he wrote:

> In these days of desperate conflict and struggle with the disastrous, though not unexpected, invasion of neighbouring countries across the water and with no victorious triumph to reward our efforts as yet, let us remain resolute and undismayed. We are standing for what is right and just and we will not waver in our confidence in God's grace and power. We will faithfully carry on with our daily duties avoiding the rumour mongers and scare gossipers so that we may maintain a calm and confident outlook. While our hearts are filled with pride in the courageous exploits and achievements of our airmen, sailors and soldiers; day by day they carry on amid these dangers and ordeals: let us then do the same, and if the demand is made, share in facing lesser dangers. (June 1940)

Mr Cowland-Cooper left the parish on February 1st 1942 after almost fifteen years. He had said previously that he did not believe a minister should stay too long in any one parish because he felt it was not good for either the man or the congregation but he had done his best to stay at St Laurence until the end of the war feeling that the people required a stable pastoral lead in the time of emergency. Unfortunately, his wife's ill health rendered this impossible and he had his ninety year old mother living with him too, both ladies being at risk in air raids because they were unable to move quickly to a shelter. A parish which was less on the front line was clearly in order. Mr Cowland-Cooper's humility was shown at his farewell when he refused to accept anything other than a cassock from the parish and insisted on putting the remainder of the sum collected into the Day School Rebuilding Fund. Although his words on that occasion went unrecorded, they were probably on the lines of what he wrote when he left his previous parish in 1927:

> The great and chief function of a Parish Priest is surely to bring God - His reality, His power, His will - to bear upon the lives of parishioners. Inasmuch as any of you have come, through my ministry, to know God better, to love Him more earnestly, to follow His bidding more faithfully, so have I succeeded in my work here: but if it should be the reverse of this, then I have undoubtedly failed in my position and duty.[88]

His parting gift to the parish was the hour-glass which today sits on the pulpit. He bought it, as he said, to keep his successors on their toes to ensure that their sermons were neither too short nor too long and that services did not over-run.

Mr Cowland-Cooper was one of the most beloved of all the clergy to serve at St Laurence during the century and he continued to visit it after his retirement when he always received a warm welcome. He died in 1964 and his obituary in *The Beacon* said: "He was a practising Christian in the true sense of the words. He was forthright, jovial and kind and for this reason he was liked by all who knew him."

The task of replacing him fell to **John Hartley Roundhill**, a Yorkshireman and widower of fifty-one who had been vicar of Holy Trinity, Sittingbourne for the previous twelve years. He turned out to be one of the most remarkable incumbents in the church's nine hundred year long history, a man of immense dedication who faced difficulties which would have destroyed many a man. He was known as Father John.

He arrived in the midst of the war on 1st May 1942 when there was no Sunday School, no bell-ringing, no choir, no services at Ebbsfleet and no parish magazine. From a pastoral perspective, things were challenging to say the least. The vicarage had been requisitioned by the Fire Service so Mr Roundhill found himself living in St Mildred's Road until April 1946. Enemy action saw bombs landing across the parish with seven landing on the cemetery at Cecilia Road within a month of his arrival. The church escaped a direct hit but had three stained glass windows damaged, two on the north side and the great east window.[89] There were difficulties planning events and publicising them. The

---

[88] Sturry Parish Magazine, November 1927
[89] The east window was taken away for repair September 1948 and returned a year later. One on the

Archbishop came to confirm twenty-one parishioners in December 1942 but his visit had to be kept secret for fear he become a target which meant the sight of him processing round the church came as a great surprise to everyone. Mr Roundhill had lost his car when the Germans attacked his previous parish of Sittingbourne in 1940 which caused him to try to get to and from Manston and Cliffsend by bicycle or on foot or rely on loans. With no assistant clergy, he had difficulties in scheduling services. Not only did he have three services to conduct each Sunday at St Laurence but there was one at the hospital, one at Manston and from 1943 onwards, one at Cliffsend. The blackout meant that during winter Evensong had to be held mid afternoon directly after Sunday School and since it was physically impossible to repeat the service in three churches before dusk this meant having to try and fit in a celebration of Matins in either Manston or Cliffsend, the other having Evensong. No bells could be rung until May 1943 though a shortage of ringers meant they were rarely heard before VE day. Fund raising was challenging and even traditional events such as the annual parties for choir boys and Sunday School became difficult as they had to depend on members of the congregation surrendering some of their rations in order that a spread could be produced. Yet Mr Roundhill refused to be downhearted. At Christmas 1942, he was determined that there should be a Midnight Service but how was this to be achieved without any light? His answer was to have the radio broadcast service relayed into church. People had no hymnbooks and the organist could not play as it was pitch black inside the church but he reasoned that people knew the words of the carols off by heart anyway. He did the consecration himself alongside the broadcast – it being a Book of Common Prayer service, he did not need to read it – with the communion table brought from the sanctuary to stand under the tower as in the seventeenth century. When it came to distribution, it was too dangerous to have people trying to move around in the dark, so Mr Roundhill took the bread and wine to each pew accompanied by a server with a single candle. The whole service was a demonstration of his ingenuity and dedication.

Moreover, he did not let the war stop his evangelism. In the spring of 1943, he accepted an offer from the Primitive Methodists at Cliffsend to use their empty premises and started services in them. Shortages and rationing prevented the purchase of curtains for the communion table there so Mr Roundhill gave them a set of curtains which had been boxed up when he left the vicarage.

On 19th May 1943, Mr Roundhill became the first vicar in the church's history to marry at St Laurence. He married Patience Cowland-Cooper, the daughter of the previous vicar and the service was conducted by her father. Afterward the couple departed for a celebratory tea in the Parish Hall to which everyone on the electoral roll was invited. They had been given a number of coupons before the day to help them provide a feast and the parish gave them a cheque for £27. Mr Roundhill promptly deposited this under the War Loan scheme and said: "your generous gift has had the immediate effect of helping the country and the extended effect of providing us with

---

north was too badly damaged and remained plain glass until 1998.

something to buy necessary things when we move into the vicarage at a time when it will be more patriotic to spend."[90]

The war ended in 1945 and on VE day, Mr Roundhill held four services of thanksgiving because the crowds were so great, there was not room for everyone in the church. After the VJ day celebrations, a white silk chasuble was purchased for his use in honour of peace. Mr Roundhill was also delighted to obtain the services of a volunteer lay reader in September. The question of a memorial was raised and Mr Roundhill suggested moving the vestry and restoring the Lady Chapel but the PCC were not enthusiastic and the demand that the parish raise £840 (over £200,000 in today's terms) for the Archbishop's Thank-offering Fund meant that there was no money to erect any form of parish memorial. Mr Roundhill wrote regarding the fair arranged in 1947 toward this appeal: "Those of us who lived in Kent during the war are fully aware of our cause for thanksgiving. The fact that we shall be able to sit on the Vicarage lawn without fear of sirens, shells, bullets or bombs is itself a good reason for thanksgiving."

It was Mr Roundhill who gave the parish magazine the name, *The Beacon* in 1951. He edited it and always wrote a letter for it regarding the magazine as a form of outreach to many who did not attend church and an aspect of pastoral ministry. Keeping spirits up in wartime was essential and so was helping people come to terms with loss and hardship. Later, he had to address fears raised by the development of nuclear weapons and the descent of what Churchill termed "the Iron Curtain." His communications show a gift for words and illustrate his personality. He took his role as a teacher seriously and was always keen to lead from the front, consistently portraying problems as challenges to be overcome and often using sporting imagery. A selection from his letters shows this:

> "The Church is not primarily for consolation of individuals in distress but rather for the consecration of those who are willing to take up the stress of living. It is not an ambulance unit to pick up the wounded only but a complete fighting force, attacking, defending, saving. Its function is not merely to save the victims of a sinful and frustrating word but to attack the causes of sin and frustration." (February 1949)

> "If we are mature Christians, we are drawn by His love and driven by His Spirit, There are far too many who call themselves Christians who want to be drawn but would hate to be driven." (June 1952)

> "You go to church to be the church." (January 1960)

---

[90] *Parish Magazine,* July 1943. In order not to interfere with his work, the couple married on a Wednesday.

"The meaning of worship is worth-ship. No worship – no worth. Worship is no mere pastime or hobby, it is something which is due from man to God. It is a duty, a debt. It can be a pleasurable duty but should be offered not as a pleasure but a due. Our services in church are our collective offering to God, His worthship. When Jesus founded the Church He did not provide a form of entertainment for the few but a way of salvation for all. (January 1950)

"Extra services are not intended to give you a wider choice but extra opportunities for extra prayer and worship." (March 1944)

"Material power without spiritual power is a very dangerous thing. This is clearly demonstrated for us by the destructive power of the atomic bomb. It is as plain as a pike staff that the world and the human beings in it can only be saved by men and women who have sufficient spiritual power to handle material power to the glory of God and the good of all His people. There are too many apathetic and ineffective Christians. The Church and the World suffer in consequence." (September 1946)

"If all the time, thought, skill, money and material which is being put into the defence of peace could be put into the creation of peace, it would then be well spent." (April 1951)

"I very much enjoy taking my place in the pew. It is a thing I cannot do at home. I do not expect everything to be done exactly as it is at St Laurence but so long as the service is according to the BCP I can worship and feel at home." (August 1951)

"To write Xmas may be an economy in the use of letters but we use X to cross something out and reduce it to nothing. Do not let them cross Christ out of Christmas for you. The commercial Christmas season is of recent development. This business trend has its influence on some Christians and is responsible for the singing of Christmas carols before the Advent season of preparation is finished. The commercial scheme is all excitement in the selling but when Christmas

> comes it is all a flop. This puts Christmas in reverse. Christmas is the dawning of great light. It is the beginning of something very wonderful not the end." (December 1957)

> "Laurence was a Saint and a Martyr, a man with a courageous faith for which he would rather die than deny. He was a man, no flabby jelly or driftwood about him." (August 1958)

When Mr Roundhill first arrived, the main service on a Sunday morning was Morning Prayer or Matins. Immediately the war was over, he changed this writing: "The service of the altar is the peak of Christian worship, the mount of transfiguration. Our Lord Himself has made it for us the place of cleansing and enrichment, He gives himself for us and to us. In Holy Communion we offer ourselves for His infusion that His redeeming life may be carried wherever we go." Thereafter Holy Communion was celebrated at 8 a.m. and also at 10.30 a.m. with recipients sitting in the Side Chapel but it was repeatedly made clear that it was expected that all those who were able bodied should attend the early service.[91] He wrote in April 1943: "the lateness of the hour (10.30) gives a good opportunity for those who are old or invalid to make their communion. It should not be regarded by the young and strong as an easy opportunity, they should make the effort in the early morning." Assuming that everyone would fast before receiving the sacrament, he refused to countenance the idea of having Matins first and the Sung Eucharist after saying people "would not be prepared or able to wait until after 10.30 for their breakfast."[92] His success in encouraging early Communion can be seen by the figures: an average of 49 received Holy Communion at 8 a.m. during his incumbency compared to just 7 at 10.30 a.m. He expressed his anger at members of the congregation who chose to leave immediately after receiving to go home to prepare either breakfast or lunch in December 1947 saying: "If you intend to receive at the service, please stay for the whole of it, remember Jesus is the Host and you the guest. When Jesus instituted the Sacrament of Holy Communion one of His disciples went out before the end, it was Judas." With regard the form of service, Mr Roundhill celebrated facing east in the High Chancel, except for during the very cold weather from the late 1950s onward, when he started using a mobile altar under the tower. This table had been supplied for the use of St Christopher's when it was first built but not used as two were given. In 1948 he introduced the custom of ringing the bell to mark the consecration of the elements. Sadly, having Holy Communion in the middle of the morning meant that Matins was moved to 11.30 and it ceased to be a sung service. The inconvenience of the time led and loss of music reduced attendance and saw it being dropped at Easter 1960.

---

[91] They sat in the Side Chapel because it was assumed that being frail, they would not be able to undertake the longer walk from the nave.
[92] *The Beacon*, March 1953

As with every clergyman, Mr Roundhill's work involved teaching, meetings, visiting and work with the school and organisations. He also conducted on average seventy-six baptisms every year. When he took a baptism, he would always take each child in his arms – or lead an older child or adult – on a tour through the church to show them what he hoped would become their home and to stress that baptism was the first step on the journey toward confirmation and becoming a communicant, so that the service finished with prayer in the high chancel.

Mr Roundhill's incumbency was characterised by serious financial problems. When he arrived, the parish still had a large debt from the rebuilding of the Girls' and Boys' Schools in 1938 and the war not only meant all money raised had to go to the war effort but that there was a reduced population to contribute. This was graphically displayed on the front of the parish magazine in March 1943:[93]

An Appeal from the Parochial Church Council to all who value St. Laurence Church

There is no need to labour the point that the Church has been badly hit by the war. Many of our members and friends are, for the time being, living in other parts of the country. We are living in a "front-line" town. The Church to which we belong is a bastion of defence against the powers of barbarism. If we are to have a better world when the scientific slaughter is over, the Church must also be a strong point for attack now. To be ready is not an alarmist cry but practical commonsense. The Church's methods are, of course, spiritual but in this life, spiritual forces must find material expression. Money is a sacrament, that is to say, the money given by Church people for the necessary material support of the Church is a measure of their spirit of sacrifice and sincere desire to strengthen the Church for its spiritual task. Funds are to the Church what the supply columns are to the morale of a fighting army. Will you belong to the "supply column"? The following figures indicate our need.

	1939			1942		
	£	s	d	£	S	D
Collections in church	563	11	4	284	13	2
Free Will Offering	19	17	2	15	17	8
Donations	19	4	0	7	0	0
Boxes in Church	10	17	8	3	19	0
Total	**613**	**10**	**2**	**311**	**9**	**10**

The debt on the schools continued until 1950 when the final £109 19s was paid. That was followed by problems with the roof and organ, the estimates being £180 and £1175 respectively. In 1951, work was begun on the roof but unfortunately, when the plaster boards in the north aisle, transept and chancel were removed, death watch beetle was discovered and the estimate shot up to £3000. Mr Roundhill wrote in the March

---

[93] Moreover, prices rose by a third between 1939 and 1942 so this represents a 62% drop in income.

parish magazine: "We are the trustees of a priceless heritage. As such we must not fail those who have done so much in the past to provide and preserve it, we must not fail those who are yet unborn. We have received a beautiful church with a rich history, we must not hand on a ruin." To give an idea of the scale of the challenge, annual collections at the time were about £460 so the church needed to increase its income sevenfold at a time when shortages remained rife and inflation was running at around 9%.

Inevitably, fund-raising began. The Young Wives group led by Mrs Roundhill started a worm box where people could deposit a farthing to "slaughter a worm" in the roof. People collected newspapers, bottle tops, stamps and jam jars which raised £49. Whist drives and square dances were held and choral concerts arranged. By the summer of 1952, £766 had been collected. Work was completed in spring 1953 and the final bill was £3,571.19s.6d – the equivalent of almost £95,000 today. Further collecting meant that at the end of 1952 £2,370 had been raised but it took until January 1955 to clear the debt. Paying for the roof was a monumental achievement and it was the more impressive because it was achieved almost entirely by the congregation. The church received just two grants: £500 from the Historic Church Preservation Trust and £100 from the Diocese. It also received £629 from the Church Commissioners who were legally responsible for the costs in the chancel area. The general public's disinterest was made evident in 1951 when two thousand appeal letters were printed and distributed by hand to homes in the parish and just fifteen responses were received.

Before the war, there was a vicar and curate to seven thousand people. From May 1943 to the end of September 1950 Mr Roundhill worked alone and with the post-war rebuilding, the parish grew rapidly reaching ten thousand in 1948 and twelve thousand people in around four thousand homes in 1953. There was absolutely no doubt that Mr Roundhill needed a curate but where was the money to come from? In 1947, a curate in his first year was entitled to £300 which increased by £20 per annum up to £360. He was to get a further £25 per dependent, £50 if married and either a rent-free house or £50 for accommodation. The Diocese would pay £40 toward this but the parish had to find the rest.[94] In January 1949, the Crusade was launched, the objective being to raise enough money to pay for a clergyman to come. They were told that if they could raise the entire first year's pay for him plus a bit more for recruitment and moving expenses, (£450), the Diocese would in future contribute up to 30% but they would have to raise the rest.

By September 1949, the parish had collected enough money to allow Mr Roundhill to start advertising for a curate. He did so with alacrity but kept finding candidates withdrawing as soon as they found that there was no accommodation with the job. The level of pay – which was set by the diocese – was too low to enable anyone to rent a house or to pay for storage of their furniture. Mr Roundhill came up with the idea of splitting the vicarage into three flats with himself, his wife and son having the middle one, a curate having another and the last being rented out with the income acting as a contribution toward the costs of having the curate in the first place. He put the idea to the PCC in May 1950 and they turned him down flat saying they could not afford to have the work done. Mr Roundhill was understandably hurt and in desperation decided to cash in his National Savings Certificates to get the work done himself. As he commented, this was a very serious step because the money had been set aside to make some provision for his family after his death, clergy widows inevitably being made homeless when their husbands died. It was also an act of faith. As he explained, his income was £615 per annum of which £345 went in Compulsory Expenditure (rates, taxes, pension, insurance), £395 on Essential Expenditure (housekeeping, domestic help, fuel and car) which not only meant he was having to rely on his savings which were now "pretty well used up" for daily life but also for Necessary Expenditure (clothing, garden, subscriptions, holidays, hospitality, sundries and savings).[95] The alterations were duly made and on 28th September 1950 the much desired curate arrived. Ever humble, Mr Roundhill said he rejoiced "not because it will make life easier for an overworked Vicar but because it will make possible greater pastoral care of this great parish."

At first things seemed to go well and the new curate spent lots of time visiting as well as taking services and assisting with the various parish groups but in July 1951,

---

[94] *St Laurence Parish Magazine* December 1946, May 1947. The *East Kent Times* in 1947 showed a considerable shortage of housing in the area. Bedsits were about £2 a week unfurnished or £5 or more if furnished so the curate's £50 per annum housing allowance was woefully inadequate hence the demand made by clergy for actual accommodation.

[95] His income was equivalent today to £18,800. At the time, a police constable earned £594.

Father Roberts announced that he was leaving as the flat was too small and he needed a house. A despairing Mr Roundhill accepted that his hopes of obtaining help were now non-existent and announced that the money the Crusade team had raised would be given to the roof restoration fund.

Yet all was not lost. With the prospect of a new church at Newington, the diocese stepped in and the Reverend Stanley Bounds arrived on 1st September 1952 moving into 2 Auckland Avenue. In November, the local council accepted building plans and fund raising began. The parish had to raise £6000, about £170,000 in today's money. With the money still owing on the roof, this undertaking was an act of real faith but Mr Roundhill was ready for the challenge. St Christopher's was dedicated on 26th September 1955 with money still owing and Mr Bounds having left. This time, however, Mr Roundhill was not left without assistance and the Reverend Francis Coveney arrived the same month though he only lasted a year. He had also, by then obtained the services of Deaconess Hilda Howard who arrived in May 1954. The parish really needed a curate who could take Holy Communion services but could not afford one. A curate would have cost the parish between £400 and £450 a year, she cost them £250 thanks to a Diocesan grant.[96] She soon made herself useful, however, taking over much of the youth work and women's groups.

In April 1957, a Free Will Offering scheme was started at St Laurence which still faced a debt of over £3000 on St Christopher's and needed a further thousand to repair the organ and £750 for a new heating system, the coke stoves being as Mr Roundhill remarked "dirty, expensive and inefficient." Plans to introduce a microphone system at £140 had to be shelved for lack of money. The same year saw the inauguration of the Quinquennial inspection scheme which found problems in the tower roof which were expected to cost a further £1500. A report by the masons Foster and Barber in June 1958 noted: "The old stone is falling away in pieces bigger than a cricket ball at the least vibration." The battlements themselves would have to be replaced as well as the lead on the roof and internal timbers.. Mr Roundhill told the next PCC meeting: "We could be very sorry for ourselves because we have the burden of a new church to be paid for and the burden of an old church which requires a lot of money for repairs because it is an old church. We ought to accept it as a challenge. We have got this lovely old church. We inherit a long history and we also inherit the death watch beetle. We have to decide whether we are going to be a victim of self pity or be braced by the challenge." The estimate for tower repairs came in at £2340.4s.9d plus a further £40 to repaint the clock faces whilst the scaffolding was in place. Mr Roundhill had hoped that the parish might install hot water at the vicarage but he agreed to forego this saying "we ought not to have it with so many other pressing needs."

In April 1959, something that seemed a miracle occurred. The Diocese decided to give a further £2000 toward the cost of building St Christopher's which meant they had been responsible for seventy-three per cent of the bill. Grummant's then took pity on the church and chose to make a substantial donation themselves toward the remaining £300

---

[96] PCC Minutes 14th December 1957

and the last payment of £39 was made from the Church Building Fund. Mr Roundhill wrote: "our natural jubilation at being free from debt is tempered with humility by the recognition that we have needed and received so much help from the Diocese. After being submerged in debt for over twenty years, we are about to come to the surface."

The financial problems and difficulties caused by either a lack of curates or in two cases, the behaviour of them, created some tension and Mr Roundhill chose to tackle this head on saying that if people had something to say, they should say it to him. He wrote in May 1957: "There has for a long time been a "fifth column" in the parish. A "fifth column" is a number of people who belong to an organisation but work for its enemies, For a long time now there have been people injecting poison into parochial relationships by unruly tongues giving an evil twist to quite normal and ordinary happenings. The trouble makers have succeeded in making difficult work more difficult. I do ask those who love God and His Church and parish of St Laurence to strengthen the good in the parish and starve and wither the evil." The letter created an outcry and the PCC Secretary took the opportunity of the AGM to support the vicar saying: "An atmosphere has been created entirely inconsistent with Christian principles and fellowship which has resulted in the whole foundation of our religious doctrine being undermined." It was evident that the problems still existed a year later when Mr Todd advocated starting all meetings with the intercession from the Litany: "From envy, hatred and malice and all uncharitableness Good Lord deliver us." However, the arrival of the Reverend Stanley Evans who was to stay for almost six years did help generate much needed stability.

Like most ministers, Mr Roundhill took a keen interest in youth work. He maintained the traditional afternoon Sunday School for the hundred or so infants but got rid of those for older children and replaced them in August 1946 with a Junior and Senior Guild. The idea was that children would attend church on Sunday with either their parents or their leaders and they would then have Guild meetings on a weekday evening. Meetings involved Bible study, craft activities, filmstrips, competitions and games and there were also outings to places like the zoo, the theatre or train rides into the country for tea and sports. Only those who attended church were allowed to attend the Guild meetings. Members were also encouraged to work for badges, rather like the Guides and Scouts, these covering areas such as Church history, lives of the saints, books of the Bible as well as practical tasks such as visiting the sick and helping with younger children. The Guild rules were:

As a loving child of God I must try always

1. To be present at Holy Eucharist each Sunday
2. To pray to God morning and evening
3. To read part of my Bible each day
4. To attend my weekday church activity regularly

> 5. To give part of my pocket money each week to help the church's work for God[97]

By 1947, there was a waiting list for Guild membership and he was attracting over a hundred children a time to Lenten and Good Friday services. In 1950 he started an afternoon service for the benefit of junior school age children and their parents so they had something productive to do whilst the infant family members were at Sunday School. His encouragement of children at the Sung Eucharist service was, as he admitted, something entirely new in the church's history and there was some criticism amid fears they would disrupt the service but he found they were generally well behaved and felt it was important that they should be there and not shut away in a Sunday School.

He was also deeply interested in Remembrance Day. He had joined up in Rotherham in September 1914 just after becoming a Lay Reader and before he could start ordination training. He served in the York and Lancaster Regiment during the First World War at Ypres and Passchendale and then from November 1917 as Second Lieutenant in the West Yorkshire Regiment. He was gassed in 1915 and also received shrapnel wounds to both legs and lost two fingers. In November 1953 he wrote: "Our remembrance is one of proud thanksgiving. Some have sacrificed their lives, some their health. The latter go through life handicapped in the battle of life in which they have to compete with those who have no such handicap to carry. After a few years this is so easily forgotten. When you remember with thanksgiving the dead, remember also those who are partially dead because they served. Remembrance is in grave danger of being sentimental and ineffective." The annual garden of remembrance where people could buy a cross was inaugurated in 1947.

Despite being an old man by the 1960s, Mr Roundhill still had enthusiasm for new projects. In 1960 he asked the PCC to consider creating a memorial chapel on the north side and moving the children's corner over by the font but this scheme never came to fruition. In 1955, he introduced a half hour of favourite hymn singing to follow Evensong once a month as well as an adult Bible study group.

Nonetheless, expecting one vicar with a single curate to minister to four churches, each of which naturally expected services every Sunday, was a tall order. There were five services alone at St Laurence every Sunday, each involving an address, plus three mid-week, a figure which rose during Lent and Advent. Moreover, Mr Roundhill also had to take Holy Communion to the sick in hospital at 7a.m. once a month. At the Annual General Meeting in 1960, the church secretary Mr Todd said "How the vicar has managed to carry on up till now is beyond one's understanding." Mr Roundhill managed by sheer force of will but the strain was affecting his health, something that was not helped by the

---

[97] There were children from eighty separate families in the Sunday School in 1946 when the scheme was introduced. Mr Roundhill asked all the parents to a meeting to discuss the merits of Sunday Schools versus Guilds in the spiritual development of their children and was unimpressed that only five adults from two families turned up. *St Laurence Parish Magazine*, August 1946

severe damp to be found on all the vicarage walls.⁹⁸ He was, after all, almost seventy and a sick man. Later that summer, he decided it was time to pass the reins to a younger man, but ever the dedicated priest, instead of simply retiring, he moved on to a smaller parish.

Mr Roundhill's last service was on 30th October 1960. He accepted a gift of money which he said relieved the worry about the cost of moving. He then presented the parish with the gift of a pyx: for the past eighteen years he had been forced to use his own because the church had never supplied one. When he left, Mr Roundhill said that "The years I have spent at St Laurence have been the most worry laden years of my life." The Reverend Stanley Evans, curate at St Christopher's went to visit him in his new home at Stanford just a few weeks later and came back saying that already Mr Roundhill looked years younger.

The Reverend John Roundhill retired in 1965 which gave him time to enjoy his hobbies of reading, painting, walking his dog and music. He died at Folkestone on 5th May 1977 aged 86. His wife Patience passed away in 2000.

His successor, **Clemments Hartley Bird** was almost as much of a contrast to Mr Roundhill as it was possible to get. He was outgoing to the point of exuberance and announced his arrival on 6th May 1961 in the parish with the simple words "the Bird has come home to roost." He was generally to refer to himself in this manner.⁹⁹

One of the first things to happen when Mr Bird arrived was the erection of a new vicarage. The Manston Road one was sold for £5500 and consequently demolished and a new four bedroom one built in Newington Road. The cost was £8652 5s. 3d of which £2000 was contributed by the Church Commissioners. The remaining £1172 came from a twenty-five year mortgage at a rate of 5% interest. Mr Bird was able to move into his new home in 1963, just after his marriage, though he warned the parish that it was a lot smaller than the old vicarage and that all meetings would in consequence have to be held in the Parish Hall.¹⁰⁰

---

⁹⁸ 19th June 1958 Dilapidation Report. It also noted extensive cracks in the walls due to war damage and that the garage was in extremely poor condition.
⁹⁹ Mr Bird announced at the start that he did not use his first Christian name, just Hartley.
¹⁰⁰ Mr Bird married Margaret Bushell at St Laurence on 21st September 1963, the second incumbent in history to wed in the parish church.

Mr Bird was an academic. He had a first in Classics and Theology from Keble and had become a Cambridge don at the age of twenty-nine. He served on the advisory committee of the New English Bible, the first complete new translation of the Scriptures into English since 1611, and parishioners were impressed by his habit of closing his eyes and putting his head back in the pulpit and quoting long passages of the scriptures as if he had memorised the entire text. Indeed, he did know substantial amounts of it and that in Greek, Hebrew and English. He also enjoyed discussing the Bible, religion, and any aspect of life in general which a parishioner wished to ask him about. He would settle down on the floor of someone's home or pace up and down as he thought, never using his learning to browbeat someone but simply to educate or exchange ideas.

Following Dr Cotton's popularisation of the 1062 myth, the church celebrated its nine hundredth anniversary in 1962. The whole year was packed with special events from a celebration ball on 10th January to a service of re-consecration at midnight on December 31st. Particular highlights included a pageant, an exhibition and the Founders' Journey, a two day re-enactment of the journey made by monks from St Augustine's at Canterbury to Thanet with parishioners in period costume and treated to an eleventh century meal. Both the Abbey and the Cathedral gave the party souvenirs. September 1962 was devoted to a Parish Visitation. Mr Bird had announced his intention of visiting every home in the parish – there were almost five thousand – in June 1961 and had been working hard toward this. He decided that during September, himself and the Reverend Stanley Evans, would go and bless them all. Mr Bird led the way, striding out with his staff, and later recalled:

The warm welcome everywhere, the sacred needs and yearnings I have been privileged to share and together offer up through Our Lord to the Father of all; the intimacy of those household Communions where more than ever we could feel the presence of the Lord to bless… and those unforgettable hushed Complines when we brought the needs of all on whom we had called in general terms before the Throne of Love.[101]

It was not a surprise that his charismatic personality and efforts to make himself known to people, resulted in an increased congregation. At the AGM in 1962, just eleven months after his arrival, the Parish Secretary noted that communicants were up by twenty per cent and congregations at all services were "greatly improved." He attributed this to Mr Bird's inspiring leadership and said: "We have in the vicar a born leader capable of extracting from everyone a desire to follow his lead. The vicar is not only a born leader

---

[101] *The Beacon*, October 1962

but a great optimist."[102]   Service registers show that during his incumbency, communicants at 8 a.m. averaged fifty-six and at 10.30 a.m. nineteen. On 5th February 1961, the PCC voted to buy fifty new Prayer Books as there were not enough to go round. A fifty per cent increase was also reported in Sunday School membership, though here it is difficult to say whether this was due to Mr Bird's influence or the fact that the evening Guilds had been replaced by conventional morning Sunday Schools.[103] In 1962 Mr Bird wrote:

> Children abound. Some 100 a year brought for baptism and they fill children's churches and Sunday Schools…and this year's number of confirmation candidates dwarfs any of the past. …Better times have brought us a new "young middle aged" congregation and thriving men's and women's societies testify that many now stay and are attracted to these parts. The professions are well represented, the teaching profession especially. There are clerks and secretaries, shopkeepers and hoteliers, the police and armed forces, technicians from the Sandwich road, agricultural labourers from Manston. There is little heavy industry in the parish but we result in many industrial workers, colliers, transport workers, jostling with enchanting survivals of the past such as blacksmiths and fishermen.[104]

At Christmas 1965, the church was so full for the midnight service that people were turned away.

With regard to churchmanship, Mr Bird announced at the start that he was a High Churchman. [105] He continued the eastward celebration but discarded the portable communion table under the tower and also dropped the idea of calling the clergy Father. In his first letter he said that he expected to see people kneeling for prayers rather than sitting unless they were ill and added: "I'm sure we'd all be helped if we kept the church and its precincts as hushed as possible before a service that we might approach Our Lord with inner calm and holy awe; afterwards, when we have been renewed by Him in joyful fellowship, we should express it in much greeting and cheerful conversation." His next move was to start a tidy up of the church, announcing: "a clean, free, open church rid of all fussiness is a standing parable of a Christian soul." The manorial banners and screen at the rear of the side chapel were all removed as part of this exercise. He expressed his views on faith in the parish magazine:

---

[102] *The Beacon*, March 1962
[103] At the time he left, there were seventy in the infant Sunday School and eighty in the juniors.
[104] *Nine Hundred Years*, (Ramsgate, 1962) p.7
[105] The PCC had requested a married man who was of moderate churchmanship.

"For every parish as for every Christian things go wrong, we get out of our depths. Despondent and depressed we rediscover our weakness and our failures, then we find the stone is rolled away, life begins anew from death, richer than ever. We wonder how on earth we did it till in a moment of joyful mirth we find it's all the doings of the risen Lord and all He asks of us is our penitence, our prayers and our very open hearts." (April 1964)

"We cannot paddle in Christianity – we must swim or sink." (March 1963)

"There is no obstacle that gentle, unselfish cheerfulness cannot sweep right aside when it is founded on prayer." (July 1961)

He also used *The Beacon* and the pulpit to promote right behaviour, challenging the commercialisation of Sundays saying: "We should never take part in, promote or attend any function that clashes with the generally accepted hours of Church worship – morning or evening. Only Christians can keep Sunday holy and only Sunday worship can keep England Christian." He criticised the liberalisation of ethics: "Even within the church there are voices denying that there is any moral law absolutely binding in all circumstances save that of love. True no doubt, but love needs definition and application and the Ten Commandments appear to me as a good a guide as any we shall be granted…A condition for grace is a readiness for mortification, a rediscovering of joy through austerity and stringent self discipline."[106] It was an attitude which, though scriptural, was not entirely in line with the mood of the Swinging Sixties. Mr Bird saw *The Beacon* as a means of evangelising so sadly removed the reports on church council meetings and summaries of the accounts which Mr Roundhill had believed an essential part of stewardship.

Changes made to the building during his incumbency include the loss of the chimneys over the vestry and south-west porch and the introduction of a new heating system and boiler house at a cost of £3300 in 1963. The external staircase to the belfry was renewed, the church was re-wired and work continued treating death watch beetle in the nave and south aisle. The triptych was moved from the south transept to the north. Amongst gifts, Mr Hingston gave the extension to the list of incumbents in the porch in 1964, Mr and Mrs Maynard gave an alms plate, Deaconess Hilda Howard gave two processional candlesticks, Miss Wotton a set of crib figures from Oberammergau and Miss Morris gave carpet for the communion rail. The side chapel also got renamed Becket. Mr Bird also introduced the sale of church postcards as a contribution to finances.

With regard groups, a branch of the Church of England Mens Society was formed

---

[106] *The Beacon*, February 1965, May 1964

in 1961 and also a '61 Club which in 1967 was renamed the Ladies' Fellowship.

Although a man of restless energy who had once played rugby and cricket for Cambridge, his health at St Laurence was not good. He completed the Founders Journey despite being in great pain and was hospitalised in both 1962 and 1965. Severe mental exhaustion caused him to forget names and tasks and this upset him. He was also dismayed that it was proving impossible to escape the burden of administration and this work was interfering with his pastoral duties which he believed should be paramount. In October 1966 he left saying that he hoped he would be well enough to return to parish ministry one day but he was unsure. His final letter showed the anguish that he felt that he had failed. He had not overcome apathy on the part of the congregation and despite having over four hundred people confirmed in five years, barely any of them were regular worshippers. He worried too about the fifty or more people who had departed to other parishes because they wanted to attend Matins and not Holy Communion. He felt he should have made a greater effort to fit in such a service for them although he had started a children's service which meant he now had three services at St Laurence every Sunday morning. He wrote: "The needs of youth must never over-ride the requirements of the faithful old." His questioning and guilt were typical of the man who set such high standards for himself but he was much loved as a vicar and his departure came as a shock and disappointment to many. He returned briefly to the parish to take Christmas services that year as the church was in interregnum.

Almost nine years later on March 19th 1975, Mr Bird died suddenly aged just 56. Les Dunbar prepared the obituary for him at St Laurence saying: "Compassion was the keynote of his ministry. Many a person of the parish, perhaps worn out after nursing a dying relative, was given a few nights welcome sleep by this man arriving, unasked, at the door and taking over. He had a happy attribute of being able to talk to anybody but never down to anyone, able always to find common ground on which to build a friendship."

The task of following the extrovert Mr Bird fell to **Francis Bospidnick Yarker** whose induction took place on 22nd January 1966. He was a very different character and came from a completely different school of churchmanship.[107] One of his first acts was to replace the 1662 Book of Common Prayer with the 1928 Prayer Book and during the course of his incumbency, he was to introduce westward facing celebration of the

---

[107] In a letter to the author, Mr Yarker admitted that he was not made to feel welcome when he arrived and noted that it took some time for the parish to accept him as he was so different from Mr Bird.

Eucharist and a communion table under the tower. He also ceased the formal hearing of confessions in the church which his three predecessors had all adopted and he got rid of the angel topped riddel posts which made the high altar look like a communion table once more.

Perhaps reflecting the spirit of the age and the fact that he had grown up in the era of parochial church councils, Mr Yarker's attitude to ministry tended to be more democratic. He arranged parish meetings almost every month on different topics to give the clergy an opportunity to offer teaching and people the chance to express their views. For the most part, these were positive events although Mr Yarker was disappointed that at the meeting set up to discuss sermons, the popular view was that they should be shorter and that his proposal to preach series based on books of the Bible was rejected.

Mr Yarker's ministry took place at a very difficult time in the church. There was a lot of desire for modernisation, particularly in liturgy. There were demands also for liberalisation of teaching with the 1960s seeing the birth of free contraception and much easier divorce as well as the sex equality movement. In July 1969, he tackled the subject of the permissive society writing: "You do not help people much by judging them; you help them by understanding them. Still to refrain from judgement need not mean that we have abandoned all standards….Love is the fulfilling of the law. It does not abrogate the Ten Commandments but transcends them. The trouble is that for so many the term love is both vague and sentimental. When driving a car benevolent intentions are not enough: a knowledge both of the car one is driving and the rules of the road are necessary. So we need to know ourselves and the basic rules which govern human behaviour if we are to behave in truly loving way." In May 1972, in response to growing calls for the church to remarry divorcees he stated: "To allow remarriage in church for any reason would blur the church's witness at a time when it is greatly needed."

Another problem with the church faced in this period was vandalism. Faced with recurrent instances in the church building and the graveyard, the decision was made just before the school summer holidays in 1970 to lock the doors.

Alongside these difficulties, Mr Yarker had to face two major catastrophes. In the early hours of 6th February 1967 the Parish Hall burnt down due to an electrical fault. The roof was totally destroyed and the contents badly damaged by smoke and water. Not only did this mean the loss of meeting space used by parish organisations and paying customers, the hall had been used for some years by the church schools for lunchtime meals. It was also revealed that the hall had been substantially under-insured with estimates for a replacement coming in at £17,000 for a new building – the old had been insured for £4000 – and new contents expected to cost £710 – the old having been insured for £500. Even with the PCC opting to rebuild using the existing foundations to save money, it was clear that the parish would have to raise at least £8000.[108] Fund raising duly began but the problem was exacerbated just a few weeks later on 2nd May when part of the wall at the Girls' School collapsed causing some of the children to be evacuated to the Concorde Youth Centre and others to St Christopher's. Repairs to this cost £3195 and then there was the cost of hiring alternative premises whilst the school could not be used. The new Parish Hall opened on 22nd March 1969 but the girls were not able to return to their building until the start of 1970.

Financial difficulties relating to the above and the rising costs of the clergy saw staff levels reduced in 1970 and all but essential visiting stopped. At this point, the church had to raise £2010 a year toward its curates plus pay £457 in Quota. Collections were then about £450 a year whilst Planned Giving raised about £1200.

As if these concerns were not enough, the church continued to have problems with beetle in the roof. In 1968, work began on repairing the chancel and north aisle roofs at a cost of just over £1200.

Yet Mr Yarker supported schemes both to beautify and repair the church writing: "Whilst we have a responsibility to future generations to hand on the fabric of our church

---

[108] PCC Minutes 28th February 1967, 19th July 1967

intact, we have a responsibility to God and to the present generation to make our church as beautiful as possible. There is a tendency nowadays to regard expenditure on anything not strictly utilitarian as wasting money on frills. This is not the way Our Lord regarded the "waste" of the precious ointment which Mary poured upon his feet at Bethany: he said "She has done a beautiful thing." Money spent to the glory of God on things which help others to realise that glory is not wasted."[109]

Mr Yarker's biggest achievement was the rise of the parish communion. When he arrived, there were on average forty-nine people at the early communion and fifty-six at the later. Keen to see as many people as possible gather together as a family at one service, he encouraged people to move to the later service and said that fasting was not essential. As a result, by the time he left, early communicants averaged seventeen whilst the main service had almost ninety. He was, however, unhappy at what he referred to as the "regrettable long standing tradition" of up to half the congregation leaving before the final hymn and blessing. [110] Mr Yarker's ability to bring people together in the parish communion was the more remarkable because his ministry coincided with the Church of England's infamous liturgical reforms – series one, two and three with the threat of there being a series four.

Other achievements during his incumbency include the introduction of the Planned Giving scheme in 1967, the establishing of a board for prayer requests in 1966, the setting up of a drama group which put on a play about the nativity as well as *An Inspector Calls* and the creation of Project C for children in 1969. Around the church, the vestry was re-ordered and the whole building was treated for damp and repainted, a new font was given in 1972 and an aumbry installed in the side chapel in 1969. This last was designed by Colin Shewring and showed the early Christian symbol of a fish above a chalice and wafer. A bookcase for hymnals and service books was built in 1973 beside the porch. The practice of recording services was introduced so that the housebound could feel a greater part of the congregation. He also revived the tradition of the rogation day procession. Gifts included the sanctuary chair with the cross and gridiron from Mr Knivett in 1969 and the Paschal candlestick given by Miss Butcher and her brother in 1970. The Manston brasses were remounted in the summer of 1969 and placed at the rear of the side chapel. Also during his time, the Garrett Almshouse was sold in 1970 as being uneconomical to repair.[111] Female servers were introduced in 1970.

A highly articulate man, Mr Yarker enjoyed editing the parish magazine and some of his comments there illustrate his goals and style of preaching:

> "There are many who think that belief is unimportant but if you thought you were sitting on a £5 note your belief would soon influence your actions." (September 1970)

---

[109] *The Beacon*, February 1966
[110] *The Beacon*, September 1973
[111] It had passed to parish control in 1916, CCA-U3-19/5/5

"We need to recover the sense that prayer and worship is offered with all the company of heaven. In the Holy Communion the narrow dividing wall between living and departed falls away and our environment is not time but eternity." (November 1967)

"My great concern is to help the church to be the church not just a collection of people with similar interests" (January 1972)

"Every Christian is a potential superman in that he has a strength beyond his own freely available for the work of the kingdom. If only we believed and acted on this men would say as they did of the disciples in the Acts that the men who have turned the world upside down have come here also." (June 1968)

"There are two things which can paralyse a church; complacency or satisfaction with things as they are and despondency or disillusionment. We must adapt ourselves to the present existing world or die out – or linger on as a quaint anachronism…We must not rush into changes in order to be up to date. We have to weigh the disruption caused by change against the actual benefits likely to accrue." (January 1967)

He was indeed a most spiritual man with a habit of preaching while gazing heavenward and frequently saying: "Activity without prayer is worthless." His style of ministry could best be described as supportive leadership in that he neither sought to place himself so far ahead of his congregation that they could not follow, nor to the rear where he would be always responding rather than instigating, but rather he walked alongside them offering encouragement and suggestions and set a pace at which the slowest could walk.

Mr Yarker was created an honorary Canon of Canterbury Cathedral on 22nd May 1976 and he retired on 2nd October 1977. He died at Rye on 22nd December 1993 aged 81. He had said that his goal was to create a congregation at St Laurence which was "converted, instructed, united and evangelistic" and to a large extent he had done this.

The next vicar was the Reverend **Philip Norwood**, aged thirty-nine, a Cambridge educated man who had trained in theological seminaries from Jerusalem to Geneva as well as Cuddesdon and who had spent three years as chaplain to Archbishop Michael Ramsey, an experience which gave him a particular appreciation of the wider church.[112]

---

[112] He was originally appointed priest-in-charge rather than vicar as the diocese was considering

The Archbishop came to license him on 13th January 1978 and over four hundred attended the service.

At the time of his arrival, work was in process on creating an upper vestry for the choir. This scheme had been devised by Mr Yarker in 1974 with a view to not only improving the use of space but of eliminating the need for an external staircase to the belfry which was a constant source of vandalism. It would take until Easter 1979 for the scheme to be fully achieved.

One of Mr Norwood's first changes was to introduce the laying on of hands which he described as "the forgotten sacrament." Although of Biblical origin, it is likely that this had never before taken place in the church.[113] Rather than have separate healing services, he had this carried out during the Sung Eucharist on third Sundays saying: "it is the cornerstone of the ministry of healing that we support one another in love."[114]

Continuing on from Mr Yarker's idea of parish meetings, Mr Norwood held one on June 29th 1978 to decide on how the church should best bear witness in the area. It decided to: encourage Bible study groups, increase youth work, install an amplification system, create a literature area, have an annual festival.

Over the coming decade, all of these things happened. In the case of the literature area, this was almost immediate. Mr Cowland-Cooper had originally installed a stand for missionary literature and Mr Yarker the Bray library, so this was a building up of that tradition but with a new stand in the south west corner in memory of George Miles, one of the parish's lay readers who died in 1979. Regarding youth work, a new group was set up for teenagers and the Sunday School flourished so much that by the time he left, there were four separate groups comprising some two hundred children meeting at different times and locations to cater for the demand and there was a waiting list. Mr Norwood wrote: "The future of Christianity depends to a large extent on encouraging children and

---

benefice changes at the time but the role was the same. He legally became vicar in 1982.
[113] Luke 9:2, Mark 16:18
[114] *The Beacon,* April 1978

young people now to feel at home in church."¹¹⁵ A crèche was established for the benefit of parents with very young children who wished to attend the Sung Eucharist and week long Bible based activity schemes were held each year in the Parish Hall for junior school age children. A sound system was installed in 1980. Bible study groups were set up across the parish with at least half a dozen meeting for most of each year and at Lent, up to twenty-one existing. Mr Norwood also stopped the annual dedication festival which had taken place on the first Sunday in October since 1536 and replaced it with a week long celebration of St Laurence tide in August. The programme of events varied each year but normally included special tours of the church and tower, an exhibition, often a concert and a Sung Eucharist with parish meal.

In January 1980, Mr Norwood was joined by his father, Canon Clarence Norwood, who had just retired. The Canon soon proved a most useful addition to the staff taking over St Catherine's in the summer of 1981, running a Bible study class which met for nine months of every year, assisting with preaching and taking baptisms and generally supporting his son in every way possible.

During the same year, the first stewardship campaign was launched. Mr Norwood wrote: "Although we appeal through the fayre for the community at large to help keep the church building standing, it is the worshipping community which must be responsible for the work and witness of God's church. The Church must never go begging for people to support it." By contrast, the offertories were for "clergy stipends and expenses, heating and lighting, service requirements, youth work and missions, Diocesan costs etc."¹¹⁶ The need for money was acute. In the year he arrived, the quota was £2912: a decade later when he left it was £16,968. By the end of 1987, the church had had deficits running into thousands for three years running and the general fund which had been used to pay bills was exhausted. Planned giving had increased substantially to £9,508 in 1986 but the church needed that figure to reach £17,219 in 1988 just for the church to break even. Asking people to increase their donations by over eighty per cent when wages had not risen by this amount was seeking a miracle.¹¹⁷

It was in 1979 that Mr Norwood transformed the confirmation course system by introducing a two year course for young people and one year for adults. This comprehensive system involved a detailed study of the Creed, the Lord's Prayer, the nature of sacraments and the structure of the liturgy together with an outline of Church history and the organisation of the Church of England. Young people also spent several months studying the Holy Bible, working through a Gospel, an epistle and selections from the Old Testament. In terms of subject matter, it was fundamentally the catechism without the need for rote learning and it provided a valuable groundwork for faith and Christian life. It might be understood as the gold standard of confirmation courses and

---

[115] *The Beacon*, November 1979

[116] *The Beacon*, August 1980, September 1986

[117] *The Beacon*, November 1987. Inflation over the ten years saw prices double, the quota rise sixfold.

typified Mr Norwood's ministry of teaching.

In 1986, the Isle of Thanet played host to the Down to Earth Mission. For three weeks, Eric Delve preached in the tent at Margate while the worship was led by Hugo Anson. It was a memorable occasion and one which St Laurence embraced to the full. Mr Norwood wrote: "Our mission in 1986 is not just someone coming to speak in a tent in Margate, important though that is. Mission is to bring others in our neighbourhood and amongst our own friends to come along to hear the Word of Life, to receive spiritual food and to grow to maturity in the worship and love of God our heavenly Father."[118] In preparation for the Mission, in April 1986 Mr Norwood set up a new Sunday morning service to follow the Sung Eucharist called Morning Praise. This soon proved very successful and started to attract people from outside the church who sought a non-traditional service which did not regularly include Holy Communion. Music was supplied by its own band consisting of two keyboards, one oboe, one clarinet, three tenor recorders, one cornet, one flute and one guitar. The hymnbook used was *Mission Praise*.

Arguably Mr Norwood's greatest achievement was the creation of the new church school in 1984. This required a considerable amount of effort over five years with regard to obtaining the site, securing permission to build and integrating what had been two single sex schools into one mixed. The new school opened in 1985.

Other achievements include introducing Thought for the Month to the parish magazine in 1978, setting up the Book of Remembrance in 1980, establishing a tradition of parish walks and harvest suppers, and introducing monthly coffee after worship in 1982 to promote fellowship. Taking advantage of the rise of car ownership, he introduced united parish wide family services in 1978 and sought to encourage opportunities for the congregations of the four churches to get to know one another. He also led a number of pilgrimages to the Holy Land enabling people to see for themselves where Biblical events had actually taken place and to meet with Orthodox Christians as well as Jews and Moslems in a spirit of brotherhood. Concerned at the rising divorce rate, he set up marriage preparation classes for those seeking a wedding in the church. During Holy Week, he held services of Compline, the first time the order had been used and he started the annual Christingle service in 1981. He also introduced the weekly news sheet for the pews complete with suggested topics for prayer during the administration of the sacrament. In addition, he established the Prayer Partners scheme in 1986 and started the Lunch Club in February 1988 in the Parish Hall for the benefit of the elderly, lonely and sick in the parish.[119]

There were no major changes to the church during his incumbency though new lighting was installed just before Easter 1987 designed by Denys le Fevre and the cross

---

[118] *The Beacon*, February 1986
[119] The Lunch Club closed in April 2016.

over the Victorian porch was removed in 1981. However, plans were drawn up to develop the north east corner of the church in his time, a project completed by his successor. Also started in his time was the parish office which began life in a portacabin in the vicarage garden in 1986. He laid the foundations too of the Team Ministry by setting up the new parish constitution which came into operation in April 1987 and gave each church in the parish its own District Church Council.

Mr Norwood left on 26th September 1988 to minister in Spalding. He was one of the most beloved vicars in the church's long history and he certainly attracted the largest post war congregations. He took his role as a pastor seriously, always making time for those in need. He was known for his unheralded acts of kindness, such as taking posies of flowers from the vicarage garden to the sick or accompanying those who were alone and frightened to hospital visits and staying with them to reassure them and prompt necessary questions. He was open to the new but keen not to abandon valued traditions. He had expressed his goals as encouraging greater unity, making the church more welcoming both through its people and its worship, replacing narrow conservatism with forward looking positive and fighting evangelism, developing piety and improving knowledge amongst church members of what the Church of England actually believed. His ten years in the parish were spent promoting these ideals.

After an interregnum of two months, **Peter Cotton** became vicar on 20th November 1988. He was forty-three and had been ordained eighteen years earlier. He wrote of his hopes:

> What's my vision of the local church? A community of people with the God of Jesus Christ at the centre of their lives; a God who stands for justice, peace and love; a God who urges his people to witness to him at home, in their streets and at work; a God who reassures his people through the power of the risen Christ that God's love cannot in the end be beaten.
> My vision of the local church has its members concerned for one another's needs not as an end in itself but so that together and separately we can be strengthened to serve God in His work and join in the bringing in of His kingdom. One and all we are called to take up our cross and follow Christ.
> My vision of the local church sees a great diversity of membership – diverse in age, race, occupation, education, political allegiance, religious tradition. Yet a community of people mature enough to tolerate, to understand, to value the differences as a sign of God's reconciliation brought about in Christ.[120]

Amongst the changes which he made was the introduction of marriages in church

---

[120] *The Beacon*, January 1994

for divorced people. Stating that it was the Church's duty to show "genuine compassion" he laid down guidelines that at least one party must live in the parish, that the decree absolute was at least a year old, that any past children had been adequately provided for and that "the couple are able in their own time and way to ask God's forgiveness of all that they have done wrong in the past." He further required that couples give six months' notice of a wedding as a minimum and be invited to attend marriage preparation classes.[121] In the first year of this policy, nine of the forty-three weddings involved a dicorced person- 21%.

He was very aware of living in a society where lifestyles were changing and moral attitudes which had been held for centuries were being challenged. In February 1995 he spoke of how he found labels such as heterosexual and homosexual "unhelpful" adding that he had recently attended a conference where people had been invited to divide into two such groups when "it was surprising how many of us were in the middle." Advising readers that Biblical writers were men of their time and that people in the twentieth century should be "more flexible" he asked for an "openness to the possibility that in the committed love two people of the same sex may have for one another there is something for the church to encourage and support."

Peter Cotton was a firm supporter of women. He wrote in *The Beacon* in November 1989: "That men are more influential in shaping the life of our parish than their numbers in our congregations suggest they should be, presents us with a challenge how we might we find ways of ensuring that women's gifts are fully used in forming policy for our common Christian life of worship, witness and service." When the Reverend Ivan Howitt left St Christopher's in July 1990, he apologised that he could not replace him with a woman because the Church as a whole had not yet decided to ordain women. By the time the Reverend Brian Sharp left in January 1996 the situation had changed and the vacancy was made accessible to women.

It was Peter Cotton who inaugurated the Team Ministry. He had proposed this originally in July 1991 and it finally came into being on 7th June 1993. Instead of St Laurence being the mother church and St Christopher's, St Mary's and St Catherine's being the daughters, they were now sisters. Where there had once been curates, there were now Team Vicars who instead of being directed by the vicar, shared fully in all decision making processes. Peter Cotton's expressed hope was that this change would attract more experienced clergy to the parish and those who would be willing to commit for seven years rather than the usual three served by curates. It would also enable people's gifts to be utilised more fully with the possibility existing of specialisation. The

---

[121] *The Beacon*, January 1990. In the first decade of the twenty-first century, one in six grooms and one in ten brides was divorced.

vicar himself took on the title of Team Rector, an historical anomaly which still exists.

His second major achievement was the creation of a formal Parish Office. Since 1987 there had been a portacabin in the vicarage grounds but this was replaced by an extension to the vicarage itself in May of 1993. It was designed by Maureen O'Connor and built by W.W. Martin.

Other innovations during his incumbency included the launch of the annual Charities Fair in 1990, the move from a typed to word processed parish magazine in 1991, the introduction of lay pastoral assistants in 1992 to assist with bereavement counselling and preparation for baptism and marriage, the replacing of *Hymns Ancient and Modern* with the *New English Hymnal* at Easter 1996 and the creation of a business style mission statement in 1995. The establishment of the Thurstin Room and toilet was also achieved in this period and the loop system was installed in July 1994 in memory of Jimmy Deakin. The 11.15 Morning Praise service was stopped on 25th November 1989 though it was reborn in 1991.

Peter Cotton left on 5th January 1997 and it was to be nine months before a new minister was appointed. Given the requirements listed, it may be surprising that anyone applied:

> The leadership skills of Moses, the musical talents of King David, the wisdom of Solomon, the missionary zeal of St Paul, the prophetic insight of Isaiah, the strength of Samson (for chairing meetings), the speaking skills of Aaron, the patience of Job, the courage of Elijah, the loyalty of Ruth, the heart of the Messiah.
> Persons lacking any of the above talents need not apply.[122]

Peter Dewey, age fifty-nine, was instituted on 16th September and he introduced himself saying: "My personal mission in the church has been to teach the presence of the Lord both in creation and in ourselves and our neighbour. In this simple understanding the seeds of a deep and lasting relationship are sown and a church of trust is built." The encouraging of a deeper spirituality was to be a hallmark of his ministry, both through a growth of meditation and developing the understanding of traditional forms of worship.

His arrival in the parish came at a difficult time. The church bells were due to go away three days before his institution so it was planned to give a welcome peal a week before as Mr Dewey's first hearing of the bells. The sudden death of Diana, Princess of Wales followed by Mother Teresa and the mother of one of the bell ringers caused this plan to be revised with a half muffled peal being rung in memory of those ladies the day before. The bells were returned on 15th November with eight of the ten being rung that year for Christmas and all ten at their re-dedication on 17th January 1998.

It was Peter Dewey who was vicar at the time of the millennium.[123] This

---

[122] *The Beacon*, January 1997

landmark event was seen worthy of commemoration and St Laurence church decided to get a new font, although this did not arrive until his successor's time.

A believer in developing the ministry of the laity, Mr Dewey continued to encourage those who felt called to the work and in February 2000, the Archdeacon recognised the creation of ministry teams across the parish. Four people trained as Lay Readers during his incumbency and two as priests. He was a keen supporter of the team ministry "respecting my fellow Clergy as fully trained, experienced clerics, equal in all ways with me and with each other. It prevented authority issues and permitted proper discussion and sharing in decision making thus allowing a harmony amongst all the team members and the Team itself. It was a happy place to be and to work in."

July 2002 saw the 450th anniversary of the 1552 Prayer Book, the precursor of the 1662 Book of Common Prayer and the volume which showed most truly Archbishop Cranmer's determination to return worship to a state of simplicity and scriptural integrity without the accretions of tradition and Romanism. For the first time in centuries, Holy Communion was celebrated at St Laurence church in exactly the manner prescribed. It was a memorable occasion. In his sermon, Peter Dewey said that the marriage of scripture with Cranmer's sublime language was indeed a match made in heaven. The church also revived Sung Matins on the fifth Sunday of each month.

Other work during his incumbency included the installation of the window showing St Augustine's Cross at Ebbsfleet in 1998, the restoration of the flagpole and weathervane in 2000 and the introduction of educational tours of the churchyard for young people in a bid to deter vandalism. Most importantly, copies of the Holy Bible were provided for the pews.[124]

Peter Dewey retired from being a parish priest on 29th December 2002 although he continued in the ministry. In one of his last letters to the parish, he turned to the subject of how the Church was failing to reach people who were searching for a spiritual dimension in their lives. He warned: "The problem of what the Church really believes and the differences between churchmanship of many groups have exasperated those seeking spiritual guidance and leadership. So many people are put off by the Church and the growing fundamentalist attitudes of many of its ministers that a search for spiritual help, love and comfort has to be made in new directions. Unless as a church we are prepared to preach and be ministers of a God of love and forgiveness, we shall decline into an early grave."[125]

---

[123] Although Rector of the parish, he was also vicar of St Laurence.
[124] St Laurence DCC Minutes 2nd October 1997
[125] *The Beacon*, November 2002

His successor, appointed six months later, was unique in a number of ways. Firstly, she was the first woman to serve as vicar of St Laurence as well as Team Rector. Secondly, she was already working in the parish having been licensed as Team Vicar of St Christopher's and St Catherine's on 3rd December 2001. She was also only the second vicar in three hundred years to have been trained outside Oxford or Cambridge. Moreover, she introduced a new form of address by calling herself Reverend Sharran rather than following the practice of her predecessors who were either Mr, Vicar or Father or simply known by their Christian name.

Sharran Ireland became Team Rector and Vicar of St Laurence on 3rd October 2003 and stayed ten years.

Mrs Ireland did a great deal to encourage the development of lay ministry and to support those who felt called to ordained ministry. Training was offered to those who wished to participate in work with the bereaved, sick and children. She introduced "Visioning Days" and from one of those came the mission statement "Together we serve reflecting God's glory."

She contributed extensively to *The Beacon* and was not afraid of tackling difficult issues speaking out against same-sex relationships and abortion. She even tried to encourage the congregation to smile a bit more often: "It's not that worship should be based on laughter all the time – we have to have a sense of occasion – but there is nothing wrong with looking a little happier from time to time!"[126]

It was during her incumbency that the church got the font from Lydd[127] and the Burma Star cabinet. In 2006, as part of a desire to see the church used more as a community space, the summer fair was held in the church itself and in the churchyard, something which had never happened before.[128] The Sunday School, which had been renamed Junior Church, became Rock Solid in 2011.[129] She also oversaw a variety of celebrations in 2012.

She encouraged healing services and the development of the churchyard as a wildlife friendly eco-system. The Friends of St Laurence Churchyard was set up in April 2008. She introduced a wider variety of evening services, maintaining Prayer Book Evensong generally monthly but also including praise services and a Celtic format. She tried to persuade more people to attend study groups and to read their Bibles arguing that those not "well versed in the scriptures" would be unable to proclaim the Gospel effectively.

---

[126] *The Beacon*, March 2004
[127] Stated by Mrs Ireland to be Victorian in *The Beacon* December 2003
[128] In the first year of this practice, there was also the traditional fair in the school field but that subsequently lapsed.
[129] The 11-14s were renamed Faith Builders.

Following a review of baptismal policy, she set up Little Angels to try to foster relationships with the families of those seeking baptism for their children. Parents would then attend a group preparation session and get a home visit from a pastoral assistant. In cases of imminent death, baptism could be performed sooner.[130] Footprints was set up for the bereaved at the end of 2006.

In 2011, she created a two page spread sheet for *The Beacon* to explain her job. This included:

> prayer – twice a day and weekly with other clergy
> administration – correspondence, Orders of Services, service rota, meeting reports
> writing – for the Beacon and other talks
> school – taking assemblies, working as a school governor
> visiting – the sick, bereaved and housebound and taking Communion to them
> meetings – attending deanery meetings as well as chairing PCC and DCC meetings
> teaching – confirmation classes, house groups, faith courses, preparing sermons
> spirituality – preparing and leading retreats and prayer gatherings
> worship – planning and leading regular services and occasional offices such as baptisms, weddings and funerals
> training – attending courses and also training staff in the parish
> outreach – involvement in fairs, uniformed organisations, parish clubs and activities

Inevitably she was concerned about falling numbers in the church. Membership of St Laurence had halved between 1982 and 2002 whilst the Quota had risen sixfold.[131] She wrote: "We need to think differently about "doing church" in and among the community. It's no good looking around outside expecting people to walk in through the door, they won't unless you go out and get them. Look around you in your church seats, these are the worshipping community today. Where is the worshipping community of tomorrow?"[132] She continued: "The world is changing, the parish is changing, and we must be forward looking and think outside the box of four walls if we are to be relevant in people's lives and a vibrant worshipping community into the future."[133] She added: "this

---

[130] *The Beacon*, October 2005.
[131] Electoral roll for St Laurence district was 239 in 1982 and 126 in 2003. Regular Sunday communicants were 143 in 1986 and 76 in 2006. In 1982, the Quota was £6942: in 2002 it was £40,954.
[132] *The Beacon*, August 2007
[133] *The Beacon*, August 2011

doesn't necessarily mean that we will increase our numbers coming into church but it does mean that we shall be the church working for Christ in the community which has always been our aim."[134]

Following Mrs Ireland's retirement in July 2013, the parish experienced a long period of interregnum until the Reverend **Andrew Jacobson**, a powerful preacher of the Word, was appointed in January 2015. Under his ministry, St Mark's in Pyson's Road has become part of the parish and modern language services with new booklets have been introduced.[135] Coming from more of a business background than many of his predecessors, Mr Jacobson has sought to address the financial crisis in the parish as well as to encourage a greater participation in its running. Lay committees have been set up to consider worship, administration, youth work and fundraising. He has also sought to encourage closer links between the parish school and the church, particularly with regard to worship and there are signs of some growth with the Sunday School. As with some previous vicars, Mr Jacobson has also been Area Dean.[136]

As with every minister, he faces some problems which were shared by his predecessors and some which are unique. A decline in church attendance has taken place across the UK and St Laurence is no exception. In 1750, eighty-five per cent of the parish population attended regularly with a further twelve per cent attending non-conformist worship: just one in thirty-three people missed church on Sunday. A century later, one in every two people were to be found at St Laurence each week with a further one in twenty-five at the non-conformists. In 1891, around a fifth of the population was at St Laurence each Sunday. In 1981, one in thirty-three attended. Today, around one in every one hundred and sixty-five parishioners in the St Lawrence area attends St Laurence church, though the congregation is augmented by those who live outside. The numbers of those in the parish who attend other churches is unknown.

There are many factors which have contributed to this decline, most of them beyond the control of the parish church. Many of the men who went to serve in the First World War were so shaken by what they had seen that they lost their faith and consequently did not pass it on to their children. Others could not believe that God would reject those who had sacrificed their lives and so the belief in salvation by works rather than faith was reborn. The idea that being a good person is enough remains prevalent and multiculturalism has made Our Lord's claim to be the only way to salvation (John 14:6)

---

[134] *The Beacon*, April 2010

[135] St Mark's had been established as a parish on 1st March 1982 with part of its land being taken from St Laurence.

[136] In the time of Messrs. Sicklemore and Norwood, the title was Rural Dean.

politically incorrect.

In the past, life was hard and comforts were few for most people so the dream of heaven to come was comforting and aspirational. Today, most people enjoy a much higher standard of living and they are able to enjoy existence on earth and their aspirations are for material things. Unlike the authors of the Prayer Book, they are not concerned on a daily basis with fears of plague, sudden death or even war. Belief in an after life has diminished. The idea of hell as a real place of torment has virtually disappeared and concepts of heaven have more to do with family reunions than worshipping the Lamb. Many people are quite content to see this life as all there is so Our Lord's promise of eternal life (John 6:54, 10:28) means nothing to them. As George Bernard Shaw once observed: "our conduct is influenced not so much by our experience as our expectations."

Belief in God has declined, particularly in God as an interventionist being. Even where agnosticism exists, the idea of Jesus as God has proved hard to believe. Many of those who do accept the idea of a higher power do not see any necessity of responding to that. Expressing wonder, for example, at the birth of a child or a glorious sunrise, does not provoke any obligation to worship, particularly day in and day out for a lifetime.

The development of contraception and encouragement of it has increased sex outside marriage and made Church teaching on fornication seem outdated. Christians who value celibacy are more likely to face referral for inhibition than be praised for their commitment. Rising divorce levels have challenged Church teaching on marriage being for life. Peer pressure has led to weddings being seen as an expensive luxury – even though the church fees are generally a fraction of what is likely to be spent on the dress or honeymoon. Few activities today are seen as always wrong and even the Church has largely dropped reciting the Ten Commandments. Most people do not regard themselves as sinners and as Our Lord Himself said, the healthy have no need of a physician (Luke 5:31). Without sin, there is no need for a Saviour. (1 John 1:8)

The role of the church has changed. A century ago, the church was almost the only provider of entertainment and the principal provider of education. Through charity, it provided medical care, food for the hungry and practical assistance to those in need due to sickness, old age or pregnancy. Today those functions are met by the state or private, secular organisations which has reduced opportunities for outreach. Alongside this, the idea of the quiet Sunday devoted wholly to God has been lost. Not only are shops and places of entertainment open but sporting fixtures are increasingly held on Sunday. For those less active, there are the attractions of television and computers. An increasing number of businesses see fit to open on Sundays forcing Christians increasingly to choose between their faith and their career.

In general terms, there has been a decline in membership of organisations from political parties to trade unions. People have become more inclined to value their freedom and there is a widespread cynicism about institutions. Respect has declined. Just as less people bow or curtsey to the Queen as the embodiment of the country or use words like

"Sir" outside school or the army, so less Christians kneel, and visitors to the church accept this as the norm and see nothing to inspire awe.

At a community level, there has been a breakdown in local ties. Few members of the congregation were even born in the parish let alone can trace their membership of the parish back through three or more generations. This tends to lead to a reduced commitment to the building itself and a willingness to move on if the parish church does not suit. The Church of England as a whole has encouraged such a response. Common Worship is structured around the idea of meeting the needs of congregations, a total contrast to the Prayer Book which saw worship as God centred. Pandering to people's preferences and worrying about whether they are getting something from church membership may represent a more business like approach to "selling" the product, but it is the antithesis of duty and discipline which are essential to maintaining attendance.

Those who have sought spiritual solace have found difficulties too. The rise of Biblical criticism unsettled some and the growing liberalism of the Church has been a deterrent for those seeking clear answers. Surveys of Anglicans have consistently found dissatisfaction with Church leadership and concern at their failure to speak out on issues such as abortion. Other surveys have shown large numbers of clergy expressing doubts about the physical resurrection or virgin birth, something hardly likely to inspire confidence in worshippers. Traditionalists have been left feeling ostracised by the ordination of women and liturgical changes. Evangelicals are perturbed about the way the modern lectionary and services edit out almost all references to judgment or original sin and include Roman ideas like prayers for the dead. The rise of Holy Communion has caused the church to be associated with what appear to outsiders as strange rituals which talk of alien concepts like human sacrifice and eating flesh and as a member only rite, is not user friendly to visitors. Attendance at non-eucharistic services was always substantially higher than at eucharistic and that option has been lost.

Theologically, there have been changes too in teaching about the nature of God and the atonement. Since the Holocaust, God has been portrayed more as a fellow sharer in suffering than as the Almighty. The stress on Our Lord's humanity has seen Him portrayed more as friend than master – and if Jesus is shown as just a good man and wise teacher, there is no more reason to worship Him than any other good man or wise teacher. As Christians have become a minority, focus has shifted to the incarnation and resurrection rather than grace and the implications of the crucifixion.

Nonetheless, the fact remains that hundreds of children have been through the Sunday School and day school at St Laurence or confirmation classes and they have not remained in the church as adults. Similarly, contact is made each year with many couples approaching marriage and with the bereaved but they, for the most part, have just attended the one service never to be seen again. Reaching the totally unchurched has always been more difficult since they are not in church to hear a sermon or to experience worship and they are likely to have little if any Bible knowledge to build on. It is arguable that one of the biggest mistakes ever made by the Church was when it decided that conversion should no longer be its aim but rather the development of good citizens.

Our Lord did say that the door to salvation was narrow and only a few would find it (Matt. 7:14) and the size of the congregation at St Laurence today bears this out. Yet He also called the Church to be a light in the darkness – a proclaimer of the Gospel, not a heritage centre or social club - and the task of guiding the parish through this difficult time rests with the Reverend Andrew Jacobson.

PEOPLE, EVENTS AND PLACES

1992 Survey

The Reverend Peter Cotton was keen on statistics and surveys and in 1992 he commissioned a survey of the parish congregations. Of the 220 forms distributed at St Laurence, 161 were returned, 73.2%. The details covered 281 adults and 51 children. Amongst the findings were that the adult congregation was 26.3% male and 73.7% female. In terms of age, 36% were aged 65 or more, 8.2% were under 30, 16.9% were aged 31 to 44 and 38.3% were aged 45 to 64. In the youngest age group, 92% were female whilst amongst the over 65s, it was 32% male and 68% female. Not only were females more common in the church but they were more regular in their attendance with 74% worshipping at least once a month compared to just 47% of the men.[137]

With regard to occupation, 47% were retired, 38% were in paid employment, 9% were homemakers, 1% were unemployed, 3% were students and 2% classified themselves as other. Amongst the paid workers, 48% were professional or managerial. Amongst those who were retired, 54% were professional or managerial. These results formed a considerable contrast to the island as a whole where 9.1% of the population was unemployed according to the 1991 census and 21% were classified as being in professional or managerial jobs.

One of the most interesting findings of the survey was that everyone available attended church in only a quarter of the households which contained more than one occupant.[138] Amongst couples, 24% saw both attend, 12% saw neither attend although their offspring might go to Sunday School, 46% saw only the wife attend and 18% only the husband.

In terms of households, 35% had no car compared to 55% on the island as a whole according to the 1991 census.[139] Of these households, 80% were occupied entirely by

---

[137] The 1991 census showed 46% male and 54% female and that 21% were aged 16 to 29, 22% aged 30 to 44, 26% aged 45 to 64 and 30% over 65.

[138] Households where there was an invalid requiring full time attendance were excluded.

[139] At Manston, car ownership was 92%, at Cliffsend it was 85%, at St Laurence 65%, at Newington it was 38%.

pensioners. A third of households consisted of a single pensioner and just under a fifth, 19%, had children. These rates were similar to the local population as a whole. By contrast, 93% of the congregation were owner occupiers compared to 73% across the island. Also different was the fact that 3.9% of households on the island were headed by a single parent but 0.9% of those in the parish church.

At the time of the survey, the church had four services each Sunday of which two were Holy Communion (8 a.m. and 9:45 a.m.) and two were not. The 11:15 a.m. was a modern praise service with the emphasis on informality whilst the 6.30 p.m. service was traditional Evensong according to the Book of Common Prayer. The breakdown of those attending these services was as follows:

Age Group	8 a.m.	9:45 a.m.	11:15 a.m.	6:30 p.m.
0 to 15	0%	10%	32%	4%
16 to 30	7%	4%	10%	9%
31 to 44	15%	11%	26%	9%
45 to 64	30%	37%	27%	39%
Over 65	48%	38%	5%	39%

Overall, 38% of worshippers under 16 attended Holy Communion, 46% of young adults, 50% of those aged 31 to 44 whilst 70% of the 45 to 64 age group chose to attend Holy Communion and 84% of those above pension age. It was clear that despite the efforts of confirmation classes, younger people generally preferred a non-Eucharistic service whatever the format that took.

The survey provided a fascinating snapshot of those attending church, their backgrounds and preferences. It demonstrated the areas where the church was succeeding in its outreach and those where it had failed.

St Laurence Summer Fair

The twentieth century saw the resurrection of St Laurence fair though this was not originally regarded as an annual event. The first was held at Southwood House in 1909 to raise money towards the rehanging of the bells and repairing the Parish Hall. It was a big event and clearly well attended as over eleven hundred teas were served. Considerable attention was paid to field events. There was a tug of war competition involving six teams which represented Manston, Holy Trinity, St Laurence, the police service, the fire brigade and the brewery. There was a "komic kricket" match played by members of the Lads Club. Children's races included the traditional egg and spoon, three legged, sack, wheelbarrow and general running and skipping. Cyclists were invited to dress their bicycles for a fancy dress contest and also to compete across an obstacle course. The band of the 4th Buffs provided music throughout the afternoon. Donkeys were brought from the beach for a polo match. The fire service brought one of their two ambulance litters across from their base next to the Parish Hall – a stretcher on a wheeled frame with a canvas roof like a tent – and demonstrated a mock rescue. The most spectacular display came from the 21st Lancers – the heroes of Omdurman - who rode in from Canterbury to give a display of tilting, wrestling on horseback, lance and bayonet charges, before engaging in a mounted tug of war. Around the field were stalls selling various home made items and the sideshows included a coconut shy, character reading and a shooting gallery. Swings were set up for children and there were shows of Punch and Judy and of marionettes. The event ended with the Boy Scouts performing a gymnastic display and first aid demonstration before showing how to light a campfire. Once it was lit, they cooked themselves a meal and sang a selection of songs.[140] The presence of the Scouts is particularly interesting since the organisation had only been started the year before and the troop at St Lawrence was one of the first in the country, even having the distinction of being started by someone who was with Baden-Powell at Brownsea Island.

The next fair was in 1924 but that was held in December as part of the fund raising toward the bells. Another winter fair followed in 1927.[141] Fairs were held in 1930 and 1931 in aid of church restoration but on 6th April 1932, the PCC voted against having any more. It was then revived by the Reverend John Roundhill in 1947 as a vicarage fete which was held on the nearest Thursday afternoon to St Laurence day with normally five or six stalls.[142] Takings varied according to the weather but were normally between sixty and a hundred pounds. The fair continued to be held in this location until 1958 when it was moved to the school playing field in Newington Road.[143] In 1975 the custom developed of having the fair on the last Saturday in July rather than that nearest August 10th. Under Les Dunbar's management in the 1960s and 1970s, the fair became a major event with roundabouts, a fairground organ, donkey rides and fireworks. At this time there were usually about sixty stalls. There was traditionally a social event in the evening for those helpers who still had energy to dance. Competitions were incorporated from traditional three legged and sack races to fancy dress and cookery. In 1968 they inaugurated a Miss St Laurence competition to be judged by two men and two women from outside the parish on the basis of their "feminine attributes including personality taken together with the style and elegance of the summer dress that must be worn." In the later 1970s the fair changed but income remained high and a mainstay of the church's income. In 1972, the profits reached £1000 for the first time and they continued to rise with the 1985 fair making £2303. In today's money, the fair generated around £6,500 to £7000 per year unless it rained.

The erection of the new school in the playing field saw further change and from 1990, half the space each year was given over to private traders as a boot fair. In 2006 the

---

[140] *Thanet Advertiser*, 14th August 1909. The amount raised was not recorded in the newspaper and the lack of any Parochial Report or Accounts for the year means that the receipts are unknown.
[141] CCA-U3-19/5/5
[142] Thursday was early closing day.
[143] No fair was held in 1955 due to fund raising for the building of a church at Newington..

fair was moved to the churchyard and parish hall with stalls even being erected inside the church. This was something totally new in the church's history but the change reflects the desire today to see the church used as multi purpose community space rather than purely as a consecrated place of worship or "house of prayer."[144] Christmas fairs are also now held in the same manner. The income has declined in real values by about seventy per cent since the 1970s and 1980s. The August date has been revived.

The church has also had other fairs over the years including Christmas fairs in the 1920s, a Charities Fair in November from 1989 and a Candlemas Fair in the twenty-first century.

Parish Hall

At the outset of the twentieth century, the parish hall was in use almost every day but chiefly for church organisations. The Parish Magazine of January 1902 noted that it was considered too small for requirements but there was no money to enlarge it and limited space particularly following the erection of the Fire Station.[145] Nonetheless, it was able to cope with cooking dinner for six hundred elderly pensioners for the coronation in 1902, even though it had to do this over twelve days at fifty people a day.

Until 1930, the hall was controlled by a management trust but this was changed following a PCC resolution of 20th December 1929 that they would take over responsibility. Various improvements were made to the hall in the 1930s including a new kitchen and the erection of a proscenium arch for the stage with a gilded G in the centre, the parish's project to honour the Silver Jubilee of King George V. The Secretary's report to the 1935 Annual Meeting recorded: "The Parish Hall is a very essential means of carrying on much of the work of the parish e.g. meetings, lectures, day school physical drills. The hall is furthermore a means of bringing parishioners into close touch with one another by means of whist drives, socials, concerts, scouts, guides, Girls' Friendly Society. We have arranged it for badminton. The hall is gradually getting clear of debt and becoming self supporting."[146] The whist drives were certainly popular with an average attendance of more than 150 per week. The hall was also used for meals by the parish boys and girls schools, something interrupted by the fire of 1967.

Mr Bird's arrival saw a campaign to improve the external appearance of the hall. The area in front was then walled off from the pavement and he had a flower garden planted around the yew tree that stood there.[147] Inside, the meeting room at the back was redecorated by TocH in 1962.[148] His hard work was destroyed in February 1967 when the

---

[144] The term used by Our Lord in Luke 19:46 quoting Isaiah 56:7.
[145] The accounts show that from 1901-2, the fire service paid a 5s ground rent to the Parish Hall.
[146] The decision to create the badminton court was made by the PCC on 24th July 1934
[147] PCC Minutes, 29th September 1961, 5th February 1962
[148] This room had fallen into disuse early in the twentieth century and Bible classes and PCC meetings had tended to be held either at the vicarage or in the school. The demolition of the old vicarage and its replacement by smaller premises was the spur to this redecoration.

hall burnt down.

Rebuilding the parish hall presented an opportunity to rethink the design in terms of current requirements but opportunities were limited due to a lack of money. It was decided to rebuild using the existing foundations to save money and to work in two stages. The first step would be to create a hall which could be used and let to generate income. The second step would be to add an upper room for meetings and the design of the new hall deliberately left space for the stairs to such a chamber. The PCC also decided to remove the yew tree at the front and to tarmac over the ground rather than to set up a new garden.[149]

The new hall was opened on 24th March 1969. It looked airy and modern but the vicar was horrified to discover on a routine fire extinguisher check just eight days later that every one of the eight extinguishers provided was defective. Whether they had been at the time of the 1967 fire or whether they were damaged in the fire was not revealed but they all had to be replaced very quickly.

In 1971, four years after the fire and two after the new hall was opened, the final payment was made. To celebrate, letters were put up showing the name on the front of the building. In the same year, the stage was extended to provide extra storage space.

In 1976, Frank Brown, who had been hall manager, died and left a sum to the church for development work on the hall. It was hoped to use this to carry out the initial plan of adding a meeting room on top to be accessed by a set of stairs from the lobby. It was discovered in 1977 that the funds did not extend to this so the PCC decided instead to add a meeting room at the rear which would be the full width of the building and have its own entrance so that it could be used independently of the main hall, thereby enabling the church to have meetings or study groups whilst the hall was in use. This scheme, which would have restored the hall to its pre-fire flexibility, also failed for want of funds. The Works Committee on 10th May 1978 approved a scheme to extend the hall at the rear for storage and to add a new food preparation area on the right between the ladies toilets and the main hall and with the PCC's consent, this is what was built.

---

[149] PCC minutes 21st February 1968 16th October 1968, 20th February 1969. The hall was designed by Francis Shea of Margate. The upper room would have been in line with the folding partition so 28' by 20'.

Over the years, various changes have been made to furniture and fittings. These include a loop system installed in 2003, double glazing in 2005, a ramp added to the front in 2002 and a disabled toilet in 2015.

Both old and new halls have found it difficult to make ends meet. In 1904, for example, costs were £22 6s 4d and income was £13 6s – a loss equivalent to £990 in current terms. In 1907, income was £15 12s 2d and expenditure was £42 11s 8d, a loss of £26 19s 6d, around £3000 today. In the early 1930s, it was losing on average £20 a year – just over a thousand pounds in today's values. The situation in the 1950s was a lot better. In 1951, for example the costs were £153 1s 11d but income was £155 8s 2d of which £75 was paid by Kent Education Committee due to the hall being used for school meals. By 1955, bookings from private organisations were generating over £200 a year and at the end of the decade, the annual profit was some £30 a year – worth just over £600 today. The 1990s, however, saw it in regular deficit, a loss of £1646 recorded in 1991 alone – around £3300 today. In 1994, it lost £4522 – over £8000 in modern money. The same decade saw the quota double and the congregation shrink by a third.

By the start of the twenty-first century, changed requirements had affected the situation. Couples were more likely to have their wedding reception in a hotel than the hall, small groups found it cheaper to meet in somebody's house and were able to do so since living room sizes had grown considerably since 1885, a number of organisations had closed, jumble sales had been replaced by charity shops and boot fairs, the belief in home grown entertainment such as amateur dramatics or whist drives had fallen foul of the rise of television and electronic devices. There was also the issue of parking, something which the builders in 1885 had clearly not needed to consider but which was a factor a century later. With the hall currently in deficit, its future is uncertain.[150]

St Laurence School

The twentieth century saw continued development of the parish schools. The process began in 1902 with the passage of the Education Act which set up Local Education Authorities who took on the costs of paying teachers, and providing books and equipment whilst the church remained liable for the buildings and religious education. [151]

The growth of the population caused the schools to be extended several times. Just before the First World War, the house occupied by the headmistress of the girls school was knocked down to make room for an additional classroom but the war prevented the work taking place and space remained tight.[152] In the early 1930s the Local Education Authority decided to build a new infants school at Ellington and as this would mean the closure of the church infants, plans were made for modernisation and expansion. The vicar, Mr Cowland-Cooper said that they needed to get rid of the system

---

[150] Accounts presented at the 2016 AGM showed hiring receipts covered only two thirds of the costs.
[151] The Act was very unpopular with many because it meant non-churchgoers were supporting church schools through their rates.
[152] *Thanet Advertiser*, 29th March 1913

which left two teachers trying to teach over a hundred children in a single room separated by just a curtain, something which was unfair to staff and children. He described the desks in the girls school as appearing to have come "from Noah's dump when the ark grounded!"[153] He wanted to see the boys and girls integrated into a mixed junior school with modern facilities but an "old world appearance" but despite a lot of fund raising in the 1930s whilst the church waited for the infants to move into the new building, there was not enough money to completely rebuild the Victorian schools. Instead, at the boys school, the two classrooms were divided into three classrooms separated by a folding partition. A corridor was created behind and the classroom opposite extended. A separate room was set aside for the headmaster to the right of this with additional space for children's coats. Toilets remained outdoors. The cost of the work was £944. The girls school was extended to take over the 1885 infants building. The two were linked with a new lobby and the entrance was switched from the porch facing Newington Road to the side. The infants building became the school hall and was extended at the rear to create a fourth classroom and land was purchased from the laundry so that new toilets could be built. The cost of work on the girls school was £468.

The changes were made during the summer school holiday of 1938 but already the prospect of war was looming and the Vicar was forced to deal with issues of air raid shelters as part of the building plans. The original idea had been to fund the developments by money raising exercises in the parish and by selling off Manston school for £375 which had been declared redundant. The war prevented the sale of Manston and stopped most of the usual fund raising activities. Rationing prohibited most cake baking and jam making and the blackout prevented evening events whilst war duties meant people had other concerns. The result was that the church was faced with a huge bill for the schools which did not get paid off until 1950.[154] By this stage, another Education Act had been passed which affected the schools. In the summer of 1949 they were granted Aided status which meant that they remained Church schools but that the county council took over responsibility for all internal maintenance leaving the parish with just the exterior.

---

[153] *East Kent Times*, 6th November 1935, CCA-U3-19/8/A/9

[154] The estimates for the work had been £310 for the girls and £843 for the boys, total £1153. The actual cost was £1412 but with the additional land purchased for the girls toilets, the final bill was £1640. At the outbreak of war in 1939, the church had raised £798 which left Mr Cowland-Cooper making an appeal for donations toward the remainder. CCA-U3-19/25/10

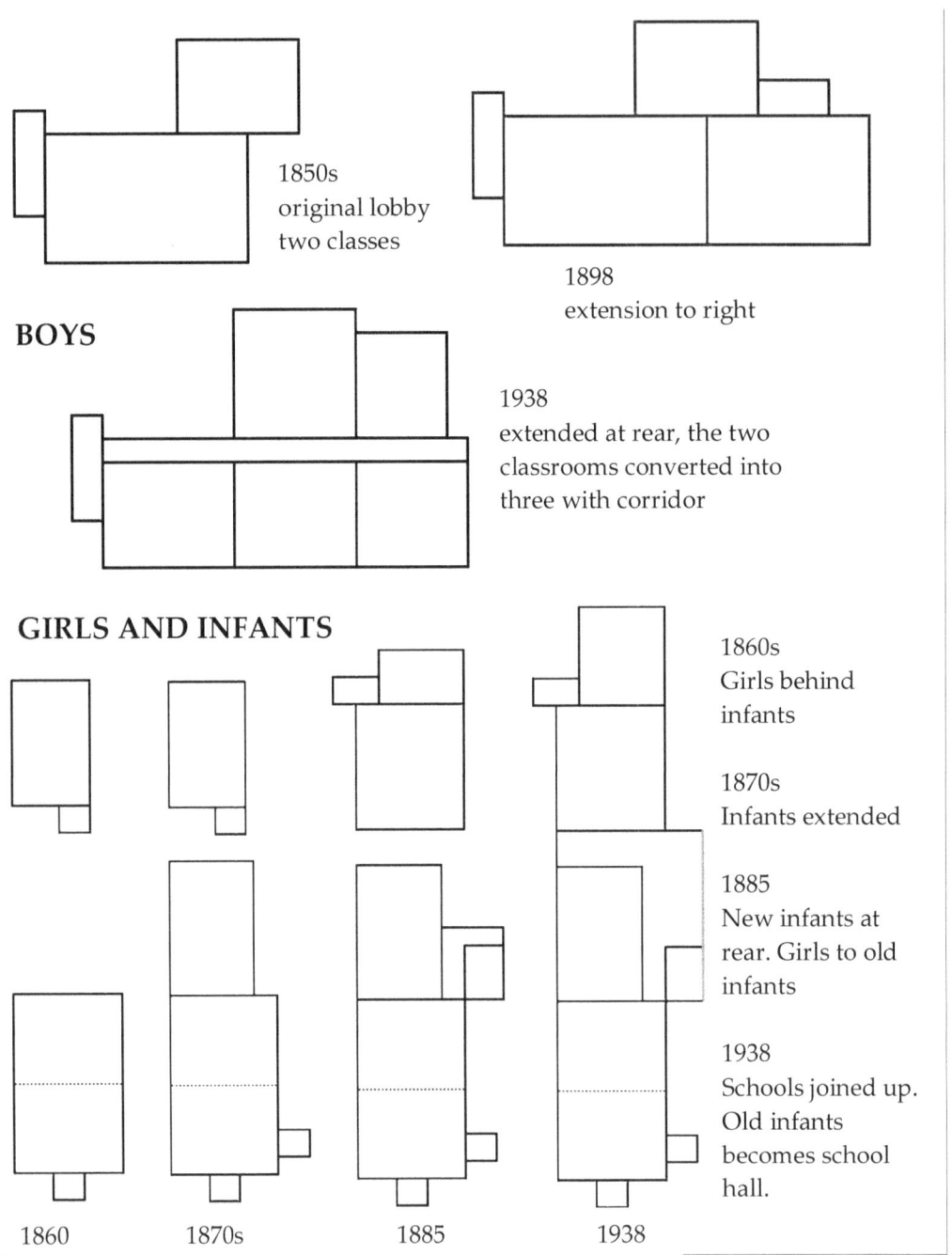

Ironically given all the dedicated hard work which had gone into the 1938 changes, both schools were listed for closure in 1948 as they did not meet modern standards but a lack of money to do anything about this meant that they remained open. The government inspector visiting the boys in December 1960 noted that the building lacked hot water and much in the way of storage. but despite the cramped conditions and need for redecoration, he was impressed:

> This is a school with a tradition – a tradition for sound, hard work especially in the basic subjects and for good behaviour based on mutual respect and secure relations. It is in no way pretentious but the range of its references and of its interests is wider than appears at first sight. It is a good place for young boys.[155]

The situation changed when part of the buttress on the north east side of the girls school collapsed in a fierce gale on 2nd May 1967. The children had to relocate, two classes to the Concorde Youth Centre and one to St Christopher's and considerable pressure was placed on the church to agree to the school's closure with the pupils being moved to Dame Janet. The church opposed this strenuously but it was clear that something would have to be done. The cost of repairs was estimated at £5000, and this was just weeks after the Parish Hall had burnt down and whilst the parish faced the cost of building a clergy house at St Christopher's. In the end, Kent County Council provided two portacabins for classrooms and the Diocese sent a portable toilet block so the girls were able to return to the school whilst repairs began.

The dream of rebuilding and combining the schools remained and in 1980, the laundry premises came up for sale being offered freehold for £70,000 or leasehold for £9,500 per annum. The Reverend Philip Norwood moved quickly to secure the site and a planning application for a new mixed school was submitted - TH/78/50H. This was approved and in September 1983 the girls moved into portacabin classrooms in the boys school playground whilst their own buildings from 1841 and 1885 were demolished. On April 4th 1984 the foundation stone of the new school was laid by Canon Pollard together with a time capsule and on January 9th 1985, the children moved into their new building. The architect was Kenneth Waite and the cost of the building was £500,000 almost all of which came from the Diocese, the church contributing just £10,000. The official opening was performed by Archbishop Robert Runcie on 14th June 1985 who said that he hoped it would be: "a homely happy place, a place of hard work and discipline, a place of which everyone is really proud and a place which you are all determined to make even better."[156] It was designed on the open plan scheme which meant there were no walls or doors between classrooms nor even curtains. This was a return to the Victorian layout

---

[155] It then had 153 boys, a headmaster, three masters and a part time female teacher.
[156] *The Beacon*, August 1985. The Archbishop had been at St Paul's cathedral earlier that day at a service to dedicate the South Atlantic Campaign Memorial, the event being attended by the Queen, the Duke of Edinburgh. the Prince and Princess of Wales and, of course, Prince Andrew who had fought in the Falklands on the front line. For more details of his war service see Bolton, *Seven Centuries* op.cit. pp.424-429

and caused the same difficulties which resulted in the building being later changed and conventional walled classrooms established. The decision was made to call the new school St Laurence rather than St Lawrence to reflect the fact that it was the church's school rather than the village's.[157]

---

[157] In the mid Victorian period, the church had generally been spelt Lawrence so the founders had not intended to make any distinction.

Church Finances

Undoubtedly, the biggest change made in the parish across the century was the inexorable rise of the quota, or parish share as it was renamed. This was the contribution made by parishes toward the cost of their clergy. Officially a voluntary payment, the increase was eye-watering and this was made the more difficult by the fact that the size of the congregation fell sharply during the same period.

The following figures show data gathered from church accounts across the century and annual meetings. The current value of the sums is shown italicised in brackets afterward.

From 1916 to 1921, the quota was £23 7s 2d *(£2158)*. The electoral roll in 1921 was 402 and annual collections were £161 7s 11d. St Catherine's paid £4 toward this. From 1922 to 1926, the quota was £52 7s *(£2309)* and annual collections were around £235. Following the death of Mr Wilcox and the loss of the curate, the quota did go down temporarily. In 1931, the quota was £37 10 *(£2209)* whilst collections were £396 12s 4d. However, in 1933 the quota shot up to £60 *(£3792)* but this was covered by an increase in collections to £452 6s 6d. The electoral roll was then 530. The PCC of the time did request an explanation from the diocese for the new figure but they never received one.

The quota was still £60 in 1948 (£2118) but it rose to £103 *(£3378)* in 1949. By 1956 it was £162 *(£3839)* with an electoral roll of 443.

The situation thereafter is complicated by the existence of four active churches and neither the accounts nor the annual meetings always detailed the share across the parish.

Between 1961 and 1966, the quota went from £190 *(£3990)* to £393 *(£6878)* across the parish whilst the total electoral roll fell from 520 to 461. The 1970s saw enormous changes. In 1971 the quota was £381 *(£5194)*, in 1972 it was £661, in 1975 it was £1200 *(£11,292)* and in 1976 it was £2000 *(£15,160)*. From 1977 to 1986, the quota rose six fold whilst the electoral roll remained steady at around 330 people. The 1990s saw the quota rise from £21,156 *(£47,601)* to £41,961 *(£66,718)* whilst the electoral roll fell to 267.

The twenty-first century has seen the quota double again reaching £81,996 *(£102,495)* in 2008 although the electoral roll has continued to fall. In 2015 it was 155.

The reasons for the increase are complex and the method of calculation used by the diocese has altered across the years. The figure is affected each year by the number of clergy working in the parish and this has risen not just in line with extra churches but with the move from Matins to Holy Communion which has meant an ordained minister is needed to take the service rather than a Lay Reader. It is also affected by numbers on the electoral roll which do not always bear a close parallel to the number of regular worshippers. In fact, at times the electoral roll has been almost double the size of the average congregation. Parishes have been forced to accept a greater part of the burden than in the past and there have been complicating factors such as the introduction of pensions for which parishes became responsible in 1998: previously, most clergy had worked until they dropped dead, often into their eighties or even nineties which was clearly undesirable. Moreover, it is important to remember that parishes used to pay significant amounts toward their clergy in the days of lower quota charges. In 1930, the vicar was without a curate and the church was faced with having to raise an additional £300 *(£17, 190)* per annum if it wished to secure one. In 1950, the parish paid £150 toward the vicar and £335 for a curate whilst the quota was £103. The total contribution was thus £588 *(£18,757)*: in the same year, church collections were £466 *(£14,865)*. In 1969, the curates got £800 *(£12,560)* of which £325 was paid by the parish. This changed in 1974 when parish contributions to vicar's stipends and vicarage expenses ceased and in 1976 when similar contributions to curates were stopped, the money thereafter being paid fully by the diocese with the costs being added to the quota.

Regardless of the politics which surround the Church of England's overall income and financial policy, the result has been to create a greater burden on individual worshippers and it has caused the church to concentrate its energies on raising money for the quota rather than for other projects as would have been the case in past years. With the amount needed from each regular worshipper per week at St Laurence just to cover the quota – and clearly churches have many other costs such as heating, lighting, insurance, administration, maintenance – now being the equivalent of 10% of a single pensioner's income, the scale of the problem is evident. In 1921 it was 0.5%,

The church's financial difficulties have dominated PCC and DCC meetings. For many years, the church has run at a loss. The annual deficits between 1987 and 1994, for example, were £2797, £1970, £4082, £2727, £7101, £3006, £6370 – a total of £28,053. Of the expenditure, two thirds was quota. During the same period, collections dropped by 3%, planned giving increased by 14% and inflation rose by 44%. Communicant numbers also fell by 21%.[158]

The problems have affected policy too, particularly during the 1970s. When the war memorial was erected after the First World War, the money was raised entirely by parishioners in honour of the dead. When the decision was made to add a reference to the Second World War in 1974, the church pleaded poverty and got the British Legion to pay for it. Similarly, with the clock. This was installed by the church of its own free will, the money raised by parishioners, but in 1978, an audacious suggestion was made that the council should pay for its maintenance, despite the fact that they had not asked for its installation and the vast majority of the ratepayers were not church supporters. Perhaps surprisingly, the council accepted the request although this use of public money was not publicised. There was also the closure of the churchyard, a move that stemmed from lack of money. Notwithstanding the problems that resulted from the Parish Hall burning down when under-insured, this practice was also continued. In 1975, it was revealed that the church was insured for only 38% of its value and the Parish Hall for 48%.[159]

By the start of 2015, the church owed over £30,000 on the quota alone and with

---

[158] Rector's report to Annual Meeting 26th March 1996, Treasurer's Reports
[159] PCC Minutes 20th March 1975. A decision was taken on 2nd June to increase cover despite the higher premium.

the Parish Hall running at a loss, a declining congregation and rising costs, the twenty-first century is clearly not destined to be any easier than the last. The current deficit, as stated by posters in the church, is almost £2000 a month.

St Christopher's, Newington

The desire to have an Anglican place of worship on the estate was expressed not only by the clergy of St Laurence but the residents over five hundred of whom signed a lay organised petition to the Archbishop requesting that one be built.[160]

It was on 16th November 1952 that St Laurence church began its formal work on the Newington estate. On that date, the Reverend Stanley Bounds, together with Miss Dora Waters, opened a Sunday School in Newington Infants school, itself a new building having been opened by Edward Heath two months earlier. By the end of the month, it had over 130 children, by Easter 1953 it was 200 strong. By Christmas 1953, the Sunday School occupied one whole wing of the school, the dining hall and four classrooms and there were fourteen teachers and 250 children. In November 1954 membership reached 300 and the church was renting twelve classrooms, effectively the whole school.

The new church was designed by Messrs Denman and Son of Brighton and it was intended from the start to be multi-purpose.[161] The sanctuary was behind a screen which could be closed when the building was being used for a secular purpose. The pulpit and lectern were located to the sides so they would not intrude. The seats were stackable. It was designed to seat 265 people with room for 40 more in the gallery and the cost of building was £15,000 of which the Diocese would contribute £9,000. In May 1954 the Archbishop approved the name of St Christopher, "a very proper name for the new church that will bear the Gospel of Christ to the new suburb that has sprung up in the fields of Newington."[162] Work began on 19th September with over two hundred people coming to lay a brick, all accompanied by the Ramsgate Silver Band. Fund raising involved the buy-a-brick campaign, the mile of pennies and the Mammoth Fair in 1955 when Ramsgate churches gave up their own individual fetes to have one in Ellington Park to raise funds toward the building of St Christopher's. Each church set up their own mini village with St Laurence creating an Elizabethan scene – no doubt using costumes from the 1934 pageant – Holy Trinity made a Tyrolean village, Christ Church took on a Spanish theme whilst St George's adopted a Dutch style complete with home made windmill. The fair raised £1300 which was badly needed as over £3,500 was still required. The congregation of Christ Church came and put on a play in St Laurence Parish Hall as an extra contribution. The building work was done by Grummant's of Ramsgate and completed in time for the Archbishop to dedicate it on 26th September, 1955. One person

---

[160] They represented 436 houses – almost half the estate.
[161] The original plans show the intention was to have the church on the left of the current position with room for a vicarage on the right and an area for cars in the middle. Instead, the church was built in the middle with gardens either side so that it was more visible on the estate.
[162] The legend of St Christopher is that he carried the infant Christ on his shoulder.

who missed this event was the Reverend Stanley Bounds who had done so much to establish the Sunday School at Newington and to raise funds. He was called to move on to South Ashford. In his farewell address he said: "St Christopher's is more than a mere building. It is a symbol of greater things. it is an expression of faith. Let St Christopher's be to you not a building alone but the centre of everything worthwhile in your life while you live at Newington."

The first curate to serve at Newington was the Reverend Francis Coveney. The service plan was 7.30 a.m. Holy Communion, 10.30 a.m. Family Service, 6.30 p.m. Evensong with Sunday School in two shifts from 2.30 p.m. The church had a choir of around a dozen boys and was given a cross and candlesticks by St Lawrence College. St Laurence donated a chalice and paten. Almost one hundred attended the first Family Service and over two hundred Evensong. With a Sunday School that was close to five hundred and a teenage Youth Fellowship that had sixty to seventy regular members, the future seemed bright. The church was reaching around one in three children and one in eight adults in the neighbourhood, an incredibly high proportion. Within a year, those who were contributing to the Free Will Offering Scheme numbered 298.

After the initial excitement of opening the new church, there was a decline in enthusiasm. When the Reverend Stanley Evans arrived in October 1957, he found no choir and that communicants normally numbered just a couple of dozen. On Christmas Day 1959, only twenty-two attended Holy Communion though eighty-two were at Matins. Yet slowly but surely he started to build the congregation and by Easter 1962, there were ninety-two communicants. Inevitably, much of his time was spent on fundraising. He wrote in August 1958: "We must give up relying on bazaars, fetes and jumble sales for paying off our debt and live instead off the Gospel. We can pay it off by direct giving if we really believe in God. If we continue to rely on worldly methods we shall be just a worldly church with a fair amount of treasure on earth but little (if any) in heaven."

In October 1958 St Christopher's got a bell from St Paul's and a month later it got choir stalls and two clergy stalls from the same.[163] Mr Evans started a new choir which was given some cassocks and surplices from St Augustine, South Croydon and from Canterbury Cathedral. In 1961 it got its own processional cross, designed by the Reverend Stanley Evans and made by Arthur Sullivan of St Laurence. As Mr Evans noted, the shape

---

[163] The bell was given to an overseas church after the ringing apparatus was vandalised in 1966.

was a reminder of Our Lord's arms stretched out on the cross, the red was a reminder of the blood He shed for us, the gold of His glorious resurrection, and the orb it stood upon represented the world.

The church was finally paid for in Easter 1959.

At Christmas 1965, the church had a new organ dedicated. Restored in 1975, this sat in the gallery until replaced by an electronic keyboard.[164] In the summer of 1967, a flight of central steps was made to stand in front of the stage by Mr Porter to avoid people using those on the side. In August 1970, the cross on the east wall was dedicated in memory of Bill Gristock and the reading desk in memory of six year old Peter Debling.[165] The flagpole was given by Jackey Baker's in 1984. The banner was given for the church's twenty-first birthday in 1976, the Reverend Roger Parsons saying at its dedication: "Like St Christopher we represent Christ wherever we go; we are Christ bearers. our vocation is to introduce Christ's way where it is not known, to carry Him to others, treading fearlessly our hand in His." In 1999 the chancel was refurbished and in 2000 the gallery and upper room were redeveloped, a glass screen being placed at the front and a computing centre set up behind, the space later being used for meetings and a charity shop. The room was named after John Bosco, a nineteenth century Roman Catholic priest who worked with underprivileged and delinquent children in Italy. The votive candle stand was given in 1998 and new chairs arrived six years later. A new kitchen and central heating were installed in 2012, a loop system in 2005.

The church gardens were originally laid out at Easter 1956 by TocH. The grounds were used for the annual fair and in June 1967, this was opened by the actor Jack Warner, famous for his role as Arthur Huggett and then as Dixon of Dock Green. His presence ensured a record turnout and profit. In 1982, chickens and ducks were introduced alongside a scheme of people paying for a tree to be planted in memory of a loved one. In 2015, Newington Big Local was given permission by the DCC to place an office in the grounds.

---

[164] The church had purchased a 1930s Compton pipe organ from the Palace Cinema in 1960 but this had proved too expensive to rebuild and install.
[165] Both were designed by Mr Tulley

In 1967, St Christopher's House was built for the resident curate with the garage added in 1973. Clergy serving in the area have included: Stanley Bounds 1952-55, Francis Coveney 1955-56, Stanley Evans 1957-63, Brian Kerley 1964-69, David Maple 1969-71, John King 1971-76, Roger Parsons 1976-81, Anthony Christian 1981-84, Roger Knight 1984-86, Ivan Howitt 1987-90, Brian Sharp 1992-96, Matthew Hughes 1996-2001, Sharran Ireland 2001-2003, Brian Griffiths 2003-09, Shola Aoko 2010-date.[166]

With regard to worship, westward celebration was introduced in May 1967 but only for parade services when it was thought it would be helpful if children could see what was happening in the service. On 1st July 1970, the PCC voted to allow the use of vestments for great festivals, although their first use had been by the Reverend Stanley Evans in 1961. Both became general in the 1970s. Modern language worship in the form of Rite A began in 1988, replacing both Rite B and Prayer Book Matins, and has remained in use.

From left to right: Roger Parsons, John King, Roger Knight, Ivan Howitt

St Mary, Cliffsend

The west of the parish was an area which had no tradition of separate Anglican worship because for centuries, the population was too small. A chantry chapel dedicated to the Holy Cross existed in the middle ages but this would have been privately owned. Rate assessments of the 1640s show just five households at Cliffsend, a figure which scarcely varied from the sixteenth to mid eighteenth century.[167] The nineteenth century saw some growth and by 1861, the population was 90 of whom just fifty-two were adults.

The Methodists began missionary work in 1868 and soon had a congregation of sixty adults and sixty-five children which must have been virtually the entire population plus some from elsewhere. Concerned at the loss of this area to the Church of England, the vicar of St Laurence began services at nearby Pegwell in December 1889 but this initiative ended in June 1892 due to lack of support.

In September 1934, the Reverend Charles Cowland-Cooper, aware of further

---

[166] In the case of David Maple and John King, they came to the parish as general curates before being placed in charge of St Christopher's. Sharran Ireland moved on to St Laurence.
[167] CCA-U3-19/5/2. Two farms of 132 and 76 acres held by Dadds and Rigden respectively and three cottages which were almost certainly occupied by their workers.

homes being built in Cliffsend, began services in the Upper Room but these were suspended as the threat of war loomed. At Whitsun 1943, St Laurence was offered the use of the Methodist Mission Room which had opened in 1871 provided that it was prepared to accept the cost of repairing it.[168] Despite the difficulties involved, the Reverend John Roundhill seized the opportunity and decided to start services at Whitsun. He was without a curate and blackout restrictions meant that initially services could only take place monthly in the afternoons, Mr Roundhill cycling down after lunch. By the summer of 1944, weekly services of Evening Prayer were being held with monthly celebrations of the Eucharist. A management committee was formed and the first churchwarden appointed. A communion set was bought for £7 and dedicated that year in memory of Reginald Quick and the first baptism took place on 12th June 1949.

When the church first started using the chapel, it was intended to be a temporary measure just to establish a congregation. The plan was to build a new church with either a hall attached or as a multi-purpose building on the lines of the later St Christopher's. A fund was started and a possible site viewed in the summer of 1949 but the plan fell through. In January 1953, the church was offered the chance to buy the chapel and this it decided to do. The final payment was made in the spring of 1954, the Cliffsend treasurer proudly noting that the full cost had been raised by their own congregation so there was no cost to St Laurence itself.

For many years, the chapel was known as Cliffsend Mission Chapel but in the 1960s, it was decided to give it a more conventional Anglican name. On 11th January 1963, the subject was discussed at PCC. Three names were suggested, Gregory, Mildred and Mary. The votes were cast: Mary 9, Mildred 6, Gregory 5. The matter was passed over to Cliffsend and they voted in favour of Mary and hence the chapel was dedicated as St Mary's church on 17th April 1964 by the Archdeacon of Canterbury.[169]

Gifts to the church have included a hymn board in memory of Mrs Britton in December 1946, a pulpit in 1959 in memory of Mr Fisk, a font and painting of the Madonna and child from the

---

[168] *Thanet Advertiser*, 28th October 1871. One of the donors was Mr Thomas Noel Harris who was the donor of four panels in the west window at St Laurence church. For conditions of usage see *St Laurence Parish Magazine*, March 1943.

[169] The original scheme to name it St Mary had been agreed in May 1959 but the Archbishop of Canterbury has refused to sanction the name so the plan was shelved.

Reverend John Maynard in May 1964, portable communion rails in 1968 and a second hand organ in the same year.[170] A burglary in 1982 meant that new chalices, a paten, baptismal shell and silver wafer box had to be purchased. The church banner, dedicated 8th September 1988, was made by Barbara Wingrave and given by Joan Frenken in memory of her husband.

The building itself has been developed over the years with a new entrance door being created in 1976 whilst the earlier doorway was converted into an east window which was dedicated on March 25th 1977. A vestry was created and an extension was opened by the Archbishop of Canterbury on 11th October 1981. In 2005 the kitchen and meeting area was refurbished. A large white cross was made and affixed to the front for Easter 1959 by Mr Ellery.

The Sunday School began in August 1955 and the church has continued to put a lot of stress on its youth and missionary work having regular family services since 1977, regular Alpha courses from the late 1990s and a number of trips to Spring Harvest.

Clergy who have served at Cliffsend have included John Maynard 1963-67, Ron Harris 1968-73, Andrew Watson 1974-75, Stephen Parsons 1976-79, Bob Jones 1981, Clinton Davis 1984-87, Bob Coles 1987-93, Neil Perkinson 1993-2001. The last left when a pastoral re-organisation by the Diocese meant that one position in the parish had to go. The clergy house at 1 Sandwich Road, bought in 1984, was sold and has not been replaced.

St Catherine, Manston

The start of the twentieth century saw St Catherine's church flourishing. In August 1901, the church bought its first organ, a small manual one made by Walker of London which had previously been in a church at Sheldwich. They paid £37 13s for its restoration and dedicated it in memory of Queen Victoria who had died at the start of the year. Just eleven years later, this organ was replaced by a tubular pneumonic one built by Browne and Sons. The church had been raising funds for a memorial to Edward VII who died in 1910 but they had not got enough money for a new instrument until the philanthropist Andrew Carnegie offered his assistance. The organ was dedicated on September 20th 1912 by the Rural Dean, Canon Molineux of Minster. Although details of the cost are unknown, the fund was sufficient to purchase in addition a new reading desk which was dedicated the same day.

Also in 1901, the church gained gas lighting and two extra pews. These were rendered necessary because the congregation had been sharply increased by the arrival in the village of the children from Thanet Union workhouse at Minster who were housed in the Cottage Homes, the idea being that bringing them up in a more relaxed environment rather than an institution would benefit their development. A hundred children arrived in 1900 and their regular attendance led to a new surpliced choir, a branch of the Girls

---

[170] The rails were removed in 1986 and an electronic organ used from the 1990s.

Friendly Society and a Band of Hope opening and a Sunday School that had 133 members in 1902. By 1901, the number of communicants had increased sixfold and at Advent 1902 the church launched its own extension appeal. During the winter of 1901-2, a club was started in the church school at Manston so that adult men could spend their evenings reading newspapers, smoking, playing board and card games and drinking coffee – an alternative to time at home or in the public house. A year later, SPCK provided seventy books to establish a lending library in the church. A Lads Club was set up for young farm workers and soon had twenty members.

This growth continued through the Edwardian period and in 1909, the church was given the services of its own resident curate, the Reverend Richard Bevan Pyper. He stayed until 1913 and is the only clergyman to have lived in Manston village.[171] His successors, Lionel Perry-Ayscough 1914-18, George Barnwell 1918-24, Alexander Weemyss 1924-28, were all given special responsibility for Manston but lived at St Lawrence.[172]

The first world war saw the establishment of the airfield. The Royal Naval Air Service arrived in May 1916, becoming part of the newly formed Royal Air Force in 1918.[173] This led to a further increase in population as well as a change to parish boundaries as the airfield extended over Pouces which was part of Minster. The RAF were to remain at Manston until March 1999.[174]

At the end of the 1960s, the Cottage Homes were still sending fifty or so children to church each Sunday their presence so outnumbering the adults that the PCC referred to the church as "mainly a chapel for the children's home."[175] In 1969 this situation changed with the clergy thereafter visiting the Leys instead of the children attending church.

---

[171] The 1911 census showed he lived at Highlands, a nine room house where he employed a housekeeper and a parlour maid.
[172] Perry-Ayscough and Barnwell were both in their forties so neither was called up in the war.
[173] *East Kent Times* 13th May 1936
[174] The arrival of aircraft – RAF and civilian – caused a red light to be affixed to the top of St Laurence church tower to aid navigation. It was removed as technology advanced and rendered it superfluous.
[175] PCC Minutes 24th October 1960, 29th March 1967.

Various changes have been made to the original church building. Three stained glass windows were added during the time of the Reverend Thomas Crosse (1899-1904). Dedicated on St Laurence day 1904, they were designed and made by Hemming of London who had made the East Window at St Laurence two years before and the cost was met by public subscription. They show the crucified Christ flanked by his mother on the left and St John on the right.[176] An oil painting of angels by the celebrated local artist Henry Weigall was given by his daughter.[177] The west window was given by Ernest Philpott in memory of his wife Catherine who died on December 13th 1924 aged fifty-four. She had been a major benefactor to the church providing it with a lectern, sanctuary lamp and a processional cross, the last of which was in memory of one of her relatives who died in the First World War. The beautiful carved figure of a lady with a cross in St Laurence churchyard, now sadly broken, remembers her. [178]

Other changes include the installation of electricity in 1964, a professional sound system with loop in 2007, a memorial garden in 1997 and a lavatory in 2015. Wooden collection plates were given in 1978 in memory of the organist's wife, Hilda Bolton, and William Hawkins gave the church its banner in 1959 in memory of his wife. Mr Hawkins had come to the village initially as headmaster of the village school in 1901. He stayed in this role until 1936 and from 1952 served as a Lay Reader, taking services at Manston until 1965 when he was ninety. An additional banner was given by the Sunday School in 2009. In 2012, the RAF standard was laid up in the church. In 1995 the harmonium was sold and the space used to create a refreshments area for after worship fellowship.

The war memorial was unveiled on 24th May 1921 by the Reverend Thomas Crosse, the ex-vicar and a man who had lost two sons in the war. It was designed by Mr T Garrett of Haine and made by Mr A. D. Sackett of Ramsgate. It remembers seventeen men from the First World War including Private Charles Terry of the Royal Army Medical Corps who died of typhoid caught whilst treating men in an outbreak of the same, Ernest and Thomas Lodge, sons aged twenty and twenty-one of the publican at the *Jolly Farmer* and Private Reginald Bingham who was killed with the Gordon Highlanders on the Somme. At the time, it was hoped that this would be the war to end all wars but that was

---

[176] *Thanet Advertiser* 13th August 1904
[177] For more on Weigall's works, see the National Portrait Gallery.
[178] The Philpotts married at Christ Church, Ramsgate. The bride had an eventful trip to the church for on leaving her home of Ferndale in Manston with her father, the horse bolted and had to be chased through the village before being caught and calmed down, *Thanet Advertiser,* 16th October 1897

not to be and Manston was to incur further losses during the Second World War and to find itself on the frontline in the Battle of Britain. The church was damaged and it was some years before it was repaired.

In October 1933 a pair of wrought iron gates were dedicated by the Reverend Charles Cowland-Cooper in memory of Edmund Martin who was superintendent of the Cottage Homes for 27 years as well as choirmaster and organist of the church.[179] These were replaced in 1964.

In the post war period, considerable effort has gone into restoring the church, particularly in the late 1960s. The organ was restored between 1980 and 1984, most of the money coming from the Reverend Roger Parsons who had served as curate there and who was a skilled organist and musician.

With regard to worship, modern language services were introduced in 1985. The church was licensed for marriages in 1968 and saw its first wedding in 1969.

Over the past forty years, St Catherine's has ordinarily shared its clergy with either St Mary's or St Christopher's except for 1981-85 when they had Canon Norwood, father of the Reverend Philip Norwood and who had retired to the parish to assist his son.

Perhaps the last word on Manston should be given to William Hawkins who wrote in 1953: "No one can measure the influence that services in this small house of God have exerted over countless lives…Hundreds of souls have found spiritual consolation within its walls and have gone forth to fight the battle of life with braver hearts and stronger purpose."[180]

[179] *Thanet Advertiser*, 20th October 1933
[180] CCA-U3-239/28/1

Appendices

John Johnson alias Anthony
c1497-1566

The story of John Johnson is the story of a self made man who made his fortune in the reign of Henry VIII and was intimately involved with the early Reformation in Kent.

John Johnson was born around 1497, the only son of Anthony Johnson. He spent his childhood in Canterbury where his father appears regularly in the records of St Andrew's parish from 1505 onwards contributing to the bells, the rood, and paying various cesses. Of a routine fifty or so taxpayers, Anthony Johnson's name generally comes about tenth down the list in terms of amount.[1] He was not the wealthiest man therefore but the family was certainly not poor. When Anthony died in 1508, he left his children £6 13s 4d each (approx. £ 5,100 today) and made arrangements for his son to be educated by Sir John Pesemeth, the vicar of Lyminge whom he would have known through Pesemeth's work in St Andrew's Canterbury.[2] John spent at least three years with Sir John before being apprenticed to a haberdasher. John's sister meantime was sent to live with her uncle, John Sowte, a wealthy skinner with property in Antwerp,[3] suggesting that although Anthony Johnson had a wife living, she was not the mother of the two children. This sister died shortly afterward.

---

[1] Charles Cotton, 'Churchwarden's Accounts of St Andrew, Canterbury', *Archaeologia Cantiana* vol. 32 (1919) pp.225-44

[2] PRC17/11/4

[3] John Sowte or Sweet is listed as living in the Burgate area of Canterbury from 1494 until his death around 1511. His widow appears at the property in 1512. See J.A. Cowper *Canterbury Intrantes* (Canterbury, 1904) p. 160. Sowte was the husband of Anthony Johnson's sister. His will (PRC17/12/239) mentions various fur lined robes and a house in Antwerp.

It was with his master, the haberdasher John Anthony, that Johnson returned to Canterbury in 1517. Johnson was presumably very happy with his master and close to him because he adopted the surname Anthony as an alias, something he was to use for over twenty years. Most likely, Anthony lacked a son to take over the business so Johnson took the name together with the trade. Johnson's links to the Anthony family were evident as late as 1550 and it is quite possible that he spent the years prior to marriage living with his master's brother in law Paul Richmond, who seems to have regarded Johnson as a surrogate son.[4]

Around 1520, Johnson married Sybil, daughter of John Crouch of Canterbury, a baker who had been one of the witnesses to Anthony Johnson's will.[5] The couple had two children – Paul and Margaret. Sybil evidently predeceased her husband because when John passed away in 1566, he left a widow Beatrice who survived him by at least twelve years.[6]

It is very difficult to know what happened during those early years of marriage. Johnson may have been trading in fabric because an entry in the St Dunstan's parish records shows 5/- paid to his wife for a surplice in 1523.[7] He certainly developed links with Christ Church, the cathedral priory, probably initially as a supplier given that the records reference him as Anthony. Johnson developed a close relationship with Prior Thomas Goldwell which lasted over many years and it is likely Goldwell tried to help the young man out with work and contacts where he could. Johnson was clearly increasing in stature because in 1529 he appears as a business partner of the Hales family[8] and in 1532 he was elected Sheriff of Canterbury.[9] It was in this period too that Johnson became connected with Henry VIII's chief minister, Thomas Cromwell. A month before he became Sheriff, he was taking messages regarding horses to and from Cromwell and Sir Christopher Hales, the Attorney General.[10] Exactly when Johnson started this work is not

---

[4] See will of Paul Richmond (PRC17/27/248) whose sister was Joan Anthony, widow of Johnson's master. This includes money bequests to Joan and silver artefacts to Johnson to whom he also entrusts care of his widow both personally and in her business affairs. Presumably Richmond had no son of his own. It is likely Johnson named his son after Richmond and was responsible for introducing him to John Crouch, his father in law, with whom Richmond was later to do business, see Michael Zell (ed.) *Kent Feet of Fines for Henry VIII* vol. 2 part 2 (KAS 1996) no 1079.

[5] Crouch arrived in Canterbury in 1483, see Cowper op.cit. p. 136

[6] C. E. Woodruff *History of Fordwich* (Canterbury, 1895) p. 79. Beatrice was asked by Fordwich corporation in 1578 to return two tablecloths which they alleged she had of theirs.

[7] J. Cowper, 'Accounts of St Dunstan's Church', *Archaeologia Cantiana* vol. 17 (1887) p. 83

[8] *Kent Feet of Fines for Henry VIII* Part 2 no 923 *op.cit.* Thomas Hales was cousin of Sir Christopher and brother of Sir James. Peter Heyman was a further partner in this transaction. He had connections with Hales back to 1523 and his daughter married Johnson's only son and heir. The other party to this land deal was Paul Richmond

[9] William Urry *The Chief Citizens of Canterbury* (Canterbury, 1974) p. 64

[10] PRO *Letters and Papers foreign and domestic of the reign of Henry VIII* (hereinafter referenced as L&P) vol. V, nos 1354, 1386

clear for messengers are not often named in letters but it was a role he was to continue to fulfil until the summer of 1540 when Cromwell fell from power. During this time he met and had correspondence with people such as Thomas Cranmer, Lord Lisle (uncle to Henry VIII), the Boleyns and Dr Rowland Lee. He was also involved in the administration of major diplomatic visits.

It is easy to suppose that Johnson would have been attracted to the messenger position on grounds of the help the contacts could give him in building his business and the benefits he could accrue, but why did Cromwell select him? The Hales connection would have helped but most likely it stemmed from his position at Christ Church which was the pre-eminent monastic establishment in England. Johnson was a senior lay servant there[11] and his brother in law was a leading monk, later Chancellor.[12] Upon the death of the Archbishop of Canterbury, the Prior of Christ Church was meant to take over the role until a new appointment was made. The first mention of Johnson in the state papers is just a month after the death of Archbishop Warham. This was six months before the appointment of Thomas Cranmer, a time when Henry was still locked in a battle with Rome and romancing Anne Boleyn. The outcome of the Reformation was not then certain. Supporting the view that Johnson obtained his role through Goldwell is the fact that Cromwell and Goldwell were the only people who consistently referred to him as John Anthony even though both knew his real name was Johnson. [13]

In January 1533, Johnson was taking messages from Cromwell to Prior Goldwell. Convocation, the parliament of the Church, was due to meet and Prior Goldwell should have chaired the assembly but he did not want to do so and tried to persuade Cromwell to appoint someone else. His reluctance was hardly surprising. He was 56 years old which was relatively old by Tudor standards[14], and the last two years had seen the clergy accused of treacherously supporting Wolsey as an envoy of the Pope and forced to subject themselves to Henry. Furthermore, the business of the coming Convocation was to deny the Pope's claim to have authority to issue dispensations in contradiction of Holy Scripture.[15] For a leading Churchman of the Roman tradition and one who had known

---

[11] L&P vol VII no 763 where Prior Goldwell includes Johnson among "the chief servants of this house" noting he earned 26/8. This letter dates from 1534 showing that Johnson did not immediately surrender his position there upon joining the royal service.

[12] Will of John Crouch (PRC17/21/43) confirms Sybil's brother had taken the name John Ambrose upon joining the monastery. His first mass was in 1523, C Woodruff. 'The Sacrist's Rolls of Christ Church, Canterbury', *Archaeologia Cantiana* vol 48 (1936) p 71. See also Patrick Collinson *A History of Canterbury Cathedral* (Oxford, 1995) p. 126 for details of Ambrose's education at Oxford.

[13] Cromwell always refers to Johnson as Anthony, even though Johnson replies as "Johnson alias Anthony", e.g. L&P vol VII appendix 27.

[14] L&P Vol XII no 437

[15] Henry's claim was that the marriage he had conducted with Katherine of Aragon was not valid because it had only taken place after Pope Julius II in 1503 had issued permission for the scriptural prohibition on a man marrying his brother's wife (Lev. 20:21) to be ignored. If, as Henry now argued, the Bible was the Word of God and therefore above the authority of man, the permit to

Wolsey well, this would have been a very difficult situation.

In May 1533, Johnson was in Faversham at the bedside of Henry Hatch, a merchant who was dying. Johnson wrote the will out on his behalf. The conflicts over this will were to continue for over twenty years and centred around the issue of whether the will accurately reflected the wishes of the deceased, some alleging that Hatch was beyond speech at the time the will was actually written.[16] Some months later, Sir Christopher Hales, the Attorney General, advised Hatch's widow to bring the will to his house at Canterbury which she did, staying at the home of John Johnson. Together they went to Hales' house where Hales and Johnson apparently sought to persuade Widow Hatch to marry James Hales, Christopher's cousin. She declined and left the house with the will. Another suitor of Widow Hatch decided to get involved by complaining to Anne Boleyn's father that Henry Hatch's next of kin was Boleyn's servant and that he had been unlawfully cut from the will. This ultimately resulted in a lawsuit claiming that the will held by the Widow Hatch was a forgery. Johnson himself did not profit from the will and it is not obvious why he should have wished to change the terms, but it was a significant and public test of his integrity, the importance of which can scarcely be overestimated given the value placed on reputation in Tudor times.

The autumn of 1533 was a busy time for Johnson. The government was concerned with the case of Elizabeth Barton, the Nun of Kent. She had spoken publicly against the King's marriage to Anne Boleyn and since 1526, had enjoyed a series of high profile meetings with people including Cardinal Wolsey, Bishop Fisher, Archbishop Warham, Sir Thomas More and even King Henry VIII.[17] She had attracted a large number of followers and was assisted by Dr Bocking of Christ Church as well as Father Risby of the Observant Friars[18]. It was a dangerous time for such talk. The King had been excommunicated in July 1533 and there was talk of a war to depose him and who might replace him, the Nun favouring the claim of Exeter.[19] Cromwell set in motion the process to destroy Barton and her adherents, a prospect which must have alarmed many including Prior Goldwell who, as superior to Dr Bocking, could have been blamed for the situation. Johnson, however, was at hand not just to carry messages but to take an active role in the

---

marry was without value. For this reason, Henry did not need a divorce from Katherine just an annulment. Katherine's argument was that as the marriage to Prince Arthur had not been consummated, there was no need for a dispensation so the validity of the document was irrelevant.

[16] A detailed account of the story appears as Appendix 20 of Patricia Hyde *Thomas Arden in Faversham* (Faversham, 1996) pp. 480-5. The statement that Johnson was a Protestant at this date (p.282) cannot be substantiated and he did not purchase the property at Fordwich until 1553. Although Johnson had links to Cromwell from at least 1532, he did not join Cromwell's payroll until the summer of 1534, L&P vol VII no 763

[17] E. F. Rogers, *Correspondence of Sir Thomas More* (Princeton, 1947) Letter 197. Alan Neame *The Holy Maid of Kent* (London, 1971) p. 68 discusses contemporary accounts of Barton being surrounded by thousands of people wherever she went.

[18] Henry Hatch had left money to them in his will, Hyde *op. cit.* p.482

[19] Neame op.cit. p. 198

suppression of what was seen as a movement that endangered the Crown and the security of England. Into Johnson's hands was surrendered the vital and extremely confidential dossier on the Nun's activities and he was also given the task of making the inventory of Barton's property at St Sepulchre's following her arrest. [20] Johnson's enthusiasm attracted praise from Dr Rowland Lee who was chaplain to Henry VIII and widely believed to have been the man who conducted the private marriage with Anne Boleyn in January 1533. Dr Lee wrote to Cromwell: "We beseech you to be good master to John Anthony for he hath showed as much kindness unto us as a man of his behaviour might do and hath always become diligent to further our cause as much he might…John Anthony has furthered our causes much."[21]

Cromwell obviously did this for Johnson is seen making a number of journeys between Canterbury and London at this time, not just carrying letters but passing on verbal instructions which Cromwell clearly did not wish to commit to paper.[22] That Johnson had the ear of the King's chief minister was not in dispute.

1534 saw Johnson continuing his role of messenger and collector carrying letters, gifts and quite large sums of money.[23] He was involved in business at Sittingbourne, Canterbury and Dover and the arrangements for the visit of the Admiral of France who spent time at Canterbury with Prior Goldwell and George Boleyn before being escorted to London.[24] He was being given gifts and asked for help, signs that others saw him as a man of influence whose favour they wanted.[25] He seems also to have been involved in administering the Oath of Supremacy for he writes to Cromwell in June 1534 advising that most have taken the oath except for two observant friars at Canterbury and the vicar of Sittingbourne noting ominously "I shall do with the said parties as you command me."[26]

In 1535, Johnson became involved in the visitation of monasteries prior to Dissolution. He was involved in the inspection and subsequent surrender of Langdon, Folkestone and Dover. At Langdon, he accompanied Dr Layton who wrote a vivid account:

> A good space knocking at the abbot's door neither sound nor sign of life appearing saving the abbot's little dog that within his door fast locked bayed and barked, I found a short pole axe standing behind the door and with it I dashed the abbot's door

---

[20] L&P vol. VII nos. 192 and 763
[21] L&P vol. VI no 1512, G. Cook *Letters to Cromwell and others on the Suppression of the Monasteries* (London, 1965) p. 30
[22] ed. J. E. Cox *Miscellaneous Writings and Letters of Thomas Cranmer* (Parker Society, 1846). Letter LXXXII from Archbishop Cranmer to Cromwell dated 16th December 1533, pp. 271-2.
[23] L&P Vol VII nos. 763, 1125, 1507, 1520
[24] L&P Vol VII nos. 1427-8
[25] L&P Vol VII nos 739, Appendix 27
[26] L&P Vol VII Appendix 27

in pieces and set one of my men to keep that door and about the house I go with the pole axe in my hand for the abbot is a dangerous, desperate knave and a hardy… His whore … bestirred her stumps … and there Bartelot took the tender damsel … Your servant John Anthony and his men marvelled what fellow I was.[27]

The whore was clearly a frequent visitor for her clothes were found in the abbot's chamber. She was taken to Dover and put in a cage whilst the abbot was sent to contemplate his sins in Canterbury jail.[28]

Clearly regarded as a good administrator, Johnson took the inventory of the Maison Dieu and was made Receiver-General of the property of the disgraced Bishop Fisher of Rochester.[29] He also sought to advise Cromwell on appointments.[30] From at least 1534 to 1546, he served the Crown at Dover being involved with wrecks, royal visits, harbour development and Cinque Port affairs.[31]

There is no evidence that Johnson was involved in the election scandal of 1536 though given his closeness to Cromwell and Goldwell's knowledge of Bryges, he may have been somewhere behind the scenes. Canterbury elected two MPs only to be told by Thomas Cromwell that the men elected were not those he wished to see and therefore they must hold another election. Cromwell's letter is indicative of the style of government being employed: "the King's pleasure and commandment is that Robert Darknell and John Bryges[32] shall be elected …. You…have chosen other at your own wills and minds contrary to the King's pleasure and commandment …whereat the king's highness doth not a little marvel. Wherefore in avoiding of further displeasure that might thereby ensue, I require you on the King's behalf that, not withstanding the said election, you proceed to a new and elect those other … to avoid his highness' displeasure at your peril. And if any person will obstinately gainsay the same I require you to advertise me thereof that I may order him as the King's pleasure shall be in that case to command. Thus fare you well."[33] Unsurprisingly Canterbury promptly elected those named. As an insight to the way Johnson's boss worked, it shows the dangers of his role and his need to accept the

---

[27] Cook op.cit. pp 56-7. Anthony was the name Johnson used during his employment with Cromwell, see note 22

[28] L&P vol IX no 668

[29] L&P vol VIII nos 96 and 888. The property of the Bishop was found to include copies of letters sent between Johnson and Cromwell.

[30] L&P vol IX no 828

[31] L&P vol. VII no 1428 and vol. XXI part 2 no 390

[32] Like Johnson, Bryges was a business partner of Thomas Hales, purchasing land with him at Wingham in 1530, see *Kent Feet of Fines for Henry VIII* part 2 no 1020 *op. cit.* Bryges had also served with William Goldwell on the 1524 commission to raise money for the King, see L&P vol IV no 547

[33] Merriman *op. cit.* vol 2 p. 13 Letter no 148 dated 18th May 1536, the day before Anne's Boleyn's execution.

principle that the end justified the means. Serving Cromwell was not for the squeamish.

Another curious incident which may or may not have been connected to Johnson occurred in 1538. Allegedly fearing examination of his opinions, the sub-cellarer of Christ Church, one Robert Anthony, ran away. Letters from Archbishop Cranmer to Cromwell refer to the suspicious letter he left behind and the rumours of Anthony apparently being seen en route to Rome.[34] It might be supposed that this would be the end of the story but in August 1538, Anthony returned and much to Cranmer's horror, far from being disciplined or cast out, was welcomed back by Prior Goldwell with open arms. The episode raises the obvious question of why. Was Goldwell so weak that he did not know how to say "no" or was he actively demonstrating his independence and commitment to the Christian principle of forgiveness by publicly giving shelter to someone who was clearly opposed to government policy? Cranmer's comment that Goldwell was easily led has often been quoted but Cranmer also complained about Goldwell openly defying orders which was a dangerous thing to do and correspondence shows Goldwell was not afraid to refuse Cromwell's requests.[35] If the legend of the monks hiding Becket's body before the Royal commissioners arrived is ever proved, that too would be Goldwell's work. There is no evidence for Johnson being related to Anthony[36] and no sign of him interceding for Anthony's life but it is strange how the sub cellarer survived his escapade in a monastery where the Prior's close friend was John Johnson alias Anthony who had contacts in high places. It is reasonable to suppose that any other monk who had done the same thing would not have been so fortunate. Other monks at Christ Church had been sacrificed by Goldwell without a fuss when they were accused of treasonous ideas.

Johnson continued his career as messenger through to 1540 when two events in quick succession caused a major change in his life. In April 1540, Christ Church Priory was dissolved and over half the community were pensioned off including Johnson's brother in law, Dom John Ambrose, and his friend and former employer Prior Thomas Goldwell. Johnson was also granted an annuity.[37] In June 1540, Thomas Cromwell was arrested with execution following a month later. Not only had Johnson lost his job but by October he was being summoned to appear before the Privy Council to answer charges that he had colluded with Prior Goldwell to hide property from the Royal Commissioners.[38] No minutes survive of the meeting but the idea that this might happen had been voiced as early as 1535 when Christopher Levyns wrote to Cromwell saying Goldwell "will alienate out of the same house into the hands of his secret friends

---

[34] Cox op.cit. p. 334 letter CLXXXIV and p. 373 letter CCXXXIII

[35] Cox op.cit. p. 334 letter CLXXXIV, also L&P vol XIII no 756, vol XIV part 2 no 575

[36] Looking at the names of the monks present at the Dissolution, approximately half had adopted alternative surnames on joining Christ Church so it could be that Anthony was a false name. See SP1/116 pp. 44-46

[37] W. E. Flaherty, 'A Help toward a Kentish Monasticon', *Archaeologia Cantiana* vol. 2 (1859) p. 59; L&P vol XVI no 1500.

[38] L&P vol XVI nos 146, 229

thousands of pounds which is well known he hath to his comfort hereafter to the great hindrance of our sovereign lord the king."[39] That Johnson was questioned suggests that the Privy Council may have interpreted this statement as a reference to him but Levyns was not a reliable or independent witness. He had been involved in an acrimonious legal dispute with Goldwell back in 1519 which Wolsey had been asked to settle[40] and was one of those replaced in the Canterbury re-election of 1536 for which he may also have held a grudge. It appears the case against Johnson was dropped as no evidence was produced to support the allegation.

For the later part of Henry's reign, Johnson kept a much lower profile. He was never restored to his former position of favour but he did continue to serve the government. In 1542, together with Thomas Arden, he was made responsible for collecting wheat at Faversham to provision English troops.[41] It would appear that Johnson generally resumed his career as a merchant and landowner. He had never ceased from these roles even whilst working for Cromwell. He had sold oats to Cromwell, vestments to St Martin's, and his vessels had carried corn and maybe herrings.[42] His income seems to have fluctuated somewhat, possibly due to the fact that he could not supervise his own business adequately whilst working for Cromwell. In 1537 he was described as "poor" and in 1534, Prior Goldwell intervened with Cromwell to urge him to pay the expenses Johnson had incurred working for him.[43] Nonetheless, Johnson bought almost 3,500 acres of land including property at Canterbury and Thanington in 1536, pasture on the Isle of Thanet in 1538, woodland in Sturry and Westbere in 1540, the estate of Nethercourt in St Laurence in 1541 with more property in the same in 1546 and 1550.[44] His purchases continued with him buying the manor of Fordwich in 1553 and Upper Court, the neighbouring estate to Nethercourt in 1558.[45] He also sought to buy the Priory of the Black Friars in Canterbury in 1557 but the sale was never completed with Johnson having his £132. 12s returned six months later.[46] In 1554 he took a lease on Stonar from the Crown though he had owned the rectory there from at least 1537.[47] Other properties

---

[39] Cook op.cit. p. 70. Levyns was one of the men elected to Parliament by Canterbury in 1536 to whom Cromwell objected, see note 30.

[40] C1/491/8

[41] L&P vol. XVII no 738. This was the same Thomas Arden whose murder was to be made famous through the play *Arden of Faversham*.

[42] L&P vol IX nos. 478 and 756, vol. 16 no 1524; Hyde *op. cit.* p.175

[43] L&P vol XII no 573 where Cavendish seeks to give Johnson the position of royal rent collector saying: "It will be a good deed for the poor man and provide the king with a true man to execute the office." See also L&P vol VII no 763.

[44] *Kent Feet of Fines for Henry VIII* op.cit. nos 517, 923, 1375, 1376, 1384, 1535, 1689, 1753, 2572, 2579, 2586. Nethercourt was purchased with 183acres of land for £200, around £115,000 today.

[45] C. Woodruff, 'Fordwich Municipal Records', *Archaeologia Cantiana* vol. 18 (1889) p. 87; Hasted op.cit. vol. 10 p. 383

[46] C. F. R. Palmer, 'The Friar Preachers or Black Friars', *Archaeologia Cantiana* vol. 13 (1880) p. 95.

[47] F. W. Hardman, 'Stonar and the Wantsum Channel', *Archaeologia Cantiana* vol. 54 (1941) p. 54;

which Johnson held included a house in Canterbury, a sheep farm at Braddon and Bayhall Manor at Pembury.[48] Given the time he spent living and working in Dover, he must have had property there too. He also had property on the Isle of Thanet from at least 1534.[49] Such landholdings allowed Johnson to take his place in society and he served as Mayor of Fordwich in 1561.

John's prestige was instrumental in the marriages made by his family. His son Paul married Margaret Heyman whose brother in law was the Protestant Bishop of Winchester and Rochester, John Ponet. His grandchildren married into the landed and generally Protestant gentry families of Crispe, Hales, Bletchenden, Honywood, Mann, Knatchbull, Aucher and Claybrook.[50] He had come a long way from the orphaned boy sent to live with a clergyman in Lyminge. He was now a gentleman with his own coat of arms.[51] He had certainly profited from the Reformation but whilst it is possible to trace many of the details of his career, the question remains, why did he do what he did? Did he become a committed Protestant and use his connections within Christ Church to seek to undermine it or was he an opportunist whose efforts to make friends with Cromwell and to destroy the Nun were motivated by a desire to protect his friends and family at Christ Church? His father was clearly a very devoted Roman Catholic. In his will of 1508 he leaves money for 90 masses and a priest to pray for his soul for a year.[52] His father in law was of similar persuasion. In June 1534 he left money for 15 masses and also for candles to be burned before relics plus money for prayers to be said for both his and his

---

L&P vol 12 no 780. Johnson ceased to hold Stonar in 1558.
[48] J. Wadmore, 'Knight Hospitallers in Kent', *Archaeologia Cantiana* vol. 24 (1900) p. 132; L&P vol 18 no 449
[49] His letter to Lord Lisle was written from the Isle of Thanet on Trinity Sunday 1534, see L&P vol VII no 739. This probably indicates he leased Nethercourt prior to purchasing it.
[50] John Johnson married Jane Crispe 8th January 1570 Birchington, Elizabeth Johnson married William Hales in February 1574, Mary Johnson married Bartholomew Mann, Agnes Johnson married on 1st July 1566 at St Laurence in Thanet William Claybrook the Presbyterian who called Archbishop Whitgift the "pope of Lambeth" *Archaeologia Cantiana* vol 89 p. 191 in 1566. He was the great-nephew of the Rev. William Claybrook who served Wolsey, Cromwell and Cranmer, Roger Merriman *Life and Letters of Thomas Cromwell* (Oxford, 1902) p. 326, Cox op.cit. p. 254. Lydia Johnson married Robert Blechenden. Timothy Johnson married Elizabeth Knatchbull. Anne Johnson married Henry Aucher, grandson of John Johnson's colleague amongst Cromwell's servants, Sir Anthony Aucher who was descended from Geoffrey Boleyn and a cousin of Anne. Henry Johnson married Mary Honywood whose sister, aunt and uncle had all married into the Hales family. The Honywoods were also cousins of Prior Thomas Goldwell. Johnson's only daughter Margaret married Nicholas Fish of Fordwich who does not appear to have been a man of special stature.
[51] The College of Heralds have no record of the date of grant of arms to Johnson but it is probable that it was during Cromwell's period of power. Johnson selected for his arms a pelican vulning herself, the same symbol as both Cromwell used and Ponet. Merriman op. cit vol 2, p. 284, Papworths *Ordinary of British Armorials* (London, 1874) p. 1038
[52] PRC17/11/4

deceased wife's souls, these prayers being addressed to "our blessed lady the virgin." [53] His surrogate father, Paul Richmond, even in 1550 when the Protestant Edward was King, wrote a will which clearly demonstrated his Roman opinions.[54]

Of Johnson's own opinions, we know nothing until relatively late in his life. The fact that his uncle lived in Antwerp, home of Tyndale and the pioneers of English Bible translation, means Johnson may have been an early Protestant and smuggler of the scriptures from the 1520s. In 1557, aged around 60, he was arrested for "casting street earth" against the home of Cardinal Pole in Canterbury.[55] This would seem clear indication that by then he had adopted the reformed faith and his own will of 1566 with its very Calvinist preamble, Biblical quotations and appointment of a "learned preacher" supports this.[56] However, in 1543 he was indirectly implicated in the Prebendaries' Plot. It was noted that he had welcomed into his home at Nethercourt, William Gardiner, John Milles, Edward Shether and Robert Serles who had decided to conduct a preaching tour of the Isle of Thanet. Johnson was not part of the plot but it is often said that a man is judged by the company he keeps and Gardiner described Johnson as "our friend."[57] Johnson would have known Milles and Gardiner from their time as monks of Christ Church, but all four men were conservatives who sought to see Cranmer, a man Johnson had served both before and after, in jail or even executed for heresy.[58] Was Johnson's friendship with them innocent in that he did not understand the issues or was he still at this stage a Roman at heart? If so, what converted him? Was it the burnings? As a resident of Canterbury, he could not have failed to see or smell the Protestants burnt alive there. In his long life, Johnson had seen immense changes and knew many of the people who had been responsible for those changes. He must have drawn conclusions about the characters of people like Cranmer and Cromwell from personal observation. He had also seen people he knew threatened and sometimes executed as government policy swiftly changed. For historians with the benefit of hindsight, its easy to judge but he had to make decisions without knowing from month to month what Henry's policy might be. Ultimately he chose to side with Reform and his descendants did likewise, a number serving on the Parliamentary side in the Civil War[59].

---

[53] PRC17/21/43

[54] PRC17/27/248

[55] Canterbury Court of Quarter Sessions CC/JQ/356/9. The document is undated but it is likely that the act was in response to the burning of Protestants in the city. Johnson appears to have sold his house in the Northgate immediately afterward, see ed. Michael Zell *Kent Records vol. 4: Kent Feet of Fines Philip and Mary* p.134 no 31

[56] PRC17/39/49

[57] L&P vol XVIII no 546. p. 341

[58] Brian Hogben, 'Preaching and the Reformation in Henrician Kent', *Archaeologia Cantiana* vol. 101 (1984) p. 175, L&P vol XVI no 779, vol XXI no 390

[59] Details of the career of Johnson's grandson, Sir Edward Hales, and other kin such as Peter Heyman. Henry Heyman and John Honywood can be found in Peter Clark *English Provincial Society from the Reformation to the Revolution* (Hassocks, 1977) and other histories of the Civil War in Kent.

The Sum of the Whole Scripture

From the Geneva Bible

The books of the Old Testament do teach us that the same God whom Adam, Noah, Abraham, Isaac, Jacob, David and the other fathers, did worship is the only true God, and that He the same is Almighty and everlasting: who of His mere goodness has created by His Word heaven and earth, and all that is in them: From whom all things do come; without whom there is nothing at all: And that He is just and merciful: who also works all in all after His own will: to whom it is not lawful to say, wherefore does He thus or thus?

Moreover these books teach us that this very God Almighty, after He created all things, shaped also Adam the first man, in the image and spiritual similitude of himself, and that He did constitute him lord over all things that He had created in earth. Which Adam by the envy and fraud of the devil, transgressing the precepts of his creator, by this his sin brought in such and so great sin into the world, that we which be sprung from him by the flesh, be in nature the children of wrath, and thereupon we be made subject and thrall to death, to damnation, to the yoke and tyranny of the devil.

Furthermore, we are taught by these excellent books that God promises to Adam, Abraham, Isaac, Jacob David and to other fathers of the old time, that He would send that blessed seed, His son Jesus Christ our Saviour, which should deliver all those from sin, and from the tyranny of the devil which by a lively and working faith should believe this promise, and put their trust in Jesus Christ, hoping that of Him and by Him, they should obtain this deliverance.

Also they give us to understand, that in the mean season, while those Fathers the Israelites looked for the salvation and deliverance promised (for the nature of man is such, so proud and so corrupt, that those would not willingly acknowledge themselves to be sinners which had need of the Saviour promised) God the Creator gave by Moses His Law written in two tablets of stone: that by it, sin and the malice of mans heart being known, men might more vehemently thirst for the coming of Jesus Christ who should redeem and deliver them from sin: which thing, neither the Law, nor yet the sacrifices and oblations of the Law did perform. For they were shadows and figures of the true oblation of the body of Christ: by which oblation all sin should be blotted out and quite put away.

By the books of the New Testament we be taught that Christ so afore promised, even He, I say, was shadowed in the books of the Old Testament in sacrifices figured, that He was sent at the last from the Father, the self same time which the Father did constitute within Himself: I say, at that time when all wickedness abounded in the world, then He was sent: and this Jesus our Saviour being born in the flesh, suffered death and rose again from the dead. Which acts of His were not done by Him in respect of the good works of any man (for we were all sinners) but that this God our Father should appear true, in exhibiting the abundant riches of His grace which He promised and that through His mercy He might bring us to salvation.

Whereupon it is evidently shown in the New Testament that Jesus Christ, being the true Lamb, the true sacrifice of the world, putting away the sins of men, came into this world to purchase grace and peace for us with the Father, washing us from sins in His own blood, and should deliver us from the bondage of the devil, whom by sin we did serve: And so we should be adopted by Him to be the sons of God, made heirs with Him of that most excellent and everlasting kingdom.

Now that we should acknowledge this singular and excellent benefit of God towards us, almighty God gives us His Holy Spirit: the fruit and effect of which is faith in God and in His Christ. For without the Holy Ghost, by which we are instructed and sealed, neither can we believe that God the Father sent Messiah, nor yet that Jesus is Christ: for no man (says Paul) can say that Jesus is the Lord, but by the Holy Ghost. The same spirit witnesses to our spirit, that we are the children of God and pours into our bowels that charity which Paul described to the Corinthians. Furthermore, that holy Spirit doth give us hope, which is a sure looking for eternal life, whereof He himself is the certain token and pledge. Also He gives us other spiritual gifts, of the which Paul writes to the Galatians. Therefore the benefit of faith is not yet to be despised or little to be set by. For by the means, this trust and faith in Christ, which works by charity and shows itself forth by the works of charity, moving man thereto, we are justified and sanctified: that is to say, God and the Father of our Lord Jesus Christ (which is made our father also by Him being our brother) does accompt us to be just and holy through His grace, and through the merits of His son Jesus Christ, not imputing our sins to us, so far forth that we should suffer the pains of hell for them.

Finally, Christ himself came into the world, to the intent that we through Him being sanctified and cleansed from our sins, following His will in good works, should deny the things pertaining to the flesh, and freely serve Him in righteousness and holiness all the days of our life: and that by good works (which God hath prepared for us to walk in) we should show ourselves to be called to His grace and gift of faith: which good works whoso has not, does show himself not to have such a faith in Christ as is required in us.

To Christ must we come, and follow Him with a cheerful mind, that He may teach us: For He is our master, lowly and humble of heart: He is to us an example, whereby we must learn the rule to live well.

Moreover, He is our Bishop and our high Priest, which did himself offer up for His own blood, being the only mediator between God and men : Who now sits at the right hand of God the Father, being made our Advocate, making prayer and intercession for us: who doubtless shall obtain for us whatsoever we shall desire, either of Him, or else of His Father in His Name, if so be that we thus desiring shall believe that He will so do: for thus has He promised. therefore let us not doubt, if we sin at any time, to come with repentance (to the which He does invite and stir us at the very beginning of His preaching) and with sure trust to the throne of His grace, with this belief, that we shall obtain mercy. For therefore He came into the world, that He might save sinners by His grace.

This is verily Christ Jesus which shall come at a certain time appointed by His Father, and shall sit in great majesty to judge all men, and to render to every man the works of His body according to what He has done, whether it be good or evil: And He shall say to them which shall be on the right side, which in this world did look for the good things to come (that is to say, life everlasting) "Come you, blessed of my father, enjoy the kingdom that has been prepared for you from the beginning of the world: but to them which shall be on the left side, He shall say, depart from me you cursed into everlasting fire prepared for the devil and his angels. And then shall the end be, when Christ having utterly vanquished all manner of enemies, shall deliver up the kingdom to God the Father.

To the intent that we might understand these things, the sacred Books of the Bible were delivered to us by the goodness of God through His Holy Spirit, with the preaching of that doctrine which is contained in them, and with His sacraments, by which the truth of His doctrine is sealed up to us: that we might understand, I say, and believe that there is one only true God, and one Saviour Jesus Christ whom (as He had promised) He has sent: and that we believing might have in His Name life everlasting.

Besides this foundation, no man can lay any other in the Church of Christ: and upon this foundation the Church does stand sure and steadfast. And Paul wills him to be accursed which shall preach any other faith and salvation, than by JESUS CHRIST, yea, though he were an angel from heaven.

For of Him, through Him, and for Him are all things: To whom with the Father and the Holy Ghost be all honour and glory, world without end, Amen.

The Churchyard

People have been laid to rest at St Laurence since 1275 but initially the space was reserved just for the poor. The deeds of consecration for the churchyard read:

> All parishioners of the said chapel, holding land, are to be buried at the mother church of Minster as parishioners of the said chapel were formerly accustomed to be buried, nor shall it be allowed for anyone, a parishioner of the said chapel holding land to be buried in the cemetery of the said chapel except he has proceeded with the consent and the declared wish of the vicar of Minster although in his will he has chosen burial therein.
>
> Children however and the poor parishioners of the same chapel not holding land, and the rest of the household, may be buried at the same chapel provided that all fees, offerings and bequests accruing by reason of the said burial or of bodies buried at the same chapel shall be honestly, fully and without fraud or guile divided equally between the said vicars of the church of Minster and of St Laurence.[60]

The reason for this regulation was simple: the vicar of Minster wanted to secure his income. It was not until around 1400 that those who were not paupers or children were allowed to be buried at St Laurence. At this stage, the churchyard consisted just of the ground immediately about the church.

On 14th November 1766, the vestry meeting unanimously agreed that owing to the "great increase of inhabitants": "The old churchyard being small and so full of corpses that it is with great difficulty any room can be found to dig graves

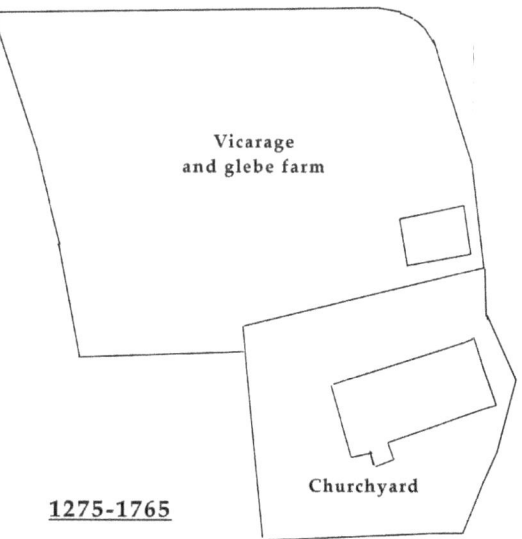

1275-1765

---

[60] A H Davis (trans), *William Thorne's Chronicle* (Oxford, 1934) pp.260-262. The consecration took place on 9th September.

without greatly disturbing the bodies interred", the vicar would therefore give half an acre of his glebe in order to extend it. The vicar and his successors would be paid £1 10s per annum for this by the church and the parish would incur the cost of erecting a new "substantial brick or flint wall." In May 1769, the rent payable to the vicar was increased to £2 and it was reported that the wall had been duly built but there had not been any burials. This was because the vicar refused to permit any until the church actually paid him the due rent. It was further agreed that no new vaults or double graves were to be dug without the vicar's permission anywhere in the churchyard due to space constraints.

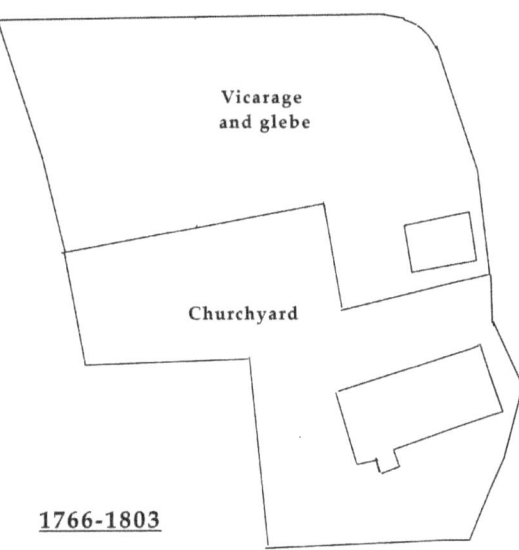

In March 1794, the road was widened on the north east side where the roundabout now is and this necessitated building a new wall. Three years later, a committee was set up to discuss the necessity of further extending the churchyard. In 1799, land was leased from George Hardy and William Hooper for eight guineas a year. The vicar was required to sign an undertaking that he would not "permit any horse or cow to be fed or pastured or on any account to go into the churchyard or new burial ground."

In 1803, it was extended again when land was purchased from Thomas Garrett, partly for burials and partly to recompense the vicar for the loss of glebe. A new six feet high wall was built around the whole and strong gates set up to prohibit anyone using it as a thoroughfare. In 1824, the area which had been rented from the vicar since 1766 was purchased and consecrated by the Archbishop.[61]

It is easy to see why the parish needed to extend the churchyard. Through the sixteenth and first half of the seventeenth century, the church had averaged fifty-five burials a year. In the second half of the seventeenth century, that rose to seventy-one. From 1700 onwards it increased sharply. By the 1780s, it was averaging ninety-three a year and with the outbreak of the French Revolutionary and Napoleonic wars, this rose to one hundred and forty. The rate of burial only started to drop at the end of the 1820s when St George's was built.

---

[61] *Canterbury Journal*, 3rd September 1824. The changes are evident today by the wall mounted monuments which now stand in the midst of the churchyard. The consecration took place on August 28th, a week after the Archbishop had laid the foundation stone for St George's. The Archbishop had been rather shocked to learn that burials had been made for some years before the ground was consecrated.

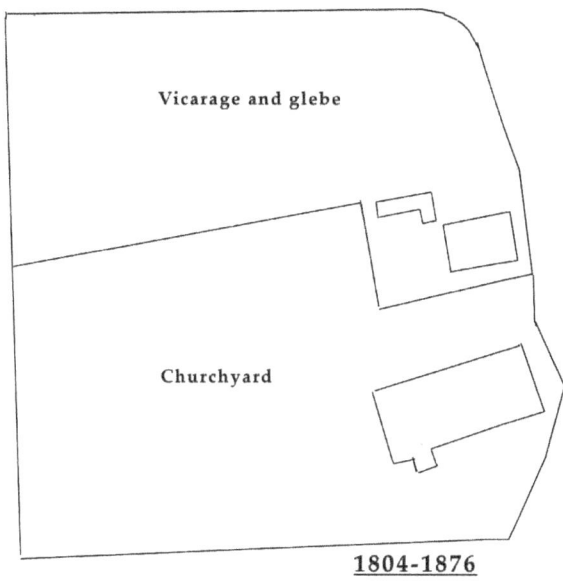

1804-1876

The final extension to the churchyard was in 1877 which took the churchyard out as far as Manston Road.⁶² This was made possible by the church buying part of the glebe from the then vicar, the Reverend George Sicklemore.

Maintenance of the graveyard has always been a concern. The churchwarden's accounts show regular payments to people to weed the site, such as Thomas Pamphlet earning a shilling in 1621 and Edward Philpot the same in 1704. At this time, there were scarcely any memorials so the ground was mostly left to grass with areas of flowers and trees. It is impossible to know what plants grew in the churchyard but it is likely that rosemary was grown. In medieval and early Tudor times, it was traditional to give brides and godparents a sprig of rosemary to carry at weddings and baptisms as it was thought to help them remember their vows.⁶³ There was also at least one yew tree, the branches of which were cut and used in Palm Sunday processions in the middle ages. The will of John Curling, written more than a century after such processions were stopped, refers to his wish to be buried "nigh to the palm tree."⁶⁴

In the mid nineteenth century with a larger churchyard and more stones, the problem became a lot worse. In the summer of 1873, the *Thanet Advertiser* received a number of letters about the state of the churchyard, all of them uncomplimentary. One parishioner wrote: "Instead of impassable tangled grass let us have dry paths; let trees

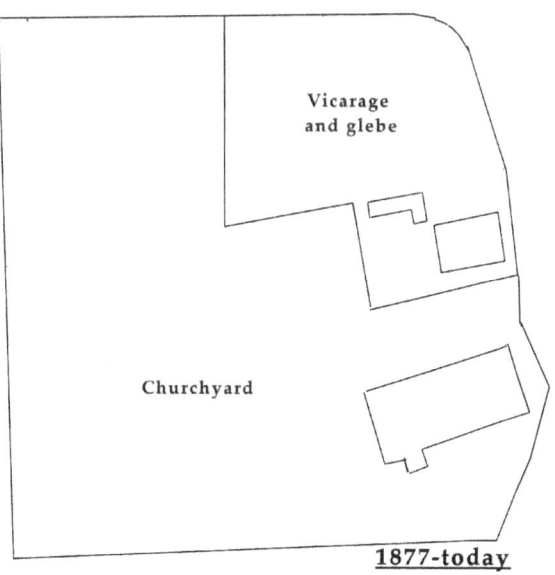

1877-today

---

⁶² CCA/DCb-E/F/St Lawrence in Thanet/6
⁶³ Ruth Goodman, *How to be a Tudor* (London, 2015) p.29
⁶⁴ PCC 11/230/277 dated 1652.

be planted which, while adding to the solemnity of the place will also carry off the noxious vapours from the ground; let us no more see sheep grazing on herbiage nourished by our ancestors remains and despoiling remembrances placed by pious hands on the graves of the departed."[65] The organist responded by saying that sheep were only let in for a few weeks each year and that this was because the "mass of hillocks" made mowing impossible. He further pointed out that hurdles were erected around graves which had no railings to keep the sheep off. The vicar also replied saying that he did not like having the sheep in there either. His parents and child were laid to rest in the churchyard. He was open to any scheme which would avoid sheep but meanwhile could see no alternative.[66]

With the development of new mowers, the sheep were discarded. In the 1890s, it was costing almost ten pounds a year to have the grass cut in April, June and October – this at a time when the total collected at services was around £170 per annum. [67]

The early twentieth century saw the situation deteriorate despite efforts being made. Extending the churchyard to Manston Road had meant people using it as a thoroughfare and that created issues with litter and damage. In 1909 a noticeboard was erected reminding people that they were on consecrated ground and asking them to respect the resting place of the dead by passing through quietly and without dropping anything.[68]

It was not until the time of the Reverend Alfred Wilcox (1922-1927) that the churchyard was taken fully in hand and restored. An avenue of remembrance was laid out lined by roses and considerable effort was spent in trimming around every grave and planting new shrubs.

Only the most essential maintenance was carried out during the Second World War and it was not until 1948 that the Churchyard Care Committee resumed. Since then, various tidying up campaigns have been run. At one point children were given the task of caring for stones, at another the Mens' Society took over the grass cutting and clearing. With a reduced and aged congregation and amid increasing episodes of vandalism, the problem of keeping the churchyard clear grew. PCC Minutes record a number of complaints from irate relatives who were upset that they were paying money for annual maintenance of graves and then visiting the churchyard to find them overgrown.[69]

It was the Reverend Francis Yarker who first sought to close the churchyard to

---

[65] *Thanet Advertiser* 6th September 1873. It may be presumed that the writer was not a worshipper since he also condemns the "enormous yearly sum" earned by the vicar. In fact, the majority of the vicar's income came from the fortune inherited by his wife and not his stipend.

[66] *Thanet Advertiser* 16th August and 23rd August 1873. The iron railings attached to the buttresses on the north side were probably erected against livestock.

[67] Parochial Reports 1890-1892

[68] *Thanet Advertiser* 17th April 1909, 5th December 1914

[69] The usual response that they should make an individual agreement with a local gardener instead was unlikely to have impressed.

burials. His predecessor had stopped the digging of new graves because he was concerned that with no record of burial locations, they could not dig a new grave without risk of disturbing an old. Mr Yarker's decision was based on cost. At the time, the church had debts for rebuilding the Parish Hall after the fire, owed money on major structural repairs to the Girls School which had partially collapsed in 1967, had a large bill for repairs to the church roof and it was forced to reduce staff in order to pay the Quota. He wrote in January 1970: "The churchyard ought to be accepted as a public responsibility and the vicar and congregation should be relieved of financial responsibility for its upkeep which is quite beyond us." Whilst a practical solution to the problem, it was not uncontroversial. Church teaching maintained that the dead were still part of the church congregation and for centuries, people had entrusted their loved ones to the care of the church, not some civil authority. Admitting that the church could not cope was a source of shame and reflected church decline. He did, nonetheless, manage to get the local council to take over the maintenance in 1972 with them taking on the war memorial as well in 1973.

In November 1975 a public notice was issued proposing that the main churchyard excluding the section added in 1877 would be closed for further burials, except where someone already owned a plot with sufficient space for further interments. The Manston Road section could not be closed because of its age and the fact that it was not full but it would pass to the Diocesan Pastoral Committee for maintenance and governance. A resolution regarding this was passed by the PCC on 19th April 1978. The closure order became operative on 18th December 1978 and was presented to the PCC three months later. The order received included a map showing that the Manston Road end was also being closed, something which had not been discussed or agreed and was actually contrary to all previous debate. Given that the church was keen to surrender its responsibilities for maintenance, nothing was said about this error and nobody has yet challenged its legality. At the time the churchyard was closed, around 25,000 people had been buried in it.[70]

With the main churchyard closed, plans were made for re-development. On 16th February 1978 the church voted to remove most of the memorials: "the main tombs and historic monuments should be kept…kerbstones and other rubbish should be removed." They were advised against this. Such a policy would have made maintenance easier but disturbed graves and gone in the face of Biblical teaching that all are equal in the eyes of God. Instead, they cleared a small area to make room for a Garden of Remembrance and concentrated on tidying the site. Another scheme to clear the Manston Road end and build twelve homes there was also discarded.

In 2008 the Friends of St Laurence Churchyard was set up to encourage ecological development and heritage appreciation.

---

[70] From 1560 to 1980 there were 21,532 burials. It is likely that there were around four thousand in the middle ages also.

The Monuments

Over the years, 1408 monuments have been erected of which 106 are listed. The vast majority are of sandstone not least because anyone wishing to use marble or a polished stone had to obtain a faculty. Approximately a sixth have been lost due to vandalism, brambles or poor construction and over half are no longer legible. Amongst stones erected since 1876, the damage rate is over a third, largely because the foundations are much less deep than in earlier periods. Amongst eighteenth century stones, the loss rate is one in ten.

Inscriptions

Recording the inscriptions began in 1978 when the task was given to children and other volunteers. The contents demonstrate not only changing lifestyles but tastes.

A great many of the graves have an inscription which is beyond the necessary length to describe the inmates. Some have verses from the Holy Bible, one has the 'Save us 0 Lord while waking" prayer from Compline (234), a few tell a story, but most are compositions - some original, some from stonemasons stock - which express the faith and aspirations of the family. One of the reasons why inscriptions were long was because until the 1920s, the most popular Sunday afternoon activity was walking round churchyards, often with a picnic, reading memorials. People sought therefore to entertain and educate in what they wrote.

One of the earliest stones from 1706 (1069.1) is to Elizabeth Giles of whom it says: "whose exit sudden was, whose life was pious. She loved all of each denomination that feared ye Lord, acquaintance or relation. Sincere in all her ways, Heaven was her aim; her self denying temper shewed it plain. And now we hope she's in that place above where's nothing else but joy, peace and love"

The earlier stones tend to stress the suddenness and inevitability of death. One to an eighteen year old girl in 1773 (1256) reminds people that "youth, fair prospects, parental fondness cannot reverse the sentence: To dust thou shalt return" Another of 1789 advises "repent in time, make no delay, for now you see I'm snacht away" (1110). A cheerless one from 1804 describes the world as where "dangers stand thick through all the while, to send us to the tomb, and fierce diseases wait around, to hurry mortals home" (1134).

The Victorians did sometimes repeat these attitudes. In 1899, one notes "a sudden change, I in a moment fell, I had not time to bid my friends farewell. Think not strange, death comes to all. This day was mine, tomorrow ye may fall" (641). Another from 1882 reads : "We cannot know who next must fall, beneath thy chastening rod; one must go first, so let us all; prepare to meet our God" (183). Despite these reminders, the overwhelming attitude is one of confidence. This is especially true with children. One to a 17-month child in 1850 claims "when the archangels trump shall blow and souls to body join, thousands shall wish their lives below, had been as short as thine" (718). To an 11-year old was attributed the sentiments "I left dear mother weeping. Weep not, dear mother far me. I am in heaven with Jesus, as happy as can be" and it ends, "what think ye of Christ?" (544).

Typical Victoriana is the verse to a 10 year old who died in 1872 "Only a little maiden, only a few years old, Gone down to the grave with her heart untouched and the tale of her life untold. Far away in the Holy City, she sings to harps of gold, in music of sweet thanksgiving, that she died when a few years old" (415).

It is sometimes tempting to smile at these verses but it must always be remembered that each stone represents a human tragedy. One stone talks of "a bud so young and fair cut short by early doom, how sweet the flower in paradise will bloom" (1125). The couple who raised it, Charles and Mary Ann Home, had by then lost three children aged eighteen days, eleven months and twenty-four months. They probably intended to be laid to rest themselves in this plot but they went on to lose more children all of whom died between seven and ten months. As a result, the inscription recalling the toll of losses continued to grow and the parents were buried in another part of the churchyard with their eldest son who died at just twenty. If the parents in such circumstances had not possessed a strong faith that their children were being specially favoured in their selection to live with Our Lord, they would have gone mad. In total Charles Home, a builder who lived in Denmark Road, had eighteen children with his wife Mary Ann, thirteen of whom died young.

The inscription to William Emery who drowned in 1914 seems to sum up the attitude of acceptance : "I know there are no errors in the great eternal plan, and all things work together for the final good of man, and I know when my soul speeds onward in its great eternal quest, I shall say as I look onward, whatever is - is best" (101).

One husband in 1843 expressed total confidence that his wife would get to heaven, saying 'she was too good on earth to dwell with me' (745) but he added a postscript : 'You now can come to me, but I to you must go", and legend says he spent many a night in the graveyard awaiting the rustle of her skirts as her ghastly form rose from beneath the silvered stone. How much this legend owed to the effects of the large number of public houses nearby is not known, but nobody has ever claimed to see her.

Only a couple of stones have ambiguous messages. A husband in 1790 says of his wife and children "I hope that God will them repay for I am mouldered with the clay' (1267). A group of children in 1818 said of their parents at resurrection day 'what manner of persons they were, that day will discover" (893).

Poetic verses are rare. One of the better examples is that of a husband in 1946 who said his wife had 'ascended with the sunrise' (1061). A sailor penned this in 1830 : 'An anchor laid remote from home, toiling I cry, sweet Spirit come; celestial breeze no long stay but swell my sails and speed me on my way. Fain would I mount, fain would I flow. Thou then must breathe th' auspicious gale' (1024). More typical and from 1785 was "The God that lifts our comforts high, or sinks them in the grave, He gives and blessed be His name, He takes back what He gave' (521).

On some stones, the tributes are fulsome. A draper had this to say of his wife who died in 1795 : 'She was a good wife and faithful friend, who opened her mouth with wisdom and with her tongue uttered she laws of kindness. She looked well in the midst of her troubles and eschewed the bread of idleness. She bore her many afflictions with fortitude and patiently waited till her time came. Favour is despised and praise is in vain, but worthy she stands before the Lord.' (1241). Sons of Robert and Susanna Witherden in 1774 went even further in lauding their parents claiming: "Fame will convey their virtues down through ages yet to come. 'Tis needless since so well they're known to crown them on the tomb, Indeed to engrave them on our hearts rather demands our care. Ah! could we stamp in every part the full impressions there. In life to copy thee we strive (439).

For those men and women opposed to long verse or great tribute, the message could be simple : 'Praises on tombs are but vainly spent, a man's good name is his true monument' (707). Although, for most with the money to spare, a final comment was in order as in this from 1826 (1187) :

> Farewell vain world, I've known enough of thee
> And now care not what thou sayest of me,
> The smiles, the frowns, I neither fear nor dread,
> My body is easy, and silent lays my head.
> What faults ye saw in me take care to shun,
> Look well at home, there's enough to be done

Types of memorial

Overall, six per cent of the memorials are vaults of some description be they brick based or marble chests. Ten per cent are crosses, fifteen per cent have some sort of decorative motif and almost sixty per cent are traditional plain inscribed stones, a quarter of these having bodystones attached. The remainder include kerbstones, wall mounted memorials and ledgers.

Imagery

A third of eighteenth century memorials have motifs compared to just ten per cent of nineteenth century ones. Clear fashions in illustrations can be seen. In the early eighteenth century, skulls and crossbones were popular. There are twenty-three stones so inscribed and one stone has four sets along the top. The motif was chosen to signify mortality and had no relation to piracy. Less popular but equally distinctive to that era was the hour glass showing time had run out. One stone has a winged hour glass ascending to heaven (878). The imagery reflected the sense that people had that they were living in a dangerous world where illness could strike at any time and a bad harvest could result in hunger and death.

Urns made their appearance later in the century as an interest in classicism emerged. They are often shown draped to represent the mourning veils that accompany the deceased's return to dust. One stone near the church entrance shows a pair of classical Greek women posing about the urn (821).

The most popular motif of the late eighteenth century was the cherub. Some are on the graves of children but not all. They seem to have been especially popular with sailors. The ideal of innocence and life in heaven was one all ages were keen to claim and by including the image on the stone, they were making a statement about their belief that the deceased was now so blessed.

Two anchors also survive from this century representing faith, Christ the anchor.

In the early nineteenth century, motifs became less popular as literacy grew but as the century progressed, a fashion arose again for images. Flowers became popular, especially lilies for purity and resurrection, roses for remembrance and their association with the crown of thorns, and also ivy, this last shown especially clinging to the cross in a gesture of steadfast faith. In the late nineteenth century, sheaves of corn were sometimes used to remind how God had harvested another soul (13).

Human beauty is also portrayed, notably in the girl's head an the stone remembering the two wives of John Wilkinson (212). A second head on the Bubb grave is now missing (159).

Animals are extremely rare and of the four examples, all are birds, three being of a dove which is a traditional symbol of the Holy Spirit. A fine eagle appears on one to an 18 year old man from 1800 (1213).

Extremely popular from the late Victorian period into the 1930s was the cross. One hundred and fourteen were erected in the churchyard though less than a quarter of that number are currently standing. Six of them are Celtic crosses which were chosen as part of the revival of interest in the Isle of Thanet as a site of major historical significance. Most appeared within twenty years of Lord Granville's monument to St. Augustine at Ebbsfleet. One such cross, and a little later is to the Reverend Alfred Wilcox, vicar of the parish who died in 1927. There are no pre Victorian crosses and this is because prior to Catholic Emancipation in 1829, the cross was very much associated with Roman Catholicism which conjured up memories of Gunpowder Treason, Bloody Mary burning Protestants and absolutism. The Oxford Movement reclaimed the cross as a symbol acceptable to Anglicans.

The finest stone showing a Biblical scene is the portrayal of Adam and Eve in the garden of Eden which dates from 1756 (839). Another stone from 1799 shows the day of resurrection (961). Greater interest in Biblical themes had been aroused by the Wesleyans.

Ramsgate being a port, there are a few nautical connections. A set of navigational instruments and compasses appear on two (541,282) and one sailor had a flag at half mast on his stone (30). Another has an illustration of a bell labelled 'wreck' with an angel sitting upon it (347). The inscription says it is to mark the 'wreck' of a sailor "launched 15th April 1826 and sunk 30th August 1903" and claims that "when resurrection guns fire, the wreck will be raised by the angelic salvage company, surveyed and found worthy, refitted and started on the voyage of eternity".

Two other images appear toward the close of the nineteenth century and into the twentieth, that of the scroll or open book, to link the deceased with 'those in the Lamb's book of life, and that of the joined hands, particularly popular with married couples to show reunion in heaven.

Also of interest, in terms of art is the set of musical instruments on an officer's grave from the Napoleonic war (517).

	1701-1750	1751-1800	1801-1850	1851-1900	1901-1950
Angel					3
Biblical scenes		2			
Cherub	27	43	3		
Inscribed crosses			1	11	2
Standing crosses			1	79	53
Floral			4	34	5
Human			1	3	2
Skulls and hour-glasses	30	3			
Occupational			2	1	
Religious symbols	4	1	3	5	
Urn		6	1		

Costs

In terms of cost, in the eighteenth century it was generally a penny per letter and three shillings a foot for the stone. In modern values, that means that a short plain stone with a simple inscription naming the person, their age and date of death would have cost around £200. If they had wanted a cherub or skull or similar, that price would have doubled. Most stonemasons would have had their own pattern books and in the later Victorian period it was possible to buy books of designs. There is evidence that some of these were used at St Laurence. A tall plain stone would have cost around £400, a cross some £1500 and a vault about £5000 depending on complexity. Railings would have been extra. This might be compared to a wall mounted marble monument inside which could have cost anything from £4000 to £10,000. In addition, there was the cost of the plot. In 1848, the fee for a vault in the churchyard was set at four guineas, around £400 today. Although this might sound cheap by comparison with modern costs, it is important to remember that the average labouring man at the time earned about eleven shillings a week which was the equivalent of about £70 today.

Although no earlier information exists for St Laurence, a table of fees for Margate shows they were charging in 1577, six pence for burial in a sheet or a shilling for a burial with a coffin.[71] It is likely that fees for St Laurence were the same or similar.

---

[71] Lewis op.cit. 1723 edition pp. 103-4

War Memorial

The War Memorial was unveiled by Rear Admiral Clinton Baker, C.B. C.B.E on Sunday 14th November 1920 following dedication by the Archdeacon of Canterbury who spoke of the need to remember all those who had given their lives in the Great War. He reminded those present of the need to remember those left behind as well, warning that they should beware the temptation to just feel sorry for themselves. Men had died because they thought the world worth dying for and it was up to those left to ensure that it was a place worth living for. They should recall the tremendous odds against which they had fought and maintain the spirit of duty, service and self sacrifice in their honour which had brought them to victory and to use these to build a new world. The Rear Admiral used his address to warn of the perils of Bolshevism. [72]

It was designed by Sir Charles Nicholson who was the architect of Portsmouth Cathedral and Alton Abbey. Nicholson also did the layout for the side chapel at St Laurence.[73] It was built by Elliott, the local stonemason at a cost of £105 16s with a further £6 being spent on the path around it.[74]

There are also a number of Commonwealth War Graves in the churchyard including one bearing a maple leaf which remembers one of the Canadian soldiers who died here.

Mausoleums

The D'Este Mausoleum dates from November 1847.[75] It was erected by Augusta Murray's son – a bastard grandson of

---

[72] *Thanet Advertiser* 20th November 1920. At the dedication, the Vicar read the names from the Roll of Honour which is kept in the church archives. The memorial at Madeira Walk was given three weeks later.

[73] His wife's nephew was Sir Laurence Olivier

[74] CCA/DCb-E/F/St Lawrence in Thanet/ 15. That would be about £5000 today.

[75] *South Eastern Gazette*, 18th November, 1847

George III - and he had her remains together with his grandparents moved from the church into this.

There used to be a second mausoleum also to the Abbott family but this was demolished and the panels placed along the wall that backs on to the vicarage or rectory. Only one image of the Abbott mausoleum survives and that is from 1805 where it can be seen almost opposite the vestry door where the path now leads to the house and parish office. As late as 1895, it was possible to walk into the mausoleum to see the tablets inside.

The Forgotten

The majority of people, of course, were laid to rest without ever having a memorial stone although this proportion has varied.

Period	*Number buried*	*Remembered*	*%*
1701-1750	2548	201	7.9
1751-1800	3821	581	15.2
1801-1850	5441	868	16.0
1851-1900	4338	986	22.7
1901-1950	1259	525	41.7

Christian faith teaches that they are no less valued than those who might be more famous. Some of those without a stone include:

Henry Elmore – soldier's son

That there was an influenza epidemic at the end of the First World War which killed thousands across Europe is well known: a family in Church Road show the human cost locally.

Henry Elmore, born in 1886, had been a carpenter before the war. In 1914 he married Ethel Baker, daughter of the headmaster of St Lawrence Boys School and a year later they had a son whom they named Henry. Henry senior joined up on 11th December 1915 and served with the Bedfordshire Regiment on the Western Front. Sadly, Ethel died a week before Christmas 1916 aged thirty-two so his baby son was cared for by his parents and her sister. At the start of November 1918, less than two weeks before the Armistice, Private Elmore came home on four days leave. Unbeknown to him he must have been carrying the influenza bacterium for on Monday 4th November he died as well as his father and his sister-in-law. Two days later, his mother died. Henry junior, then aged three, also died of influenza in Ramsgate Hospital during the night of November 6th/7th. Unlike his father and grandparents, he was not buried at the cemetery but laid to rest with his mother Ethel who had been buried with her parents(48).[76] Henry's name was

---

[76] *Thanet Advertiser*, 9th November 1918. The elder Elmores were active members of Cavendish Baptist Church hence they were not buried at St Laurence.

never inscribed on the stone. After all, there was nobody left to make the arrangements.

George Moyne – Napoleonic sailor

George "Old Trip" Moyne was a colourful character who departed this life in October 1863 at the age of ninety-three. Born at Dover, he was a sailor most of his life and as a young man he served in the wars against France. One day, Captain Moyne took his boat with its six crew from Deal across to Dunkirk. This was a dangerous mission but he had managed to land supplies before and escape again without being captured by the French. This time, he was not so lucky. Bad weather forced him into Calais where he was taken and thrown into jail. For five weeks, George tried to find a means of escape but the bars were firm, his cell was in a tower and security was tight. He then had an idea. George was a Freemason and working on the theory that brotherly support should transcend national borders, he decided to let down one of his shoes on a piece of twine with a masonic symbol chalked inside it. The next morning he hauled it back up and saw some paper in it. Hoping someone may have given him something useful like a map, he opened it eagerly and twelve francs dropped out. This might help him bribe one of the guards into giving him some extra food or tobacco so he was encouraged. The next night, he repeated the exercise but when he went to haul the shoe up, he found it was empty. All was not lost, however, for he then had a visit from two French officers who advised him that not only were they Freemasons but so was Napoleon Bonaparte. Another week passed before George and his crew were suddenly dragged from their cells and told they were free to leave by order of the Emperor himself. Not only were they given a lugger for the journey but they were given an excellent dinner at a local hostelry. When George asked for the bill, he was told that the French officers had paid for the meal. The next morning, George and his crew set sail for home. As they approached the beach, a man there called out to ask their identity. George replied, "Old Trip." The man shook his head: "Old Trip and his crew were all drowned and the families are in mourning." George replied: "dead or alive, here we are, now make haste and get some help!"[77]

John Penney Philpot - sexton

John was baptised at St Laurence on 17th July 1763 and when he was thirty-one he became sexton, responsible for digging graves, tolling the bell at funerals and for cleaning both the church and the churchyard. On 28th October 1819 he was about his duties as usual when it was reported that, despite being a "stout, hale man" who had barely had a day's illness in his life, he simply dropped down dead into the freshly dug grave of four year old Charles Goodyear as he shovelled earth over the body.[78] The vicar, who had seen him only a few minutes or so earlier during the funeral and who had escorted the family from the churchyard afterwards, must have been extremely shocked to come back and see a grave which had not been filled with a spade beside it and no sexton. This shock

---

[77] *Kentish Gazette,* 13th October 1863

[78] *Gentleman's Magazine* vol. 89 part 2 (1819) p.475

would have turned to horror when he looked down and saw John's body crumpled on top of the corpse. John's body was recovered and duly laid out. He was buried in the churchyard where he had worked for a quarter of a century on 1st November 1819.

Sarah Hughes – unfortunate widow

Sarah Hughes née Carden was born at Chislet in 1797. She married the agricultural labourer Stephen Hughes on August 20th 1815 and the couple had seventeen children many of whom were named after Biblical characters, including David, Noah, Adam, Job, Samson, Rachel. In 1859 she was widowed and for a time she lived in High Street, St Lawrence where she took in washing to make ends meet. In the early 1870s she was granted a place in Garrett's Almshouse where she was regularly visited by the vicar, George Sicklemore. On 1st March 1876 she sat down to dinner as usual. At the end of the meal, she picked up her scissors and used them to cut the wick to extinguish her candle. It was about 9pm and she was about to prepare for bed. A spark flew up and caught her clothes. She tried to swat at it but she was old and frail. Within seconds, her clothes had caught fire. She collapsed in her armchair and cried out "Oh, dear!" The lady who had the room above her, Eliza Gibbens, heard her and came down the stairs. She saw Sarah sitting panic stricken with her dress blazing. Eliza took the water from the wash-stand and threw it over Sarah, following it up with another pail of water brought from downstairs. Eliza was fifty-six at the time and had lived next door but one to Sarah before they were granted accommodation in the almshouse. She succeeded in getting the flames out but Sarah was barely conscious. A charity doctor was called but Sarah had suffered severe burns to the legs, abdomen and arms and she died the next morning. She was buried in a pauper's grave in the churchyard by the vicar who said he had lost "a dear friend."[79]

James Adson – the Pegwell hermit

Born in Yeaxley in 1803, James Adson married twice and had nineteen children before coming to the parish in the 1850s. By then he had spent over a quarter of a century paving the streets of London and some time working for one of the newly established rail companies. It was during the last period that he had a major accident at work which left him unable to work again. His wife died so he decided that rather than become a burden to his children or enter a workhouse, he would travel. He walked along the coast from London and came to Pegwell Bay and was so enchanted by the place that he decided to make it his home. For fifteen years he slept in a sack under the trees at the foot of the cliff. He survived by combing the beach for debris or seaweed which he could sell, walking each day into Ramsgate to see if he could get a penny or two for food. In 1869, he decided that he wished to go to Aberdeen so he spent two years walking to and fro. On his return to Pegwell in 1871, he decided that he ought to build himself a shelter since he was nearing seventy and starting to feel the cold a little. He built himself a wigwam. A visiting

---

[79] *Thanet Advertiser*, 4th March 1876

journalist described this in February 1875: "The ground plan of the structure is not larger than seven feet by four and a man of average stature might use the roof as a stand up desk...A wood fire blazed in the little grate, a few boards roughly joined together with a thick rug for a coverlet served the purposes of a bed at night and a bench in the day. There was one or two shelves filled with old cigar boxes and gallipots in which my host had stored away certain shells, fossils and petrifactions." His only other possession was a copy of the New Testament and he said that he read and re-read just two books of that, the Gospel of St John and the Acts of the Apostles. He was still supporting himself the same way though he admitted that sometimes parishioners would come and bring him a meal. He said that though some days he went hungry, he was never lonely: "I always did love solitude. I never fall out with myself, When the wind blows from the south west and the rain comes down in mighty torrents there is a mighty row about this little house of mine but it weathers the storm." Predictably the locals called him Robinson Crusoe or the Hermit of Pegwell. Despite being very stooped, James was said by the journalist to be "far and away the most contented and therefore the happiest man it has ever been my good fortune to meet."[80]

Ironically, for someone who had stated he would rather die than live in a workhouse, that is where James ended his days. He died at Thanet Union and his body was returned to St Laurence for burial on 13th July 1882.

Garden of Remembrance

The Garden of Remembrance for cremated remains was set up in 1981.[81] Initially people were invited to purchase shrubs as a memorial but in February 1990 the system was changed and people were allowed to place small stone tablets instead. Denys le Fevre donated the path to the garden in memory of his aunt in 1995.[82]

The first cremated remains were laid to rest in 1941 but there were no more until 1971 when there was one further case. Two more appeared in 1978. This pattern reflected the fact that burial was considered the norm for centuries.

---

[80] *Thanet Advertiser*, 27th February 1875
[81] CCA/DCb-E/F/St Lawrence in Thanet/ 48
[82] *The Beacon*, December 1995

World War One Roll of Honour

The following individuals were killed during the Great War and are remembered on our War Memorials or within the churchyard. Some were parishioners, some were men who died in the parish, others were men whose association with the parish went back further, perhaps to childhood. Honour is, however, due to all who served and it is important to remember that nobody came back unaffected. In addition to those named, there were some other deaths who were excluded at their family's own wishes.

The summary statistics are:

Year	Died	Army	Navy	Other
1914	3	1	2	
1915	21	18	3	
1916	22	19	2	1
1917	23	22		1
1918	34	28	4	2
1919	3	1	2	
1920	1	1		
Total	107	90	13	4

- Of the army deaths above, 59 lie buried in France and 17 in Belgium.
- Eight of the men died after the armistice of wounds or influenza.
- One casualty was a civilian killed in the explosion at Kent Munition Works in Faversham.
- Seven died in the Battle of the Somme, two on the first day.
- There are five sets of brothers and one father and son.
- Two of the Royal Naval deaths occurred on HMS Hampshire which was targeted because it was carrying Lord Kitchener.
- The first casualty was one of the 'Old Contemptibles' killed in the retreat from Mons.
- Seventeen of the men are also remembered on the memorial at Manston.

Name	Served	Age	Died
Corporal William Southee	Royal Field Artillery	28	27/08/1914
CPO Alfred Assiter	HMS Aboukir	37	22/09/1914
Able Sn William Emery	HMS Cape of Good Hope	32	01/11/1914
Stn PO John Henderson	HMS Formidable	24	01/01/1915
Petty Officer George West	HMS Formidable	30	01/01/1915

Name	Served	Age	Died
Corporal Oliver Smith	Yorkshire Regiment	28	07/01/1915
Private Frederick Phillpott	The Buffs (East Kent)	39	21/04/1915
Private Herbert Hopley	Canadian Highlanders	26	26/04/1915
Private Joseph Hambrose	The Buffs (East Kent)	34	03/05/1915
Private John Fordham	The Buffs (East Kent)	28	03/05/1915
Private William Mancktelow	City of London Regiment	19	25/05/1915
Corporal George Smith	Australian Imperial Forces	28	07/08/1915
Private Robert Lambert	The Buffs (East Kent)	26	11/08/1915
Corporal Alfred Pomeroy	City of London Yeomanry	25	08/09/1915
Private Henry Dadd	Royal Army Medical Corps	20	08/09/1915
Private Jacob Mancktelow	Winnipeg Grenadiers	25	25/09/1915
Private Edward Spain	Royal Sussex Regiment	21	25/09/1915
Private Charles Wheeler	The Buffs (East Kent)	19	26/09/1915
Private Harry Beer	The Buffs (East Kent)	18	29/09/1915
Private Cecil Packer	Coldstream Guards	27	08/10/1915
Private Edwin Laker	The Buffs (East Kent)	19	13/10/1915
Private William Petts	The Buffs (East Kent)	30	24/10/1915
Sergeant Albert Chantrell	Grenadier Guards	28	17/12/1915
Ldg Seaman Thomas Jervis	HMS Natal	23	30/12/1915
Private Charles Riches	South African Infantry	36	10/02/1916
Mr Alfred Southam	Kent Munition Works	34	02/04/1916
Private Sidney Woodward	Queens Royal West Surrey	26	30/04/1916
1st class stoker Frederick Bean	HMS Hampshire	24	05/06/1916
Ldg Tel John Bear	HMS Hampshire	22	05/06/1916
Private Ralph Gifford	Royal Field Artillery	23	01/07/1916
Corporal William Pomeroy	London Regiment	24	01/07/1916
Private Charles Terry	Royal Army Medical Corps	22	10/07/1916
Private Reginald Bingham	Gordon Highlanders	21	19/07/1916
2nd Lieut James Earl	Essex Regiment	24	26/07/1916
Gunner Albert Constable	Royal Field Artillery	26	30/07/1916
Private William Stokes	Royal Fusiliers	21	04/08/1916
Lance-Corp Henry Maxted	The Buffs (East Kent)	20	04/08/1916
Private Ernest White	The Buffs (East Kent)	37	07/08/1916
Private Clarence Reid	Royal Fusiliers London Reg.	21	16/08/1916
Rifleman Eric Layton	London Regiment	26	05/09/1916
Sergeant Arthur Culmer	The Buffs (East Kent)	20	07/10/1916
Private Harry Harrison	The Buffs (East Kent)	42	07/10/1916
Private William Gardner	The Buffs (East Kent)	38	07/10/1916
Private Cuthbert Winslow	Royal Warwickshire Reg.	23	16/11/1916
Private Thomas Lodge	The Buffs (East Kent)	21	18/11/1916

Name	Served	Age	Died
Lance-Corp Albert Willey	The Buffs (East Kent)	37	01/12/1916
Sergeant William Lawrence	21st Lancers	36	06/04/1917
Private Herbert Hammon	Royal Fusiliers London Reg.	32	10/04/1917
Albert Martin	Mercantile Marine	24	10/04/1917
Private Ernest Lodge	Tank Corps	20	20/04/1917
Private George Culver	Northumberland Fusiliers	31	26/04/1917
Lance-Corp Archibald Orders	Royal Fusiliers London Reg.	28	29/04/1917
Lance-Corp George Drage	Royal Fusiliers London Reg.	27	03/05/1917
Private William Page	Queens Royal West Kent	21	03/05/1917
Trooper James Neeves	Household Battalion	26	03/05/1917
Private Ernest Burchett	Queens Royal West Surrey	31	07/06/1917
Private James Curtis	Royal Berkshire Regiment	24	10/06/1917
Private Sidney Spratt	Royal Army Service Corps	34	28/06/1917
Lance-Corp George Brockman	The Buffs (East Kent)	24	04/07/1917
Private Charles Harty	Hertfordshire Regiment	36	31/07/1917
Captain Arthur Sherren	The Buffs (East Kent)	38	03/08/1917
Gunner William Smith	Royal Garrison Artillery	23	05/08/1917
Gunner John Radford	Royal Field Artillery	20	07/09/1917
Private Herbert Curtiss	The Buffs (East Kent)	18	04/10/1917
Private William Ellen	The Buffs (East Kent)	18	12/10/1917
Driver John Wood	Royal Field Artillery	33	14/10/1917
Private William Tompsett	Lancashire Fusiliers	20	22/10/1917
Private George Eve	The Buffs (East Kent)	22	30/11/1917
Private Walter Wilmoth	Sherwood Foresters	30	01/12/1917
Private Leonard Mirams	Lancashire Fusiliers	19	10/01/1918
Private Wilfred Beer	The Buffs (East Kent)	25	21/03/1918
Private Frank Smith	The Buffs (East Kent)	29	21/03/1918
Private Reginald Clark	Royal Fusiliers London Reg.	26	23/03/1918
Private Herbert Howland	The Buffs (East Kent)	21	23/03/1918
Private Robert Nixon	13th Batn Canadian Infantry	38	23/03/1918
Sapper Samuel Woodhall	Royal Engineers	39	27/03/1918
Gunner Christopher Stanner	Royal Horse Artillery	24	04/04/1918
Private Britton Wilkinson	Coldstream Guards	32	18/04/1918
Private Charles Clark	The Middlesex Reguiment	18	24/04/1918
Signaller Harold Bear	HMS Submarine Group 12	21	06/05/1918
Edward Southam	Mercantile Marine	61	03/07/1918
Sapper Arthur Dennett	Royal Engineers	39	19/07/1918
Private Arthur Petley	Sherwood Foresters	24	21/07/1918
Private Percy Boskett	Machine Gun Corp	30	26/07/1918
Sapper Harry Martin	Royal Engineers	30	27/07/1918

Name	Served	Age	Died
Sapper Walter Goodwin	Royal Engineers	35	29/07/1918
Private Cyril Grainger	The Buffs (East Kent)	22	30/07/1918
Private Stephen Drayson	Royal Fusiliers	25	31/08/1918
Private Charles Pittock	Lincolnshire Regiment	21	05/09/1918
Private Ernest Bootes	London Regiment	20	08/09/1918
Private Walter Diddams	The Buffs (East Kent)	25	21/09/1918
Driver George Hammond	Royal Field Artillery	29	26/09/1918
Private Sidney Darby	Sherwood Foresters	28	05/10/1918
Private John Debling	Sherwood Foresters	28	07/10/1918
Lance-Corp William Howland	Royal Engineers	25	09/10/1918
Private Ernest Studham	Royal Fusiliers	36	20/10/1918
S.R.A Percy Petley	HMS Pembroke	37	23/10/1918
Private Henry Southey	Northamptonshire Regiment	37	26/10/1918
Private Austin Pegden	Northamptonshire Regiment	35	29/10/1918
3rd Acting Maj Sidney Pointer	Royal Flying Corps	28	13/11/1918
Corporal William Bruce	The Buffs (East Kent)	31	21/11/1918
Ldg Seaman George Baker	HMS Ursa	33	29/11/1918
Stoker Edward Lincoln	HMS Endeavour	43	12/12/1918
3rd Hand Henry Goldring	H M Armed Smack, Ivanhoe	31	09/01/1919
Able Seaman William Tottman	HMS Indomitable	33	01/04/1919
Staff Sgt Ernest Beer	Royal Army Service Corps	41	04/05/1919
Captain Hugh Sherren	Royal Army Medical Corps	37	28/02/1920

World War Two Roll of Honour

According to the Parish Magazine, these were the parishioners killed on active service during the war.

1. *William John Farley*

Just 18, he was an Ordinary Seaman on HMS Ajax. The ship was lost in the Battle of River Plate off Argentina on December 13th 1939. In tribute to him as the first victim of the battle on that ship, a road was built in Ajax, Ontario and named Farley Court and in 2000 a tree was planted in his honour.

2. *Victor Thomas Church*

A Private in the Buffs, 21 year old Victor was killed as part of the British Expeditionary Force in 1940. His body was not recovered so his exact date of death is unknown but he was probably lost in the retreat to Dunkirk and the confusion on the beaches.

3. *John Denis Harold Cunningham*

Aged 21, Denis (as he was known) served in the RAF Volunteer Reserve. On 8th April 1941, he was pilot on a de Havilland Mosquito which was participating in a Bomber Command raid over Yugoslavia. The plane disappeared with all crew killed. He is buried in the St Lawrence section of Ramsgate Cemetery. Denis had been a chorister and sang in the Ramsgate Pageant of 1934 and he later became a server.

4. *Sidney Griggs*

Sidney was an Able Seaman on HMS Juno which was attacked by Italian aircraft on its return to Malta in April 1941 as it prepared to join the liberation of Crete. Another attack saw the ship sink in just 97 seconds with the loss of over a hundred crew. Sidney, was 25 when he died.

5. *Stephen Robert Castle*

A 17-year old Mess Room Boy, he was serving with the Merchant Navy on S.S. Cortes when it was torpedoed by a German U-boat in the early hours of 26th September 1941. There were no survivors.

6. *Albert George Isaacs*

Buried in the St Lawrence section of Ramsgate Cemetery, he served with the Heavy Anti-Aircraft Artillery in Blantyreferme, just south of Glasgow. A married man, he was 39 when he died.

7. *Leslie Cotton*

Leslie was an air gunner in RAF Volunteer Reserve 78 Squadron. He was on board a flight from RAF Breighton in Yorkshire for Monchengladbach when the aircraft developed problems and crashed near Wisbech with the loss of all seven men on board. His body was brought back for burial in our churchyard alongside his grandparents, John and Fanny Darby. He was 37.

8. *Glynne Parsons*

A Welshman by birth, he attended Chatham House School and sang in the choir before becoming a server. He was confirmed at St Laurence in 1936. From school, he went on to study at Guy's Hospital though he was at King's when he was called up. He served as a Lieutenant with the South Wales Borderers and died of wounds in Italy in 1943 aged 21. A stained glass window in his honour was dedicated on 8th March 1956 at Holy Trinity, Corris, Merionethshire.

9. *Donald Frederick Butler*

A Sergeant in the RAF, he was on an Avro Lancaster which took part in a Bomber Command raid on Berlin on 16th December 1943. The mission was accomplished successfully and the aircraft was returning home when it was shot down. The crew ditched in the North Sea and only one person was recovered. Donald was 19 at the time.

10. *Reginald Norman Quick*

A Leading Seaman on HMS Janus, he was killed aged 23 when the ship was hit off Anzio in January 1944. The ship had been involved in landing troops to liberate Italy. He had been intending to train for the ministry at the end of the war and a Communion set was given in his memory.

11. *Nigel Coombes*

A 31 year old Sergeant, he was serving with the Royal Canadian Armoured Corps at the time of his death on 26th February 1945. They were engaged in the brutal fighting to liberate Groesbeek in the Netherlands.

12. *Rodney Hawkins*

Son of William or Bill Hawkins, the schoolmaster and regular sidesman, he was a gunner with the Royal Artillery. He died on 20th July 1945 aged 26 and is buried in our churchyard.

Although not a parishioner at the time of his death, it would be appropriate to add Michael Cowland-Cooper, son of the vicar at the start of the war who was killed on 19th October 1944 when instructing his men about use of hand grenades. Both him and his brother appear in the list of church members published in the November 1944 Parish

Magazine as serving, the news of his death being received after the parish magazine went to print.

David, Michael and Patience Cowland-Cooper on the vicarage lawn.

Roll of Honour

We print below our list of men and women who are away from their homes in the service of their country. They are each mentioned by name on one of the Sundays in the month. They are also remembered at the altar on the mornings of the week following. We give this list in the hope that:

(1) You will help us with any necessary corrections;

(2) You will add to our list those who are dear to you, if they are not already there;

(3) You will join in the family prayers on Sunday at Evensong, and/or at the altar during the week.

The Men and Women from our Church and Parish who are serving in the Forces

Esther Allan
Joseph Barnes
Sydney Barnes
Ruth Bolton
George Bolton
Albert Boxole
Frederick Boyes
Cyril Boyes
Royston Burton
Horace Burton
Sydney Bushell
Peter Britton
Alfred Brenchley
Frank Carthew
Stephen Castle
Alfred Church
Lionel Clack
Cyril Clark
William Clark
Eileen Claw
John Claw
Alan Claw
Frank Coombes
Nigel Coombes
David Cowland Cooper
Michael Cowland Cooper
Vera Cunningham
Sheila Cunningham
Roy Curtis
Nora Dearlove
Olive Dennis
Noel Edis
Leonard Foord
Harold Frost
Bertram Futter
Stanley Gee
Henry Griggs
William Griggs
Leslie Griggs
Charles Hall
Wilfred Harris
Rodney Hawkins
Peter Henzell-Thomas
Harold Horton
Victor Horton
Charles Horton
Harry Hurst
Walter Hurst
Frank Inge
William Jarvis
Francis Jennings
Vyvyan Knivett
Phyllis Laming
Harold Lott
William Madgewick
Sidney Maple
Gladys Marsh
Charles Mayhew
Frank Mayhew
Michael Mayhew
Leslie Mettam
David Miles
Alfred Miller
Fred Morecroft
Jessie Munday
Ralph Neat
Cyril Nichols
Arthur Nichols
Freda Page
Dennis Parkinson
Frederick Philpott
Ernest Pidduck
Cecil Pittock
Frederick Pitcher
Frank Pitcher
Reginald Pitcher
Douglas Pointer
Leslie Pointer
Doreen Pointer
Edwin Purkess
Arthur Purkess
Leslie Quick
Ronald Quick
Douglas Quick
Henry Simmonds
Ralph Stanley
Cyril Stanner
Kenneth Startup
Eric Startup
Walter Taylor
Richard Tombs
Nancy Tombs
Albert Turner
Ronald Warner
John Watler
Harold Wells
Marjorie White
John Wright

The Church at Rest
Victor Church
Robert Castle
Dennis Cunningham
William Farley
George Isaacs
Glynne Parsons
Reginald Quick
Donald Butler
Sidney Griggs

St Laurence and St Lawrence

Today there is a clear tradition of spelling the name of the church with a "u" as Laurence and the name of the village with a "w" as Lawrence and the question is often asked why this should be so.

There is no doubt that the church was founded as St Laurence because it was named after the Roman saint of that name and Latin has no "w." Medieval documents which refer to people living in the vicinity therefore use this spelling, for example, John of St Laurence was witness to a land deal in 1272 and Ralph of St Laurence made a contract regarding land in Chislet in 1300. [83]

The rise of English in the fifteenth century saw the Anglicisation of words but this took many years. Tudor books and parliamentary rolls invariably use laues where we would use laws. Lawrence was the English way of spelling the Latin Laurence and as time went by, use of the English form became a sign of patriotism and anti-Roman sentiment.

However, there is no clear date of any change and this is largely due to the lack of any concept of right and wrong spelling in the days before Dr Johnson produced his dictionary in 1755. William Shakespeare, undoubtedly one of the most literate men of any age, variously wrote his surname as Shakspeare, Shakspere and Shaksper and in our own parish records we see variations of names like Maxted and Pullen.

Authors have varied in the way they have spelt the name of the church. Those who have used the "u" include:

      Richard Kilburn, *A topographie or survey of the county of Kent* (1659)

      John Harris, *The History of Kent* (1715)

      John Dart, *The history and antiquities of the cathedral church of Canterbury* (1726)

      John Walker, *The Itinerant* (1799)

Those using the "w" include:

      Andrew Ducarel, *A repertory of the endowments of vicarages in the Diocese of Canterbury* (1763)

      Samuel Palmer, *The Nonconformist's Memorial* (1777)

      John Boys, *A general view of the Agriculture of the County of Kent* (1796)

      Joseph Hall, *New Ramsgate and Margate Guide* (1792)

John Lewis in his *The History and Antiquities of the Isle of Tenet* (1723) speaks of the church of St Laurence on p.123 but then lists the monuments of the same on p95 of the appendix where he writes church of St Lawrence.

Similarly and surprisingly, Charles Cotton who wrote the famous *History and Antiquities of the Parish of St Laurence* in 1895, published a leaflet in 1900 entitled *St Lawrence Church, Isle of Thanet* which was taken from his article in *Archaeologia Cantiana*

---

[83] George Turner, Herbert Salter (ed.) The Register of St Augustine's Abbey, Canterbury, commonly called the Black Book (London, 1915), pp.129, 605

vol 24. He offered no explanation for his change of spelling.

In the churchwarden's accounts, it can be seen that "u" was used in 1590, 1633, 1640, 1648, 1704 and "w" in 1611, 1627, 1635, 1690, 1698, 1705, 1727. In 1703, one churchwarden used "u" and the other "w." In early seventeenth century accounts, the spelling Larence also appears and in 1721 it was Larancs in January but Lawrence in July. In the vestry books, it is "u" except for 1756, 1758, 1777 and 1794 when it is "w." Amongst the parish registers it is Laurence for those starting in 1560, 1754, 1813, 1830 and 1882 but Lawrence for those starting in 1843, 1867 and 1890.

Until 1880, headed paper used by the clergy showed the title as vicar of St Lawrence. Thereafter, they used paper which read vicar of St Laurence but the Parochial Church Council which began in 1921 chose to have Parish of St Lawrence on theirs.

The church silver which is inscribed shows Lawrence being used in 1721, 1742, 1833 and 1890 but Laurence in 1798 and 1840.

In newspapers, articles about the church using "u" appeared in 1788 and 1805 whilst articles using "w" were published in 1809, 1821, 1824, 1845, 1856, 1858, 1862, 1875 and 1889. Meanwhile, articles on the village spelt with a "u" appeared in 1783, 1848 and 1872. The local press consistently used St Lawrence for the church from their inception in the mid Victorian period through to the 1920s. They reported that Charles Cowland-Cooper became vicar of St Lawrence in 1927 but that he left the church of St Laurence in 1942. Since that time, the "u" form has been used.

In parliamentary acts, it is St Laurence parish in 1785, 1796, 1827 and 1835 but St Lawrence in 1838, 1875, 1878 and 1884.

The parish yearbooks which began in 1880 were Laurence until 1888-9, Lawrence from 1889-90 to 1893-4 (although the Parish Magazine was Laurence), Laurence in 1894-5 and 1895-6, Lawrence in 1896-7 and 1897-8 and thereafter Laurence.

Amongst the many wills made by parishioners, Valentine Holt in 1618 used "u" whilst John Fairman in 1603 and Thomas Philpot in 1658 used "w". John Tickner in 1646 used both spellings in the same document.

Canterbury Cathedral Archives uses St Lawrence for all parish records even though the Diocese of Canterbury recognises it as being St Laurence.

The church schools were originally named St Lawrence when they were built 1840-50 but this was changed in to Laurence in 1985 when they were amalgamated into one new junior school. The reason given was to stress their link to the church although Lawrence had been used in the nineteenth century because the church used this spelling at the time.

These instances serve to underline the differences that have occurred over the years. The variation today is not a result of mis-spelling but reflects the development of English language and changing attitudes to the church's Roman Catholic origins.

Vital Statistics

Parish registers for the church commence in 1560. The table below shows the number of baptisms, marriages and burials performed between 1561 and 2010 at St Laurence church. Although burials stopped in the churchyard, clergy were still involved in taking funerals: 1421 from 1981-1990, 998 from 1991-2000 and 792 from 2001 to 2010 though these cover the whole parish including Newington, Cliffsend and Manston. The rate of baptisms today is equivalent to those at the end of the seventeenth century when the population was about 900 compared to over 6,500 today.[84] Marriages have declined since the 1994 Marriage Act authorised a wider range of authorised venues and, despite a broadening of the rules governing marriage, are now on a level with the mid eighteenth century when the population was about 2000. The table otherwise shows increases in line with population growth and decreases when new parishes have been created, such as St George's in 1827, Holy Trinity 1845, St Luke 1875. It is impossible to know the number of baptisms, marriages and burials in the medieval period but it would be reasonable to suppose that in total, since 1275, there have been around 35,000 baptisms, 10,500 marriages and 25,000 burials.

Decade	*Baptisms*	*Marriages*	*Burials*	*Decade*	*Baptisms*	*Marriages*	*Burials*
1561-70	229	68	191	1791-00	1365	358	1109
1571-80	294	99	253	1801-10	2038	518	1578
1581-90	326	84	206	1811-20	2232	587	1341
1591-00	301	97	245	1821-30	1868	475	1297
1601-10	351	91	238	1831-40	735	199	633
1611-20	388	122	254	1841-50	693	244	592
1621-30	431	105	328	1851-60	555	243	701
1631-40	484	133	287	1861-70	528	197	760
1641-50	519	111	263	1871-80	527	210	1132
1651-60	537	82	202	1881-90	455	158	1019
1661-70	569	124	372	1891-00	549	208	726
1671-80	640	161	406	1901-10	494	246	562
1681-90	646	136	454	1911-20	591	210	401
1691-00	614	137	328	1921-30	710	240	109
1701-10	582	134	394	1931-40	710	278	116
1711-20	673	95	506	1941-50	612	249	71
1721-30	665	126	532	1951-60	756	248	51

---

[84] *Parish Profile, 2003*. Cliffsend had 1800, Newington 6650, Manston 500 plus 160 RAF creating a parish population of around 15,450

Decade	Baptisms	Marriages	Burials	Decade	Baptisms	Marriages	Burials
1731-40	732	126	551	1961-70	923	402	25
1741-50	751	116	565	1971-80	591	347	22
1751-60	685	181	592	1981-90	1080	394	
1761-70	751	204	702	1991-00	531	274	
1771-80	740	224	663	2000-10	307	141	
1781-90	862	255	755	Total	31620	9437	21532

It is interesting to note the changing patterns of weddings as evidenced in the charts overleaf. In the sixteenth and seventeenth century, most marriages either took place just before the harvest or around November by which time the crop had been sold, wages paid and young men had money in their pockets. A ban on sexual intercourse during Lent and Advent which was of medieval origin meant weddings in February, March and December were virtually non-existent. There were few weddings in May as this was the peak of the mackerel fishing season and late September and October saw similarly low numbers due to the herrings. As the parish became more economically diverse and the medieval prohibition faded, the seasonality changed and weddings became more evenly spread throughout the year. The current pattern of the bulk of weddings taking place in the summer, is of relatively recent origin. In the first half of the twentieth century, Christmas and Boxing Day were both extremely popular with up to a fifth of weddings taking place on these two days, most likely to the chagrin of the vicar's family.

Fees have always been charged for marriages and burials but not for baptism which is a sacrament. However, the 1783 Stamp Act introduced a charge of 3d to have a baptism entered into the register. Previously, baptism had ordinarily taken place on the first Sunday after birth but after 1783, many couples delayed having their children baptised for six to eight weeks, a period which they obviously felt was enough to see whether the baby was likely to survive. For a poor family who knew they might face the cost of a funeral for their infant, the 3d registration fee was something they could save and use the money toward a shroud.

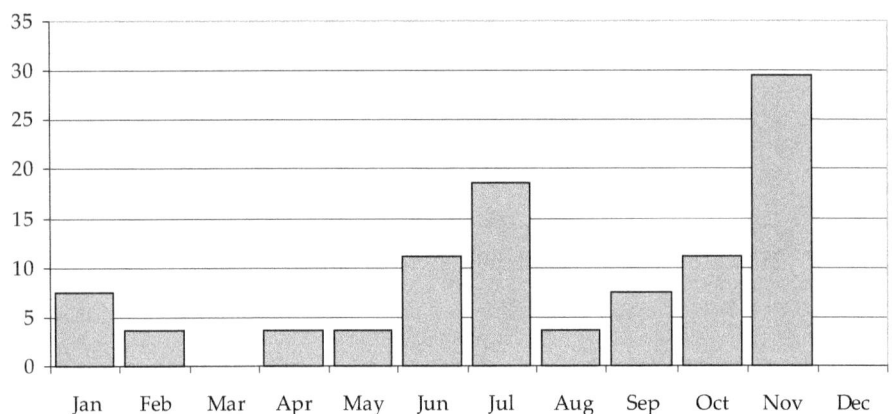

1590s

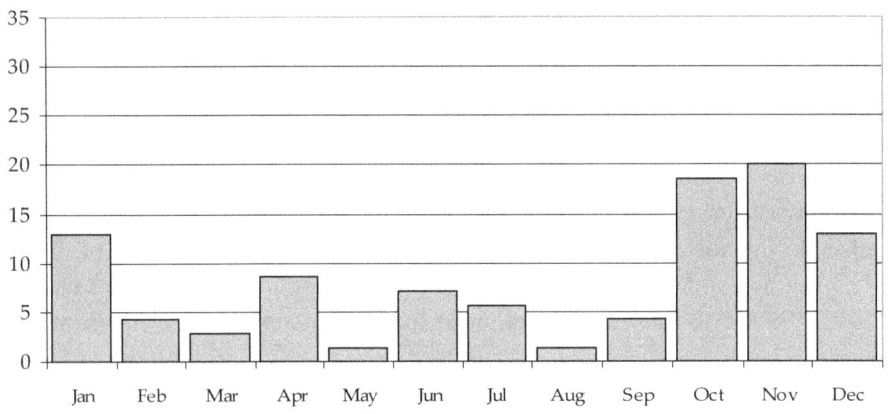

1690s

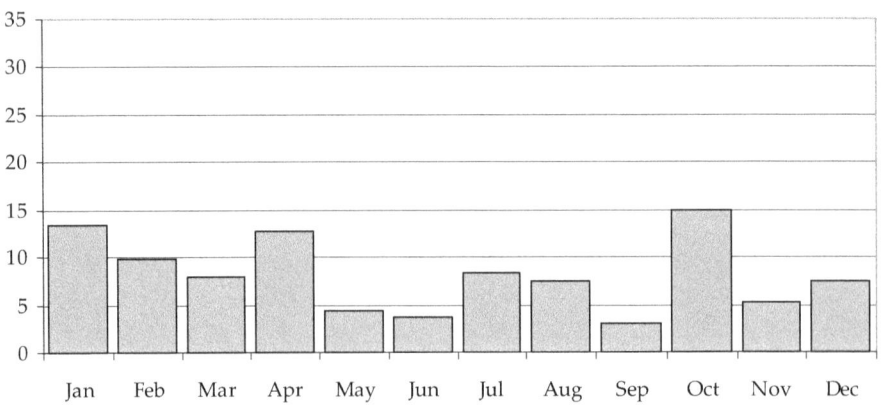

1770s

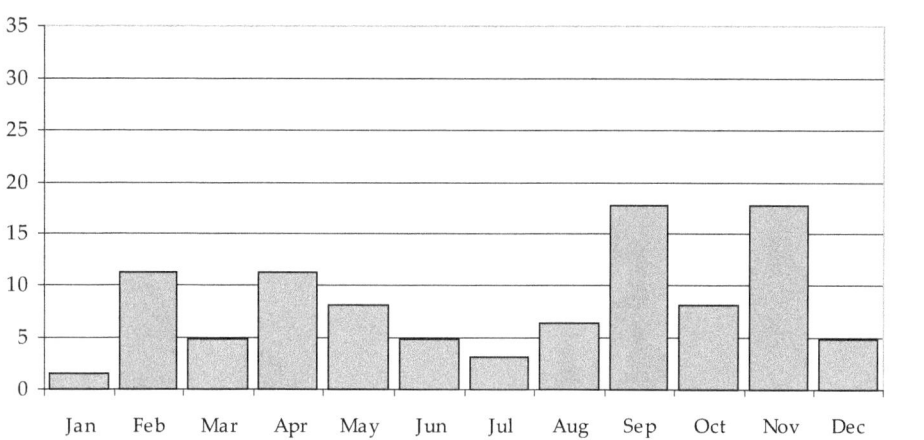

1870s

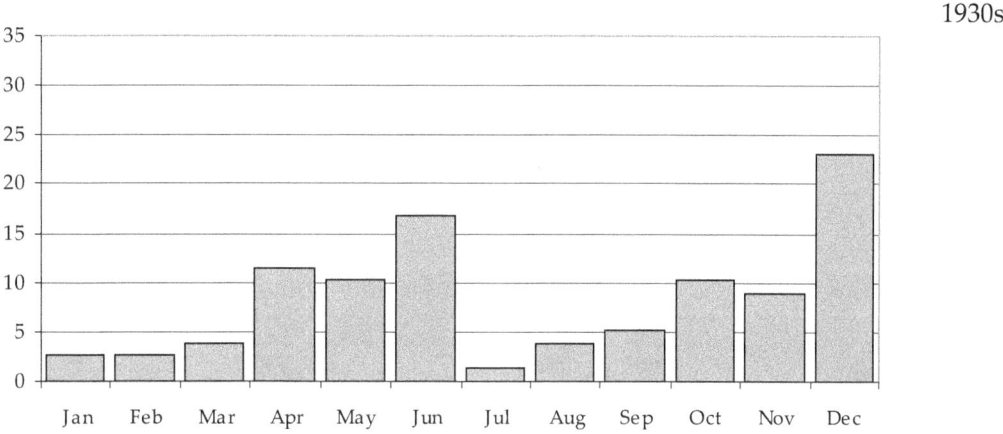

1930s

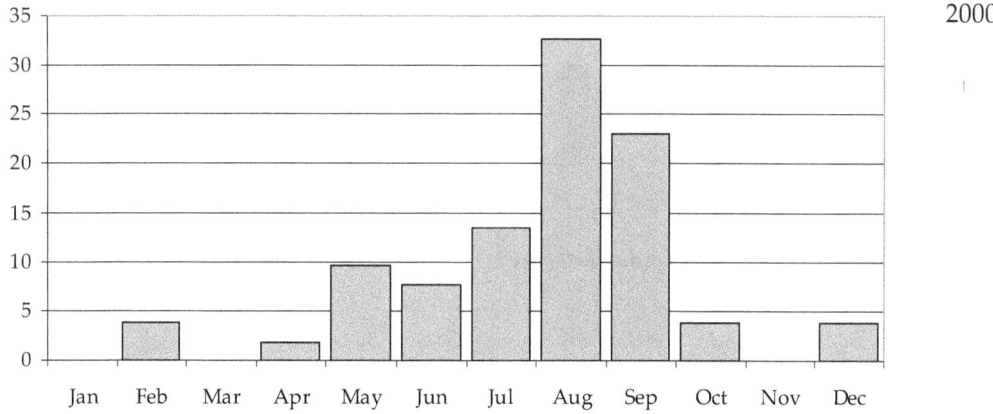

2000s

Floor Plans

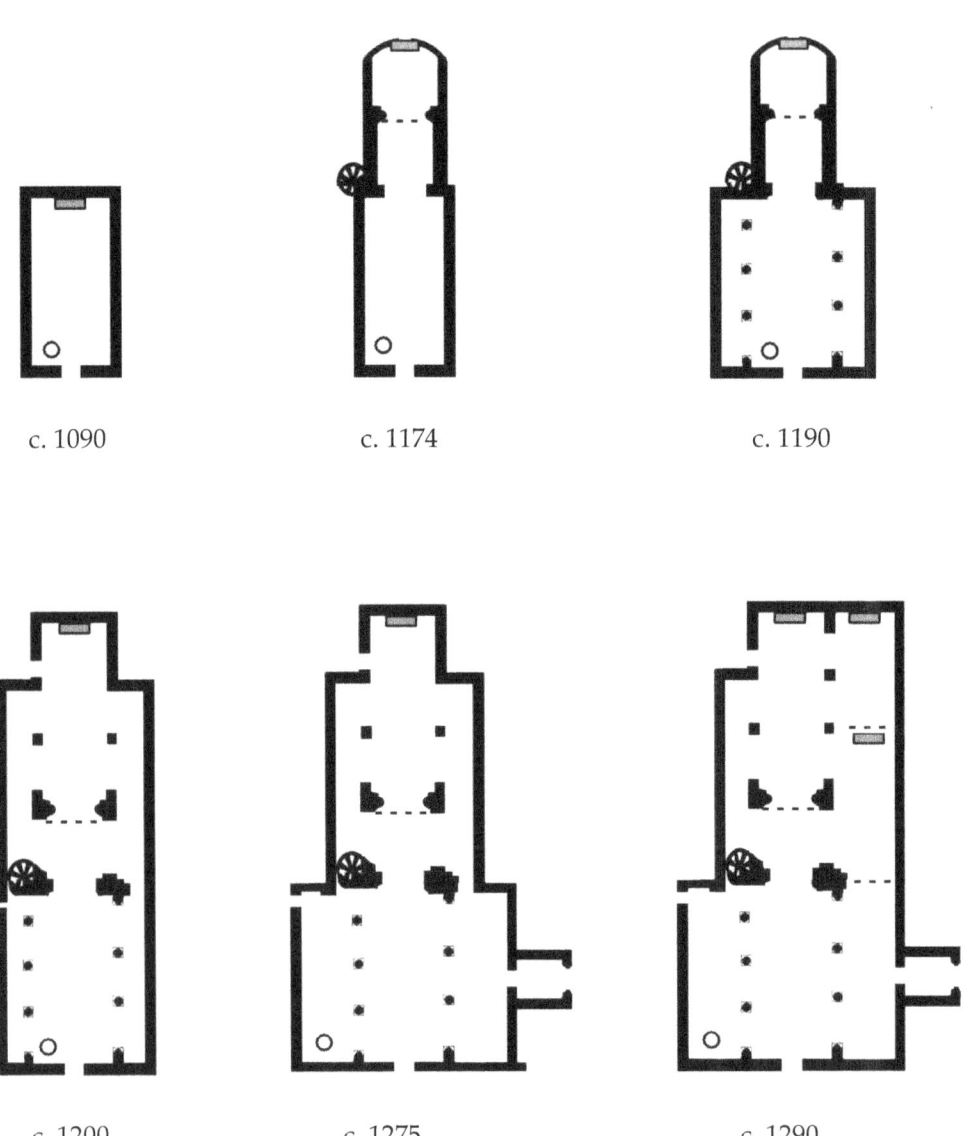

430

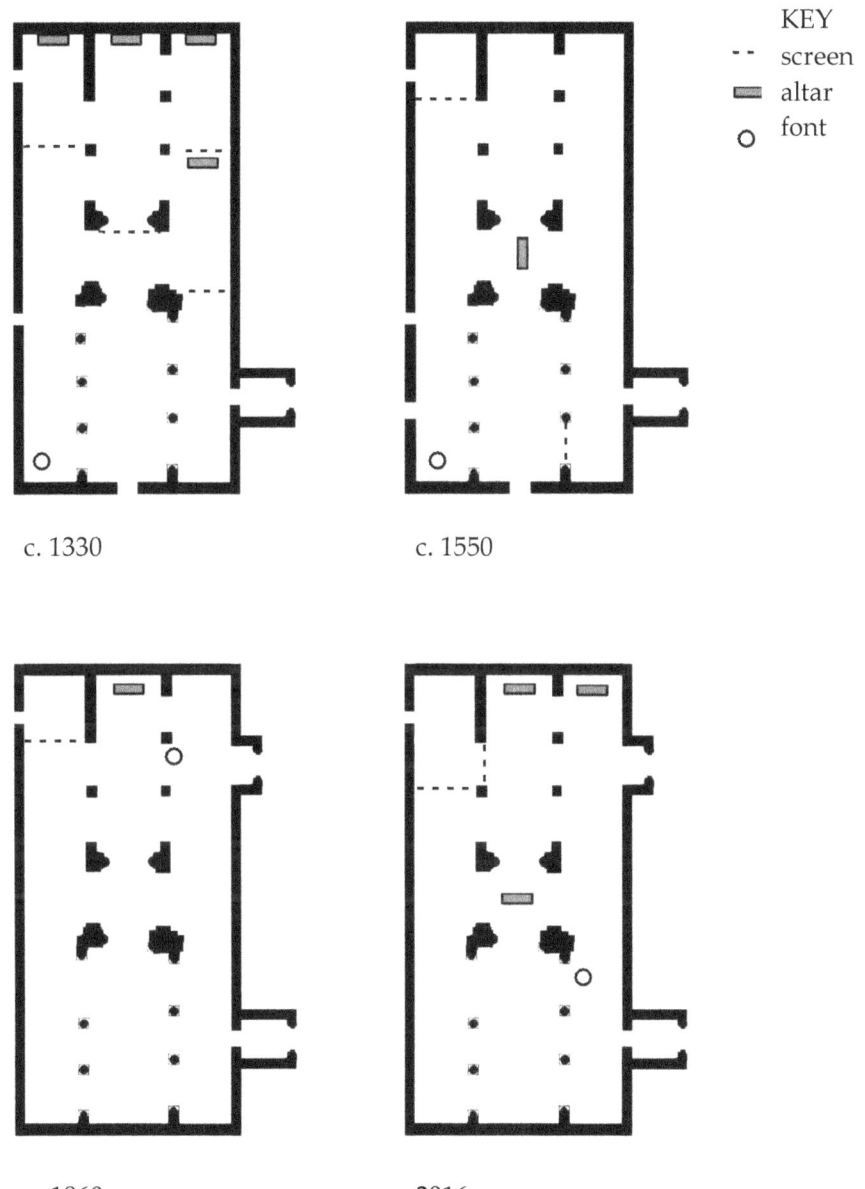

Hymns about the Church

Over the years, at least five hymns have been written in honour of St Laurence and this parish church. They include:

Within thy sacred portals, 1890

words   Ada Fowler
tune   Passion Chorale (*O sacred head surrounded*) or Aurelia (*The Church's one foundation*)

Within thy sacred portals
Oft have my footsteps strayed
Along the solemn transper
Where honoured dead are laid
Where through some painted window
Of saint or angel bright
Like jewels rare, lie scattered
The rays of heavenly light.

As slow the twilight gathers
On wall and oaken screens,
I see the past unfolding
Its long forgotten scenes.
I see the monks of Minster
Who loved thy walls so well
And sweet and clear o'er many years
I hear the Vesper bell

Through the low porch approaching
Come village maid and lad
And knight with stately lady
In fur and velvet clad.
From cottage and from manor
They gather day by day
Tis meet and right ere night
To rest awhile and pray

Oh may their echoing voices
Float o'er the tide of time
And raise with ours the anthem
Of harmony sublime
And may the lingering memories
Of all thy glorious past
Speak peace and love from Heaven
Where'er our lot is cast

And if our faith should falter
Or fear our heart appals
Oh teach us solemn lessons
By thine unshaken walls
As through thy rich hued windows
So may God's love divine
Like halos bright of Heaven
Through us His servants shine

Hymn of St Laurence, 1934

words   unknown.
tune   Melita (*Eternal Father, strong to save*)

Ye watchers and ye holy ones
Bright seraphs, cherubim and thrones
Raise the glad strain, Alleluia!
Alleluia!
Cry out dominions, princedoms, powers
Virtues, archangels, angel's choirs

For Laurence who with jest could lie
On fiery bed and smiling die
Christ we laud Thee, Alleluia!
Alleluia!
Pray we, that girt by holy faith
We too may smile thro' pain and death

For this Thy sacred house we raise, 1962

words   Robert Todd
tune   Ar hyd y nos (*All through the night*)

For this Thy sacred house we raise
Lord God of Hosts
Our thankful hearts in hymn of praise
Lord God of Hosts
Nine hundred years thy children here
Have brought before Thee joy and care
Gladness, sorrow, hope and fear
Lord God of Hosts

This ancient building bears the scars
Lord God of Hosts
Of ravages of time and wars
Lord God of Hosts
For grace to glory to maintain
For strength to labour in Thy name
We will not turn to Thee in vain
Lord God of Hosts

We pray and listen for Thy voice
Most Holy One
For spiritual food our souls rejoice
Through Thy dear Son
No eye hath seen Thee, Blessed Lord
But those of faith heard Thy word
And with saints in Heaven adored
Lord God of Hosts

All glory to the Father Be
And to the Son
With Holy Ghost, Blest Trinity
The Three in One
Forgive us sinners we implore
Thy sevenfold gifts upon us pour
That we may love Thee more and more
Lord God of Hosts

Thanks be to Thee, O God most holy, 1951

words   Lancelot Sykes
tune   Picardy (*Let all mortal flesh*)

Thanks be to Thee, O God most holy,
For the life of blessed Laurence;
Who served Thee a deacon lowly
Christian faith was then an offence,
Told the soldiers he would wholly
Trust in God instead of man.

When they asked him for the treasure
Wanting silver, jewels and gold
He stood firm ignoring the pressure
Sold it to help poor, sick and old,
Said to them in church, this is the true treasure
Pointing at the people there.

Laurence knew in his last hour,
He was chosen for God's blessing;
As the flames his body devoured
Died at peace, Our Lord confessing
Knowing neither death nor earthly power
Can take us away from God's love.

Give us grace as children of light
To walk boldly, not in fear
Reaching out to those mired in night
Showing them that God is here.
Strengthen us O God, to do whatever's right
And to always worship Thee.

This is our festal day, 2009

words   Alex Hallier
tune   Harewood (*Christ is our corner stone*)

This is our festal day
In praise of Him we sing
And as we gather here
Our thanks and love we bring

To Laurence, martyr for our Lord
Who died in God's pure holy word.
He loved the sick and poor
Who had no power or might

The wretched, sick, outcast
And those who had no right
But all he had to these he gave
But his own life he would not save

Christ's word he followed true
With every act and breath
His faith stood firm and strong
He loved Christ to the death

God grant that we if called the same
Will follow in His martyred name
So while we worship now
Our Christian faith to share

God grant that we will all
Show others that we care
And bless our saints to whom we come
In God the Father, Spirit, Son

Parish Magazine

The parish magazine was introduced by the Reverend Montague Fowler in 1890. He had produced a Parish Paper in December 1889 just over a month after his arrival in the parish. The magazine has been published every month since then barring two years in the Second World War when the paper shortage prohibited its production, July and August 1959 when the printers were on strike and from March to September 2001 when no editor was available.

Over the years, the size, price, format and content of the magazine has changed. The earliest magazines were simply text. By 1900, the magazine had a picture of the church on its cover. In the 1930s, the Reverend Charles Cowland-Cooper invited an artist friend of his, Thomas Noyes-Lewis to prepare a series of images which could be used for the covers and these continued in use until 1961. The Noyes-Lewis covers were based upon historical reconstructions of how the church would have looked in centuries past and were supplemented by sketches made by Charles Armstrong and the vicar himself.

In January 1951 the magazine's name was changed to *The Beacon* and the size altered from crown quarto to A5. The vicar of the time, John Roundhill, explained the reasons for the new name:

> When St Laurence church was first built the Isle of Thanet was indeed the Isle of Beacons. Beacons were lit to call the men of Kent to action to defend their freedom. Beacons were lit on high ground. You will have noticed that St Laurence is on high ground towering over all Ramsgate. More than many parish magazines it reflects the life and activity of the parish. The greater the intensity of heat within the beacon, the greater is likely to be the range of light. The hotter it is inside the further it reaches outside.
>
> We believe that The Beacon is an apt description of the Church. It has held up the torch of Christian faith and practice in this part of Thanet for nearly nine hundred years. The warmth and radiance with which it burns depends upon the worshippers in each generation. What of our generation? How brightly does the beacon radiate the love and power of God? What is its candle power? Are you adding or with-holding your candle power? We can only reflect the light and power of God if we first of all receive it from him. If we worship Him we shall offer ourselves to Him and that means consecration. He will then use us to win others to His service and fellowship.

Aside from the war years, the parish magazine had an inset, a magazine within. Initially this was the *Church Monthly* but in 1900 that changed to *Home Words*. These insets were professionally produced at national level and provided a range of material such as short stories, recipes, church news, poems, gardening advice, puzzles and educational features on matters of doctrine, missionary activity, nature study and science. *Church Monthly*, for example, included articles about how electricity worked and the development of air travel. Often the insets were more extensive than the parish magazine. In 1890, the magazine cost 2d and that was made up of four pages about St Laurence and Manston plus twenty-four pages of *Church Monthly*. In 1944, the magazine still cost 2d but was just four pages about the parish, three pages of advertisements and a cover.

After the war, the inset was *The Symbol*, a Tractarian offering with features on hymns, the sacraments and points of church law as well as recipes and a crossword. From 1950 to 1969, the inset was *The Window*, a regular eight pages of news about the wider church with an answers to correspondents section. This was clearly not aimed at the family like the earlier insets but was aimed at what might be termed the thinking Christian. The responses to questions were more forthright than would be seen today. In June 1953, a woman who complained that she was not allowed to receive Holy Communion because she was divorced even though it was her husband who had left her for another woman was told: "I hope you will try to understand what defects in your own character and behaviour may have contributed to your husband's unfaithfulness. There must have been something you could have done that you failed to do." Another writer who objected to her vicar saying the congregation should bow to the altar which she thought was idolatrous was told: "Instead of trying to instruct your vicar, you should have requested him to instruct you. I note that whilst he merely advised his people, you took up a much less tolerant attitude and this puts you completely in the wrong." Fairly typical was the exchange below from January 1951:

> Q- It has been propounded to me that the Trinity is a false doctrine and is not found in the Bible. Could you please enlighten me?
> A. Why don't you enlighten yourself by reading the Bible? Start with St John's gospel and the Acts of the Apostles and if you have any difficulties I shall be delighted to deal with them for you. Your request as it stands is a lazy one which I feel I should be wrong to accede to. If you care about the answer you will make the effort I suggest and if you don't nothing I could say would be likely to influence you

With regard circulation, the parish magazine started off at around 240 copies a month. Within a decade, that had grown to around 350. In the 1950s, the average was around 530 sales a month. The publicity of the 1962 anniversary saw circulation boom to a record 800 but by the 1980s sales were just over 620. By 2003, circulation had dropped to 400. Today, the monthly circulation is nearer 350.

The method of production has varied across the years. Until 1976 the magazine was printed but rising costs meant that it was then typed and duplicated. In 1991 it changed to a photocopied work which enabled the use of external material as well as the introduction of a lot more humorous items and also controversial ones such as the following from April 2000.

> Heavenly Father, we come before you today to ask Your forgiveness and to seek Your direction and guidance. We know Your Word says, "Woe to those who call evil good,," but that is exactly what we have done. We have lost our spiritual equilibrium and reversed our values. We confess:
>
> We have ridiculed the absolute truth of Your Word and called it pluralism.
>
> We have worshipped other gods and called it multiculturalism.
>
> We have endorsed perversion and called it alternative lifestyle.
>
> We have exploited the poor and called it the lottery.
>
> We have rewarded laziness and called it welfare.
>
> We have killed our unborn and called it choice.
>
> We have shot abortionists and called it justifiable.
>
> We have neglected to discipline our children and called it building self-esteem.
>
> We have abused power and called it politics.
>
> We have coveted our neighbour's possessions and called it ambition.
>
> We have polluted the air with profanity and pornography and called it freedom of expression.
>
> We have ridiculed the time-honoured values of our forefathers and called it enlightenment.
>
> Search us, Oh God, and know our hearts today; cleanse us from every sin and set us free.[85]

Since 2002 it has been word processed using Publisher.

Sadly, almost all the early issues of the parish magazine have been lost. There are copies of 1891-2 and 1900-3 but almost nothing otherwise until 1943.[86] To give an idea of past magazines, one has been reproduced in full (January 1891) on the following pages

---

[85] The prayer of Pastor Joe Wright before the Kansas House of Representatives on January 23, 1996.
[86] If anyone has copies of any of the missing volumes, the church would be pleased to receive copies, even as a loan so they can be photocopied.

together with the black edged cover which followed the death of Queen Victoria, extracts of *Home Words* and *Church Monthly*, some advertising from 1927, a staff list from 1930 and the vicar's letters which appeared at the outset of the Second World War and on the occasion of VE Day. Owing to the frailty of the originals and the coloured papers used, the quality is imperfect but the images represent a unique chance to see these rare works.

St. Laurence-in-Thanet.

1062   1930

Clergy : Rev. C. COWLAND COOPER, M.A., Hon. C.F. (Vicar).
Hon. Lay Readers : *Mr. H. Stead, *Mr. Martin-Martin, *Mr. W. T. Layton.
Churchwardens : *Mr. E. W. Barnes, *Mr. F. Harris, *Mr. F. Bax (*St. Catherine's*).
Deaconess : Miss H. Feild.
Organist : Miss S. Wilkinson, A.R.C.O., L.T.C.L. (22, Hollicondane Road).
Verger : Mr. A. Startup (Queen's Avenue, Newington).
Parish Treasurer : *Mr. E. Spencer-Payne (4. Chapel Place)
Hon. Secretary : *Mr. C. H. D'Eath, 72, Southwood Road.
Diocesan Representatives : *Mrs. A. Cowland Cooper, *Mr. A. Thompson.
Deanery Representatives : *Mr. F. Harris, *Mr. W. Layton, *Miss McCleesh *Miss Weigall.
Parochial Church Council : Those marked * and Mrs. Anderson, Col. C. Bamber, Capt. H. Boorman, Mr. E. Clarke, Mr. Foat, Mr. Gentry, Miss Gardner, Mr. Hawkins, Mr. R. Impett, Mr. F. Jarvis, Miss Simmers, Mrs. Stock, Mr. G. W. Watson, (ST. CATHERINE'S)—Mrs. Burton, Mr. G. Church, Mr. Clackett.
Sidesmen : Messrs. A. Butcher, E. Clarke, W. Clarke, J. Daniels, C. D'Eath, S Foat, C. Gentry, W. Hawkins, T. Howard, W. Hudson, R. Impett, W. Layton, C. Peyton, F. Rapp, W. Stanner, H. Stead, A. Thompson, C. Whitling, (ST. CATHERINE'S)—Mrs. Burton, Mrs. Clackett, Mr. G. Church, Mr. W. Clackett, Mr. E. Hawkes, Mr. H. Patterson.
Day Schools : *Headmaster.*—*Mr. G. Watson. *Headmistress.*—Miss O. Huggard. INFANTS : *Headmistress.*—Miss E. Agnew. *Hon. Correspondent.*—Mr. Martin-Martin (Cuddesdon, Queen's Avenue, Newington).
Churchyard Committee : *Hon. Sec.*—Mr. E Spencer Payne (4, Chapel Place).
Orchestra : *Hon. Sec.*—Mr. W. L. Alexander (108, Grange Road).
Choir : Messrs. L. Bolton, P. Black, S. Gee, E. Harrison, F. Jarvis, J. Leonard, H. Oliver, J. Parren, A. Siminson, P. E. Videan, H. Wells, H. Williamson, Capt. Stableford, Mrs. Butcher, Mrs. Videan, Miss Andrews, Miss Arthur, Miss Butcher, Miss Brunus, Miss Carley, Miss D'Eath, Miss Foad, Miss E. Gardner, Miss Hallums, Miss Oliver, Miss Riches, Miss Stanner, Miss Thompson, Miss Williamson.
Bell Ringers : Messrs. S. Twyman (*Conductor*), A E. Jarman (*Deputy Conductor*), W. Birch (*Hon. Sec.*, 9, Vale Road), C. Bird, P. Black, J. Blythman, H. Foster, A. Friend, S. Gee, W. Hollands, J. Jarman, F. Philpott, L. Porrit, T. Scott, N. Staynes, L. Twyman, H. Wickens, H. Williamson.
S. School Teachers : *Seniors*—Miss Andrews, Miss Allen, Mr. G. Watson, Mr. Bolton.
Juniors—Miss G. Williamson, Miss Thompson, Miss Holloway, Mrs Butcher.
Infants—Miss Tomlinson, Miss P. Hallums, Miss Iddenden, Miss Moys, Miss P. Sivil, Miss N. Sivil
Bible Class : WOMEN.—Miss F. E. Kennett in the Parish Hall at 2.45. YOUNG WOMEN.—Mrs. Howe, at 18, Vale Square at 3 p.m. LADS.—
Parish Hall : *Hon. Sec.*—Mr. W. G. Lawrence (48, High Street St. Laurence).
Caretaker—Mrs. Harlow (31, High Street, St. Laurence).

S. Laurence Parish Magazine

VOLUME II. JANUARY 1891. PRICE TWOPENCE.

Services at Parish Church.

Sundays.—Holy Communion (every Sunday) at 8 a.m.; 1st and 3rd Sundays, after Morning Service, 5th Sunday, at 10 a.m.
Mattins and Sermon (with Litany on 2nd and 4th Sundays) at 11 a.m.
Service for Women only (1st Sunday); for Men Only (3rd Sunday); Children's Service (2nd, 4th, and 5th Sundays) at 3 p.m.
Holy Baptism every Sunday afternoon.
Evensong and Sermon at 6.30 p.m.

Week-Days—Mattins daily (except Wednesday and Friday) at 8 a.m. Evensong daily at 7 p.m.
Holy Communion on Wednesday at 8 a.m.
Mattins and Litany on Wednesday and Friday at 11 a.m. instead of 8 a.m.
Churching of Women is taken immediately before, and Holy Baptism is administered after, any of the Week-day services.

Saints Days.—Holy Communion at 8 a.m. Mattins at 11 a.m. Evensong and Sermon at 7 p.m.

A Service is held in the Church Club at Pegwell every Sunday Afternoon at 4.10 p.m.

A Mission Service is held in Southwood Hall every Sunday Evening at 8 p.m.

CLERGY.

REV. MONTAGUE FOWLER, M.A., The Vicarage. | REV. J. CAMPBELL, M.A., The Lodge. St. Mildred's Rd.
REV. W. STUART YARDLEY, B.A. | REV. H. L. DAVIS, M.A., Tenterfield House.
Licensed Lay Reader: COL. LOWE, 2, Heather Villas, Dundonald Road.

CHURCHWARDENS.

MR. J. FROST. | MR. W. PERKINS.
Organist: MR. ABRAM, 58, Queen Street. | Clerk and Sexton: MR. W. GIBBS

DISTRICT VISITORS.

NAME	DISTRICT
LADY ROSE WEIGALL, Southwood House.	Haine, Spratling Street, Coleswood, and Ozengell.
MRS. CAPES, 2, Cambridge Villas, Grange road.	Ellington Cottages.
MRS. COLEMAN, St. Laurence House.	Alma and Greenfield Cottages, and Workhouse Yard.
MRS. COOK, 8, Northumberland Villas, Dundonald Road, and Miss DAVIDSON, Prospect Lodge.	High Street (both sides).
MRS. FOWLER, The Vicarage.	Manstone, Poleash, Vicarage Cottages, and Manstone Road.
MRS. FOX, Cheshunt, Crescent Road.	Southwood Terrace.
MRS. LOWE, 2, Heather Villas, Dundonald Road.	Chapel Road (both sides).
MRS. PORT, Elm Lodge.	Ellington Triangle.
MRS. REEVES, Southwood Villa.	Southwood: Ashburnham Terrace, Cottages by French Laundry, Australian, and Southwood Cottages.
MRS. SHEPPEY, Ferncott, Ellington Road.	Chapel Road (High Street end).
MISS CASTLE, 3, Ballure, South Eastern Road.	Lorne Road. Bell Alley.
MISS F. KENNETT, Nethercourt Farm.	Great Cliff's End.
MISS M. KENNETT, Nethercourt Farm.	Chilton Terrace, Villas and Cottages.
MISS MASCALL, Chapel Cottage, with MISS WILLIAMS and MISS HILES.	Whitehall and Newington Terrace; Southwood from Collard's shop to Southwood Tavern (both sides). Claremont Gardens, Bella Vesta Terrace, and Forge Alley.
MISS NOWERS, Gothurst, South Eastern Road.	Jubilee and Grosvenor Roads, and Seafield Road.
MISS SALE, St. Laurence.	Almshouses.
MISS TAPSELL, Grosvenor House, Grange Road.	Part of Southwood, King Harman Terrace, and Hesse Villas.
COL. LOWE, 2, Heather Villas, Dundonald Road.	Pegwell, Coastguard Station, and Little Cliffs End.

MY DEAR FRIENDS,

Mrs. Fowler and I take the opportunity, through the Parish Magazine, of wishing you in the truest and highest sense "A Happy New Year."

The past year has been full of interest and blessing in the work, and has led to many true and trust lasting friendships amongst us.

The chief event of the year is the completion of the restoration of our grand old Church (the greater part of which was so ably done by you and Mr. Molony), by the recent work in the Chancel which Ecclesiastical Commissioners have carried out. When Mrs. Barber's munificent gift of carved choir stalls is in its place, we shall indeed be proud of St. Laurence Church.

I do not propose in this letter to indulge in a retrospect of the year 1890, as I hope to do that greater length in the Year Book, which will be published about Easter. But I cannot refrain from expressing my deep gratitude to Almighty God for the encouragement He has given us in the increased spirit of devotion and earnestness in so many branches of the work.

The measure of success in the spiritual work of a parish is the prayerfulness of Christ's flock. you all help on the work by this means?

I am deeply sensible of your liberality to the Master's work during the past year. "God loveth cheerful giver."

Once more within six months a great sorrow has fallen upon Mrs. Fowler and myself. On Christmas Day the Archbishop of York (my wife's uncle, to whom she was deeply attached) passed away. We his death very keenly, not only as a personal bereavement, but as a loss to the Church at large. you pray for us in our sorrow, and for the widow and family whom he leaves to mourn him?

May the New Year dawn brightly on you all, and as each stepping stone to eternity is passed, it bring you nearer to your Saviour is the prayer of

Your Affectionate Servant in Christ Jesus,

MONTAGUE FOWLER.

NOTICES.

On Thursday, Jan. 1st, being the Festival of the Circumcision of our Lord, and Tuesday, Jan. being the Festival of the Epiphany, there will be the usual Holy Day services.

GUILD OF ST. LAURENCE.—The monthly meeting of the Guild of St. Laurence will be held Wednesday, Jan. 28th, at 6 p.m., in the Parish Hall. Guild service and sermon at 7 p.m.

SERVICE FOR WOMEN ONLY.—The monthly service for women only will be held on Sunday, 4th, at 3 p.m. The Vicar will give an address on "Women's rights."

SERVICE FOR MEN ONLY.—The monthly service for men only will be held on Sunday, Jan. at 3 p.m. The Vicar will give an address on "Money."

DISTRICT VISITORS.—The monthly meeting of the District Visitors will be held on Friday, 23rd, af 6.15 p.m. in the Vestry.

SUNDAY SCHOOL TEACHERS' MEETING. — The fortnightly meetings will be held on Thursday Jan. 8th and 22nd at 6.15 p.m. in the Vestry.

PEGWELL MOTHERS' MEETING. — Miss Warre holds this class every Monday at the Pegwell at 2.45 p.m.

CONFIRMATION CLASSES. — The classes for preparation of candidates for the Confirmation March 3rd are held as follows : For men and lads, Friday, 7.30 p.m., at the Vestry ; for women girls, Tuesday, 7.30 p.m., at the Vestry.

BIBLE CLASSES, &c.—The following classes are held weekly throughout the winter :—

Sunday—Bible class for young men, 2.30 p.m., Parish Hall, taken by Mr. Everitt.
      "   "   mothers, 2.45 p.m., Southwood Mission Hall, taken by Miss Warre.
      "   "   girls, 3.30 p.m.,   "   "   "
Monday— "   men, 7 p.m., Parish Hall, taken by Rev. W. S. Yardley."
Thursday—Mother's meeting, 2.30 p.m., Southwood Mission Hall, taken by Mrs. Warre.

Mrs. Reeves has kindly undertaken the Clothing Club in place of Miss Sale.

OFFICIAL YEAR BOOK OF THE CHURCH OF ENGLAND. — This most valuable record of work of the Church is published annually by the Society for Promoting Christian Knowledge (Northumberland Avenue, Charing Cross) at the cost of 3s. 0d. It is well worth possessing.

ACKNOWLEDGMENTS.

ALTAR DECORATIONS.—In addition to her generous gift of the new violet altar cloth, Mrs. Campbell has presented the church with some beautiful lace for the superfrontal and re-table, and a " linen cloth," for which we offer her our sincere thanks.

CREDENCE TABLE. — The Misses Campbell have given a very handsome oak credence table which the Vicar desires to return his sincere thanks.

FOR THE POOR.—Mr. J. Sebag Montefiore has again this year presented the Vicar with a cheque for £10 towards the relief of the sick and poor. He has also sent Mrs. Fowler £3 3s. 0d. for use the parish. These gifts are in addition to the £10 which Lady Rose Weigall distributes for Montefiore, and it will thus be seen that the poor in St. Laurence have in him one of their best kindest friends.

ALTAR FLOWERS.—Mrs. Campbell has generously paid for the altar flowers for the first three months of last year. The Vicar wishes to thank those who have responded to the appeal he made through Miss Williams, who kindly undertook to collect subscriptions for this fund, for the £1 15s. 6d. which has been handed over to him.

SUNDAY SCHOOL TREAT.—The gifts have not yet all come to hand, but we acknowledge with sincere thanks the following :—Towards the clothing : Mrs. Shippey, £1 ; Miss Sale, £1 ; a gift of flannel from Mr. and Mrs. Jones ; a large parcel of warm clothing from Miss Williams, Mrs. Gibbs, Mrs. Boulton, Mrs. Darby, Miss Ayres, and Mrs. Tapsell ; and scarves from Miss Ellerm. Towards the treat : Miss Ellerm, 10s. ; Mrs. Davidson, 10s.

C. M. S. COLLECTING BOX.—Mrs. Gibbs sends us 6s. 7½d.

PARISH HALL.—Mr. C. Lethbridge has handed over to the Treasurer of the Parish Hall the sum of £4 2s. 6d., the proceeds of the entertainment on Nov. 19th and 20th.

CHURCHYARD FUND.—Mr. and Mrs. Hall have kindly given 5s.

BAZAAR.—We have received a beautiful gift of woollen and crewel work for the Bazaar from Miss Hobley.

FOR CHURCH WORK IN THE PARISH.—The Vicar desires to convey his sincere thanks to Mrs. Ansley Robinson, of Bath, for £1 ; and to Mr. H. Gordon Roberts, for £2.

CHURCH BELLS RESTORATION FUND.—The Vicar acknowledges with many thanks: J. H. Warre, Esq., £10 ; the Vicar, £10 ; Mr. Hall (2nd donation), 2s. 6d. ; Miss F. Ofield, 2s. 6d. Amount already acknowledged, £182 15s. 3d.

SOUTHWOOD MISSION HARMONIUM —The Vicar acknowledges with many thanks : Mrs. Twigg, 7s. 6d. ; Mrs. Hall, 2s. 6d. ; Miss Maxted, 2s. Amount already acknowledged, £1 16s. 0d.

MAGIC LANTERN.—Mrs. Ansley Robinson kindly sends us 2s. 6d.

WANTED.

CHURCH BELLS RESTORATION FUND.—The Vicar has now in hand £203 0s. 3d. The contract for £273 8s. 6d. has been signed, and the work will be commenced early in January. The Vicar urgently appeals for the £70 still required, so that the restoration may be completed without delay. The bellringers are taking round cards which we hope will bring in the amount needed.

MAGIC LANTERN. — Will some of our friends who are interested in the Southwood Mission Work help towards the £7 required to purchase the magic lantern, so that it may belong to the parish ? Please send donations to Mrs. Fowler.

HARMONIUM FOR SOUTHWOOD MISSION HALL. — We have received £2 8s. towards the £6 required. Please help us to clear off this debt.

VESTRY.—We want a good clock for the Vestry, and a new inkstand. Will one of our many friends give us these?—The clock would be a useful "Christmas box" for the clergy..—[Vicar's note.]

BOOKMARKERS.—Who will give us bookmarkers for the Bible and service books ; white and gold ?

ALMS BAGS.—Mrs. Gibbs has kindly given us our white alms bags. We want the green and violet.

MANSTONE CHURCH IMPROVEMENT.—We have had to "do up" Manstone Church, and repair the fabric at a cost of £16. Will any friends interested in Manstone help us with a donation towards this object ?

CARPET FOR THE SACRARIUM.—Who will give us a handsome carpet, at a cost of about £7 (velvet pile), or double that amount for a turkey carpet ?

PARISH MAGAZINE.—We want new annual subscribers. Please send 2s. 0d. (or 2s. 6d. including postage) to the Vicarage.

Notes of the Past Month.

RE-OPENING OF THE CHANCEL—VISIT OF THE BISHOP OF DOVER.

The chancel of our dear old parish church was re-opened on Thursday, Dec. 11th, by the Right Rev. G. R. Eden, Bishop of Dover. The Sacrarium has been raised to what was in all probability its original height, and the floor has been inlaid in walnut and oak. The entire roof of the chancel, which was formerly white-washed, has been lined with oak, the carvings of the roof have been restored, and in certain parts new carving has been added in exact imitation of those portions which were missing. A delicately carved oak screen has been introduced in the arch between the chancel and south chapel where a handsome oak sedilia has been placed. The altar rails of oak with simple brass standards are in keeping with the other alterations, and the graceful brass coronas look well and are a satisfactory means of lighting the chancel. The quaintly carved old communion table has been placed in the side chapel. It was formerly used as a rest for the temporary altar and was of necessity hidden from view by the altar frontal. [To make the restoration of the chancel quite complete, we now require handsome oak choir stalls (promised by Mrs. Barber), a nicely carved oak litany desk (cost, about £5 10s. to £6), a carved oak bishop's chair, and a really good carpet for the sacrarium.]

The service of reopening commenced at 7 p.m. with the processional hymn "The Church's one foundation." Amongst the clergy present were Rev. H. Bartram (Vicar of Ramsgate); Rev. J. E.

Brenan (Vicar of Christ Church); Rev. B. Burrows, Rev. A. Lyne (Westgate), Rev. J. B. Parker (... Andrew's, Deal), Rev. J. Campbell, Rev. T. A. Easterling, Rev. H. L. Davis, etc. The Rev. S... Yardley acted as the Bishop's chaplain.

The service was taken by the Vicar; the first lesson was read by the Rev. H. Bartram, and... second lesson by the Rev. J. E. Brenan. The special collect was read by the Bishop of Dover, who... preached an impressive and eloquent sermon from Psalm xxvii. v. 8. "When Thou saidst, Seek ye... face, my heart said unto Thee, Thy face Lord will I seek." The Bishop's delivery (which is at... simple and powerful) and his clear and musical voice lent additional charm to his stirring address,... held the attention of his auditors throughout. At the close of the service the choir rendered a... recessional the hymn. "Now thank we all our God."

The clergy of the neighbourhood, the churchwardens of St. Laurence (Alderman Frost and M... Perkins), and Mr. Abram (organist), were presented to the Bishop. Later in the evening Mrs. Fow... held a reception at the Vicarage, at which from 70 to 80 guests assembled. The Bishop left St. La... rence for Canterbury the following morning at 8 o'clock. Our only regret was that Mrs. Eden w... unable to be with us also.

C.E.T.S. ENTERTAINMENT.—An amusing entertainment was given in the Parish Hall on Tuesda... Dec. 16th. The Vicar presided and gave a reading. Rev. W. S. Yardley, Mr. Alderman Frost, a... others were present. An excellent programme was provided, and the Temperance choir as usual s... with spirit. The dialogue given by the Misses Waller, Lawrence, M. and A. Kingsmill, deserves espec... praise. Messrs. M. Tucker, W. Graham, C. Saunders, E. and A. Mirams, A. Parnell, &c., took part.

MAGIC LANTERN SERVICE.—The second magic lantern service was held on Friday, Dec. 12... and was well attended. The Vicar opened the service, and Revs. W. S. Yardley, J. Campbell, and C... Lowe took part. The slides represented scenes in the life of our Lord.

BAPTISMS.

Dec. 7—Stanley Austen.
7—Caroline Mary Sutton.
14—Laura Darby.
14—Walter James Cole.
14—Rosa Edith Wood.

MARRIAGES.

Dec. 9—John William Sydney Howe and Clara Alexandra Kennett.
14—Richard Thomas Foster and Agnes Harriet Watts.
20—Stephen Henry Cardwell and Emma Goodall.
20—Harry George Marsh and Emma West.

BURIALS.

Dec. 3—Bertram Spicer Sutton.
4—Mary Elizabeth Ofield.
8—John Edward Peal.
10—Annie Winifred Delo.
13—Mary Ann Rowland.
13—Emily Dugwell.
18—Sidney Dugwell.
20—Deverson Douglass.
20—Maude Gertrude Mirams.
24—Elizabeth Annie Stonehouse.
24—Selina Pollard.
27—Sophia Bradley.
29—Emily Wheeler.

OFFERTORIES.

PARISH CHURCH.

Date	Time	£	s.	d.	Fund
November 30 (Advent Sunday)	8 a.m.		3	9	Alms account.
	11 a.m.	1	12	8	Churchwarden's Account.
	6.30 p.m.		17	0	"
December 7 (2 S. in Advent)	8 a.m.		3	9	Alms account.
	11 a.m.	1	8	4	Organist and Choir Fund.
	6.30 p.m.	1	1	5	"
Dec. 11 (Re-opening of Church)	7 p.m.	4	4	4	Churchwarden's Account.
December 14 (3 S. in Advent)	8 a.m.		2	6	Alms account.
	11 a.m.	1	13	3	Churchwarden's Account.
	6.30 p.m.	1	8	6	"
December 21 (4 S. in Advent)	8 a.m.		2	10	Alms account.
	11 a.m.	1	13	3	Churchwarden's Account.
	6.30 p.m.	1	1	1	"
December 25 (Christmas Day)	7 a.m.		4	2	Church Embroidery.
	8 a.m.		18	0	Alms Account.
	11 a.m.	3	9	0	National Schools.
	3 p.m.		4	4	"
December 28 (Holy Innocents' Day)	8 a.m.		3	3	Alms Account.
	11 a.m.	2	17	9	Churchwarden's Account.
	6.30 p.m.	1	1	6	"

CHRISTMAS SERVICES. — We have again to thank the many kind friends who supplied us with evergreens, &c., and assisted in the decorations. Mrs. Campbell arranged the altar flowers; the Misses Warre undertook the font; the Misses Kennett took the reredos in hand; the Misses Reeves decorated the choir stalls; while Miss Tapsell and Miss Ayres shewed their skill in ornamenting the pulpit.—The belfrey sent forth a merry Christmas peal at 6.30 a.m. At 7 a.m. the Vicar celebrated. At 8 a.m. there was a choral celebration, at which most of the men and some of the boys of the choir were present and communicated; the Rev. J. Campbell being the celebrant.—The Vicar preached and celebrated at 11 a.m., when a large congregation were present.—At the Carol Service at 3 p.m. the Rev. J. Campbell gave a short address.—Our Christmas joy was clouded over by the sad news of the Archbishop of York's death. The flag was lowered, and the passing bell was tolled.

Pegwell.

MY DEAR FRIENDS AT PEGWELL AND CLIFFSEND,—

I wish I could meet you all to offer you my best New Year's greetings in person. But I cannot be everywhere at the same time!

I do rejoice at the blessing which has attended our work among you during the past year. And I hope that we may see still greater fruits of our labour in the year on which we are entering. With our good Colonel to lead the Pegwell battalion, we are sure under God's blessing to prosper.

Your sincere friend and Vicar,

MONTAGUE FOWLER.

ANNIVERSARY.—The members of the Pegwell Church Club and Reading-room celebrated their first anniversary on Wednesday evening the 17th Dec., by a select entertainment, in which the Vicar, Revs. W. S. Yardley, E. H. Hardcastle, the Misses Warre, Hickson, Adult, Rhodes, Robinson, N. La Fargue, and Messrs. Beynon, G. Weigall, W. H. Port, S. Port, S. Banger and Bicknell kindly gave their assistance. Tea and refreshments were provided by Col. Lowe, to whom in a great degree the success of the entertainment was due. There were present upwards of 95 persons, who expressed themselves much pleased with the admirable programme arranged for them. The room was tastefully decorated with flags, and the singing and recitations were excellent throughout. The meeting closed with the singing of the National Anthem.

Manstone Church.

The Services on the Sundays in January will be as follows:

Jan. 4.—Mattins, Holy Communion, and Sermon 11 a.m.; Evensong, Litany, and Sermon 6.30 p.m

" 11 —Mattins, Litany, and Sermon 11 a.m.; Children's Service, 3 p.m.; Evensong and Sermon 6.30 p.m.

" 18.—Mattins, Holy Communion, and Sermon 11 a.m.; Evensong, Litany and Sermon 6.30 p.m.

" 25.—Mattins, Litany, and Sermon 11 a.m.; Children's Service, 3 p.m.; Evensong and Sermon 6.30 p.m.

NOTICES.

BIBLE CLASS FOR MEN.—This Bible class is held every Monday at 6.30 p.m., in the Schoolroom.

CHOIR PRACTICE.—The choir practice is held every Monday at 7.30 p.m.

MRS. FOWLER'S CLASS —Mrs. Fowler's class will meet on Wednesdays, Jan. 7th and 21st, at 3 p.m., in Mr. Britton's house.

CONFIRMATION.—Confirmation classes will be held—for women and girls, and for men and lads. The days and time will be published next month.

MY DEAR FRIENDS AT MANSTONE,

Mrs. Fowler and I feel we must send you a letter through the "Parish Magazine" to wish you all a very happy New Year. God has blessed our friendship with you in many ways, and with your prayers and ours, He will continue to bless us in the work for Him.

Your Affectionate Friend,

MONTAGUE FOWLER.

Notes of the Past Month.

CHILDREN'S ENTERTAINMENT.—An excellent entertainment was given on Dec. 9th and 10th which reflects great credit on Miss Skinner and Miss Maxted for the careful training of the child[ren] The Vicar presided the first evening, and the Rev. J. Campbell the second. The dialogue "Se[rving] him out," was splendidly rendered. The wax works were most amusing. Mr. Port and Mr. S. P[ort] enlivened the proceedings by a duet, which caused much laughter.

ADVENT SERVICES.—The Rev. J. Campbell took a course of sermons on the Friday evening[s in] Advent. Some of our people seem to appreciate these weekday sevices, and we feel sure that gra[dually] others will come to do so.

CHRISTMAS SERVICES.—The little church looked beautiful on Christmas Day. The decoration[s] were carried out with great taste. We are indebted to Mr. T. Chandler, Mr. Solly (of Preston Far[m) and other friends for the evergreens. Miss Emptage, Miss L. Bingham, E. Nutter, and A. Whitehe[ad] took the lion's share of the work. Mrs. T. Chandler arranged the altar flowers. The pulpit from S[t.] Laurence Church, which is a most handsome addition to Manstone, was prettily wreathed with ivy. T[he] new brass standards at the altar rails greatly add to the dignity of the Church. Two beautiful banne[rs] and a text made of gold letters on pale blue foundation, relieve the east wall, and are a great improvement. They were kindly made for us by Col. and Miss Lowe. The Rev. W. S. Yardley preached morning a[nd] afternoon to good congregations. The Vicar greatly regretted being prevented by the sudden news o[f] the death of the Archbishop of York, from being with our Manstone friends on Christmas Day.

OFFERTORIES.

December 7 (8 a.m.)	1	1 (Alms Account)	December 21	6	0 (Church expenses)
„ (11 a.m. & 6.30 p.m.)	6	7 (Church Improvement Fund.)	„ 25 Christmas Day	8	3 (National School)
„ 14	7	6 (Church expenses)	December 28	6	11 (Church expenses)

Haine.

MY DEAR FRIENDS AT HAINE,—
I wish you all, most heartily, a very happy New Year.

It has been a great pleasure to me to see the earnestness with which so many of you have joi[ned] with us in the services. I should like, if you agree, to hold them more frequently.

I have many friends in Haine, and I hope before the year is out, to have many more:

Your affectionate Vicar,

MONTAGUE FOWLER.

SERVICE.—The services on the Tuesday evenings in Advent were well attended, and much app[re]ciated. The Vicar took the first, when Mrs. Fowler sang "I heard the voice of Jesus say," as a s[olo]. The Rev. W. S. Yardley took the others. It is hoped to continue these services on the Tuesday eveni[ngs] throughout the winter.

Lady Rose Weigall's class meets on Wednesday, at 3 p.m.

ADVERTISEMENTS.

The Advertisements in this page include only such as are personally recommended by the Editor.

W. H. PORT, Builder and Contractor, St. Laurence.—All kinds of Sanitary Work efficiently carried out. F[unerals] conducted.

RICHARD EVENS, 43, Baker Street, London, W.—Those of our readers who wish to purchase really pretty and inexpensive lamps should pay a visit to Mr. Evens' depot in Baker Street. Every pretty novelty in shades and la[mps] from the delicate cl ina fairy lights to the tall standard lamps can be seen at the Baker Street depot at modes[t prices.] Mr. Evens also supplies an exceptionally pure photogen oil quite colourless and transparent and free from the inflamm[able] spirit benzolline. It gives a bright white light, 1/3 a gallon. To save the expense of frequent deliveries five gallo[ns can] be charged at 1/2 a gallon; ten gallons and upwards at 1/1½ per gallon for cash. This oil is specially recommen[ded for] school-rooms, mission churches, and other crowded buildings, as it gives off no inflammable vapour at 120° and fo[rms no] impurities in the air.

S. Laurence Parish Magazine.

Vol. XII. FEBRUARY, 1901. Price 1d.

Clergy: REV. T. G. CROSSE, M.A. (Vicar and Surrogate).
REV. C. G. T. SALE PENNINGTON, M.A., Parkside, Ellington Rd.

Churchwardens: MR. T. SNOWDEN, 27, Grange Road.
MR. W. H. PORT, Elm Lodge.

Sidesmen: Messrs. Bowley, Browne, Bushell, Chapman, Cook, Dodsworth, Jarrett, Longley, Ofield and Tucker.

SERVICES.

PARISH CHURCH.

Sundays:—
8. 0 a.m., Holy Communion (every Sunday).
11. 0 a.m., 1st, Matins and Holy Communion; 2nd and 5th, Matins and Sermon; 3rd, Matins, Sermon and Holy Com.; 4th, Matins, Litany, and Sermon.
3.45 p.m., Litany, Baptisms and Churchings except 4th Sunday.
3. 0 p.m., 4th, Children's Service, Baptisms, etc.
6.30 p.m., Evensong and Sermon.

Saints' Days:—
10. 0 a.m., Holy Communion.

Week Days:—
11. 0 a.m., on Wednesday and Friday, Matins and Litany.
7. 0 p.m., on Wednesday, Evensong with Address.

Organist: Dr. A. T. Froggatt.

Clerk and Sexton: Mr. W. Gibbs.

MANSTON CHURCH.

Sundays:—
8. 0 a.m., Holy Communion (1st Sunday.)
11. 0 a.m., 1st, 3rd and 5th, Matins, Litany, and Sermon; 2nd and 4th, Matins, Holy Communion and Sermon.
3. 0 p.m., Children's Service.
6.30 p.m., Evensong and Sermon.

Thursdays:—
6.30 p.m., Evensong and Sermon.

Organist: Mr. W. J. R. Gibbs.
Clerk: Mr. Measday.

Notices of Banns, Weddings, Funerals, &c., can be sent either to the Vicar or to Mr. W. Gibbs.
Baptisms and Churchings taken at any of the Services if notice be given.
All seats are free, but they can be allotted on application to the Churchwardens.

Copies of Magazine may be procured from the District Visitors, from Mr. Saunders (Stationer), High St., or from Miss Williams, High St.

REMARKABLE REMEDIES	CUT FLOWERS, FLORAL WREATHS
For Most Ailments, are Sold by	Supplied to Order on Short Notice at Popular Prices.
A. H. SIMINSON, THE CHEMIST,	FRESHNESS AND STYLE SECOND TO NONE
ST. LAWRENCE.	**J. W. CHAPMAN,**
	171, HIGH STREET, RAMSGATE. Tel. 279

F. HARRIS,
FAMILY BUTCHER,
141, GRANGE ROAD, RAMSGATE.

Home-made Sausages a Speciality.

A. A. JEZARD
Newington Grocery Stores.

GROCERY, PROVISIONS, NEWSAGENCY.
LICENCE FOR STAMPS.   PATENT MEDICINES.
TOBACCO, Etc.   Agent for Perry's Celebrated Coals.

LAWRENCE BROS.,
BAKERS, CONFECTIONERS AND CATERERS
Excelsior Machine Bakery, St. Lawrence.

Respectfully Solicit a Share of Your Patronage

Tel. 128.

A. H. JANES,
FISHMONGER.   Telephone 181
7, SOUTHWOOD ROAD & 152, KING STREET
WET, DRY AND FRIED FISH DAILY.
FRIED FISH DELIVERED TO ALL PARTS.

GEORGE HARMAN,
FLORIST AND SEEDSMAN,
24 & 26, GRANGE ROAD.
FLORAL DESIGNS A SPECIALITY.

Established 1884.

T. HOBDAY,
PRACTICAL BOOT AND SHOE MAKER
37, HIGH STREET, ST. LAWRENCE.
Best Material and Workmanship. All Work done on the Premises. Special attention paid to HANDSEWN Work.
SOCKS, LACES AND POLISHES ALWAYS IN STOCK.

PORTS for
ALL BUILDING AND DECORATING MATERIALS.
GLASS cut o size.   PAINTS ready for use.
66, BOUNDARY ROAD, RAMSGATE.

B. G. ARTER,

VEGETABLES.   CORN.   GROCERY.

GRANGE ROAD STORES.

A. G. ELLIS,
46, GRANGE ROAD, RAMSGATE

NEWSAGENT, STATIONER & TOBACCONIST.

Established 26 Years.

FRANK FINCH,
54, HIGH STREET, ST. LAWRENCE

GENERAL DRAPER, HOSIER AND
OUTFITTER.

District Agents for the famous James Motor Cycles.   A.A. Official Repairers.   Officially Appointed Dealers in Wolseley Cars.

Morrison & Siminson
Next to the Church.   Phone 189 Ramsgate.

MOTOR, MOTOR CYCLE & WIRELESS ENGINEERS,

Any Make of Car or Motor Cycle Supplied   Accumulators Charged.   Repairs Carefully Executed.

We offer a free service scheme, including tuition in driving, with every Car or Motor Cycle supplied by us. Our service is both liberal and genuine. Ask for Particulars.

Our Bible Questions.

By The Rev. Percy Nott, M.A.,
RECTOR OF ROMA, QUEENSLAND.

7. By whom was it announced that an ambassador (from the Lord) was sent among the heathen? 8. Where do we read that distribution was made unto every man according as he had need? 9. What king twice spared the life of a man who threw stones at him? Who was the man? 10. On what occasion did some men speak of a national scourge as the "finger of God"? 11. Where is it said that Our Lord healed the sick that prophecy might be fulfilled? Quote the prophecy. 12. Find the first prophecy that the power of Satan should be broken.

COTTAGE COOKERY.

Maccaroni Soup.

3 pints of stock.	A sprig each of marjoram, thyme, lemon thyme, and parsley tied together.
1 turnip.	
4 leeks.	
2 carrots.	¼ lb. maccaroni.
2 onions.	½ teaspoonful salt.
2 cloves, 1 blade of mace.	A little pepper.

Put the stock in a saucepan, and place over the fire to boil, pare the turnip, and cut in quarters, wash, scrape, and cut up the carrots, shred the leeks, pare the onions and stick the cloves in one of them. Put all these into the boiling stock with the mace, herbs, pepper and salt, and let all simmer quietly for two hours. Put another saucepan, half full of water, over the fire to boil the maccaroni in, which should be put in as soon as the water boils, and cooked for about half an hour, or until tender. When quite soft, strain through a colander, and cut into pieces half an inch long. Put these into the soup tureen, and strain the hot soup over them.

Barley, vermicelli, or rice may be used instead of maccaroni if preferred; but barley takes two hours to boil after being soaked overnight in cold water. Vermicelli will be cooked in ten minutes, rice in from twenty minutes to half an hour.

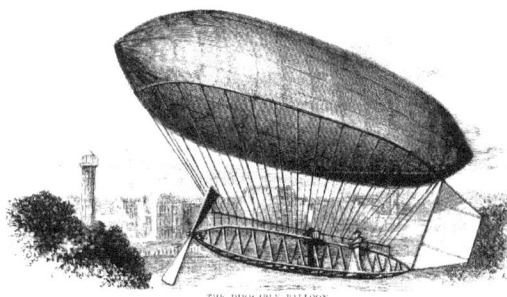

THE DIRIGIBLE BALLOON.

THE WIDOW'S MITE.—At the close of a sermon in Manchester Cathedral, Bishop Welldon said: "Copper coin was not valueless, if it was given in the spirit of the widow's mite; but when he looked at the weight of copper coin in the offertory plate he could not resist the thought—or at least the charitable hope—that there must be an unusual number of pious widows in Manchester."

GARDEN WORK FOR FEBRUARY.

Kitchen Garden.

CABBAGE plants may, if the weather is mild, be planted out into the beds in which they are intended to remain. Strong plants should be selected. The ground should have a good dressing of manure. If weather permit sow cabbage and savoy seed about the end of the month. Sow also radish, spinach, and lettuce. About the end of the month ground should be made ready for sowing carrots and parsnips, trenching at least one spade deep. Prepare ground for sowing leeks and onions, digging in well-rotted manure.

Fruit Garden.

Prune apple, cherry, pear, and plum trees, thinning out branches in espaliers when too close. These should be about ten or twelve inches apart. In standard trees thin out and cut branches which cross one another. Prune also gooseberry and currant trees, and raspberries, removing all decayed wood.

Flower Garden.

In mild weather plant edgings of box, daisies, London pride, pinks, and polyanthuses. Also ranunculus in rich soil, covering up well to protect from frost. Prune thorn and privet hedges.

A QUAINT GRAVESTONE.

"A House she hath it's made of such a fashion

The tenant ne'er shall pay for reparation

Nor will the landlord ever raise her rent

Or turn her out of doors for non-payment

From chimney money too this cell is free

Of such a house who would not tenant be!"

Parish Church of St. Eanswythe, Folkestone.

OUR·WEEKDAY·PAGES·FOR·WOMEN·WITH·HOMES

Monday's Washing.

WHEN washing woollen stockings, if you have no mangle, or don't wish to use one, do not *wring* your stockings. When well rinsed roll them up tightly, beginning at the toes, pressing against side of basin and spreading out creases. When rolled, squeeze out as much water as possible, and hang to dry toes uppermost. The stockings will dry much quicker than if merely left to drip, and will not require ironing. (M. E. WIDNELL, Beckenham.)

I have found that men's soft collars (not *silk* ones) look much smarter and keep their shape better if they are put through thin boiled starch, then ironed in the usual way. (Mrs. G. BRADFORD, North Finchley.)

To minimize the labour of ironing by making one flat-iron do a whole afternoon's ironing, first place an asbestos mat on the ironing table, then on the mat put an ordinary gas ring. Connect this with the gas burner by a length of rubber tubing, and light the gas ring in the usual way. Put the iron over the gas ring. When it is hot enough to use, turn the gas down to a glimmer, and use the ring as you would an iron stand. By this means your iron is always kept hot. (Mrs. HANKS, W. Hampstead.) (Fig. 1.)

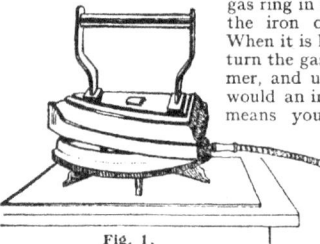

Fig. 1.

When ironing, fold the sheets and place flat under ironing blanket. When you have finished ironing the other things, you will find the sheets pressed and ready for the airing cupboard. (Mrs. BOWDEN, Basingstoke.)

Tuesday's Sewing.

HANDKERCHIEFS are expensive to buy, but good ones can easily be made from fine lawn or mull bought by the yard, neatly hemmed by machine. They can be trimmed with lace, or have an initial embroidered in one corner. (Mrs. BRISTOW, King's Lynn.)

When cutting out a pattern, it is always best to outline the pattern pieces on the material with a tracing wheel, instead of just cutting round the pattern. A tracing wheel costs about 1s. and is a capital investment. But before you start tracing, pin your *material* firmly to the table with strong pins or drawing pins, putting them at the top and bottom of the selvedge edges, or of selvedge edge and fold if your material is doubled. Don't try to use the tracing wheel on material just laid on the table, or it will probably move. (ELEANOR FENTON, Leytonstone.) (Fig. 2.)

Every woman who has to do with men's overall trousers knows how quickly the buttons pull off the back, often tearing pieces of overall with them. This may be prevented by taking two pieces of elastic 3 inches long and ¾ inch wide, doubling them, and sewing each piece where the buttons go. Leave the double end an inch above the top of the trousers, and on this sew the button. As the wearer bends over his work the elastic gives. The saving is obvious. (L. WILSON, St. John's Hill.) (Fig. 3.)

To make a jumper fit higher at the neck, I find an excellent plan is to get a piece of tape about 8 inches long, and sew it inside the jumper at the top of the back, leaving the ends open. Then get a piece of elastic about half the length of the tape, and sew firmly to one end of the tape. Thread through the slot with a bodkin, and fasten securely at the other end of the tape. By this means the neck will be made to fit close at the back, and the front raised higher, so that it will fit more closely all round. (H. S., Bolton.)

Wednesday's Nursing.

REMEMBER that milk is a food as well as a drink, and that by giving an undue amount of milk you may overtax the patient's digestion. At times, therefore, substitute plain water, or, if ordered, barley water or fresh lemonade.

Put two tablespoonfuls of the selected beverage into an ordinary feeder, which is preferable to a glass, as it conceals from the patient how little he is being given. Urge him to hold the fluid under the front of the tongue or at the back of the throat. The effect will be a refreshing sensation of coolness, whereas a long draught induces flatulence, and does not allay the thirst so well. (Mrs. E. SPENCER, Darlington.)

Fig. 3.

To keep fomentations hot, have a steamer over a saucepan of boiling water, put in the fomentation, and it will be kept moist and hot without needing wringing out. One can be kept in while the other is in use, and quite a small gas jet will keep the pan boiling. (Mrs. M. JONES, Helsby.)

If you should lose your voice with a cold, you will find butter and sugar beaten together a very good remedy. Take a teaspoonful at a time. (L. TUCKER, Copplestone.)

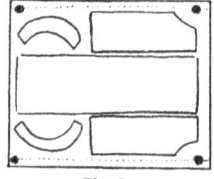

Fig. 2.
(Diagram only intended to show pinning down.)

To-day's Thoughts.

God never imposes a duty without giving the time to do it.

To live is nothing, unless to live be to know Him by Whom we live.

There is nothing the body suffers that the soul may not profit by.

To-day's Thoughts.

It is not the cares of to-day, but the cares of to-morrow that weigh us down.

We kneel—how weak. We rise—how full of power.

Those who bring sunshine to others cannot keep it from themselves.

FROM MY STUDY CHAIR

And so it has come. Those gradually darkening clouds which gathered so persistently, while faithful hearts still hoped and prayed that the light of reason and good-will would break through, have now crashed into the storm and conflict of war, the effects of which will be felt increasingly by us all. So from September 3rd a new world has begun, as past history abundantly testifies. We had hoped for a new and better world to follow 1914, but the lesson was not learnt or practised. There has been no true peace since 1919; only resentment, fear and selfish ambition. Now Europe is again to be battered and wounded, and out of the bitter travail, a new world will be born, a world where Faith and Love and Brotherhood may more truly rule and reign. God grant that such a hope and purpose may ever remain in our hearts, and keep us strong and steadfast in all our sufferings and hardships.

* * *

The Church Times (in its issue of September 8th) referred to the words of S. Augustine of Hippo—" Remove righteousness, and what are kingdoms but great bands of brigands—," the truth of which is as evident to many to-day as it was to S. Augustine. Just as S. John wrote of the " New Jerusalem " when it seemed that the Christian Church was to be annihilated by its persecutors; and as Bunyan produced his " Pilgrim's Progress " from within the bars of Bedford gaol, so Augustine was moved to write his great treatise " concerning the city of God " at a time when the Huns and Vandals were sacking Rome and spreading ruin and death throughout the land. Such men were the possessors of a robust faith and courage in God's eternal purpose and reality, which no worldly disasters or misfortunes could hide or destroy. Let us take that to heart ourselves in these days.

* * *

But let us also notice that the real quality of life which lasts, and which is immune to the infection and decay of an evil world, is righteousness, the very quality of God Himself. Unless this true quality of Life can be grafted on to the old stock, whether of nations or of individuals, there is no hope of redemption : men live merely as brigands. So then must the children of God and the servants of Christ pray and worship and live in order that righteousness may be preserved, and the world redeemed from its chains of selfishness and pride.

* * *

In these days then we shall find, I hope, in our church membership and its worship a great refreshment to mind and spirit : and though of necessity the present desperate needs of the world, and of our fellow-men, will have a constant place in our prayers, yet the object of our worship will be to draw near to God, to hear his message, to lift up our hearts to the realms above, and to follow more carefully in Christ's way of life. We shall, alas, get plenty of war news and war talk every day outside, but in church we shall thankfully come together to get our minds set on something else, something more steadying, and which will, please God, enable us to be a steadying influence on others.

* * *

Obviously we shall have to forgo many of our customary social gatherings : but we propose to hold our Family Breakfast on Sunday, October 1st, after the Parish Communion, when the Bishop of Dover hopes to be with us, as our Father in God; and I know that many of us will value such a gathering. We rely moreover on every member of the family remembering to mark our Birthday Festival by their generous gifts on the Thank-offering Day, October 6th, to help us meet our church expenses, which face us in war as in peace.

May God's blessing and love rest upon us all.

11 St. Mildred's Road,
Ramsgate.
June, 1945.

My dear People,

These are great days. Days of deliverance, victory, and hope, which provide sufficient grounds for a continuous thanksgiving. They are days of deep emotion, and so they should be, for without emotion, life would be very cold and dull. That is why we indulge in flag-wagging, and other forms of expression. It is good to give expression to what we feel so deeply, but emotion is not enough. Our emotions are warm whilst they last, but they do not last long. Our thankfulness must be built on something more abiding. That is why our thankfulness should always carry with it, self-dedication. All that we are thankful for has been achieved by service and sacrifice of a high and noble order. If there is to be no slipping back to the conditions which produce war, we must resolutely dedicate ourselves, our emotions and our wills, to a high and noble purpose. The fine qualities which are necessary to win wars, are also needed to win peace. As the war has been everybody's business, so must the business of peace be everybody's concern. For most of the years of the war, members of the Mothers' Union have made use of a suitable prayer, "God give me peace in my heart, that there may be peace in my home, that there may be peace in the world." Peace can begin with each of us, and its range is the whole world.

Perhaps we are first of all conscious of a great deliverance, which has restored to us, personal safety, some measure of comfort, and some degree of freedom which should steadily increase.

In 1939 we sacrificed these, in a struggle which we had been compelled to see as inevitable. It was inevitable in 1939 and the few years before it, but there was a time when something could have been done to prevent it, and it was not done. The majority of people just could not be bothered. Our deliverance means that we have been given another chance so to order our world that men and nations will not go to war again. War is not necessary, if constructive action is taken in time, to prevent it. Human nature is the weakness, but human nature can be changed. That is the Gospel, the good news, without which, the world would be in a sorry plight.

We have cause to be thankful, not only for deliverance but also for Victory. Victory which means that all the service which has been given, and all the sacrifice made, has not been in vain. It is for us, who have been spared to see this day of Victory, to see to it that it shall never be in vain. This victory means the triumph of right over wrong, and that in spite of the overwhelming power of evil forces in the early days. Right is might, providing there are enough people who believe it. It is the high calling of Christian people to believe this and act accordingly. The power of right was demonstrated in the life, death and resurrection of our Lord Jesus Christ. It is in His power that right becomes might. He chooses to invite ordinary human beings to co-operate with Him and demonstrate it.

If all the service and sacrifice is to be worth while, right must be might, even in peace-time, with all its comforts and pleasures.

In times of war we do things under the stress of fear, and for self-defence. However hard the demands which are made on us, we know that if we do not respond, things will be worse, and so we are impelled by fear.

When war is over, and immediate fear removed, some other urge must be found, for wise, resolute action is still necessary. Is there anything else that will inspire men to serve and sacrifice?

Many of us have seen the films showing the horrible treatment meted out to prisoners in the concentration camps in Germany. No doubt we recoiled with disgust, and probably were more impressed with the sufferings of the victims, than with the sin of their persecutors. It is a human tendency to be more concerned with suffering, than with the sin that causes it. It is the persecutors who have debased human nature, their own. The sufferings of the victims show what degraded human nature can do to other human beings when in power. Our victory has taken power from people who were not fit to have it. For the glory of God, and the good of men, those who have power must also have character.

When I was watching one of these films, the commentator said that the victims of the camps were there because of their political and religious convictions. I think that is very significant. We have known days of peace when politics and religion were thought of as the interests of a crazy minority. Those who were keen were tolerated, and pitied. At the time of an election we are goaded by the keen ones to realise that we are important, we have a vote. We cast that vote, and then slip back into political slumber until the next election. In the meantime we leave politics to those who happen to have a taste for that sort of thing. In other words we leave them to manage or mis-manage our world. Politics is not a hobby for the few, it is the science and art of government, and governments make conditions or war, or conditions of peace. We know from costly experience that war in these days is everybody's business, and so is peace. In times of peace we must be ready to cut out those things which lead to war. It is more commendable to prevent your house catching fire, than to risk your life saving your relatives and goods, when, through your neglect, the house has been allowed to catch fire. It is more commendable, but less spectacular. Politics good and sound, make for peace.

It is significant that those tyrants who set out to enslave the world found their way barred by people of definite political and religious convictions. Apparently religion is not a mere hobby for old ladies, an ineffective past-time for childhood, and a form of entertainment for a few other people who happen to like that sort of thing. It is something vital, powerful, and compelling. That is why there were so many in the concentration camps for their political and religious convictions.

Politics and religion form the crosspiece of sound community life. Politics has to do with our relationship one with another, Religion with our relationship with God. Politics alone, are not enough, but they are very necessary. If we make our religion our dominant passion, we shall cleanse and strengthen our political action. To men who believe in God and try to serve Him, Dachau, Buchenwald and Belsen are unthinkable. When men leave God out of their lives, this is what they can sink to.

For the glory of God, and the good of man, politics and religion go hand in hand. But the politics must be good and sound, the religion true. All who know something of the Bible are familiar with the following passage, " God so loved the world that He gave His only begotten Son to the end that all that believe in Him should not perish, but have everlasting life." Jesus came to live on earth that we might know the truth about God, and about ourselves. In this knowledge and faith there grows up a relationship with God which cleanses and strengthens all other relationships.

Jesus also showed us how to live. Fear had no place in His life. The circumstances in which He lived, the opposition roused by His teaching, were enough to create conditions of fear. He served men, suffered for men, made the supreme sacrifice and died for men, all without fear. His motive for action was love.

The motive for the demolition of evil (war), may be fear, but the motive for building the good (peace), must be love.

Somebody's blood is beginning to boil, and angry words are being framed. How can we love the Germans after all the suffering they have so cruelly caused? You cannot love them with deep emotion, it can only be that kind which is achieved by the will. Christian love is not something soft and sentimental. Love does not require the absence of sin before it can operate, " Whilst we were yet sinners, Christ died for us." It operates in spite of sin.

Again Christian love does not say that sin must be forgiven and forgotten under all circumstances. Repentance and amendment are required of the sinner, in the matter of sin, Christian love is stern. In more peaceful and settled times the Christian Church has often been criticised for " continually harping on sin to be confessed," and in times like the present there are those who charge the Church with a soft sentimentalism when she proclaims the gospel of love for all mankind. In times of peace the Christian Church requires confession of sin, in war and just after it the Church still requires confession of sin as the prelude to forgiveness, but in peace and in war the Church must proclaim the gospel of God's love for every man. God loves, though man does nothing to deserve it. Love works like that, it is not something we earn, or deserve, we just receive it.

The love of God is constant, however sinful we may be, but that love cannot save us in spite of ourselves. There are steps to salvation, and these steps rest upon the sure basis of God's unwavering love. The steps themselves are no soft and easy way, Contrition, being sorry, not for self but for sin, Confession, owning up to it, Amendment of life which serves to prove sincerity, and then Reception into the Fellowship, that is the state of salvation.

The days that lie ahead are beset with many problems and perplexities, let us not lose sight of what the Church has to teach us around VE-Day. Ascension Day, May 10th, was overshadowed for some, by the thrill of VE-Day. Its message of the ascension of Jesus above all human limitations, His presence with His disciples everywhere, and the promise of His Spirit to guide and strengthen, a promise fulfilled on the first Wiht-Sunday and ever since.

May the God of wisdom, love and power, grant us now and always, His Peace.

Your friend and Vicar,

John H. Romdwell.

Children's Services in the 1880s

PROCESSIONAL HYMN

Come ye children, hearken unto me: I will teach you the fear of the Lord.

Let us pray

O God of Abraham, God of Isaac, God of Jacob, bless these thy servants, and sow the seed of eternal life in their hearts; that whatsoever in thy holy Word they shall profitably learn, they may in deed fulfil the same. Look, O Lord, mercifully upon them from heaven, and bless them. And as thou didst send thy blessing upon Abraham and Sarah, to their great comfort, so vouchsafe to send thy blessing upon these thy servants; that they obeying thy Will, and alway being in safety under thy protection, may abide in thy love unto their lives' end; through Jesus Christ our Lord. Amen.

Our Father, which art in heaven, Hallowed be thy Name. Thy kingdom come. Thy will be done in earth, As it is in heaven. Give us this day our daily bread. And forgive us our trespasses, As we forgive them that trespass against us. And lead us not into temptation, But deliver us from evil. For thine is the kingdom, The power, and the glory, For ever and ever. Amen

O Lord, open thou our lips.
And our mouth shall show forth thy praise.

Praise ye the Lord
The Lord's Name be praised

O praise the Lord of heaven : praise Him in the height.
Praise Him, all ye angels of his : praise Him, all his host.
Praise Him, sun and moon : praise Him, all ye stars and light.
Praise Him, all ye heavens : and ye waters that are above the heavens.
Let them praise the Name of the Lord : for He spake the word, and they were made; He commanded, and they were created.
He hath made them fast for ever and ever : He hath given them a law which shall not be broken.
Praise the Lord upon earth : ye dragons, and all deeps;
Fire and hail, snow and vapours : wind and storm, fulfilling his word;
Mountains and all hills : fruitful trees and all cedars;
Beasts and all cattle : worms and feathered fowls;
Kings of the earth and all people : princes and all judges of the world;
Young men and maidens, old men and children, praise the Name of the Lord : for his Name only is excellent, and his praise above heaven and earth.

He shalt exalt the horn of his people; all his saints shall praise Him : even the children of Israel, even the people the serveth Him.

Glory be to the Father and to the Son and to the Holy Ghost: as it was in the beginning, is now, and ever shall be, world without end. Amen

READING

ADDRESS

I believe in God the Father Almighty, Maker of heaven and earth :
And in Jesus Christ his only Son our Lord: Who was conceived by the Holy Ghost, Born of the Virgin Mary: Suffered under Pontius Pilate, Was crucified, dead, and buried: He descended into hell; The third day He rose again from the dead: He ascended into heaven, And sitteth on the right hand of God the Father Almighty: From thence He shall come to judge the quick and the dead.
I believe in the Holy Ghost: The holy Catholic Church; The Communion of Saints: The Forgiveness of sins: The Resurrection of the body, And the Life everlasting. Amen.

CATECHISING

My soul doth magnify the Lord : and my spirit hath rejoiced in God my Saviour.
For He hath regarded : the lowliness of his handmaiden.
For behold, from henceforth : all generations shall call me blessed.
For He that is mighty hath magnified me : and holy is his Name.
And his mercy is on them that fear Him : throughout all generations.
He hath showed strength with his arm : He hath scattered the proud in the imagination of their hearts.
He hath put down the mighty from their seat : and hath exalted the humble and meek.
He hath filled the hungry with good things : and the rich He hath sent empty away.
He remembering his mercy hath holpen his servant Israel : as He promised to our forefathers, Abraham and his seed, for ever.
Glory be to the Father and to the Son and to the Holy Ghost: as it was in the beginning, is now, and ever shall be, world without end. Amen

O Lord, we beseech thee mercifully to receive the prayers of thy people which call upon thee; and grant that they may both perceive and know what things they ought to do, and also may have grace and power faithfully to fulfil the same; through Jesus Christ our Lord. *Amen.*

Almighty God, who hast given us thy only-begotten Son to take our nature upon Him, and as at this time to be born of a pure Virgin: Grant that we, being regenerate and made thy children by adoption and grace, may daily be renewed by thy Holy Spirit; through the same our Lord Jesus Christ, who liveth and reigneth with thee and the same Spirit ever, one God, world without end. *Amen.*

O Almighty God, who out of the mouths of babes and sucklings hast ordained strength, and madest infants to glorify thee by their deaths; Mortify and kill all vices in us, and so strengthen us by thy grace, that by the innocency of our lives, and constancy of our faith even unto death, we may glorify thy holy Name; through Jesus Christ our Lord. *Amen.*

HYMN

The Blessing of God Almighty, the Father, the Son, and the Holy Ghost, be upon you, and remain with you for ever. *Amen.*

PROCESSIONAL HYMN[87]

---

[87] In accordance with the Act of Uniformity Amendment Act, 1872, the service was composed solely of elements taken from the Holy Bible or Book of Common Prayer. The sources in order were: Ps 34:11, Marriage service, Matt. 6:9-13, Morning Prayer, Ps.148, Evening Prayer, collect for first Sunday after Epiphany, collect for Christmas Day, collect for Innocents Day. In the case of a service aimed only at Infants, the Catechising and Magnificat could be omitted. Ps 100, the Jubilate from Morning Prayer, could be used in place of Ps. 148.

O be joyful in the Lord, all ye lands : serve the Lord with gladness, and come before his presence with a song.
Be ye sure that the Lord he is God; it is he that hath made us, and not we ourselves : we are his people, and the sheep of his pasture.
O go your way into his gates with thanksgiving, and into his courts with praise : be thankful unto him, and speak good of his Name.
For the Lord is gracious, his mercy is everlasting : and his truth endureth from generation to generation.
Glory be to the Father, and to the Son : and to the Holy Ghost;
As it was in the beginning, is now, and ever shall be : world without end. Amen.

Epilogue

St Laurence church was standing when:

- ✠ Richard the Lionheart went on Crusade
- ✠ King John signed Magna Carta
- ✠ England defeated France at Crécy and Agincourt
- ✠ Henry VIII married Anne Boleyn
- ✠ Charles I was beheaded
- ✠ Nelson won the Battle of Trafalgar
- ✠ The first trains started to run
- ✠ Machine guns fired across the Somme
- ✠ Man walked on the moon

It still stands.

Our history is no gaudy pageant of self glorification. It has been the drama of countless souls who have lost their lives to find them, who have gone the way of the Cross to glory. The Church's driving power has been that of the Holy Spirit tapped by prayer.

The faithful of past ages are not dead and gone. They are with us, not just in memory; they inspire us by more than their example. They are with us alive; for they are with Him and they have their place in His perpetual intercession.

And He is with us. We will go forth in the name of the Lord and in His power we will do great deeds for He will make us mighty in love. Nothing can be good enough for St Laurence because nothing can be good enough for God.

The Reverend Clemments Hartley Bird, Vicar, 1962

Signing Out

Subject Index

1851 Religious Census 256–57
Attendance 113, 136, 217, 256–57, 306
Banners 295
Bells 33, 65, 89, 130–32, 140, 192–95, 288–92
Black Death 24
Carvings 14, 15, 18, 21, 25
Cecilia Road cemetery 226
Chancel 14, 18, 179, 283
Children's Corner 296
Choir 126, 172, 184–86
Cholera 258
Church Plate 128, 179, 199
Church Wax House 46, 90, 118, 126, 151
Churchyard 96, 318, 362, 401–16
Clock 182–83
Compton Census, 1676 113
Demography 84, 119–20, 258–61
Elizabeth I 322
Fair 46, 52, 264, 368–70
Fire escape building 226
Font 30, 181, 215
Galleries 90, 124, 171
Geneva Bible 67–73, 398–400
Hatchments 189–90
Icon 297
Laud, Archbishop 99
Lectern 180
Manston 217, 267
Model 295
Monuments
    Coppin 95
    Eason 132
    Freeling 133
    Froude 190
    Gillow 95
    Manston 30–32
    Rogerson 134

  Smith 232
  Sprackling 66, 94
  Vince 191
Music 59, 62
Music book 33
Nelson, Horatio 231
North chapel 23, 26
North door 29, 174
Organ 183–84, 298–99
Pageant, 1934 321
Parish Hall 272–74, 308, 352, 372
Parish magazine 219, 337, 438-51
Parish office 358, 360
Peasants' Revolt 46
People
  Austen, Jane 239
  Ayton, Bertie 277–78
  Browne, John Collis 267–69
  Coppin, Richard 113
  Cotton, Charles 276–77
  Cranmer, Thomas 79–81
  Fox, William 238–39
  Garrett, Robert 261–64
  Garrow, William 250
  Johnson, John 81, 388–97
  Joy, William 120–23
  Kyriel, Thomas 43
  Manston, William 43
  Massey, Cromwell 242–47
  Murray, Augusta 157–63
  Noel, Sarah 274–75
  Pugin, Augustus 247–48
  Regnier 270–72
  Sprackling family 102–11
  St Laurence, Ralph, Thomas 40–41
  Victoria, Princess and Queen 239–40
  Warham, William 81
Pews 58, 174, 257
Porch
  south-east 170
  south-west 20, 28, 63, 215, 227, 292

Poverty	86, 116–18, 219, 258
Pulpit	58, 79, 88, 127, 172, 174, 179, 180, 335
Reformation	47–61
Registers	52
Reredos	127, 172, 175
Residents	
Austen	132, 147, 148, 190, 192
Curling	24, 27, 44, 46, 84, 85, 93, 97, 114, 116, 117, 118, 146, 148, 150, 231, 239, 322, 403
Guillum Scott	180, 286, 287
Maxted	91, 92, 95, 148, 149, 418
Montefiore	82, 251, 255, 265
Noel Harris	187, 234, 251, 265, 383
Philpot(t)	386, 403, 414
Siminson	288, 289, 293, 299
Warre	188, 189, 191, 199, 217, 226, 240, 250–55, 272, 273, 288, 298, 308
Weigall	178, 186, 188, 208, 220, 273, 283, 308, 316, 386
Rood	27, 52, 60, 285
Roof	292
aisles	89
chancel	30, 179
chapel	25
nave	28
Royal coat of arms	129
Schools	75–77, 372–76
Sexton's piece	111
Shipping	114–15
Side chapel	21, 26, 276, 288
Sunday School	234–38, 256, 344, 362
Thurstin room	294
Tower	14, 28, 175–79, 343
Triptych	329, 349
Vermin	91
Vestry	23, 195
Vicarage	36, 78, 134, 138, 204, 206, 335, 342, 343, 346
War memorial	292, 405, 412
War with France, 1793-1815	228–34
West door	13, 25
Windows	90, 187–89
east	28, 175, 281
north aisle	29, 297
south aisle	261

    west 174, 187
Witchcraft 85, 115
Worship
    Children 452–54
    Eighteenth century 128
    Nineteenth century.. 196–98, 217
    Seventeenth century 92, 94
    Sixteenth century... 60, 62
    Twentieth century 302–7

www.ingramcontent.com/pod-product-compliance
Lightning Source LLC
Chambersburg PA
CBHW080721300426
44114CB00019B/2453